CW00376708

STRANGERS
NO MORE

BOOKS BY SANJOY HAZARIKA

Strangers of the Mist: Tales of War & Peace from India's Northeast
Rites of Passage: Border Crossings, Imagined Homelands, India's East and Bangladesh
Writing on the Wall: Reflections on the North-East
Bhopal: The Lessons of a Tragedy

BOOKS EDITED BY SANJOY HAZARIKA

Hope Floats: The Boat Clinics of the Brahmaputra (with Bhaswati Khaund Goswami)
Gender Poverty and Livelihood in the Eastern Himalayas (with Reshmi Banerjee)

STRANGERS NO MORE

NEW NARRATIVES FROM INDIA'S NORTHEAST

Sanjoy Hazarika

ALEPH

ALEPH BOOK COMPANY
An independent publishing firm
promoted by *Rupa Publications India*

First published in India in 2018
by Aleph Book Company
7/16 Ansari Road, Daryaganj
New Delhi 110 002

Copyright © Sanjoy Hazarika 2018

The author has asserted his moral rights.

All rights reserved.

The views and opinions expressed in this book are
the author's own and the facts are as reported by him,
which have been verified to the extent possible, and
the publishers are not in any way liable for the same.

No part of this publication may be reproduced,
transmitted, or stored in a retrieval system, in any form
or by any means, without permission in writing from
Aleph Book Company.

ISBN: 978-93-84067-44-1

3 5 7 9 10 8 6 4

Printed by Parksons Graphics Pvt. Ltd., Mumbai

This book is sold subject to the condition that it shall
not, by way of trade or otherwise, be lent, resold, hired
out, or otherwise circulated without the publisher's
prior consent in any form of binding or cover other
than that in which it is published.

For
Meghna, Ralf and Preeti

CONTENTS

AUTHOR'S NOTE

For years, I have wrestled with the idea of this book; stuttering efforts to start it came to naught. While I felt that I was not yet running out of time, I was certainly running out of ideas.

There have been acute challenges. The writing has been halting, arduous, especially after my wife Minal suddenly fell ill and then left us, all in a space of three months in early 2009. She was only fifty-six, and a powerhouse of energy, planning, curiosity and ability. For months after she passed away, I was unable to put pen to paper or even think of writing. A few months later, my son-in-law Ralf faced a challenge with cancer. My daughter Meghna's strength and love enabled him to overcome that crisis, as much as good treatment and early diagnosis. I was around to provide support in any way possible, keeping my sanity with daily walks, pranayama and yoga. Ralf's parents came from Germany at this difficult time and kept our spirits up with their energy and good cheer.

It takes time for people like me to realize that such challenges spur us to tell our stories better, weaving details and facts together, merging, mixing and remembering.

After years, my interest in the book revived. And as I began to resume writing, I was humbled by the vastness of what I do not know. I cannot but recall the words of that intrepid British explorer and botanist who walked into history with his legendary treks in search of fabled lands and rare plants—Frank Kingdon-Ward. He wrote: 'I am fully conscious that a complete account of the regions visited is a task beyond my power.'

One of his unfinished tasks was the exploration of the Tsangpo Gorge through which the Yarlung Tsangpo—known as the Brahmaputra in Assam—hurtles. This, too, is an incomplete challenge for me although I have travelled along the river through Tibet, Arunachal Pradesh, Assam and Bangladesh into the Bay of Bengal.

As the book developed, I realized it was important to weave stories of legend, imagination, future challenges and perspectives as well as personal experiences into a narrative flow. I have tried to do this as part of a frank introspection of where things have gone wrong or right and where they can be nudged to change. I felt that it would be useful to look at how, in my limited view, our region has both grown and unravelled after 1993–1994. Why those years, why this particular benchmark?

Because it was in the fall of 1993, possibly November, during a fellowship at the Joan Shorenstein Center at Harvard University, two decades ago, that the proof copy of my first book landed at the Center's reception and into my excited hands. I am aware that two decades and more may not be a long time in the history of a nation but it does give us an opportunity to look back, introspect and consider the future.

◆

This is a deeply personal book, for it reflects what I regard as the core issues facing the eight Northeastern states of India: politics, policy, law and disorder, violent uprisings and painful reconciliations, offence and defence, conservation and oppression, history and the contemporary reality, stereotyping and breaking out of the mould, hope and despair.

I spend a fair amount of time looking at how new frontlines are emerging, of the new battlegrounds of discrimination and communalism, of the dangers of Islamic radicalism born out of prejudice as much as mobilization. There is too the relentless and ruthless exploitation of natural resources in the name of 'development' and 'management', profiting a handful and pauperizing the vulnerable. In this I have focused on the struggle between political and commercial lobbies on one side and environmentalists, human rights campaigners, social scientists, researchers and writers on the other.

The structure of the book has developed along the following lines: a long introduction looks at borders, histories and notions of identity with a detailed study of the region's place in history and the struggles within and between Whitehall, New Delhi, Beijing and the 'Northeast' itself, reflecting on intricate and opaque lines, frontiers and borders. These remain sharply contested and hugely problematic, especially in the India–China sector, underlined by recurring clashes on the disputed border between the Asian giants. The first chapter begins with a death, the killing of Thangjam Manorama Devi in Manipur that provoked a public outcry and forced the Government of India, for the first time in its history, to review a national security law after a popular agitation. That was a democratic response to a democratic demand. However, the same cannot be said of what happened afterwards and the centre's pusillanimous failure to follow up on the Justice Jeevan Reddy Committee's report reviewing the Armed Forces

(Special Powers) Act (AFSPA). That incapacity and official inchoateness has democratic incontinence stamped all over it. These are studied in detail, with personal narratives, official texts and a range of responses and documentation. AFSPA is a brief yet ponderous and powerful law, widely reviled as draconian. It has survived the wrath of Supreme Court judges who have virtually shredded the official position in powerful judgments. Yet its removal remains implacably blocked because the centre hasn't shown the guts, vision or trust that's needed for its revocation. I look at different aspects of conflicts in Manipur and provide a historical context to developments in Nagaland, bringing in personal experiences and interviews with the Naga militant leaders as well as ordinary people and peacemakers. The craft of peacemaking must be one of the most difficult in the world. Later in the book, I look at one example of it in Nagaland, unheard, unheralded, unsung and yet one that celebrates the triumph of courage and humility over hatred and suspicion in one of the state's most influential villages.

I move to Mizoram, fleshing out the Mizo story of rage, resistance, retribution and reconciliation with many dramatis personae, building it around numerous figures and phases. Central to the narrative are Laldenga, who led the revolt, Lalthanhawla, the man who was Mizoram's chief minister at the time of writing, and Sangliana or Lal Sangliana, the charismatic guerrilla leader. Sangliana's father, T. Sailo, was an Indian Army brigadier who went on to become chief minister of the state. We move to Assam and look at issues of migration and discrimination and the ubiquitous Bangladeshi—both in Nagaland and Assam, issues of prejudice come vividly to the fore as do questions of defining who's an Indian, an outsider or an immigrant. We revisit the fear of being overwhelmed by the 'illegal immigrant', an issue that I had looked at in depth both in *Strangers of the Mist* and *Rites of Passage*. There's a chapter on the secret killings, patronized by the system, which maimed Assam and struck fear into the lives of many. A long look at the United Liberation Front of Assam (ULFA) follows, its connections to Bangladesh and the Bhutanese crackdown on it. The ubiquitous Paresh Baruah, who has managed to stay one step ahead of the security forces in India and Bangladesh, strides through these pages. The nature of the state at local and national levels as well as of armed groups and 'civil society' actors are on test here and emerge clearly. I look at the new Indians and the impact of discrimination and prejudice towards them and also at how they respond in places such as New Delhi and 'back home'. What is the trigger for the out-migration and who is moving out of the Northeast?

There are two chapters on border issues, one on Arunachal Pradesh, and the other combining Sikkim, Meghalaya and Tripura. The Arunachal chapter talks of how Tawang became part of India through the initiative of the feisty and forthright Major Bob Khathing. It examines the emerging crisis of corruption and power based on an exploitative approach to natural resources, especially, water. The segment on Sikkim looks at its royal past but as in the chapter on Meghalaya, I reflect on the themes of abuse of power and abuse of nature that resonate across state and national boundaries. I also show how Tripura, despite its size, has carved out a unique space for itself. This it has been done through good governance and delivering healthcare, education and communication to its people. But there's another factor—it overcame more than thirty years of rebellion with a combination of political tact and mobilization and extraordinary armed interventions in insurgent camps in Bangladesh, taking the fight to the rebels in a foreign land. Tripura has turned the clock back by lifting the Disturbed Areas Act, which essentially ends AFSPA rule and sends the troops back to their barracks. It has shown confidence in the capacity of its police to handle armed groups.

The final chapter looks at the psychological distances which still need to be bridged, discriminations which need to be addressed, differences which need to be accepted and a sense of shared humanity, going beyond citizenship, that has to be built. Yesterday's strangers have become today's migrants. The challenge lies in the transition to becoming tomorrow's neighbours, not through an overweening embrace but a process of engagement. If this doesn't happen, then we could see a dangerous slippage to the past, with different and abler leaderships, armed with better ideas, practices and informed by the experience of the past decades. A greater fracturing would then be upon us.

In addition to this author's note, there is an introduction, an epilogue and a list of appendices which includes some documents that have so far not been made public.

◆

I am deeply conscious of how much more needs to be written, documented and disseminated. I take comfort in the fact that there are many competent and reflective writers who could meet these gaps far better than I can.

My writing has been influenced by deep, intense connections to the Northeast, through travel, work, marriage, relationships and relatives, love and inspiration, friends, life, death and acute sadness. There are the boat clinics which I've designed and built to take health services to the poor and marginalized on the Brahmaputra; a campaign to save the Gangetic dolphin, including a film on those exquisite, endangered, childlike creatures which gambol, play and approach us as we cheer and exclaim at their tossing, turning and peeking. There have been treks to isolated villages through thick forests, where leeches have feasted on us. Exhaustion has been a constant companion.

In some ways, this is an impatient book, having heard insurgents and their opponents in government, as well as those who have suffered at the hands of security forces and non-state armed groups, conversations with activists, government leaders and the underground. I've also used my work as an editor and journalist, researcher, filmmaker and activist. I place value on my tenure in Justice Jeevan Reddy's Committee to review the AFSPA, in the Constitution Review Commission and the National Security Advisory Board.

I have been privileged to meet an extraordinary range of people in the course of my journeys to Tibet, Bhutan, Nepal, Bangladesh, Myanmar, China and Southeast Asia, over bumps and curves of the highways of the Northeast as also by river. In all these journeys, the decision to travel has been mine.

These journeys have reinforced a fundamental conviction: that despite all their troubles and challenges, the margins have proved that they are becoming a part of the mainland, if not 'the' mainland. The impact of sweeping technological, economic, social and political change is visible in urban areas across the Northeast, spurring rural–urban migration, creating both success stories and inequalities. Rising aspirations fan a desperate determination to move quickly out of the past.

◆

There is another factor that provoked me to make this book as comprehensive as possible: the dominion of shortsighted punditry in newspapers, social and broadcast media. These pundits make laughing stocks of themselves. Mixing up Manipur with Mizoram or Meghalaya or confusing one chief minister with another is not just frustratingly annoying. What is unacceptable is that they make difficult situations worse by taking sides and imagining that they know better without even living in or visiting the areas that they write about, broadcast or discuss. That they don't speak a local language or know people beyond intelligence agents, media persons or political leaders speaks volumes of their incapacity. Poor information is the bane of understanding, especially of a complex region.

Hate talk and vitriolic, prejudiced, unmoderated outbursts on social media create both imbalance and outrage, leaving those targeted, angry and thirsting to hit back. Many in the media, not to speak of government, professionals and the world of academe, have hardly understood the subtle changes that have been taking place as the marginalized become the mainland.

The media is significantly to blame for misunderstandings that persist about the region and its people, the stereotyping that persists, the gaps that have endured if not widened. This is inexcusable when vast amounts of information are accessible at the tap of a finger on a smartphone, an iPad or a laptop.

Sanjoy Hazarika
Cambridge, New Delhi, Shillong, Guwahati, Badem
October 2017

INTRODUCTION:
DISPUTED BORDERS, DIVIDED PEOPLES

In the Mishmi Hills in Arunachal Pradesh, as the Lohit River's sparkling waters gleam and shimmer below in a torrent of streams that spread like lines on the palm of a hand, gusts of wind force the tall grasses, the few trees and all visitors to bend. A conversation has to be shouted, hats and caps have to be firmly clutched otherwise the wind would toss them into the great valley below where strong currents of air and water flow.

A short distance from this point, known as Hawa (Wind) Camp—for obvious reasons—lies the India–China border or what India calls the LAC (Line of Actual Control) where, in places, barbed wire fences, border posts, signs and heavily armed and heavily clad soldiers stand, patrol, wave, stare or glare at each other.

The Indian line, ingrained in the imagination of many, with not-so-imaginary posts staked into frozen earth and snow, runs along the watershed and below; the Chinese command many heights. The line snakes along the Tibetan Plateau that lunges at the skies across six Indian states and two other nations—from the northwestern heights of Ladakh in Jammu and Kashmir, across Himachal Pradesh, Uttarakhand, Uttar Pradesh, Sikkim, Nepal and Bhutan—finally surging into a windswept space of luminous, extraordinary beauty in Arunachal Pradesh.

Susan Conway describes the region with a felicity of language:

If you look at a topographic map of Asia, you will see that four great rivers have their origin in a tight cluster at the eastern rim of the Himalaya. To the west lies the Brahmaputra, in the centre the Salween and Mekong and to the east the Yangtze. From this common origin, the rivers spread out to form an almost perfect fan, although they meet the mountain ranges before descending to the flood plains and then on to the Bay of Bengal or the South China Sea. The apex of the fan in the Tibetan Plateau encompasses the hinterlands of the great Asian cities of Dhaka, Yangon, Bangkok, Phnom Penh, Saigon, Hanoi, Canton and Shanghai. It is the middle swathe of the fan that is less familiar. Here the original rivers are joined by their tributaries and by the Irrawady, the Chao Phraya, the Ho and the Hongshuii. Together they dissect the mountain ranges into small valleys, forming a distinctive landscape which extends over thousands of square miles.[1]

It is at this confluence of mountains, rivers and plains that our stories are located, where our origins lie, where the histories of British India, post-Independence India, China and Southeast Asia intertwine and—strangely enough—where our futures are connected to one another, beyond margins, borders and nations.

The extraordinary reality of Northeast India—a triangular shape of land wedged between Myanmar, Bangladesh, Bhutan and Tibet—is that it has longer borders with its neighbours than it has with India. Nearly 96 per cent of the region's borders are with other countries; only 4 per cent of the border is connected to the rest of India. Thus, its physical links with India, not to speak of other connections, are limited and its proximity to other countries is far greater. The larger region we are surveying sweeps down from the eastern edge of the Himalayas, through the Chittagong Hill Tracts below and across the Chin, Kachin and Karen Hills, into the rich, humid Shan Valley and Yunnan Province of the People's Republic of China as well as to the northern lip of Bhutan and Tibet. It is part of a vast tropical rainforest that stretches from the eastern rim of the Himalayas to the Gulf of Tonkin and the South China Sea on one side and the warm waters of the Bay of Bengal on the other.

One part of this magnificent tapestry lies at a border whose Indian interpretation has been long unacceptable to the Chinese. It runs along the ridges of the greatest mountain chain on earth for over 1,000 kilometres; the entire section of Arunachal Pradesh is disputed between India and China, a quarrel that began during British times among colonial offices in India and London and with the Chinese Foreign Office in Peking.

The issue of disputed borders and divided peoples comes up time and again, and has set nation against nation and pitted communities against each other. By the early twentieth century, China was already pressing its claims to strategic points along the border with British India, still not demarcated but stating its sovereign demands.

By drawing an incoherent line, scripting an incomplete story and then adding fuel to separatist zeal (then or for the future) in a last-minute pre-Independence effort, the British essentially laid the ground for the million mutinies that have fallen on the heads of New Delhi and its minions in the provinces of the Northeast.

As far back as 1910, the British were disinclined to interfere between the Tibetans and the Chinese, despite their own intervention and capture of Lhasa under Major Francis Younghusband. They underlined this point: 'On the 3rd July, the Secretary of State was informed that the Government of India proposed to reply to the representation from the Dalai Lama that His Majesty's Government were unable to reconsider their decision not to interfere between the Tibetans and the Chinese.' That sentence needs to be read about three times to understand its negativity and see through the opaqueness.

The Chinese had laid claim to the strategic Chumbi Valley in today's Tibet Autonomous Region, at the tri-junction of the then independent kingdom of Sikkim,[2] Bhutan and Tibet. At that time, it was a wilderness unexplored.

Today, Indian military specialists say:

> The tri-junction of India, Bhutan and China is like a Chinese dagger held at India's throat. At this point the Chumbi Valley which is part of southern reaches of the Tibetan Autonomous Region along the Line of Actual Control is like a pointed kris dagger thrust between Sikkim and Bhutan, giving access to China directly into West Bengal.
>
> China has been trying to maximize this geographical advantage because it is aware that it is through Sikkim and the Gaygong-Geegong gap that India can pose a threat by a lateral manoeuvre that will cut off the Chumbi Valley from the rest of China.[3]

Did the Chinese really think so? In 1908, Captain W. L. Campbell, the British trade agent at Yatung, sent details of a proclamation by Chinese officials to the political officer in Sikkim. The announcement, he said, had been postered widely in the area. The note dated 21 February 1908 was marked confidential.[4] Follows a transcription and translation of a proclamation posted by the Chinese Popon on the 17th or 18th instant [this is in Tibetan]:

> Translation of a proclamation posted at Pipitang in the Chumbi Valley on the ninth day of the Chinese month, corresponding with the 10th February 1908.
>
> A proclamation by Ma, the Trintang of Chumbi, wearer of the fourth button and the peacock feather &c, and officer appointed by the Chinese Emperor on the Indo-Tibetan frontier. Whereas, according to a telegram received from Chang the greater minister empowered by the Emperor of China to discuss a Treaty between

Tibet and Great Britain, it is notified to the Tungloing and the Popon that I, Chang, have noted the news contained in the telegram received on the 7th day of the 11th month. Now the Indian Government have actually withdrawn the troops from Chumbi, therefore you, the Tungloing and Popon, with the Customs commissioner, Chang, and the various Tibetan officials should consult together and do all that you do with care. Further after the troops have been withdrawn the administrative power in different places will be in the hands of the Chinese, as in former times [Chang's telegram ends. Trans].

In a blunt warning to local leaders, the proclamation added:

According to the letter received from Chang Yin Tang on the 7th day this proclamation is issued to you, all the Genpos and people under my orders, should bear in mind the clemency of the Chinese Emperor and should serve the Chinese and Tibetans with open mind and not follow your own inclinations. Let all the headmen and people understand this.

The threat was unambiguous—you are under our rule; ignore this at your peril.

◆

The boundary between Tibet and India was named after Sir Henry McMahon, who chaired the 1914 Simla Convention where India, China and Tibet were represented at a dialogue at the then Viceregal Lodge[5] in the hill station. But over the years, the British commitment to the McMahon Line[6] appeared to falter. At one point, riposting to a British diplomat who declared that the area north of Assam should be included in Szechuan Province, that is, recognizing the Chinese claim to the same and thus inserting a Chinese segment between Tibet and Assam (British India), a senior British official suggested that the cartographers use their imagination to draw the lines well north of the administrative frontier of Assam. He was emphasizing that the McMahon Line was not sacrosanct, unlike what New Delhi has been holding for decades.

The extreme sensitivity with which His Majesty's Government regarded the border issue extended to covering up and refusing to share information with the public. It was especially worried about the media getting hold of material that could be extremely embarrassing to Britain even if it did not place the future of the realm in jeopardy.

In one such case, the Imperial Government dispatched Olaf Caroe,[7] who was to become foreign secretary in the External Affairs Department of the Government of India, to meet with and placate Peter Fleming of the editor's office at *The Times* of London. Fleming had written on 20 April 1937 that 'you [Caroe] had some interesting information about the loss [on paper] of some 40,000 square miles of the British Empire, somewhere north of the Brahmaputra'. After dealing that stunning blow to the Foreign Office Fleming added, with acute sarcasm: 'It is, no doubt, a trifling loss; but the editor feels that our readers would be interested in an accurate presentation of the facts regarding this cartographical lacuna.'

Fleming was referring to the failure of official maps to include the area south of the McMahon Line in the British Empire.

The Times then threw Caroe a lifeline: 'It is perhaps presumptuous to bother you; but if you are ever in London and have a few minutes to spare, the editor would be most grateful if you would come in and see us.'

The Times's letter filled the Foreign Office with alarm as 'we do not want the correct presentation of the facts to be "splashed", as the F. O. [Foreign Office] and the I. O. [India Office] are agreed as to the desirability of avoiding unnecessary publicity; and will ask them not to publish anything without consultation with the I. O.'

The following year, a flurry of letters was dispatched to the Royal Geographical Society, *The Times* and John Bartholomew's of the Geographical Institute ('Cartographer to the King', proudly says Bartholomew's insignia). What followed was a major coup for the Foreign Office: all of them agreed to publish the latest map of 'Highlands of Tibet and Surrounding Regions' sent out on 26 August 1938 with a detailed letter saying:

> [The dispatcher had been] directed by the Secretary of State for India to say that his attention has been drawn to the fact that the north-eastern frontier of Assam in the neighbourhood of Assam has hitherto been incorrectly shown on many maps published in this country. I am therefore to enclose herewith, for your information, a copy of a map... which has recently been published by the Survey of India. This map shows correctly the Indo-Tibetan frontier in this region, although, since it is intended mainly for the purpose of showing physical features, it will be observed that all the frontiers of the various states are not marked upon it.

On 9 January 1939, the *Evening Standard* of London carried a three-paragraph news item issued from New Delhi by Reuters headlined 'New Map of India has been issued'. The crucial lines here refer to 'all the changes brought about by the introduction of the Government of India Act...

involved the grouping of new provinces and the regrouping of states into different political charges, and rendered all previous maps out of date'. It concluded significantly: 'Included for the first time on a map of this scale is a definite boundary between the tribal areas of Northern Assam and Tibet. Hitherto this frontier was undefined. The new demarcation shows that the Assam tribal tracts cover a much larger area than was generally imagined.'

Caroe, later knighted and made governor of the North West Frontier Province (NWFP), was still battling away. He wrote from New Delhi, objecting to a map published by George Philip and Son Ltd in London, saying that the map 'follows Chinese cartography, not ours and might be used in support of Chinese claims against India or Tibet'...and drawing the publishers' attention 'to the importance of Sino-Tibeto-Indian boundaries being drawn according to the British reading of them (boundaries). Any British publication issued under the authority of public or quasi-public firms and institutions and depicting boundaries otherwise than as read by HMG is likely to be used as evidence against us.'[8]

In addition, a note at the end of that year referred to the Simla Convention that established boundaries between Outer and Inner Tibet, Inner Tibet and China and relations between China and Tibet. Outer Tibet was to be autonomous, while Inner Tibet was to be under Chinese control. At the same time the convention recognized China's suzerainty over the whole country. The Chinese refused to ratify the convention mainly because of the boundary question.

> The Tibetans have since maintained that as the Chinese rejected the convention they (the Tibetans) are not bound by its provisions especially in respect of Chinese suzerainty and are free to assert their complete authority which in fact they have done by all means at their disposal. The position...is indeterminate and it is advisable that it should be so shown on British maps.[9]

The note added: 'Care should be taken to show the international frontier between Burma and Tibet as running not along the northern administered border of Assam but a considerable way to the north along the main ridge of the Himalaya.'

Map making and enhancing the notions of nations, nationhood and sovereign right cannot be left to bureaucrats and surveyors alone. As always, politicians, politics and security officials—as well as armies—play key roles. People or citizens come at the end of the story. But the British were not done yet with the Northeast and its incomplete borders. They were interested in doing more damage: carving out a totally new territory, directly answerable to London, for the tribes of the periphery, declaring that these had no connection to the plains below, either of India or Burma. This was what came to be known as the Crown Colony Plan.

Historian David Syiemlieh speaks of it in his book, *On the Edge of Empire: Four British Plans for North East India 1941–1947*. Were the Nagas and Mizos encouraged by these British proposals to retain a slice of empire at the end of the war and even after Indian independence to declare their own 'independence' later? The Naga and Mizo stories of differences with the Indian state are strengthened by their firmly held belief that 'we are not seeking independence because we were never part of you'. They present their world views as complete in themselves, different and unique.

The British plans for Northeast India did not close with the plans to transfer power. As late as 1946, there were detailed efforts and extensive reports by governors and their advisers (known as agents) including anthropologist-administrators such as J. P. Mills, on why the region, including the plains of Assam, needed to be protected from mainland India. The idea proposed, most precisely by Governor Robert Reid, was that an area on the border of Assam's eastern tribal belt and the forested, mineral-rich Sagaing-China-Kachin provinces of Burma could be carved out and put under the protective care of British administrators since the hill tribes had nothing in common either with the Congress or the anti-British movement, that many of these from the Naga-Lushai (Mizo Hills) had sided with the British in World War II and could expect neither justice nor economic and social equality from the dominant plains dwellers of Assam, India or Burma. The proposed area could be ruled directly by Whitehall, a continuum of the colonial power of the past.

Reid was blunt about the future of the hill areas: 'It cannot be left to Indian political leaders with neither knowledge, interest nor feelings for these areas.' He developed upon the ideas of the legendary J. H. Hutton, whose pioneering work in anthropology and administration in the Naga Hills is well known, proposing a crescent-shaped political unit running from today's Arunachal Pradesh down to the Chittagong Hill Tracts, and areas inhabited by the Nagas, Chins and Shans of Burma as well as the Khasis and Manipuris. A great arc would be carved starting from the Balipara Tract (now in Arunachal Pradesh), Nagaland and Mizoram to the Sagaing Division and Chin Hills state of Burma. This would, in effect, have carved out a large state under the nomenclature of a North East Province Agency headed by a chief commissioner. It would be a Northeast version of the

North West frontier.

Hutton's key recommendation was on the role of the commissioner who 'would, I imagine, have to be divorced...from the control of the Government of India (presumably a federal body by then) and put perhaps under some appropriate department at Whitehall'. This was the famous Crown Colony Plan that was subsequently wrongly attributed to Reginald Coupland and came to be known as the Coupland Plan.

Discussed at various levels of the colonial administration, this World War II mystery has many other elements to it, including high secrecy and top officials from the British Foreign Office flying in and out of Assam on stealthy missions. Officials and the single scholar-officer among them toyed with what seemed to some to be an extremely attractive idea. But with Indian independence drawing near and the forces of nationalism clamouring across the subcontinent, the British realized that they had left it too late. The administrators in Burma rejected the idea in mid-1946. Finally, Whitehall and those pressing the Reid–Mills Line, if it could be called that, had no choice but to drop it.

Mills also supported Reid on the whole and suggested a series of sub-states such as the Naga, Lushai, Abor and Khasi (this would include the Garo and Jaintia) and saw practical advantages to the union of states as a colony along the lines of South African protectorates such as Basutoland and Swaziland.

Mills's successor Philip F. Adams wanted each tribe to be consulted individually before developing a policy towards it. He even proposed an interesting phrase, to 'constitutionalise autocracy' or, in other words, keep the traditional system of chiefs— such as Syiems, Khasi rajas, and Dolois, chiefs of the Jaintia tribe—alive but place the burden of administrative costs for the hill areas on the shoulders of the central government.

All these points are still relevant for the best (or worst) practices in governance. Government processes remain fiercely contested in the Northeast—for example, one point of sharp debate has been whether the Sixth Schedule, which seeks to protect tribal rights over natural resources, traditions and customary entitlement, was the way to go. Nearly six decades after it found a place in the Constitution, the central government under the BJP (Bharatiya Janata Party) said that it would provide a lump sum to the states of the region and let them manage their own affairs instead of doling out funds, as the powerful centralized Planning Commission had under the Congress and the centrists.

Nearly seventy years after the idea was first tossed about the issue has come to public notice, giving further grist to the conspiracy theory about independence movements among hill tribes in the Northeast. Many of the Naga and other pro-sovereignty groups were in all likelihood completely unaware of these papers as they were kept in government archives away from the public domain. Even contemporary leaders of rebel movements show little interest in these papers, revealing their disinclination to engage with significant new material on the history of the region and their determination to stick to the known.

Of course, all authors of the four reports or notes assert their commitment to the welfare of the hill tribes who they felt were unfairly lumped with the people of the plains, placing the former with their limited exposure to the 'modern' world at a huge disadvantage. Thus, the hill groups with their lack of education, disconnect with financial transactions and naïvety had no understanding of one of the most deadly representatives of the march of empire—the usurious middlemen. They were simple, easy prey, low-hanging fruit.

Mills's twenty-six-page proposal said: 'The practical advantages of treating the union of States as a Colony till such time as they are sufficiently advanced to unite with India are so great that the ideas should not be rejected out of hand.'

He even quoted the precedent of Basutoland, Bechuanaland and Swaziland in Africa to protect the inhabitants against exploitation. These sweeping thoughts were framed following two events. The hills that came under the direct control of the Raj were categorized by the Government of India Act, 1919, as Backward Tracts. While the majority of the tribes acquiesced to the term, the progressive and modern Khasi-Jaintia were unhappy at being lumped into this category. Consequently, the Government of India Act, 1935, applied different nomenclature for the tribal areas.

The hills were categorized as either Excluded Areas or Partially Excluded Areas. Hence, Reid, then governor of Assam, wrote the first piece in November 1941 as a confidential note—*A Note on the Future of the Present Excluded, Partially Excluded and Tribal Areas of Assam*. His note, according to a University of Tokyo scholar,[10] underlined the strategic importance of India's Northeast frontier in relations with Tibet, China and Burma.

Many of these ideas originated in 1928 while the concept of amalgamating the 'Backward Tracts' of Assam and Burma under the control of the central government was initiated in 1925. Following the recommendation of the Simon Commission to separate Burma Province from the Indian Empire, N. E. Parry and. Hutton, who served in Assam, suggested establishing a new 'North-East Frontier Province', or the later Crown Colony, on the lines of the North West Frontier Province of Pakistan which till today borders Afghanistan. Hutton held that the tribal peoples in the hills had nothing in common with the plains people of Assam racially, historically, culturally or linguistically.

Parry and Hutton's concept of amalgamation developed for several reasons. If the separation of the hill areas of Assam was accepted by the Simon Commission, it would reduce the difficulties inherent in the creation of so small a unit; the peoples of the Assam Hills were ethnologically more akin to the peoples of the adjoining Burma Hills; and the distribution of these hill tribes ran across the political boundary.

The above suggestion found no place in the final plan of constitutional reforms, which resulted in the Government of India Act, 1935. In addition, the British government showed no interest in Assam's frontier at that time. As we have seen, the scheme of amalgamating the backward tracts of Assam and Burma was revived by Reid, who was inspired by Hutton and Mills, Reid's secretary from 1937–1942.

Although the ideas of Hutton and Parry were not adopted in 1935, they were to become controversial during the last period of British rule in India.

As mentioned earlier, under the Government of India Act, 1935, the Backward Tracts of Assam were divided into partially excluded areas and excluded areas. The administration of excluded areas became the sole responsibility of the governor of Assam. The partially excluded areas were placed under the ministers and were subject to the governor's discretionary control.

Indian nationalists criticized the whole system of exclusion and the governor's arbitrary 'safeguards' because these were inconsistent with true self-government and any real merger of the hills and plains, while the constitutional premises endorsed a future fusion of backward tracts with Assam as the ultimate goal. For accepting the backward tracts as part of Assam already, the Government of India Act, 1935, contemplated the conversion of the excluded areas into partially excluded areas and the conversion of the latter to ministerial areas, but did not counter the reverse process.

Burma, as suggested by the Simon Commission (a controversial reform committee set up in 1028), separated from India when the Government of Burma Act, 1935, came into force in April 1937, with Ba Maw as the first prime minister. L. S. Amery, secretary of state for India and Burma, suggested that the separation of Burma from India was the natural consequence of the introduction of self-government. He said the racial type, culture and geographical position of Burma belonged not to India but to the projection of the main bulk of Asia and the Indo-Chinese peninsula. Following this outlook, Reid wrote that Amery's point of view applied just as closely to Assam's excluded and partially excluded areas as to the 'Tribal Areas'. Reid said that no other line could fulfil British duty to the primitive peoples without separating them from the ministerial control of the plains of Assam, and concluded that he was in favour of Hutton's idea of a Northeast.[11] These were key ideas that shaped perceptions in the region and elsewhere.

It was left to Sir Andrew Clow, governor from 1942–1947, to shoot down both ideas. He believed that the hills and plains of Assam were interdependent on each other, dismissing his predecessor Reid's 'grandiose plans' of a crown colony/protectorate/agency. Snubbing the geographical shape of the proposed colony as 'fantastic' and incoherent, he said it would push the region into primitive economic self-sufficiency. Opposing both Reid and Mills, he added that it was unlikely that a British government which was setting out to give independence to India and Burma 'should now undertake the administration and financial responsibility for a patchwork of sparsely populated hills…Indian opinion would be equally strongly opposed to the constitution of a foreign territory within its natural boundaries'.

THE WINDS OF WAR

While these deliberations were under way, the region was also at the heart of an epic struggle that was pivotal not only for the future of the region, but the world. The British were at war on two fronts, fighting not only for the survival of their empire but also of their country. Although the battle on the Russian front was finally turning against Hitler, in Asia, the Japanese were rushing through Southeast Asia towards India.

Given its strategic geographic position, the Northeast witnessed its share of action in the China-Burma-India (CBI) theatre of war. The CBI theatre was notorious for the high number of aircraft that were lost on the 'Hump' route between US airbases in northeastern India and airfields in China.

The Hump was so called because it best described the natural saddle in the Eastern Himalayas which enabled pilots to cross over from Ledo in Assam to Kunming and Chengdu in China's Yunnan and Szechuan provinces as the transport aircraft launched repeated sorties to keep supply lines intact and the Japanese at bay. Having to fly through nightmarish, brutal air turbulence, a staggering 1,556 Allied aircraft with their crew (over 4,000 Americans lost their lives in that extraordinary struggle to help China and the World War II effort) went down in those conditions, attacked also by Japanese fighter planes and battered by winds so fierce that they could shear engines and wings off aircraft.

The peaks on that route rose to 19,500 feet (about 5,910 metres) and the lowest pass in that region was 10,500 feet (about 3,180 metres) above sea level. Scores of aircraft and their crews remain 'missing in action' and reports come in regularly from Manipur, as well as Myanmar's Chin State and Sagaing Province of 'new' discoveries of old crashes.

The crashes add poignancy to the epic scale of the conflict. The US Department of Defense said in 2004 that more than 500 US aircraft and 1,200 crew members and passengers remain missing in the CBI theatre, with an estimated 416 Americans still missing in India alone. Many of these aircraft have never been found, and their crews and passengers have since been declared administratively dead, unrecoverable or missing in action. The CBI theatre and its Hump route might have more US airmen missing in action than any other World War II theatre of operations.

◆

As far as the war was concerned, the situation was improving for the Allied forces, with the slow but steady turnaround in the Asian, African and European theatres of war: the Japanese got tangled, slowed down and turned back at the Assam borders, the Nazis failed to bomb out the heart of the British and the Russian winter overwhelmed the ambitious German push into the Soviet Union.

The Indian National Congress was opposed to the war and the Muslim League under Muhammad Ali Jinnah, in its own battle against the Congress, aligned with the war effort through its 'Grow More Food' campaign, especially in Assam.

At the time, barring Assam and parts of Manipur and Tripura, the rest of the region did not play a role in the anti-British, pro-Independence movement. In fact, there was a clear division between Assamese leaders who fought for their province and its peripheries to remain in India and the sharp irritation of leaders like Jawaharlal Nehru and Vallabhbhai Patel who felt that the eastern front was slowing India's tryst with destiny. Thus, the shape and size of the northeastern border with China, one of the most critical issues in pre-Independence India, remained undiscussed, unfocused upon and consequently unresolved by the new leaders of India, who, unwittingly or otherwise, had left the whole complex and messy business in the hands of British civil servants. They were handed an indigestible pottage.

In the years between 1940–1944, the border issues—or rather the question of how the line with China should be drawn, where and with what coordinates—were a reason for close combat between the India Office in London and the Foreign Office (both part of the Foreign Ministry of His Majesty's Government), between the latter and the Viceroy's Office and the India Government Office in New Delhi, and finally between His Majesty's Government and the Republic of China. Intense correspondence between these sides took place at the height of the war.

With London and other British cities under heavy bombardment, coping with the accompanying psychological stress and the spectre of defeat, with news from different fronts far from good, how did British officials manage to apply their minds with such detail and focus to issues that were thousands of miles away? There is wit, humour, research, exasperation and friendship that comes through in these letters that helped decide the shape of the borders. And perhaps, being so intensely wrapped up in their preoccupation with detail, the greater unfolding story of India's relentless fight for freedom from the foreign yoke had simply passed them by, especially the babus in London. Similarly, the khadi-clad fighters for freedom remained so determined and focused in their struggle for Independence, that they missed out on the minute details of defining the border and the strategic significance of its political and military implications.

This is true for leaders like Mahatma Gandhi, Jawaharlal Nehru and Vallabhbhai Patel who were at the forefront of the Independence struggle. However, the issue did not escape the attention of the pre-eminent Assam Congress leader Gopinath Bordoloi, later premier and chief minister of the province, and his core group who came to know of the Crown Colony scheme in the fading years of the war. But more on that later.

The Muslim League and the Congress were locked in mortal combat over India's future. They had been at each other's throats in electoral politics for years, including over the issue of support or opposition to the war. The glimmer of a growing possibility of freedom from colonial rule also fuelled agendas and campaigns on both sides.

TRYSTS WITH DESTINY

While the war was being won or lost, the skirmishes over what should constitute India's northeastern border with Tibet was continuing in the catacombs of Whitehall. Much light is shed on the inner workings of government on the issue of disputed and undemarcated borders by the study of correspondence over a decade between various figures in the British Foreign Office, the India Office in London and the Government of India in

New Delhi. ·

The review here is of India's northern border or that between India and Tibet and later India and China, which still remains hotly contested despite negotiations that have continued for over half a century. I have selected this slice of history to illustrate how colonial concerns, lack of clarity and arbitrariness have left both Asian giants with a legacy that is difficult to resolve.

Many of the current internal challenges faced by the existing states and communities (ethnic groups) in Northeast India lies, for the centre, anyway, in these unresolved border questions. From that perspective, it is completely understandable why the state needs to beef up soldier strength, weaponry and bases even if there was extensive peace.

This, in my view, is the crucial link in the border dispute that has endured for nearly a century and eluded resolution.

Take just one recent capricious fact: the borders were drawn arbitrarily by the British before leaving India, without consulting the most affected groups on these uplands. In that partition of the subcontinent into two, one nation, Pakistan, with its eastern and western wings, was separated by over 2,000 kilometres of a populous India; yet, the inclusion of the Buddhist majority Chittagong Hill Tracts into Muslim-majority East Pakistan stood the theory of Partition on its head. For when Sir Cyril Radcliffe drew his line, fuming at the heat and dust of India and wishing to get out of the country as quickly as possible, he took into consideration religion and geographical contiguity of the religious groups as key factors for the line he drew, slashing, in blood, a nation in two. That was the basis of Partition to which the Muslim League of Muhammad Ali Jinnah and the Congress of Jawaharlal Nehru had agreed (Mahatma Gandhi remained deeply opposed to the idea). The fact of a village, a town, a district or province being dominated by one religious majority or the other was reason and sole reason for being on either side of Sir Cyril's sweatily drawn line, cementing those of the same faith and exorcising those from a different church.

In the Census of India, 1911, a Major H. R. Davies remarked with exasperation about Burma: 'It is safe to assert that in hardly any part of the whole world is there such a large variety of languages and dialects as are to be heard in the country which lies between Assam and the Eastern border of Yunnan and in the Indo-Chinese countries to the south of this region.' The reason for this is not hard to find. It lies in the physical characteristics of the country. It is the high mountains and the deep, swift, flowing rivers that have brought about the differences in custom and language, and the innumerable tribal distinctions which are so perplexing to the enquirer into Indo-Chinese ethnology.

If we change the geography of Davies's remarks and locate them west of Assam and move eastwards, we would then include the swathe of countryside, river, stream, lake, jungle, hill, plain and peak that we spoke of earlier. To the mind of the 'mainlander', in all the countries of the region, whether it is the Han of China or the 'Indian' of northern and central India, the Burman of Central Burma, the Bangladeshis or the Drukpa or the dominant ethnic group of Bhutan, the tribes or distant groups on their international borders, at the frontier of nationalism and national consciousness, constitute the 'other'. They represent this complex innumerability, these ethnic distinctions 'which are so perplexing to the enquirer' and to the non-enquirer, who gets most of his information (or disinformation) from the burgeoning mass media, preferably noisy television channels, especially if it's in his or her 'mother tongue' or the language of the majority.

Indeed, we are still governing ourselves and especially our peripheries—those borderlands inhabited by what many see as 'the other', the 'tribals', those opposed or disinterested or ignorant of our ideas, our ways, our country, our people, our cities, our growth, the 'us' about ourselves—in the twenty-first century through nineteenth-century laws and legislation, acts of Parliament or Gazettes Extraordinary, judicial but not judicious.

These margins and borderlands spread across the great ranges that span like the fingers of two hands, their palms touching, outstretched and pointing both northwards and eastwards—from Tibet and across Bhutan, across the northeast of India and Myanmar into China's southwest; the lower palm lies in the Assam valley and the Bangladesh plains.

TRIBALS TAKE A STAND

While the Crown's cooks stirred the broth of a new colony and Partition, an extraordinary event took place in Assam. It was extraordinary against the background of mutual political hostility and suspicion and as the campaign for independence from Britain rushed into its final phase. Expediency and the need for a common cause on a few issues pioneered a coalition politics that spanned nationalist discourse and religious barriers.

In 1945, for the first time in India and in the history of the Indian National Congress, a coalition government took shape with the Congress, the Muslim League and an independent group led by a firebrand Assamese nationalist, Rohini Kumar Chowdhury. That such a hybrid could be born in such stressful conditions was an example of the power to innovate and seize political advantage. The experiment was short-lived, but for Bordoloi, the Assam Congress leader and his party, it had a specific goal—it forged a land settlement agreement under which the Congress ensured that the League-led provincial government, which was on the brink of collapsing before the sudden coalition, would end its policy of encouraging and settling East Bengal Muslims on open and reserve forest lands. This strengthened the Congress's nationalistic image on the home ground and came in handy during state elections in 1946 where it won a handsome majority.

This was one of many parallel and constant struggles. On the eve of Partition, there was a strong push by the British under the Cabinet Mission Plan of Sir Stafford Cripps to develop Muslim and Hindu majority provinces which were first placed into sections and then based on similarities were grouped together. Technically, these would then be free to draw up their constitutions, depending on the religious group with numerical clout in the provincial assemblies. Everything was to be reduced to the religion of the individual, the party and the land. If this were to happen to Assam, a C category state (the more 'important' provinces were designated 'A' and 'B'), was at risk of being dominated by Muslim-majority Bengal, which would brush aside any Assamese sub-nationalist hopes of protecting its special place and that of the hill groups.

Bordoloi, seeing a future rimmed in blood and despair, refused to submit and called for a revolt. The resistance by the state's Congress workers and leaders, in total opposition to their central leadership, perplexed and angered men like Nehru; even Patel lost his patience. India's Independence, they snapped, could not be held hostage to Assam's feelings. In a strange way, their views and those of the Muslim League were identical. Neither wanted Assam on its terms, only on theirs. Bordoloi sent special missions to New Delhi to the Congress leaders to make them understand his concerns. But more critically, he asked two lieutenants to visit Mahatma Gandhi in riot-ravaged Noakhali, and ask for his blessings. Gandhi was categoric: quit the party and quit India, if necessary; fight for your rights, unfurl the banner of revolt, refuse to bow to the dictates of Bengal.

Bordoloi's unswerving conviction and the steadfast support of his people and party, but especially Gandhi, swung the tide in favour of Assam in this battle of survival. The Cabinet Mission Plan, also known as Grouping, fell through. That is why today's map of India is the way it is—because of one man and his determination, a man few Indians have heard of but whose image, nationalism, integrity and energy are impressed in the minds of generation after generation of Assamese. The irony is that many from the 'nationalist' BJP party that rules this nation are also unaware of this gigantic contribution: take Bordoloi out of the picture and you would have to take the Northeast out as well and leave behind what Jinnah once called his partitioned Pakistan, a 'moth-eaten' nation.

It was with Independence that the various tribal groups started taking positions on either being with India or veering away from it. During the drawing up of the Constitution, Bordoloi tried to accommodate the deep and legitimate concerns among the hill tribes. His subcommittee created the Sixth Schedule to protect tribal rights over natural resources, traditions and customary entitlements. His dream of integrating the region into India was complete when Tripura, Manipur and the Khasi states signed instruments of accession and merger agreements with New Delhi. Tripura and Manipur were accorded Union Territory status in 1950.[12] In addition, the protective power of the Bordoloi-fathered Sixth Schedule and its district councils were placed in what was then known as the United Khasi and Jaintia Hills and Garo Hills as well as Mikir, North Cachar and Lushai Hills.[13]

As the relentlessness of daily events underscore, the process of greater divisions within the region, raising the question of integration, re-integration or disintegration of the 'idea of the Northeast' is still a work in progress. The issue of separateness appears to be subsumed in a pan-India context. It was fear of the latter that was raised by insurgency after insurgency between the 1950s and the 1980s. Yet, this appears to have become a matter of rhetoric, played for public approbation, triggering agitation after agitation that rise and ebb.

The silent accommodation with India is taking place. This is seen in the diasporic sweep of communities from the region that have settled not just in the burgeoning metros but in smaller, quieter places such as Goa, Bhopal and Satara over the past three decades. The violence of discrimination may continue but the answer is also equally vibrant and open: the 'outsiders' are saying, 'We are here and we're not going back. This is as much our place as anyone else's.' In place after place, local communities and migrant groups try to talk with and understand each other just as in a smaller number they protest, abuse or harass each other. In the former lies a better future, if not a predictable one.

But the intractable divisions within the region continue to grow, separating tribe from tribe, community from community, over issues of rights and entitlements, plains and hills, about who's 'more' indigenous than others, making a lethal combination of unrequited anger and suspicion. The non-finalized borders rather like a door with a broken hinge, lacking the stability and legitimacy that would accrue from the third hinge. The sense of palpable disquiet and uncertainty among its many communities will grow unless this unease is put to rest—it is not a very safe feeling to know, every day, that the state or the region in which you live is shown as the property of a hostile neighbour (which China remains despite all the surface bonhomie: they don't overdo things like we do, they walk silently and carry a big stick, they push their country forward, not their leaders[14]) on its maps, whose troops (and ours) criss-cross the border reasonably frequently, although they are not yet shooting at each other and where the land frontier is called the LAC, where there are fixed positions and forces.

THE CHINA FACTOR

For a brief period following Indian Independence in 1947, all appeared quiet on what is today's Line of Actual Control until 1950, when Chinese troops first went into Tibet, and its iconic religious and temporal leader, the Dalai Lama, came under the control of Beijing. In November 1950, Prime Minister Nehru declared that the McMahon Line was 'our boundary—map or no map. That fact remains and we stand by that boundary and we shall not allow anybody to come across that boundary.'[15] This brave statement did not go unnoticed in Beijing as it built up its case and, on the ground, dismissed the notions of both Nehru and the McMahon Line. China had already invaded Tibet, overwhelming it with vast force in October 1950, an act which New Delhi called 'aggression'. It triggered an alarm in India about whether the Chinese would honour past Tibetan agreements, especially those about the borders. Among the most suspicious of Chinese intent was Deputy Prime Minister and Home Minister Vallabhbhai Patel, a formidable lawyer who, along with Nehru, Gandhi and other figures, was among the founders of free India. Unlike Nehru, a man who trusted the Chinese, Patel was unswayed by the former's emotionalism or his international dreams. He was a pragmatic, tough-minded politician who read the Chinese game correctly. While denouncing 'Chinese perfidy' in taking over Tibet, Patel remarked:[16] 'Even though we regard ourselves as friends of China, the Chinese do not regard us as their friends.' Also, he predicted to Nehru that 'very soon they will disown all the stipulations which Tibet had entered into with us in the past'. This would, in his view, throw 'into a melting pot all frontier and commercial settlements with Tibet on which we have been functioning and acting during the last half a century'. Step by step, point by point, the Chinese approach over the years proved Patel's fears to be true even as it belied and then destroyed Nehru's hopes of a better relationship between the Asian giants. First of all, they imposed a 17-point agreement on Tibet, which proclaimed it as an integral part of China.[17] This changed the entire course of events as Patel had forecast.

Within months the 1954 Panchsheel Agreement that Nehru and Zhou Enlai, the Chinese premier, signed,[18] China demanded that New Delhi hand over a trading post which the former had even recognized in a trade agreement as being part of India! Military incursions by Chinese army units followed. India protested to little avail.

The situation became more critical. In 1957, China began building a high altitude highway from Tibet to Sinkiang across the Aksai Chin region which New Delhi regarded as part of Ladakh in Jammu and Kashmir. This later was to become the Karakoram Highway, the highest all-weather road in the world. Zhou Enlai ominously pointed out to Nehru, who was urging a settlement of the border issue, that 'conditions (had not been) yet ripe for settlement and the Chinese side, on its part, had no time to study the issue'.[19] Beijing was being dismissive of India's insistence on an early settlement of the border. Relations worsened after 1959 when the Dalai Lama fled to India after a failed public armed uprising and was given shelter by Nehru.

Following the Dalai Lama's flight, the antagonism between Beijing and New Delhi erupted into border incidents, with both sides firing at the other numerous times, Indian soldiers being taken captive and a sharpening of diplomatic missives which each side hurled at the other, with accusations of fraud, violations of boundaries, trust and dignity. In the winter of 1962, the two countries fought a war at the highest point of the world. The Indian Army got a battering, outgunned, outmanoeuvred and outmanned. There were several places where the Indians, in the words of an officer who survived, were 'simply sitting ducks'. That humiliation runs so deep that India, a nation that commemorates events and historic dates with lavish celebrations, proclaims 'surgical strikes' against Pakistani forces or Kashmiri militants holed up on the Pakistan-held side of Jammu and Kashmir or assaults against Naga militants on the Myanmar border, rarely acknowledges the defeat or the gallant soldiers who lost their lives. A seminar to mark the war's fiftieth anniversary brought together memories but barely a hundred former and serving officers. Not a single media person or television crew, student or independent scholar barring one[20] was present. No one thought it was important enough to pay heed: there was not one politician, minister, MP or MLA, leave alone senior officials from the defence and home ministries, the critical core of India's security systems.

Nowadays, without the other's knowledge, Indian and Chinese intelligence agents as well as army patrols slip into the territory of the other across the LAC. The Chinese do this more often than the Indians, who don't advertise their entries. In 2014, a unit of the People's Liberation Army walked into a mountain patch of desert in Ladakh, Jammu and Kashmir, raised flags and tents before diplomats persuaded them to retreat after several rounds of talks. It was one of several incursions that year. But the Indians don't lag far behind in such interventions either.

Some years ago, an intelligence officer posted on the front told me that he was about to shave in a 'forward' post when he noticed some movement in the mirror. A check with his binoculars showed a Chinese patrol heading his way. He quickly packed up and left. After all, he was a few kilometres inside the Chinese side of the LAC and the Chinese soldiers were en route to occupy their summer post, abandoned in winter because of the cold and snow. The Indian officer was on a recce to check the play of things before the Chinese interrupted his sojourn.

These are games that many nations play, across the world, on either side of their borders. The fusillades of words continue, tempered with moderation. They show the dangers and challenges of having a border that is neither properly demarcated nor agreed to by the contesting sides.

In a significant book on the India-China boundary issue, the scholar and editor A. G. Noorani pointed out that this has been the case for at least over a century, no matter what Indian historians and officials speak of as their natural boundary.[21] A sense of traditional borders cannot take the place of demarcated ones, which are placed on mutually agreed maps, with geographical certitude and legal clarity. Until the second decade of the twentieth century, the British empire-Tibet border north of Assam had not been demarcated. This was pointed out by the secretary of state for India in a memorandum in 1913: 'It should be observed that Tibet is nowhere coterminous with the settled districts of British India, but with a belt of country which, though geographically part of India, politically is a no-man's land inhabited by aboriginal savages, partly the territorialities of states, independent (Nepal) and subordinate (Bhutan and Sikkim).'[22] Is it surprising then that there should be problems of nation and nationality, of nationhood and concerns among smaller populations about their place in the world and history?

◆

Seventy years after Independence, this region—especially along Arunachal Pradesh's border with Tibet and China—remains one of India's most isolated pockets. It is also witness to one of the most remarkable efforts by the Indian State to maintain a regular and very expensive connection to its mountain redoubts. Thus, almost every day, giant Russian Mi-26 helicopters, used elsewhere as deadly gunships or to ferry stranded villagers struck by natural disasters such as earthquakes and floods, lift effortlessly into the sky from Mohanbari Air Base on the edge of Dibrugarh in the steamy Assam plains. Following a northern trajectory but sticking to the vast marker of the sprawling Brahmaputra below, the helicopters lumber on a steady path some 3,000 metres above the ground as they head to the hilltop villages of Tuting and Gelling. At times, they stop in Pasighat, across the river, where the Brahmaputra gathers pace as it dips towards low-lying Assam.

Their cargo is neither weapons nor ammunition, yet the khaki-coloured helicopters are critical to the security of the region and the survival of communities and Indian armed posts in Gelling and Tuting, the former right on the border with China. They carry 'rations': rice, flour, dal, cooking oil, vegetables, tinned milk, fuel and other goods. They also carry people—villagers taking a trip to the plains for medical treatment, others for a visit to the larger markets, taking goats and chickens with them. There are students returning to schools and colleges. Without these regular sorties, these last outposts of India would have a rough time. The drone of the choppers is interrupted when the weather packs up in the high hills, as mist, high winds and rain swarm across the terrain, making flying difficult, even hazardous, for elite helicopter squadrons such as the Siachen Tigers. This is one of the most unheralded missions of the Indian Air Force (IAF), which binds border and distant people to the plains of the 'mainland nation' below. Actually, the service is strictly not that of the IAF but of the Arunachal Pradesh state government's Department of Supply, located at Mohanbari base, which has contracted the IAF for a fat fee. Of course, the state government is not paying the fee—the centre is, through a complex network of arrangements involving the Ministry of Defence and the Ministry of Home Affairs, arguably the most powerful arm of the Government of India. Mohanbari is part of the civilian airport that serves Dibrugarh and the prosperous tea belt of upper Assam. Between 1998 and 2003, the IAF transported over 26,000 tons of goods to Arunachal and was paid more than ₹2 billion (about US $12 million) by the Arunachal government's Supply and Transport Department.

Tuting and Gelling have long been the last posts of India's border with

China. There are no highways leading here although successive governments have made brave announcements about building one across Arunachal Pradesh's many river valleys. Trekking paths, rugged, single lane roads and the helicopter service remain the only sure sources of communication and transport in the twenty-first century. Building a highway would be an extremely challenging task given the geological barriers (soft sliding sediment) as well as the very geography of the place with its deep valleys, swift rivers and fragile ecosystems. The Chinese, on the other hand, have had a much smoother run of things: the large expanse of flatlands on the Tibetan Plateau has meant that they could lay hundreds of kilometres of specially strengthened railway track, able to survive the extreme Tibetan winters without cracking or falling apart, and connect Lhasa to the Middle Kingdom. They have improved road connections and mobile access but haven't bothered about the environment. Today, Tibet is being pillaged for its raw materials in the manner of a colony, with minerals being mined and the upper reaches of the Brahmaputra, the Yarlung Tsangpo dammed and used for producing energy. Their infrastructure drive has meant that they have brought their rail and land bridge to the lip of the Himalayan edge, overlooking the Arunachal foothills and the Assam plains, for long the object of their desire and interest.

To China, this remains the unresolved question and one on which it is not prepared to budge, for the boundary problem has over a century of political negotiations behind it. Let us for the moment, leave aside the Tibetan declarations of sovereignty from the eighth to the nineteenth centuries; those are matters for the history books. It is not what we wish to discuss here. What we will be looking at, to a degree, is how an unsettled problem grew out of years of incomplete discussions for which the British are squarely to blame. It is on the cusp of that irresolution that many of the Northeast's internal problems lie for it is part of the arbitrariness of one-time great powers that they drew lines without considering the consequences and rarely by consulting the people whom those lines affected.

The high degree of sensitivity of Chinese governments, whether Nationalist (Kuomintang or KMT) under Chiang Kai-shek or Communist under Mao Zedong and Zhou Enlai, to map-making and border definitions was clear even in 1943 at the height of World War II, when China was struggling for survival under Japan. Chiang Kai-shek and his forces had been driven to Yunnan Province in the southwest where they survived as a result of Allied missions flown over the Hump of what is today's Arunachal Pradesh bringing supplies to his beleaguered forces, landing at airfields built out of freshly dug and levelled fields. On 20 April that year, the Chinese head counsellor of the European Department of the Waichiapu (foreign office of the KMT) sent for the British counsellor at Chungking and pointed out that one of the maps at an exhibition at the Charing Cross underground station in London showed 'Mongolia, Tibet and three eastern provinces as if they were not part of the Chinese Republic' and the Chinese government believed that those responsible for preparing these and similar maps 'had acted through ignorance and without any intention of giving offence. The Chinese Government could not however let these maps pass without a process or the Chinese people would receive the impression that their government acquiesced in the alienation of these territories which the Chinese people and their government had every intention of recovering.' Those last words are ominous and worth repeating: '...alienation of these territories which the Chinese people and their government had every intention of recovering'.[23]

To the Chinese, maps were not cartographic exercises or creations as much as historic assertions of righting perceived wrongs by other powers, a delineation of their political power and a proclamation of their place in the world. Even under a Nationalist government that hated the Communists (the latter went to war over the disputed territories in 1962), this fierce conviction, contestation and commitment to perceptions of inalienable borders and sovereign lands was unshakeable. This lies too at the heart of the cartographic and political dispute over which India and China have gone to war once and massed half a million troops on either side of the border or the Line of Actual Control in 1987 over Chinese efforts to build helipads in Sumdorong Chu in Arunachal Pradesh.[24]

There is another issue here: were India's freedom fighters and its entire leadership—from Mahatma Gandhi to Pandit Nehru, Vallabhbhai Patel, Maulana Abul Kalam Azad, C. Rajagopalachari and others—so caught up in the quest for Independence that they did not pay attention to this critical aspect until it was too late? Barring Nehru and to a degree Patel, they appeared too busy throwing out the British, battling the Muslim League, building a new nation and securing their own positions within the party and the system to be concerned about such matters. Thus, a region that turned history on its very pivot because of its role in World War II was completely ignored as far as precise territoriality, mapping and hence inclusion in the larger nationalist narrative were concerned.

After all, the defeat of the Japanese on two fronts in Asia is directly attributable to the Northeast, if for no other reason than for the simple fact of geography and where it was located in time and space: first, the land frontier with Burma in the battles of Kohima and Imphal and then in China, thanks to the great air bridge over the Hump, connecting China to Assam. It is not as if foreign policy questions were not debated or views were not formulated during the Independence movement, not only by the Congress but also by other parties including the Muslim League. The issue of Burma's freedom, of Ceylon and its Tamil tea garden workers, knowledge and concerns about the spreading movement against colonialism across the world, especially in Asia and Africa, spurred the imagination of many. Palestine was an issue that was strongly debated as was the creation of Israel; the creation of states on religious lines did not sit well in India with its history of a bloody Partition.[25] But there seemed to be a lack of understanding of the complexity of the Tibet issue and how it could develop in the future.

Foreign policy statements of the time by the Congress Party made numerous references to China's struggles for freedom from Japan's occupation as well as expressing hope for a time when it would be united and able to work with India, Burma, Malaya, Indonesia, Ceylon and the Middle East and formulate common policies for trade, defence, cultural and economic growth. Clearly, Nehru was the driving force behind such grand ideas. Yet, at the Asia Relations Conference in New Delhi in July 1947, a month before Independence, he found China fiercely contesting India's position on the border and causing not a little embarrassment. The Chinese delegation refused to enter the conference hall until a map of Asia showing Tibet as an independent country was removed. Although the Tibetan delegation remained in the conference, the Chinese insistence undermined India's position as host and clearly defined Chinese goals of restricting New Delhi's influence and ambitions of a leadership role in Asia. Thus, apart from abstract statements about the need for Asian unity and so on, the conference was unable to come up with anything substantial.

Years later, when the Chinese Communists had driven the Nationalists out of the mainland to Formosa (now Taiwan), the official position towards Nehru was extremely hostile, dubbing him a reactionary and bourgeois, deeply suspicious of him and India's future plans and opposing any middle road between the Communist Bloc and Western Alliance, which Nehru tried to develop by launching the Non-Aligned Movement.

PARTITION'S LEGACY

While we're on geography, it might be good to look at the Northeast again, that triangular shape of land wedged between Myanmar, Bangladesh, Bhutan and Tibet, with longer borders—and greater affinity—with its neighbours than it has with the rest of India. Partition's legacy is a landlocked region, without hinterlands and markets, distant from any major manufacturing centre and saddled with both huge natural resources and rich soils but few industries barring those brought by the British (tea, oil and gas) and the newer ones of a renter economy with infrastructure building, including the extractive ones of energy (hydroelectricity), limestone quarrying (for cement) and coal. A thin sliver of land connects it to mainland India, a point that all scholars are fond of referring to and which one of them described as the Chicken's Neck. This narrow corridor hosts highways, railways and oil and gas pipelines.

It is home to not less than 210 minority languages or languages spoken by populations ranging from 10,000 to a million. In fact, in 2010, a National Geographic expedition, which climbed steep hills, passed through misty valleys and forded frothing mountain streams, located a new language in a pocket of Arunachal Pradesh. The new language is Koro, part of the Tibeto-Burman language family (of which there are 400 languages), and it is spoken by fewer than 1,000 persons. Indeed, of the 325 languages listed in K. S. Singh's monumental *People of India* series, the largest number belong to the Tibeto-Burman group and of them 175 are found in the Northeast. The number of dialects is vaster. There are twenty-two scheduled languages mentioned in the Constitution of India. One study says those enumerated in the census are but a linguistic subtraction of the 1,600 identified by Indians as their 'mother tongue'. To give another taste of the complexity of the place, if you travel several kilometres in any direction in Assam, the most populous state of the Northeast, apart from Assamese, you could also find other minority language speakers—Rabha, Deori, Bodo, Mishing, Khasi, Tiwa, as well as major ones like Bangla, Hindi and Nepali, to mention a handful. All this within a span of 30 to 50 kilometres from the principal commercial hub of Guwahati. A survey says that forty-five languages or dialects are spoken in Assam alone. This was one of the earliest places in South Asia to be 'globalized': tea and oil made those connections in the nineteenth century under the British and the East India Company. The inland waterways provided a major link to the outside world, with vessels taking Assam tea and jute down the sprawling Brahmaputra to Calcutta through East Bengal and bringing in commodities from Bengal. These connections were weakened by Partition and closed by the 1965 Indo-Pakistan war. A natural advantage was lost. After nearly half a century, India and Bangladesh are trying to make up for lost time and huge economic losses caused by the folly of Partition and conflict by reviving and renewing those trade routes.

What is also not often understood is that the Northeast suffered the impact of not one but two Partitions. The first was the 1947 separation of Burma (annexed by the British in 1885 and the third Anglo-Burmese war which was no war but a devastation and loot of Burma); this split the Nagas and Mizos between two sovereignties, devastating kinship relations and trade connectivity. Then the Radcliffe Award divided the Khasis, Garos, Hajongs and Rabhas of Assam from their kin in East Pakistan and also the Reang of Tripura. Today, the Mizos are in three countries: Bangladesh, India and Myanmar.[26]

Such disruption was disastrous for the local economies and people: connectivity was broken, not merely fractured. A truck takes seventy-two hours from Agartala, one of the southeastern-most points of the region, to Kolkata. It takes only half this time to reach Chennai. The easiest route is the most commonsensical—via Dhaka: as we learnt in school, the shortest distance between two points is a straight line, not a series of zigzags and U-turns. Because of political mistrust and sharp differences between India and Bangladesh, especially in the non-Awami League time—or more than half of Bangladesh's freedom since 1971—the first Kolkata-Dhaka bus route began in 1998, the one from Agartala to Dhaka in 2003 and in 2015, Mamata Banerjee, chief minister of West Bengal, flagged off the first bus to connect Kolkata to Agartala via Dhaka. For Bangladesh, the key no-no word has been 'transit' because, according to Dhaka, it connotes concession; 'experts' have transformed that word into a wonderful diplomatic phrase: 'transshipment'. Making a straight line has many hurdles; it took forty-four years of trust building to enable a simple route to emerge.

Today a language that is spoken from the India border in Pangsau Pass to the Kachin heartland of Mannerplaw is not Hindi, nor is it Burmese, Chin or Kachin. It is Nagamese, a pidgin of Assamese and local Naga dialects, developed by plains traders and evangelists who brought it there to enter 'native' lands and access and use their products and markets. In time and in turn, it was expanded and expounded by the Naga guerrilla fighters under Angami Zapu Phizo and then by Thuingaleng Muivah and his followers as they trekked to Ruili and the China border to what they thought was their promised land. Accounts say that the Indian Nagas behaved at times with brutality when they enforced a rigid form of Christianity on the poorer, uneducated Nagas of Burma, often unshod, poorly fed and fearful in that hostile terrain.[27]

THE FANTASY AND THE REALITY

So, where do we go with the litany of abuse and injustice that we have uncovered? These reach back in time and there are many more stories to be told. What we have heard and read so far are just a sudden slash of the wind (for does not the wind have claws?), a whisper of the harm that has come and gone over the decades, if not centuries. These stories are a talisman for our age and a reminder that all that is brutal is not behind us yet and persists every day in the many lives in the region we inhabit and the neighbourhood around—in Myanmar that was Burma, in Bhutan, in Bangladesh that was East Pakistan, in the Tibet Autonomous Region that was Tibet and now is part of the People's Republic of China.

There are old histories and experiences that are also of recent vintage. So where do we begin, for there seem to be many beginnings just as we cannot end now, for this is not yet a time for closure.

James C. Scott[28] of Yale University reflects on this in his book on the restive groups of Southeast Asia, where he talks of how for hundreds, no, thousands of years, 'the disparate groups that now reside in Zomia (a mountainous region the size of Europe that consists of portions of seven Asian countries) have fled the projects of the organized state societies that surround them—slavery, conscription, taxes, corvée labor, epidemics, and warfare'. Zomia is a name coined by Willem van Schendel, a Dutch scholar and social historian. It remains an imaginary land, for the different groups are too disparate to form a nation, and have remained isolated among their many hill ranges, not just separate from each other but often in conflict with each other. This was explained by a Naga friend who said that his village had been 'at war' with another village of the same Chakhesang tribe for decades over a disputed boundary line—whether it began at a stream or along the wall of a particular farm.[29]

Of course, these groups do not speak a common language, not that one would be acceptable to all. Yet, the name is perhaps derived from the demands by the Mizo and Chin groups of Mizoram state in Northeast India and of Myanmar respectively, who are the only ethnic groups who have demanded a separate land by a similar name: Zomiland, with a vision for a Zomi people or hill people. This land is to be carved out of existing territories that span national borders. Mizo translates into highlander, to differentiate themselves from the people of the plains, who are obviously resented. Scholars like James Scott, Bengt Karlsson[30] and others also refer to hill people as 'uplanders'. Indeed, Scott's book is intriguingly titled *The Art of Not Being Governed: An Anarchist History of Upland Southeast Asia*, where he looks upon many ethnic groups which are divided by national boundaries as stateless people who are seeking self-determination in a rugged, rich but unforgiving landscape. And he describes their strategies at remaining stateless, assuming, incorrectly in my view, that despite their history of migration, movement and straddling hill ranges and new nations, they have sought to remain so: 'physical dispersion in rugged terrain; agricultural practices that enhance mobility; pliable ethnic identities; devotion to prophetic, millenarian leaders; and maintenance of a largely oral culture that allows them to reinvent their histories and genealogies as they move between and around states'.

◆

Thus, apart from the Crown Colony Plan, the stuttering efforts at delineating frontiers and borders in the Northeast, there is a history from earlier times of resisting the state that cannot be denied, of the divisions between hill and plain, hill dweller and plains resident. This demonstrates that here in the highlands of the Eastern Himalayas and the lands in between lie the natural homelands of Scott's and van Schendel's Zomia, where the reach of the state is constrained by geography. Flowing from the hills of Northeast India into those of Southeast Asia, a large number of ethnic groups reside in Zomia—a mountainous region comprising parts of Burma, Cambodia, China, India, Laos, Vietnam and Thailand. Scott describes it as the largest remaining area that has not been integrated into a nation state. However, this is not one set of people or places located in one contiguous nation. And divergent geographies ensure that there are many Zomias, not one.

A review of Scott's book on the uplands of Asia remarked that:

...for over two thousand years, the people living in the highlands of Zomia have lived outside the reach of the lowland government. The standard view of these 'hill people' is that they are remnants of the pre-state period and represent a primitive form of living. In contrast, those that have moved into the lowlands and become part of the state system have progressed and become civilized. It should be noted that governments and those involved in international development efforts tend to hold a similar view towards those living outside the reach of the state in other settings as well. Indeed, this view underpins the efforts to 'fix' the various institutions (economic, legal, political and social) in societies around the world in the hope of bringing modernity to people who are viewed as primitive.[31]

Given the possibility of being subject to predatory behaviour by states—including conscription, slavery, excessive taxes, forced labour, and war—people make the deliberate choice to move into the hills as an act of state avoidance. Indeed, geography has become a strategic resource that can be used by ordinary people to avoid the grabbing hand of the state. In the case of Southeast Asia, migration to the mountains not only creates space in the form of distance, but also friction in the form of terrain between the hill people and the state. Settled rice cultivation was also an effective means of consolidating political power in the lowlands of Southeast Asia prior to the twentieth century. The underlying logic is that a sustainable state requires concentrated manpower, which in turn requires flat expanses of land that can be used over long periods of time to grow sedentary agriculture.

There is another reality that drives these different peoples who were 'there before us'. Their swidden or slash and burn cultivation techniques go back to an ancient time as do their oral narratives, fashioned through storytelling of families, villages and heroes down the centuries. In fact, not less than five million families in five countries—Nepal, Bhutan, India (Northeast), Bangladesh and Myanmar—are dependent on swidden agriculture for both livelihoods and survival. These have flexible kinship structures and similar community exercises such as jhum or slash and burn. This form of agriculture remains, much to the frustration of national and state planners, outside the system of government and the settled, sedentary cropping that most governments of these countries seek to promote. That sedentary cultivation (largely growing rice with other cereals and a range of quick-growing vegetables) is in the valleys shows where the power of the state lies, where its authority vests and where it draws its loyalty from. Rice cultivation of the plains of northern and southern India, of Bangladesh and Nepal, of Myanmar and Thailand, Cambodia, Laos and Vietnam were assertions not just of settled agriculture but of state formation in those areas which organizers of empires, kingdoms, companies and nations sought to push upward and outward to the outer reaches and boundaries, including the uplands or hill areas. In all of these countries, the colonizers were the people from the plains, constantly seeking new acquisitions, populations and resources.

While the hills of Zomia provide a safe haven for people wishing to avoid state activities driven from the plains, they cannot escape it altogether with the state and its overwhelming security apparatus seeking aggressively to lock communities into national structures by laws, taxes, handouts, buyouts and buy-ins, fences, borders and sheer force. In state after state or nation

after nation, from the edge of the Northeast of India through Myanmar
and Thailand, Cambodia, Laos and Vietnam, this is a visible, lived reality.

Yet, people have been part of both upland and plains communities
for centuries with other ethnic groups with a mixture of accommodation
and tension. Take, for example, a pocket of my home state of Assam: small
communities of the Bodo tribe are to be found in Dhemaji and Dibrugarh
in the north; there are Yadava milk producers originally from Mithila in
Bihar, hundreds of kilometres to the west, on the islands of Jorhat and
Dibrugarh who supply milk to the bustling towns on the riverside. In
the distant Tin Mile Ghat on the edge of Arunachal Pradesh, thinly clad
Nepali herders scurry across the roiling waters in flimsy-looking dugouts
with cans of milk to be loaded on to the ferry: this is part of a daily ritual
of the passenger ferry—picking up their produce between Oriamghat, a
nine-hour ride upstream, and taking it to the tea capital of Dibrugarh.
Despite all the violence and harm that armed groups and the state's forces
have inflicted on each other and on ordinary people over the decades in
Assam, the 'milk ferry' or 'milk special' is part of an economic and trade
network that works on one core cashless principle: trust. This has not come
easily but it has developed over the decades as people learnt the nuances
of business and interdependence, through migration, settlement as well as
transporting goods.

Some communities such as the Santhals, Orans and Adivasis of central
and eastern India were shifted there like cattle, hustled to labour camps in
Calcutta and then sent by boat on the Brahmaputra to Assam where they
were conscripted to work as tea labour. Many died in the malarial swamps
and forests of the state, without access to medical care or basic living
conditions. Others moved on their own. They were not always settled in one
place. With new communities came new settlements, languages, ethnicities
and identities, which positioned one group against another except where
the latter accepted assimilation into a larger group.

The concepts of borders and identities changed with the coming of the
British and the colonial determination to fix locations, map and name people
and exploit resources for commercial use. The map as well as the physical
ecology and geography of the Northeast, and of all of India, underwent
overwhelming changes. At the root of much of today's disputations are older
disagreements transposed onto a nation-state that is seventy years old and
on federal units that are even newer. The sharp border problems between
Assam and Nagaland go back to the giving, of what are seen as original
Naga homelands and forests in the Brahmaputra Valley to Assam by the

British in 1826. This was the area between Golaghat, Sivasagar and Jorhat, where Nagas hunted, lived and foraged and went on pillaging expeditions. Today, they are neighbours in a nation. But we still have to deal with the old animosities, of Zomia coming into confrontation with the state of the plains and the mainland.

The centre treats the borders as its frontier, where its sovereignty begins and the rights of others end. These borders are boundary stones to its integrity and existence—those who challenge it, no matter where they're from, no matter that they lived and existed with their own ways of life for hundreds perhaps thousands of years before the 'modern state' came into being, are not to be tolerated. It will brook no challenge, countenance no threat, accept no divergence of view, oppose every divergent strand and seek to bind every 'separate' ethnic group into a nationalist theme that only it can dictate, design and develop. Any opposing view is a threat to the state and is to be met with utmost force to crush, curb, intimidate and humiliate the opponent or those holding an opposing view to the point of capitulation or acceptance of a superior power.

What began in colonial years as an imposition by foreign occupying powers has become a mandate of national government, independent of the past yet beholden to it in terms of its use of force and the provisions of law, harking back to that very colonial past. We do not live down our colonial legacy or denounce it; instead, we revel in it, using the very laws used to browbeat and humiliate us to do the same to those who oppose us, who believe they are right and, this, in the view of the state, is both their wrongdoing and undoing.

It is interesting that in all the countries I have travelled to bordering the Northeast—Myanmar, Nepal, China, Thailand, India and Bangladesh—it is the weaker, poorer, fragmented and 'different' border people who are bearing the brunt of being 'different', by raising their voice against insensitive and insensate states and their uniformed and un-uniformed minions, uninformed media and scholars who toe the government line. As recently as the 1960s, the Naga and Mizo armed groups fighting against India were called 'hostiles' by the government and the media: they were not dignified by being described as insurgents or even by the name of their organization. They were just dismissed as a bunch of bandits up to no good and bent on harming the interests of government, which, of course, was determined to 'protect' the rights of its citizens—or rather, its own rights and interests. It is hardly surprising that in area after area, ranging from Assam to Burma's hill states, Bangladesh's Chittagong Hill Tracts to

Bhutan's plains, the victimized and vulnerable groups were ethnic minorities compared to the larger 'mainland' groups and population. These groups often lived on top of vast natural, mineral, forest and agricultural resources that the centre wanted to control. It would not countenance the existence of a fragmented or discontented periphery.

Laws are used to control, intimidate and divide. The legal restrictions in place are, unsurprisingly, similar in non-democracies like China and Myanmar as well as in a 'democracy' like India. The Armed Forces (Special Powers) Act which has been in place in the Northeast since 1958 and is one of the most reviled and hated laws in the region and the country with the power to snuff out individual lives, destroy homes and detain people (all on suspicion that they are part of an insurgent or terrorist group) resonates with similar legislation in Burma, Bangladesh and China. But our focus is closer home, in India, and that is where we begin the larger journey. In all these areas, conflicts arise between a reactive centre and a pro-active periphery. And in this violence, women became the primary, most vulnerable and easiest targets.[32]

Perhaps the concept of Zomia can be linked with the idea of ethnic divergence, of appearances, of what many speak of as race, to emphasize differences but also to strengthen the affinity between groups of a particular phenotype. This spans national borders with ease. The Swiss scholar and linguist Georg van Driem emphasizes how perceptions matter:

> As a species, we have always been obsessed with how we look and in which ways we appear to be similar or different from one another. The ancient Hindu caste system and the apartheid system of South Africa were just two of many systems based on our perceptions of caste, tribe and race.
>
> [The] Eastern Himalaya from the Dhaulagiri to the Liángshan, and more particularly the region comprising Nepal, Sikkim, Bhutan, southeastern Tibet and northeastern India, furnished the cradle for the ethnogenesis of all East Asian language families: Trans-Himalayan, Hmong-Mien, Austroasiatic and Austro-Tai, i.e. every major language of East and South East Asia as we know it today emerged from this little carpet of Asia, basically not more than 1,000 km on an east west axis and 700 km on a north south axis.[33]

This lies, significantly, within the very tapestry of the 'fan' of rivers that Susan Conway spoke of.

In ethnic matters relating to this region, the issues of race and racism, of discrimination and exclusion also come up. So do processes of inclusion and inclusiveness and what can be described as the nazar or gaze of the 'other'. For in a region that is as complex as the Northeast with over 220 communities and almost as many dialects and languages, each group can safely be described as 'the other' in the view of a second, third or fourth person. On top of that is the nature of the public perception, the gaze, from the 'mainland' to the periphery, always seeking to keep it peripheral and perhaps obsequious, a role that Zomians[34] find hard if not impossible to accept. Dominance is met with resistance and resistance with organized violence. The state survives, conflicts endure, ordinary people suffer and receive no justice. Inequity grows, poverty thrives, hatred and violence are energized. Suspicion sweeps the land and its people.

These reflect the visible divergences between the mainstream Indian narrative and that of its periphery in the Northeast. What is often ignored is the fact that the British government made not one but three efforts in rapid succession to hive the Northeast away from the rest of India, almost at the very end of World War II. In contrast, successive Indian governments have made many efforts to attract, pressure, brush aside, support and embrace the region. This has taken many forms of major, medium and minor political and economic efforts apart from changes in social structures that have evolved over decades. There have been army interventions to crush armed uprisings and challenges to the state, massive economic packages and infrastructure projects to raise basic conditions, though these are received with extensive cynicism. There are also innumerable committees and commissions to address the grievances—real or imagined—of the people of the area. While many leaders speak glowingly of the area's natural resource wealth and the opportunities before it, few have articulated a vision for the area that has distance, depth, resonance and sensitivity. Just one of these qualities is not enough. The tossing of money into projects and the ideas of a few are unlikely to work. They seek to connect a dominant statist narrative to the complex concerns and issues of the people of the region. The latter figure but little in the architecture that is sought to be built.

Jawaharlal Nehru, much derided and criticized by contemporary politicians and others, perhaps put it most elegantly when he spoke of the need to consider the needs of the communities of the Northeast and strongly advised against straitjacketing them, believing that 'integration' and 'mainstreaming' would create more problems than anything else. He declared at one point:

The problem of these areas is to make the people feel that they have

perfect freedom to live their own lives and to develop according to
their wishes and genius. India should signify not only a protecting
force but a liberating one. Any conception that India is ruling them
and that they are the ruled, or that the customs and habits with which
they are unfamiliar are going to be imposed upon them, will alienate
them, and make our frontier problems more difficult.

We shall see how this went awry, including in Nehru's time and with his
knowledge. In the clash between Nehruvian idealism and Northeastern
complexity, both suffered grievously.

As we have seen, the British also added to the bubbling cauldron with
one plan after another. The first was the Crown Colony Plan; the second
was the Cabinet Mission Plan of Sir Stafford Cripps that sought to lump
Assam with Muslim-majority Bengal. The third was Britain's failure to
draw a specific border formalizing Tibet's boundary with Northeast India,
an uncertain legacy that haunts a frozen and embittered frontier.

Could it be that an opportunity for change lies not in what India and
China say to each other but in what the new Tibetan leadership in exile
says? Is there escape from the 1914 Simla Agreement that even the British
Foreign Office, within a couple of decades of its signature, was disinclined to
take seriously? Although an introduction is hardly the place to speculate on
a way forward, perhaps there is merit in the remarks of the Tibetan prime
minister in exile, Dr Lobsang Sangay, who has discussed a treaty between
China and Tibet (821 CE) and reflected how in the thirteenth century, Tibet
'stood at the junction of two competing empires, Imperial China and the
Mongol Empire'. He talks about the Panchsheel Treaty, which was in reality
a trade convention and byproduct of the Simla Convention, which was
renewed every decade from 1914 onwards until 1954 when the Chinese
only agreed to renew it for eight years. At the end of the eight years, they
attacked on two fronts and inflicted a humiliating defeat on India.

Dr Sangay raised a simple point: China has consistently rejected the Simla
Convention or Agreement of 1914. Yet its leaders still speak glowingly of
the Panchsheel Agreement:[35] If the Panchsheel Agreement is valid even after
the 1962 war which violated each of the agreement's five principles, then it
becomes evident that the Simla Convention is equally valid... If governments
claim the legitimacy of the Panchsheel Agreement, then they cannot escape
the fact that it originated from its mother, the Simla Convention.

What do neighbours across borders, strangers who glower at, spy on,
trade with, snap at, threaten, walk in and out of each other's 'disputed
territory', yet also smile, chat and wave at each other have to say about

that? Even China's supremo has declared that these principles have not just stood the test of time but also have been the bedrock of his country's foreign policy for over half a century.

Chinese President Xi Jinping said the five principles have served as the cornerstone of China's independent foreign policy of peace during the past six decades. He said the principles have withstood the test of international vicissitudes and have been widely accepted and observed by the international community.[36]

If this is so—that China truly accepts Panchsheel and the five principles, how can it deny the essence of Lobsang Sangay's logic?

A. G. Noorani fiercely faults Nehru's approach in the negotiations with China: for his failure to turn to history and facts instead of relying on 'historically untrue' positions which have put India in a negotiating and diplomatic bind for decades, what he calls 'a total disconnect between the facts of history and India's policy on the boundary problem and later boundary dispute'.

India's conflicts on its eastern borders with the Nagas and Mizos, with Manipur and groups in Assam stem from a different reading of history, facts and perceptions as well as the differing idea of borders, nations and nationalities. These were one-time smaller neighbours, especially the first two without much intercourse with the mainland, which were absorbed into British India and then subsequently into Independent India. Each side, the majority and the minority, the government and the 'underground', the army soldier and his guerrilla opponent, the officials in power and their rivals, the parallel governments which existed as virtual entities in cyberspace and in different places wherever the insurgents were located—each became the 'other' in multiple forms, at the district, village and state levels as well as at the 'national' level. The following chapters tell their tale when resistance abounded, how approaches informed by power and ill-informed by facts on the ground drew a robust response. And how, in order to sustain assumptions of an overweening nationhood, one law was used to dominate them all, one law to bind and control them.

The issue of borders has many interrelated layers, each more complex than the other, whether it is Tibet, China and India or the southern border of the United States or between Ukraine and Russia. Deeply disparate and embedded ideologies are described by Stephen E. Flynn, with reference to the US. Reconciling the demands of a globalizing economy that relies on greater openness with security concerns that have an opposed imperative is a policy dilemma that many governments face today. 'There is a potential train wreck in the making,' says Flynn. 'Moving in one direction are those who would like to see national borders become as seamless as possible, while coming from the opposite direction are those charged with homeland security who would like to stop would-be terrorists, contraband, criminals, and illegal migrants at border crossings.'[37]

Chapter 1

A CRY IN THE DARK: AFSPA, MANORAMA AND IROM

impunity[1] *(noun) exemption from punishment or freedom from the injurious consequences of an action: the impunity enjoyed by military officers implicated in civilian killings; protestors burned flags on the streets with impunity.*

—Collins English Dictionary & Thesaurus

As dawn crept slowly across the Manipur night, the armed men took aim at the small figure running away from them. A few short bursts of automatic gunfire, and the lone woman fell with a hopeless cry, crumpling to the cool earth below.

A few days later the sentries at the main gate to Kangla—the historic fort that was once both royal capital and spiritual centre of power before the British snuffed out the independence of Manipur's kingdom towards the end of the nineteenth century—curiously but casually watched a group of women walking towards them. Moments afterwards, their faces were flushed with horror, embarrassment and helplessness as they averted their gaze. For the women, several middle-aged, a few elderly, some young, most of them activists and veterans of many protests, had ripped the clothes from their bodies and now stood naked, with sagging breasts and flowing hair, some thin and others heavy hipped, before the stunned soldiers, and unfurled banners abusing the army. 'Indian Army, Rape Us, Kill Us' read one banner. The searing images flashed across India and the world, shaking the edifice of power and silencing even the strongest of votaries of military power, shaming, scorching, outraging. Human rights groups, civil society leaders, women and other activists called for justice for Thangjam Manorama.

For those weeks after her death, Manorama became as well known a symbol of state oppression and the ugliness of the AFSPA as the other icon of the rights struggle in Manipur—a frail woman with a nasogastric feeding tube, then in the third year of a hunger strike demanding the law's repeal. The hunger striker was Irom Sharmila, who had gone on a fast on 2 November 2000 to protest the killing of twelve civilians who were waiting at a bus stop at Malom, near Imphal. They just happened to be in the line of fire of angry soldiers of the Central Reserve Police Force (CRPF), blinded by rage and thirsting for revenge after the deaths of colleagues in a deadly ambush by Manipuri insurgents a short distance away.

While the Manorama incident is well known and is often cited as an example of human rights violations in the Northeast, it needs a brief recantation. On a night in June 2004, a unit of the Assam Rifles surrounded and entered Manorama's home in Imphal. They knew exactly whom they wanted to get and pulled her out of her room, sleepy-eyed and frightened, wearing a phanek, the Manipuri-style sarong, and a blouse. The household was terrified; the soldiers slapped the men, shouted at them and then hit the girl and poured water on her. They took her into another room where the family could hear more sounds of beating. This was in total violation of a code of conduct laid down by the Supreme Court of India[2] and of laws existing across all Indian states. Throughout India, if a detention, arrest or interrogation of a woman was being planned by government authorities, it was mandatory for a female civil, paramilitary or police officer to accompany the unit (army, police or otherwise).[3] After some time the sounds of hitting from the small room stopped. The uniformed men emerged, dragging a fearful Manorama and pushed her into a waiting vehicle. They were, as the havildar who led the operation in the absence of an officer said, trying to get her to rat out fellow comrades in the banned, pro-independence People's Liberation Army (PLA), people they could pick up during the course of the night and put through a process of inquisition. The cycle of pressure and fear was to continue but not much longer for Manorama that night.

The twenty-four-year-old woman had been a member of the PLA, one of the small active rebel units in the Manipur Valley with a history of guerrilla warfare of over twenty years. She had been a low-level courier within the organization but, unable to endure a tough life in rough terrain and uncertain conditions, had returned to her family. The calm was not to last.

The unit had gone to Manorama's house that night after an underground informant or spotter, in the pay of the Assam Rifles, had told his handlers that she had returned. He placed her as a prize catch, Number 3 in the PLA hierarchy. That Lieutenant General Bhopinder Singh, the head of the Assam Rifles in Shillong, had fallen for this line was clear as we sat in his large and sumptuously decorated drawing room, with its lush sofas, cane chairs and sparkling glass, bamboo and brass mementos. I remember being surprised that though such a senior army man, he was a teetotaller who sipped a nimbu pani while I nursed a whisky. 'Can you imagine how excited they were?' said Singh, then director general of the force which was headquartered in Shillong. He had recently taken over and was scornful of demands by human rights groups for an investigation into Manorama's death.

Through that night, the unit took Manorama from place to place, hoping she would help them nail other 'UGs' as underground activists were called. She didn't. Perhaps she didn't know. As dawn approached and their task remained incomplete, frustration was setting in among the captors. Manorama wanted a bathroom break: she wanted to urinate in privacy and a short distance from the unit. She was bound, like a domesticated animal, by one hand to a long thick rope, the end of which was held by a soldier. She walked to the side of the road and then, shaking off the rope, began to run. We don't know what desperation impelled her, what knowledge pushed her. She probably knew what was going to happen, she certainly didn't want to be raped before she was shot (one report says that she was not raped before being killed although most people do not believe this, citing postmortem reports that showed bullet wounds to her vagina and lower parts of the body).

I wonder what the havildar had shouted to his unit, seeing their captive trying to escape. Did he cry out: 'The bitch is escaping, stop her'? Or did he possibly shout: 'She's escaping, kill her'? Both are conjectures. But what happened afterwards is not: two soldiers opened fire with their AK-56s on Manorama, an easy target, her back towards them, unable to flee swiftly in her phanek. Two short bursts slammed into her, killing her instantly, tossing her into a nearby ditch by a rice field. They later pulled her out and dumped her body in the field. That is where the villagers, who fearfully crept out of their homes after the misty light had dawned and the jeep and its killers had left, found her.

To date, Manorama's killers have not been brought to justice. Not in a civil court. We do know that they faced a court martial but the quantum of punishment is not easily accessible. What I did find out later was that at least one of the men involved in the incident was more concerned about the reactions of his family to the rape charge.[4] They were suspended from their posts, transferred and later dismissed with their pensions and allowances intact. We do not know their names. Yet everyone knows Manorama's story. But no one knows who killed her.

I am reminded of Edgar Allan Poe who writes of impunity in *The*

Cask of Amontillado: 'I must not only punish, but punish with impunity. A wrong is unredressed when retribution overtakes its redresser. It is equally unredressed when the avenger fails to make himself felt as such to him who has done the wrong.' Manorama's case is a clear example of what Samir Das, a political scientist from Kolkata, calls the existence of 'exclusivity zones' of law and justice, where different individuals and organizations are treated differently to the general population and where what are regarded as 'normal' civil and criminal justice laws, used across India, are not functional in zones of exception such as Manipur, Assam and Nagaland.

Indeed, these conflictual conditions remind us of the three elements of conflict induced deaths across the world, an index that has been developed by the Uppsala Conflict Data Programme (UCDP) of Sweden, which has been working in these fields for years and is respected internationally for its methodology and accuracy of research as well as the depth of its analysis. These three segments, relating to deaths in such conflicts, were defined as state-based violence (the use of armed force between the government of a state and one or two organized armed groups; one-sided conflict where the government of a state or a formally organized group (or groups) uses violence against civilians. And third, non-state violence, which witnesses the use of force between two (or more) organized groups, neither of which is the government of a state.[5] All three conditions have prevailed in the Northeast for decades though they appear to be abating, as we shall see later in the book.

◆

And though we still do not know, many years later, who killed Manorama, we do know that her death and the public reaction to it was like a punch to the solar plexus of the centre followed by an upper cut to the jaw. New Delhi was reeling and groping for solutions. In a masterly stroke, seeing light through the haze, it did what all governments across the world do, especially in India and South Asia, to buy time, divert attention and cool public anger. At the initiative of Prime Minister Manmohan Singh, it bowed to public pressure and appointed a committee, under a retired Supreme Court justice. The committee would review the draconian law that protected Manorama's killers from prosecution. This was the arbitrary AFSPA, an Act dating to 1958. The Justice Jeevan Reddy Committee, the government said, should suggest how the act could be made 'more humane'.

The committee did not follow the well-trodden path of many similar government-appointed groups. It bucked the trend and, in the words of a top security official, gave the centre a 'report we can't implement'.

On a sunny but chilly November afternoon in 2005 in Imphal, the capital of Manipur, witnesses and victims of conflict and atrocities of the state began their testimony before the committee against a law that the committee itself was to describe as a 'symbol of hatred and oppression'. The Act had been extensively used, especially in Manipur, and its neighbours, Assam, Nagaland and Mizoram. It is here at the edge of the nation that the idea of its political civilization hangs, connected to the mainland, by bunches of alternating slim and thick threads, some frayed, others strong, yet buffeted by uncertainty and human rights violations. It is also here that the law was first tested and then used across the region to curb risings for separation and independence. There were five of us on the committee, including Justice B. P. Jeevan Reddy, a calm and reflective judge, who had earlier been chairman of the Law Commission of India. The others were three former senior government officials—Lieutenant General Vasantha Raghavan, a highly decorated army officer who had seen action in three wars and had headed the army's military operations wing; P. P. Shrivastav, a veteran of administrative service in Assam and Arunachal Pradesh with a stint in Manipur as adviser to the governor; Professor S. B. Nakade, a former vice chancellor of Marathwada University and a friend of the home minister, the ever dapper Shivraj Patil. I was the fifth and the only non-government member. Also I was in a minority—the only person with an unambiguous position on AFSPA—that it needed extensive review at the very least and repeal at the most.

The situation in Imphal Valley was characterized by a bandh that greeted us on arrival at Imphal airport. Effigies of the committee were being burnt and 'Go Back' slogans were peppering the empty streets at crucial points where we were bound to see them, though we had been driven in a long convoy with heavy security. There was a deep and palpable sense of unease, suspicion and anger. It was into this fog of rhetoric and bitterness, alienation and anger that we had flown in.

At hearing after hearing, we listened to stories of pain and loss accompanied by a bitter sense of injustice. At a later hearing, among those present was an elderly Manipuri woman had come with her son, daughter-in-law and their child. She waited in dignity and silence as her son and daughter-in-law testified before the committee. The young woman's husband, the elder son of the family, had gone to fish in a pond early one morning. He did not return. His body was found near the pond, shot in one of the unending 'encounters' between security forces and 'underground' cadres.

Or at least that was the official version. The victims are always silent and silenced. There are no witnesses. Or, if there are, they are too fearful to speak out. We listened. What can you say to such pain and loss? It was the end of another long day of hearing testimony from victims of armed oppression under AFSPA. Justice Reddy thanked the family and as they got up to leave, the older woman stopped, swung her shawl over her shoulders and declared in a voice that brooked no interference and which commanded our attention: 'I too wish to say something.' She spoke in Hindi, so that everyone could understand: 'You are all wise people, you will listen to us, you will write a report and I hope we will get justice. But even if nothing happens, I wish to say just one thing to you. I wish simply that no mother of this country goes through what I have gone through. That is my only wish.'

We sat in silence, stunned by the power, urgency and emotion in her words. That, in my view, was the tipping point for the committee, which compelled it to demand the repeal of a 'hated' law. Even today, I cannot speak of her dignified declaration, either in private conversation or public interaction, without my eyes smarting. Some images and words endure.

Manorama wasn't the only figure whose unseen presence cast a shadow over the committee and reminded us of its mandate. Another woman, who had lived for years in a small room of a government hospital not far from the location of the hearings, preceded Manorama as the face and voice of opposition to AFSPA. Irom Sharmila had been on a hunger strike for nearly sixteen years, from 2 November 2000 until 9 August 2016. For all those years, the 'Iron Lady' of Manipur, as she is known, was force-fed through a plastic nasogastric tube and kept away from visitors and media, from whom the Manipur and central government wanted to 'protect' her. Her prison term was renewed every six months as she was charged with an attempt to commit suicide. Hers was a fast for a political cause, not an effort to kill herself as the government kept saying. The demand was for the repeal of AFSPA. Having repeatedly stated that her fast would end the day AFSPA was repealed, her decision to call off her hunger strike in 2016 and contest elections while the act was still being enforced in Manipur came as a surprise to her supporters. Sharmila's battle for the removal of AFSPA continued, but shifted to the political arena where she launched a political party ambitiously called the Peoples' Resurgence and Justice Alliance (PRAJA). The party was crushed in the March 2017 elections and Sharmila herself met a humiliating defeat, brushed aside by her rival, Okram Ibobi Singh, the state's chief minister. She got only ninety votes, showing that support for her cause didn't translate into trust in her as a politician.

Manorama's story is also that of impunity, enshrined in the laws that endow army and paramilitary personnel with the capacity to inflict extreme harm on men and women, laws that have existed in one form or another since the times of the British. These laws apply the principle of maximum use of force to restore public order and security and what the state justifies as decisive and often necessary use of deadly coercion.

Impunity cannot be measured. But it is a demonstration of how the state and non-state actors react to each other, at times in opposition, at other times conniving with each other to oppress the weak and vulnerable who must survive both (the state and non-state actors) in order to simply live. New Delhi invariably seeks to assert its dominance over a peripheral centre[6] like the Northeastern region, which also calls for special treatment in terms of laws and policies because of the area's 'difference'. AFSPA represents another strategy to tackle the region which, in the view of this dominant narrative, is necessary to protect national integrity.

Of the six clauses of the law, among the most controversial is that which states:

> Any commissioned officer, warrant officer, non-commissioned officer or any other person of equivalent rank in the armed forces may, in a disturbed area, *if he is of opinion that it is necessary so to do for the maintenance of public order* [my emphasis], after giving such due warning as he may consider necessary, fire upon or otherwise use force, even to the causing of death, against any person who is acting in contravention of any law or order for the time being in force in the disturbed area prohibiting the assembly of five or more persons or the carrying of weapons or of things capable of being used as weapons or of fire-arms, ammunition or explosive substances.[7]

It also states that no criminal case can be brought against a soldier if he has taken action under the Act that has resulted in loss of life or otherwise, except by the express sanction of the central government. Such sanction has not been given in a single case since the Act was instituted in 1958.

At the heart of the debate about AFSPA is the well-articulated view among its opponents that it is 'lawless', undemocratic and unconstitutional and that it has further alienated communities and groups that did not anyway feel deeply attached to the 'idea of India'. There is virtually no legal redress in these laws because no courts of law have any right to take up any case, even against civilian personnel, unless express permission is granted by those authorized—in other words, usually by the persons who should be held accountable for the act(s) of commission or omission.[8]

There is no equality before the law because the laws themselves were made to 'legalize' inequality. In most laws, an individual is presumed innocent unless proved guilty. Under these laws, a person is guilty unless he can prove beyond doubt[9] that there is no ground for authorities to 'suspect' him. And anyway, by the time the case goes before a court, the person may not even be alive.

Discussion often arises as to why normal powers under civilian control would not have been adequate to deal with the Naga situation in the 1950s and whether it was necessary to have brought in the armed forces, a situation that has continued for well over half a century. AFSPA originally asserted New Delhi's reluctance to deal with armed rebels through a process of dialogue. Efforts to seek mediation and peace while significant were brief and not sustained.[10] Today, this reluctance has changed to an official recognition that only dialogue and political settlements, not military force, can sort issues out. Yet it took over forty years to establish, although there were two ceasefires in the 1960s and 1970s, the first in 1964 between the two sides and the second after the 1975 agreement between the Government of India and representatives of the Naga underground.

Although the first ceasefire was followed by several rounds of discussions between Prime Minister Indira Gandhi and leaders of the Naga National Council (NNC), the political organization that set up the Federal Government of Nagaland (FGN), the talks fell apart. The central government accused the Nagas of bad faith, of retaining their connections to Pakistan and the People's Republic of China, where the Nagas were sending groups for training in arms and guerrilla tactics.

Attacks on trains in Assam gave the centre a reason to abrogate the ceasefire. Meanwhile the Indian government was messily involved in dividing the Nagas along tribal lines in order to weaken the movement and create schisms. It's a strategy that continues to this day. This strategy ran parallel to the extensive use of AFSPA, underlining a fact that New Delhi continues to ignore: state power, armed even with an omnibus law like AFSPA which has the capacity to instantly decide issues of life and death, can diminish but not extinguish either armed or political opposition, especially if there is public support for the fight. In other words, AFSPA was, even at an early stage, far less effective in crushing the opposition than New Delhi had wanted or expected it to be.

India sought to lessen the damage and the threat through a political initiative aimed at reducing the influence of the 'underground'. This took the form of what is widely known in Nagaland as the 16 Point Agreement, in 1960, with the Naga People's Convention (NPC) comprising those who were opposed to the armed movement led by the NNC and its 'governmental' wing, the FGN. The pro-India group were either local officials or politicians from the NPC; most of them later crossed over to the Congress Party of Jawaharlal Nehru. The agreement ensured that Nagaland would become a full state three years later, with special rights. One of those special clauses was inserted in the Constitution as Article 371A. It said that Naga customary laws would be untouched by any act of Parliament and that laws passed by Parliament would not apply to the state unless ratified by the local legislature. Even the natural resources of the state would be under the control of village and tribal councils as well as the state assembly, unlike other parts of the country where underground mineral and other resources were classified as the property of the central government.

The accord continues to be known as the 16 Point Agreement although not all sixteen points of political discussion were agreed to. Nehru rejected several including a demand for the integration of the contiguous Naga-inhabited areas, by including districts from the neighbouring states of Assam, what was then the North East Frontier Agency (now Arunachal Pradesh) and Manipur. This specific issue was deferred for discussion at a later date at Nehru's insistence and not unsurprisingly remains a prickly, unresolved issue in four states—Assam, Manipur, Nagaland and Arunachal Pradesh.

No elections were possible in the Naga Hills until 1964, a year after the state was carved out. However, Naga scholars say the creation of the state, conduct of elections, emergence of a political elite and middle class and subsequent formation of elected governments have still failed to assuage basic demands, although these are more muted today. The new comprador class established close financial and political connections to New Delhi, a relationship that has grown with the years.

In the early years of Independence, the reality was that the central government was unsure, despite the growth of the Naga elite, of whether representative democracy would work in Nagaland. It knew that it could depend on the army, an all-India organization that served the state without asking too many questions. But it was not prepared to trust even its own administrative structures in the state, such as the police and civil administration, and viewed even political organizations with suspicion, concerned that these could again fan revolt. Such suspicions are visible in the central government's approach to pro-Naga nationalist groups, and reflect what Sanjib Baruah, professor of political studies at Bard College, New York, describes as a policy supporting army rule through the back door in the Northeast. 'Generals as governors' is a much-quoted phrase of Baruah's, who referred to the military mindset of New Delhi that for decades appointed either retired generals or former intelligence officials as governors to sensitive states like Nagaland, Assam and Manipur and to Arunachal Pradesh. Baruah sees this approach as reflective of New Delhi's mistrust of the region and the need to have a strong representative to intervene on its behalf should a crisis arise.[11]

In Nagaland, the first pro-NNC government took office in 1974, in the teeth of opposition from the Ministry of Home Affairs. The Vizol government lasted barely two years before it was dismissed by the centre. Thirty years later, when Neiphiu Rio, a renegade Congressman, formed his own state-level party and led it to a decisive victory over the Congress Party, the central government did the same thing. Barely two months before Rio was to complete his term, New Delhi dismissed him, only to face embarrassment when he captured power again, partly on a sympathy vote.

Even in the Indian Army, although there is resistance at high levels to repealing the Act, there is an acknowledgement that things cannot remain as they are and that AFSPA needs change: the army wants the Act to be made 'more humane'.

Rio, who was elected as a Member of Parliament in the 2014 elections after an eleven-year stint as the state's top elected political figure, says that there was a need to 'appreciate the special circumstances of Nagaland as well as the security concerns of Government of India', yet 'at the same time, we are against these (extraordinary) laws as today we are living in a civilized world. We cannot win over the people with such laws.' Rio, who assumed office in 2003 and ran the regional coalition known as the Democratic Alliance of Nagaland (DAN), said that the state government had repeatedly declined to extend the Disturbed Areas Act, which empowers AFSPA and the use of the army. Every time, he said, the centre would override the local government.

Other political figures like the veteran S. C. Jamir,[12] a three-time chief minister of the state from the Congress Party and later governor of Goa, Maharashtra and Odisha, are also bitterly opposed to AFSPA. In this, their views run counter to the fact that it was the Congress Party government under Nehru in New Delhi which instituted the law. Since then the Congress has, for the most part, helped keep it on the statute books all these years.

Jamir, known for a combination of diplomacy, craftiness and blunt talk, says: 'These laws have blatantly denied all fundamental rights to the Nagas and treated them worse than animals, many innocent people were killed and/or herded to jails, traditional villages were uprooted and grouped into well stockaded "concentration camps" under the pretext of denying food to underground cadres, etc'.[13]

◆

It was with this political background of opposition to AFSPA from within Naga politics that the Reddy Committee began its work. The committee noted that while the Supreme Court had upheld AFSPA's constitutional validity in a 1997 ruling that deeply disappointed human rights activists and organizations around the world, it pointed out that this ruling was not an endorsement of the law. In addition, the committee said that legislative shape should be given to many of these riders; its concern here was that security forces should not be allowed to hide behind the cloak of rules that empowered them to conduct themselves as they wished and in violation of the basic tenets of justice and the rule of law.

The committee did not merely stop with recommending the removal of AFSPA. It formulated a structure that aimed at undoing the draconian aspects of the Unlawful Activities (Prevention) Act, 2004, by proposing clauses that could curb the sweeping powers of the states and its functionaries. The proposals were aimed at what committee members described as bringing the armed forces under the law instead of allowing them to remain above it. This has been misunderstood by legal pundits in New Delhi and human rights activists as an effort that could technically enable the government to enforce AFSPA on a national scale. Prominent lawyers have said that it substitutes one offensive and unacceptable law with another. However, the committee's suggestion was aimed at democratizing the Unlawful Activities (Prevention) Act, 2004, which has the same objectionable clauses and protections of AFSPA. The proposals were based on a realistic understanding of the political establishment in India and its concerns: that it would not be possible, given the conditions in Jammu and Kashmir and the Northeast, as well as the problems in neighbouring Pakistan, Bangladesh, Sri Lanka and Nepal, to do away with anti-terrorism laws. The AFSPA review committee took the view that 'it would be more appropriate to recommend insertion of appropriate provisions in the Unlawful Activities (Prevention) Act, 1967 [as amended in the year 2004] instead of suggesting a new piece of legislation' because it considered the Unlawful Activities (Prevention) Act to be a law that was sufficiently broad and comprehensive to curb terrorism.

The committee made a proposal that could meet many of the basic grievances laid at the door of the armed forces by proposing a chain of grievance cells that could be managed by army and police officers and the civil administration. The goal was to deal effectively with the complaints of people who were picked up and detained, and with the cases of those who had disappeared or ended up dead or badly injured. There is a need for a mechanism that is transparent and quick and that involves authorities from concerned agencies as well as civil society groups to provide information on the whereabouts of missing persons within twenty-four hours.

Although this may be regarded as a proactive approach to preventing the abuse of power by the armed forces by insisting on transparency, accountability and a rigorous time frame in which accountability has to be delivered, it drew criticism from Amnesty International, which reluctantly welcomed only one 'aspect' of the report, referring to the committee's call for AFSPA's repeal. Amnesty opposed the committee's suggestions to amend the Unlawful Activities (Prevention) Act.

The committee wanted to resist state power and to enforce greater accountability on the armed forces and the government. The current method of simply extending the Disturbed Areas Act every six months by a decision of the Ministry of Home Affairs should be done away with. Although this power is now concurrent, the centre overrides the state government, which may not want the Act to be applied.

AFSPA becomes operational only after the promulgation of the Disturbed Areas Act: an area must be declared 'disturbed' by either the state or central government and requiring the deployment of the army and other central security forces because local law enforcement authorities are regarded as inadequate to deal with security conditions. The committee wanted control to be enforced on both the time and the conditions of deployment so that it did not become a permanent feature of government and governance, because this, in effect, was what AFSPA had enabled the army and paramilitary forces to do.

The Reddy Committee[14] went so far as to propose its own full draft legislation for a bill that Parliament could enact as Chapter VIA of the 1967 Unlawful Activities (Prevention) Act 'to serve as a guide in drafting the legislation to be introduced in Parliament'. Surprisingly, despite the great interest in the Manorama case, apart from occasional statements and articles or uncoordinated meetings and conferences, there was no debate worth the name over the committee's report. Civil society in Manipur began focusing on other issues after the report was submitted, and the central government has deflected every effort to make it public. Although it has not been made public officially, *The Hindu* posted the report on its website. But the strong views of civil society towards the government's inaction on this issue remain unchanged. *The Sentinel* of Guwahati remarked caustically on the first anniversary of the committee's report that the government 'stubbornly refuses' to place the report in Parliament.

The Reddy Committee report tried to break new ground and offer a way out of the conundrum in which Nagaland and other parts of the Northeast find themselves. The lack of official response highlighted the lack of government interest in taking a broader perspective on issues and in continuing a business-as-usual approach.

All this despite the high-sounding intentions of government leaders. Thus, Manmohan Singh who was then the prime minister called for amendments that could make the act more 'humane', a view that had the approval of the Ministry of Defence, the army leadership and the Ministry of Home Affairs. This was echoed by A. K. Antony, the then defence minister, who said that AFSPA would remain in force but could be amended to make it more humane. Antony even went so far as to say that the army would accept such an amendment, raising serious questions about who called the shots in the Indian defence establishment and whether India needed the army to approve political decisions.

The review committee's recommendations and report were stalled by the inability of the United Progressive Alliance (UPA) government to get a consensus within the cabinet on the issue, as well as by strong opposition from the army and the defence ministry. The non-implementation of the report indicates the power of the latter two institutions to dictate government policy in the name of 'national security'.

After the report stayed wrapped in files for nearly a decade, in 2015 the centre quietly appointed a new committee of former bureaucrats, a journalist and a junior academic to look at the issues of Manipur and how these could be handled. On the day that this group headed to Imphal for its first set of meetings, the home ministry leaked a report to the media that it was rejecting the Reddy Committee Report. However, there was no follow-up after the initial reports quoting unnamed officials in the ministry, saying they had decided to bury the Reddy Report.

◆

It's worth revisiting here the hearings of the committee because apart from the determined manner in which in presentation after presentation, civil society groups—whether students, women's organizations, human rights activists, lawyers, media, professionals and even businessmen—came before the Reddy Committee to demand the law's repeal, two state governments also took positions which flew in the face of New Delhi's arguments. In unambiguous terms, Nagaland and Mizoram, which have suffered the most in the conflict with the state, demanded repeal; they spoke the same language as those of the human rights movements. It is worth repeating what the additional chief secretary of Nagaland shared with the committee. He came with an array of officials and police with a well-prepared note which he read out to us in the conference hall of the Hotel Japfu, a sprawling monstrosity which claimed at its reception that it had received an international hospitality award—I would say for poor service and bad food.

This representation by the Nagaland government on 22 March 2005 represents the anguish of a people and a government emasculated by the lack of power, angered and frustrated by their own helplessness in the face of arbitrariness, yet determined to salvage some dignity and authority and in the process, perhaps, get some justice for their people.

It was a formidable group, representing the leadership of the civil administration—the additional chief secretary, the additional director general of police in charge of vigilance, the state's public prosecutor, an inspector general of police and the special secretary (home). I am paraphrasing from the Reddy Committee's report of that account. The state government of Nagaland said that this Act should be replaced with some more humane legislation as it had generated a great amount of hatred and suspicion between the Nagaland people and others. He (reference is to the additional chief secretary) said that the law and order position had tremendously improved and as such the state government had not recommended further extension of this act yet the central government deemed it fit to issue extension order for another six months, they complained. He said that political necessity should not be weighed as far as this act is concerned.

The additional DGP mentioned that prior to the ceasefire, there were allegations of human rights violations but thereafter such incidents have reduced considerably. He said that the draconian provisions of the Act needed review and it had to be made acceptable to the people. He was supported by another officer (IG) who said time had come to review this Act as we have to live together. Proper amendments needed to be made to hand over the suspects within twenty-four hours as stated in the Code of Criminal Procedure (CrPC.) The public prosecutor mentioned the problems faced by the investigating agencies in the cases registered under AFSPA as the prosecution never cooperated in producing evidence in the courts. He mentioned various cases of abuses/misuse of the Act. Special Secretary (Home) M. V. Chagsan gave certain suggestions for amendments regarding Section 3—that it should be the state government to issue the notification and not the central government

This is significant because the official was challenging the right of New Delhi to unilaterally declare an area disturbed or extend the period of 'disturbance' without bothering to consult the state government or allow the state government to decide on the matter. The Nagaland government report added that the powers under Section 4 should be vested only in commissioned officers and not in non-commissioned officers. In addition, it said that AFSPA and the CrPC should be similar. The CrPC informs and governs the police on a wide range of issues including legal processes of detention and action against alleged criminals. But if AFSPA is 'brought' to a level of conformity or uniformity with the CrPC, it would essentially take away the right to kill, barring the most exceptional of circumstances. Regarding Section 5: Time given to hand over the accused should be more specific. Regarding Section 6: Immunity given to the armed forces for action under AFSPA should be removed and they must be made accountable for their illegal actions. Summing up the debate, the additional chief secretary said that this Act was a bad law which had been misused/abused and the people were against this act. As such, it should be amend(ed) and made... friendlier. The security forces should be more friendly with the people.

There, in a nutshell, we have it—clearly but firmly, the Nagaland government was expressing its opposition to central authority. The additional chief secretary was explicit: AFSPA was 'a bad Law which had been misused/ abused'; the Special Secretary (Home) was even blunter: remove the immunity given to the security forces—they must face the consequences of their actions. This assertion lies at the heart of opposition to AFSPA's repeal from the security forces and the defence ministry.

The objection to the centre intruding on the space of the state government and overstepping the fine constitutional line defining power sharing with the states was interesting especially as it came from Nagaland. It should be remembered that the Nagas were the original rebels—they had raised arms against India and its Constitution. Ironically, half a century later, senior Naga officials from the state were reading the riot act to New Delhi for failing to follow its own constituted principles. Nagaland was officially telling New Delhi that the latter's unilateral amendment of AFSPA in 1972 for the sake of 'national security' was unwarranted. The additional

chief secretary told the committee that the state government opposed the
continuance of the Act because there was an improvement in the law and
order situation. But every six months, the centre, without even a by your
leave, would renew the Act for Nagaland (as it does for Assam, Manipur
and Tripura and the other peripheral states where it is applied). He snapped:
'(although) the State Govt. had not recommended further extension of
this Act yet the Central govt. deemed it fit to issue extension order for
another six months'.[15]

On that day, the state government found itself on the same page as
groups which had often opposed it. The path had been eased by leaders
of the Naga Students Federation (NSF), known to be supportive of the
militant National Socialist Council of Nagaland (I-M). Achumbemo Kikon,
former president of the NSF and Neizokhotuo Belho, its general secretary,
described AFSPA as 'a threat to Indian democracy'. It was quite illogical
and irrational to retain it because 'other existing laws were adequate' to
deal with the situation. Belho also criticized the Supreme Court judgment
of 1997 which upheld the Act's validity. Justice Reddy swiftly stepped in
here, clarifying that the Supreme Court had examined AFSPA, as it did
other laws and Acts passed by Parliament, only from the perspective of
their constitutional validity and correctness and 'not from the angle of the
desirability'. This was a major point he would underline later.

Justice Reddy's views, which he set out in jurisprudential but clear
language in the final report, were not influenced by the political turmoil
or social challenges in the states that the committee had visited and which
surprised, even stunned him. However, the narratives and testimony of
witnesses did make a mark. It was not that the independence demand of
the Nagas or Meiteis was unimportant or not or whether their armed
groups held sway in pockets of India, raising their own flags, running their
fiefdoms, collecting taxes and doing all this under the nose of the centre
and the state governments. These positions and external conditions did not
sway his thinking on the rightness or otherwise of AFSPA. This approach
underlined the importance of critical thinking and considering the limits
of coercive state force, of what was necessary not just what was acceptable,
what level of force was important to use decisively and when. The issues
of checks and balances, the right of equality before law and the desirability
of the state to use maximum force as a deterrent in the rarest of rare cases
were at the heart of his concerns.

This also reflects a view of which I often speak and which I believe finds
resonance in many hearts and minds: a law may be 'legal' and 'constitutional'

but is it just? That is the key. It is not just whether theory precedes practice or vice versa. Both are equally important to find a stable balance.

I am reminded of the remarks by Mizoram Chief Minister Lalthanhawla that a spirit of give and take, a willing bureaucracy and total involvement of civil society can make peace accords succeed. 'Peace, development and governance are closely related. Imbalance in one disturbs the other,' he said, adding that if the mindset of people could be changed, half the battle for peace would be won.[16]

That mindset needs changing as much in New Delhi—some would say more so there than anywhere else—as I have argued earlier,[17] as in places such as Nagaland and Mizoram which had borne the brunt of official wrath.

The Mizoram government supported the Nagas in the democratic revolt against AFSPA, supporting a peaceful framework that would bring justice and not carve the rule of arbitrariness in stone.[18] Then as earlier with the mautam (famine caused by bamboo flowering), its pleas have been of little avail, its assertions have fallen on deaf ears. Mizoram was even sharper in its criticism of AFSPA than the Nagaland government, saying that all sections of people irrespective of political affiliations were against the act, that its misuse during the time of insurgency had left 'a scar on their mind(s)' and that it had been unused for two decades since the signing of a peace accord that brought calm to the hills, ending years of insurgency and bloodshed that lasted from 1966 to 1986.

Speaking of the scars of that time, C. Ropianga, the officer who signed the submission to the committee, said:

> So far as Mizoram is concerned, there is no reason for reviving the operational validity or applicability of the Act. The State Police Forces and other Para-military Forces presently stationed in Mizoram are able to manage the affairs of the State with regard to maintenance of law and order without Special Powers envisaged in such Special Powers Act.

The army had quit its anti-insurgency role after the accord and even if the law was not repealed or amended, Mizoram wanted nothing to do with it—it was opting out. 'Just leave us alone, we've had enough of this,' was the message. There are valid reasons for this allergy to AFSPA in the Mizo Hills as well as elsewhere.[19]

◆

We were at breakfast when Justice Reddy who was reading a local newspaper looked up and said, with some alarm and extreme surprise: 'Sanjoy, what is this?' He was pointing to a front page news item about Naga forces celebrating their national day and a photo of a Naga militant leader taking the salute in an open field, with armed cadres marching smartly by. 'How can this be?'[20] I smiled and said: 'Sir, there are no less than four governments in this state. Besides the central and state governments there are two "governments" of competing armed Naga groups, with the same flag which bear the same name and have the same nomenclature for their "administration"—the Government of the Peoples Republic of Nagalim (GPRN). Although it is a notional government and operate loosely, they collect taxes regularly from government officers (up to 25 per cent of their salary and demands "taxes" from several groups, which incentivizes opportunities for corruption). Every business in the state, small or large, dhobi, trucker, tea shop and professional, pays according to their annual turnover. They are issued a tax receipt. As far as the march past was concerned, it was the founding day of the Naga National Army and that's why they were celebrating.'

'But surely they are not legal?'

'No, but they exist and everyone lets them be.'

I added: 'Despite the existence of the unofficial "governments", Nagas participate enthusiastically in state elections. They vote for their candidates in large numbers—partly based on clan affiliation and village loyalties as well as simple cash delivered at home, allurements of liquor, sewing machines and other consumer goods. In fact, villagers expect great feasts—the Feasts of Merit—which men of wealth and prominence are supposed to give to honour their own villages and kinfolk. This has been converted in the present day to ensure they vote for the right candidate. The problem crops up when there are competing Feasts of Merit. So there's a simple factor to choose the person worthy of support—he (for few women, if any, contest elections in Nagaland) who gives the greater feast, slaughters the greater number of pigs, provides the greatest amount of liquor, usually wins: add to that clan, kinship, village and tribe loyalties, not necessarily in that order.

By this time, Justice Reddy's eyes had acquired a glazed look. 'But they're taking part in a democratic process in India?' he asked with an air of desperation, seeking some sort of assurance. 'Yes, but they're electing a government that is supposed to deliver them basic services and help them live comfortably. They're not voting for democracy in India or for an Indian party or an Indian cause. But even this is changing with the generations that are coming up—for this is the first generation now which has seen a semblance of peace and normalcy: to them the stories of their parents and elders, of house searches, shootings, terrible fights and acute violence, seem to be mere stories. But they remain deeply aware, sensitive and alive to their "uniqueness" because often when they venture into "India", they're reminded of it by the discrimination and treatment they face.'[21]

He asked another question, with utter frankness: 'But how can they parade in their own uniforms and arms so openly? Doesn't the government do anything or can't it do anything?' It was more than that, I explained: the fourth government—that of India—chooses not to do anything that would upset the apple cart.

P. P. Shrivastav, who was taking in the conversation nearby, his agile eyes twinkling behind powerful glasses, chipped in. 'Sir, the Government of India knows everything. But they don't interfere because if they act too abruptly, the peace talks can get disrupted, so there is always that at the back of the government's mind and the militants are taking full advantage of it—although under the ceasefire ground rules[22] they're not supposed to parade openly with arms.'

He would know, as someone who served for nearly thirty years in the region, speaks Assamese fluently, has many close friends there and, as a top official in the home ministry, had helped run matters and policies related to the region.[23]

◆

As we talked, I was reminded of a discussion in that very town a few years earlier with a group of Naga women,[24] both in government and out of it. The topic was similar—the impact of conflict on women. Daisy Mezhur, a trim, energetic Naga official, was talking and the room had fallen silent. 'Every time a door closes with a bang, I jump in fright, because I think someone is attacking,' said Daisy. 'Every time a car backfired, I used to dive under the table in the office. I felt I was going mad,' she said, as everyone listened. One could only describe the atmosphere as one of collective pain. Then she explained the roots of that fear: 'As a child I remember our parents shouting to us to hide under the table when there was firing in the street, when there were clashes in town between the security forces and members of the underground.[25] That is one of my strongest memories.' At this point, a senior member of the Naga government who was there representing the education department (because social welfare, which handles issues of women's and children's rights, fell under that bureaucratic section) wanted to speak. I wondered whether he would try to rebut some of the things that we had been hearing. This is was what he said. 'I just wanted to share, after listening to all of you, that I too have suffered, my family has been through pain—my brother used to be a "national worker" and he was shot dead by the army. It is a grief I live with every day and it is not something that I have shared, it is not even something that people in my office know.'

That was all he said and all that he could say, in that state of emotional tumult. But for him and for all of us, it was enough.

That year, despite all the harm that had been inflicted, all the sharing that had taken place, all the hurt that had accumulated, the state of Nagaland was still without a women's commission that could record the wounds of women and provide if not some corrective action and compensation at least some healing, to try to restore their lost sense of honour and dignity. A report to the National Commission for Women recommended the establishment of such a state commission. To those of us who wrote that report, it is a matter of some satisfaction that this was subsequently set up and is functional. Some balance of equality and justice or a semblance of it has been restored.

How much of this could I share with the committee, how much of this would they appreciate?[26] I was wrestling with these thoughts that morning after breakfast with Justice Reddy when we went to listen to officials of Nagaland and heard their attack on AFSPA.

◆

After the official visits to the states were over and hearings completed in New Delhi, the time came to sit down and write the report. The lead was taken by Justice Reddy, who, as much as anyone else, was appalled by the misery and tragedy that AFSPA had inflicted. We discussed the experiences, considered the different viewpoints and each one gave written and oral inputs, which went into an initial draft. I wrote a separate note which finds place in the appendices.

What Justice Reddy and our team tried to achieve, I believe, was to defang AFSPA, to ensure that the bond of impunity and immunity from prosecution for the security forces was challenged and those guilty of serious human rights violations would be prosecuted. Not taking action would worsen the hatred and feeling of both distance and anger against the army and New Delhi. The sum of these emotions, in the lives of countless victims and their relatives and friends, was a formidable force and could create a large bank of ill will, which could be repeatedly tapped and funnelled towards violent rebellion against the state. Stories of bitterness and angst get better (or is it worse?) by their repeated telling.

Justice Reddy was clear on the core issues. He believed that the army, though protected by AFSPA, could not take shelter behind the garb of arbitrariness. They were covered by specific aspects of the Constitution, which was binding on all individuals and organized bodies, especially the government and those who serve it (even though they may be under the illusion that they serve the nation too). Therefore, Justice Reddy intoned, the army had to bend before Article 22 of the Constitution; this is something it refuses to accept or even take cognizance of.

In all its discussions, responses and a particularly sharp exchange I had with the former judge advocate general (or chief legal officer for the army) on a television programme,[27] the army has been unrepentant even though some have acknowledged that there had been excesses.[28]

Reddy was scathing: although Section 4, Clause C of AFSPA empowers 'an officer of the armed forces to arrest any person, without warrant, who has committed or who is reasonably suspected to have committed a cognizable offence', he said that such powers were comparable to those enjoyed by a police officer under Section 41, Clause A of the CrPC. The power of arrest that the army officer has is expanded to 'prevent a person who is about to commit a cognizable offence'. Should force be required to handle the person or situation, the armed forces are authorized to do so.

But he pointed out that Section 5 of the same Act places a restriction on the arbitrary use of such clauses because it says that any detainee under AFSPA had to be handed over to the officer in charge of the nearest police station 'with the least possible delay, together with a report of the circumstances occasioning the arrest'.

In the main, the army takes 'least possible delay'—which does not circumscribe the length of time that a suspect had to be held in its custody—to often mean that it could do as it wished and hand over detainees at its own whim to the civil administration. It was not required, it believed, as has been argued by its officers and defenders, that the period of detention cannot be in excess of the mandatory twenty-four hours.

However, the Constitution is clear on this as is the CrPC:

> We do not think there is any basis for such a doubt inasmuch as Clause (2) of Article 22 of the Constitution of India does cast such a duty. Indeed, the said clause in the Constitution *confers a right upon the person arrested and detained in custody* [italics mine] to be produced before the nearest Magistrate within a period of twenty-four hours of such arrest

excluding the time necessary for journey from the place of arrest to the court of Magistrate and further declares that such person shall not be detained in custody beyond the said period without the authority of a Magistrate. The constitutional right so conferred upon the person arrested is available whether the arrest is made by an officer of the armed forces or by the police. It is, therefore, clear beyond doubt that a person arrested under clause (c) of Section has to be produced before a Magistrate within 24 hours excluding the time taken for journey from the place of arrest to the court of Magistrate.

Justice Reddy put it simply so that there could be no ambiguity:

...the person arrested under clause (c) of Section 4 has to be produced before a Magistrate within 24 hours of his arrest (excluding the time taken for journey) and it is within this period that the officer of the armed forces who made the arrest shall hand over the person to the police and the police shall produce the person before the Magistrate. In this connection, it would be appropriate to notice Article 33 of the Constitution of India, which, as amended in 1984, reads as follows:

Power of Parliament to modify the rights conferred by this Part in their application to Forces, etc.,

Parliament may, by law, determine to what extent any of the rights conferred by this Part shall, in their application to: (a) the members of the Armed forces; or (b) the members of the forces charged with the maintenance of public order; or (c) persons employed in any bureau or other organization established by the State for purposes of intelligence or counterintelligence; or (d) persons employed in, or in connection with, the telecommunication system set up for the purpose of any Force, bureau or organisation referred to in clauses (a) to (c); be restricted or abrogated so as to ensure the proper discharge of their duties and the maintenance of discipline among them.

Yet, despite having such potential powers, Parliament has not passed any law that either modifies or qualifies the right that a detainee enjoys or is understood to 'enjoy', if such a word is appropriate for someone held in shoddy and frightening circumstances, 'conferred by clause (2) of Article 22 upon the person arrested where he is arrested by the members of the Armed forces or of the Forces charged with the maintenance of public order'.

Under this clause, Parliament is empowered to make a law determining 'to what extent any of the right conferred by this Part shall, in their application to (a) the members of the armed forces or (b) the members of the armed forces charged with the maintenance of public order', be restricted or abrogated so as to ensure the proper discharge of their duties. But Parliament has not made any such law.

'It is, therefore, clear that the right conferred by clause (2) of Article 22 upon a person arrested to be produced before the Magistrate within 24 hours (excluding the time for journey) remains untrammelled and unaffected and has, therefore, to be obeyed.' How have the army, the defence ministry and the Government of India responded to this? Ignored it with a blanket of silence. Therefore, one could argue that the government, by not accepting Article 2(C) in the application of AFSPA, is guilty not just of dereliction of duty but of a far worse offence—of wilfully violating the very Constitution of India that it is pledged to defend and which takes precedence above all else by denying its citizenry the right to be set free, if legally approved by a magistrate, within twenty-four hours of arrest or detention under Article 22.

◆

These questions are at the heart of the AFSPA debate. As in all debates, there is another side as well. What do the much-maligned government and its security arms have to say in their defence? A major question is that raised by the security specialist Praveen Swami,[29] albeit on a different issue about a Saudi diplomat in New Delhi who was recalled by his government after a storm broke around him alleging rape of housemaids. Swami pointed out that the 1961 Vienna Convention on Diplomatic Relations which protects diplomats, is aimed at stopping punishment and counter-punishment of envoys without which 'for all practical purposes, diplomats would be at constant risk of becoming hostages'. He cites Article 31 as saying that diplomats 'shall enjoy immunity from the criminal jurisdiction of the receiving state' and that they would also not fall under the local government's 'civil and administrative jurisdiction'.

This sounds familiar when we consider AFSPA. The argument by the security forces—and others in their favour—for retaining AFSPA is similar. It is that should the protection enjoyed under Clause 6 be withdrawn, they would face an impossible situation in which to work. They see themselves as vulnerable to all manner of cases and legal harassment, going back years if not decades when they may have conducted an operation or an action that caused harm to a civilian or civilians. The functioning of the army, its efficacy and attraction would slow and diminish. In other words, the point being made is that it would not be a fit fighting force. That argument appeals to most nationalists and those who value the army—which would include virtually everyone in the country. But the question remains: should there be punishment for heinous crimes that have nothing to do with the purpose for which the security forces had been called to action? How can acts of rape, molestation, torture, damage to homes and theft in any way be seen as being conducted in the 'line of duty'? But this is the fig leaf under which the government and the security forces function. Another argument is related to the issue of 'vague and baseless allegations' being hurled against the security forces, especially when they claim to be on a winning wicket and have the militants on the run. The arrogance of senior officials is reflected in the disdain with which state governments are addressed: 'There is a tendency amongst the weakened leadership to encourage the locals and media, to highlight the perceived wrongdoings of the security forces (SF) to show that it still has some modicum of control.'[30] In an article about AFSPA, General Umong Sethi also says that the armed forces and civil society 'best co-exist in mutually exclusive domains' and that they share a dynamic division for eventually 'civil society seeks to recall its natural freedom and space while the armed forces are still in the process of consolidating the gains'.

What Sethi and others rarely indicate is *how long* the process of the consolidation of 'gains' should take. Both AFSPA and the Disturbed Areas Act are silent on this although the Disturbed Areas Act needs to be renewed by Parliament every six months. These gains could mean anything from capturing rebel strongholds to decimating the leadership or forcing them, having weakened their strike capacity to such a degree, to come to the negotiating table. But even when this has happened, conflict has ceased and peace has returned, both Acts have continued to apply, barring in the case of Mizoram.

Sethi describes two conditions which he considers are paramount for the army to operate effectively: 'the requisite freedom of action and...be safeguarded against motivated investigations and being prosecuted for the legitimate actions undertaken in good faith, while conducting operations'.

While he says that the local police have greater powers under the CrPC in most states and what is known as the Ranbir Penal Code in Jammu and Kashmir, he does not address a fundamental point. The CrPC and Indian Penal Code (IPC), set out in detail the manner in which suspects may be arrested, the procedures involving magistrates, police and even the summoning of armed forces, who in exceptional circumstances, may even disperse an unruly assembly on its own if it is not possible to contact an executive magistrate. But they only have the powers to arrest and confine. At no point are the civilian forces or the armed forces operating under the Act allowed the privilege of 'using force to the extent of causing death' as AFSPA does. The civil law is very clear on this point. But AFSPA, which is a bald Act of six clauses, does not have any rules set out during its passage or even through amendments later. It gives the power of inflicting death, without trial, detention or interrogation, to a non-commissioned officer. The power to inflict death can be instant, for the officer has the power to open fire on a person or persons, to the extent of causing death, upon mere suspicion, without knowing whether the person is armed or unarmed. Of course, it stands to reason that soldiers will fire at people who represent a perceived threat or who fire upon them first. Survival is the instinct of the fittest.

What the defenders of AFSPA don't say is that the forces can kill a person—as in the case of the young man who went fishing only for his wife to get a phone call to come to the morgue, or the group standing at a bus stop who were gunned down by CRPF personnel hungry for revenge after a few of their own had been killed nearby by insurgent fighters, or twelve-year-old Azad Khan, reading the newspaper, who was snatched from his house and shot—not suspected of an offence that includes heinous crimes and could be punished by death or life imprisonment.

In other words, it doesn't discriminate between the innocent and the not-so-innocent. The CrPC doesn't just define the nature of gatherings which could harm public security but it lays down very clearly how arrests are to be made and only gives the police officer a chance to 'use all means necessary to effect the arrest', if the person sought seeks to evade arrest. And even this use of force rules out the infliction of death 'unless they are accused of an offence punishable by death or life imprisonment'.

While piloting the bill in Parliament in 1958, G. B. Pant, the home minister at the time, said that the security personnel 'have the authority to act only within the limits that have been proscribed generally in the CrPC or in the Constitution'. If this was the intent, then it should have been written out clearly with precise rules and regulations, like other security laws. Unlike the CrPC, which defines the rank of officers that can disperse what are seen as unlawful assemblies, AFSPA simply hands over this power to non-commissioned officers.

There are other significant areas where public vulnerability is high and the accountability of the security forces is low. The reason why AFSPA is promulgated is one such grey area. The decision to declare an area as disturbed is ostensibly to bring conditions back to 'normal', so that the civilian administration can work without fear or favour and the people can go about their daily work freely. The declaration of a state or any part of it as disturbed is a precursor for AFSPA's use. It also means that the civil administration has collapsed to the extent that it cannot function without the armed forces or security forces playing a direct role in the restoring of 'normal' conditions. If the centre declares a state or part thereof as disturbed, should there not be a limit to how long this situation should be allowed to last? Or is there an inherent assumption by the centre that local communities, leaders and governments are so untrustworthy that the Disturbed Areas Act and AFSPA should continue in perpetuity? The view obviously is that lack of robust governance or even failure to deliver minimal governance could create insecure conditions. As a result, this argument goes, law and order problems would grow and pose greater challenges to the State. In which case, it would be better for AFSPA and its twin, the Disturbed Areas Act, to be in place—just in case something happens so that the army is neither caught on the wrong foot nor suddenly summoned from 'peacetime conditions' into combat.

Former home secretary G. K. Pillai says that the army's deployment for a limited period is what's necessary, pointing out how Nagaland has remained designated as disturbed 'despite the fact that hostilities have been suspended for over a decade and no security personnel have been killed in this period'.

The 1997 Supreme Court judgment, while upholding AFSPA as constitutional, put out a list of dos and don'ts for the army going into insurgency operations, saying that they had, among other things, to approach women with respect and that rape, one of the principal complaints against the security forces, was unacceptable.

The judgment said the law was constitutional and hence valid, a cause for celebration in the establishment and for disconsolation among those opposed to it. The list was not part of the main judgment but only a set of recommendations which were not enforceable by law (although a lawyer could perhaps argue that since they were issued along with the main verdict, they formed part of the judgment). This is important for there are international covenants to which India is a signatory. Do these not place a greater responsibility on the central government on doing the right thing? The act violates non-derogative provisions of international human rights law, extinguishes the right to life, the right to remedy and the right to be free from arbitrary deprivation of liberty and from torture and cruel, inhuman or degrading treatment or punishment. That being the case, it also violates this essence enshrined in the International Covenant on Civil and Political Rights (ICCPR), to which India is a state party since 1979, and other treaties and standards. The UN special rapporteur on extra-judicial killings said in his report that the act has no place in a democracy. But, as on many other occasions, New Delhi does not heed wise counsel.

There's another set of statistics which should alarm us. We discuss this elsewhere also: Assam's maternal mortality ratio (MMR)—the number of women who die in childbirth per 1,00,000 live births—is the highest in India. This record damns all facile talk about respecting women's rights, speaking about the 'traditions' of gender equality in the state and upholding their dignity there and elsewhere in the Northeast. Assam's MMR is 300, a sharp drop from the staggering 490 of 2003–2004. The improvement has been substantial, but it is not enough. India's overall MMR rate is 145; this means that Assam's situation is more than doubly worse than that of the overall national picture. It represents a statement of the government's failure to reach the margins and the most vulnerable groups. Despite the best improvement rates in the country in the decade between 2003–2004 and 2012–2014, Assam remains at the bottom of one of the most important human development indices, one that guarantees the right to life of women who are about to give birth to new life.

◆

One could argue that the lack of access and the failure of governance is linked to a vast range of factors, many of which are interlinked. Thus, the collapse of institutions, the inability or disinterest of officials in tweaking existing systems to improve the quality of life for ordinary citizens, the climate of fear and foreboding, of anger, suspicion and despair that has ruled different parts of the region are strongly connected. As is the inability of local governments to deliver basic services at a time when conflicts rage and agitations surface, when street protests erupt and there are repeated crackdowns by the military and paramilitary occur, who move about unquestioned, heavily armed and in powerful vehicles that roar through towns and villages, scattering local traffic: a daily display of power that asserts their seeming invulnerability and the desperate inequality of those on whom they gaze. AFSPA and such laws—but there are no other laws quite like this—ensure that this can happen, time and again.

During 'peacetime' when the guns are silent but people are not, they're tense and watchful of each other, of the underground and the military and non-military, of the politicians and the businessmen in cahoots with each other. No one is quite certain of what is happening in one's own area or what could happen at any time to disrupt, harm and strike fear.

Decades after the initial incidents that troubled his childhood, a pastor in Dimapur tells visitors the sound of a jeep engine at night, when he is asleep, is enough even today to wake him up in a panic and a sweat. It brings back memories, he says, of army sweeps through his village when the family would be asleep and his parents would tell him and his siblings to run to the paddy fields and forests and return only when the elders called out to them. Of course, one has to treat some stories with caution. Victims' tales become embellished with repeated telling. The writer and human rights activist Salil Tripathi says that 'victims tend to exaggerate'[31] and that their claims should be verified closely.

Such conditions and continuing pressure are assured as long as AFSPA remains in place. The army and the police support and protect each other. The rot is deep and the question remains: is it irreparable or can it be healed?

Seen in this light, the killings in Manipur, Assam, Nagaland, Punjab of the 1990s as well as Jammu and Kashmir take on a different dimension. This is why AFSPA remains immutable and irrevocable for the armed forces: they cannot agree to its repeal. If they do so, they fear the opening of a huge can of worms that would expose the deep graft, deceit, pettiness, bloodthirst, ambition and corrupted mess which exists. Which government is prepared to do that? But which government wants the legacy of such brutal indiscipline?

So, here's the conundrum: while they want to protect their own and also operate with a legal protective mechanism, the armed forces and the police by extension cannot regain lost ground or lost integrity without removing AFSPA. And what happens when courts start demanding the imposition of AFSPA because of the failure of state governments? This happened in the Garo Hills of Meghalaya where a brutal armed group, the Garo National Liberation Army, has let loose a reign of terror, attacking police patrols and government officials, kidnapping traders and others for ransom, looting and even killing women in front of their families (in one case, a man used an automatic weapon to blow a young mother's head off; she was suspected of being an informer).

The critical situation is not improved by the fact that the chief minister of Meghalaya, Dr Mukul Sangma, was from the Garo Hills. Sangma, a medical doctor, was accused by rivals of connections to militants while his cabinet colleague was charged in a police case for using members of an armed group against electoral rivals in 2013. The politician, Social Welfare Minister Deborah Marak, has denied the allegations saying she cannot be blamed if some cadres of the local unit of the Congress Party used the help of such groups.[32] This is a strange view, indeed. As a result of a political-militant nexus, the latter has surged in influence and power, terrorizing civilians and targeting both merchants and the police.

One account gives a detailed report of well-oiled machinery that has a finger in many pies and is well sourced and connected:[33] Analysts say that politicians use insurgents to terrorize people and control their votes. They pay insurgents to protect or run business ventures designed to cash in on development projects funded by the central government, such as road construction and social welfare schemes for rural residents. Contractors and distributors handpicked for public works projects act as fronts for terrorist outlets. Insurgent-controlled businesses collect income from coal mines in the Garo Hills. 'Officials also enlist militants to protect them from Opposition political factions and rival terrorist groups. In return, insurgents reap hundreds of thousands of dollars that they then spend on weapons, terrorist acts and sustaining their cadres,' said the late Purno Agitok Sangma, a former speaker of the Lok Sabha of the Indian Parliament, who represented the Tura Lok Sabha constituency of the Garo Hills until his death. His son, Conrad Sangma, succeeded to the parliamentary constituency.

The situation was so critical that the Meghalaya High Court did something quite extraordinary in November 2015. While the centre was used to getting brickbats on AFSPA and unending demands for its repeal, review or amendment, the judges went in the opposite direction: they demanded its imposition in the Garo Hills. The centre was stunned—it was not prepared for such a move and instead of welcoming the demand, said it would do everything to prevent AFSPA from being used in Meghalaya. For a change, the government found itself on the very side of those it had been opposing and contesting for decades, the civil society organizations wanting AFSPA's repeal! And, caught napping, it tried to wriggle its way out of it.

The high court called upon the central government to brush aside the state and impose AFSPA in the Garo Hills to battle the violence. It said that the state government had failed to control the violence and, according to media reports, the court issued an order saying:

> The central government can enforce Armed Forces (Special Powers) Act, 1958 for the purpose of deployment of armed forces in the aid of civil administration in order to restore public order and maintain the

law and order. Such deployment of armed forces of the Union would be only for the purpose of enabling the civil authorities in the state to deal with the situation effectively so that there is a regime of rule of law.[39]

It was not a request but a direction:

> We have no option but to direct the central government to consider the use of Armed Forces (Special Powers) Act, 1958, in the Garo Hills area and deployment of armed and para-military forces to control the situation in the aid of but certainly not under the command of civil and police authorities till life becomes normal and the incidents of rampant kidnapping and killing totally stopped.

The situation in the Garo Hills, once one of the most peaceful parts of the Northeast, underlines the contradictions that emerge within the Indian system, undermining the democratic approach and fabric further, when laws like AFSPA continue without change for decades. It is woolly-headed to think that changes for the better will happen by chance or relying on hope. They won't. It will need robust action and the government and especially the leadership of armed forces will have to agree that this is the right thing to do and is in their interests to do so. Without their consent and support, any effort to remove or change this law will not happen.

Yet, without its removal, the social, human and political dimensions which need to be restored will remain untouched. Communities and individuals are living in trauma, anger and fear, their futures jeopardized, their hopes crushed. That is why it is as critical to bring these rights to the forefront as it is to 'protect' the nation from external threats and the old idea of restoring 'order'. The health and honour of the armed forces and the true security of the country demands these changes.

◆

There is the occasional glimmer of hope in this grim scenario. That the tyranny of impunity can be ended was shown by what Manik Sarkar, the schoolteacher-like chief minister of Tripura, did in 2015. The earlier conditions of violence had improved to such a degree in Tripura, that Sarkar was able to declare the state insurgency free. He chose to walk out of the AFSPA club on his own, with the support of his party and colleagues and take the courageous step of saying he didn't need Tripura to be a disturbed area. But more of that later.

Elsewhere, the need to change AFSPA has become a constant refrain.

An inflection of this was seen in the meeting of a group called the Peace Consultative Committee in Kohima with Justice Reddy. They said that the 'government was looking at insurgents and was not worried about the general public. The general public, in fact, was bearing the brunt of both the militants as well as the Armed Forces.' The Nagaland Bar Association said the Act has created 'a fear psychosis in the minds of the people'. In Assam, a representation to the committee by a group of lawyers led by a former Member of Parliament spoke of AFSPA as 'draconian, cruel and barbaric. It is creating panic among innocent people.'

Prasant N. Choudhury, a boyish-looking senior lawyer in the Guwahati High Court, told the committee that AFSPA should not conflict with existing constitutional provisions and special laws. He proposed that the armed forces should be given pre-induction training or that they should be better prepared for their role. In addition, he proposed two other major amendments to the law: the power of arrest should vest with an officer of the rank of captain in the army or deputy commandant of the concerned central police organization. Choudhury also suggested that the absolute immunity clause provided under Section 6 needed to be diluted and that sanction for prosecution should be transferred to civilian hands. This should not rest or vest with the army. Such sanction could be granted by the joint secretary of the home ministry or finance ministry as had been done in the case of Northern Ireland.[34] In other words, he was arguing for civilian control of the military and bringing it under the law, ensuring that army officials did not remain above it. Justice Reddy and the committee returned to this issue time and again in parts of their report which are frequently quoted by civil society groups and human rights defenders. One refers to the 1997 judgment which upheld AFSPA's constitutional validity and the other is an indictment of its shallowness. The report stressed that 'constitutional validity...is not an endorsement of the desirability or advisability of the Act'. The act, it said, had become a 'symbol of oppression, an object of hate and an instrument of discrimination'.

Remarks by a senior central government official reflect this too though he was speaking in a different context and specifically about health:

> The fundamental right to life is the most basic capability. One has to first exist before one is able to make choices about his or her life. However, if we only made available the capability to exist/survive, without a care as to the manner in which people exist, then it hardly even qualifies as a capability. The Supreme Court of India has already established this for us, thus reading into the right/capability to live,

the capability to live with dignity and the capabilities of nutrition, education and health. These are interconnected and therefore the status of each capability has a bearing on all the others. Any effort towards empowerment—towards the freedom to choose by making available one or more of these capabilities—must treat them as a system.[35]

The fundamental right to life remains suspended where AFSPA exists today, a slap in the face of the Constitution and its upholder, the Supreme Court, as well as Parliament. Life, as the official note so cogently noted in the preceding paragraph, has to be lived 'with dignity'. Such conditions, so basic to the notion and practice of liberty, do not and cannot exist where draconian laws prevail.

The pain and grief that people suffer in these situations is often unheard. Their trauma, personal or suffered as a group, remains unaddressed, their many experiences rarely documented; they continue to be untouched by the healing of counselling and often carry their sad secrets to the grave. Those who go to unearth these stories, unwittingly become caregivers in whom they entrust their stories in the hope that these may be told and retold but also as an effort to release themselves from years of indignity, remorse, feelings of guilt, bitterness and anger.

I recall a project in Nagaland where the research team recorded how it had responded to the need to provide care to victims of violence and trauma.[36]

To bear witness has been a challenging and disturbing experience; listening to and reading the testimonies of the victims has been particularly painful and saddening—especially as we are deeply aware that virtually none of the victims have had access either to compensation or justice by getting the legal system or even the administrative system to take care of the harm they have suffered. To some, the nightmare persists because they remained unhealed and unreached; for others the nightmare is renewed when they see the killers of their relatives walking around free and unfettered. The research teams have been privileged to have been included in some of the most personal and difficult situations those women and other individuals have faced.

But will impunity go? Will immunity be erased? Will inequality and injustice be addressed? I gained an insight through two interactions in which I was involved.

In the first, columnist Siddharth Varadarajan talked of an encounter with M. K. Narayanan, then national security adviser to Manmohan Singh. This was soon after the Reddy Committee had submitted its report and

Varadarajan, one of India's finest journalists, had published details of it in *The Hindu*,[37] where he then worked. They were old family friends and Varadarajan asked the top cop why the government didn't implement the report; after all, the journalist said, it seemed to be a good report. Narayanan replied: 'When we picked Reddy, we thought he was a "safe" judge. General V. Raghavan would represent the army's interests; Dr Nakade was a friend of the home minister and P. P. Shrivastav was a home ministry person. Sanjoy Hazarika was in a minority. How were we to know that he would turn everyone to his side? Now, we're stuck with a report we can't implement.'

I thought Narayanan's remark was one of the greatest compliments I had received.

Some time later, I met Narayanan at an official banquet for a visiting Bhutanese dignitary at Hyderabad House. I went up to him for a chat, aware of the exchange with Varadarajan. 'So, what's going to happen to AFSPA?' I asked.

He was categorical: 'Governments may come and governments may go, but AFSPA will remain.'

Given this view by a person who was the highest ranked adviser on national and international security matters for the Government of India, who had headed the Intelligence Bureau not once but twice, was close to the Gandhi family, and highly regarded in security circles, we should not be surprised by the centre's vehement opposition to the repeal of AFSPA. Others take a different position but they appear to be a vocal minority. Former home secretary G. K. Pillai spoke of the connection between the law's future and the integrity of government. The repeal or extensive repeal of AFSPA was necessary, Pillai said, to 'restore the credibility of the Government of India and the (then) Prime Minister. [Manmohan Singh] whose assurances on this issue remain unfulfilled more than six years after they were made in Imphal'.[38]

There's a reality of rising aspirations, of engagement and alienation with India among the younger generation that the government needs to be far more acutely aware of than it appears to be. These subterranean movements, reviewed in detail later in this book,[39] are being driven virtually without prompting, pushing or coercion by New Delhi. Yet as long as AFSPA remains in place, the centre must be prepared to face more atrocities under its imprimatur and the unleashing of many furies. Each new blow against the public will hurt efforts to bring peace not to speak of the official campaign to 'mainstream' the region. Though physically closer through improved infrastructure and communications, New Delhi would still be viewed as a distant, implacable, an unjust foe—distant for its inability to understand the nuances that drive young and old in lands where some guns have fallen silent but many remain ready for use.

Chapter 2

THE MANIPUR CAULDRON

Alexander Solzhenitsyn, that greatest of Russian writers, spoke of the human qualities of impunity and licence, each more arresting than the other:

> They can take anyone's freedom from him, without a qualm. If we want to take back the freedom which is our birthright—they make us pay with our lives and the lives of all whom we meet on the way... By taking up the sword, the knife, the rifle, we quickly put ourselves on the level of our tormentors and persecutors. And there will be no end to it...there will be no end.

Manipur is a hard scrabble poor but beautiful, culturally diverse, historically rich pocket of the world, far from Solzhenitsyn's Gulag, between India and Myanmar. It is, as we have seen, home to two of the most potent symbols of revolt against state oppression and AFSPA—Manorama and Irom Sharmila, who began her hunger strike in November 2000 to protest the killing of twelve civilians by the Central Reserve Police Force at a bus stop at Malom, near Imphal.

When the resolute Sharmila ended her hunger strike against AFSPA in August 2016, many of her followers were aghast, angry and inconsolable. She left her hospital room, which had doubled as a prison cell for over a decade, only to return to it at night the same day she ended the strike, because no one would take her in. But that initial misunderstanding and animosity to her decision has dissipated. Sharmila realized she could not defeat New Delhi or get the revocation of AFSPA by a hunger strike in Manipur. So she decided to take on the state government itself at its own game of politics and elections. There was much anxiety among those who once supported her robustly whether the anti-AFSPA campaign would flicker out as she tried to reach out to ordinary people, activist groups, scholars and politicians in Manipur and outside, seeking clarity on her own role and whether politics was the way.

Prior to the March 2017 elections in the state, she met with small groups and family gatherings, listening to the concerns and pain of ordinary people who had suffered loss and harm. In September 2016, she travelled to New Delhi and Chandigarh without raising even a whisper of media attention, in marked contrast to the high decibel coverage which accompanied her on earlier trips when she had to deal with a court which was asking her why she was trying to die by suicide. She used to say that she was merely a democrat on hunger strike for her beliefs, an echo of what Mahatma Gandhi, the man who probably played more of a role in the creation of an independent India than any other individual, did.

A few months later, her campaign was in tatters, her political career had stalled, her hopes were crushed. Sharmila won just ninety votes in her low-budget campaign against Chief Minister Okram Ibobi Singh in his stronghold of Thoubal district. It was a complete humiliation but she said she would continue with the political campaign. Singh steamrolled the opposition with 69 per cent of the vote and 18,649 ballots.

Pradip Phanjoubam, the founding editor of the *Imphal Free Press* and one of the region's most thoughtful writers, said what many believed of Sharmila's politics—that it was naïve. The vote was on that aspect and not on her battle against AFSPA. Her tragic hubris, he said, showed that politics is much more complex than a one-agenda resistance campaign.

> The elections were not just about liking or hating the AFSPA. People's voting decisions are determined by issues pertaining to multiple insecurities, such as unemployment, falling standards of living, a drop in the quality of education and the existential threat to the state on account of deep divisions between ethnic communities—AFSPA is just one among several insecurities.[1]

Yet, as Anubha Bhonsle reflected in *Mother, Where's My Country?*, there is another side to the story of this frail pro-democracy fighter who writes poetry, sought love, and yearned to smell the flowers, live life again and taste real food after so many years of the nasogastric tube that had been keeping her alive. She seemed to have found love in the company of a Goan expatriate who was fiercely opposed by the Meira Paibis or 'guardians of civil society', a women's social movement in Manipur, who used to support her; Bhonsle writes of how Sharmila and her friend sat quietly in the courtroom, during her many court appearances defending the charge of attempting to commit suicide, holding hands before the proceedings began.

The *Imphal Free Press* commented sharply on the insensitivity of the

New Delhi media to her concerns:

> ...the only question that the television journalists seem to have is a 'How do you feel?' Words are virtually put into her mouth to suit their premeditated stories. This is not to question their professional commitment...[But] sensationalism must be checked. In our attempt to get the best story, one should not trample upon the subject. Sharmila did not descend from the heavens in a supernatural phenomenon. She rather emerges from the clutches of an oppressive apparatus, which has dislocated the people in their own land. What is extraordinary about Sharmila is that she is an ordinary human being albeit with an extraordinary spirit. Let us give her some more breathing space.[2]

It could not have been better put.

Sharmila chose to continue her struggle against AFSPA, without the hunger strike, and find a normal life. Surely, sixteen years of a hunger strike was enough to shame not just the Government of India and the states as it is to challenge civil society? But perhaps that is not so. The dependence on one person weakens any campaign or cause. Perhaps, as a strategy it would have been better to have had more hunger strikers who could have done it in relays so that Sharmila could carry on with her battle. There is no shame in this, no contradiction.

Sharmila's story is heroic and tragic: heroic in the scale of her endurance, being fed through the nose for more than fifteen years throughout which she and her relatives, her supporters, the government and the doctors attending on her knew that if she were taken off the nasogastric tube, she would have died in a matter of days. If that had happened, Manipur would have erupted on an unimaginable scale, making whatever had occurred in terms of violence in the past a mere shadow; this could have pitted all of Manipur and its communities against the Indian state, forcing the redeployment of a reluctant army and paramilitary in full force and a crackdown on civilian populations. The army hates this kind of deployment; it wants to be out of it for good because its officers know that apart from the body blows they take, the hatred that the public bears towards them grows manifold. This is not a situation in which an army, under political control, likes to be placed. To be seen as the enemy in its own nation is not just uncomfortable but surely repugnant. In such conditions, the 'people' on the streets would no longer be alone, they would be supported by well-armed cadres of various militias and both urban guerrilla warfare and rural violence would explode.

Sharmila became symbolic (a word she says she dislikes) of opposition to ruthlessness; her single-minded commitment to the righteousness of her cause won national and international praise and she was even nominated for the Nobel Peace Prize. But there was tragedy and despair too: she wanted to breathe the fresh air outside the confines of her room, to be with her family, to savour the pungency of home food, to chat till daybreak with friends and family, to find a sense of normalcy and love. In the last few years of her protest, she was released for a few hours or days every six months and then rearrested on charges of trying to die by suicide. The Government of India, in an effort to blank her out of the public eye, developed a complex set of rules that imposed conditions on media and activists who wanted to meet her. This tangle of regulations included a deposit of ₹1 lakh for an interview or visit. There were penalties for not abiding by the rules although the state government was empowered to change them.[3]

How long can AFSPA resist the thousands like Sharmila who have fought and opposed it? It would make eminent sense for the government to accept the basic demand—repeal the most obnoxious parts of AFSPA for conditions, times and communities are different. As a former army official pointed out to us: 'We are no longer in the 1950s, those times have changed.' But perhaps the Government of India hasn't yet realized that.

◆

It was Manorama Devi's death in 2004 which sparked off the demand for the repeal, the naked protest and the surge of both activism against AFSPA and official resistance to demands for change. But hers was not an isolated case, as we will see in other chapters. Take the case of Mohammad Azad Khan, a twelve-year-old boy in Imphal. On 9 September 2015, a news report spoke of the 2009 case in the Supreme Court involving Azad. Family and neighbours say Azad was reading the papers with a friend on his veranda when he was dragged away by security forces. His relatives were reportedly locked up as he was beaten up and shot dead.[4]

According to the Manipur police, officers of the Assam Rifles claimed they had information about armed militants hiding in the area. Security forces closing in on the house said they saw two boys fleeing into the fields beyond. When they were pursued, the boys apparently broke cover and opened fire as they ran in two different directions. So the soldiers returned fire. But an inquiry by a district court found an FIR had already been filed against Azad before his death. It accused the pre-teen of grave offences under the Arms Act and claimed he belonged to a banned militant organization.

Azad died in 2009. Five years later the Manipur High Court ordered the state government of Manipur to pay ₹5 lakh in compensation to his family. But no security personnel have been held to account for his death. The police reportedly refused to register a case against security forces. As the Supreme Court told off the Manipur government on 10 August, it asked if payment of compensation was the end of the matter.

It also asked a more fundamental and awkward question: 'If you think it was a valid encounter then why are you paying compensation?' After all, the commission said, the major leading the assault did not even know who he was looking for, neither his features nor his age.

◆

Journalist Kishalay Bhattacharjee writes of an extremely disturbing phenomenon of 'marked up kills', secret encounters and the ratcheting up of murders of innocents in the Northeast as well as other states by the army in connivance with the local police in order to gain medals.[5] In one case, the Ashok Chakra, the nation's highest military gallantry award, was given to an army officer who was later investigated by the National Human Rights Commission (NHRC). The NHRC found that the officer had himself written the report of 'heroic action' which recommended the award. Another police officer who was awarded the President's Medal for courage in action was found to have been recommended for an 'encounter' he did not conduct for he arrived at the spot after it was over. No official action has been taken against these individuals and their lies.

But the most troubling accounts from Bhattacharjee show how the murders are conducted after meticulous planning, especially when the victims are either petty criminals or people who don't have relatives or associates who would go after the police to get information about a missing relative or friend. An army officer asks for a 'loan' and the policeman arranges it: the loan is, in the language of the killers, a live human who is brought to a unit and then dispatched after being investigated, with recycled weapons and Bangladeshi currency or 'incriminating documents' dumped on the corpse. The younger officers need to placate higher ranks, meet targets of kills (as in the Punjab in the 1990s)[6] in order to get promotions and awards. It's an unending vicious cycle. The victims, he says, are often men detained for theft or cattle rustling across the border and, in a large number of cases, Muslims.

The implication of these killings are huge for it involves a chief of army staff who served in Nagaland before he took office, the writer says.

But it is not that such incidents are the norm. They remain exceptions; most officers, I believe, are not part of this but the network of killers and their influence is growing. These deeds are known and are seen, according to Kishalay, as an accepted form of swift justice, settling scores as well as moving up the honours list.

Let's go back to the young Muslim boy, Azad. He is picked up from the veranda of his parental home by a joint team of army personnel and police commandos with an Assam Rifles major leading the operation.[7] The commission appointed by the Supreme Court says in its report that he is beaten and his family is locked up in a room. But the room has a window from which they can see that the child is taken to a field, beaten and shot and a pistol tossed near the body. The major's version is that they heard that a Muslim underground group was moving in the area, that two cadres ran away across the paddy field, one of them engaged with the unit and was shot. There were twenty hunters with AK-47s and INSAS rifles, including ten army soldiers. A lone prey, a twelve-year-old child. They fired sixty-five rounds.

That's how it's done, says the officer who confessed to Kishalay. The former points out what we've known all along—and what the courts have also commented upon: the attacking force, soldiers and police, are always unharmed in the life and death struggle which they describe and for which they get gallantry awards.

◆

In a news article in May 2011, *The Telegraph* of Kolkata had a curious and piquant headline: 'Scrap AFSPA', it said, 'help tourism'. It was quoting the official draft of the Manipur state government's Tourism Policy Report and it went on to say:

> A draft Manipur tourism policy has proposed removal of the controversial Armed Forces (Special Powers) Act, 1958, and also the restricted area permit system to boost tourism in the state. While the department of tourism is acting on a new tourism policy for promoting tourism as an economic sector in the state, hurdles imposed by the restricted area permit[8] and the Armed Forces (Special Powers) Act, 1958, have to be removed.[9]

The draft policy added that tourists required a peaceful environment, free from the 'uneasy presence' of armed forces. In addition, it commented that 'the number of tourists, both foreign and domestic, has been increasing gradually during the past few years. But the prolonged economic blockade along the Imphal-Dimapur highway by the All Naga Students Association, Manipur, reduced the number of domestic tourists last year, although the number of foreign tourists had increased.'

Then categorically and unambiguously comes the demand: 'The policy also said the tourism department should move the centre to lift the permit system and vacate armed forces from tourist destinations.' How was such a request from the most unstable and, in terms of local and 'outside' public perception, an extremely unsafe state, received in New Delhi?

With deafening silence, of course.

That silence is not new. It is part of the set of strategies that the centre adopts over time towards what it sees as its central peripheries[10] and therefore their peripheral demands—not just in terms of how it seeks to assert full sovereignty over these margins and their small populations.

Four years down the road, in 2015, Manipur was as far from the removal of that uneasy presence as possible: the state struggled with another round of protests, counterstrikes, police firings and road blockades that brought men and women, school students and teachers, villagers and urban dwellers, young, old and the middle-aged, to the streets. For weeks the government was paralysed and New Delhi just watched.

There were different reasons for the crises in the hills and plains which pitted one against the other. In the valley, the demand was for the imposition of the Inner Line Permit, a rule that would bar outsiders from beyond the state—specifically non-Manipuris—who wished to settle in Manipur from acquiring permanent assets and settling. They would require formal and legal permission. In addition, bowing to the demand of protesters, the state government passed three bills, one of which empowered it to enable settlement of the tribal-dominated hills by the Meiteis of the plains. This outraged both the Nagas and Kukis, the dominant hill tribes, who began their own counter protests, saying that their rights were being trampled upon by the majority Meiteis and that their legal access to control of land in their hill areas was inalienable and should not be infringed.

One Meitei view is that while the Naga, Kuki and other tribes were not hindered in purchasing lands in the valley and many have homes in Imphal and other towns, the Meiteis had been barred by law from accessing purchase of property in the hills. There was one ugly incident in Churachandpur in the Kuki areas where nine persons were gunned down in police firing on an agitating crowd. The nine bodies were placed in the morgue as a commemoration of their 'sacrifice' against Meitei nationalism.

The police and law enforcement authorities were portrayed as protectors and purveyors of the majority Meitei cause, an interesting window of viewing the perceptions of smaller and vulnerable groups in relation to a larger social and publicly more powerful group within a state, not just a region or the country.

In a scathing criticism of AFSPA and its license to use all means necessary to enforce the law, Bimol Akoijam asked: Is the conduct of the military personnel under (AFSPA) a part of a military campaign against an enemy combatant or a law-enforcement operation against a criminal?[11]

In Manipuri usage, obviously the phenomenon that has disturbed normal life in Manipur is referred to as 'khutlai-paiba lalhouba' (literally 'armed rebellion'). Yet the Supreme Court ruling of 1997 on the Act says that 'there is no material on record to show' that the 'disturbed condition' is due to 'armed rebellion'.

Akoijam said that the court's ruling allowed the military to operate as a law-enforcing agency without the restraints imposed on law-enforcing agencies, a point we have noted earlier and that 'such a military law with military style powers have shaped a culture of unbridled violence that has destroyed the normative and institutional mechanisms of a civilized polity in Manipur and [the] Northeast over the years'.

◆

On 27 January 2016, an unsmiling Manipuri policeman in civilian clothes made a stunning confession to the media. Head Constable T. Herojit Singh, his face taut and eyes expressionless, told a group of television and print media interviewers that a story (which few had believed at the time anyway) of a 2009 encounter in which a young militant was allegedly shot dead in a gun battle with local policemen was a complete lie, a fabrication. 'I shot him, six, seven times,' Herojit said, without blinking. The young man only had a cell phone, no weapon. The policeman repeated the story several times to different media, triggering an uproar in Manipur and forcing the central government to call for an explanation from the state.

The policeman said he had been ordered to 'finish off' young Sanjit Meitei by a senior officer. Sanjit had been picked up for allegedly trying to extort funds. Herojit said there were several policemen who were milling around Sanjit, supposedly a member of the People's Liberation Army, one of many rebel groups in the state, who then took him inside a pharmacy in the crowded bazaar.

Herojit told the others to leave and, as the door closed behind them, picked up the 9 mm revolver. At that time the youth's mobile rang repeatedly. Finally, Herojit picked up the phone and put it on speaker mode. A voice said: 'We know you have Sanjit, don't do anything to him, we will give you anything you want. Don't harm him.' Herojit switched the phone off, then turned to his quarry, who was resigned to his fate, and opened fire. The first bullet knocked the boy to the floor, and the gun was fired at least five more times as he lay prostrate. The gunshots were clearly audible to the crowd outside the pharmacy. At the same time, a lone policeman's gun went off, whether in nervousness or a calculated effort to divert attention is not clear. That gunshot smashed into the head of a young pregnant woman, Babina Leishram, killing her instantly. She just happened to be standing nearby. Death comes to those who stand and stare in such situations.

A video recording of the incident clearly captured the rapid fire of shots when a troop of police rushed into the building amid the flurry of activity. First Babina's body and then Sanjit's bleeding corpse are lifted and tossed, like sacks of vegetables, onto the cold floor of a van.

He felt nothing, said Sanjit's confessed killer. He was just following orders. And as *Indian Express* reporter Esha Roy noted, the 'swagger' of a Manipuri police commando was missing in his interview. 'His hands shook' and he nervously and 'repeatedly brushed his forehead'.[12] But there is a catch here as well as a horrible realization of how deep and rapid has been Manipur's descent into the depths of despair and lawlessness. A police officer, of whatever rank, under the laws of the land, is supposed to protect the person who has been delivered into his or her custody. Of course, that this rarely happens in the Northeast or any other part of the country is of little consolation to us. A policeman is not supposed to kill a person under his custody and hence under his protection. But then all of us know how much of a seemingly 'normal' circumstance death in police custody is anywhere in India.

Of course, the man accused by Herojit of ordering Sanjit's killing has furiously denied the charge as 'motivated, concocted and baseless'.[13] Herojit was unmoved and even declared that his immediate boss had claimed that the top police officer in the state as well as the then chief minister (Ibobi Singh) had okayed the execution.

The Central Bureau of Investigation has had an enquiry into the case since 2009 in which Herojit and nine others are named as accused. The suspended policeman says that none of the others were involved and that he was the only one who pulled the trigger. But why did the issue surface six years after the incident? Herojit said that he feared for his life. So it wasn't a desire to make a clean breast of things or a burst of conscience or to ask for the forgiveness of the family he had destroyed. It was a simple survival tactic, a ploy to stay alive, a chance that he did not give Sanjit, if his account is to be believed. There is no reason to disbelieve the accuracy of his statement, about himself, anyway, if not about the other officers and the chief minister. But as we have seen before, perhaps the most awful and ugly aspect of such incidents is the seamless manner in which impunity travels across borders of security and government structures, processes and organizations. It infects civilian organizations. AFSPA and its continuous use endows those who do not have its legal protection, such as the police, with the belief that they actually not only hold powers of life and death over citizens but also cannot be called to account, just like the army soldiers.

When I called the NHRC about the case, an official there was more interested in brushing me off, saying that I should speak to someone else. 'We have to go through due process,' he declared pompously over the phone. But hearing the anger in my voice, he hastened to say: 'But I understand your anguish.' It wasn't a question of anguish, I snapped, appalled that a human rights organization like the NHRC was behaving like a slothful, disinterested bureaucracy.

Luckily I had shot off a couple of emails to another NHRC officer—those were taken up as an official complaint. Due process was followed but it remains egregious that such pitiful responses signal the incapacity of India's principal human rights protector, which appears as flabby as any part of a vast government and just as unable to respond swiftly to issues of urgency.

The Commonwealth Human Rights Initiative called the shooting, if true, an act of 'premeditated murder'. Maja Daruwala, its director at the time, asked for the protection of Herojit as a 'key witness'. Daruwala said in a statement:

> The core issues at hand are whether there was an order to murder an unarmed person, who gave it, and how far up the chain of conspiracy action and intent went. Unfortunately, the usual pattern we see is that the public discourse will subvert the main issue. Motives will now be questioned, character vilified. None of this has any bearing. The state must not allow talk of insurgency to mask murder, subversion of justice and impunity.[14]

In this conundrum, Manipur's official system and that of the Government of India will be found lacking, time and again. Without removing the scourge of AFSPA, such unacceptable conduct will remain business as usual, raising anger and outrage when they are reported but fading away in the face of greater furies elsewhere.

The sequence of events makes fascinating reading: Herojit's confession came six years after Sanjit was shot. The shooting itself took place five years after the murder of Manorama Devi. And when Manorama Devi was killed, a young woman named Irom Sharmila was already in the fourth year of a hunger strike to remove AFSPA from the statute books. By January 2016, when Herojit made his blinding confession, Irom Sharmila had completed fifteen years of her solitary battle. She had fought much of this struggle alone in the isolation of a hospital ward and away from the support of family and friends.

The number of dissenting voices is growing. For example, there's Leika Yumnam, a firebrand, energetic activist from Manipur, who describes herself on her Facebook page as 'A high functioning neurotic running on caffeine, nihilism and a pinch of inner peace' who courageously takes on those who discriminate against outsiders in her home state of Manipur, apart from robustly challenging the might of the Indian state. This is especially tough in her state's cloudy, ruffled waters and no less so since she's the daughter of a former senior police official. Her father, Yumnam Joykumar Singh, contested elections in March 2017, won a seat and was picked as deputy chief minister by the new BJP boss of Manipur, N. Biren. And therein lies a new story of the threads that seem to be unravelling and being woven together constantly in a place that is always in flux and ferment. The script of this story is still being written and it will take a few years to see how and whether it will change some of the narratives that drive Manipur or the perils that hem it in, seemingly from every side. While a few lines of the script have been penned, the role and future of contestations by those who oppose the 'mainland' narrative by Leika and many others like her, such as the anti-dam crusader Ramananda, who seek inclusive growth and not an economic paradigm which is pushed by corporates and multilateral institutions in league with governments, are not yet clear. And what of the Naga demand for a homeland that includes parts of Manipur, Assam and Arunachal Pradesh, which has the potential to unleash egregious violence by all three sides and involve ordinary people in the crossfire? How will that play out?

We may be able to suggest what could be done in this and other situations but a clearer picture will develop over time and depends on actors within the state as well as outside. This is how it has always been and perhaps this is how it may be for some time to come.

Take the case of Biren who was the former right-hand man of Ibobi Singh, who broke away from his one-time mentor, joined the BJP and led the party to a feisty second-place finish. But Biren wasn't content with that. He had other plans. A former journalist and Opposition legislator who migrated to the Congress, as many politicians have done in states across the country these past decades, to become part of the ruling hegemon and be on the safe side of New Delhi, he strategized an alliance with the crafty Himanta Biswa Sarma, who burst onto the national stage in 2016 by designing a stunning BJP victory in his home state of Assam, the first time the saffron party had been able to win enough votes to form a government. Sarma knew the politics of the state and of the Northeast like the back of his hand. A one-time lieutenant of another powerful Congress satrap, three-time chief minister Tarun Gogoi of Assam, he had bolted from the party in anger along with a bunch of supporters after Gogoi brought his son, Gaurav, into politics and gave him the family parliamentary pocket borough of Koliabor. Sarma, deeply ambitious, tireless and extremely capable, saw this as a threat to his hope of succeeding the elder Gogoi as Assam chief minister, perhaps a step up to greater things.

The break-up was bitter. Sarma swore to do his best to make the entire region, not just his state, 'mukt (free)' of the Congress. After winning Assam for the BJP, he went about his goal methodically, first toppling a Congress government in Arunachal Pradesh. Although he had the mortification of seeing the defectors go back to the Congress, he manoeuvred to bring the entire flock back to the BJP fold, no mean feat. All of this happened in the space of a few months. It was to Sarma that Biren turned, having established connections with the Naga Democratic Front and the Nationalist Peoples Party of the late Purno Sangma which had won a clutch of seats.

Deals were brokered, ministerial posts were promised, mobile phones in New Delhi and Imphal hummed and the Congress with twenty-eight seats, and the biggest party in the sixty-seat assembly, found itself out of a job. Biren sewed up a coalition and got Governor Najma Heptullah's nod to form a government. An immediate result of the new government taking office was the end of a long and bitter blockade in the Naga hill areas, imposed by the United Naga Council (UNC), which had opposed the creation of new districts and special laws that they said undercut the rights of hill tribes, especially the Nagas (their tribal rivals, the Kukis, with whom there had been a bloodletting in the 1990s, said exactly the same thing for their areas). One of the leaders of the agitation was picked for the new cabinet—clearly the blockade became politically and otherwise unviable. Biren had set the end of the blockade as one of his priorities.

In the past years, such blockades had created an increasingly sharp divide between the Nagas and the Meiteis of the Imphal Valley, with the latter having to cope with acute fuel shortages (especially of cooking gas) and subsisting on coal-fired or wood stoves, a surge in prices for essential commodities and long queues at petrol stations. The anger was palpable and grew, finally exploding into an attack on a convoy of vehicles heading for the hill areas by mobs which pulled the passengers out—but didn't harm them. The police escort was overpowered and twenty-one vehicles and the luggage and property of passengers were torched. Although many Manipuris came out to give succour to the victims, the bitterness and memories of that day and other days have come to stay.

The centre dispatched contingents of paramilitary troops to ensure the violence was not repeated. It was a small gesture but thanks to the immense patience of the Meiteis, it was not too late.

Phanjoubam reflected on the complexity of his state's condition and the difficulties in arriving at any formula which would be acceptable to different sides. As he pointed out:

> ...the UNC's insistence on consolidation and the political autonomy of Nagalim (the larger Naga homeland) corresponded with the NSCN(IM)'s pursuit of an exclusive sovereign Naga nation carved out of neighbouring states, including a huge chunk of Manipur, and merged with Nagaland. It is ironic that the NSCN(IM) and UNC, who are pursuing grand themes of 'shared sovereignty' and 'shared competencies' with the Government of India are averse to any idea of a shared homeland with tribes and communities who also have been inhabiting the same tracts of lands as them.[15]

Chapter 3

THE NAGAS: A ROCKY ROAD TO PEACE

The fundamental right to a life of dignity was something that statesman and Prime Minister Atal Bihari Vajpayee thought about and spoke of eloquently during his first visit to Nagaland in 2003. In two speeches that I helped draft, Vajpayee, who moderated much of his earlier Hindutva beliefs during his tenure, spoke the following memorable lines in Kohima, trying to obliterate the hurt of the past and even bury Nehru's anger of half a century earlier when he was snubbed in the same town.

> Unfortunately, too much blood was shed in Nagaland in the decades gone by. A lot of people suffered. The wheels of development stopped. Mistakes were committed. Now the time has come to leave the sad chapter of conflict and violence behind us. Rather than remaining tied to the past, we have to take care of the present and look to the future. This is the time for reconciliation and peacemaking. This is also the path that Mahatma Gandhi and Loknayak Jayaprakash Narayan wanted us to follow. Both were true friends of Naga people. It is true that, of all the states in India, Nagaland has a unique history. We are sensitive to this historical fact.[1]

His government, Vajpayee said, wanted 'to achieve permanent peace with honour and dignity' with the Nagas. Then he spoke some more powerful lines; I take pleasure and not a little pride in reproducing them because I had penned some thoughts in an earlier draft and handed them over to one of his speech writers a few days earlier.[2] The prime minister used them extensively.

> Let us leave behind all the unfortunate things that happened in the past. For too long this fair land has been scarred and seared by violence. It has been bled by the orgy of killings of human beings by human beings. Each death pains me. Each death diminishes us. My government has been doing everything possible to stop this bloodshed,

so that we can together inaugurate a new era of peace, development and prosperity in Nagaland. The past cannot be rewritten. But we can write our common future with our collective, cooperative efforts.

◆

The 'sad chapter of conflict and violence' had begun long before India gained Independence. On 14 August 1947, a young Naga walked to the only post and telegraph office in a small town and dispatched a telegram to the secretary general of the United Nations in New York.[3] According to the popular story, the telegram simply said that the Nagas on that day had declared their independence as a free and sovereign nation. But official British records show that the deputy commissioner of the district rebuffed numerous efforts by villagers from the legendary village of Khonoma[4] to send the telegrams. Later that day, in the garden of the official bungalow of A. Kevichusa,[5] the leader of the Naga National Council (NNC), the blue flag of the NNC, with a rainbow and star, adopted later even by bitter rival factions in the Naga movement, fluttered for the first time from a simple bamboo pole. Not many in India paid attention to these two acts of civil disobedience because the country was getting over the horrors of Partition and preparing to launch its own momentous celebrations of Independence from the British, when the inspirational words of Jawaharlal Nehru would ring across a nation and touch it at a moment of breathless hope and aspiration, troubled by pain, tears and bloodshed: 'At the stroke of the midnight hour, as the world sleeps, India awakes to life and freedom.' And he spoke to his fellow countrymen as 'your first servant', with kindness and humility.

The Nagas, even if they heard and were touched by Nehru's speech, had a different world view of themselves and their future—and it was not a future with India or in its tight embrace. Xavier Mao,[6] a teacher of philosophy at the North Eastern Hill University and an ardent Naga nationalist, spoke of this perception. Tracing the creation of the Naga Club, the first political association among the Nagas after World War I, following the return of Nagas who had been with the Labour Corps in Europe and had seen a little of the world and nascent political awakenings, Mao said that the club 'had (the) limited purpose or aim of representing Naga interests to the British Government without having a very clear picture of what later came to be known as Naga Nationalism'.[7] He noted that 'the consciousness of nationhood was not explicitly present' in the club's submission of a memorandum to the Simon Commission which visited

Nagaland in 1929. The memorandum essentially called on the British to leave the Nagas as they had been before colonial power came upon them. The Nagas took this to mean as 'free people...and not to include them within the Indian Union'. 'The outcome of the memorandum was the declaration of the Naga areas as a Special Backward Area later changed into an Excluded Area status by the British India Act of 1935 which became effective in 1937, since the Nagas objected to the word "backward".'

The Nagas, one of the most robust, reflective and remarkable communities in South Asia, have challenged every Indian government since Independence, through a war of weapons, ideas and words. The gauntlet was tossed down in 1918 with the formation of the Naga Club, followed by a presentation on 10 January 1929 to the statutory commission named the Simon Commission after its chairman, Sir John Simon.

The commission was looking at future constitutional structures under a possible reforms package. Members of the Naga delegation included a range of government employees who were mostly interpreters and teachers as well as a doctor, an overseer and a clerk. It demanded that the Nagas be placed under direct British rule and rejected the reforms plan which sought to bracket them with the rest of India.

The memorandum's closing paragraph has been at the core of Naga political mobilization since:

> ...we pray that the British Government will continue to safeguard our rights against all encroachment from other people who are more advanced than us by withdrawing our country that we should not be thrust to the mercy of other people who could never be subjected; but to leave us alone to determine ourselves as in ancient times.

A member of that commission from the British Parliament was the Labour Party leader, Sir Clement Attlee, who succeeded Sir Winston Churchill as prime minister after World War II and played a key role in India's Independence.

The impact of the visit to Kohima, then little more than a village and not the bustling town that it is today, on the MPs and especially on the future premier of Britain has not been closely documented. But it was substantial enough for the commission to propose that the Nagas along with other hill tribes such as the Mizos, Garos, Khasis, Jaintias and parts of Lakhimpur and what is today's Arunachal Pradesh be placed in an 'excluded area', directly administered by British officers who were responsible to the governor and not the chief minister of the province (Assam). 'Nowhere in

India is the difference between the life and outlook of the...hill-men and the totally distinct civilization of the plains more visible,' the commission's report said. Referring to the need for change, it prophesied: 'If progress is to benefit and not to destroy these people, then it must come about gradually and the adjustment of their needs with the interests of the immigrant will provide a problem of great complexity and importance for many generations to come.'

Then came a sentence which was submerged in the tumult of the anti-colonial sentiment sweeping the subcontinent: 'It is a matter for the most serious consideration that whether the British Government which found the hill tribes independent can leave them dependent.'

When the commission's report was debated in the British Parliament in 1935, its members said that they were advocating protection for the hill groups, not independence. Later, Attlee himself was to tell Parliament in 1947 that as far as the 'hills in the Northeast Frontier are concerned, they come into the Province of Assam and will be dealt with by the constitutional assembly of which Assam forms a part'.

Over a decade later, political conditions were dramatically different. World War II was over and the British were preparing to leave India. But how were they to leave the backward and excluded areas? There was serious consideration of the Crown Colony Plan mentioned earlier, devised by Sir Robert Reid, who served as the governor of Assam, which would have ensured direct British rule of a large swathe of territory from parts of Western Burma across the Chittagong Hill Tracts up to the Tibet border. Naturally, this was unacceptable to the Congress and fell through.

Then followed a set of intense discussions over the years within the club and a group of senior Nagas who were closely linked with J. P. Mills, the anthropologist-administrator of the Naga Hills district, his successor Charles Pawsey, and Philip F. Adams, the adviser to the Assam governor.

In a collection of fascinating notes, British officials wrote to each other about developments in the Naga Hills during the run up to 1947. Pawsey sent a note in 1947 about divisions within the Naga fold among the various Angami tribe groups, Sema, Ao and others.

The British officer W. H. Archer, Pawsey's deputy, heard from his senior administrator that 'Khonoma [was] still making trouble over the independence racket and Kevichusa has resigned from Govt. service. But their influence is not increasing and Kohima is very angry with them. The Southern Angamis vacillate and the others are all against them.'

These divisions were to weaken the Naga coalition against India in the decades to come and become sharper with time, instead of being easier to manage.

Kevichusa was appointed along with the Ao educationist Mayangnokcha Ao by the Kohima Tribal Council[8] to represent the Naga views to the Cabinet Mission 'should a call' come.

According to official notes, there were also differences on whether the Naga leaders should go to meet Sir Akbar Hydari, the governor of Assam, who had drafted a nine-point agreement on behalf of the Government of India. This was discussed with the NNC and finally signed in Shillong on 9 June 1947. The agreement, according to Xavier Mao, 'reflects the willingness of the Naga people to enter into a peaceful settlement of their political status'. While Mao said that it included 'experimental coexistence with India for a period of ten years', to be reviewed at the end of that period, New Delhi viewed it completely differently. Signing on a clause that said specifically that the Nagas would be with India for an initial period of ten years meant, to the Indians, very clearly and simply that they had made their choice. Although the Nagas say that this was 'misunderstood' as 'a permanent settlement', India viewed it simply as a closed chapter, an accomplished fact of integration with the Indian union.

After meeting Mahatma Gandhi at New Delhi in July 1947, Naga leader Angami Zapu Phizo announced that the Nagas would declare independence on 14 August, one day before India unfurled its own flag of freedom. Archer's own notes[9] followed a series of events, each perhaps less known than the other, even among the Nagas: for one, it says clearly that the Naga flag was raised at the Kevichusa residence but taken down by Pawsey and that Mrs Kevichusa was 'in hysterics'; one note says that there were twelve efforts by the 'Khonoma group' to send telegrams announcing Nagaland's freedom but Pawsey intercepted all of them and ensured that no telegrams were sent. And finally, since they were unsure about how to proceed after the declaration of independence, the major Angami village of Khonoma and the Mao tribe on the border with Manipur agreed to join the nine-point accord. Sir Akbar agreed to their view asking them not to insist on saying that they would leave the Indian union at the expiry of the ten-year period.

Thus the phrasing of the ninth point of what became known as the Hydari–NNC Accord was always ambiguous because it was ambiguously drafted—it said that the Nagas would have the right to determine their future after a period of ten years. But, then, which country, having absorbed a small nationality or ethnic group into its midst, would willingly let it go?

Charles Pawsey,[10] the knowledgeable administrator of the Naga Hills, who had been in the area throughout the critical war years, foresaw trouble. Pawsey had served Assam for decades with distinction and dedication. Assistant commissioner in Assam in 1919, he became director of land records in 1932 and was made a deputy commissioner in 1935. He was deputy commissioner, Naga Hills, during the Burma campaigns of 1942–1944.

In a note to a junior officer shortly before Independence, Pawsey remarked pensively: 'I don't know what the eventual fate of the Nagas will be, there's nothing more to help them that we haven't already done. But it seems a pity that we couldn't have had a few more years to get things straight.'

But the leader who was to be in charge of India appeared to be very clear on where the Nagas were to be. On the eve of Indian Independence, Nehru made his views about the Naga demands known in a letter on 1 August 1946 to the NNC. This is Nehru's earliest and most comprehensive policy statement on Naga issues. He declared that it must continue to form part of India and Assam, when India became independent. He said:

> It is obvious that Naga territory in Eastern Assam is much too small to stand by itself politically or economically. It lies between two huge countries, India and China, and part of it consists of rather backward people who require considerable help. When India is independent, as it is bound to be soon, it will not be possible for the British Government to hold on to the Naga territory or any part of it. They would be isolated between India and China. Inevitably, therefore, this Naga territory must form part of India and of Assam with which it has developed such close associations.[11]

After his election as president of the Naga National Council on 11 December 1950, A. Z. Phizo called for 'non-cooperation' and 'civil disobedience' and held a limited 'plebiscite' where he proclaimed people had overwhelmingly voted for independence (an unbelievable 99.9 per cent in favour. Of course, there were no election commissions or independent observers to assess the veracity of the claims). In 1952, the Nagas boycotted the first Indian general election and two years later, Phizo announced that the Sovereign Republic of Nagaland would be replaced by the Naga Central Government which was again to change its name to the Federal Government of Nagaland in 1959. By this time, a full-scale conflict had exploded in the Naga Hills against Indian security forces and the Assam police. However, the first seeds of division and discord within the Naga family had already been sown. Phizo's aide and then principal critic T.

Sakhrie, from Khonoma village, was killed by extremists for saying that it would be better to come to a peaceful resolution of the issue through talks with New Delhi since they would not be able to defeat the Indian Army by force of arms. The subsequent bad blood resulted in killings and counter-killings and decades of hatred and suspicion between the two families until the violence was peacefully resolved more than fifty years later.[12]

◆

The second incident with the Nagas directly involved what Jawaharlal Nehru perceived as a personal affront. On 30 March 1953, Nehru, along with his Burmese counterpart, Thakin Nu, popularly known as U Nu, visited Kohima. They were to address a public rally together, the kind of grand gesture Nehru enjoyed. U Nu was not just the leader of a neighbouring nation but also an ally of India's policy of non-alignment of equidistance from the two superpowers, the United States and the Soviet Union, and their respective 'blocs'. Bureaucratic insensitivity led to a missed opportunity.

Several Naga elders sought a meeting with the Indian prime minister. Fearing a possible confrontation and concerned about Nehru's famed temper, the deputy commissioner of the Naga Hills district informed the elders that there could be no audience. At the meeting ground, the public had been waiting patiently for Nehru and U Nu to appear. As word spread that their elders would not receive an audience, the Nagas in the crowd turned their backs to the leaders. What Nehru saw, to his everlasting chagrin, was hundreds of Nagas whacking their backsides as they left. In a towering rage, angered by the insult in the presence of the Burmese statesman, he vowed never to visit the Naga Hills again. He kept his word.

For a variety of reasons, not limited to the 'insult', the surge of violent activities against the Indian state started soon after that ill-fated visit. As did the increasingly harsher responses by the state. First, as attacks on police officials, parties and stations grew and Nagas began snatching weapons, the Assam government promulgated the Assam Maintenance of Public Order (Autonomous Districts) Act, 1953 (Act XVI of 1953) just two months later.[13] It was the first of a series of successive and increasingly draconian laws that were to be used to govern the Naga Hills and then other parts of the Northeast, as group after ethnic group rose in revolt against the state. By the 1990s, such laws were in place in no less than five states, including Assam.[14]

The 1953 Act specifically mentioned that it 'shall apply to the Naga Hills

District' and come into force 'at once'. It was meant to be an amendment of the Assam Maintenance of Public Order Act of 1947. The provisions are sweeping in their scope: the movements and activities of individuals and associations are regulated. It was discriminatory and placed enormous powers of discretion and arbitrariness in the hands of officials who were mandated to discharge their duties. Thus, an executing officer, not necessarily a magistrate, needs no proof except his own personal 'opinion' to proceed against a suspect. According to another provision, even if a person's life and activities were 'restricted', the authority needed only to inform the person of the order 'without disclosing facts which the said authority considers it would be against the public interest to disclose'.

A third clause allows 'the inhabitants of any area' to be 'collectively' fined in any manner the 'authority' thinks fit. A sub-inspector of police can arrest anyone on suspicion, without warrant. The Act makes no mention of requiring an arrested person to be produced in court, although the maximum penalty for not appearing is up to two years' imprisonment or fine or both. To protect the police, no suit, prosecution or other legal proceedings were allowed against any officer acting under the act.

This last clause is crucial because it was to form the core of AFSPA five years later, providing omnibus protection to any soldier or officer who may have violated the human rights of a citizen by what otherwise would have been illegal and forceful entry into homes, damage to property, detention without a warrant or custodial deaths. AFSPA wiped the slate clean, all was forgiven, all was acceptable, all acts of omission and commission were justified. What is truly extraordinary is that these conditions and clauses have continued without change, brushing aside legal challenges, for six decades and appear to be set in stone.

The Assam Maintenance of Public Order Act, 1953, laid the foundation for other extraordinary legislation, which followed in quick succession. These laws have successively denied basic rights to citizens and cloaked judicial proceedings. In recent years, with the growth of civil society movements, especially in the human rights sector, the media have begun to function as both investigators of abuse and disseminators of information about such violations.

The 1953 Act was followed by the Assam Disturbed Areas Act (Act XIX of 1955) in December, which became operational on 1 January 1956. The Act itself was preceded by an ordinance of the same name (Ordinance V of 1955). This legislation and the Assam Maintenance of Public Order Act, 1953 were applicable to the Naga Hills district.

The origin of such draconian or restrictive legislation should pique our interest. I was hardly surprised when a little research revealed that the Disturbed Areas Act was promulgated at the time of Partition in 1947 when the Government of India enacted four ordinances to tackle extensive and extremely brutal communal rioting. These were the Bengal Disturbed Areas Ordinance (Special Powers of Armed Forces); the Assam Disturbed Areas Ordinance (Special Powers of Armed Forces); the East Punjab and Delhi Disturbed Areas Ordinance (Special Powers of Armed Forces); and the United Provinces Disturbed Areas Ordinance (Special Powers of Armed Forces). They were designed to confront the Hindu-Muslim riots of the time, when India and Pakistan were born in blood. The Assam Disturbed Areas Act empowered authorities to:

- Declare any area 'disturbed';
- Empower any magistrate or police officer of sub-inspector rank or havildar in the case of a police armed branch, including the Assam Rifles, to fire upon or use force to the extent of causing death, if he 'thinks' such a step is necessary to maintain 'public order';
- Block processions and legal proceedings against any person acting under this law except with the previous permission/sanction of the state government (executive) that first ordered the action.

Less than two years later came the law that is one of the most hated in contemporary India—the Armed Forces (Special Powers) Act, 1958 (Assam and Manipur) was enacted, embracing the second and third clauses in the Assam Disturbed Areas Act, which empowered soldiers to shoot to kill and then protected them against any prosecution. A specific paragraph was written into AFSPA, which said that immunity against civil and criminal process against security personnel was guaranteed. None other than the central government, by precise sanction, could overturn this permanent protection.

The promulgation of AFSPA was also important in other ways: it assigned specifically to the military the major role in combating insurgencies and armed struggles against the state. Till this time, the police and paramilitary units such as the Assam Rifles were the main tools of defence. AFSPA changed that equation in the 'disturbed areas' for all time.[15] The army and other central forces were now to become the principal weapons of war, following their own leadership, strategies and procedures. There were no other options at the time.

This was a turning point in policy formulation and field action for, in my view, it represented a pivotal moment, one when civilian power to deal with a political challenge was 'transferred' in an extremely sensitive and complex region to the army and paramilitary forces. The latter were not equipped to deal with political nuances or complexities but only with conflict. The stage was set for a disaster.

As a result, a military response to a political problem became embedded in the system and in New Delhi's approach. The number of efforts to stifle the armed struggle by the Nagas grew. In 1961, the central government passed the Nagaland Security Regulations Act (NSRA) (Gazette of India Extraordinary Part II, Section I, 11 April 1962); this and the Disturbed Areas Act are still in place. Over and above AFSPA, the Nagaland Security Regulations Act put more sweeping powers in the hands of police and civilian authorities. It cannot be but an irony that in Nagaland, where the first shots against the 'idea of India' were fired over six decades ago, Naga politicians and officials use both AFSPA and the NSRA against their opponents, perceived and real.

The Nagaland Security Regulations endowed officers with the right to:

- Use force to the causing of death if an officer suspects a person was likely to commit an act of 'looting' in a riotous situation; control the production, sale and purchase of any commodity—including transport, modification, repair, etc.;
- Evict any person from his own property; such property can be confiscated/requisitioned; enable the governor to take a range of additional actions, which included the arbitrary relocation of villages.

In addition, the judiciary could not interfere with the powers or processes pursued by the government. AFSPA transformed the government's approach to the problem, substituting central security forces for the police. This signified a new phase in the conflict—an acceptance that the challenge from the Nagas was far more serious than previously thought and that armed forces required 'special powers' to deal with the situation. Local police and constabulary were thus viewed as not being able to deal with the Nagas who, though not trained in insurgency, had a tradition of fighting against intruders, rival villages and tribes in their forested hills.

At the time, the areas covered by the new law were the Naga Hills district in Assam and three subdivisions (Ukhrul, Tamenglong and Mao) in what was then the union territory of Manipur. What started as a temporary measure to deal with the Naga movement was invoked in the Lushai Hills district of Assam (currently the state of Mizoram) in 1966; in the 1980s, the law was extended to Tripura and the largest state of the region, Assam, following insurgencies there, and expanded to the whole of Manipur.

In addition, as originally enacted, the Act conferred the authority to declare an area as 'disturbed' only on the state government. This is the enabling provision that legalizes the use of AFSPA; without it, the act cannot be used.

In 1972, however, the same authority was given to the central government to enable its armed forces to exercise the special powers. What are perceived widely as emergency and draconian powers are dressed up as normal procedure. Consequently, there have been instances in which the state governments of Tripura and Nagaland wanted to lift the 'disturbed area' status and the central government wanted to reimpose it. All it requires is for the central government to propose to Parliament an extension of the use of the act before it expires in the specific state—even if the concerned state has not asked for it or has opposed such extension. A great deal of ennui has set in: casualness on the part of the government, and a feeling of helplessness on the part of the states and people's organizations.

If this were not enough, a whole slew of all-India legislation was enacted between the 1960s and 2004. These laws were targeted at problems of internal security, which the police were viewed as incapable of handling because the uprisings constituted an armed insurrection against the whole state, not just a part of it, and hence justified the use of the army or paramilitary forces. These included the Maintenance of Internal Security Act and the Unlawful Activities (Prevention) Act, 1967, which lapsed and was reintroduced in 2004 and then passed virtually unanimously by Parliament that year.

The Unlawful Activities (Prevention) Act was the first comprehensive legislation passed by New Delhi that dealt with the problems of secession. At the time, the Naga armed movement and the Mizo insurgency were viewed as major threats, and the new law strengthened AFSPA by defining unlawful organizations and facilitating bans on them. In addition, it empowered the central government to control the use of funds by such groups. In other words, the central government had created a legal framework to target the political associations and support systems that sustained the insurgencies. AFSPA was intended to be just a military tool, although it was used extensively against civilian populations. The Unlawful Activities (Prevention) Act buttressed that power by hitting at the basic freedoms that were constitutionally guaranteed to all Indians but which it sought to deny to those living under the pall of

AFSPA: the freedoms of expression and association as well as of movement.

In 2004, Unlawful Activities (Prevention) Act was repealed, following much criticism over its use and abuse in the nearly forty years of its existence. However, bowing to national security concerns in the wake of an attack on Parliament and an India-Pakistan standoff that had lasted almost a year, a new law, the Unlawful Activities (Prevention) Act, introduced specific clauses to battle 'terrorism'. In this new law, enacted post-9/11, lawmakers took pains to define terrorism in detail. Yet despite all these laws and a large presence of the armed forces, some forty armed groups—most little more than a band of irregular mercenaries with a group tag—have continued to function in most states of the region, except Sikkim.

Again and again, we see the power conflict between different forms of social and political authorities, within the state and its processes as well as outside of it.

◆

If you go to the hills of Benreu and trundle down a narrow path outside the village, you'll come to a place where a high stone slab commemorates the centenary of the coming of the Christian missionaries to Peren district and specifically Benreu. You'll notice a cluster of small gravestones with epitaphs to individual soldiers 'of the Naga national army who laid down his life for national cause, mourned by his wife and family'. And so on. I asked our guide: 'They were fighting the Indian Army, right?' That's a standard assumption when one comes across such graves along remote roadsides and busy paths.

Of course not, came the response. They were fighting Gaidinliu's people. And herein lay the complexities and multilayers of Naga nationalism, competing and collaborating with Indian nationalism. Gaidinliu, or Rani Gaidinliu, as Pandit Nehru called her, had, along with her leader Jadonang, founded a sect that rejected Christianity and espoused the Heraka faith with vague connections to Hinduism and idol worship. The movement was also a rough and ready reckoner to the rejection of colonialism as they raised the flag of revolt against the British. The Heraka group led an offensive against the Kukis, whom they regarded as ultra-loyal to the British. Jadonang was captured and hanged on charges of murder and violence and inciting rebellion against the crown. Gaidinliu continued her struggle against the British whom she regarded as oppressive. She was especially opposed to their forced conscription of villagers. Gaidinliu was just seventeen when she was imprisoned.

In 1937, Nehru met her in Shillong Jail and, in his incurable romanticism, portrayed her as 'this brave Naga princess pining away for freedom in a distant jail' in his prison diaries which were published as *The Discovery of India*. Released only when India became independent, she became a Member of Parliament while government awards too came her way, including the Padma Bhushan,[16] given to some distinguished figures (and others not so).

But Gaidinliu's importance does not lie in her resistance to the British but, as Benreu shows, to her struggle against her fellow Nagas who were fighting the ideas espoused by her mentor Nehru and his daughter Indira Gandhi. The fact that the Heraka faith resisted the Church and the NNC was reason for the BJP and its acolytes, including Prime Minister Narendra Modi, to celebrate her birth centenary with a big exhibition in no less a place than the Nehru Memorial Library. The BJP, with Modi repeatedly calling her 'Rani Ma', thus appropriated a Congress legacy without a whisper of protest from the Nagas, the Congress or anyone else. In fact, even the Nagaland chief minister of the time, T. R. Zeliang, himself a Rongmei Naga from the Peren area, was present and made supportive remarks at the event. Everyone conveniently forgot that for the Kukis this was a painful and difficult chapter of their lives which involved issues not just of community and custom but also of land and resources, which lie at the heart of multiple contestations between different ethnic groups in the region.

Gaidinliu's importance was that she had a following, no matter how much the anti-Heraka Nagas would deny it, and it made perfect sense for the BJP and Congress to claim someone who was opposing those fighting the nation state. She had all the right qualifications: she was Naga, had fought against the British and the NNC. As far as the opposition to the Kukis was concerned, it was papered over. How else is the nationalist narrative otherwise to be understood? There is no further explanation of this.

Although many Nagas deny her, the effort is to commemorate Gaidinliu in perpetuity, through awards and celebrations. There's need for caution when one walks in Naga history, for scattered across the landscape are both old and new graves. On some of them, the earth has not yet dried.

◆

The Indian Army came to the village on the high ridge of the Naga Hills after a brief mortar attack. The first mortar shell blew to bits a young mother who was nursing her child. Every man, woman and child, barring one old man, fled into the jungles. The old man stayed behind because in the tradition of the Zeliang tribe, villagers do not return to a settlement that they have abandoned completely. Instead, they set up a new one. The harvest remained uncut for months; the women would stealthily slip down to the stream at night, babies strapped to their backs, to collect water; there would be no fires lit to cook for fear of alerting the soldiers.

The granary bins in every home of Benreu were ransacked. Vegetables, pots and furniture were destroyed by the intruding forces. Only when the fear had abated after three or four months—nobody is sure exactly how long because it happened a long time ago and those who remember it are old—did the villagers return to their homes. 'When the forces came, they would beat and harass anyone, either on suspicion or just like that, it was a time of great fear for everyone,' said one village elder. The humiliations were constant as patrols came, hunting for insurgents and informers.

This was the last village to fall to the Indian Army after A. Z. Phizo, the charismatic leader of the movement against India, had called upon his people to revolt. Phizo was from the Angami tribe but held the support of other tribal groups—there are sixteen in Nagaland—as he forged an alliance of the Naga National Council and what it called the Federal Government of Nagaland.[17] The fighters had held their ground but retreated in the face of superior forces, armed with better weapons and mortars. The guerrillas faded into the jungle, to ambush and harass the security forces or SFs as the army and paramilitary forces came to be called. To the government, its media as well as the independent press,[18] the guerrillas were simply 'hostiles'—an ugly, anachronistic term that conjures up images of a shadowy group of evil intent, bent on bloodshed. By designing and persisting with this caricature of the Naga opponent, the media, both government and independent, and India's existing and soon to become even larger gargantuan bureaucracy, especially its intelligence and security agencies, pitted India against its tribals, without considering a madhyam, a middle path. The 'for us or against us' ideology, so simplistic, patronizing and nationalistic, immediately strengthened the resistance to the 'idea of India'. For if as Gandhi said, India was a garden with many flowers, then were the tribals, because they thought and lived differently, thorns to be plucked out?[19]

Benreu, like many parts of the Naga Hills, had little contact with the rest of Assam and the plains, let alone the Indian mainland. Like other upland groups in South and Southeast Asia, spanning the entire Himalayan range and the fingers of ranges that radiated southeastward from India's east, from Afghanistan to Vietnam, they had rarely been conquered but sometimes defeated. They were brutally oppressed by Siu-Ka-Pha, the first Ahom king, who mercilessly tortured his captives as a lesson to other Nagas when he crossed the Patkai and ran into resistance. That treatment silenced them, historians say, for over 150 years although they began raids afterwards. They held ownership and control of the salt mines near Namrup, which they traded with the Ahoms.[20] There was a time when various Ahom monarchs, irked by the harassment, led punitive expeditions against the hill groups but to little avail, for their adversaries vanished, as did the ones at Benreu and elsewhere in the twentieth century, into the forests. Atanu Buragohain, the premier of one Ahom king, counselled the ruler against such campaigns, comparing the effort to that of an 'elephant entering a rat hole'. So the Ahoms settled for a patchy peace with the hill tribes, giving them a pusa or tax to keep away from their territories.[21] There are also references in historical accounts to social relations between the Ahoms and other Assamese groups and the hill tribes. One example that is frequently cited to underscore the good relations between the two is that of the fugitive Ahom king Godapani, who was protected by the Nagas in the seventeenth century when he was briefly overthrown. Godapani, while in exile, is said to have married a Naga woman.

So, given the long history of non-relations between India and the Nagas, it was hardly surprising that army soldiers were the first 'Indians' that the Zeliangs of Benreu were to encounter. This unfortunate chain of events set a counter-image in their minds—as across the Naga Hills—that the 'armies' as the security forces are referred to in conversations in villages, were representative both of Indians and their country. Just as the word 'hostile' imprinted a stereotype on the Indian psyche, among the Nagas and other hill groups, a different and equally powerful stereotype of India emerged.

Benreu, like many other Naga villages, hugs an escarpment and commands the strategic heights on four sides. Even today, thick green jungle, washed by spring rains, covers the plunging hillsides and a journey from Kohima, barely 100 kilometres away, can take six to eight hours because of the slush on roads and frequent landslides which block travel.

There was one saving grace, in the form of a Captain Dorairaj of the Garhwal Rifles, who reached Benreu before three other army units—the Manipur Rifles, the Rajputana Rifles and the Sikh Light Infantry—which rushed the heights from other sides. No one could tell me Dorairaj's initials or first name. He was just 'Captain Dorairaj' and they respected him because, to his lasting credit, he refused to allow soldiers to burn the village, as had many others in the Naga Hills. That was, if not a tradition, a practice followed by the army at the time.

That was fifty-four years ago and it was the Indian Army that went in to control the first armed revolt against the 'idea of India' in the hills of Assam. Of course, it's not as simple as it sounds. It wasn't just an occupation. It was a military response to the holding of Benreu by the Naga fighters, members of the Naga National Council of A. Z. Phizo, who headed the Federal Government of Nagaland, fired by the vision of an independent homeland where they could live free of the institutions and power brokers of a foreign land.

In the words of a teacher from these parts: 'This was the last village held by the Naga fighters to fall in this district.'

Benreu was lucky: many other villages were razed, residents killed and women raped. It's a long painful history of which we should be ashamed— and for those who dispute this, it's well documented. Nari Rustomji, who served in Bhutan and later became chief secretary of the state of Meghalaya, described that time as 'a dark and senseless' period.

Conditions are now better, there is no harassment; electricity and mobile phone connectivity have reached this remote outpost of the Indian nation. Yet the nightmare and horror of those days still haunt the people of Benreu.

For our elegant young researcher, Lungshang, who looks more like a college student than a mother of two and a teacher at Nagaland University, it was a traumatic return to her roots. She discovered that the woman who had been blown apart by the first mortar shell lobbed into Benreu was her aunt, and the child she had been feeding, her cousin. For many years, this information had been held from her by the woman's brother, Lungshang's father, concerned about the impact it would have on her. Her father had been a member of the Naga underground, who to this day, no matter which faction they belong to, are called national workers. Lungshang cried that day, as she listened to this story and other stories of beatings and harassment, in the hearth of a village home, in pain and deep abiding grief for two lives she had never known, for the hurt of not knowing, of that knowledge being kept from her. 'I'm sorry,' she kept saying as she wept, 'I don't know, I did not know, I can't help myself.'

It's not easy to get to Benreu—it took us over six hours from near the capital of Kohima. Scattered showers welcomed us on our journey through hill and plains, including a decapitated forest that was now a rice bowl. At one point, the Bolero in which we were riding got stuck in slush caused by incessant rain and a landslide on a narrow, bumpy, winding road through thick forests and a spectacular view of the hill ranges that stretch across Nagaland and sweep into northern Manipur.

We tossed twigs, branches and stones in the creased muddy lane to help the tyres get a grip. After much sliding and complaining, the jeep got onto firmer earth and with the car and our shoes caked in mud, we bumped our way into Benreu's little square. Below the square stood a great traditional thatch home, not less than 75 feet long, smoke rising peacefully from the hearth, as villagers waited on the veranda of the village council building, protected from the gusting cold wind and rain showers.

To understand why the idea of separation from India remains so attractive for so many in Nagaland and other parts of the Northeast, it is important to listen to their stories of grief, their songs of sorrow and to realize with horror that for decades here and in countless villages of this state, of Assam, Mizoram and Manipur where the conflict has been sharpest, few have come from anywhere in India to listen; there has been no counselling to enable them to cope with their trauma and the nightmares which haunt their waking and sleeping hours.

In fifty-four years, we were the first independent group to come to Benreu.

◆

There are ways out of these tragedies, to reduce the levels of anger and expand the opportunities for peace and better understanding. Sometimes they work, perhaps incompletely, incoherently and inchoately. Dialogue and conversations by a mediator or mediators, who have no personal stake in the matter, can play a role in bringing two or more opposing sides closer together even though that closeness or better understanding may not result immediately in an agreement. But it can help create conditions which can eventually help such a concord.

The story below is an example of one such effort, however incomplete, of the role that all such small stories have in a bigger picture, in a larger peace process. The Prime Minister walked out of my great-uncle Dev Kanta Barooah's small ground floor apartment in Lodi Colony that wintry February morning, surrounded by bodyguards and lackeys; he had come to commiserate with my great aunt on DKB's passing. More than twenty years earlier, P. V. Narasimha Rao, before he became prime minister, had been a joint secretary in the All India Congress Committee, which was then headed by Barooah as party president. Rao had inherited a country riven by caste and Hindu–Muslim division, a party shattered by the assassination of Rajiv Gandhi at the hands of a Tamil suicide bomber, a minority government and a collapsing economy driven into the ground by a fractious polity and rump governments which lasted barely a few months.

More than three years later, in the autumn of his rule, the Prime Minister, ever courteous and scholarly, had come to call on my great-aunt, the kind and gentle Priyalata Barooah, to remember a leader with a photographic memory and a prodigious intellect, who developed the concept of the Other Backward Castes to shore up the Congress Party's ebbing support among the middle and upper castes. My great-uncle had among the best libraries in Delhi and loved to engage in debates.

I had positioned myself at the door, and as the Prime Minister got up to leave I introduced myself. 'Ah, yes,' Narasimha Rao smiled. 'I've been wanting to see you. Rajesh has been talking about you. When are you free?'

Rajesh was Rajesh Pilot, then minister of state for environment in the central government, and a man in a great hurry to tackle issues whether in the Northeast or in Jammu and Kashmir. He had a lot of energy and wonderful ideas but was always running up, in his earlier role as minister of state for internal security, against Shankarrao Bhavrao Chavan, the doughty Maratha senior minister for home affairs, who did not approve either of his junior's haste or his penchant for upstaging his boss.

I was astonished at the Prime Minister's courtesy. 'Sir, I am not the busy person; you are. Please ask your office to give me a time and I will come.' Narasimha Rao turned to one of his secretaries, instructed him to take my numbers and to fix an appointment. Within a few days, the Prime Minister's Office called, asking me to come to 7, Race Course Road. My direct involvement in the Naga story had begun—but it had been in the making for some time.

◆

The meeting that was to follow as well as the conversation at the Barooah residence had been preceded by weeks of phone calls, discussions and talks with Pilot. It started with a strange call late at night from Pilot who said he wanted me to meet someone who was interested in issues related to the environment in the Northeast. This turned out to be a man called Roger[22] from Shillong, whose family were Armenian Christians and ran a large school there.

It was just too pat, I reasoned to myself and turned to Minal, my wife. 'Pilot will never call me at home for an environmental story (I was then with the *New York Times*); this has nothing to do with the environment.' I had a gut feeling that it had something to do with the Nagas; don't ask me why: it was just a gut feeling, one that as a journalist with decades of experience, you learn to trust.

The next evening I went to see Roger who was staying at the Ashoka Hotel. That made me even more suspicious: why would he be staying in a five-star hotel, offering me drinks at the bar and spending so much money? Not to talk about elephant corridors in Meghalaya and what a great job they were doing in conservation. I evinced polite interest, sipped my beer and waited for Roger to get to the point. And it happened so suddenly and without finesse that I was quite surprised.

'Look, Sanjoy, do you know how to contact the NSCN? I need to get in touch with them,' Roger said, in a rush. As we know, NSCN was the National Socialist Council of Nagaland, the most powerful armed group fighting against India in the Northeast (the Nagaland in its name was later to be changed to Nagalim, which meant essentially the same thing but was a fallout of the group's aversion to anything that smacked of a connection to the Indian state). The fact that he was out of his depth was clearly visible. He probably had given a commitment to Pilot and realized that he could not deliver, he did not even have a number to reach the NSCN. Not that I did either at the time. But I made some general excuse about having to check it out and that I would get back to him. Of course, I didn't. I would have been an idiot to share the information—but anyway at the time I didn't have it.

I called a journalist friend in Bangkok with Naga contacts who worked extensively on insurgencies in Southeast Asia. We knew that the NSCN leaders Isak Chishi Swu and Thuingaleng Muivah lived in Bangkok with their families and aides and had been there for some time. Let me check, said my friend. When I rang back, he gave me a number: this, he said, was Muivah's contact point, a guy called James. I decided to wait and see what would happen to the bumbling Roger, whose efforts at contacting me came to naught, and to his puppeteer, the extremely likeable and ambitious Pilot. The game needed to be played a little more.

◆

After a few days, I called Pilot. I thought that he would now be ready to talk a bit more openly. And so he was. He called me over and I asked him how Roger's mission had gone. 'Arre, kuch bhi nahi hua,' he snapped. 'He just gave a lot of big talk, spent our money and did nothing.' Well, I said, you should select your people with a bit more care and research into their background. Pilot asked me if I would contact the Nagas and see if they would talk. 'On whose behalf am I supposed to be doing that? They won't talk just like that.'

'Say that you are speaking on behalf of the government, on my behalf as internal security minister and that of the prime minister.'

'I needed time to think about this,' I said. And I needed to talk to two of my closest friends, whose counsel I trust implicitly and who knew the Naga situation well. One was a Naga friend and civil society leader, a man I had known for over twenty-five years. The other was a school friend who worked in the central government. I needed to go to Shillong to talk to them.

Both were encouraging. My Naga friend and I spoke for over two hours, walking in the forest above my mother's lovely bungalow in Motinagar. He said that this was a chance for Assam to play a role in bringing the Nagas and India together; it sounded rather lofty because I have never claimed to represent anyone except my own views. This was a tremendous opportunity and much good could come out of it, he said. If it didn't work, that was also fine—'you would know that you had tried to do something truly positive'. My school friend also said that this could be something that could work for both sides. For one, I was a reasonably well-known journalist without a political agenda, I had worked with an international newspaper, and I had published a book, *Strangers of the Mist*, on the Northeast as well as numerous articles and essays. Two, I was not connected with the government although I came from a family whose senior members had served both at Delhi and in Assam, in politics and the bureaucracy.

I returned to Delhi and told Pilot that I would take the assignment.

After much hesitation, I called the number that my journalist friend in Bangkok had given. I was tense: suppose it's a wrong number, suppose they don't answer, suppose they just disconnect the phone or worse listen to me and say: 'We're not interested'? All of these were acute possibilities and it was the first time I had done anything of this kind although, while studying in London, I had gone to see Phizo and listened to him with a mixture of awe and cynicism as he expounded on the need to be independent of India and how the Assamese one day would realize their mistake of being with Delhi and also raise the banner of revolt. 'We're Indians,' I remember telling Phizo, 'I don't think we'll go that way.'[23]

A man answered the Bangkok number. I introduced myself; he was instantly suspicious. He said his name was James and asked how I got his number. The answer is pat for most journalists: 'I'm a journalist, I managed to get it through my contacts.' James was non-committal when I said I was speaking on behalf of the government. I had asked to speak to either Muivah or Swu. I don't know, he snapped, you'll have to call back later.

We ended the conversation. Not a very auspicious one, I thought to myself. The only thing that James appeared to indicate with some positiveness was that he would talk to the 'uncles', as he called the two Naga leaders. But I had also told him that my understanding was they had communicated to the Indians, in some way—I'm still unsure of that—that I would be acceptable as a facilitator.

Over the next months, James and I became phone buddies. We talked, he spoke of how often the uncles travel and how little they're in Bangkok. He opened up a bit but didn't let on too much except to say that their families were with them, that he and the younger ones missed home food but were committed to the cause for which the uncles had pledged their lives. But the conversations didn't seem to be going anywhere. We had started talking in about June, and by the beginning of December after conversations that were sporadic (at times once a week, at other times twice a month), I was getting a bit fed up. The uncles hadn't appeared or come on the line and it was time to move on to other things. I was tired of being kept on almost perpetual hold, nice though it was to talk briefly with James. Meanwhile, Pilot had moved from internal security to environment, to put some distance between him and the senior home minister S. B. Chavan, but he continued to be on top of the Naga talks. I had other travel, writing and work to do apart from the family. Minal knew of the conversations but only as much as I told her, no point getting her worried.

So in December, in a conversation with James, I gave him a deadline: 'Do your uncles want to talk or not? Do they want to meet me? If so, let me know within a week. I am speaking not on my behalf but at the request of the prime minister and the home minister and I need answers; otherwise, thanks a lot, let me get on with my life and work. I don't even know, James, whether you represent them or whether you have even told them about these discussions on the phone.' James sounded rattled. 'No, no,' he said. 'Of course they are interested. Please call in a few days and I will give an answer.'

As all this was playing out, I had my own little disagreement with Pilot. He kept saying that the 'old man' wanted to meet me; that he had told Rao everything and I would be seeing him soon. But no appointment came through or word from the Prime Minister's Office and I got the strong feeling that Pilot too was playing me for as long as he could without making a commitment. 'How on earth,' I said to him, 'could you say I represent the PM in these telephone conversations if I don't even know if he is familiar with what I was doing?' Pilot smiled in his affable way:

'Arrey, Sanjay, don't worry, milwa denge.' No commitment, I thought to myself, typical political bombast.

It was shortly after this that Rao came to visit my great-aunt in the Lodi Colony flat that wintry morning and direct contact was established with the PM. I didn't need to depend that much on Pilot any more and a senior officer on special duty, seconded from the Foreign Service (this is a long-standing tradition in the Prime Minister's Office, that a middle-ranking officer from the Foreign Office is deputed there as a special assistant), became the contact person. I had known the officer earlier when he worked at the External Affairs Ministry handling Indo-US relations. Then, as now, he was courteous, cheerful and extremely efficient and helpful.[24]

Soon afterwards, I'd had the meeting with the Prime Minister. It seemed positive. He said: 'Just listen to them and see what they want'.

A few days later, I called James again. He was excited. 'The uncles would like you to come and meet them as soon as possible,' he said. Could I come in a few days to Bangkok? I was taken aback by the sudden enthusiasm and thought to myself, there's nothing like a little pressure and a deadline to get things to work. 'Let me get back to you,' I said.

Of course, I called next day to accept but negotiated a date a couple of days later than they had set. Both Pilot and the Prime Minister were pleased with the response. I obtained the visa. Though Thailand issues visas on arrival at the airport, I didn't want to take chances. At the airport, I fixed a hotel which looked quite nice: neither expensive nor flashy. 'The uncles will come to see you at 5 p.m. at the hotel lobby,' James said, when I contacted him after checking in to the hotel. I started getting tense. Would I recognize them? After all, the pictures I had seen of them were a few years old and they might have changed. What on earth was I doing here, trying to talk to two of the most wanted men in India?

I would be wearing a blue jacket and slacks, I told James. This was, I thought to myself, sounding more and more like something out of a spy movie and I was playing more than a bit role.

Well before 5, I positioned myself in the lobby, so that I could get a view of those entering. Suddenly, there they were—dressed casually, in slacks and batik shirts, smiling and at ease, with a young silent Naga behind them, obviously a minder, whose name turned out to be Robert.

I had rehearsed for this moment: 'Mr Muivah, Mr Swu, a pleasure to meet you. It's wonderful to meet two living legends.' Then I added, 'Most legends are usually several feet underground.' They laughed at that, at what seems now a poor joke (Isak Swu died in June 2016). We moved to the bar/coffee shop at the same level.

'What would you like to drink?' I asked, and then almost bit my tongue off for not remembering that both were teetotallers. 'We don't drink, I'll have a coffee,' said Muivah. Big mistake. We talked for a few minutes and then I said that I had read so much about them, it was a privilege to meet them and that I was grateful to them for agreeing to the meeting. 'We will talk at length tomorrow,' said Muivah, while Swu smilingly nodded. I had written about them in *Strangers*. Yes, said Muivah, he had read the book. 'You referred to me as ruthless.' I was startled: I don't think I said that, although I remember my publisher advising me to cut out a very trenchant paragraph on Muivah: it could cause legal problems. I followed his advice but retained some descriptions. 'Read the book again, look at that passage,' Muivah advised me, as they got up to leave. Later, in my room, I checked it out. And sure enough it was there, leaping at me from pages 105 and 106. I could have kicked myself. But what I wrote then on page 104 remains true:

> Muivah was a true trailblazer of Asian insurgency. A student of St. Anthony's College in Shillong, he was among the few Naga rebels to have studied and understood Marxism and Maoism. Yet nationalism and Phizo's mesmeric appeal drew him relentlessly to a destiny that made him, after Phizo, the most important of the true Asian rebels in the Eastern India-Bangladesh [I would add Myanmar here in this book] theatre of war and insurgency. And among its most feared.

Not a good start, I thought, to the dialogue and wondered how the next meeting would go.

◆

The next morning I waited for them in the hotel room, wearing slacks and a casual blue shirt. The bell to the room rang and this time I felt positively under-dressed: Swu was in a smart, deep blue two-piece suit and Muivah in a brown jacket and trousers. Both wore ties. They looked more like prosperous businessmen than insurgent leaders who had carved out a space for themselves in the annals of guerrilla war and struggles in Asia, people who had met with Zhou Enlai, presidents and prime ministers of Pakistan and with armed groups and political organizations in Myanmar and other parts of Southeast Asia which battled their governments. Robert again accompanied them; he, I was relieved, like me, wore casuals.

The reason I am dwelling on the sartorial side of things during the discussions in the Bangkok hotel is because both clothes and body language are critical in conveying impressions, attitudes and positions in discussions.

Robert, I was to learn, was Anthony Shimray, the head of the Alee Command, or the chief weapons procurement arm of the NSCN, and one of Muivah's closest aides. One of his achievements is celebrated in an annual report of the NSCN which talks about how the Alee Command, which is the external intelligence wing of the group, under Robert's direction, negotiated and delivered major arms consignments both at sea (in this case, transferring the weapons from one vessel to another) in the Bay of Bengal and landed another one in the Cox's Bazar area of Chittagong in Bangladesh. Later, he told me that he had lived in Kunming, capital of China's Yunnan Province, for four years with his family.

The Yunnan has long been a staging and training place for the rebels of the Northeast, apart from a celebrated theatre of World War II through which ran the famous Stillwell Road or the Old Burma Road, a key supply route in the last phase of the war for the Allied forces and the Kuomintang Army under General Chiang Kai-shek who were desperately fighting the Japanese.

Yunnan was where, in 1966, Muivah and General Thinsolie Keyho of the Federal Government of Nagaland had travelled with their band of 100 men across leech-infested, tropical forest and high ridged valleys in Burma from their home region seeking Chinese political solidarity and armed assistance for the war against India. That desperate journey lasted over four months, hiding from relentless Burmese troops (among the toughest in the world when fighting insurgencies—they've been doing it since the country gained independence from Britain in 1948) and connecting with the Kachin Independence Army (KIA). KIA is the military wing of the Kachin Independence Organization of Brang Seng, loved by his people as a revered teacher, a small stocky man who led them in a ceaseless struggle for greater autonomy (not the independence that the Nagas have sought for so long and remain so far from achieving).

The trek through Burma into China became the stuff of legend and the passage to leadership and fame for Muivah and Keyho, although the former outshone the senior general in the years and decades to come. It was the Naga equivalent of the Long March of Mao Zedong and Muivah was eulogized by many young Nagas as their equivalent of Mao.[25] As we sat down for talks at the small dining table in the room, Swu asked to pray. I remember being taken aback but quickly agreed. Swu, a deeply religious man, prayed for divine blessings on our conversation, for the good of the

Naga people and appreciating my presence. I find this religious side of matters hugely contradictory in an approach that is based on armed warfare, not the love of persuasion or by embracing peaceful methods for its goals. But this is not seen as such, as Muivah once explained to me—it was important to be courageous and take up the struggle for rights instead of being soft and cowardly and letting the other side walk all over you. He played on the traditional fighting role of the Nagas, who opposed oppression and outside control. His faith was couched in an interesting combination of Naga pride and the Marxism of old, not the religious virtuosity of Swu.

Indeed, a journalist remarked that Muivah's ideology was a curious mix of Naga evangelism and leftism, a cocktail combination that remains at the core of the NSCN's struggle. It is difficult to follow especially as most Nagas, including the NSCN, swear by Christian values but see no flaw in taking up guns and fighting for their cause and taking the lives of others, not to speak of risking and often losing their own. Muivah's explanation of this contradiction has not convinced me: that conditions come or are created where the oppressor must be confronted by the power of arms, not just good intentions and virtuosity. 'I believe in political realism,' he said to me once in a separate conversation in another country. But Swu was a different persona altogether. I was to find that Swu would pray on many other occasions in the next two days—he prayed when we were served coffee and lunch on both days.

Swu then began to speak on Naga history and their struggle from unrecorded times, for the Nagas have a rich history of oral traditions, on their refusal to be under anyone's yoke, on their relations with Assam's Ahom kings and how the fugitive King Godapani was protected by the Aos when the Burmese attacked and swept over his kingdom, how even the British could not crush them and developed a political system that ruled them lightly. Swu was an experienced orator but I was getting a sense of déjà vu since this kind of oration was something I was quite used to from my Naga friends and contacts, both at conferences in the Northeast and in private conversations. Whenever I tried to interrupt the flow and say that I was familiar with a certain part of the story, Swu would continue regardless.

It was a virtuoso performance but one that at the end of three hours was beginning to get on my nerves and test my patience, since the latter quality, in those days, was not an established virtue in my life. And I don't particularly enjoy being addressed, as Queen Victoria said of her Prime Minister Gladstone, 'as if I was a public meeting'. Muivah too was showing signs of tiring, as his colleague's presentation of the case was something that he was pretty familiar with[26]—also, in me, they were not talking to a foreign audience or someone unfamiliar with the Naga case. I have followed the Naga issue closely not only after my one-off meeting with Phizo in London in 1972, but also since developing friendships with a group of Nagas in the 1970s who were deeply connected to their independence movement and were wonderful individuals.

So three hours into the political harangue, as Swu had just demolished the Indian political puppets in Nagaland (men like S. C. Jamir, the former chief minister, are objects of the NSCN's collective wrath) and spoke of the continued depredations of the Indian Army and security forces on Naga men, women, children and property, especially churches, Muivah stepped in. Without even a hint of an apology to Swu (they had, at that time, worked together for over forty years and were strong friends; without that bond of friendship through times of grave adversity, their different approaches based on very different personalities would have seen the collapse of the organization), he said it was time to move from history to the present. His intervention brought to mind a description by a fellow journalist and writer some years ago referring to a photo of Muivah, which was the only one around for years with the Indian media: 'qualities of intelligence, shrewdness and ruthlessness could be detected. It was probably this combination of traits that had enabled him to survive and prosper throughout the turbulent decades... A shrewd man, but with a chilling cut to his charm.'

Muivah's flow of ideas underlined the observation. However, by this time, I was feeling the need for some sustenance. As Muivah started speaking, I suggested that we take a lunch break. They agreed, I ordered lunch and when it came, Swu said grace once more. Robert ate and lounged about; we chatted briefly and he talked about living in Kunming and how nice it had been and also how he had been captured by the Indian Army in Assam, tortured and then escaped from prison in a major jail break. He had not been caught again and I doubt if the Indians knew the importance of the man they had had in their custody because he was obviously a tough nut, who would not crack under duress or even third degree.

◆

In a well-defined overview of the contemporary Naga situation, Muivah dwelt at length in our talks in Bangkok on the nature of the Indian state as well as the idea that the Nagas had never been subjugated by any power. New Delhi, he remarked, had shown neither good faith in negotiations in the past nor an ability to understand the Naga mind and demands. The

Nagas had fought for nearly fifty years and were prepared, he declaimed with force, as I listened impassively, and not with a little cynicism, that they were prepared to fight for another fifty if the Indians did not heed their demands.

His basic line was that the people and resources of the Nagas had never been under any power and that India was ruling through a combination of force, deceit and local collaborators, who were corrupt. Muivah said that while he was grateful that the Government of India had sent me as an emissary, he wondered what New Delhi could do since it had not shown sincerity in the past. India, he said, was difficult to trust.

I seized the chance to speak: that I appreciated the chance to listen to them, without necessarily agreeing with their perspectives. I also told them frankly that I had been apprehensive about meeting them because I was not sure of how they would receive me, despite my good intentions. Although the government had been keen for me to travel, my family had not. I had taken the chance because I wanted to meet the legends and, as an Assamese and an Indian, wanted to see if there was anything that I could do to reduce the pain of the people, because their movement was the 'mother of insurgencies' and anything that would abate the conflict in the Naga Hills would have a significant effect on other parts of the region where political demands were backed up and met by force of arms.

I said that the prime minister and the internal security minister had met me and I had their trust; but my mandate, while it was specific, was also limited. It was to find out what the Naga leadership wanted and to convey it to the Indian government. I was not a negotiator, I was a chowkidar, someone who could stand at the door and open it for them. Whether to pass through or to stay outside was their choice. If they wanted to pass through, I could inform the government and the two sides could then take it forward directly.

Both Muivah and Swu appeared pleased with my little speech. They seemed prepared to talk but said that they had specific issues and problems which needed to be resolved. Would I convey their questions and problems to the government? I said that I would write down their points and hand these over to the prime minister. As it had been a long day, I suggested we meet the following morning to wrap up the discussion when I would write down their points and travel to Delhi to report back to the prime minister.

◆

We began the next morning with grace recited by Swu, hoping for fruitful conversations. I hoped that this would be a brisk and businesslike session so that I could take a break and see a bit of the city. Both Muivah and Swu, however, reiterated that past experience of dealing with the government had not been fruitful but they were prepared to talk on the Indo-Naga issue as they defined it. Their conditions, as it were, for laying the ground rules for the negotiations surprised me. I wrote them down and still have them: The first was that negotiations would have to be with their group only, not with the rival NSCN faction headed by S. S. Khaplang, who commanded a fiercely loyal organization that comprised his own tribe, the Konyaks, the largest Naga tribe, and others. Muivah's group was completely dominated by his tribe, the Tangkhuls, geographically located in the northern hills of Manipur. Khaplang, who passed away in June 2017, was a Naga of the Hemi sub-group, whose home area was in Burma; he described himself as a simple soldier unlike Muivah whom he regarded as a Machiavellian politician. The NSCN (I-M) was positioning itself as the sole representative of the Nagas, ignoring Khaplang, whose fellow tribesmen were derided as simple and ignorant by their rival faction.[27]

The second was an extremely astute demand, which bore Muivah's stamp of political acumen in undermining his opponents: the NSCN leaders said that S. C. Jamir, the powerful chief minister of Nagaland, whose dislike for Muivah was as distinct and visceral as the latter's loathing of him, would have to go. Jamir would block any and every effort to bring the NSCN into talks with the Government of India since he was supportive of Khaplang. Although Jamir, a wily old fox, rarely spoke of his support of Khaplang, he made no secret of his opposition to Muivah and challenged the latter's claim to represent the Nagas. His rebel opponents had authorized at least four attempts to assassinate Jamir, including one in Nagaland House, on New Delhi's Aurangzeb Road, where government officials stay on visits to the national capital. Two more had been in Nagaland, including a bomb blast on his convoy, and a shooting assault. Each time, Jamir survived, and his opposition to Muivah, understandably, grew more resolute, making his association with Khaplang a natural course of action. In addition, Jamir was a significant factor in Delhi's politics and wielded clout in the Congress Party, of which he was a member, as well as in the gargantuan bureaucracy of the Ministry of Home Affairs, the nodal ministry for conflict zones. The MHA, as it is known, has long seen the need to put a 'Made in India' stamp on every part of India, especially the truculent and recalcitrant areas. The roots of Jamir's influence are not hard to understand. In the 1950s, having decided that his lot was with the Congress and India and not with Phizo, a dashing young Jamir was appointed parliamentary secretary to Jawaharlal Nehru. From that point on, he never looked back. He opposed the Naga demand for independence and always asserted his commitment and loyalty to India and the Nehru-Gandhi dynasty. The home ministry and Congress saw him as a bulwark against anti-India forces and cited his courage. If they were to not support him, it would be dishonouring a loyal soldier of the party and of India, who had withstood physical and political assaults at times when for a Naga to call himself an Indian was seen either as an act of treason or one of absolute folly that could result in his elimination by militants. Chief minister of Nagaland three times, Jamir was a member of the apex Congress Working Committee and familiar visitor to the offices and residences of India's prime ministers and power brokers. He could not be brushed aside easily, as developments in Nagaland were to prove.[28]

The National Socialist Council of Nagaland's Khaplang (K) faction under the leadership of Khole Konyak and S. S. Khaplang, and the Tangkhul faction, the Isak-Muivah (I-M) faction led by Swu and Muivah, regularly battled each other with automatic weapons in the state, with internecine killings, which sucked in ordinary villagers as well as rival cadres, becoming a norm. The Government of India, of course, knew exactly what was going on but made no effort to intervene. The NSCN (I-M)'s point was easy to understand—without the dominating presence of Jamir, the organization could have a free run of Nagaland.

The third demand was even more fascinating: the Indian Army would have to call off its boy scouts in the Kuki underground and stop using the Kuki groups against the Nagas. As with Jamir's tacit support to Khaplang, the army backing of the Kukis after the 1992 bloodletting between Nagas and Kukis, led by insurgent groups on either side, that gouged Manipur's hills, was talked about extensively, in whispers and conversations in closed rooms, but rarely made a public issue. In those brutal intra-tribal incidents, women were raped and killed, children butchered and villages torched. Each side accused the other of ethnic cleansing. But I was surprised, again, that the Naga leadership would insist on the army breaking its Kuki link, at least then.

Yet, with the few insights that I have gained over time, as I look back at these basic demands, I realize that they reflected Muivah's political sharpness, honed over many years of dealing with governments and rival groups. He had defined the core areas which would give advantage to the NSCN (I-M), weaken its political enemies and enable it to face New Delhi on a more equal playing field. On this wicket, while it could not dictate the fate of the game, the NSCN could certainly influence the state of play by insisting on its own ground rules. On what I would call his basic platform of demands, he had ensured three major gains for his organization and by interpolation for the Naga cause that he espoused.

- Political realism: this is Muivah's mantra—political realism dictates that governments or stakeholders talk to the principal and strongest adversary not the weakest or even the most loyal. It was a point he made time and again in our marathon discussions.
- Territorial expansion: the NSCN could not be limited to Nagaland and instead should be recognized as a major force that the government had to contend with in his home state of Manipur.
- Limiting the role of the Indian Army: the army, that holy grail of the Indian system, was to be pulled back from supporting his ethnic and political foes and asked to toe his line, no mean achievement for a man who was leading barely 3,000 armed followers at the time.

We shook hands. I flew back to New Delhi the next day after a much deserved break enjoying the street food and walking around Bangkok's smart and shining malls.

◆

The formal political engagement between the Naga leaders and the Government of India is not yet over. After over two decades of talks, both sides are impatient to get it over and done with but a full agreement is elusive. As always, the devil is in the details. There's an important point to be recognized—without the powerhouse of the I-M, its armed forces backed by clear political determination, could the Nagas have come anywhere close to achieving what they have or are on the verge of securing? The Government of India understands the power that flows from the barrel of a gun. The questions that the prime minister's representative and his Naga counterparts raise continue to be the same that successive negotiators have struggled with since the talks began on real issues in 2000 with K. Padmanabhaiah, the second interlocutor: Will the Naga Army merge with Indian paramilitary forces?[29] Will a third Member of Parliament flag the concerns of the state and its people adequately?

Talking about flags, there's a demand for a separate Naga flag that won't go down well with either Parliament or other states, either of the region or across the country. Why should, the argument goes, a state with a population of less than two million be rewarded with a special flag just for fighting the system and causing extensive bloodshed, apart from economic losses as well as social and political disruption? Manipur, its Meitei population always sensitive to special deals with the Nagas and anything that might hurt its own interests, would probably be the first off the block to oppose this. So would Assam and larger states like Uttar Pradesh, Maharashtra, Tamil Nadu, Madhya Pradesh and Bihar.[30] The issue of the larger homeland of Nagalim, the dream of the Nagas to hold sway over swathes of Manipur, Assam and Arunachal Pradesh, is just that, a dream. They've been told categorically that the government is not going to concede on this issue. There's too much at risk here and the other states whose lands are being eyed are not going to take this lying down. The risk of civil conflict is very real with the states determined to exercise their right to protect their identity and oppose any claims.

In a future agreement, there'll be a peace dividend too, with cash payouts to those who fought the Government of India; corporates wishing to invest in the state would receive handsome rebates, tax holidays and be given land on long lease in return for substantial fees, bringing cash into households and villages and resolving a perennial hurdle to investment in traditional communities like the Nagas. Tribal groups hold tight control of property through a multilayered web of individuals, clans and communities, seeing their identity in the soil they till or hold; this is a process and a fabric which is woven into their lives by myths[31] as well as generations of families. What is rarely spoken of is the myth of gender equality: for one, women are shut out of inheritance processes by traditional codes, except in a handful of families. This was also one of the issues central to the movement for political representation by Naga women over the years, which peaked in the winter of 2016 and saw a furious blowback by dominant male groups which led to rioting, torching of public and private properties and intimidation. In firing incidents, at least two persons were killed in Dimapur.[32]

For some time now, Muivah hasn't been running all rounds of the dialogue directly, as in the past. He comes for discussions when substantial issues are on the table. But otherwise, his trusted lieutenants V. S. Atem, the former army chief, and R. S. Raising, a smaller version of Muivah himself, both members of his Tangkhul tribe, hold the fort. They know their leader's mind and consult him before and after the talks.

Age is beginning to tell on the legendary guerrilla who walked a thousand kilometres with a hundred fighters to Yunnan to win Chinese support. As we have seen, Muivah marched his men through Burma's leech-infested forests and over high hill ranges, evading deadly Burmese Army patrols, snakes and malaria. Isak Swu died in 2016 after suffering for a year with damaged kidneys and coming in for dialysis regularly at Fortis Hospital in Delhi. Swu's passing was a stunning blow to his comrade of over fifty years, who had seen the summits and the valleys of life as a rebel. 'We were together for 52 years facing fire. Never have we had any disagreement over anything. Never did we doubt each other's intentions. I can't help but get emotional.'[33] The Sumi leader was, Muivah recalled, his closest friend and ally to whom he would turn for advice and guidance.

It was Swu's sudden deterioration in health in 2015 that provoked the government to sign a hastily drawn up framework with the NSCN leadership because, as Swu told a friend: 'I want to sign something before I go.' He wanted this to be his legacy. But, alas, there wasn't much flesh on the framework. Swu signed the brief statement from his bed in the intensive care unit at Fortis with his wife by his side, supporting him. It was this statement that was taken to N. Ravi, the interlocutor, and Muivah for their signature at the prime minister's official residence at 7, Race Course Road on 3 August 2015. A year down the road, Swu was dead, having outlived the dire predictions of medical advice which pressured the hasty signing of the 'Framework Agreement', the talks were still on and the agreement was still secret because Muivah said that a separate flag and passport for Nagas was not just a 'demand' but a right as the 'Nagas were never under Indian rule... No, no. The understanding on shared sovereignty has been arrived [at] because the uniqueness of Naga history is recognized. We are not giving up on the demand of sovereignty,'[34] Muivah said in an interview after the death of his colleague. He also said that the framework had to be kept secret 'to save the course of the talks'.

The shared sovereignty idea, which surfaced in 2012 and has gained momentum since, is a part of official documents used during the negotiations. It is, after all, a matter of interpretation. Many of the details from the nomenclature of the governor and chief minister, all part of the thirty-one points submitted by the NSCN a decade back, have been thrashed out and finalized. What has been left unsettled is the explosive and interminable issue of garnering land from other states—which no government in Manipur, Assam or Arunachal Pradesh can part with at the risk of inviting public wrath and political denouncement. In addition, negotiators have got down to the nitty gritty about who would have the power to transfer deputy commissioners of districts and superintendents of police. The shared sovereignty clause would enable the creation of a pan-Naga traditional

body which would include all tribes located in different states but which
would not have control over territory; it would be a cultural group that
could rule on questions of custom, tradition and community. Even this is a
challenging proposition that is open to wide interpretation; those opposed
to it will assert that it is an informal or back-door way of tackling the
issue of land. It would have the impact of ethnic mobilization if not
of territorial acquisition. According to one account, Muivah told a large
gathering at a resort owned by former chief minister Neiphiu Rio on the
edge of Dimapur town that 'the government of India had accepted it as
part of the competencies. He said the "Pan-Naga Hoho" will be a statutory
body with certain powers having separate budget, and very unique for the
Nagas.'[35] The problem is that Naga 'customary law' is not written down or
codified and hence is a tradition not a law. Each tribe has its own codes
and traditions, making codification even more complex. Each tribe disputes
the capacity of the other to lay down the law. How the Government of
India and the NSCN will resolve this problem is anyone's guess. It's like
peeling an onion, layer after layer, with the accompanying tears. What
could happen is to turn to the tried and trusted way of all governments
when faced with a problem: appoint a committee of various individuals,
well versed in the issue or respected by different sides (however, it would
be close to impossible to get a set of consensual candidates which would
be accepted by the NSCN). That is a labyrinthine task. To provide an
understanding of its vastness although we are speaking of a tiny state that
has a population of barely 1.5 million, as we have seen, there are not less
than sixteen recognized tribes in Nagaland. Of this list, four—the Garo,
Kuki, Kachari and Karbi, with a total population of about 1,00,000 largely
in the Dimapur area—are not accepted by some Nagas as 'indigenous Naga'.

So how do we define shared sovereignty? After all, to rephrase the
Bard, what's in a word? It boils down to a matter of interpretation, not
even of law but of language. Do you share my sovereignty or do I share
yours? Or do we share each other's, rightfully, legally, dutifully, fully or in
part, and for how long? Till death do us part? But isn't shared sovereignty
part of the way the constitution has been written and how the union of
India is constituted—a centre and states in a federal structure? Whether
the states have a fair share or not is not the issue here. What matters is
that even small states like Nagaland can make their own laws and impose
taxes. Nagaland is protected by Article 371A of the Constitution[36] which
says that no law passed by Parliament will be binding on the state unless
it's passed by the state legislature. This is unique but it has been around for

decades. Shared sovereignty is not a new concept. It is seen in the daily practice of constitutional functioning in India. It's a catchy phrase for an old process. Trust the mandarins in New Delhi to cook up something as sweet-sounding as this. But the taste can't be terrific and it has taken more than a year to digest.

Is it all about a republic within a republic? Or is there something more? It boils down to a simple question of how we live with others. This is especially challenging in a predominantly rural society where 80–90 per cent of the population lives in villages where groups and individual family units depend on each other for help and interaction, both economic and social. One of the byproducts of urbanization, structured living—with guilds, religious and state origin groups as well as ethnics dominating specific neighbourhoods—is still a slow phenomenon. The issue of living peacefully with one's neighbours, whether close or distant ones, is an issue that engaged the ancient Romans and Greeks, the Indian and Chinese civilizations as well as the Native Americans, Africans and the Aborigines of Australia.

It is that simple, yet so critical and difficult.

Chapter 4

A TROUBLED PEACE IN MIZORAM

The Indian Army brigadier stood by the recently dug up grave. Two highly decomposed bodies, which had been pulled out of the pit covered by grass and shrubs on a hillside, lay by the open grave. The officer was in deep emotional distress, for one of the bodies was supposed to be that of his son. He was no ordinary army officer and one of the bodies that had been exhumed was of no ordinary soldier. It was of a soldier all right, but one who had been in the service of the very forces fighting those represented by his father. It could have been a scene out of a movie. It wasn't; it was an episode from hard knuckle life and the father was mourning his son. He had come from Shillong, then capital of composite Assam, in a helicopter, bearing an empty coffin. Earlier that day in 1967, his wife was scheduled to undergo surgery. But when they got news of their son's 'death', the operation was cancelled; his wife went home in tears and the brigadier took to the air to reach the Mizo Hills.

'It's all in the game,' the brigadier had told a compatriot earlier in the day. 'This was an operation against the underground. The troops have done their duty.'[1]

But he was not that composed, he recalled in his memoirs. Musing on the fifteen-minute road trip from the helipad to the village where the bodies had been interred, he recalled: 'It was a long journey. Here was I sitting all by myself by the side of a coffin at my feet meant to carry back the dead body of my son.' For this slightly built, kind-faced but incredibly tough professional soldier, who had been in hand-to-hand combat with the Japanese in World War II, carried out strikes, espionage and organized a guerrilla campaign against the Japanese in the Chin Hills of Burma, the written words were akin to a cry of utter despair.

Some twenty-two months earlier, his son had left his home, college and the town where he had been living, Shillong, in response to a call to arms by a rebel leader who had proclaimed independence from India in the Mizo Hills district. Then a teenager, he had been fascinated by the exploits and campaigns of the Palestine Liberation Organization (PLO) and its armed resistance to Israel. Denounced as terrorists by the United States and much of the Western world, the PLO got support from the Organization of Islamic Countries and other pro-liberation governments in Africa and Asia. India was a big supporter of the PLO, pushing its case in international fora and at every opportunity, inviting leaders like Yasser Arafat, the PLO chairman, to the country and treating him as a state guest. Partly, this was due to geopolitics and was aimed at getting enough oil and financial support from the oil-rich Arab world. But what the young man recalled in his father's home nearly forty years later, was the PLO's resounding call to fight for freedom, for the liberation of their land from an unwanted ruler, one they had not invited and which had been placed there by colonial rule and diktat.

The young man 'loved', he said, the idea of a homeland, taking up arms for it, of fighting against India, the juggernaut. Even in his travels to New Delhi and Calcutta and elsewhere in the country, he had felt the sting of discrimination and racial slurs despite being an army officer's son, his family being part of the elite of their people. That sting continues to be felt by countless others from his state and their region decades later when they are snubbed, teased, abused and the women molested and groped in New Delhi and other parts of the Hindi heartland.

He stayed in a college hostel in Shillong, capital of undivided Assam, where other Mizos also lived. They talked among themselves, about hopes and aspirations, of freedom and the rights of people; those were interesting days but they turned exciting when they learnt of stirrings of revolt in the district, of arms training being given to volunteers. In January 1966, several of his friends left Shillong to join the struggle. They had been called, they told him. He also wanted to leave. But they restrained him, saying his time would come.

Fretful and unwilling to wait while his 'seniors' organized the liberation movement, the strapping youth also went a few weeks later to Aizawl, the district capital. At the time, he stood 6 feet 4 inches, very tall for a Mizo or any person from the Northeast, inhabited by mostly small statured people. Renouncing his Indianness, the teenager enlisted in the Mizoram National Volunteers and then trained with a growing number of Mizo youth under a group of tough instructors, men who had been discharged from the Assam Regiment a couple of years earlier. They had been sacked because of a mutiny in the regiment and nursed a sense of grievance against the government and the army. The supporters of the rebel leader Laldenga located this group of embittered but trained men and tapped them to fight the Indian state. In the valleys of the Mizo Hills, they trained the youth to hide in the terrain, crawl through undergrowth, fire at moving targets, master close combat, survive the jungle.

A date for the uprising was set.

On 28 February 1966, the call to arms was sounded under the biblical name of Operation Jericho. An army of not less than 20,000 men, both armed and unarmed, overran the district, almost captured all of Aizawl, including the treasury, all government offices and the office of All India Radio, the government broadcaster. Only one little hillock resisted the power of the young Mizos as the doughty Assam Rifles unit fought back and refused to surrender.

Within a few days, the Government of India, stunned and angered by this challenge, slammed its mailed fist on the rebels, ordering air strikes with the air force's Canberras, which dropped incendiary bombs and strafed Aizawl and other towns and villages. Lalsangliana (better known as Sangliana) the brigadier's son, and the others from the Mizo National Army and the Mizo National Volunteers got out well before the strikes as they had had had an inkling of what could be in store when helicopters dropped water and other supplies to the beleaguered Assam Rifles garrison, with air cover from jet fighters.

As the Indian Army sent to relieve the Assam Rifles made its way up from Silchar, in the Assam plains, the jets returned, authorized by the Indian cabinet under Prime Minister Indira Gandhi to do something that had never been done in the history of free India—and hopefully will never be repeated—drop bombs and strafe civilian-inhabited towns. Aizawl as well as the villages where the Mizo nationalists were said to be located, near Burma, were repeatedly attacked. They were turned, as the historian J. V. Hluna says, 'to ashes'.

But this had happened a year and a half earlier, before the army officer had received word of the casualty.

◆

At that time, the idealistic young fighter Sangliana was nineteen. His parents learnt (from a source that the brigadier did not specify), that Sangliana was missing from home and was suspected to have joined the Mizo National Front (MNF). The eldest of five children, Sangliana, in his father's view, had 'apparently succumbed to the pressures...by many college student friends to join the Mizo National Army...fighting for independence—a very formidable underground movement with their sanctuaries in East Pakistan'. Concluding that his son had joined the anti-India forces, the soldier returned to his brigade posting in the freezing heights on the Himalayan border with China. There was, he said, 'nothing else I could do'. The statement takes on an added poignancy when we return to the scene this chapter opened with—Brigadier Thenphunga Sailo, in the uniform of the Assam Regiment, and with shoulder tags of the Paras, one of the toughest fighting groups of the Indian Army, standing by the grave of the young men and mourning his son.[2] The military honours were from his younger days and action in World War II in Burma where he was deployed twice, first with the HASFORCE in Falam under the Chin Levies unit and then as the head of a spy mission deep in central Burma. His orders: collect intelligence, organize rescues of pilots shot down over Burma and 'stay alive as long as possible'. As the tide of war turned against Japan, he and his colleagues came out of hiding and joined the victorious rush through the Burmese plains with the Assam Regiment in 1945. The older Sailo was a tough cookie. He had been captured twice but secured his release and that of his compatriots after convincing his Japanese captors of their Burmese nationality. He once sent the head of a Japanese soldier in an empty ghee tin to their immediate commanding officer, a General Cowans, head of the 17th Division. What the latter thought of the gift is not known, even if it was recorded.

◆

Brigadier Sailo was surprised by the voice of the village chief who had approached him. As the bodies were lifted out, the village elder whispered into the army officer's ear: 'This is not Sangliana, these are the bodies of Lazika and Rozidinga. Lalsangliana is alive.' The startled father decided not to say anything for he knew this could bring the local army unit's wrath down on the village. He was well aware of what his compatriots were capable of doing. 'All hell would be let loose on the villagers,' the informant feared. So Sailo said nothing, though he realized immediately that neither of the highly decomposed bodies could be that of his son, as Sangliana was 6 feet 4 inches tall. These MNF fighters were much shorter. He took one body with him for a proper church burial to Aizawl in the same helicopter in which he had come.

The drama was not over. The real Sangliana was not only alive but was present, a short distance from the crowd, watching through thickets as his father arrived, first stoic but grieving, and then stunned and relieved before leaving. Sangliana had told himself when he went to the jungles that he would be lucky if he was alive the following Christmas.

Forty years later, burly but weakened by two strokes, the former guerrilla fighter said he still believed in the rights of the Mizos to a separate homeland and to unite with other Mizos and ethnic kin in Manipur, Assam, Bangladesh and Burma. This remains an imaginary land that he and others who believe in it call Zomi and their movement is for Zomi reunification. His father passed away, at the age of ninety-two, peacefully in his own bed in Aizawl, in 2015. Today, Sangliana lives in that house with his wife, sons, daughter-in-law and two huge St Bernards.

Dreams don't die.

◆

My initial understanding of the sadness and trauma that has gripped so many individuals and communities in the area we call the Northeast came from a young Mizo blessed with a beautiful voice, Joseph Zokunga, who was a rock singer in Shillong, where he also studied. He was twenty-two when I first met him and I was not a little in awe of him, especially because of his popularity as a singer. He was not good-looking, stocky with a walk that resembled a bird hopping and a mop of sharp hair. As I travelled with him to a students' conference near Bombay in 1970, I remember him telling me the story that started my journey to learn about our region and why things are the way they are and whether they can become any better.

On the bus journey from Shillong to Guwahati, where we were to catch a train on the long journey to Bombay through the blazing May heat of central India, Joseph told me about how his father, a man who earned money repairing radios and transistors, had been picked up by an army patrol from his shop in Aizawl on suspicion of being a supporter or informer of the Mizo National Army. He was beaten severely and tortured; the soldier crushed his father's fingers, Joseph said, by stamping on them, destroying the fingers which sustained a family.

Guantanamo Bay, the Gulag, Robben Island—we've been there and back, and we do all this without the inconvenience of prisons too, thank you. Joseph's father could never again work and support the family. I recall that conversation as if it was yesterday just as I also remember my anger at what governments and soldiers do with such seamless impunity. But I also found it hard to absorb. I had relatives in political power, the fathers of several friends were high officials. In my naïvety, I kept thinking: 'How could this happen? Surely they could not know of it? Could they be associated with such events?' And 'they' were people whose children were in class with me or my brother; 'they' were 'uncles'. I wanted to believe Joseph but at the same time did not want to. There is a great helplessness when you are a teenager, coming to terms with the world and its ugliness, while dreaming of great visions of reshaping society.

Another thing was important to me—the shame of not knowing that such brutality was inflicted on our neighbours. The media was silent on these issues, concentrating on battles and skirmishes, ambushes and surrenders. Joseph talked about regrouped and protected villages, people pushed into new settlements at gunpoint, their old villages burnt by the army.

When I went to meet Joseph in the summer of 2015, he was not there, having lost a battle with cancer. In the modest wooden home, which he had shared with his siblings and nephews in Aizawl, I spoke with his brother. What appeared to be church pews were stacked up against the wall, an old television and a frayed sofa set were placed in the room. We talked about earlier days, Joseph's singing and work at the State Music Academy where he trained a new generation of young singers. 'We' were my friend, L. R. Sailo, portly and constantly cheerful, a bit like Friar Tuck of Robin Hood fame, and I. Sailo has been press adviser to many chief ministers including Brigadier Sailo (yes, he did become chief minister) and Lalthanhawla.

'He kept talking about you all the time and always referred to your book,' Joseph's sister said. She went to a cupboard and pulled out a copy of *Strangers*. I would be happy to inscribe it, I said. But I found, leaping from the pages of the book, lines I had written more than twenty years earlier, thanking Joseph for starting me on this journey. It was moving and strange. It felt as if he was there.

That journey may have ended for the singer with the silken voice— but on YouTube, that voice lives on. You can hear him crooning a Tom Jones favourite, 'The Green, Green Grass of Home,' at the Aizawl Club. His life experience had shown that the path least, not less, travelled was the way to go.

Responding to the years of turmoil, he used to sing the incredibly moving 'Prayer of St. Francis of Assisi' at performances across India and abroad by Song of Asia, a musical group from Moral Re-Armament[3] that propagated social change through reform in individual conduct. It is a hymn, not easy to sing, and his voice would soar effortlessly over the impossibly high notes:

Lord, make of me an instrument of your peace
Where there is hatred, let me sow love;

where there is injury, pardon
where there is doubt, faith
where there is despair, hope
where there is darkness, light
where there is sadness, joy.

O Divine Master, grant that I may not so much seek to be consoled as
to console
to be understood as to understand
to be loved as to love.

For it is in giving that we receive
It is in pardoning that we are pardoned;

And it is in dying that we are born to eternal life.

This chapter started with a burial, an exhumation, two deaths, a non-death
and now, Joseph's passing. The Mizo story is complex, its triumphs and
tragedies, its hopes and aspirations are many. The arbitrariness that changed
and continues to change the balance between these elements remains
constant at the personal, community and government levels.

◆

Around the time that Sangliana and his comrades fled through the jungles,
an eleven-year-old schoolgirl arrived in Aizawl for her winter vacation. She
had come by bus from the hill town of Haflong in the Cachar Hills. She got
down and walked into a ruined town. 'I could see there was nothing there,
everything was burnt,' she recalled, thirty-nine years later, sitting in the large
polished wooden drawing room in the sprawling hillside bungalow that she
shares with her husband and their children. The house is well hidden from
the road below and in the evenings, Aizawl appears like a fairytale town
with twinkling lights sprawling across hills and valleys. In the conversation
with me, she sat with her ninety-one-year-old mother beside her.

Margaret Zama, daughter of Chhunga, the head of the ruling Mizo
Union which controlled the district council that governed the hill district,
had grown into a respected scholar, professor of English at the new Mizoram
University and author of several books but known to close friends simply
as Maggie. Even now, she remembers, the 'strangeness' of it all.

They went not to their home but to an uncle's house where Margaret's
other siblings (there were nine of them in all), cousins and her parents were
packed in. The fun of being together as children, the novelty of sleeping

on the floor on mattresses and tucked into thick quilts to keep the hill chill out, chatting and playing games with her relatives: these eased the stress of the situation. But outside, it was war. And her father, the burly Chhunga, was on the MNF's hit list. The Mizo Union, which Chhunga headed, was a target of the MNF because they professed loyalty to the Indian Constitution. But this did not prevent their family business, the largest pharmacy in town and the printing press below, from being destroyed as the Indian security forces went about their work of demolition, without caring who was on their side or otherwise.

It has emerged that the insurgency was as much aimed at Chhunga as anyone else for he had thrown the rebel leader Laldenga out of the district council seven years earlier for allegedly fudging accounts. Laldenga was an accounts clerk at the time and Chhunga was his boss. The MNF had not always been an armed force; it used to be the Mizo National Famine Front, aimed at saving the Mizos from an artificial food scarcity in 1959 when a strange natural phenomenon, known as the mautham or bamboo flowering, took place. When the bamboo flowers, every half century or so, there is a sudden proliferation of the rat population. Hundreds of thousands of these pests invade homes, stores, fields and granaries, eating everything that is possible. The Assam government in the plains slept over the warnings until the situation became too critical to ignore and international agencies and church alliances started sending food relief. The word spread that the Assam government was blocking these supplies because it wanted to cover its tracks and to inflict greater suffering on a minority community. Resentment was building up.

Laldenga, a brilliant orator, had got his Mizo National Famine Front going, taking full advantage of the plethora of political opportunities that the Assamese leadership, by their infinite insensitivity to the mautham, had handed him. A few years later, he changed its name to the Mizo National Front while he sought to oust Chhunga and the Mizo Union from power in the district council. In this effort, he was assisted by the Assam government which even gave funds and held secret meetings with him. The MNF didn't win seats but was slowly becoming a force to reckon with. Assam gave cash stealthily to Laldenga because it thought he would play ball in their effort to dislodge the Mizo Union, a party founded in 1946, from power. Of course, Laldenga had no intention of doing anything that would eventually upset his secret plans to rise against Assam and India. But he played his cards close to his chest, never revealing his greater plans.

Chhunga's people accused B. P. Chaliha, Assam's chief minister, of being soft on Laldenga even when there was clear evidence of him consorting with India's enemy, Pakistan. On Christmas Eve 1963, Laldenga and two aides were detained when they were surreptitiously returning from East Pakistan. They were in jail for a couple of months and released upon an assurance of 'good conduct' and their commitment to work within the Indian Constitution. Laldenga persuaded Chaliha that all he wanted was to seize control of the district council which had once tossed him out.

◆

As Laldenga and his fellow fighters vanished into the jungles of the rugged countryside, his wife Biakininga, or Pi Biki as she was known, stayed behind with their four children, including the youngest who was just an infant. This was a time of uncertainty for there was no news of the man of the house. A month later came word that they needed to move to East Pakistan.

As they slipped through the night and the forested trail, word of their movement had reached the security forces who set up an ambush. The latter thought that Laldenga was in the group and he had come to spirit his family away. As the group stumbled into range, the soldiers opened fire.

'There were bullets whizzing around, it was a nightmare, we just held on to each other, hid behind trees, I don't know how we escaped unhurt, but we did,' said the older of the sisters, as they sat on either side of their mother, now eighty. They talked in the living room of their home in Aizawl; the house was built into a hill and can't be seen from the road above. The wooden and cement structure is cleverly disguised and entering it, said the younger daughter with a laugh, is almost like going into a bunker.

But that incident was no laughing matter—although they got away without being injured. Later, they reached a point where they were to float down on boats to a rendezvous where Sangliana and others were to meet them and take them to safety across the India–East Pakistan border. They floated down in the dugouts, but got lost. Again, it was providential, they say. The rendezvous point was being monitored by troops and the Mizos who had gone there were fired upon.

A different date was set. The escort party found them and eventually, they crossed the Kalodyne River which forms the India–East Pakistan (now Bangladesh) and India–Myanmar border at different parts of its journey to the Bay of Bengal. They walked into East Pakistan where they were briefly reunited with Laldenga before he went on to his own work.

Throughout all this, as well as the many years that were spent in exile first in East Pakistan, then Myanmar and finally West—or the only—

Pakistan that survived the Indian-Mukti Bahini assault of 1971, the children and their parents changed their names numerous times, went to different schools, weren't allowed to invite too many friends to the safe houses where they lived. But apart from that, it was a pretty normal, peaceful existence. They liked the mystery of the name changing, the role-playing and fitted seamlessly into a life in exile. They also said they were bound by the love that their parents had for each other and the children: that bonded them together and made them feel safe.

When I asked Pi Biki whether she had ever questioned her husband about the crises that the family had fled from, the danger to the children and the disruption to their lives, she smiled. 'When I married him, I thought it was a safe marriage: he was an accounts officer in the district council. I did not expect any of this.' But then her philosophy was surprisingly like that of a middle-class Indian woman—to follow her husband unquestioningly. 'He was much older than me, he knew better, he was not just my husband but like my father.' She also believed that whatever he did was for the betterment of the Mizo people, not just the family.

'I never asked him those questions because I also believed in the cause.'

As the Laldenga family and their aides created new lives in new circumstances, with new names and in a new country, the land which they had fled had fallen into a shambles with darkness, fear, harm and hatred sweeping across its hills and homes.

◆

The connection between the Mizos and the Indian union has been wrapped in a cloak of ambiguity for which the British were not a little responsible. The same is true of the Naga case[4] too and the wording of the controversial clauses was similar.

In 1946, the administrator or superintendent of the Lushai Hills was Major A. MacDonald. That year, on 6 April, the first political party in these hills called the Lushai Commoners Union (later to become the Mizo Union) was formed. The following year, MacDonald's successor L. L. Peters called a meeting of citizens in Aizawl to which some 200 persons turned up to consider the future of the Mizos. The meeting called for independence as the Mizo political goal. The Mizo Union objected to this approach, having boycotted the meeting, and instead opted for the status of an autonomous district in Assam.

When the advisory subcommittee for Assam areas and 'fully excluded and partially excluded areas' of the region, under the chairmanship of Assam

Premier Gopinath Bordoloi went to Aizawl in April 1947, the Mizo Union submitted a detailed memorandum outlining the origins and clarifying that they had nothing in common with the Nagas or Manipuris nor did they accept being bracketed under the Kuki nomenclature[5] and that they resented being called by the latter name. It added that the Government of India should do 'the just and proper thing and grant the Mizos their just demand for territorial unity and solidarity'. It then placed three clauses (of territorial unity, self-determination with Assam and financial support by the centre) based on these essential points, closing with the caveat that 'all above items shall be subject to revision according to the future trend of events to the extent of seceding after ten years'.

This ambiguous document was signed by Khawtinkhuma, the president of the Mizo Union, and Vanthuama, its general secretary, on 26 April 1947.

The similarities between the Naga and Mizo 'agreements' of 1947 are striking: both had the crucial ten-year clause, after the completion of which period the groups could seek their place in the sun (or so they thought). But both statements also mentioned that that was to be after an interim period—those ten years would be spent in India. I have said there are few recorded cases in history of a small group accepting their absorption into a large entity and then the latter being generous enough to let the smaller one walk away after a few years.[6]

But what is important to note about the Mizo document is that it was drafted by a British officer, who then shared it with Mizo leaders at a meeting. Upon their approval, it was submitted to the Bordoloi Sub-Committee which later drew up the Sixth Schedule to protect the rights of tribal minority groups. The committee's mind was already made up as British officers discovered to their dismay in the spring of 1947, as India lurched towards Partition and freedom. It was coming with a premeditated framework though it was prepared to listen to formal memoranda, written statements and presentation of historic and legal documents. It wanted to mark its visit and discussions as official and as fair as seemingly possible. But it would not take on board any effort to revive the dead Crown Colony concept or flog the idea of separation from India and independent homelands.

Thus, unsurprisingly, there's always been a bit of a mess and an element of dodginess about Mizoram's links with the Indian union. As in the case of the Nagas, once inside the union, there was no going back—neither for the Nagas nor for New Delhi.

♦

This burden of recent history could not have been weighing on the mind of the eleven-year-old Margaret Zama during the initial disturbing days of insurgency and counter-insurgency. But Margaret intuitively sensed the stress of the situation. She remembers waking up at night and seeing a small red light burning some feet away. When her eyes familiarized to the darkness, she could make out the profile of her father sitting on a chair, smoking silently into the night, unable to share his deepest worries and pain with anyone.

'He was a politician, a leader, he had many things on his mind, the condition of his people, their suffering, the violence of the security forces, the difficulties with the family,' she said, remembering those days. Her mother, Isabella Rothangi, was blunter in the conversation at her daughter's sprawling wood-panelled home.

'When I think back to that time, I feel anger, not sorrow, yes, anger,' said the white-haired, firmly erect woman in a puan, the traditional sarong of Mizo women, and a shirt with a light shawl draped over her shoulders to keep out the monsoon evening cool. Her eyes were bright and full with tears but they did not shed any.

'Their fight was with those who were against them, why destroy the homes of those who had nothing to do with the insurgents or who were on the side of the government?' After retaking Aizawl, the Assam Rifles went through neighbourhoods telling residents they would return to burn the homes and stores. And so they did. One of the homes singled out for official arson was the Chhunga household. As they set the place on fire, its owners and others stood about numb and helpless.

Women like Rothangi were sent away by male relatives to the safety of the hills a couple of kilometres away. 'When we saw the flames and the houses burning, we cried, in helplessness and in grief, in anger.'

Her husband, Chhunga, was a kind but firm man. He had seen the uprising coming and made a desperate, last-ditch effort to calm and prevent the horrors which were to be visited on his people. He reached out to his greatest foe, the man behind the MNF. A few days before Christmas 1965, two months before the MNF seized most of the district, Chhunga and another Mizo Union leader went to see Laldenga. The MNF boss, who had demanded independence from India, was uncertain: 'Even if we decide to change our plan, our boys will kill us.' To which Chhunga responded: 'If Zoram (Mizoram) can be saved...by the deaths of Laldenga and Chhunga, we should both be ready to make the sacrifice.'

Laldenga wasn't prepared to make that sacrifice. The peace mission

failed and the war erupted. Yet, although an MNF marksman once had
Chhunga in his sights, he didn't pull the trigger. The explanation was simple:
'I didn't have a reason to shoot him; he was doing what he thought was
right for the people and the country. So were we. Did that mean that I
should kill him?' Chhunga later became chief minister of Mizoram when
it was upgraded from a district to a union territory.

However, others were not that lucky. More than 200 members of the
Mizo Union and their associates were to die at the hands of MNF fighters
in the long-drawn out conflict.

When the peace accord was signed in 1986 and Laldenga became chief
minister, he was once asked if he would apologize or seek forgiveness for
those civilians killed by the MNF and for the casualties suffered in the years
of trouble. 'Why should I?' he snapped. That was the difference between
him and the large-heartedness and courage of Chhunga. Laldenga seized
the opportunity to take his people to the promised land of freedom and
equality but only ended up putting them through hell.

◆

The 1 March 1966 Declaration of Independence[7] had sixty-one names with
Laldenga's at the top and proclaimed a style which was resonant of the US
Declaration of Independence and church lore. It actually copied verbatim
entire sentences of the former, without giving any credit.

Accusing New Delhi of bad faith and discrimination against the Mizos
for their Christian faith, the appeal which was printed as a two-page
pamphlet, proclaimed:

> We hold this truth to be self-evident that all men are created equal,
> and they are endowed with inalienable fundamental human rights and
> dignity of human persons; and to secure these rights, Governments are
> instituted among the men deriving their just power from the consent
> of the governed... We, therefore, the representatives of the Mizo people
> meeting on this day, the First of March in the Year of our Lord 1966
> appealing to the Supreme Judge of the world for the rectitude of our
> intention. So, in the name and the authority of the good people of
> this country, solemnly and publicly declare that Mizoram is and out of
> rights ought to be free and independent, that they are absolved from
> all allegiance to India and its Parliament.[8]

The appeal said as did the US declaration of 1776 that 'we mutually pledge
to each other with a firm reliance on the Protection of Divine Providence,

our lives, our fortunes and our sacred honour'. It called on 'independent countries' to recognize the 'independence of Mizoram' while seeking the backing of 'freedom loving nations and individuals' to back their demand for self-determination.

For three days, the MNF controlled the town—and overran every other town of substance in the district, brushing aside resistance from police and the few paramilitary troops present—barring the Assam Rifles garrison which was under huge pressure from a flood of young and battle-hungry Mizos. The MNF army was then at its peak, and whether fully or partially armed, was estimated by Sangliana, the brigadier's son, to be a fighting force of not less than 30,000 overall, a huge number for a guerrilla army. Others say it was much less, probably not more than 3,000. Time, attrition, the harsh life in the jungle and the difficulty of surviving in such conditions, accompanied by death and disease, forced many to leave and slip into 'normal' lives in an abnormal situation.[9]

Under attack, the beleaguered deputy commissioner, T. S. Gill, and other civilian officers took refuge in the Assam Rifles camp, the only area under Indian control for those first few chaotic days. In the chaos, the MNF finance secretary Lalkhawliana led a raid on the district treasury and, it is said, removed huge amounts of cash and treasury papers. At a discussion in 2014, he smilingly denied the remark by a friend, saying: 'Oh, we only took a few papers!' But Lalkhawliana asserted his powers by ordering the detention of the young Denghnuna, an outspoken member of the District Information and Public Relations Department, considering him a bit of a nuisance. He later released the officer.[10]

There weren't many casualties in the fighting for the town. There were thirteen dead, of which several bodies were kept in the jail which was turned into a mortuary. The stench was awful, Denghnuna remembers, and they got the municipal workers to bury the dead.

At the time, the MNF had declared in an internal communication that its physical 'effective control over the entire Mizoram' needed to last 'at least eight months'. This was the time and breathing space given for the insurgent leadership to campaign for recognition in international capitals. Reflecting on the conflict, the legendary Field Marshal Sam Manekshaw remarked that '100 or 200 guerillas can effectively tie down a vast number of the army, especially when the terrain is extremely difficult as in Nagaland or Mizoram'.

Four days after the rebel assault erupted on 1 March 1966, fighter jets of the Indian Air Force came screaming over Aizawl.

The Indian bludgeoning was not wholly unexpected by the MNF. It had believed that there would be retaliation but not the scale of the counter-strike that followed, which smashed and burnt villages, molested and raped women, virtually displaced the district's entire population, destroyed property and tortured elderly men and youth. The violence was unprecedented in the history of India and its already nascent struggle against the pro-freedom group in Nagaland which had erupted over a decade earlier.

One of the key figures in the Mizo movement was a man called Vanlalngaia. Small, and quick to laugh, this unlikely head of the insurgency's intelligence arm spoke of how he went to China in 1968 to establish contact with the Communist Party and the army. 'I walked to Kachin area in Burma and spent two months with the Kachin Independence Army, you know; you have heard, no, of KIA?' he chortled. Then, in the company of Kachin scouts, he crossed into China where he met with officers from the People's Liberation Army. He was there for over four months but did not have much success in extracting Chinese support. That was to follow a few years later and according to Bertil Lintner: 'China's only interest in the Mizo rebellion was that it needed a fifth column in India. It was part of the Great Game that was being played out in north-eastern India's borderlands, nothing more.' But certainly, nothing less.

This diminutive man had many distinctions. Born near the Burma border,[11] Vanlalngaia went to school in Burma, and spoke Burmese fluently. At twenty, though Indian by birth, he was picked to train for Burma's Royal Air Force at Halton Base. He was inducted into the Burmese Air Force but eventually returned home, to the Mizo Hills district. And as the MNF took shape and gained strength, Vanlalngaia became one of Laldenga's trusted lieutenants and advisers and was made the organization's intelligence head.

It was Vanlalngaia who designed and carried out one of the most audacious attacks in the history of insurgency in South Asia, though little has been recorded or reported of these events.

Soon after Aizawl was nearly overrun and the battle for the future of Mizoram began in earnest, Vanlalngaia, relying on his deep knowledge of the Burmese terrain, expanded the theatre of conflict and internationalized it by taking the war across the border into Burma. They hit at the towns of Falam and Tiddim and the hamlet of Tuibual in Chin State in a well-coordinated assault early on 1 June 1966. Mizo soldiers took over Falam, crushing the opposition from a Burmese Army post with ease. Vanlalngaia pressed on with an even more audacious plan: he wanted to capture Kalemyo airport, also known as Kale.

When he first suggested the idea to a small group of fighters and MNF strategists, Sangliana, who was there, said he just couldn't understand it. 'I could not locate it, so I asked him, "Where is this place?"' The intelligence chief pointed to a spot on the map that said Kalemyo. The pronunciation had led to the puzzlement. Vanlalngaia's plan was simple and, in the eyes of Sangliana, totally mad: attack the Burmese air base and seize a few aircraft, fly to China (better than walking for months through jungles, streams and over hills, in foul weather and fair, with leeches, other wildlife and the predatory Burmese Army always in pursuit, ready to attack).

'I thought that if we had two or three planes, we could fly them and use this as a base against both India and Burma,' the MNF leader said. But although he had been with the Royal Air Force, he was an engineer, not a pilot. So the point of striking at an air base would have been to capture publicity and shake government confidence. Sangliana said later that he had all along thought that the idea was hare-brained. 'If we had the planes, who would fly them? How would we keep them running? Where would we get the fuel, who would maintain them? There was no way the Burmese or the Indians would allow this to continue. They would blow everything up.'

The effort to hold on to the base was botched because of a simple logistical problem. Vanlalngaia planned to buy 1,000 automatic rifles from the Kachin Independence Army to carry out the assault on the air base. The consignment didn't come through. The plan was dropped.

The rebels knew they could not overstay their other gains. The Burmese Army was a tough customer and hated reverses, especially at the hands of insurgents. In this case, to add insult to injury, they had been slapped across the face by an Indian rebel group from a little spot from across the border. Vengeance would be theirs and it would not be kind. The Burmese were known to be brutal in their treatment of ethnic minorities, including prisoners of either sex. Villagers were often forced to work without pay, clearing jungle paths, carrying army provisions, helping to set up camps. They would be beaten, given poor pay (if at all) and light rations—perhaps one meal of rice gruel and vegetables in a day.

The Burmese Army retook the towns swiftly by force. Its soldiers fanned out, hunting the rebels. With the advantage of time, the latter managed to scoot and escaped retribution by scattering across the border.

Meanwhile, on the Indian side, four months into the conflict, the central government was planning another major blow, one that has remained in the hearts, minds and lived experiences of Mizos since. It was aimed at crippling the insurgency and denying the rebels food, shelter and manoeuvrability.

The Rambuai had begun in real earnest with a campaign that, fifty years down the line, should make every Indian ashamed of the government and what it did to a civilian population during a time of conflict.

◆

The regrouping of villages was an idea that was first implemented by the British and its loyal Malay forces from 1948–1960 in the Malay Peninsula to crush a Communist insurgency. The British strategy was called 'emergency' or 'counter-insurgency', and it was the first time that the phrase 'regrouping of villages' was used. It was based on forcing massive displacement of the local population from their original homesteads; the army moved villages and their inhabitants from interior locations to near the highways. The villagers were resettled in officially built villages, surrounded by barbed fencing and heavily armed guards, 'protected' from the rebels.

In truth, the entire process was aimed at denying the rebels access to food, water, shelter and health care for the wounded and sick: the place was especially notorious for virulent malaria. The idea was two-fold: starve the insurgents and put them under such intense pressure, that without access to the basic necessities of life, the movement would collapse and they would surrender.

It worked in Malaysia under the relentless pressure exerted by General Sir Gerald Templer, nicknamed the Tiger of Malaya, and his combined force of Malay and British troops. There was no quarter given or taken. The brutality inflicted on rebels taken captive was extensive and frequent. The Malay situation and the strategy to deal with it evolved after World War II when Britain announced and then was forced to abandon a constitution which had abolished the role of the sultans in the Malay Peninsula, converted the place from a protectorate to a colony, offered citizenship to anyone born ten years before the passing of the constitution and triggered a backlash of anger and fear that the Chinese and Indians would overwhelm the ethnic Malays. The resistance and the capitulation by the British made many anti-colonial fighters realize that a weakened Empire, drained by World War II as well as the surge of independence that had swept India and Pakistan and was rushing across Asia and Africa, would not be in a position to fight on too many fronts.

The campaign was led by the Communist Party of Malaya and had three goals or rather three phases of a plan to demolish British rule. The first was to drive British business interests (by targeting its nationals) into urban areas after raiding isolated tea and rubber estates, tin mines and government offices in the rural hinterland. A second was to seize the psychological high ground of such successes by proclaiming these areas as 'liberated zones' and recruiting extensively from the public. Finally, the resurgent army would attack towns and urban settlements and eventually have a direct showdown with the British on the battlefield.

Of course, it did not quite go according to plan.

◆

Accounts of the time say that the attacks began on 16 June 1948 in the Northern Malay state of Perak, with the shooting of a British estate owner followed by other attacks on the same day on other plantations. Unarmed persons were taken prisoner and shot. Sir Edward Gent, the British high commissioner or senior-most civilian official, declared a state of emergency. The police were granted extensive powers, quickly armed and a major recruitment drive launched.

In 1949, Lieutenant General Sir Harold Briggs was appointed director of operations and decided to strike at what he regarded as the heart of the Communist base, Chinese migrant communities. These were settled into new villages, surrounded by fences and police posts cutting the communists off from their source of food, supplies and manpower. It also gave the settlers more faith in the Malayan government and made them less prone to support the communists. Five hundred new villages were created forcing the communists out of the jungles where the British forces could defeat them more easily.[12]

Despite these efforts, the rebels assassinated Sir Henry Gurney, the high commissioner who succeeded Sir Edward, but were pushed back steadily by his ruthless replacement, Sir Gerald Templer.

British colonies like Fiji and East Africa as well as allies from Australia and New Zealand Corps (ANZAC) added troops and muscular support to the crackdown. The campaign saw the use of air support including helicopters and a strategy that included the building of permanent garrisons and forts. Special forces skilled in close combat and guerrilla tactics struck deep against the perceived enemy. Pushed on the defensive, the Communists lost the initiative, retreated to deeply challenging terrain, the thickly forested tropical jungles, where access to basic facilities was negligible and public support nonexistent. They never recovered.

By the time Malaya (United States of Malaya and Borneo, at the time) became independent in 1957, the Communists were not much of a threat. The emergency continued however till 1960, when the rebellion was said to be finally quashed. One of the lessons of that conflict appeared to have been lost on the MNF and especially Laldenga.

According to Dugdale-Pointon,[13] the British succeeded in Malaya because of three factors: well-organized authorities, the influence of leaders like Briggs and Templer and the 'communists thinking they could win by military means'. The last point should have echoed with Laldenga but one doubts if he ever read the history of other insurgencies. The Malay situation was different to that of the Mizos in India. The Mizos were fighting against a newly independent nation whose political leadership, army and officials were determined not to allow further vivisection, especially after the bloody partitioning of the country.

The issue of collateral damage, if it was ever raised, and its handling was never high on the government agenda.

Thus B. P. Chaliha, chief minister of Assam, who felt betrayed by the MNF and especially Laldenga, supported the crackdown, saying ominously: 'The army will move into the Mizo Hills. When the army moves, it means what it says.'[14] The historian Sajal Nag says that Chaliha was aware of the MNF's 'military and secessionist intentions' and that he 'willfully chose to ignore it'.[15] Upon their release after the East Pakistan episode, Laldenga and Lalnunmawia, his vice president, wrote a letter to Chaliha on 14 February 1964, which was almost schoolboyish in nature, seeking forgiveness from a stern headmaster for their mischief. This was two years before the uprising and the letter emphasized that they were aware:

> [it] would be entirely wrong for any one of the Mizo National Front or otherwise to meet or discuss political matters with the Pakistani authorities...we beg to confirm that it was our intention to meet our Mizo brethren in Pakistan on the border, but not in any circumstances to meet or discuss matters with the Pakistani officials.

This was clearly untrue. By the time, over 200 Mizos had already been trained by the Pakistanis in armed combat and tactics.

The letter went on: '...we wish to state that the programme and policies of the Mizo National Front are not anti-state and we would not take a course of action...against the Constitution of India'.

So what did Laldenga and his colleagues really want? This confusion has not been cleared up, fifty years later, despite numerous detailed interviews, discussions, essays, books, seminars and research. Did they really want the 'development of our beloved Mizo district' or did they want to break away from the Union of India? It appears, from new material that has emerged over the past years that Laldenga was never really interested in a protracted war and was unsure of himself much of the time, seeking to open talks with the centre even before the insurgency was launched! The new material shows a man who was more concerned about the safety and comfort of his own family than the future of his people or the suffering that they were being put through.

Thus, when the Malay experience was sought to be replicated in the Mizo Hills by a team led by one of India's most decorated, astute and courageous soldiers, Sam Manekshaw,[16] Laldenga was nowhere in sight. Manekshaw, a Parsi general with a bristling moustache and delightful English accent, was part of the Gurkha Regiment and perhaps its most distinguished member. From Calcutta and New Delhi, he planned the operational counter-strike in detail with his aides and the army brass. Whether he envisaged himself as an Indian version of Templer is not known.

But the fact of the matter is that the Malaya transplant was a human disaster on an epic scale. People still remember those days with sadness and bitterness although it did damage rebel morale significantly as surrenders within a year of the uprising showed.

◆

J. V. Hluna and Rini Tocchawng have come out with a significant account on this period, which draws heavily on the debates about the uprising in the Assam Legislative Assembly. It is unique, for it captures in detail the actual anger, frustration, unhappiness and duplicity of government and the opposition, people from the plains and the hills. While Hluna and Tocchawng's overall emphasis is a stinging denunciation of the manner in which the Government of India and the Government of Assam used subterfuge, deceit and huge pressure and intimidation which harmed the lives of ordinary people, they remarked trenchantly on the nature of the insurgent movement and especially its leadership:[17]

> Those who had set up insurrections in Nagaland, Mizoram, Tripura, Manipur and Assam soon become elusive shapes, like phosphorescent creatures of the deep oceans, directing their confused struggles from the safety of foreign sanctuaries, while the village folks, most of whom knew very little about anything, have received the brunt of an exasperated, and often clueless, system of government.

First of all, the military retook Aizawl, Lungleh, Kolasib and other towns. In Lungleh, over 200 kilometres from Aizawl, the Indian armed forces had capitulated during the first MNF surge after having fought for five days, bowing to pressure after the water supply was cut. Chaliha stressed that:

> there had been no bombing but there was machine gunning and strafing... I would submit that the use of aircraft was a necessity; it cannot be said to be unnecessary. I would not agree with the honorable members that excessive force was used and they could not manage without the help of the Air Force.[18]

But Stanley D. D. Nichols-Roy, the tall, tennis-playing Member of the Legislative Assembly from Sohra (Cherrapunji), and later a cabinet minister from what is today's Meghalaya state, was not one to silently sit by and listen. That same day, he spoke of his visit to Aizawl with legislator colleagues and denounced the government for bombing the town, dramatically waving large bullet casings, fragments of what he said was a bomb and showing photographs of an unexploded bomb:

> It is very interesting that even the Military people were afraid of this bomb because nobody knew at what time it would explode. We touched it, we measured it and we took photographs of it... We have the testimony of a hundred people who have heard the explosion the moment the planes flew over in Mizo hills they saw something like dust and from which fire broke out in the houses. Sir, rockets were also used.[19]

He urged that 'such weapons should not be used', that if such bombs had fallen on the assembly it would 'destroy the whole House... it would have been enough to destroy so many people and so many homes'. And when the government spoke of airdropping supplies for the civilian population, he responded by holding up the bullets and the photographs: were these edible?

Thus began the Rambuai, or the Years of Trouble, as they came to be known.

The poet Cherrie Changte's translation of a prominent poet, Suakliana, rings out sharply, capturing the misery of the time:

> Children, women, people from everywhere
> Starve under the noonday sun, lost like the riakmaw (thirsty bird).[20]

◆

In the Assam Assembly, the chief minister did agree with the Opposition that helpless villagers were 'caught between the devil and the deep sea',[21] a remarkably honest statement in today's context when most leaders deny either the reality of state violence or the plausibility of government involvement in criminal conduct. While he acknowledged that the security forces and the 'hostiles'[22] both demanded the loyalty of the villagers, it was the latter who subjected them to torture and extortion. He was silent on the charges against the army and paramilitary. But when the outspoken Opposition leader Gaurishankar Bhattacharyya asked him to identify which was 'the devil and which side is the deep sea in between the security forces and the hostiles', Chaliha merely said that it was a matter for the legislators 'to interpret'.

Speaking of the need for a new effort to break the back of the movement, Chaliha said: 'it was felt [by whom he did not say] that a new initiative had become necessary as much in the interest of the villagers as that of the satisfactory conduct of the operations for bringing the hostiles back'.

Then Chaliha spoke of the regrouping scheme, perhaps officially for the first time, saying that while it was not a new idea, it had also been tried 'with considerable success in some other countries under similar conditions and even at home in the territory now known as Nagaland'. He did not say that the government had dropped the Naga experiment after it was stoutly resisted locally. The chief minister added that 106 villages on the 'Vairengte-Aijal and Aijal-Lungleh roads' with a population of 50,000 had been regrouped into eighteen larger villages, known as Progressive Protected Villages (PPVs). He referred to some of the accompanying trauma briefly but tried to brush it off saying that this operation initially met with considerable local resistance. No one could, he said paternalistically, be 'enthusiastic about leaving his own hearth and home for a new place even for his own good'.

But later, they had settled down 'cheerfully', forgetting the anger and trauma that still prevails among those who were force marched and driven like cattle to these camps, often sleeping in the open, without food or medicines and unable to understand the reasons for the harsh treatment. In a later discussion, Bhattacharyya was to refer to the regrouped villages as 'concentration camps'[23] while Nichols-Roy, the Khasi leader, asked: 'Who (do) they protect?'[24] Nichols-Roy, known for his blunt talk, also cited the deaths of children from poor sanitation conditions in one regrouped village.

The 'hostiles', the political leader said, reacted sharply to the move to cut off supply lines and refuge, attacking the resettlement operations, inflicting 'considerable casualties' on the security forces. 'This was mainly because the forces had to function in smaller parties than usual for conducting the villagers heavily laden with their possessions to the new centres and could not adopt the necessary tactical measures in all cases.' In other words, without air cover or sufficient strength in this ill-advised move to uproot eventually two-thirds of the entire Mizo population in the district, the soldiers were sitting ducks for the guerrillas. And they took their wrath out on the innocents.

Yet, Chaliha added, the experience gained in these months would be used in the extension of the grouping plan. He also admitted that the insecurity of the situation meant that movements were heavily dependent on air support, that conditions were far from normal and the administration had collapsed in the interiors.

He also referred to the way the MNF went after small ethnic groups like the Chins, Chakmas and Lais; at one time some 10,000 Chakmas 'had been uprooted from their homes' in villages and fled to the main town of Demagiri.

The Opposition lashed out at Chaliha. In a stinging reproach, Rathindra Nath Sen referred to the operations by the British in Malaya and by US forces in Vietnam:

> It seems unbelievable that India has in the Mizo Hills anything like the problems which the British imperialism faced in Malaya or the American invaders still have on their hands in Vietnam. We hope the Government will appreciate that grafting a large number of population on unfamiliar lands is a very grave and disturbing process. Let us remember that history is merciless. It is no respecter of persons or personality.

But apart from such brave and striking words, how did regrouping actually work in the Mizo Hills?

Nichols-Roy told the Assam Assembly:

> Had not the Home Minister[25] said 'Crush them'. We thought that… the MNF would be crushed. But…we have seen that the 'Crush them' policy has been faithfully implemented by the Armed Forces, not against the MNF Volunteers but against the innocent and defenseless Indian citizens of the Mizo Hills.

The following, in the voices of those who were affected by it, and others who implemented the process should give us an idea of what happened. It makes the fact of peace-building in Mizoram even more significant, including the lack of hatred and the determination to move on, leaving the past behind.

Vijendra Singh Jafa of the Indian Administrative Service, who was an additional district magistrate at the time in the district, recalled the Rambuai and quoted extensively an army officer[26] who was involved in the regrouping.

> Darzo was one of the richest villages I have ever seen in this part of the world. There were ample stores of paddy, fowls and pigs. The villagers appeared well-fed and well-clad, and most of them had some money in cash. We arrived in the village about ten in the morning. My orders were to get the villagers to collect whatever moveable property they could, and to set their own village on fire at seven in the evening. I also had orders to burn all the paddy and other grain that could not be carried away...so as to keep food out of the reach of the insurgents. For about three hours, I tried to convince them that they would have to shift bag and baggage to the Hnahthial Protected and Progressive Village, as the Group Centres were officially known. They argued with me endlessly, until I had no choice but to tell them that the soldiers would deal with them if they did not obey my orders. [27]

Out of pity, the officer offered the shaken villagers time to hide their excess paddy in nearby caves and assured them that they could later come back and collect it.

Then it was time for the villagers to set fire to their homes. This was the other, brutal side of the Indian operation. People were expected to set fire to their own homes. Who in their right minds would do such a thing? All this was also part of a psy-op effort, of psychologically weakening and stressing out the opponent even if the victim did not have anything to do with the event. Another factor in the minds of the Indian security planners was that this would also turn the anger of the victims onto the insurgents for placing them in this predicament and their suffering. To a degree this worked.

In Darzo, when the villagers refused to burn their homes, the soldiers were told to drive people out of their houses. The officer set fire to the first house.

'I knew I was carrying out orders and would hate to do such a thing if I had my way. My soldiers also started torching other buildings and the whole place was soon ablaze. There was absolute confusion everywhere.' Women were weeping and cursing, the children were frightened, but the men 'were silent, not a whimper or a whisper from them'.

After the burning, the men, women and children were forced into a column and marched at gunpoint with soldiers leading from the front and blocking any escape from the rear. They walked 15 miles (24 kilometres) through the night to Hnahthial. 'I tell you, I hated myself that night. I had done the job of an executioner.' Children barely three years old carried heavy loads up hillsides as did pregnant women. At the end of this horrible journey, the officer summoned the village council head and his associates and told them to sign two documents, one saying that they had burnt down their own village and that no coercion had been used against them. The second claimed that they had moved voluntarily since their village was backward and did not have proper education, health and communication facilities and that they were being harassed by the rebels.

The villagers refused to sign. They were asked to leave and after some time summoned again, one at a time. The officer had laid his revolver on a desk and two jawans stood inside the tent pointing loaded sten guns at the villagers. Out of fear, the villagers signed.

Similar stories were repeated in village after village, home after home until two-thirds of the Mizo Hills district was in Protected and Progressive Villages, clearing hillsides, shrub and forests to make a new home for themselves and live with complete strangers as neighbours and eventual friends.

One doubts whether the officer or his comrades who razed Darzo felt they had done something courageous and in the true 'service of the nation'. Such stories of brutality and excess are endless. It was not the civil authority which called for the burning of the villages; it was the army high command. And not a single official or officer has been called to account or justice.

Why? Because they know that such acts cannot be tackled in law for these are protected by AFSPA. The best-known part of the Act is perhaps Section 4A, which gives the power to fire at persons if the officer is 'of the opinion that it is necessary to do so' and 'after giving due warning as he deems is necessary fire upon or otherwise use force, even to the causing of death, against any person who is acting in contravention of any law or order for the time being in force in the disturbed area'. Then there's Section 6, which provides immunity from criminal prosecution to anyone who takes action under the Act: without the clearance of the central government, no such prosecution can be cleared. Not one case has been approved since 1958 when the Act was passed by Parliament.

But there is also a Clause 4B (as there is a 4C which empowers the state to arrest people without warrants) which covers a key aspect of security operations. It empowers an officer if he is of the opinion that it is necessary so to do, to destroy any arms dump, prepared or fortified position or shelter from which armed attacks are made or are likely to be made or are attempted to be made or any structure used as a training camp for armed volunteers or utilized as a hideout by armed gangs or absconders wanted for any offence.

Under this broad, sweeping definition, almost any place—whether a church or chapel, a hut or a paddy field, a granary bin, a grove of fruit trees, an animal shed or a stack of freshly cut wood, could qualify as the centre of subversive and unlawful activity. Thus the burning of Darzo could have come easily under the broad-brush definition provided in clause 4b.

Atrocity upon atrocity.

And though mourned by all who suffered, no compensation has been given to civilian victims, no apology offered, no recognition of the harm inflicted or justice denied.

The army went to village after village and they had standing instructions from their high command in the words of the late Lieutenant General V. K. Nayar of the Paras—one of the most decorated units in the army: 'If you were ambushed near a village, you burnt the village, no questions asked.' That continued until one day, when his team had been hit near a village and his men were thirsting for revenge, Nayar, then a young captain, locked eyes with a young pregnant Mizo.

'Sanjoy, I tell you, she looked at me with such hatred that it shook me up. I asked myself, "Damn it, what am I doing?"' Nayar recalled during a conversation.[28] He refused to let his angry men burn the village, ordered them to leave and from that day onwards disobeyed the 'standing instructions'. 'I told them,' he said, 'that I would take responsibility.' They never burnt a village again. Nor was any action taken against either the young Nayar or members of his unit.

Jafa, who served extensively in the Mizo Hills and later in Assam, Meghalaya and the central government, wrote of his views and the experience. I am quoting one specific section in full because it also underlines the dominant role of Sam Manekshaw:

In a report sent to the army headquarters in October 1966, Lt. Gen. (later Field Marshal) Sam Manekshaw, GOC-in-C Eastern Command, Calcutta, recommended that to be effective militarily, grouping must be extensive and must intern a very large portion, if not all, of the population. He, however, suggested that grouping may initially be undertaken in a 10-mile belt on both sides of the Vairengte-Aizawl-

Lunglei road. The military advantages of this action, according to him, would be to make the road axis secure and thus increase the logistic capacity as well as relatively unhampered road-construction work by the Border Roads Organisation. The grouped villagers could also be gainfully employed to work on the new roads. The 20-mile secure belt thus created would restrict movement of hostile gangs from one sector to another and to and from East Pakistan. Coupled with a 'food denial' programme based on monitoring and controlling food supplies to the grouped villages, the policy envisaged forcing the insurgents into devoting their energies to personal survival rather than armed activity. This would compel the MNA (Mizo National Army) to migrate into ungrouped and depopulated areas, thus diminishing the territory that was required to be dominated by the security forces. Manekshaw was also of the opinion that grouping of villages would enable the civil administration to exercise more effective control over a larger population than it was able to do at that time, and would eventually lead to destruction of the political infrastructure of the insurgents by isolating the militants from their support among the people. He visualised that the provision of administrative facilities for the newly re-grouped villages would include food supplies and fair-price shops, house-roofing material like galvanised corrugated iron sheets, dispensaries and doctors, and schools.

Jafa reflected in that essay in *Faultlines*, the journal of the South Asia Terrorism Portal run by the late K. P. S. Gill, who virtually single-handedly designed and led the controversial ruthless crackdown against Sikh militants in the Punjab, on the underlying issues of race and extreme prejudice in 'patterns of control of populations through concentrating in camps'.

First, they have always been used against people who are racially or ethnically different. The white races have practised control of ethnic populations in the American continent as a means to subdue the natives and to colonise their lands and resources for almost four centuries. In modern counterinsurgency warfare, too, the seminal experiment in re-settlement came with the control of the Chinese population by the British in Malaya and this provided a model for its application by other armies.

Secondly, re-settlement has often been used to maintain economic and strategic interests and to suppress struggles for democratic advance and national and social liberation... Clearly, there is a stigma attached to these tactics in their application in the Third World, where colonialism and ethnic heterogeneity have been among the most common factors responsible for insurgency. It appears unlikely that a section of white citizens in an economically stable country like the USA will take to terrorism or warfare against the state. But it is equally unlikely that, in case that happens, an entire white population would be herded into camps with barbed wire thrown around them.

For many victims who saw their dreams go up in smoke and their lives turn into a muddied shambles, away from familiar surroundings, there was refuge only in memory and song. One of the most powerful poems to emerge from the decades of violence was written at the start of the troubles by Laltanpuia and translated nearly fifty years later, at my request, by Dr Joy Pachuau of Jawaharlal Lal Nehru University in New Delhi. It is a classic that brings tears to many Mizo eyes and stirs a sharp pain in their hearts. About the village of Sialsuk, it is simply called *Sialsuk Burning*.

Sialsuk, highland village
Once acclaimed by man
Where have you gone?
I am searching for you
But you are hard to find.

You have turned to dust,
A muddy sod, cold and dead
The glorious sun, thunderous rain
Would remain with us in our yards...
With these our settlements overflowed.

Now, however, it is hard to bear
I find no one can comfort me
O, Sial (suk), you are beyond grand
Even though light may have deserted you for now.
May the Protector help us rebuild you
As the place where lovers and kindred once roamed.

Laltanpuia wrote a follow-up to this a year later, translated for me by R. Thangvuana of the English Department in Mizoram University. The following is an excerpt.

My songs have travel'd hills and homes, giving solace,
Return to us, our loved township cold and dead

To mourn in one accord.
With our sad song perhaps to cure the heart's malady.

Sad times beset our town, but life rises up again.
Turn our back on them, that way freedom may shine,
Our songs in gold display,
And sing happily, for big Saheb accord's sounded.

◆

In those early years the MNF pulled off some dramatic escapades that put them firmly in the public eye, leaping to publicity and fame. One of these incidents involved the capture and kidnapping of a young IAS officer from Kerala, R. V. Pillai, then sub-divisional officer in Lunglei. Pillai,[29] now retired, lives in his home state. He recalls that at the time he wrote extensively to the state headquarters in Shillong about the emerging insurgency situation but found it a 'very frustrating' experience since Assam had 'very little acceptance of the ground realities which I had reflected in my regular reports to the government'.

This was the time when B. P. Chaliha was chief minister and the legendary A. N. Kidwai and Nari Rustomji as well as Dharmananda Das and Bhabananda Bhuyan (all destined to become chief secretaries of Assam or Meghalaya) were the key bureaucrats, seasoned, smart and down to earth. But even they went wrong in their assessments as they found themselves unable to influence the flow of events: the centre, armed with AFSPA and the Disturbed Areas Act, stepped in directly and ordered a ferocious onslaught by the army.

Pillai said in the interview that while he could not recall many details of the time that he was whisked away and kept in the jungles, there were a few things that still remained fresh in his memory, fifty years later: 'While in captivity, I was kept for a major part of the time in different camps in the erstwhile East Pakistan (now Bangladesh), and had good exposure to the organizational structure and modus operandi of the MNF.'

Since he knew how the system functioned, the group that was holding him was reluctant to let him go and in fact wanted to shoot him. But the 'headquarters group' did not want him to be harmed in any way. 'I was allowed to leave by the headquarters group on condition that I did not set foot on Mizo soil again.' India's concerns and that of his colleagues about Pillai's safety were based on clear and growing evidence that Pakistani intelligence was actively supporting the insurgency. 'While in captivity in the then East Pakistan, close to Chittagong, I was interrogated by a Pak intelligence officer who used Tamil as the language for communicating.'

Events such as Pillai's kidnapping and subsequent release played no small role in the emergence and firing of popular imagination. It gave growth to the creation of popular culture around the Rambuai years. Those difficult decades were alternatively mourned and celebrated with a new phenomenon—the emergence of underground songs, poems, stories, novels and narratives. There was even a comic strip that's still popular, *Sudden Muanga*, based on a popular Western comic cowboy, who was feared by lawbreakers.

Margaret Zama (the same eleven-year-old daughter of Chhunga who watched her father smoke the nights away and is now a university professor) wrote of this phenomenon:

> One of the most enduring popular culture hero/anti-hero however, is the comic strip character created by Sangzuala by the name of *Sudden Muanga* after the famous cowboy hero 'Sudden' creation of Oliver Stone in his Sudden Western series. The series in comic form of *Sudden Muanga* in cyclostyled print was born in 1977 and... epitomizes and covers most of the transitions that the Mizo society has undergone...under the deceptive guise of comic sarcasm and irony lies a deeper subtext that provides a revealing study particularly of the socio-political study of Mizoram since 1977, through the 1980s and 1990s.[30]

Other popular comic book heroes, Zama says, include figures like Detective Denga by Thuamtea Khawlhring, Sailo Khawma by T. N. Vanlaltlana, and Dindin by Lianhnuna Renthlei (Sena).

Some exceptional writing emerged through the years of violence. In her commentary, Zama remarks insightfully:

> As with other conflicts throughout world history, the Mizo 'rambuai' conflict too had its supporters and detractors, the hardliners and those who tried to tread the middle path. There are also crucial questions to which there are several answers—questions such as why, where, who were the real victims, who were those responsible and the like. And as with other conflicts, there is always a suppressed voice which none dare to foreground. The sufferings caused by army atrocities were many, but so were those undergone in the hands of the underground and yet most narratives remain untold. But with the passing of time, there comes a strong desire to set certain records straight, to retell

histories, do justice to those no more, and to provide an unbiased history for the future generation.

These concerns continue to drive many people in Mizoram though they are still loath to speak openly of their experiences, the harm, sadness and pain. Although a new set of writers and published works in song, poetry, novels, short stories and narratives is emerging, people like Margaret Zama and others feel that a majority continue to hold their peace and keep silent about the past because in many cases both perpetrators and victims are still alive.

It's an extraordinary effort at living silent parallel lives with a deep faith in the healing power of the divine. Many Mizos with whom I have spoken constantly refer to this latter aspect, of being able to forgive because of the role of the Church, of its leaders and the nature of the Christian faith where the concepts and practices of forgiveness and reconciliation are deeply ingrained. Indeed, most Mizos take their religion extremely seriously, not just on the day of the Sabbath but also in their daily lives.

There's another reason for not delving into the past, says former Chief Secretary Pu Lalkhama, who signed the 1986 Accord on behalf of the Government of Mizoram.[31] 'When people heard about the peace accord and the return of the MNF, they were dancing in the streets, they were singing, they were happy. Having suffered so much, they did not want to go through any of this all over again.'

Decades after the accord, uncertain voices of concern and even anger are beginning to rise again. For several years, every March, on the day of the air assault on Aizawl, hundreds of Mizos under the leadership of the Mizo Z. Pawl, have marched in silent protest against the bombings. They demand not an apology, as in the first years of the agitation, but an acknowledgement of what happened. 'Many young people find it impossible to believe these stories, we had poor documentation and they ask, "Such cruelty, can it really take place?"' said Vanlalruata, the stocky general secretary of the Young Mizo Association, perhaps the most powerful civil society organization in the state, after the Church.

Much of the Mizo population at the time were jhum farmers, practising the primeval eco-sensitive cultivation of slash and burn. When displaced, like their brethren in the Naga Hills, they had no idea of their civil rights or of the right to compensation. It was Brigadier Sailo, the officer who mourned another man's son as his own, who broke the shackles of silence and fear. After retiring from a distinguished career in the army to Shillong, he got calls to return home and help 'his people'. Alarmed by the scale of atrocities by his own ilk, Sailo began by organizing a modest human rights movement with the help of a small group of colleagues. A meticulously organized man, he developed a simple form which could be filled in by any villager on what they had faced during the insurgency years, who had targeted them and what they sought in compensation. It unnerved the government.

When Indira Gandhi, shaken by a rising wave of public resentment against corruption and increasingly autocratic rule, declared an internal state of emergency on 26 June 1975, her Congress Party governments in the centre and the states arrested tens of thousands of democratic dissenters and Opposition leaders, the press was censored and freedom of association and movement was curtailed. The Rashtriya Swayamsevak Sangh (RSS) was banned. The judiciary was controlled, and the bureaucracy was frightened out of its wits, rushing to do the government's bidding or please the smallest whim of their political masters.

Brigadier Sailo too was arrested and taken to Nagaon (Nowgong) jail where other political leaders from Assam and elsewhere were interred. It was to transform him from a hesitant politician into a political activist. His wife was distraught and came to my mother, Maya Hazarika, to our home in Shillong, asking for advice and seeking the comfort of a friend. My mother sent word to her brother, the artist Pranab Baruah in Nagaon—the ancestral home of the maternal side of our family—and asked his help. Home-cooked food was taken to Brigadier Sailo from our place in Nagaon. It was a good gesture and a courageous one, at a time of fear and oppression.

During this period, Sangliana returned to Shillong as a tentative peace was signed between Laldenga and the centre. But the peace was neither complete nor discussed. Among those at the heart of this process was Ajit Doval,[32] then a middle-ranking official with the Intelligence Bureau (IB) who had seen action in and been deeply involved with the Mizoram process. The peace effort was initiated again by Laldenga, who by this time was tired of running; he had also worn out the hospitality of his Pakistani hosts. The MNF group in Pakistan were fed up of being virtual prisoners in a large house in Rawalpindi where their only contacts with the outside world would be visits to the market for daily or weekly purchases and then a monthly call by a Pakistani junior official who would hand over a packet containing the princely sum of ₹2,000. 'That was it, we had to manage everything on that,' Sangliana recalled.

That was very different to how they thought things would work out. Five years earlier, when Laldenga, his family and aides—protected by their own version of the praetorian guards, including the tall and strapping Sangliana—fled the fall of East Pakistan to the Indian Army and Mukti Bahini forces, they just made it across the Karnaphuli River in time. A crack unit of the army's Special Forces arrived on the former Pakistani side of the bank as the craft carrying Laldenga sped away. Sangliana and others had made enquiries and found out about a refugee camp for Pakistani tribals run by the Burmese Army. That was where they headed and Laldenga and his team passed themselves off as members of the persecuted Bam tribe in Pakistan. The storyline was that they needed succour and, as Pakistani supporters, were afraid of retaliatory violence at the hands of the Mukti Bahini and wanted to go to West Pakistan.

What he did not say was that the MNF had helped the Pakistani Special Rangers, their army's crack unit, in hunting down Mukti Bahini networks in Bangladesh. The Pakistanis told the Mizos: 'We don't know this place, you do; you know the terrain and the people, help us track them down.' And they did. It is not a period that the fighters from Mizoram are comfortable talking about for they did not exactly cover themselves with glory. Instead they were involved in assaults on Bengali Pakistanis. The Pakistani Army itself was responsible for pogroms against fighters, sympathizers, academics, students, farmers, housewives and simple, ordinary people.[33]

After weeks in the Arakan camp, the Mizos were spotted by Pakistani agents, given new identities and flown to Karachi. But there was no one to receive them at the airport, no red-carpet treatment, no space for the 'government in exile'. They didn't know where to go, what to do.

Leave this to me, said Sangliana. He had an address and the name of a person who would, he hoped, be their saviour. And it wasn't anyone in the Pakistani establishment. In their hour of need, the young man turned to one of his closest relatives, his father's own sister, who lived in Karachi and whose story qualifies to be among those which are, in a strange way, the better side of the tragedies that scarred Partition.

The long-forgotten sister of Brigadier Sailo had fallen in love with a Muslim doctor in Calcutta during World War II. They were working in the same hospital where she was a nurse. Against her elder brother's express wishes, they married and moved to Pakistan, settling in the port city of Karachi. Her husband was an army doctor and his brother was an army officer. The Mizo side of the family had excommunicated them but Sangliana had managed to contact her during his East Pakistan days and track her down during an earlier visit to Karachi. Having got to know Laldenga and his wiles, he decided to keep the family matter a secret from his boss.

Until then.

The young Mizo's aunt welcomed, fed and accommodated them for weeks in the family's bungalow, and provided them funds.

Meanwhile, Sangliana, through his aunt's brother-in-law was able to contact the Inter-Services Intelligence (ISI) agency, Pakistan's powerful and feared security wing. On his initiative, he met officers from the ISI, told them about Laldenga and the MNF (about which they had ample knowledge) and asked for their assistance. Within a few days, the Mizos were moved to a large, fully furnished and air-conditioned mansion in Islamabad, with wall-to-wall carpeting.

Laldenga was suitably impressed by his young aide's initiative. But being extremely suspicious, he was also concerned about whether Sangliana represented an incipient threat.[34]

Laldenga wanted more and got greedy. According to Sangliana, he asked the Pakistanis for funds to run his government and the army operations against the Indians. The ISI was surprised. 'Give us the name of the person and the town where he is located, in Rangoon (Yangon) or Bangkok or anywhere and we will transfer the funds to them directly.' Laldenga was insistent that the money should be given to him, as MNF president. He could have been more prudent: after all, it was a time when Pakistan had just been through the worst experience of its short life and was reeling from the humiliation of defeat, surrender and vivisection. It had been partitioned again, its right limb cut off by its worst enemy, its army had surrendered, it had 93,000 prisoners of war in Indian camps and the US Sixth Fleet had been forced to turn tail despite President Richard Nixon's high-sounding words of support for President Yahya Khan.

The ISI saw through Laldenga's plan and was equally insistent that it would give directly to the fighting units; his 'government-in-exile' dreams were to get a sudden jolt. That was when the ISI suddenly moved them to a smaller house in Rawalpindi and gave the ₹2,000 stipend. The Pakistani rationale was simple: they had virtually no bases or networks in the new Bangladesh any more, they were still bleeding from the wounds of the 1971 war and they needed to cut their losses since Mizoram—as well as the Nagas—were too far away to provide any real-time assistance. The greatest threats to India's security in the east had been neutralized by Sam Manekshaw's brilliant December 1971 campaign, although Chinese support was still forthcoming to the Nagas. Yet, the Mizos, for reasons unclear, decided to bolt for Pakistan and place themselves in its hands.

Within months, the atmosphere in the Rawalpindi house became suffocating. Laldenga wanted out to reach the Indians. But he needed new travel papers since he was thinking about slipping across the land border, through the Khyber Pass and into Afghanistan where he would connect with the Indians at their Kabul embassy.

Sangliana's ingenuity was again called upon. During his visits to Karachi, he had also established links with the local mafia. All large port cities have them. They dabble in everything, control many systems and have politicians and officials, especially the police, on their payroll. Little happens of any significance in a port city, especially of the vibrancy and scale of Karachi, without their knowledge. So, Sangliana went to a friend in the underworld who specialized in fake passports. A deal was struck and Laldenga and his family along with Zoramthanga and a few close aides, including Sangliana, were 'issued' passports. The Pakistanis were not going to make a fuss, they were quite happy to see the backs of the Mizo group. First, Sangliana and Zoramthanga went to Kabul to test the waters and check whether India was interested. They went one more time before they received a positive response.

The Pakistanis issued a passport to Laldenga in the name of Peter Lee, giving him a Chinese origin name so no questions would be asked (as in India, there has been a small but thriving Chinese community in Pakistan for generations). The idea to slip across the border to Afghanistan was abandoned as India's RAW responded, saying they would meet Laldenga in Geneva. That's where the discussion with Hassan Walia of RAW took place in August 1973. Almost immediately the MNF chief dashed off a letter to Prime Minister Indira Gandhi, which was not just polite but virtually obsequious in its tone.

On the letterhead of the Hotel du Lac, Laldenga talked about meeting Mr Singhal (which was Walia's assumed name) and declared that this 'personal letter' to the prime minister was to clarify that the Mizoram solution would have to be within the Constitution of India. To protect the 'social, cultural and religious traditions and customs' of the Mizos, special safeguards would be needed for which 'some minor Administrative adjustments would have to be made'.

The question therefore needs to be asked, if it was a matter of simple adjustments which could be sorted out through 'political talks' as Laldenga said, why had he put Mizoram through this decade of horrific pain, this trial by fire?

He went on to say in the letter to Mrs Gandhi that he was unilaterally calling on MNF to stop operating against security forces and asking for 'reciprocal action' from the security forces. To facilitate the peace process, he was prepared to come to India. But it took more talks between Laldenga and his own group, this time in Cologne in Germany, including MNF army chief Biakchhunga and Walia, before an arrangement was worked out. Under this, MNF vice president Tlangchhuaka, MNF party president K. Chawngzuala, and Biakchhunga were to precede Laldenga's arrival in New Delhi in January 1976.

Within a month, a press statement was issued by the two sides saying that MNF had accepted the Constitution of India, a set of remarks that caused consternation among the rebel ranks and confusion in civil society. But few spoke openly for they were afraid of their conversations being tapped and also of incurring Laldenga's wrath. It gave a mandate to Laldenga to settle the problem within the Constitution but the rumblings of dissension had begun.

Soon afterwards, the Government of India and Laldenga signed a three-clause agreement which acknowledged Mizoram as a part of India, adding that the rebels would suspend their activities and place their cadres and weapons inside 'mutually agreed camps', while the government would suspend operations barring those against cadres trying to cross the international border. The talks were to continue. Nothing came of it since Laldenga couldn't deliver. His army wing and many comrades were deeply divided and opposed to the accord. Security operations resumed as did activities of the MNF, the peace process went on erratically without a clear path.

The efforts continued fitfully, without much seriousness on either side, although Laldenga was desperate, his aides say, to get back to India and Aizawl. An interim accord signed in 1976 between S. L. Khurana, the home secretary, and Laldenga was broad in nature (like the Naga accord of 2015)[35] and did not go into any detail but defined the parameters of discussions. Earlier, middle-level and senior Mizo leaders were brought in from Burma and flown to Calcutta for a convention organized on their behalf by RAW and the Intelligence Bureau in a building which housed the Border Security Force. Sangliana and his colleagues were convinced that the conference room and their accommodation were bugged. They cautioned each other against speaking much. A resolution was passed to support Laldenga and the peace process leading to the announcement in New Delhi.

When the peace effort did not bear fruit, the military wing developed other plans. Fed up with Laldenga's vacillation and overweening eagerness to make peace with New Delhi, a faction involving Sangliana slipped into

Shillong and Guwahati and developed plans to attack these towns with plastic explosives. A planning unit was set up in Shillong. When Laldenga heard of it, he was furious and overrode the conspirators. There was to be no such attack. His orders were obeyed.

As the peace pendulum swung back and forth, Laldenga was at one point even arrested in this messy situation, in 1978, after Indira Gandhi was tossed out of office. Chaudhary Charan Singh was deputy prime minister and home minister, while Morarji Desai, a no-nonsense anti-Indira opponent, was prime minister. Mrs Gandhi had lost the March 1977 elections after a public surge of resentment against her authoritarian rule and the 1975–1977 state of internal Emergency. Laldenga was eventually released by the centre and sent back to London as the talks floundered and were put on hold.

Taking advantage of his absence from the stage, the anti-Laldenga group seized control of the party for nearly a year but it was finally overcome in the hills of Arakan where the MNF was based. The method of defanging them was simple yet brilliant. From his distant lair, Laldenga issued instructions.

He knew that on Sundays, all cadres and leaders would leave their weapons at home as they congregated for church services. Weapons were not allowed in the house of worship. On one such Sunday, as the anti-Laldenga group walked unarmed to the church in the main Arakan camp for prayers, they were surrounded by Laldenga's heavily armed loyalists and arrested.

Those not captured from the rival group wanted to retaliate. But Biakchhunga and Malsawma Colney, their most experienced and charismatic military leaders, refused to take up arms or authorize a counter-coup. It would have led to a bloodbath among the Mizos. 'We cannot fall into this trap, this is what the Nagas fell into, and see what has happened to them,' said Biackchhunga, the army chief, while counselling his angry young supporters.[36] He preferred detention to a bloody division that would have set Mizo against Mizo. The Mizo peace has held thanks to such wise decisions by people who are not given credit, not just those whose names are well known and celebrated.

By this time, Sangliana was based in Aizawl and a slow reconciliation was taking place between father and son. The older man became chief minister two times, his Mizoram People's Conference winning two back-to- back assembly elections, but refusing to give in to the MNF demand that he demit office. Contest the elections, was the retired officer's challenge. This became a block to the renewed peace process and the government sent Laldenga away to London. Re-elected prime minister in 1980, Mrs

Gandhi, even with her authoritarian streak, was not prepared to dismiss a leader of a rival party to accommodate Laldenga.

The latter was to come back in 1984 after agreeing to support the Congress in the local elections. Upon returning to India, Laldenga completed the eighteen-year cycle from Mizo rebel to Indian national: 'I have come back as an Indian to solve our problems and take my place...in Indian politics.'[37] But this was not a new position. The maverick had always held the avenue of negotiations open even at the time of declaring independence, going to the extent of telling his cadres: 'In case of Indian occupation of Mizoram after some time, talks with the Government of India shall be arranged through a third party.'[38] So was it an insurgency or an armed fight for more internal political power, an effort to force the centre to accommodate the ambitions of one man who had managed to convince many Mizos of the rightness of that ambition—if not cause? This always makes fascinating space for conjecture: did Laldenga unlike Muivah, the Naga leader, actually truthfully believe in liberation from India or was he really interested in settling scores with the Mizo Union, which had tossed him out of an accountant's job in the district council, and was determined to hurt them?

On 31 October 1984, India and the world was shaken by the assassination of Indira Gandhi by her two Sikh guards. There was massive retaliation against the Sikhs across different parts of India. That morning, Laldenga had had an appointment with Mrs Gandhi and was the first to give an interview to a BBC team led by the well-known actor Peter Ustinov.

Mizoram's elusive peace had to wait for another two years, until 30 June 1986, when Mrs Gandhi's son and successor, Rajiv, having stormed to a parliamentary mandate not seen before by either his grandfather Jawaharlal Nehru or his mother, approved an accord with the MNF. The terms were simple and were signed by R. C. Pradhan, the home secretary, Laldenga and Lalkhama, the Mizoram chief secretary, who had been a neighbour of Laldenga's in New Delhi for a couple of years during earlier unsuccessful efforts for an agreement.

Rajiv's electoral landslide meant that the former pilot with Indian Airlines, who had been reluctantly pitchforked into politics in 1980 after the death of his ambitious and powerful younger brother Sanjay[39] in a stunt plane crash, gave him enormous manoeuvring room for political accommodation. The hopes of a younger generation appeared reflected in Rajiv's approach as he set about trying to tackle the rot in his party and meet the aspirations of younger Indians. Trying to bring peace to regions as different and distant from each other as the Punjab and the Northeast, he signed a flurry of accords, first with the Sikhs in 1985, a year after the Golden Temple raid[40] by the army against Sikh extremists. Then followed an agreement with agitating student leaders from Assam who had campaigned for nearly a decade against illegal migration from Bangladesh, though much of their ire was actually reserved for Muslims of Bengali origin, many of whose ancestors came to Assam when it was part of an undivided India before Partition.[41]

The third was the deal with the MNF, known as the Mizoram Accord that followed secret meetings between Congress Party leaders such as the party's vice president Arjun Singh, Laldenga and Mizoram's chief minister Lalthanhawla as well as the union territory's chief secretary Lalkhama, the home secretary R. D. Pradhan and the country's top army and intelligence officials. Rajiv was kept abreast of the negotiations which moved swiftly and remains the only agreement between New Delhi and an insurgent group in the Northeast—or anywhere else for that matter—that has held.

It remains Rajiv's lasting legacy not just to Mizoram but to the region and India. In one stroke, it freed up the army to focus on other fronts, brought peace to a long-suffering people and brought the boys home. The accord was divided into three sections with a brief preamble that set out the history of efforts to bring peace. In the first section, it stressed the need for MNF to surrender weapons and for its armed cadres to abandon violence, that it would amend its constitution to accept the Constitution (although this was more seen as understood rather than specified: the clause said MNF would bring it in line with the law) and stop aiding rebels from Manipur and Tripura. The Government of India on its side agreed to rehabilitate MNF returnees and provide compensation.

It also agreed to endow full statehood on the area, making it a special status federal unit under which it would get 90 per cent of all funds as a grant from the centre. In addition, the centre committed itself to protect the rights and special traditions of its people, give the Mizo language constitutional status, set up a central university (which today is vibrant and accommodating young scholars as well as researching key issues of the Mizoram movement), a High Court and even enable border trade in locally grown farm produce.

Then comes a clause which is perhaps a niggle in Mizoram these days and hence not felt by its neighbours for it was never seriously pursued by any of the successor governments—the question of what was called 'unification of Mizo inhabited areas of other States to form one administrative unit'.

Very clearly, the centre said that while Article 3 of the Constitution enables the centre to redraw the borders of states unilaterally as well as carve out and create new ones, it was unprepared to 'make any commitment in this respect'.

The same political issue of land and greater territory, connected to identity, is highly emotive and contentious as we have seen in Nagaland, Manipur, Assam and Arunachal Pradesh. It gives sleepless nights to the political leadership in these states as well as in New Delhi. The latter's approach to the Mizo demand for a greater Zoram is something that our Naga friends would also need to bear in mind as they wrestle with the details of a possible agreement. Without the concurrence of their neighbours, this issue is as dead as a dodo, no matter how much one side cajoles, bullies, hectors and threatens the others.

In this situation, the accord also noted that victims of violence and atrocities (of course, it did not use these specific words) were entitled to financial compensation for hurt and damage and said that this would be speedily done. This had not happened in thirty years but a compensation package was being prepared for each of the 2,188 (the official figure) civilians who were killed in the conflict, taking a cue from the compensation which was paid by the centre's home ministry to two victims of rape by army soldiers; the women 'lost their sanity after being gangraped' in 1966. Of course, as in all cases protected by AFSPA, no one knows if anything happened to the soldiers involved, whether they were punished in any way. A black shroud of silence covers all such incidents as the army and other security forces scurry to cover up.

There was another substantial concession to the Mizos, which has not been fulfilled in any detail: a team from the centre had agreed to:

> ...payment of compensation in respect of damage to crop, building destroyed/damaged during the action in Mizoram, and rented charges of building and land occupied by security force. There may, however, be some claim which were referred and verified by the above team but is not yet settled expeditiously. Arrangement will also be made for payment of pending claim of rented charges or land/building occupied by the security forces.

What is not widely known is that the Congress Party, to cement the deal and ensure that the MNF kept its side of the bargain, actually signed a smaller agreement before the official concord took place between the Government of India and the MNF.

The principal clauses declared that 'to enable a smooth and orderly transition, the Indian National Congress (I) and the MNF headed by Shri Laldenga agree to form a coalition Government'. It even prescribed the way the deal would be carried out, thereby clearly emphasizing the predominance of the political wing over the executive. For the better known agreement was signed by one politician (Laldenga) who was outside the Indian system till that point and two bureaucrats (Pradhan and Lalkhama). To give it political teeth and ensure that the Congress' interests were protected when elections to the state assembly were held, Rajiv and Arjun Singh, his principal troubleshooter in those early years, pushed through a party-to-party accord. Bearing in mind the disaster of the Punjab accord where Harcharan Singh Longowal, one of the Sikh signatories of the accord was assassinated within months of signing, the party-to-party statement in Mizoram said that the political changes would follow 'soon after the members of MNF who are underground lay down their arms and join the national mainstream'.

It said that on an agreed date, Lalthanhawla would resign as chief minister but be appointed deputy chief minister under Laldenga, that Congress would have four more cabinet members while the MNF would have three. Laldenga would be elected 'leader of the Government of Mizoram', not of any party as the MNF had no presence in the local legislature.

Lalthanhawla was not happy with the arrangement. He told Rajiv: 'You are asking me to work under the man who fought against us for so long and brought misery to the Mizos.'[42] But he was persuaded to drop his opposition. Lalthanhawla, dapper and well preserved in his early seventies, was no ordinary Congressman. He had been sympathetic to the MNF cause and was restrained, he said, by his father from joining the underground. His father told Laldenga who came in a group to persuade the old man to let his son go and join the rebels: 'You will not succeed because India is too strong and I won't let my son go.' Laldenga then remarked: 'Well, he may be more useful to us overground.' And Lalthanhawla proved adept—arranging funds at short notice, sending and delivering messages.

He thought about it that day of our interview in Aizawl and then said: 'That was the only truthful thing Laldenga said during his entire political career.' Lalthanhawla, like other Mizos, had many reasons for his suspicion and bitterness towards the MNF leader. For one, within a few months of the outbreak of the conflict, he was caught and detained in what he called a 'military concentration camp' near Silchar. He was able to laugh when he thought of those days—but life was very tough. About 350 Mizos were packed into a handful of tents encircled by high barbed wire fences. He remembers the pit latrines and the food: the toilets were in the open, on a slope and they were given no water or paper for cleaning. At night, if they needed to urinate, they would shout to the guard: 'Sentry, pisab.' As his aides listened in stunned silence, he added: 'There were rows of pits.' He had never spoken of these issues before in a recorded conversation.

And the food was one mugful of gruel-like dal and two thin chapattis, served once a day. After a six-month internment there, he was shifted to Silchar and then made the critical political switch from MNF to Congress, a move that has served him well over the decades. He has been chief minister five times and is perhaps the most familiar face in his state, easy to approach and relaxed in conversation—but one of the sharpest political figures in the business. Which explains his longevity in Mizo and national politics.

Lalthanhawla's face turned sad and grim when he recounted his story, the words came spilling out in a rush. It's not a story he has told many people and his own public relations staff, including the veteran press adviser L. R. (Ruatliana) Sailo, were surprised by the details he shared.

They were moved from jail to jail and when being transported by train from Silchar to Nowgong (now Nagaon); he remembered very clearly how they were forced to kneel on the platform, handcuffed and tied to each other with a rope in groups of thirty. His wife said something in a hushed tone, as she sat and listened to a story she must have been familiar with. 'Yes, and they told us to bow our heads, kneel down.'

The humiliation runs deep. He remembers every detail, from the fact that they slept for weeks on the ground in the first detention centre which he called a POW camp. There were six to eight men in each tent and there were more than fifty tents, each with armed guards outside. The captives had only the clothes they wore and did not have a bath for weeks. Every day, they would clean the lice that had dug under their skin and infested their filthy blankets and clothes.

As he spoke, Lalthanhawla did not weep but quietly wiped his eyes with a handkerchief. It was a moment of intense grief for the state's most influential politician. Yet, after his release, he chose to align with the Congress Party and embrace the national colours, turning his back on the past but unable to close the gates of memory.

◆

Sangliana's story is different. Men and women like him remain faithful to the ideals of the MNF. To them, the peace born of the accord is incomplete. They remember their comrades who suffered in neighbouring Manipur.

The army and security forces burnt villages, homes, displaced thousands of Mizos and Kukis and their small clans in Manipur. People were killed, crops were destroyed, the pattern of repression was acutely similar to the neighbouring Mizo Hills. These victims of conflict never received any compensation for their suffering and Sangliana and a band of former MNF fighters remain deeply anguished by their inability to reach out and provide succour. 'He really is torn up by it, especially since he feels helpless,' says his sister, Laldingliani Sailo, the gregarious, blunt and bubbly Dingi, former tax official and now member of the National Women's Commission.

The lessons of the Rambuai are many and not far to seek. One is that never again in the history of independent India must such force from the air and forced displacement of populations be used against a helpless civilian population, no matter how great the provocation from an armed group. The entire episode was shameful and calls for an apology. This will take statesmanship of a very high order.

Josephine Lalbiakzuali, from Pachhuanga College's Department of English, put it thoughtfully in a free flowing conversation at her college. Pretty, composed and precise, Josephine spoke of 'a cultivated peace' where people were very careful about hurting others who may have been in the MNF or with the government during those days 'even in satirical works'. But despite this sense of abundant caution among the Mizos, Josephine appears to reflect a more robust younger approach when she says that while people were still 'very wary about uncovering hurt feelings, to me it is important that it is brought out in literature and it needs closure, to free people from the demons that are troubling them'.

That we are still to learn the lessons is obvious in the manner of the Indian state's handling of the 'Maoist' insurgency in central India where brutality, deprivation, poverty, lack of basic services and non-governance go together. Secondly, compensation, if it is to be paid at all, must be substantial and paid as swiftly as possible. Most compensation cases drag on for too long, with many complications. A third factor is that those involved in incidents of rape, destruction of property and causing bodily, emotional and mental harm and trauma need to be punished. For that to happen, AFSPA must go.

As I have mentioned earlier, the Justice Verma Committee said, rape and physical assault against civilians by the army and security forces are completely outside the 'line of duty' approach that is parroted by legal defenders of the indefensible. There cannot be protection for those who violate basic laws and rights with such impunity. Tackling the offenders would help restore the faith of people in areas where there is much opposition to the armed forces and AFSPA. In addition, it would boost the morale of the troops, not undermine it. Some army officials, politicians and bureaucrats claim the latter. But that doesn't wash.

There's another point which is relevant to the Naga situation especially: although they like to deny any similarities between the Mizo conditions and theirs, there are some. The key commonality is the demand for a greater and unified political unit spanning state and international borders which brings the Mizos and Nagas together. Mizos say their campaign is for Greater Mizoram or Zomi Reunification;[43] the Nagas say that they want Nagalim or the integration of all Naga-inhabited areas in Manipur, Assam and Arunachal Pradesh with Nagaland. The Mizos speak of Zomi or Mizo areas in Myanmar, Manipur, Tripura and Assam. Neither demand will be met by the government because broaching the idea publicly will create far more problems than those which exist. No government, either at the state or the central level, wants to add more challenges and headaches to those that it already has or has inherited.

No government, certainly not at the centre, wants to beckon the hounds of civil war where the police and people of each state will be fighting counterparts from the neighbouring state. Muivah, the Naga leader from Manipur, or men like MNF leader Zoramthanga and others will not be able to push this through, no matter how deeply they believe in it. Should they rise again with their armed groups, the full wrath of the Indian state would descend on them. This is not something the one-time guerrillas would welcome for their precise locations are known to and mapped in every detail by military, intelligence officials and local police. It may be the location of their armed and non-armed cadres (many live in what are called 'designated' peace camps which are closely monitored). Where the leadership lives, with whom, who they meet, their habits, movements, what and when they eat, when they exercise—all this is known. One-time guerrillas and their leaders have now become predictable creatures of habit.

The security forces know how to approach the camps, how to cut them off and block exit routes for the rebels.

Therefore, should a conflict take place if political negotiations fail, the outcome is unlikely to be a protracted guerrilla war, as in the past. It will probably be more in the nature of a conventional conflict where the military would have the upper hand and a huge advantage in terms of numbers and firepower. Knowledge in the information era, with satellites and snoops to capture every nuance of every sentence or every movement, is power. The government can strike from the air and from land at will, before the rebels gain any tactical advantage by slipping away.

Thus, although such outbreaks of fighting are highly unlikely, not because neither side is prepared to have a go, the practicality of such a mission weighs heavily on those who would launch it. In addition, the kind of support that was available between the 1960s and 1980s, just would not be there. Mizos are running their own affairs of state, busy with building lives, creating wealth, teaching, studying and getting on with life in the state and outside.

So even as the mist blows in the quietude of the hills and the clear water from downpours and spray of many waterfalls abound, not many are prepared to make that journey to hell and back again. In Sialsuk, where the song of pain and silence quoted earlier remembers a past horror, the cheerfulness and generosity of the villagers almost obliterate it. At the bright, small Young Mizo Association library, as the curtains were blown about by gusts of wind, a group of women sang the desolate song of the village. It is clear they don't want to travel that way again, but it's also absolutely clear that the years of the Rambuai are not going away, they are not forgotten.

The dirge recalls the village's death and its rebirth as that of countless other hamlets that were torched, demolished or otherwise damaged.

In that song and the evocation of it lies the inner Mizo story of dealing with the past—as the sad-eyed, astute and experienced Lalkhama, who signed the peace accord, said: 'The Mizos have been through hell and back and do not want to experience it again in one lifetime.' It is therefore fitting that the song's last stanza carries a message of hope:

O, Sial (suk), you are beyond grand
Even though light may have deserted you for now
May the Protector help us rebuild you
As the place where lovers and kindred once roamed.

◆

Some kilometres away, on one edge of Aizawl, not far from the central university that was a gift of the accord, lies a pocket of land where history is buried, along with the thousands who fell in the conflict with India. 'The bones and remains of about 1,500 are interred here,' said one researcher and writer. There is space for 2,000 more, many of whose remains are still in Burma as these could not be collected in time for the return journey for the survivors in 1986. For men like Sangliana, this remains the incomplete story, the reason why there hasn't been any real closure since their friends still lie far afield in an alien land. That chapter for people like him will perhaps close only when there is a full, fitting, final farewell to the lost boys.

Could hope for the future lie in the song of St. Francis of Assisi, to turn swords into ploughshares: 'For it is in giving that we receive, in forgiving that we are forgiven'? In no other part of India, certainly in few other places which have suffered so much, have those who have been harmed so deeply risen out of such a deep and dark abyss and embraced that prayer as much as they have lived the song of Sialsuk. It is in the manner of their doing so that should shame us and our governments, the men in uniform and out of it—both the security forces and the armed groups who opposed them—who hurt, humiliated, maimed and killed innocents.

The least they deserve is an apology, an expression of regret. Such a gesture will not demean the one seeking forgiveness but instead enrich and strengthen him. It takes greater courage to acknowledge one's mistakes than it does to smash a clenched fist into a villager's face, gun down a man running from his pursuers or break the bones and spirit of a captive with rifle butts, sticks and boots.

Bhupen Hazarika, the balladeer of the Brahmaputra, sang of this missing factor to his native Assam, at a time of rioting:

> If humans don't think for humans, who will, comrade…
> If a human does not become human
> A demon never will
> But if a demon turns more human
> Who will it shame more, comrade?[44]

Chapter 5

ASSAM: BATTLES FOR THE HOMELAND

Down in the plains of Assam, driving along a smooth highway with flooded green fields on both sides and cool wind on my face, I marvel at the beauty of my homeland. We reach Bokota, home of the distinguished film director Jahnu Barua, where villagers welcome us to their homes of earthen walls and tin roofs. They share tea, home-brewed rice beer and their stories. We trudge from home to home in the slippery mud, under rain and darkness, as the sounds of a million bullfrogs and cicadas fill the air, fireflies zigzag their incandescent dance. And each story fills me with anger.

This is part of what was United Liberation Front of Asom country where hundreds of recruits joined ULFA in the 1980s and 1990s, seeking a simplistic 'liberation' of their motherland from 'colonial' Indian forces, distressed by the economic backwardness and the political indifference of New Delhi and Dispur, the capital of Assam.

In one home, a father and mother mourn the death of a beloved son, picked up and beaten in front of them and then thrown into an army truck while a horrified neighbourhood watched helplessly. That nightmare in many parts of the state lasted much of the 1990s but, even today, sometimes, victims wake in fear.

'Those bad days have gone, we do not want them to return ever to Assam,' said a woman activist. Of course, the existence of ULFA in those years was a threat to the state: five cadres were killed in the village and many others died in neighbouring areas of Sivasagar district. Yet, is it worth alienating, hurting and harming an entire society to hunt down a few, even if there are networks of sympathizers and informants? Is it surprising that the opposition to the state has endured so long even if it does mean there is robust support for a weak political idea?

But we're getting ahead of our story. Let us first make a detour to the kingdom of Bhutan, whose fortunes and misfortunes have been closely linked with Assam.

◆

The prime minister looked at the men sitting around the conference table in his office. He had decided to be blunt. The Indian pressure was becoming too much for the government to bear; the National Assembly members were agitated by the presence of so many armed men and women on the soil of a peace-loving Buddhist land, responsible for conducting violent operations and deadly events in neighbouring Assam, with which his country had a long and amicable relationship ranging from culture to commerce. Most important, his monarch, the head of state, wanted tough action. Things had been allowed to fester for too long.

Acutely aware of the heavy burden he was carrying, Jigme Yoezer Thinley, head of the government of the Himalayan kingdom of Bhutan, chose his words carefully. He spoke clearly and firmly. 'Your fight,' he told the brooding insurgent leaders who had driven from their camps in Samdrup Jongkhar Dzongkhag[1] on the southeastern edge of the country, bordering Assam, 'is not with us.' Their fight was with India; they were no longer welcome as uninvited guests in Bhutan. In addition, it was becoming difficult to explain to the Indian government why his government was not able to get the rebels out.

India was Bhutan's biggest funder and long-standing friend, not just bankrolling the tiny nation's[2] five-year plans but also providing infrastructure support, weaponry and training to the modest army. Many young Bhutanese went to study in the country's top schools and colleges. The Indian Army presence is substantial in Bhutan, if not in numbers, then certainly in terms of the senior officers posted to its capital, Thimpu, and elsewhere as part of the Indian Military Training Team (IMTRAT). New Delhi needed—and still does—Bhutan's help in keeping an eye on Chinese activities in Tibet and the high Himalayas.

Every few months the issue of the insurgents' presence would come up in Bhutan's National Assembly with members from across the country but especially from Samdrup Jongkhar Dzongkhag expressing anxiety about the country's security and the potential threat from the armed groups. The king himself, the handsome Jigme Singye Wangchuck, who had by nudging and cajoling moved his kingdom from a monarchy to a constitutional democracy over thirty years, told the assembly: 'Bhutan had never faced a more serious threat to its security in the past one hundred years of its history.' In addition, there was always the pressure from Big Brother India.

Thinley is a small man with a ready smile. He was dressed in the formal gowns of office, a long, embroidered, glowing yellow and maroon coat with traditional Bhutanese stripes, a robe draped carefully on top and high boots.

'Unless you leave, this is the last time we will meet,' he quietly affirmed to the delegation, which included senior leaders from two of three rebel groups in the Northeast who had established thirty camps of tents and huts in the thick forests of Samdrup Jongkhar, clearing spaces for living quarters, ammunition stores, training facilities, general stores and kitchens. In these huts, some 2,000 men,[3] women and children, including armed cadres and their leaders, wives and families as well as other non-combatants such as nursing staff lived. The camps included the tactical headquarters of ULFA, the most powerful of the three groups and the most feared in Assam.

Its leaders, Paresh Baruah, chief of the armed wing, and Arabindo Rajkhowa, the chairman, shuttled between Samdrup Jongkhar and Bangladesh with occasional trips to Burma, where they had connections with the Khaplang group of the National Socialist Council of Nagalim/ Nagaland (NSCN-K).[4] The second significant group was the National Democratic Front of Bodoland (NDFB) of Ranjan Daimary, dreaded for its brutal strikes against civilians of non-Bodo descent as well as against security forces. The Bodos were the oldest settled community in the Assam Valley and had introduced wet rice cultivation and weaving into these parts. ULFA had fourteen camps and NDFB had eleven.

The third group was also the smallest: the Kamtapur Liberation Organization (KLO), run by Tamir Das alias Jibon Singha, its chairman, and his main aides, vice chairman Harshabardhan Barman and Tom Adhikary. The KLO was largely based in the Cooch Behar area of North Bengal and drew its cadres from the Koch-Rajbongshi community.[5] The KLO, with members in five camps, simply ignored the Bhutanese summons and did not send a representative to a single discussion. The Bhutanese were to tell me afterwards that they felt particularly insulted by this tiny faction's arrogance.

Bhutan opened discussions with the militant groups in 1998. Five rounds of talks were held with ULFA and three rounds with NDFB while Thimpu smarted from KLO's spurning. In June 2001, ULFA said it would shut four camps. But Bhutanese joy was short-lived when they found that the camps had just been relocated. Another reason for Bhutanese ire at KLO was that officials were worried by accounts of its connections to the Nepalese Maoists, who were wreaking havoc in the neighbouring country at the time, and the Bhutan Tiger Force, an incipient local anti-government group.

◆

The Assamese and Bodos who faced the prime minister of Bhutan were in no mood to bargain.[6] According to Jigme Thinley, a man of elegance and calm, they were 'quite arrogant in their responses'.

When the Indian Army hadn't been able to take them out, the insurgents virtually sneered, what could the Bhutanese do? They were perhaps recalling the fact that they had moved to Bhutan in the 1990s to escape the drives by the Assam police and the Indian military to crush ULFA in one crackdown after another. In Samdrup Jongkhar, just across the border from Assam's Kokrajhar and Darrang districts and close to Arunachal Pradesh, they had found local traders happy to supply them vegetables, fruit, chickens and meat at high prices that the armed groups were prepared to pay. Most of the money was drawn from funds extorted from individual businessmen and companies, government officials and contractors.

One account[7] quoted in *The Telegraph* of 10 October 1997 said that ULFA leaders were engaged in business in collaboration with the Bhutanese and investments were in the names of some locals. The report said that relatives of Bhutanese government officials were 'more often than not "*benamdars*"[8] in these business transactions'. It was also an open secret that a two-storeyed house in Samdrup Jongkhar belonging to a retired Bhutanese officer was being used as a resting camp for ULFA cadres. In November 1997, *The Sentinel* published a report quoting intelligence sources in which it was said that the Royal Bhutan Army had withdrawn troops of the Border Royal Task Force (BRTF) from West Deothang in Eastern Bhutan, which was known as an ULFA stronghold. They had set up their 'central training centre' in Deothang. The newspaper claimed that there was even a secret meeting between the Bhutanese king and ULFA leader Paresh Barua.

As they dismissed the notion that Bhutan could roust them from their camps, the rebels were referring to Bhutan's small army of 6,000 soldiers which had never been bloodied in action. The core of the ULFA fighting force had been trained in Burma by the NSCN (K) and the Kachin Independence Army (KIA). The latter was one of the most formidable armies around. Even in 2017, it was continuing to fight the war-hardened Burmese Army as it had for fifty years, in a struggle for independence. The Assamese fighters were well-armed, equipped with recently acquired weaponry, including mortars, AK-47s, AK-56s, grenades and hand weapons.

At some point in the discussions with Thinley, Bhimkanta Buragohain, a former schoolteacher and ULFA's main ideologue, at that time sixty-five years old and the group's elder statesman, made a statement that was to trigger a silent rage in the prime minister and define Bhutan's final response to the armed groups.

Apparently unaware of the impact his remarks would have, Buragohain, in response to a query on how long they planned to stay, said: 'We are here in perpetuity.' They wanted a base in Bhutan as long as their war of independence against India continued.

Thinley stressed the point he had made earlier—they had no business to be in Bhutan, a peace-loving country which had close relations with India and also with the people of Assam. These relations were being jeopardized by ULFA and the other groups which slipped in and out of Bhutan to conduct ambushes and other operations, extort money and then use the quick access to their bases in the Bhutanese jungles to slip away with ease. This could not go on.

He asked a simple question: how could they think that they could overcome India's huge army? And, anyway, the Bhutanese would now no longer hesitate to use force as it was a question of their national sovereignty.

'You cannot hope to win because we will be fighting for our country,' he remembered telling them. 'What will your cadres be fighting against? A country that was host to them?'

The meeting ended with the militants rejecting the Bhutanese leader's request. The prime minister was upset, not at the failure of the talks but because he knew that the die was now cast. His peaceful kingdom would never be the same again. It had faced disruption since ULFA and its compatriots had fled Bangladesh following initial but reluctant action against them by the pro-India Awami League government of Sheikh Hasina Wajed in the mid-1990s.

◆

A few years earlier, the Indian media, especially the press in Assam, had published accounts that the Bhutanese king, accompanied by senior aides, was visiting ULFA and other camps and, according to the militants even chatting over cups of tea with their leaders. Buragohain, who was affectionately known as 'mama' or uncle to his younger colleagues and followers, said the king had visited a couple of times.[9]

There were reports that ULFA and NDFB were being tacitly supported or used by the Bhutanese in their campaign of ethnic cleansing against the Lotsamphas or Nepalese who had lived in the country for decades. In return, they were reportedly being allowed to stay on, with the Bhutanese government keeping away from that corner of their nation. Thimpu robustly denied these allegations but the Government of India remained concerned by the reports that there was an unofficial 'official' connection to ULFA that went beyond the local links of buying provisions and benami transactions. These were discussed at negotiations between officials and even at the ministerial level.

According to a news report,[10] which was never denied, the king met Arabinda Rajkhowa, ULFA's chairman, on two occasions including one in Thimpu between 2001–2002. On a trip to an ULFA camp, 'the king was even accompanied by a brigadier and a colonel of the Royal Bhutan Army, besides the escort party'.

A spokesman of the Royal Bhutanese Embassy in New Delhi declined to say if the king had visited the militants' camps but would only remark that he had visited the 'security affected areas in Samdrup Jongkhar Dzongkhag and Sarpang districts'.

The visit by the king was part of a steady strategy he was developing to tackle the clear and present danger to his country and steer Bhutan to safety. His reasoning was clear: it may not take much to turn such groups, which did not hesitate to use their firepower against their own countrymen and official forces, against their small and reluctant hosts.

In a conversation with me at his simple, spacious and tastefully decorated office, with magnificent woollen carpets and silk tapestries depicting scenes from the Buddha's life and Bhutan's history, Jigme Singye Wangchuck told me how he had fooled the Indian government, the media and the rebels.

The visits to the camps were designed specifically to gain information about a few things: the first was to understand how vulnerable or protected the access points to the camps were; the second to assess the strength of the cadres and the quality of their training, fitness and weaponry; the third was to recce the exit route for the camp residents.

'They thought we were greeting them and acknowledging their presence,' said the king. What the rebels did not know was that Wangchuck was not only accompanied by his chief of staff but also by his top intelligence officer. The aim was simple: study the capacity of the fighters, how quickly their defences could be demolished and 'how to cut off their escape routes'. Attack and trap was the king's plan.

Bhutan didn't want news of the impending crackdown leaked to the media. The king, who designed the strategy to take on the militants, insisted on secrecy.

On 13 December 2003, some eighteen months after his last meeting with Rajkhowa in the jungle camp, Wangchuck called Prime Minister Atal Bihari Vajpayee and told him of the attack plan. Vajpayee agreed to place units of India's army, paramilitary and state police on the Assam and West

Bengal borders to capture any cadres or non-combatants who fleeing the assault. ULFA and the others were given two days' notice to vacate.

At his ancestral house at Ahomgaon, Dhola, Tinsukia district, Buragohain said he and his people were completely taken by surprise when the Bhutanese attacked. They were 'expecting the king of Bhutan' that day—but the visit was of a very different kind, he recalled bitterly, saying that their hosts had betrayed them.

But really, what did they expect Bhutan to do after years of persistent pressure from New Delhi, after all the bad publicity it had received from hosting not one but several armed groups which made no secret of their open if unwelcome stay on Bhutanese soil from where they planned assaults across the border, to kill, kidnap, ambush and extort? India and Bhutan had come close to an agreement on joint military operations against the armed factions a number of times. The operations would have trapped the armed groups in a pincer movement from which there would be neither escape nor mercy.

But each time, Bhutan backed out, citing domestic concerns, especially worries about a rebel backlash should some militants escape the dragnet and then target Bhutanese leaders and towns. Bhutanese officials argued that their soldiers were not well trained enough, experienced or equipped to conduct and sustain such an attack. Indian assurances didn't convince them.

After a steady stream of soldiers had been put through advanced combat training, the king summoned his twenty-three-year-old son, Jigme Khesar Namgyel, from college in England and tasked him with supporting the plans for attacking the camps. The king admitted that there was an element of risk—but it was a question of his country's survival.

The Royal Bhutanese Army struck hard and simultaneously in four districts, using mortars, automatic weapons and hand grenades as they attacked the thirty camps in Samtse, Samdrup Jongkhar, Sarpang and Zhemgang.

Bhimkanta Buragohain recalled:

> It was a morning like today—cold, with the sun struggling to break through the clouds. There was a cheer in the camp as we were expecting the king of Bhutan. The previous day [14 December 2003], I was sitting in front of my camp at our central headquarters along with my bodyguards and some of our cadres after having my morning meal when a major from the Royal Bhutan Army, whom I knew very well, came and informed us that the king would be visiting our camp the next morning.
>
> The king had visited our camp on a couple of occasions earlier,

too. The army official exchanged pleasantries and handed over some gifts, including a huge box of fresh oranges and a silver bottle of US-made vitamin pills.

On 15 December all of us—there were around a hundred of us including women and children—got up early and started preparing for the king's visit. The women were preparing Assamese pithas, while I instructed my men to tidy up the camp and line up along the three approach roads to accord a ceremonial welcome to the king. Everything was ready.

Around 8.30 a.m., I heard the first gunshots. Initially, I thought our boys were firing to welcome the king.

Quickly, though, I realized that the firing was directed towards the camp and us. Among the melee of thoughts that crowded my mind in those moments, one realization dawned with shocking numbness: we had been betrayed and attacked.

The surprise was complete. ULFA would never recover from that battering. Buragohain himself barely escaped from being blown up as a bodyguard pulled him out of his hut just before a mortar shell blasted it to pieces. Four days later, hungry, thirsty and frightened, they surrendered to the Bhutanese Army who handed them over to the Indian Army. From Buragohain's account, it appears that his group did not engage in clashes with the Bhutanese Army. The general headquarters which was under his command, as well as the tactical headquarters, the camp of the 27th Battalion and the Madhyam Manadalik were destroyed. It was the last that Buragohain saw of two men that he knew well: Robin Neogi and Ashanta Baghphukan, who had been left behind in the Bhutanese camp.

He and four other men, including the KLO's vice chairman Burman, were flown by helicopter to Tezpur where they were later paraded before the media.

ULFA was smashed as an effective army; communications between the leaders and cadres were snapped. The losses were huge.

General N. C. Vij, the chief of army staff at the time, said that no fewer than 1,000 persons had been 'neutralized' in the Bhutanese assault. The Bhutan Army suffered eleven dead and about fifty wounded, many of whom were evacuated by waiting helicopters to Indian military hospitals for quick treatment. Apart from tactical support and backup as well as closing the Indo-Bhutan border, the Indian Army did not have much of a direct role although it was prepared for action.

Non-combatants—basically the wives and children of the armed cadres as well as nursing and support staff—walked to the Assam border where they were taken into custody by local officials and police, put on buses and sent off to captivity in Guwahati. Most of them were later released.

At his home, Mama mused to the reporter:

> Till Bhutan happened, there was a proper communication between the higher-ups and the battalions. But the offensive broke this chain. More important than the blow to the organisational set-up perhaps was the pounding that our confidence took. Suddenly, our war became more difficult. Operation All Clear may have been a huge success for Delhi but for us it was a great betrayal.

In one swift surgical thrust, ULFA's firepower and fighting units had been smashed. It would take all of Paresh Baruah's organizing skills and his remarkable networks to try and put together a response that could shake India. That incipient challenge to Indian power was broken less than a year later by a tip-off from Indian agencies and the alertness of an upright officer in the Bangladeshi port of Chittagong. That fateful morning, those two elements stopped one of the biggest illicit arms deliveries to be made through the great sea routes of Southeast Asia. This was a joint ULFA and National Socialist Council of Nagaland operation under the direct supervision of Baruah and Anthony (Robert) Shimray, the latter's main weapons organizer. As we have seen in an earlier chapter, Shimray, a young, tough and smart Tangkhul who had escaped from a high security jail in Assam during the height of the ULFA movement, was one of Muivah's closest aides. He had built up an enviable list of contacts through a four-year stay in Kunming, the capital of the southwestern Chinese province of Yunnan.[11]

◆

The Bhutanese prime minister spoke bluntly after the operation. Denouncing the insurgents as 'extremely obstinate and uncompromising', and referring to their arrogance during the negotiations, he said:

> They maintained that they could not leave until they had fulfilled the objective of achieving independence from India... In effect that meant their perpetual presence in Bhutan. The KLO, which also wants to carve an independent state from India, did not even make the effort to come for talks. Quite clearly, the presence of the separatist groups from India was not only harming the interests of Bhutan but those of our friend and neighbour, India. This is something that no Bhutanese is prepared to tolerate under any circumstances.

They had given ULFA and the others a long rope: the sequence of events went something like this:

- On 19 July 2003, Bhutanese MPs proposed to raise the number of Bhutanese militia by introducing Swiss-style militia training for all citizens aged between eighteen and fifty. The motion was dismissed by then foreign minister Jigme Thinley (later prime minister), who asserted that 5,000 Royal Bhutan Army soldiers were deployed to the country's border with India.

- That year, significantly, Bhutan re-established its militia. By 15 September 2003, the Bhutanese militia consisted of 634 volunteers and was deployed in the country's south, where the armed groups operated, monitoring rebel movements, personnel and activities, sending regular reports back to Thimpu to heighten preparedness and improve attention to detail.

- On 13 December, the same day as the king called Prime Minister Vajpayee, an ultimatum was sent to the three anti-India factions ordering them to leave the territory of the kingdom within forty-eight hours.

- Two days later, the attack on the camps began. In the Bhutanese assault, the small but doughty militia played an important role as the eyes and ears of the army, guiding it along jungle routes, tightening access and escape routes, helping maintain supply lines and evacuating the sick and wounded.

Reflecting on the operation, King Jigme Singye Wangchuck spoke respectfully of the way his foes had responded, despite being outnumbered, outflanked, outgunned and out-thought. 'Many of them stood and fought, they didn't run away,' he said. His wife, Queen Mother Ashi Dorji Wangmo Wangchuck,[12] reflected on the assault in *Treasures of the Thunder Dragon: A Portrait of Bhutan*, writing that the 'war' came to 'an incredible swift and conclusive end...in one and a half days, between 15 and 16 December, the thirty camps established by the militants over fourteen years were destroyed by our army; many of their leaders were captured, and others fled to India'. There was a little hype here for the fact is that the flushing out operations continued into early January, spread over four districts.

The queen mother wrote: 'there was no crowing over victory...that is not our way. We mourned the eleven Bhutanese soldiers who died, and we lit lamps and offered prayers too for the militants who were killed, that their souls may find peace.'

After the operations, the government went after local Bhutanese who were associated with the militants, arresting over 140 people for aiding the armed groups.[13] The country's government-run newspaper *Kuensel* quoted the prime minister as saying the suspects and those convicted on charges of conspiring to assist the Indian militants included eight civil servants, thirty-six businessmen and ninety-four farmers. A number of government and private road construction workers were also charged. The suspects were accused of a range of crimes, from supplying rations to the militants to accepting money in exchange for services or just keeping quiet and not informing Thimpu about how extensively and deeply the insurgents were involved in Southeast Bhutan, especially in Samdrup Jongkhar.

As far back as 2001 when Rajkhowa met the king, the ULFA leaders had got a sense of how testy the Bhutanese were about their presence. A quiet decision was taken to move out while key figures like Buragohain would remain in the camps. Major ULFA leaders like Arabinda Rajkhowa and Paresh Baruah had slipped out of the country much earlier through the Chicken's Neck corridor and moved to Dhaka and Bangkok with their families. Some with their followers went to the lesser explored forests, hills and trails of Eastern Myanmar where they set up new networks of arms dealing, training and military camps, in collaboration with the Nagas of S. S. Khaplang and other groups, while reviving old ones.

The decision to stay on Bhutanese soil 'in perpetuity' had ended badly and bloodily for the intruders. For a number of leaders, their sojourn in Dhaka would also be interrupted far more quietly than the Bhutan adventure, almost peacefully. But it would be abrupt.

◆

India's External Affairs Minister Yashwant Singh told Parliament that the army had been deployed on the border to prevent militants from slipping into India. The Assam and West Bengal governments, which were affected by this action, had also been alerted and advised to take steps to maintain peace and security, the minister said.

> The Royal Government of Bhutan has always assured the Government of India that it will not allow its territory to be used for activities inimical to India's interests. The launch of operations against Indian insurgent groups in Bhutan has struck a blow against terrorism and terrorist activity in the entire region.[14]

When Operation All Clear wound down, it left many unanswered questions: what happened to a number of key leaders—Robin Neogi and Ashanta Baghphukan of ULFA; what about B. Erakawa, publicity secretary of the NDFB?

For the relatives of those who have vanished, life is an endless trek to find news, leave alone justice. Rajni Basumatary, who is well known in Assam as a filmmaker and actor,[15] has been searching for her brother, NDFB leader Erakawa, the group's spokesman and publicity secretary, who disappeared after the operations. All she knows is that he was seen in the custody of Bhutanese officials. A year or so after the episode, distraught by a failure to turn up answers, Rajni came to me to ask for help. I put her in touch with some officials, giving their contacts in Assam and Kolkata. The visits didn't turn up anything, deepening the anguish and frustration.

It's a feeling that emerges repeatedly in conversations, the sense of non-closure: 'I wish it was cleared once and for all even if it was to convey that he's no more,' she said. 'The toughest is for his young wife. She doesn't know whether to consider herself a widow or expect a miracle to happen some day.'

The *Times of Assam* says that five missing ULFA members had actually been in the captivity of the Bhutan government since their capture in 2003.[16] This is apparently a protective measure to dissuade ULFA from considering any counter-action against Thimpu.

'Although Bhutan authorities have never agreed or declared that these ULFA leaders are in their custody, it has been understood that Bhutan has long kept these leaders with them as a defence against probable threat from ULFA after driving them out from their camps in 2003 through army operation,' the e-paper said. Another report was much blunter. It said that Baghphukan, Neogi and at least two others were handed over to Indian security officers by the Bhutanese and driven to Shillong where they were shot after a detailed interrogation. Their bodies were secretly disposed of.

Thus Erakawa's wife and the relatives of many others—be it Neogi, Baghphukan or any of their cadres who have not been handed over to the next of kin or produced in court or before the media by either the Bhutanese or the Indians—must remain in limbo, in a state of perilous and embittered unknowing. Their lives are no different from those of the 'half-widows' in the Kashmir Valley, where married men—taken away either by militant groups or by security forces or who have gone willingly to fight or act as informers for one group or the other—have also vanished without a trace or word to their close ones. This agony is difficult to define and often leads to the psychological condition referred to as Post Traumatic Stress Syndrome (PTSS) and Post Traumatic Stress Disorder (PTSD). To mitigate such conditions, when victims go through persistent nightmares, constant reminders and memories of perceived, experienced or imagined violence leading to depression, fear and inability to work and live or emote 'normally', a period of counselling with trained caregivers as well as medication is critical.

In the entire Northeast, there are but a handful of psychiatrists who are trained and equipped to deal with stress brought on by exposure to such violence. Thus, the challenges of handling this epidemic of fear and disorders, brought on by decades of conflict and violence have grown rapidly over the long years of confrontation and intimidation. It's a situation that prevails in Nagaland, Mizoram, Assam, Tripura and Manipur and to a lesser extent in pockets of Meghalaya and Arunachal Pradesh, with tens of thousands of cases, very few of which receive the care and treatment that they need.

Providing care or counselling is not a priority of the governments of the states or the centre. The most they can think of in terms of those who've been killed or wounded is to pay cash or deposit a cheque in compensation in their bank accounts, should they have one. In many cases, there's a middleman, a local tout, who pays money to the government officers handling the funds. The compensation process moves speedily and the victim's family receives some cash, minus the tout's fee and the bribe he paid to get the payment through. At times, it's 25 to 50 per cent of the money due to the victim's closest surviving relative.

Over six decades after the first shots were fired in the battle against the 'idea of India', not a single major dedicated counselling centre exists across the region to help victims of state and rebel violence, those in need of care and specific medication. Those victims also include members of the security forces and the insurgents as well as their families, not just the visible victims. Hatred, fear and suspicion claim many invisible victims, including those who carry the weapons of terror, falling as they do into the easy snare of believing that they are above it all.

This whole process of cloaking and myth-making, of media surrealism and manufactured consent, of silent killings of those who raised arms against the state or even dissented without arms but with words and the pen, is something that comes up time and again in the constant unravelling of conflicts.

Some parts of this process have been documented by human rights activists, lawyers and journalists, but there are other spaces which remain grey areas, a no-go zone which few like to visit, let alone frequent.

To understand why ULFA developed its bases in Bhutan, one must also understand the time in Assam which was known as the season of the Secret Killings. Between 1998 and 2001, no fewer than 300 men, women and children, mostly relatives or associates of leading ULFA members, were killed by 'unknown' gunmen. The events bore the mark of organized butchery, with the implicit involvement of the local state government.

◆

The following story sounds as if it's straight out of a Hollywood thriller or a Bollywood suspense movie. It's neither. It happened, it's true and is so dramatic and filled with a sense of foreboding that one has to pause and wonder if this was really happening in the lush green plains of Assam.

On the night of 16–17 September 1998, Ananda Kalita, a mild-looking man of middling stature with a paunch, was seized from his home in Hajo, a pilgrim town for Hindus, Buddhists and Muslims in the state, by a group of hooded men. The captors slapped him around and then drove him in a Tata Sumo for two hours before they reached a secret camp. He was kept captive there for two nights, fed occasionally and interrogated briefly. He was not given any reason for his detention but was told at one point by one of the captors that if he wanted to survive he would have to kill a specific ULFA militant.

The man he had been asked to murder was a neighbour, Rupjyoti, who had been with the organization for some time. But, Kalita pleaded, he had not seen the man for two years. The man who gave him this task had identified himself as Fida Gogoi, obviously a false name. 'I am the leader, I can kill you or save your life, there is no one above us to decide,' Gogoi told the terrified victim.

Kalita thought at one point that he was in a police barracks because when he went to the toilet and had his blindfold removed, he could see police uniforms hanging from a clothesline. One person at the camp told him the place was the headquarters of the 10th and 13th Battalions, a rather unlikely scenario since these were located hundreds of kilometres apart, one in Guwahati and the other in upper Assam. The fact that he could not locate these places when he was asked to confirm his charges by the official commission probing the hundreds of killings of relatives, associates and connections of ULFA members, weakened his case. But there was no denying the rest of his incredible story for he was able to identify a few of his abductors and others involved in his case.

One of the reasons for Kalita's detention became clear at the end of it. On the second night, he was tied up again, blindfolded, made to lie down in a car and driven to a quiet hilltop. The men searched his pockets to check if he was carrying anything that could identify him, such as official cards with his name or photograph.

He was ordered to stand at the edge of the hill. As the cold metal of a gun pressed against the back of his head, Kalita screamed for mercy. The last thing he remembered as the revolver exploded against his skull was the attackers shouting abuse against the pro-ULFA Asom Jatiyadiya Yuva Chattra Parishad (AJYCP), a leftist political group of which he was a member. He fell nearly 50 metres, his drop cushioned by some bushes and trees.

As an unconscious Kalita rolled down the hill, his captors left him for dead. But he regained consciousness a few hours later, thirsty and bloodied from the head wound. Later he learnt that the bullet had entered his skull from the back and exited from the forehead, just above the eye, without damaging a single major blood vessel. It was nothing short of a miracle.

As Kalita woke, he wept and cried for water but there was no one to help. Showing incredible mental strength and physical stamina, the injured man somehow dragged himself to a nearby stream to drink water.

According to his account, he rubbed the rope binding his arms against a stone until it snapped. He crawled further to a nearby road and flagged down a vehicle. The men in the car said they couldn't take him to Guwahati because they were headed to Shillong in the Khasi Hills. That was when he realized that he was in Jorabat (literally, jor bat, a confluence of roads)— the tri-junction where one road snakes to the hill city, another towards Nagaon, Jorhat and Dibrugarh, and a third pushes to Guwahati, the region's commercial and political hub.

Kalita, even in his dazed condition, had the presence of mind to tell the travellers that he had been attacked by dacoits or armed brigands, which happened occasionally in the area. The explanation was convincing enough for them not to ask too many questions about his dishevelled state and bloodied clothes. If he had said something about the actual assault by former rebels, perhaps they may not have been that helpful. He was more than 50 kilometres from his home in Hajo. The men flagged down a truck and told the driver to take him to Guwahati where he got an autorickshaw. The rickshaw took the thirty-five-year-old man, now almost fainting from fear, exhaustion and blood loss, to the AJYCP office from where he was rushed to the Guwahati Medical College and Hospital.

He survived to tell his story and remains among the very few who escaped the nightmare of those three years. It is in the telling and retelling of these stories that they came to life for a retired judge who investigated a number of them and wrote in a blistering verdict that the crimes had the footprints and fingerprints of the army, the Assam police and SULFA (Surrendered ULFA) militants written all over them.

It's a time that's been captured poignantly by the young novelist Aruni Kashyap in his *The House with a Thousand Stories* as well as Assamese writer Arupa Patangia Kalita in *The Story of Felanee* (the castaway), a stunning masterpiece.

In his finely textured book, Kashyap writes of how a villager avoids a stretch of a path near a lamp post and brusquely advises the narrator, a young city visitor to the ancestral village, to do the same.[17] The villager tells the visitor the reason for the avoidance: he had discovered a body hanging from the electric post: 'He didn't have legs. They had been chopped off. He didn't have fingers. They had been cut off too.' The brutalized body was that of the brother of a ULFA member from a neighbouring village who had refused to surrender to the government.

Felanee's narrator talks about the seamless connections between the militants and the government, the corrosiveness of violence on society, of the struggle of ordinary people to exist in conditions where it was common to have bandhs lasting hundreds of hours:

> The bandh was a novel experience for everyone in the settlement. The days stretched and became a week. The people were getting used to the bandh. But how could they survive three hundred hours? This was absolutely unheard of. What would they do? What would they eat? Where would they go? With the army around, people couldn't even walk around freely.[18]

Did those calling such bandhs, the usually well-fed and watered fat cats, the armed groups as well as the student and other agitators, ever think of others during their brief appearances before the public or the media? It's something I've often wondered about. Suppose they had faced the same hunger and deprivation during a bandh, not being able to bring food home to feed their children—how would they have felt, how would they have reacted? What would they have done? How would they have managed? To whom would they have turned?

These questions still trouble those who need to live through protests in which they are either uninvolved or uninterested. The condition of those subsisting on daily wages—labourers, those with tiny businesses like tea shops and paan shops—is the worst. Their incomes fall to zero during such times.

But apart from hunger and deprivation, there was also fear and anger, those terrible twins.

The years from 1998–2001 were the last three of Asom Gana Parishad (AGP) rule, before the Congress returned to power in state legislature elections. It was also to be the last that Assam was to see the AGP in power for another fifteen years, before they enjoyed the fruits of a marriage of convenience with the BJP and won a junior partnership in a coalition government that grabbed a majority in the state assembly in 2016.

The violence remained embedded in people's minds as the time of the Secret Killings. Patangia used a powerful Assamese metaphor in an interview: she remarked that it was a time when the 'drains were overflowing with blood'.[19] Old and young, men, women and children, the killers spared none.

But why were the killings organized? Who gained from them? Angshuman Choudhury wrote comprehensively about this on the twentieth anniversary of the assassination of Parag Das, who was shot down by SULFA gunmen in the heart of Guwahati while taking his eight-year-old son home from school.[20] The child was injured but survived. Parag, founding editor of *Asomiya Protidin* and earlier *Budhbar*, who had been twice arrested for his advocacy of ULFA's ideals and Assam's need to be free of India, fell to eight bullets. The case was never solved although at least two of the alleged killers were later themselves killed, conveniently. They told no tales.

Human rights campaigner, radical ideologue for ULFA and witty conversationalist, Parag was remarkably prescient and I enjoyed conversing with him. During one chat at his modest home, we spoke about whether ULFA had over-reached itself. Parag smiled:

> There are three stages in a revolution: developing the idea and public mobilization; this is followed by efforts to dialogue and discuss with the State. When that second stage fails, the movement goes to the armed phase. I think they jumped from the first to the third without having the patience to go through the second!

It was a simple, brief but precise formulation—which also explained his role in that space. Because the movement appeared to be more focused on armed strategies to establish political goals, Parag more and more found himself expounding the radical theories that justified the need and growth of Assamese nationalism as opposed to Indian 'mainstream' hegemony, including extraction of resources, displacement of people and instituting a one-size-fits-all approach to the regional problems which he saw as specific to their area, economy, history and ethnicities.

His murder in 1996 came as a major blow to the rights movement as also to the theoretical base that ULFA was founded upon, which challenged the 'nationalist' assertion of the Indian state which incorporated peripheries such as Assam and Manipur. It's an outrage that more than two decades after his killing, neither the State nor ULFA has been able to bring the killers to justice in a public and transparent way.

Parag's family and friends still gather and protest publicly every year on 17 May in Guwahati to remind both sides—and the public—of his role and their rights, especially the right to know. And so this case remains, hanging in limbo, like so many others, without a conclusion or resolution, where not a day passes when family members do not think of that day and mourn silently. Both the then chief minister Prafulla Mahanta, just two weeks into his new term, and ULFA army chief Paresh Baruah had promised justice and the detention of the thugs who killed Parag within forty-eight hours. Neither succeeded. And there hangs a tale of both priorities and competence or the lack of either.

These are the foot soldiers and ideologues who are often forgotten in the haste to move ahead.

An incident that may have played on the minds of the organizers of the secret killings could have been the June 1997 failed attempt to assassinate Mahanta as he returned from Guwahati airport. This was barely a year after he and the AGP had ridden back to power on a wave of anti-Congress sentiment. The balding chief minister had authorized a surprising push against ULFA soon after assuming office—surprising to both the centre and the state security officials since in his first term in office he had been much softer towards the group as it had begun to grow in the late 1980s. It was clear to him, a senior intelligence official said, that there could not be two centres of power in the state.

◆

By the time of Parag's death, the word SULFA (Surrendered ULFA), had become a fearsome phrase that brought anxiety to the brow of middle-class urban Assamese. Conditions were to grow more precarious within a couple of years as SULFA also struck terror in isolated hamlets.

As Angshuman Choudhury wrote, the term was initially accorded to the group of ULFA rebels and top-level leaders:

> ...who laid down their arms after the Indian Army's massive 1991 offensive in Assam called Operation Rhino. These desertions of

rank, which happened en masse, were given a solid push by the state government through lavish amnesty schemes for 'rehabilitation and reintegration'. But, in reality, the government was only co-opting the surrendered militants into its elaborate security wheel as informants against ULFA.

Thus, Choudhury said, SULFA turned into an ad hoc counter-insurgency force of sorts that entered into an arrangement with the state government— 'the ex-rebels were to provide information regarding whereabouts of ULFA cadre, ammunition depots, and camp locations in return for state patronage and protection from retaliatory attacks'.

Although this seemed to work initially, Chowdhury noted that it became:

> ...a Frankensteinian monster—a dangerous crime syndicate with no real motive beyond engaging in illegal profit-making ventures. They began operating like an organized crime gang or a drug cartel— non-ideological, utilitarian, and profit-making. In return for actionable intelligence, the state offered them a carte blanche to indulge in their independent money-making ventures like extortions, kidnappings, illegal businesses and contraband smuggling. The government not only looked away from all of SULFA's wrongdoings, but also became an active stakeholder in their shadow businesses.

Under the Unified Command set up under the AGP which involved several organizations such as the army, paramilitary forces, the state police, bureaucracy and the political leadership, SULFA members were used as hit squads to 'eliminate ULFA status offenders (family, friends, and lay sympathisers)'. This triggered in turn a bloody cycle of vengeance and counter-assaults by a furious ULFA.

Scores of others were killed in this brutal orgy, which appears so completely out of place in Assam's green-drenched and sun-draped beauty, a beauty so bewitching whether in the monsoons or the dry cool winters that one can almost get drunk on it.

There are two other incidents that stand out in my mind. One was that of Dimba Rajkonwar, elder brother of the ULFA chairman,[21] who worked as a junior officer in the state transport department. Son of Uma Rajkonwar, a former Congress leader of Lakua in Sivasagar district who was involved in the anti-British Independence movement, Dimba was an employee in the state bus station in Dibrugarh. The city itself was the centre of the state's prosperous tea industry and a hub for ULFA, which had extorted huge sums over the years from individual tea planters and tea corporates based in Kolkata.[22]

Dimba, a modest, pleasant man who was widely liked, was at the workshop an August evening in 1998 when two young men on a red unnumbered Yamaha motorcycle roared into the station. One of them walked up to an unsuspecting Dimba, shot him twice in front of witnesses and dashed to the waiting motorbike and jumped on the pillion. All this while, the killer's accomplice had kept the engine running; the pair roared away. Dimba collapsed and was rushed to hospital where he died soon afterwards.

It later emerged that Dimba had been picked up at least twice earlier by security forces on charges of links with ULFA. Under stress, his health deteriorated and he had gone to New Delhi for treatment. His wife and brother repeatedly urged local officials for protection, to no avail.

There could not have been a starker message to the ULFA leadership. Nor could there be any justification for such horror where the state targeted innocent relatives of the insurgents, in much the same way as the Punjab police had targeted relatives of Khalistani fighters a few years earlier. That took place with a police force under K. P. S. Gill, then director general of police in Punjab. The similarities were uncannily close although the number of those killed in the Punjab was vastly higher. Interestingly, Gill, who passed away in May 2017, was an Assam cadre officer.

Two years earlier, the body of Dinesh Baruah, elder brother of ULFA army commander Paresh Baruah, turned up in front of his home. One after the other, close family members of ULFA leaders were cut down. Among the most macabre incidents involved the family of Mithinga Daimary, pseudonym of the ULFA spokesman whose real name was Deepak Das. Daimary/Das wrote poetry under another name, Megan Kachari. His brother, a much-loved physician, his wife, mother and sister were shot in their homes. Among those horrified by the killings was Dileep Chandan, then a reporter with the pro-ULFA weekly *Saatdin* and later editor of *Asom Bani*, the Assamese weekly.

'I can't tell you how I felt, this was a man I respected like my elder brother and even more,' Dileep said to me later, recalling how the doctor, Dharani Das, had inculcated in him a love of writing, language and literature. There were three survivors: two younger brothers, one of whom hid under a bed during the shootings while the other managed to flee, and his father, who was away from the village at the time.

Although the police denied any direct involvement in this and other killings, an additional superintendent of police of Nalbari district admitted that a group of SULFA cadres had been provided 'shelter in the police reserve' although they were not involved in the elimination of the Das family.[23]

The secret killings did not just harm individuals or families or even communities. They extracted a terrible price from Assam, which is yet to recover. The current sense of energy and seeming prosperity in some towns and urban conglomerates may lead to a superficial feel-good atmosphere and convey a sense to the visitor that all is well in Assam, or at least in urban Assam especially if he or she witnesses the mushrooming of new malls, restaurants and a burgeoning urban middle class with disposable incomes.

Guwahati is fast morphing like any other city in urbanizing India, with its unplanned growth, garbage problems and destructive approach to ecosystems, poor drainage and bad traffic management. But the reality of the past still haunts many, even though the present generation knows little of it. It remains deep-rooted, a constant yet unseen presence that rises to the surface occasionally as a sharp reminder that the past can be neither forgotten nor forgiven.

◆

In 2004, the government of Tarun Gogoi appointed a commission of enquiry into the killings, headed by Justice K. N. Saikia, a former chief justice of the Supreme Court in New Delhi. It was the Assam government's third attempt at organizing an investigation into the Secret Killings. Of two earlier judges who were asked to head the probe, one quit complaining of lack of cooperation from the state police while the second handed in a report which was rejected as not comprehensive.

Mahanta, accused of authorizing the violence, a charge he has resolutely and repeatedly denied, appeared before the commission which investigated thirty-five killings. His position was that an ongoing Central Bureau of Investigation probe needed to be completed first. The commission's three-volume report, on the other hand, was placed in the Assam Assembly on 16 November 2007 and was sharply critical of Mahanta's role. Mahanta's successor Tarun Gogoi called the period the 'darkest chapter in the history of Assam'.

Others who were pulled up before the commission but denied any role included G. M. Srivastava, who was to be director general of police (DGP) of Assam and was known as a proactive cop who advocated taking the battle to the insurgents by hitting their camps in Bangladesh. Subir Bhaumik,[24] one of the more colourful, enterprising and outspoken characters in the field of journalism in Eastern India with a penchant for bluntness and swagger, speaks extensively of Srivastava, who also served in Tripura as

its DGP,[25] in a detailed essay in his book, *The Agartala Doctrine*.[26]
Srivastava was moved to Tripura after the Congress returned to power
in Assam but his usefulness was acknowledged by Tarun Gogoi, who brought
him back as DGP in the state and later re-employed him, after the officer
retired, as a security adviser in the Chief Minister's Office.

Although it did not name Mahanta, the commission said: 'There is
enough evidence to show that the then home minister was at the helm of
these extra-constitutional killings.' Mahanta had held charge of the home
department at the time.

The report indicted the state government, the army and the police
and pulled no punches in its review of what many regard as the darkest
period in Assam's political history post-Independence.

About the motive behind the secret killings, the commission said it was
'perpetuation of the AGP rule by villainy, treachery and monstrous cruelty
and dangerous propensity'.

The common characteristics of the cases and evidence 'prove beyond
reasonable doubt, remote orchestration of killing from the Home Ministry,
through police-SULFA (surrendered ULFA) nexus using some SULFAs as
the striking arms or executioners. The authority may be held liable and
be dealt with according to law.'

It defined what it described as some common characteristics—each
killing involved an ULFA family or an ULFA related family; the investigations
into these killings would fizzle out or they would be left pending or final
reports would be submitted but there would be no real findings of what
had actually happened. Most of the killings occurred at dead of night,
and the assailants invariably spoke in Assamese to wake up the victims.
Meticulously, the commission drove home its points:

> The assailants were invariably armed with sophisticated firearms of
> prohibited bores, and masked with black wrappers or caps to avoid
> being identified. The weapons used in the killings were invariably
> firearms of different sizes, bores and calibres, mostly of prohibited
> bores normally found in police-military situations. As firearms
> with prohibited bores were used, forensic/ballistic examinations of
> exhibits were mostly avoided or unduly delayed, and the investigation
> ultimately fizzled out. The vehicles used were mostly Maruti Gypsies
> and vans and always without registration numbers. There was police
> patrolling in the crime areas prior to and after, but not during the
> killings.

It recommended that the government 'try to first keep in abeyance, and then gradually dismantle' the Unified Command structure of the army, the Assam police and the central paramilitary forces as an immediate measure to prevent recurrence of such killings.

The army, it declared, was involved in every stage of the process:

> By Army, we mean the armed forces of the Union deployed in Assam in aid of civil power. There was lurking evidence of police-SULFA nexus in the killings, some of the latter being constituted as an extra-constitutional authority and used as executioners. The modus operandi being to visit the family, ask members to persuade its ULFA members to surrender, failing which to send an advance team to survey the location and structure of the house, then to send armed and masked men at dead of night, knock at the door to wake up the inmates and then drag him/them out and shoot him/them dead, or take him/them away and secretly kill and throw the bodies somewhere.

In a lackadaisical response, the state government said it accepted the commission's recommendation to revive twenty cases for re-investigation. About the Unified Command structure, it simply said that the 'recommendation would be considered in conjunction with the prevailing situation at the time of the tri-monthly review of the structure'.

Basically, it meant nothing.

Ten years after the commission's report, hardly any prosecutions had taken place nor had the Unified Command, presided over by the chief minister, been dismantled. Three politicians from very different parties and with differing approaches, Mahanta, Gogoi and BJP leader Sarbananda Sonowal, have headed the Unified Command in the past two decades, just showing how power and security concerns override other issues and paper over party differences. There's just too much at stake and too much pressure from both the army and the central government to protect the structure of the state and block action against those who had done service by it.

◆

In this dance of death, what is lost sight of is that ULFA also retaliated in two ways.

In the first part of the strategy, it struck at those it believed were responsible for the assaults on family members. A bunch of SULFA activists and supporters died in a series of strikes. Those shot included Tapan Dutta, the man who was 'in charge' of Dibrugarh district until his capture by security forces and who turned against his former leaders. Ostensibly the reason why Dutta was shot was that he had held back or taken away ₹5 crore from what was due in collections to ULFA. A bunch of other SULFA cadres also fell to bullets.

The second part of the strategy grew around targeting innocent people from what is called the 'Hindi-speaking' population. These were the descendants of migrants who had come about a century ago from Uttar Pradesh and Bihar to work on tea estates and farms but also moved to other occupations including profitable dairy farming, fishing, or piloting ferries and boats. The attacks and bloodshed added to the atmosphere of fear and helplessness in Assam those days. The killing of those unconnected to either group was aimed at sending a message to the state government and its allies of ULFA's ability to target the vulnerable.

Showing up the Assam government's incompetence and the inability of even the security forces, including the army, ULFA killed no fewer than 100 Hindi-speaking villagers in remote villages, islands and forests of upper Assam. They fell in at least eight attacks in a hail of bullets from men armed with automatic weapons, triggering an exodus of people of Bihari origin to their original homes. This set of assaults is little reviewed or analysed in studies and research about the killings of the period and retaliation by ULFA.

That the organization hit soft targets was obvious even after the Bhutan reverses.

At Dhemaji town on 15 August 2004, thirteen persons, including ten schoolchildren, were killed when a bomb planted by ULFA exploded during an Independence Day parade in the small town on the northwestern side of the Brahmaputra. Public rage against ULFA was widespread as was its grief. Although the group apologized for the tragedy, its response came seven years after the event, too late as the tide of public opinion was turning against it.

'This was the biggest mistake of ULFA. The Dhemaji incident is a black mark in ULFA's history. I apologize,' said ULFA Chairman Arabindo Rajkhowa to the parents of the children who died in the blast. Rajkhowa had been arrested in December 2009 after being handed over to Indian security by Bangladeshi officials. He was released a year later on bail and allowed to travel to his home village and meet friends, colleagues and relatives. During that time, in interactions with the public, he decided to visit families of victims of the bombing. Initially, they declined to meet him but later agreed to receive him when he went to one of their homes.

'This incident can never be erased from my mind. I cannot forgive the ULFA from my heart, but since they came to our home and are starting a peace process, we are considering their appeal for the sake of peace,' said Jogen Gogoi, an assistant engineer in the state irrigation department, whose youngest son, ten-year-old Pradipta, died in the blast. He was the youngest of the ten children killed.

The Dhemaji blast as well as the killing of the activist Sanjoy Ghose on Majuli[27] Island, the large island in the bosom of the Brahmaputra, helped turn Assam against the organization. On top of this came the crippling 2003 assault by the Bhutanese Army that destroyed their bases and dreams.

◆

By the time the secret killings had stopped and the uproar about ULFA being driven out of Bhutan had died down, most of the ULFA leadership were ensconced safely in apartments, homes and temporary camps in what they regarded as their other safe haven, Bangladesh. Or at least under the Bangladesh Nationalist Party of Begum Khaleda Zia, whose leaders gave ULFA succour and even facilitated the safe delivery of arms shipments. More of the latter in a bit.

Some ULFA leaders shuttled between Bangladesh and Myanmar where the organization had had a presence since 1988 with its links to the undivided National Socialist Council of Nagaland (NSCN) in the forests of the country's northwest and its Somra Tract.

Within the space of barely five months of the 2003 Bhutan disaster, Paresh Baruah, working under a pseudonym, was able to arrange for funds and a huge consignment of arms, mentioned earlier, which could have restored ULFA not only to its earlier health but could unleash enough forces to tear the region apart. His planning collaborator in this appeared to be a key figure from the NSCN of the Isak Swu-Th. Muivah faction. It was none other than Anthony Shimray, ace gunrunner and head of the Naga group's Alee (foreign) Command,[28] who had on two occasions pulled off the transfer of weapons for the Nagas on the high seas from one ship to another.

That April, two trawlers arrived at a dock in Chittagong and began unloading their goods at the Chittagong Urea Fertilizer Limited, a company under Bangladesh's industries ministry, then under Matiur Rahman Nizami, amir of the Bangladesh Jamaat-e-Islami, a partner in the coalition government headed by Begum Khaleda Zia of the Bangladesh Nationalist Party. A tip-off from local and Indian sources informed the local port police and the Bangladesh Rifles of a massive arms shipment. When the paramilitary arrived, the two men supervising the operation fled.

Much later, the complex weave of that entire project began to unravel. The following is an account of what happened based on interviews, published accounts and personal discussions over the years.

According to the investigative journalist Anthony Davis, who writes in *Jane's Intelligence Review*, the shipment originating in Hong Kong, was shipped to Singapore 'where more weapons were added'. The second consignment is understood to have comprised 'weapons of both Israeli and US manufacture'; the shipment was then transported north through the Strait of Malacca to be trans-shipped in the Bay of Bengal to two trawlers, the *Kazaddan* and *Amanat*, which ferried the weaponry to a jetty on the Karnaphuli River in Chittagong.

The unloading was interrupted on 2 April by a raid conducted by the Chittagong Port Police and the Bangladesh Rifles; no less than nine truckloads of weapons were seized. It was reported that one loaded truck had left the jetty before the arrival of the port police.

The *Daily Star* recorded the details of the seizure:

> 690 7.62 mm SMG-T-56-1, 600 7.62 mm SMG T-56-2, 400 9 mm automatic carbines (model 320), 100 tommy automatic rifles, 150 40 mm T-69 rocket launchers, 2,000 launching tubes (Ugo rifles), 150 sights for 40 mm rocket launchers, 2,792 magazines of SMG T-56-1, 2,400 magazines of SMG T-56-2, 800 magazines of 9 mm automatic carbines, 400 magazines for tommy rifles, 4,00,000 7.25x25 ball pistol bullets, 7,39,680 bullets of T-56 pistols, 840 40 mm rocket heads of T-69 launchers and 25,020 NV hand grenades.[29]

This was no last-minute effort but a well-organized process involving the official intelligence agencies of Pakistan and Bangladesh, Chinese arms dealers, the principal Naga weapons organizer, funders in Dubai and a remarkable warlord from Assam. That it happened just five months after Bhutan's operation was perhaps coincidental but since Baruah had left Bhutan much earlier, he had time to renew his contacts and establish old links with Shimray, whom he had known for some years. Shimray had the expertise in procuring and delivering arms; Baruah had the finance, intelligence and political networks.

Baruah and Shimray who were overseeing the unloading had earlier checked into the Hotel Golden Inn, where the Assamese rebel had used the name Asif Zaman. It was a name that he also used with officials in

Chittagong telling one that a huge consignment of machinery was to land on the docks and that they would take care of it. He assured the officer that he need not worry since the heads of the Directorate General of Field Intelligence and National Security Intelligence had cleared the operation. It was only later that the officer, Hafizollah Khan, the prime accused in the case, found out that Zaman was actually Paresh Baruah.

They left quickly when the tryst was rudely interrupted. Security forces who raided the hotel noted that ten other rooms had been reserved for twenty Indians who were to come from West Bengal. They never showed up. But the West Bengal address showed that ULFA operatives had slipped into India from Bhutan and had access to Indian passports. They were lying low so as not to draw attention to themselves.

The funds came from a prominent business organization in Dubai with strong Pakistani connections. The *Star Weekend Magazine*'s Ahmede Hussain, in an article titled 'Selling their souls to the devil', reported:

> The ARY Group's Abdul Razzak Yaqoob (whose initials form the acronym) has been linked with the Pakistani establishment. He has offered the Pakistan government cash to bail it out. Pakistan, on the other hand, has strategic interests in funding the ULFA and other such Indian insurgent groups, as the country wants to wage a proxy war against its archrival India.

Bertil Lintner, the Swedish investigative journalist based in Chiang Mai, Thailand, provided further details for the arms deal, worth between $4 to 7 million, enough to equip a small army.

> In May 2009, after Sheikh Hasina and the Awami League had returned to power, the Bangladesh media reported that a former National Intelligence Security chief, Brig. Gen. Abdur Rahim, admitted publicly that he had visited Dubai, and there had been several meetings with a business group called ARY in connection with bringing in the arms that were seized in Chittagong. ARY, which runs an immensely lucrative gold business in Dubai and a popular digital television company, was publicly accused of acting as a conduit for funds from Pakistan's notorious spy agency, the Inter-Services Intelligence, ISI.

The scale of ULFA and Naga penetration—and by extension of terrorist penetration of the Bangladeshi establishment—was not just stunning, it was scary. The magnitude of their influence can be gauged from the fact that two cabinet ministers and two army generals (both former heads of national intelligence agencies) from the Bangladeshi side were among those arrested and later sentenced to death. The jetty where the shipment was offloaded under the watchful eyes of Baruah and Shimray, was owned by the Industries Ministry. The ministry was run by the chief or amir of the Jamaat-i-Islami of Bangladesh, an alliance partner of Khaleda Zia's Bangladesh Nationalist Party. The connection could not have been closer or more emphatic.

The court found that the former heads of the Directorate General of Field Intelligence and the National Security Intelligence were deeply involved; it also handed the death penalty to Paresh Baruah, who had already disappeared, as had the former additional secretary of the industries ministry. The collaboration within the Bangladesh intelligence network was vast. The verdicts came in the middle of a nationalist surge of anti-Jamaat outrage where Sheikh Hasina ordered the trial of scores of Pakistani collaborators who had been involved in the pogroms of 1970 against members of the Awami League and their supporters.[30]

A number were hanged, including Colonel Farooq Rahman, the man who led the assassination of Sheikh Mujibur Rahman, Hasina's father and the founder of Bangladesh. The wave of public anger against the collaborators had to be seen to be believed. At a square near Dhaka University, thousands sat in groups through the night, singing patriotic songs, chanting slogans with huge banners that shouted out their demand in huge letters, in Bangla and English: 'Hang the Killers'. And so Bangladesh did, one after the other, including former cabinet ministers and powerful leaders of the Jamaat.

The country's safety had been compromised by groups and individuals fuelled by individual lust for wealth and in the case of ULFA, if not for the NSCN-IM (which was in the middle of talks with the Government of India), revenge. The two Indian rebel groups played key intermediary roles in if not emasculating, at least of showing up the incapacity of the Bangladeshi government under Khaleda Zia to resist subornation.

It is not surprising that Bangladesh finds itself in the thick of a first-class crisis and a full-blown storm battling radicals of the right, either linked to the Islamic State or to homegrown Muslim fundamentalists, patronized by the Jamaat-i-Islami. With such persistent connivance and corruption at the highest levels of government and especially the intelligence apparatus over a sustained period of time, Dhaka is hopelessly entangled in this web of deceit with a growth in its security deficit and ensuing violence.

As top officials and intelligence operatives collaborated for over two decades with foreign armed non-state groups, Bangladesh's internal security apparatus was systematically ruined by those who should have protected it, leaving its flanks and heart completely exposed.

The Gulshan incident in which twenty persons died in an attack by young jihadists at the Holey Artisan Bakery in Dhaka in the summer of 2016 showed how acute that vulnerability was and what happens when national security is destroyed by those who are given its charge.

The *Daily Pioneer* remarking on the ULFA connection and the arms drop, said:

> ...the Jamaat-BNP coalition Government was fully involved in the crime. In fact, during Sheikh Hasina's first innings as Prime Minister (1996–2001), Ms Zia had described North-East India's secessionist rebels as freedom-fighters who deserved every support. During her two terms as Prime Minister, her Government had extended unstinted assistance to secessionist insurgent organisations of North-Eastern India like the ULFA, National Socialist Council of Nagaland (Isaac-Muivah), People's Liberation Army of Manipur and National Democratic Front of Bodoland.[31]

The court hearing the case made clear that leaders of the Bangladesh Nationalist Party and its ally, the Bangladesh Jamaat-e-Islami, who were associated in the smuggling of arms meant for ULFA, had committed treason against their own country, seeking to destabilize it as well as a friendly neighbour.

On 30 January 2014, Judge S. M. Mojibur Rahman of the Chittagong Metropolitan Special Tribunal-1, sentenced fourteen persons to death for involvement in the smuggling of ten truckloads of arms into Bangladesh.[32]

Asif Zaman, alia Paresh Baruah, had escaped—as was his wont—to a safe space. He realized, more astutely than his other colleagues, that Khaleda Zia's ouster and the return of Sheikh Hasina meant that time was running out for ULFA in Bangladesh. Media reports and public attitudes had also hardened and they were seen as a liability and even a threat. It was time to bid farewell to the country where he had lived, with his family, since 1992.

This time, Baruah headed to the border of China and Myanmar, to the town of Ruili with occasional forays to Kunming, capital of Yunnan Province. The Chinese kept it quiet as did Baruah. But his gunrunning operations continued. In December 2011, he met with greater success than the botched operation of 2004, managing the delivery of a large consignment of automatic weapons that had been smuggled through China to Myanmar, where the beneficiaries were the NDFB (Songjit faction), the

People's Liberation Army of Manipur and his own ULFA.

Lintner, who has met Baruah a number of times, told a Bangladeshi reporter that China was the only country where the Assamese rebel feels safe. Accounts in the Bangladeshi media said that he had two Bangladeshis cooking and working for him, especially to guard against efforts to poison him.

> It is my understanding that Paresh Barua spends most of his time in China. In fact, I have been told by his associates that China is the only country where he feels really safe. And I think he'll remain there. I don't think he would dare to return to Bangladesh, even if a new government came to power there.[33]

Luck has remained on Baruah's side. But it was to run out for his friend, Anthony Shimray, and his colleagues such as ULFA chairman Rajkhowa, the group's 'foreign secretary', Sasha Chowdhury, and others.

♦

On 1 December 2009, Arabindo Rajkhowa was picked up by Bangladeshi security officials along with Biswa Mohan Deb of the National Liberation Front of Twipura (Tripura) and driven to the Tripura border where both men were handed over to Indian intelligence officials. Rajkhowa was put on a special flight to New Delhi. In Dhaka, his wife Kaberi Kachari and their two children were put under house detention before being sent to India to join him.

A few days earlier, ULFA 'foreign secretary' Sashadhar Chowdhury and its finance secretary Chitrabon Hazarika had also been picked up as the noose tightened around the ULFA leadership. Those fast-moving events took place a few days before Sheikh Hasina's New Delhi visit. The time leading up to the detention of ULFA leaders came after a bilateral meeting of home secretaries of the two countries where three key agreements were signed by Hasina and Indian Prime Minister Manmohan Singh. These were on mutual legal assistance in criminal matters, transfer of sentenced persons (like Anup Chetia, ULFA founder and general secretary) and a bilateral agreement on combating international terrorism, organized crime and illicit drug trafficking.

In a few months, Rajkhowa was to start peace parleys with the Government of India, after his release and visit home. He met with Manmohan Singh, a meeting reminiscent of a previous one nineteen years earlier with another prime minister, P.V. Narasimha Rao, and agreed to settle issues within the Constitution of India. The difference was the previous time, under pressure from Baruah, Rajkhowa persuaded the centre that he needed to discuss issues with his colleagues and bring them on board. He never returned—until in 2009 as a captive.

This time, the government wasn't taking any chances and didn't let him out of its sight. Talks have taken place irregularly but a settlement eludes both sides. New Delhi's representative was for long Prodyut Haldar, the relaxed but very sharp former head of the Intelligence Bureau. Haldar later was also asked to handle talks with two smaller but deadly groups, the United People's Democratic Solidarity and Dima Hasao Daogah of Assam's Karbi Anglong district and North Cachar Hills (Dima Hasao) district respectively.

The centre has appeared to be in no hurry to push the talks through. Everything is on the table, except, of course, sovereignty. As long as the discussions kept going, ULFA would remain a divided house, with one group (pro-talks) dependent on the government for funds and security.

In the meantime, Indian security got another prize catch within months of Rajkhowa's capture. Anthony Shimray, the elusive and tough Tangkhul who emerged as the NSCN (I-M)'s top weapons procurer, fell into intelligence hands. As we have seen earlier, Shimray was the organizer, along with Baruah, of the 2004 Chittagong arms shipment that went awry for the insurgents. He was also the head of NSCN (I-M)'s fabled Alee Command and a close aide to Muivah.

Despite his involvement in the arms shipment case, Shimray had participated in peace talks with Muivah and Swu.

Indian intelligence had gotten wind of Shimray's planned visit to Kathmandu from Bangkok. He entered the long, crowded immigration hall at Kathmandu international airport but never made it past the counter. Those waiting for him outside got worried when he didn't turn up. Shimray had been hustled away by sleuths and his detention was later shown as an arrest in Bihar.

The NSCN (I-M) leadership was furious and threatened to stall the ongoing peace talks. But Shimray had been arrested by the National Investigation Agency (NIA) which filed a 100-page list of charges against him, accusing him of 'waging war' against India. It was not a bailable offence. In a First Information Report filed in a New Delhi police station, the NIA accused Shimray, who had lived abroad for many years, of meeting with arms dealers in China and Thailand to purchase weapons and conduct 'terrorist activities' in India. Like his mentor Muivah, Shimray is a Tangkhul from Manipur, the ethnic group which dominates the NSCN (I-M). The NSCN (I-M) wanted Shimray freed, saying that he was on his way to India 'to hold talks' with the organization's leadership, led by Muivah, in New Delhi.

Despite open letters to the media and civil society, a campaign by young activists who reached out to professionals, scholars, journalists and others, the government refused to budge. Shimray's hunger strike in Tihar Jail, the maximum security prison in New Delhi, had no effect and he continued to languish in custody till August 2016.

A few months after Isak Swu's death, and clearly under political pressure from New Delhi, the NIA changed its stance. The judge in a special designated court released Shimray on bail of ₹1,00,000 after the public prosecutor for the NIA stated 'that he has received an email (from the agency) directing him not to oppose the bail application of Shimray. It is submitted that the bail of the accused is important in the interest of peace negotiations between NSCN (IM) and the Government of India.'[34]

Accounts of the cases against Shimray said that he was booked under 'various sections of the IPC and the Unlawful Activities (Prevention) Act dealing with criminal conspiracy and waging war against the Government of India', serious charges which could involve a long jail term in case of conviction. At the least, he would have remained incarcerated while his trial went on.

As the organizer of two of the major arms transfers received by the NSCN (I-M) and investigators sought to assess his role in the huge arms delivery intercepted in Chittagong in 2004, which directly involved ULFA's army chief, Paresh Baruah. Not surprisingly, what has irked and alarmed Indian security officials is that despite having an Indian passport, Shimray was travelling on a Bangladeshi passport when he was caught at Kathmandu.

Shimray's wife and daughters visited him in jail or met him during his court appearances as did Naga human rights activists who campaigned for his release, saying that the government's action was harming the peace process.

Prior to its turnaround, the NIA had told the court that it had come across 'various incriminating documents/articles' in Shimray's possession 'such as foreign passports and national identity papers of multiple countries of Bangladesh, Philippines and Thailand, Indian passport, driving licence in fictitious names'. His interrogation, it said, would help it zero in on 'places and persons' being used in the trans-shipment of 'huge quantity of arms and ammunition'.

◆

Paresh Baruah, the last major holdout of the past thirty years, remains in Myanmar and China. One of the few persons to have met him in recent years was the enterprising reporter Rajeev Bhattacharyya from Guwahati. Bhattacharyya, son of a former senior Assam police officer, trekked a long way across the arduous terrain that Baruah and his followers as well as the Nagas, Manipuris and Mizos before them had trod to training centres and shelters in the Burmese hills.

For Baruah had once more, as in the late 1980s, found refuge in the forest fastness of his old friend and ally S. S. Khaplang of the NSCN (K). As always, the elusive guerrilla was one step ahead of his enemies.

In a series of interviews, rambling over a range of subjects and spread over several days, Baruah was alternately defensive, aggressive, withdrawn and calm. He defended the arms drops he had arranged, saying that struggles like theirs needed weapons 'because you cannot fight with dummy rifles'. He compared ULFA to the Indian Independence movement where 'arms consignments were confiscated by the British' but refused to speak about the Chittagong arms haul because talking about it could harm the movement. He did speak about links with Maoists and plans to firm up a new alliance of Northeastern rebel groups against India, an alliance which was finally announced in April 2015, with the unwieldy name of United National Liberation Front of Western South East Asia (UNLFW), with the main pivots being Baruah's ULFA, the NSCN of Khaplang and the NDFB.[35]

Some of the official thinking on these issues shows the gap between perceived realities of representatives of the state and those of ordinary people living in conflict zones. There's a lack of nuancing, of understanding multiple layers of issues which exist in different parts of the region. In this chapter and in earlier ones I have tried to go into depth into a few of these concerns.

Yet, as I go further, it's clear that I'm only dipping a finger into a sea of stories. There is still much that is not unknown or undocumented or unpublished. And the approach of officials as well as the official approach at times borders on the naïve.

Thus, a member of the army think tank Centre for Land Warfare Studies could write that rebels try to exploit three fault lines: 'locals versus outsiders, tribals versus non-tribals and inter tribal rivalries'.[36] There was not a whisper of the strong resentments in the region against New Delhi.

Baruah remains determined but is realistic enough to know that as age steals up on him, his life's work may remain incomplete. His planning for the future continues, his networks remain intact though considerably diminished, his old colleagues are in detention and he stays far from the reach of the Indian government or its agencies. And, occasionally from unlisted numbers, he calls journalists and officials including police officials to keep abreast of news and events and discuss the present if not the future. And to remind them that he's still around and in the great game.

◆

Sporadic incidents continue to erupt and harm vulnerable groups and innocent people. The question faces all of us—what then of the future and the Paresh Baruahs of the region? There are no clear answers: the road to settlements of grievances is rocky; grievances accumulated over the decades take long years to resolve. Their non-resolution places a huge and unacceptable burden on ordinary people, with the growing burden of financial and psychological stress. Thus the diehard supporters of 'causes' which espouse violence may continue to shed blood and spread harm. But the ideals which once inspired them and the people they led have gone. What remains is a dry and bitter shell.

Sometimes, the blood that is spilt may be their own. Militaries, intelligence agencies, political leaders, rival armed groups and secret killers are all arrayed against them, aiming to end the armed insurrections by whatever means, foul or fair. And the law, with AFSPA, remains on their side.

There are major questions of capital extraction, natural resources and human exploitation which are also at play. We've looked at these in previous chapters but will address them in the closing ones.

Another factor that will have a major influence on these developments is the Burmese role. Democracy has returned there in a fragmented way after over half a century of brutal military rule. There's a mass leader in Aung San Suu Kyi and her ruling National League for Democracy. But the military remains hugely powerful with the key ministries of home affairs, defence and border affairs. Myanmar's Iron Lady, despite the numbers on her side, cannot afford to alienate the military which, in the past, had a cozy relationship at the local level with some of the Indian rebel groups.

Until Khaplang's death in June 2017, the group remained engaged with the Myanmar government in trying to sort out a future for the Nagas in that country. As these stakes become higher, the group, now under the leadership of Khango Konyak, may lose interest in destabilizing conditions in neighbouring Nagaland and Manipur. They could even jettison their old allies who live in NSCN (K) camps if they become a burden. This would depend largely on what the NSCN (K) is offered by the Myanmar government, particularly in the realm of greater political authority and autonomy, financial powers and development growth in the Naga areas.

The future of the armed groups in the Northeast would thus depend on a bunch of factors: one would be the access to camps and support in Myanmar. That would mean access also to weapons and funds. A second would be how robustly the centre pushes the peace process and how actively the state governments and other players like civil society and rival groups are involved, making it more transparent and participative.

To date, all negotiations with the armed groups opposing the 'idea of India' have been secret. It's time this ended and a new era of openness and justice is inaugurated. We don't just need more and better roads, connectivity, growth and infrastructure. We also need a few intangibles which governments or the armed groups cannot deliver but ordinary people, mobilized by responsible civil society groups, can—that is, trust and good will.

There's been far too much ill will. It's time to break that cycle—the story of the Khonoma reconciliation which I tell in detail in the Epilogue, shows the path to real peace, one that is truly inclusive, transparent, costs both sides their pride and enables them to make up for the past. And it builds that most precious of gifts that humans can share, apart from love— trust. For trust is part of love.

Without this process, we cannot predict a real end to the fights over large issues by small groups who end up battling each other as the omnipresent state silently watches the spectacle, often without interfering. For in the inner fighting and ensuing mayhem lies the state's control—of political processes, resources and rights. The armed campaigns have turned into a predictable self-perpetuating cycle of violence and hatred as these groups, mouthing impossible slogans, turn on each other, resisting an overwhelming system they can neither hope to conquer nor be a part of.

Chapter 6

FEAR IN A HANDFUL OF DUST

Your shadow at morning striding behind you
Or your shadow at evening rising to meet you;
I will show you fear in a handful of dust.

—T. S. Eliot, The Wasteland

On 19 May 2016, the much-awaited results of Assam's elections began flowing in.

After a bitter and hard fought campaign, the electoral results turned out to be a cakewalk for the right-wing Bharatiya Janata Party and its allies. They established a winning lead early on and then cruised past the formidable Congress Party led by seventy-nine-year-old Tarun Gogoi, who was in power for fifteen years. The Congress Party was crushed, hitting its lowest tally in nearly forty years, winning only 26 seats out of 126. Gogoi himself won but most of his close colleagues fell to huge defeats or barely made it, some scraping through with a few thousand votes.

Although the BJP had expected victory, even its most tireless supporters had not believed it would win in such a stunning manner. The strategic leadership was provided by Himanta Biswa Sarma, Gogoi's right-hand man who jumped from the Congress to the BJP a few months before the election, and the ever-smiling and handsome Sarbananda Sonowal, who had been anointed chief minister nominee when the campaign had begun. Their youthful demeanour, catchy phrases and backroom planning by a smart team[1] backed by key campaign thrusts by Narendra Modi and senior leaders and undergirded by an army of volunteers from the Rashtriya Swayamsevak Sangh played no small part in the win. As did the complete sense of disconnect between the Congress leadership and the people. A strong segment of younger voters were swayed by the promise of livelihoods and development, which is critical in a state that has seen unemployment rates soar and farm production fall, triggering a rural exodus not just to towns in the state but outward migration to places as far away as Kerala, Goa and Punjab. In addition to this, the lurch towards the BJP in urban centres, in the Bengali-dominated districts of the Barak Valley and the tea garden population of upper Assam—as well as smart alliances with the Asom Gana Parishad (AGP)[2] and the Bodo Peoples Front—took them past the finishing post with ease.

If the election was won or lost on a single slogan or idea that found resonance across geographical space, ethnicities and districts barring one group—the Muslims of Bengali origin—it was the cry for 'Jati, Mati, Bheti (nationality, land and identity)' reminiscent of the heady, tumultuous and tragic days of 1979–1985 when a movement against 'illegal migration' from Bangladesh swept the state. But even at the height of its popularity, the single largest party of the 1985 state election failed to win a simple majority on its own: the AGP, which was demoted to become the junior partner of the BJP in 2016, won sixty-two seats. The AGP tally was, however, one better than its principal ally three decades later.

BJP leaders at their press conference releasing the 2016 election manifesto declared that they were determined to set right Congress policies. These had, in their view, created a demographic imbalance in the state. But a study of party announcements on how it proposed to deal with the touchy issue of migration gave rise to the feeling that it was carrying old policies forward.[3]

Significantly, nowhere does the word deportation of illegal migrants figure in the manifesto, though the party's leaders have been speaking of the election as the last battle to save the Assamese identity. Clearly, deportation was not on the agenda. This is worth discussing a little more.

For decades, deportation of Bangladeshis has been an article of faith for the party. The document speaks in general terms about issues which have been discussed threadbare since the 1980s by the AGP and other parties, as well as scholars and media. For example, the Assam Vision Document 2016–2025 says it will take a slew of actions, but is high on generalities and low on specifics. This is probably another reason why it did so well in the election even in a clutch of Muslim-dominated areas of lower Assam.

This is a practical approach born out of political realism and the knowledge that virulent campaigns against 'Bangladeshis' have led nowhere except caused acute divisions, increased mutual suspicions and fears. But for the BJP, it is a major turnaround and probably rooted in pragmatism influenced partly by its local leadership. A second factor lies in the need for New Delhi to develop a stable relationship with Bangladesh. The eastern neighbour has, in the past, taken a dim view of Indian efforts to drive out 'Bangladeshis', saying none of its citizens would migrate to India and that New Delhi was actually pushing back Indian Muslims into Bangladesh. Thus, if there is no country to 'push out' perceived illegals to, the stage would be tailor-made for a media eruption on human rights violations on one side (especially non-Indian channels and media) while the Indian side, especially the Assam and regional media, would go into overdrive about government failure to do anything on the matter especially after promising so much.

Since he came to power in May 2014, Narendra Modi has followed a carefully calibrated approach of friendship with Bangladesh combined with generous doses of economic support and political largesse. Although his overtures and conversations with the other neighbours—Nepal and Pakistan especially—haven't worked that well, as far as Bangladesh is concerned, they appear to be on track. 'We have resolved a question that has lingered since Independence. Our two nations have a settled boundary,' the prime minister declared proudly in Dhaka in July 2015 after the two governments signed no fewer than twenty-two agreements. He agreed to hand over tracts of land to the neighbouring country in a land swap[4] that ended a bitter problem of enclaves and populations marooned within each other's borders since Independence in 1947.

In addition, there is growing security cooperation between the two sides. These include better networking between their coastguards as well as combating human trafficking, smuggling and circulation of fake currency notes. The increased security collaboration became evident in 2009 during Congress rule, when Dhaka handed over virtually the entire leadership of ULFA barring the group's army chief Paresh Baruah, as well as top guns of the National Democratic Front of Bodoland (NDFB) and the United National Liberation Front (UNLF) after publicly denying that they had been functioning out of its territory. This dealt a body blow to these organizations and their terror networks. They have not been able to recover from the shock although they have managed, from time to time, to conduct some attacks on Indian security forces and state police and maintain a lower level of extraction and extortion from small and medium businesses in pockets of Assam and Manipur. But this is not a patch on their pre-2009 clout. As a result, the power of these three key organizations has been vastly slashed.[5] They lost key bases, logistical support and safe houses in an urban setting and the cadres which still held out against negotiations with New Delhi were forced to return to jungle camps and hideouts in Myanmar.

Thus it should be no surprise that a BJP government in New Delhi under Modi is not going to soft-pedal good relations with Bangladesh. It is crucial to implementing the centre's concept of secure borders and tackling perceived threats from either radicalized Islamic anti-India modules or from pro-insurgent groups of the Northeast. It also fits in significantly with his vision of an economically robust Northeast, one that has outgrown the sickly, laggardly pace that has stymied it for decades, and can connect not just to the rest of India but also to its neighbourhood of Bangladesh and Myanmar. Access to Bangladesh's waterways would enable India to connect to the port of Chittagong, one of the finest deep-water natural harbours in South Asia. Not without significance, the port is being rebuilt by China and could not only provide an immediate link to upgrading trade and commerce with Southeast Asia through the sea routes but also send goods from the Northeast to other parts of India via Paradip, Haldia, Chennai, Vizag and other major ports. For this, industrial units and agricultural centres in the Northeast would need to produce and process commodities that would gain entry and earn profits in the vast markets of the rest of India as well as Southeast Asia.

Not only that, the central government agreed during the 2015 visit to permit Bangladesh to set up a consulate in Guwahati to facilitate travel and trade between the region and its large neighbour. India was to set up consulates in Khulna and Sylhet; the significance of this can be seen from the fact that the Indian High Commission in Dhaka, overworked to the bone, issues a million visas every year, more than any Indian diplomatic mission in the world. The daily queues outside the High Commission are long and meandering, with hundreds of Bangladeshis waiting patiently for their turn for visa interviews.

The proposal for the consulate in Guwahati was not new. It had been talked about since 2000, when Farooq Sobhan, the former Bangladesh foreign secretary, visited Guwahati and Shillong at my request and spoke publicly to receptive audiences of the urgency of direct air flights, people-to-people contacts and resuming consular links between the region and his country. It took fifteen years for it to be finalized. The delays were caused by a dip in bilateral relations during the regime of the prickly Begum Khaleda Zia of the pro-Pakistan Bangladesh Nationalist Party and only picked up halfway into the regime of her successor and bête noire, Sheikh Hasina Wajed of the pro-India Awami League.

The significance of a Bangladeshi diplomatic mission in Guwahati, the political and cultural capital of Assam and commercial hub of the entire region, cannot be underestimated. The crowded premier city of the area is also the heart of the anti-immigrant movement that has triggered such deeply anti-Bangladeshi sentiments and statements. It is this management of seeming political contradictions that is important. The creation of such a relationship will reflect an aspiration to build a better understanding between the region and its large neighbour. To the people of Assam and the Northeastern region, their concerns about Bangladesh and Bangladeshis are far greater than the interest or concerns of the Bangladeshis about this area, which is little known there except as a poor and peripheral part of India.

This may be a blow to the self-esteem and ego of many in Assam. But the fact is that economic conditions in Bangladesh are actually far better than those in the neighbouring Indian states. Bangladesh is described by the World Bank[6] as a lower middle economy. Its effective transition rate of girl children who move from primary levels to secondary levels is a hugely creditable 91 per cent. In 2010, India was slightly ahead at 92.4 per cent, but the Bangladeshi figures are way ahead of Assam's which linger in the mid-60s.[7]

Life expectancy in Bangladesh is 72 years; Assam scores the lowest in India: it is 61 for men and 63.2 for women[8] while the life span of an average Indian is 66.2. According to a prominent neurologist: '...life expectancy in India as a whole has increased by five years in the period between 2001–2005 and 2011–2015, primarily due to better healthcare. In Assam, this is not the reality.'[9]

In addition, while Assam has India's worst maternal mortality ratio of 300—that's the number of women out of 1,00,000 who die giving birth—the comparative figure for Bangladesh is 162 and that too for a population of 160 million. Assam's terrible MMR is even more damning than it looks on the surface. At about 32 million, Assam's population is nearly one-sixth that of Bangladesh, making the comparative figures starker. Bangladesh's GDP is $172.9 billion compared to India's $2.049 trillion (both at 2014 levels) but what is significant is that both are defined by the World Bank as lower middle income group countries.

In the face of this, the strategy taken by the BJP to deal with issues that it considered fundamental to the future of Assam and India is fascinating, for it represents a nimble way of managing political contradictions. It also makes eminent common sense.

◆

In 2016, in the run-up to the state elections in May, the BJP in Assam spoke of 'infiltration' and strategies to stop it. The latter included shaking the dust off an old and failed idea that the border would be 'sealed permanently'.[10] Yet this woolly-headed notion was successful in fooling people for the second time in thirty years. It did not take into account that no government in any part of the world had been able to seal borders, whether it's a superpower like the US in its own backyard with Mexico or Europe's borders (by land and sea) with the Middle East.

Sarbananda Sonowal's proposal to use data from the updated National Register of Citizens (NRC) of 1951 to define who is a 'native' of the state and who isn't, is perhaps a better bet, though not free of flaws.[11] The NRC is a huge exercise involving thousands of government officers and data analysts which sought over a three-year process to establish a list of Indian citizens in Assam whose authenticity could not be disputed. It called on bona fide citizens of the state to provide ancestral data going back to 1951, including parental domicile, record of government or professional service or a mention in electoral lists or the NRC itself of 1951. Over the decades, Assam has seen India's most prolonged and tortuous efforts to prove one's citizenship—as well as to deny one's alleged illegality.

This pro-citizenship and anti-alien movement appeared to have peaked at various points from the 1940s onwards. Sonowal, one of the key protagonists of the anti-illegal movement was a former president of the All Assam Students Union (AASU) who deftly moved to the BJP in 2011 when his future in the AGP appeared dim. In July 2005, Sonowal was feted as the architect of a historic legal victory. Years earlier, he had challenged the constitutional validity of the Illegal Migrants Determination by Tribunal Act of 1983, a legal instrument which was pushed through Parliament by Indira Gandhi that year to deal with the migrants issue. It was widely seen as a law that protected illegal migrants, with clauses that made it difficult to detect them or take effective legal action.

In his motion before the Supreme Court, Sonowal had argued that:

> The result of the IMDT Act has been that a number of non-Indians, who surreptitiously entered into Assam after March 25, 1971 without possession of valid passport, travel documents or other lawful authority to do so, continue to reside in Assam.[12] Their presence has changed the whole character, cultural and ethnic composition of the area and the IMDT Act creates a situation where under it has become virtually impossible to challenge the presence of a foreigner and to secure his detection, deportation or even deletion of his name from the electoral list as they get protection on account of the provisions of the Act.

As a result of the Assam Accord of 15 August 1985, the Indian Citizenship Act was revised to include a clause to cover those who entered Assam between 1966 and 1971. Their names were to be taken off electoral lists for ten years and then reinstated. An AASU leader told me that the aim was to delete the names of Hindu immigrants from East Pakistan. In addition, the Supreme Court noted that under a special note circulated by the central government after talks between Indira Gandhi and Sheikh Mujibur Rahman in February 1972:

> ...the Prime Minister of Bangladesh had assured the return of all Bangladesh nationals who had taken shelter in India since 25 March 1971. Accordingly a circular was issued by the Government of India on 30.9.1972 setting out guidelines for action to be taken in respect of persons who had come to India from Bangladesh. According to this circular, those Bangladesh nationals who had come to India before 25 March 1971 were not to be sent back and those who entered India on or after the said date were to be repatriated.[13]

The case had the support of the AGP government under Prafulla Mahanta.[14] On the other hand, the Congress Party which handily defeated the AGP in the 2001 state legislature elections, wasted no time in labelling its predecessor's effort as unconstitutional and aimed at harming the rights of Muslim minorities. The Act was sound in law and needed to be retained, the Congress top legal troubleshooter, Kapil Sibal, declared.

However, the state government found itself under pressure from the centre, then under the control of the BJP-led National Democratic Alliance with a prime minister who had taken a keen interest in the Assam movement, the charismatic Atal Bihari Vajpayee. A middle-level official from the Ministry of Home Affairs stated the government's position in a sworn affidavit:

> ...detection of illegal migrants, who belong to the same ethnic stock as Indians is not an easy task. However, large-scale illegal migrants from Bangladesh have not only threatened the demographic structure of the area but have seriously impaired the security of the nation, particularly in the present circumstances. The need for expeditious identification of illegal migrants is more pressing now than ever. It is not a matter of dealing with a religious or linguistic group. It is a question of identifying those who illegally crossed over the border and continue to live in India contrary to the Indian law and the Constitution.[15]

The official, Jatinder Bir Singh, a director in the home ministry, showed up the vast difference between Assam where the IMDT existed and in West Bengal, where the issue of illegal migration was handled by way of the Foreigners Act, 1946. Singh and Sonowal were emphasizing the same point—that Assam had been selected for special treatment under the law: that while the Foreigners Act applied to all of India, it did not apply to the state of Assam, thus amounting to discrimination in law. Not only that but the IMDT was a hollow law and totally ineffective according to the statistics placed before the court.

> ...since the enforcement of the IMDT Act only 1,494 illegal migrants had been deported from Assam up to 30th June, 2001. In contrast 4,89,046 number of Bangladeshi nationals had been actually deported under the Foreigners Act, 1946 from the State of West Bengal between 1983 and November 1998. The IMDT Act had failed to fulfil the objective for which it was enacted which is apparent from the poor results and it places Assam in a different position from rest of the country where the Foreigners Act, 1946 is applicable.

However, this did not happen to be the conclusive end of the Government of India's position. There was to be another twist in the tale, showing how politically sensitive the migration issue is and how dependent on religious vote banks both sides are: the one opposed to the IMDT and the one supporting it.

Once the Vajpayee government had demitted office after losing the 2004 election, a new set of lawyers came to the Supreme Court, their positions reflecting the Congress view. This was that there was no illegal migration and that the BJP and the AGP campaigns were aimed at harming and harassing minorities.

The court listened to them all before coming to a decision within a year of the Congress returning to power. Its verdict came five years after the case was admitted. The Congress was stunned—the court overturned the IMDT as not just bad in law but anti-constitutional. It made a series of stinging remarks in its judgment, significant among them:[16]

- The provisions of the Illegal Migrants (Determination by Tribunals) Act, 1983 are ultra vires the Constitution of India and are accordingly struck down.
- The Illegal Migrants (Determination by Tribunals) Rules, 1984 are also ultra vires and are struck down. As a result, the Tribunals and the Appellate Tribunals constituted under the Illegal Migrants (Determination by Tribunals) Act, 1983 shall cease to function.

- The Passport (Entry into India) Act, 1920, the Foreigners Act, 1946, the Immigrants (Expulsion from Assam) Act, 1950 and the Passport Act, 1967 shall apply to the State of Assam.

- All cases pending before the Tribunals under the Illegal Migrants (Determination by Tribunals) Act, 1983 shall stand transferred to the Tribunals constituted under the Foreigners (Tribunals) Order, 1964 and shall be decided in the manner provided in the Foreigners Act, the Rules made thereunder and the procedure prescribed under the Foreigners (Tribunals) Order, 1964. In view of the finding that the competent authority and the Screening Committee had no authority or jurisdiction to reject any proceedings initiated against any alleged illegal migrant, the orders of rejection passed by such authorities are declared to be void and non est in the eye of law. It will be open to the authorities of the Central Government or State Government to initiate fresh proceedings under the Foreigners Act against all such persons whose cases were not referred to the Tribunals constituted under the Illegal Migrants (Determination by Tribunals) Act, 1983 by the competent authority whether on account of the recommendation of the Screening Committee or any other reason whatsoever. The appeals pending before the Appellate Tribunals shall be deemed to have abated.

Nothing could have been clearer. The court also noted that as far as detection of illegal migrants is concerned, whether under the Foreigners Act or laws in other countries, the burden of proof rests on those who are being complained against—that is, the alleged illegal migrants. In the case of the IMDT, this principle was stood on its head as the burden of proof rested with the complainant, the very reverse of what applied in other parts of India and the world.

The centre panicked and tried to sidestep the court's position. It hastily amended the Foreigners Act and rushed the change through Parliament. Without changing the core of the Act, the centre applied sleight of hand to ensure that the law would not apply to Assam. Another discrimination.

The centre's bête noire, Sonowal, was not to take this lying down. He rode again to battle in the Supreme Court, challenging the writ of government. The court was in no mood to be kind. It noted that instead of following the court's verdict, the central government within six months of the ruling, had amended the Foreigners Tribunal Order, 1964, making the same inapplicable to Assam. An insertion was made which said: 'This

Order shall apply to the whole of India except the State of Assam.'
The judges were outraged at the open defiance of their orders:

> Instead of obeying the mandamus issued by this Court essentially in
> the interests of national security and to preserve the demographic
> balance of a part of India, that is Bharat, and implementing the 1964
> Order in Assam in letter and spirit, the Authorities that be, have chosen
> to make the 1964 Order itself inapplicable to Assam.

Noting that there were genuine concerns about citizens being harassed, the
judges opined:

> Adequate care should be taken to see that no genuine citizen of
> India is thrown out of the country. A person who claims himself
> to be a citizen of India in terms of the Constitution of India or
> the Citizenship Act is entitled to all safeguards both substantive and
> procedural provided for therein to show that he is a citizen.

Unhesitatingly, it quashed the February 2006 order as 'unreasonable and
issued in an arbitrary exercise of power'.

Since then, Foreigners Tribunals have been pursuing cases of illegal
migrants or rather complaints relating to them. They haven't gone very
far and this is probably another reason for the BJP's steady backpedalling
on the issue.

Take the following official table, set out by the Government of India
(Assam), part of a white paper on illegal migration. This includes the cases
between 1985 and 2005 when the IMDT courts were active—a total of
42,000 cases were referred to them and about 24,000 were declared as
foreigners. That's a proportion of nearly 60 per cent. However, if we look
at comparative figures after the Supreme Court judgment, the proportion
of those detected and declared as illegals fell to less than one-fifth of the
number of cases. The system was not working as effectively as the court
or the anti-immigrant groups would have wished. However, the number
of cases had grown. From the niggardly levels of the IMDT time, over
65,000 cases were referred in the space of one year; 45,456 were disposed
of. Over a period of six years, 12,913 cases were declared as foreigners,
a better ratio than in the IMDT days. But at about 2,150 per year, the
process was still a laggard. The number of those pushed back or expelled
in that time was a bare 895. In the six years after the Sonowal judgment,
221 were driven out of Assam. That's less than 40 persons per year and
only somewhat better than 674 over 27 years or about 25 per year.

FOREIGNERS TRIBUNAL CASES[17]

Period	Cases Referred	Cases Disposed	Cases Pending (Cumulative)	Persons Declared as Foreigners	No. of Declared Foreigners Pushed Back/ Deported
1985–90	32,991	15,929	17,062	14,801	133
1991–95	482	5,909	11,635	4,005	267
1996–2000	2,986	3,552	11,069	6,026	235
2001–2005	6,094	2,216	14,947	4,593	39
2006–July 2012	65,666	45,456	35,157	12,913	221
Total	**108,219**	**73,062**	**35,157**	**42,338**	**895**

To understand why the issue has such resonance one needs to delve into a bit of contemporary history. Pre-Partition concerns about Assam being embraced by the Muslim League were high and there was also a general fear, both in the ruling Congress Party at the time as well as in other right-wing groups, that the province would be sucked into East Pakistan as a result of the Cabinet Mission Plan. The mission proposals designed by Sir Stafford Cripps and his team recommended that those parties which commanded majorities in border areas such as the north and northwest (Punjab, North West Frontier Province) or east and northeast (Bengal, East Bengal and Assam) would decide the composition of their assemblies.

Over the decades, especially since the 1920s, the British had encouraged Muslim Bengali immigration and settlement into Assam to meet a huge demand for cheap labour, settle open spaces, clear jungles for agriculture as well as infrastructure building such as roads and railways and in the process, also strengthen the Muslim League in the frontier state. The population of Muslims in parts of the state, one of its leaders boasted to Liaquat Ali Khan, later prime minister of Pakistan, had quadrupled in lower Assam which was closest to Bengal. The Muslim League opened up lands for settlement and grazing. The speed and visibility of the settlement deeply worried the Assamese as well as the smaller plains tribal groups, who found themselves competing for space and resources in their own territories.

The British first developed a system under which settlers could not progress beyond a certain 'line' which defined the borders of the indigenous. But this did not prove particularly effective. Assam Premier Gopinath Bordoloi of the Congress put in place tribal blocks as well which tightened tribal control over their own lands. Yet the spread of the Muslim population remained substantial and unfazed by lines or blocks. Unscrupulous land revenue officials and local politicians assisted the Muslims to divest tribal groups of land, especially in lower and central Assam, at times leading to clashes and growing tension.

By then the entire political situation had been communalized, divided between the Congress and the Muslim League on the basis of Hindu and Muslim populations, although the Congress also drew some Muslims and a smattering of other religious minorities such as the Christians, Parsis, Jains and Buddhists to its ranks. The parties which would draw up the constitutions for these parts of the subcontinent would do so on the basis of religious strength. Bengal would have dominated Assam and controlled how it voted.[18]

This was resisted by Bordoloi and his close aides who threw the weight of the provincial Congress against both the Muslim League and the National Congress leadership. The latter simply did not appear to understand Assam's peculiar conditions.[19] As we have seen, at a crucial juncture, Bordoloi and his team won the support of Mahatma Gandhi who underlined the need for Assam to rebel against the Congress national leadership and walk out of the mission's proposals.[20] The Congress in New Delhi under Jawaharlal Nehru and Vallabhbhai Patel came around to their viewpoint. This little-known story is the crucial reason for the map of India continuing to show Assam and the Northeast as part of the country. If Bordoloi, Gandhi and the state Congress had not revolted and stood united on the issue, there is every reason to believe that the region could have been swallowed up by East Pakistan. India's borders could have ended at Cooch Behar and the start of the Chicken's Neck corridor that connects it now to Assam and the larger Northeast.

Bordoloi's concern was so acute that the Congress manifesto for the 1946 provincial elections flagged the immigration, largely of peasants, from East Bengal as the key problem which needed to be tackled if Assam was to survive and have a future. It was this clarion call that won Bordoloi a comfortable majority in the Assembly and a chance to write his own history.[21]

In 1962, the India-China border war had flared leading to a stinging Indian debacle and Assamese fears of being sold out by New Delhi following Nehru's 'my heart goes out to the people of Assam' broadcast. Of course, it's a different thing that Nehru's was a fighting speech which called for a fight to the end till victory was assured and territory recaptured. Over half a century later, the key words of that broadcast had become so ingrained in the minds of ordinary people that they remembered only those famous nine words, not the rest.

The India-Pakistan War of 1971 resulted in the liberation of Bangladesh. But it created new problems for India with vast numbers of refugees having fled their country. A majority went back but one million are estimated to have stayed on. Post-1971, a steady stream of migrants kept coming to India especially to its east. The old problem that Bordoloi had spoken about agitatedly in the 1940s was rearing its head again.

By the end of 1979, a popular resistance movement took shape in Assam led by the vibrant students group, the All Assam Students Union (AASU) and an umbrella alliance of regional political parties, the All Assam Gana Sangram Parishad (AAGSP).

But the National Register of Citizens has its problems including the fact that there are new states where earlier districts of Assam existed in 1951: thus the Naga Hills district became a state in 1963, Meghalaya of the Khasi, Jaintia and Garo Hills districts became another state in 1970, while the Mizo Hills district first became a union territory and then a full-fledged state in 1986. So how would those who had their origins in these states and now lived in Assam find their bearings? They would need to consult old data from those states, making a tough issue even more complex.

The key lines from the strategy document on what the BJP calls 'infiltration' are bland. These have seen such widespread repetition over the years that they really count for little. It's probably a relief to the party that few people read political manifestos these days. These have a habit of springing up a few weeks before election time.

- Scrutinizing the citizenship of all suspected residents of the state in conformity with the upgraded National Register of Citizens (NRC)
- Leveraging IT like biometrics to assist revision of electoral rolls
- Identifying boats by marking them along the border areas
- Setting up ideal villages along Indo-Bangla border populated by ex-servicemen to assist the police and other security forces towards prevention of infiltration
- Strengthening the Border Wing of Assam Police in coordination with the Border Security Force (BSF)
- Enacting a law to sternly deal with industries, businesses, SMEs, or any other agencies employing infiltrators

Apart from the fourth point of setting up model villages populated by ex-servicemen, and the last one of threatening to prosecute those who employ aliens, there was little that was really new. As far as border settlements of ex-servicemen is concerned this had been done in Arunachal Pradesh after the 1962 debacle with China.

The realization that no government could throw out people on a whim has been clear to most parties, even to the BJP for some time. Before the final results were in, Himanta Sarma, the architect of the victory, told a news channel that while detection was possible, deportation was not.

Some of the reasons have been set out earlier. For one, New Delhi does not want to create problems in its bilateral relations with Dhaka and wants to protect and even nurture its security and economic ties with its neighbour. This despite the latter's consistently ostrich-like head-in-the-sand approach, that there are no Bangladeshis who leave the country for India although they work in the Middle East and other more prosperous parts of the world.

BJP leader Siddhartha Bhattacharuua[22] spoke[23] of how migration is like water and finds its own levels. He said that earlier strategies of blind anti-immigrant campaigns would not work. The best strategy he felt was the economic one—for unlike many of the right-wing, he sees the issue as essentially an economic challenge. Bhattacharyya said that the effort must be focused on improving Bangladesh's economic status so that there was less migration. But even he acknowledged that many Bangladeshis preferred to go to wealthier countries in the West instead of coming to a less developed country and that Bangladesh's own livelihoods and human development indices had much improved over the past years.

But after victory was proclaimed and defeat conceded in the 2016 elections, I was not watching victory processions or rallies but instead was walking about 60 kilometres away to a little known hamlet called Bhagduba Habi, surrounded by silence, wrapped in warmth but cooled by a persistent breeze.

◆

Three decades ago, during a tragic and brutal time in Assam, I had spent many hours in the fields of Bhagduba Habi. On one crisp winter morning, I had counted 200 bodies littering those dry paddy fields—men, women, children, victims of hate and suspicion. In many cases, they were attacked by their own neighbours, people they had lived with and known for decades, if not generations.

Soon after the incident Indira Gandhi, then prime minister, travelled to Nellie to assess conditions for herself.

That day, I found myself outside the security ring—enforced by a thick rope held by grim policemen—and literally next to Mrs Gandhi, who was visibly taken aback by the scale of the violence. I asked her a few questions including whether she took responsibility for the disaster, having called the elections in February 1983 in the face of a fierce anti-immigrant movement that had turned into a violent campaign against Muslims of Bangla origin. Her answers were sharp and she snapped them out, increasingly irked by the fact that a journalist had gotten away from the cordon and was asking uncomfortable questions.

No, she said, she didn't take responsibility because it was the fault of the agitators who had brought this on Assam and that the toll of the injured and dead was highly exaggerated. When I said that I had personally counted 200 bodies, she brushed it aside imperiously and walked away. At that point, the police intervened and I found myself face-to-face—or rather face-to-chest with the tallest man I had seen in Assam, in full police uniform—a turbanned Sikh who was very, very angry. My first reaction was one of surprise, something like: 'What's a Sikh doing here and that too in uniform?' But all notions of civility were dispelled when the officer gave me a rough shove.

In my youthful josh, I yelled at him: 'You can't do that, I'm a journalist, I'm doing my duty. Who the hell are you?' He examined me quizzically and said: 'Naam chahiye? Toh likho (You want my name, then write) K. P. S. Gill.' Then he paused and smiled: 'Ab kya karoge? (Now what will you do?)' At that point, two senior officers who knew me started chatting with him and led him away before the confrontation went any further.

They knew that a relative, Pradip Das or Montu Da as we knew him, was director-general of the Assam police at the time; I used to get my morning briefings from him on the veranda of the sprawling bungalow where he lived, on the banks of the Brahmaputra.

Gill, then deputy inspector of police (range)—or in charge of many of the trouble spots outside Guwahati—was a terror as far as the Assam agitation was concerned. It was reported that he thrashed student leaders especially during the troubled elections. He rarely carried a weapon barring a swagger stick. That reputation along with his towering presence (he stood at 6 feet 4 inches), bearded visage and piercing eyes was enough to put the fear of god into anyone who encountered him.

He dealt with illegal migrants also with the same intimidating calmness. Once as superintendent of Nowgong, he was involved in a campaign to evict migrants from East Pakistan as part of the Assam government's Prevention of Infiltration from Pakistan (PIP) scheme in the mid 1960s. He wasn't having much success till he listened to the advice of a constable from the town. The latter's suggestion was simple: call in the Muslim leaders from the villages, they would know who the new settlers were. Tell them that if they want their people to be safe from harassment and deportation, they need to come out with the list of the actual illegals.

Gill followed the advice. In a few days, the Muslim elders had brought lists of those they had identified as new migrants. Gill sent police parties out to effect detentions; the detainees were brought to the stadium in the town and put on a special train for East Pakistan.

◆

When I think of Nellie, what happened and what follows in the next pages, my mind turns to T. S. Eliot's prophetic lines that ring true again and again. I have quoted them at the beginning of this chapter, and I find in them a mesmeric quality of foreboding:

> Your shadow at morning striding behind you
> Or your shadow at evening rising to meet you;
> I will show you fear in a handful of dust.[24]

Thirty-three years later, as winners celebrated in Guwahati and losers mourned, a group of villagers at Bhagduba Habi sat quietly, pensively, under the shade provided by a tin sheet held up by bamboo poles in front of a shut store in the village. They spoke calmly and without a sense of either bitterness or grief about an earlier time of voting, and the cataclysm that blew their lives asunder. What lies under that calm surface is difficult to fathom. The feeling grew as I spoke to more and more people that the elders had decided to bury the tragedy of the past deep down so that none could see it or dig for it. Their talk appeared normal that Friday morning[25] when they chatted and smiled about daily mundane things and shared their family struggles and concerns for the future. The fields were flooded and everyone was, in equal measure, irked and saddened.

The water had not been caused by heavy rains or flooding by some of the local swift streams. The disaster was entirely man-made: the previous night, the engineers at the Kopili dam[26] project about 15 kilometres away in the Karbi Anglong hills had decided to release the water from the reservoir because the levels had risen too high.

'They had given us warning only the previous night,' said one villager.

This apparently happens on a regular basis and devastates standing crops, forcing farmers and their families to rush to the fields to save what they can of their crops. This time, some said they had lost up to 75 per cent of their rice; others were luckier with less damage.

They spoke in fluent, accented Assamese, a sharp, unmistakably Mymensinghia[27] twang betraying their origins. This cluster of villages[28] has been around for more than eighty years. It had taken us some time to get there, as the narrow dirt road to Bhagduba Habi was broken and flooded in parts. At the culvert, about a kilometre from the highway where Nellie town lies, the road was completely broken.

We walked through the slush and sun although a beautiful, soothing breeze kept us cool. That wind blew throughout our visit, calming the day, in sun and shade, as well as our own feelings as we listened to stories of sadness. On either side of the path, as far as we could see, the rice fields were soggy with the water from the dam. A few cattle grazed as we sat in the shade of the little shop where the village started, opposite the mosque. We were the cynosure of curiosity as we entered the village, though Bhagduba Habi is familiar with reporters and media types: NDTV had sent a team here in 2008, the twenty-fifth anniversary[29] of the massacre. Reporters from the nearest towns, Jagiroad, Nagaon and Guwahati, keep dropping by from time to time to see what's happening or to accompany a politician on one of his or her usual rounds to spread goodwill, create division, distribute largesse.

The men were, in the main, wiry, with barely an ounce of fat, their skin darkened by years of toil in fields under a hot and humid sun. Some were clad in lungis and long shirts or vests; others in shirts and trousers. Some bearded, others clean-shaven.

They rarely received compensation for the crop damage, they said—though I could not verify the claim. But the state of the approach road and the thatch and mud houses of the village, with few homes of brick and cement, showed how little things had improved economically over the decades for Bhagduba Habi, a place of 242 houses, and the three other settlements which are clumped together.

But there's electricity. Riyazuddin, whose father was a senior figure in the village but elsewhere that day, addressing a meeting, stopped by to distribute power bills to those at our informal discussion.

Some of the residents came at the time when Sir Syed Muhammad Saadulla, then premier of Assam, brought in Muslim settlers from Mymensingh district, East Bengal, then part of British India (and now part of Bangladesh) to cultivate wastelands and help the 'Grow More Food' British war effort.[30] Landless Bengali peasants poured in.

The British viceroy at the time noted cynically in his diaries that Saadulla's strategy appeared more to be a 'Grow More Muslims' campaign.[31]

◆

On the day of the visit, young Hojai Ali, all of fourteen and a student of class eight, was hovering about the discussion area. Why wasn't he in school, I asked. 'Oh,' he said, 'pani bandh. (It's closed because of the water).' It would be hard to better that excuse.

Jalaluddin of Basundhara village, a tall, angular man in a stained shirt and pyjamas, said he only organized one rice harvest on his twenty-three bighas of land. 'I've lost the crop in nine bighas.' Others were worried about the loans they had taken and needed to pay off.

A couple of hundred metres away, a handful of graves of victims of the Nellie frenzy lay silently, located behind a wall. At one edge of the graveyard, men and women worked briskly, drying the paddy they had salvaged from nearby fields. It was as if it was another day of saving their crops, as if nothing had ever happened here.

A small black marble slab on the graveyard's wall remembers the murders, silently. In a faded Assamese script, it speaks of 'The Pure Site of the Shaheed (Martyrs)', giving the date and year of the event, and that the foundation stone (aadarshila) was laid by two ministers of the Congress Assam government, Nazrul Islam and Bibekananda Doley, on 25 February 2011. That's twenty-eight years after the disaster. There's no mention of how many people were slaughtered or why the stone is there, apart from the bloody date. No explanation of why these are shaheeds, the same word used to describe those who died in the anti-immigration agitation who have been honoured, their families compensated and legal cases instituted against those who were responsible for their deaths.

In the killing fields of Nellie, silence speaks louder than anything else. Villagers rush to save their harvest, damaged by the unrelenting engineers of the Kopili dam, an unseen monstrous fate that decides their lives and livelihoods. But the government has not filed cases against attackers and killers, known or unknown; the Justice Tiwary Report on the violence in Assam of those dark stormy days and nights is buried in secrecy; the case filed by a few survivors drags on. The families of those butchered received ₹5,000 at the time, nothing more since.

They continue to live in the neighbourhood of villages among people who were responsible for the violence.

◆

It was hard to believe that in these very fields, hundreds of bodies were lying, felled as they fled, limbs askew, faces contorted in pain and horror on that fateful February day.

The mob of several thousands was drawn from the neighbourhood and outside, comprising Tiwas and other ethnic groups, armed with daos (machetes), bows and arrows and spears. Like a whirlwind, this huge mob swept across the rice fields, chasing the frightened and fleeing, leaving a harvest of blood, limbs and corpses.

Bhagduba Habi's older villagers speak easily, even casually, of the nightmare, almost without emotion and passion. I found this both strange and astonishing. Yet as a little probing showed, it remains an issue that brings back painful memories. And who can blame them? It is a recurring nightmare that doesn't go away. Recovery to them, it seemed, lay in denial if not forgetting.

Yet they also spoke at length of their aspirations and the need to deal with the present and look to the future. The non-telling is a way of handling the past. Their approach appears to be similar to the Mizos, as we saw earlier—where blocking out the past, the harm and indignities suffered—is an option. Here were have two communities, separated by a few hundred kilometres, living with pasts and contexts which are totally dissimilar and with no knowledge of each other—but finding similar refuge and escape from their demons in silence and silencing.

The older ones at Bhagduha Habi seem to have decided to bottle up the pain and hold it back for the sake of the future generations. They may not have found their peace but they appear to have taken a decision not to live in the past.

A sturdy white-bearded man in blue checked lungi and a vest was asked why they didn't file criminal cases. His answer was baffling: 'They attacked, not us, why should we file cases?' That's a remarkable statement of non-violence, of learning to live with one's neighbours especially after what the villagers have been through.

But before we get into this tense, stressed situation with conflict, bloodshed, the sweeping arc of glinting machetes and axes on soft flesh, the burst of muskets and lopped off limbs, the groans and tears of victims and the righteous rage of the attackers, there remains a remarkable fact: attackers and victims exist as uneasy neighbours in the same villages, even thirty years later.

In a book[32] published in 2016, Jatin Hazarika, a key official at the time of the Assam agitation and the Nellie Massacre of 18 February 1983, wrote about the slaughter. He said that 'large numbers of killed persons... were either women or children' and pointed out that though the incident was 'immediately linked with the anti-election agitation, it was in fact the result of a land dispute between local tribal people and immigrant Muslims'. This is a point that some of us have been stressing for long—that the issues were at their core economic and at the heart of that they were land related. The religious and political issues got mixed up subsequently.

But what he does not specify in his remarks is that the immigrants were not Bangladeshis but old inhabitants who had settled in the area in the 1930s, if we are to trust revenue records. 'The tribal peasants were looking for an opportunity to take revenge upon the new settlers, felt they were deprived of their lands by the immigrants, who occupied them through various manipulative techniques.'

Although he does not elaborate on the 'manipulative techniques' by which the Muslims took over tribal lands, Jatin Hazarika talks about this figuring in the Tiwari Commission Report on the reasons and magnitude of the Nellie Massacre, a report that has been shut and sealed by the state government. T. P. Tiwari, a former chief secretary of Uttar Pradesh, was asked by the Hiteswar Saikia government to investigate the violence which took place before, during and in the aftermath of the polling. Saikia, who became chief minister, won a facile victory because of the extensive rioting and fear that blanketed the valley twinned with the boycott call by the agitators which prevented voting in many constituencies. In some polling booths, only a handful of ballots were cast—often by the candidates themselves or family members and close friends.

In constituencies like Guwahati East,[33] less than 2 per cent of the total electorate of 73,780 turned up to vote. A total of 1,159 valid votes were counted. The winner, Munim Sarma of the Congress, got 687 votes, winning by a grand margin of 324 votes, edging past his nearest rival who garnered 363 votes. In nearby Hajo, about 11 per cent of the votes were cast and the unfortunate runner-up (from the Communist Party of India) got a mere 307 ballots in his favour. The winning margin was 6,327 since the victorious candidate got 6,634 votes. The total electorate in Hajo at the time was 65,567.

Yet in areas dominated by Bengali Hindus such as the Barak Valley and Muslims of Bangla origin in lower Assam, the turnouts were impressive, ranging from 45 per cent to well over 50 per cent, marking the sharp divide that would play out in the decades to come. In places such as Salmara South and Dhubri, the voting scale was above 70 per cent. People voted with a vengeance to show that they were determined not to be displaced or pressured, just as the reverse was true of Guwahati and other Assamese-dominated areas.

As far as democratic traditions go, it was a farce during Assam's dance of death. The Congress Party won no less than ninety-one seats, its best performance in decades and one which could not be matched by any party since.[34] Sixteen constituencies saw such mayhem that elections were cancelled and postponed.

The results from East Guwahati and other electoral races show how unrepresentative the process was, how outrageously unacceptable in many areas. There is no law in India's election system that could have branded this result as unrepresentative, illegal and hence liable to be cancelled.

Saikia appointed Tiwari as a one-man commission of enquiry who looked into the events of January to April 1983 with a focus, obviously, on the worst incidents such as Nellie. In Jatin Hazarika's summarization, Tiwari picked the state's adverse land-to-man ratio as the heart of the matter.

'Land grabbing and encroachments on various types of reserves and waste lands were also responsible for generating social tensions and mutual hatred among affected groups.'[35] The problem of educated unemployment has also been another cause of dissatisfaction among the people. These tensions erupted into violence occasionally. Many incidents, the commission said, could be traced to land disputes and these were deliberately fanned during the agitation.

While a large number of government staff extended their support to the movement, there was also extensive evidence to show that mass support was at times extracted by threats of coercion and violence. The commission squarely blamed the All Assam Students Union and the All Assam Gana Sangram Parishad for both the agitation and its consequences.

Analyzing three major incidents in upper and central Assam, the commission noted that while 'immigrants' were at the receiving end in two events (Chawlkhowa and Khoirabari in Darrang district), one of the worst attacks followed occupation of forest lands by Bodo tribals in Gohpur (Sonitpur district). The tribals were attacked largely by Assamese Hindus, mostly Scheduled Caste groups after the latter had faced an initial assault before reorganizing to strike back.

Bridges were destroyed and roads were dug up even in the interior, disrupting communications and making travel for rescue teams and journalists like me who were moving from place to place a nightmare. The drive from Tezpur to Gohpur, a journey of about 127 kilometres, took a team of journalists five hours. We were driven in a doctor's Ambassador car because there were no taxis available and the doctor offered to take us there to 'see things for yourself'. After some time, we lost track of the number of times we had to get out of the vehicle to remove tree branches thrown on the narrow road or while the car negotiated a dry stream bed because the road before a culvert had been dug up or a wooden bridge had been burnt. The resistance was not sporadic—it appeared well organized and planned.

Jatin Hazarika wrote: 'Hatred and dissension, accumulated over four years, had taken...a heavy toll, leaving three thousand people dead, reducing beautiful villages into ashes and destroying many roads and vital bridges.' But, he remarked: 'the biggest damage was to the values of human love and compassion which seemed to have been lost forever'.

The scale of the displacement was huge affecting more than 3,50,000 people, the largest displacement by rioting since Partition. The number of those forced to move out of their homes was surpassed only during the regime of the 'secular' Congress Party; nearly thirty years later, the Bodo-Muslim riots of 2012 saw a similar scale of displacement with over 4,00,000 living in relief camps. These makeshift shelters are usually built around a core of school buildings or large crowded tents.

Every classroom was converted into a living space, as were the corridors and patches of ground and play fields outside. Meals were cooked in the open. Toilets were few and all of them were a stinking, overflowing mess. Hardly any government official or politician seemed bothered about the unhygienic filth inherited by students, teachers and staff to clean up.

◆

At the receiving end of the violence, physically, politically and in terms of media coverage, of public rage, for the most part has been the ubiquitous Miya, the so-called Bangladeshi,[36] the Muslim of Bangla descent and origin.

The lawyer Warisha Farasat, who has worked with the International Centre for Transnational Justice in New York, said:

> Beginning, perhaps, with the Nellie massacre of 1983, the term 'communal riot' is a misrepresentation. As we saw with the anti-Sikh violence of 1984, the communal violence had become an out-and-out one-sided massacre of the Sikhs. It was a one-sided pogrom. The one-sided massacres of Muslims in 1983 in Nellie, Assam, 1989

in Bhagalpur, Bihar, and 2002 in Gujarat were also not communal riots but pogroms. If we do not acknowledge this distinction and continue to theorise under the wider umbrella of 'communal riots', we will undermine the brutality of the communal violence that has been perpetrated in the last 30 years against religious minorities, particularly Muslims. Communal carnages cannot happen without state complicity.[37]

However, the violence has not been one-sided: many other groups such as the Bodos, Rabhas, Adivasis, Karbis and Assamese and Bengali Hindus have also suffered in other clashes raging over land and identity. They too have lived, sometimes for years and more, cheek by jowl in messy settlements of tents and camps, school houses and open fields, fearful, depressed, an oppressive mix which is coloured strongly by anger and humiliation.

In a recent conversation, a relative of mine exploded when someone raised the issue of the conservation of rhinos in Kaziranga National Park. He was especially furious about Pramila Rani Brahma, the state forest and environment minister, who went to the park to energize campaigns against poachers who have been striking with brutality and impunity against the state animal. The poachers are armed with automatic weapons and the rhinos stand no chance against these vicious killers and their guns, especially since these criminals are connected to Karbi and other armed groups. Two senior officers of the park, both Muslims, were transferred.

My cousin was in a towering rage: 'She's telling us to save the rhinos, what have they done to save their forests? They've completely wiped out all the forests for the love of money. How can you save wildlife without forests?'

Brahma had earlier triggered demands for her arrest[38] when she was quoted as saying that Muslims had not voted for her party candidate, Chandan Brahma, in the 2014 Lok Sabha election. Chandan Brahma lost by a landslide to Hiranya Sarania, a former member of the banned ULFA. The results clearly showed up the complex contradictions in the Bodoland set-up where the government had tried with good intentions, no doubt, to settle extremely challenging circumstances. Sarania won the support of the non-Bodos who were a majority in the districts, although they were ruled by a tightly organized Bodo oligarchy.

The consequences were predictable in Assam's fraught, taut politics, especially in the blood-spattered Bodo council area. 'Ethnic and communal violence has struck Assam, with all its stark ugliness, once again,' wrote Abhijit Saha in India Resists[39] under the heading: 'Will we ever learn?'

What occurred in 2012, has returned, quite shamelessly, this month. Muslims of Bengali origin have been mercilessly targeted—with more than 30 persons killed in two days—and mudslinging has continued ever since, unabated. Media reports have said that the non-Bodo organisations in the BTAD [Bodoland Territorial Area Districts] which fielded a non-tribal candidate (ex-ULFA member Hira Sarania) in the ongoing General Elections, in Kokrajhar district…alleged that the minorities were targeted just because they did not vote for the Bodo candidate.

That's the starkness of how easy it is to slip over the edge of confrontation into violence, seamlessly and bloodily, ripping chunks of meat from human flesh, especially the feeble and vulnerable tearing apart lives and livelihoods.

There's drama in the facts on the ground, about the demographics of the place, contrasting with the green and lush countryside, the surging streams and rivers, which makes the violence uglier. For these are pogroms and acts of acute violence which are not being carried out by a brute majority but by a group that represents just over a quarter of the total population of the Bodoland Territorial Council (BTC).

It is widely accepted that the Bodos who run the BTC comprise a bare 28 per cent, at the very most, of the population in the area under the council. That means that 72 per cent are non-Bodos; the break-up is something like this—about 22–24 per cent are Muslims, largely of Bangla origin. Another 30 per cent or so are members of the Assamese, Bengali, Marwari and other Hindu groups. Some 14 per cent are members of the Santhal tribal group and the balance include tea garden workers and others. As a result, an extremely stressful and complex situation has developed where the majority is pitted against and dominated by a powerful minority. The political elite from this Bodo group holds the strings of political and economic (read financial) power. These are dispensed with clear discrimination favouring Bodos.

Yet, over and above the politics and finances of the place, cadres of the two former armed Bodo groups, the Bodo Liberation Tigers (BLT) and National Democratic Front of Bodoland (NDFB),[40] had access to another source of greater power: one which held the balance of life and death for many—illegal weapons. A senior police official[41] told me after the 2012 killings that these unaccounted secret arms were extremely difficult to locate.

A top security official said in an interview in Guwahati:

[Weapons] would be placed inside homes, wrapped in plastic to avoid rust and damage and buried under the house or in the fields. The location of the weapons would be kept secret and only the very small group would know about it; this made the job of the police tougher. Whenever an attack was planned, the guns and the ammunition would be pulled out by those who knew where they were and how to use them.

Pramila Brahma had blamed the Muslims for voting against the BPF candidate. Within days of her statement, no fewer than forty-one Muslims, mostly women and children, were slaughtered by armed men wearing military fatigues and carrying automatic weapons. Accounts of the assault indicated that the groups had slipped in from across the easily accessible border with Bhutan. In places, the international border is demarcated by the Manas River, small border roads but few armed patrols. The innocents didn't stand a chance. A lucky few managed to flee into the jungle nearby.

◆

In the changing context of growing armed rebellion in Assam, the connection of Bodo militants with extensive violence and organized attacks goes back some years. The earliest report of Bodo rebels using automatic weapons leapt to public attention in 1993 when groups of the Bodo Security Force attacked Adivasi, Santhal and Muslim villages, killing scores and displacing nearly 1,20,000 persons, many of whom still live in temporary settlements, in poor conditions of health, nutrition, sanitation, education and few opportunities to earn a livelihood.

The goal of the attackers was an autonomous homeland, as in the case of the Nagas and their Nagalim (Naga homeland). Clearly the strategy then, as in 2012 and 2014, was to use brutal attacks on the most vulnerable and innocent to create panic and a flight of population. As in other cases, there was another goal—to humiliate the state government and show it up as impotent, incapable of protecting the poor and innocent.

The Bodo use of explosives was deadly: a series of eleven coordinated bomb blasts within a short space of time across Assam on 30 October 2008 had killed nearly eighty persons. The strikes blew apart people in a bustling market of Guwahati and other towns of the state, set shops and persons ablaze and ripped apart cars and motorcycles. More than 300 persons were wounded. After the usual rush of blame on Islamic militants, the needle of suspicion turned to NDFB's Ranjan Daimary and his cadres although they never publicly took responsibility. But the trail of blood and gunpowder led to their door.

Interestingly, apart from the five blasts in Guwahati,[42] there were three attacks in Kokrajhar town, Western Assam, in a district dominated by Bodos in which seventeen persons died, while '12 more persons were killed in two blasts at Barpeta Road market areas in Barpeta district of lower Assam. Over ten persons were injured in a blast in Bongaigoan town in Bongaigaon district where the bomb exploded while the police were trying to defuse it.'[43] All the blasts took place within a 200-kilometre radius, showing that the striking power of the gang was limited to a certain geographical range. The death toll rose to seventy-seven in the state's worst terrorist incident in decades.

Praveen Swami,[44] one of India's top journalists on security matters, wrote: 'Evidence has emerged that a hit-team of the National Democratic Front of Bodoland (NDFB) executed the October 30 serial bombings in Assam—evidence which undermines earlier claims that the Bangladesh-based Harkat ul-Jihad-Islami (HuJI) was responsible for the murderous attacks.' In detail, Swami, who is known for his in-depth investigative work, talked about how a hit team of the NDFB conducted the attacks, received support from ULFA and that the orders for attack on vulnerable localities were issued by Ranjan Daimary, the chairman of the NDFB. Daimary, who overruled others in the group, had, Swami said, a history of 'sanctioning brutal attacks against civilians' citing attacks in 2004 in three smaller Assam towns.

◆

In this case, the aim was to strike terror into all sections of society and show up the helplessness of government to do anything to protect the ordinary citizen from harm. Both were clear political goals through the medium of terrorism. The inability of government to tackle these issues would dramatically hurt its political stature as well as its seeming capacity to enforce the law.

Thus, while these brutal strikes may have had the general goal of undermining the state government, there were others over the past thirty years and more which were aimed at one group, a specific community which is viewed with suspicion and dislike, much of it unearned. This is the Muslim population of Bangla or Bengali descent in Assam. In some places they are called Miyas, in others Mymensinghias, in yet others Bideshis. The last word means outsiders or foreigners—non-citizens—and that description is at the root of a lot of the trouble and anger that's been stoked towards this group.

Who are these people? Where are they from? Are they Indians or 'foreigners' as many would have us believe? How do these significant 'others' perceive themselves?

Professor M. Asaduddin, one of India's finest translators and a respected teacher in Jamia Millia Islamia University's English department, is originally from Assam's Barak Valley. Asad, as his friends know him, speaks with concern about the way public attitudes have hardened and literary views have narrowed over the decades, following the public process instead of broadening minds and approaches. Communities are being defined by accent, stock and historical prejudice with more and more writing emphasizing the worries of what one can only define as a 'losing community'. In broad terms, one can describe the latter as a group that sees itself threatened demographically by another group and even regards its very existence at stake, with or without hard factual evidence to prove this.

Whatever 'evidence' exists is trotted out in various reports, books, videos and media analysis by well-known figures and others unknown, by judges, lawyers, scholars, researchers, political leaders, former bureaucrats and the media, as well as the Hindu right-wing who spew venom and hatred at every opportunity.

In recent years, the rhetoric has sharpened as have official positions, of parties and governments, both at the central and state levels.

I recall Atal Bihari Vajpayee's famous statement at an election meeting in the Maligaon Railway grounds in Guwahati in 1983 when he declared that 'khoon ki nadiya behenge (rivers of blood will flow)' if the government went ahead with the elections that were to result in the horrors of Nellie and other massacres. I was at that meeting and recall being stunned by the remark from a man who was considered to be a moderate in the right-wing establishment. It was to be reflected in his attitude as prime minister towards the Gujarat riots of 2002. At a function at his official residence, I found myself in the company of the poet Anees Jung and George Fernandes, a cabinet minister and former firebrand trade union leader; the prime minister came leisurely by to chat after the event.

I was talking to Fernandes about the riots, saying it was a matter of shame for Gujarat, the Indian state and all those who believed in a united and equal country. 'Kya ho raha hain? (What's going on?)' asked the affable premier. Jung, who was by this time extremely irked by what she regarded as Fernandes's non-replies, told Vajpayee that she was appalled that the government was not 'doing anything' about the killings and riots. The prime minister looked at Jung, who was an old friend and renowned fellow poet in Urdu (though she wrote extensively and powerfully in English too) shrugged, smiled and slowly moved away. Jung, I recall, was very upset.

Twelve years later, when Narendra Modi, the robust chief minister of Gujarat,[45] visited Assam as the BJP's prime ministerial face and Vajpayee's potential successor, he spoke powerfully against the perceived Bangladeshi influx. As he exhorted enthusiastic crowds to vote for the party in places where the BJP was not known to have much of a following, whether among the Bodo tribe of the state's west or in the tea plantations of upper Assam, Modi also sent out a clear message to Muslim voters but especially those in Assam who are often derided and persecuted as 'Bangladeshis'.

At an election rally in Silchar in the Barak Valley, dominated by both Hindu and Muslim voters of Bengali origin, Modi declared in Hindi on 22 February 2014: 'The kind of governments elected here, all of Assam is troubled because of Bangladeshis.'[46] In the midst of a blistering campaign where he untiringly criss-crossed the country in an unrelenting quest for power, Modi told the meeting: 'Now you have to make the choice whether you want to tolerate the problems of these Bangladeshis or decide the future of Assam.' Two months later, *Caravan* reported, he declared at another rally: 'You can write it down… After 16 May, these Bangladeshis should pack their belongings and be ready.' The warning was stark.

On 16 May 2014, the national elections picked the BJP, giving it a simple majority, no mean achievement for Modi whose rise on the national scene was meteoric and new, enabling it to form a comfortable government with its allies. But no one was leaving just yet with bags and baggage despite the rhetoric and despite the fact that the BJP crushed its opposition in seven parliamentary constituencies in Assam, including places where the latter had not lost earlier. Even the then chief minister Tarun Gogoi's son Gaurav, Congress candidate for a seat held by the family for seven elections, got a scare.

However, after the elections there was no rush for evictions, no hasty campaign aimed at detection and deportation. Two separate strands of action followed. One was pursued by Upamanyu Hazarika, who had cut his teeth as a lawyer under the tutelage of Arun Jaitley, who rose from right-wing student leader to one of the country's top lawyers, commerce minister under Vajpayee and finance minister and defence minister under Modi. Upamanyu had started the Prabajan Virodhi Manch, which sought to launch the 'final struggle for survival' for the Assamese in the face of what he described as waves of illegal Bangladeshi immigration. The other course of action was the updating of the National Register of Citizens which would trace a person's lineage to 1947 when India became independent. We look at that area of work later in this chapter.

First, the Upamanyu effort.

After working his way up the legal ladder, with important breaks in celebrated cases like Tata Tea,[47] Upamanyu[48] carved out a niche for himself in New Delhi's corporate legal world, no mean achievement for someone from the once small town of Guwahati,[49] whose father was a respected senior scientist in the Geological Survey of India's office in Assam.

Upamanyu had founded the manch as its convener after the 2012 riots in Assam between Bodos and Muslims. He believed that the threat from a 'Bangladeshi' influx was substantial. The manch's goals were simple: to mobilize support against 'Bangladeshis' and fight for Assam's rights on this issue by providing a legal framework. The young lawyer didn't really have a base in his state, although he visited it regularly over the decades.

In turn, the court, presided over by Justice Ranjan Gogoi and Justice Rohinton Nariman, appointed him as a commissioner to investigate the issues, declaring:

> Without dilating all that we would like to say...at this stage is that the Court is left with the impression that the Union Government and the State Government of Assam have been dragging their feet in the matter of implementation of this Court's order particularly with regard to border fencing, construction of border roads, night patrolling, flood-lights, etc.

It appointed Upamanyu as the one-man commission to investigate the matter of whether the border was as poorly protected as was alleged.

Upamanyu's report became the matter of controversy when it was submitted. He conducted interviews with security and other officials, visited the border areas and interacted with local NGOs which were deeply opposed to the perceived immigration. Nowhere in the report did he speak of meeting representatives of those accused of being illegal nationals or settlers themselves. In that way, the report was predictably one-sided, for his mind was pretty much made up from the time he began to work on the issue in 2012.

In a June 2016 interview on the subject, he told a reporter:

> The violence [of 2012] was viewed as an ethnic issue rather than one between foreigners and citizens. After the National Minority Commission brought out a report that described Bangladeshis being minorities rather than foreigners first, 10 organisations got together. We worked to dispel the false impressions about the immigrants and

now aim to educate the younger generation about the issue.[50]

Upamanyu's report and views were based on a number of assumptions. However, some key issues are worth dwelling on, for they actually represent a substantial concern among the caste Hindu as well as tribal groups in Assam state. I may not be in agreement with such views but there is no doubt that they exist, even though they may be based, in my view, on sweeping generalizations and assumptions.

He took the court-mandated task seriously, collecting and receiving memoranda, listening to grievances from various groups which spoke against 'illegal' migration and encroachment, including one which posited that the Assamese groups would be a minority in their own state by 2040.

Many researchers and scholars as well as activists who have worked in this area saw little that was new or path-breaking either in the memoranda or the four reports that Upamanyu had filed for the Supreme Court over a six-month period in 2015,[51] despite the intensive work that he had done and the travel and hours he and his associates had put in. This was frankly because there was little to add to the existing body of knowledge, except opinions and recommendations.

He was clear on the legal impediments—the goal was not so much the issue of illegal migration into Assam and the Northeast but of dealing with those who were already there. The advocate spelt out the challenges with regard to the citizenship law, which is at the heart of the dispute. In the context of the 1985 Assam Accord, the two modes of acquiring citizenship in Assam are:

- Those who came from Pakistan/Bangladesh (before 1971) and citizenship by birth, which takes into account the following time frames—(a) Between 26 January 1950 to 1 July 1987: By birth and regardless of whether parents are citizens or illegal immigrants/foreigners; (b) Between 1 July 1987 to 3 December 2004: By birth with the condition that one of the parents is a citizen and implying that the other is an illegal immigrant/foreigner.
- After 3 December 2004: By birth, but both parents must be citizens, or one is a citizen and the other is not an illegal immigrant

The committee recommended a 'Sterile Zone' (on the international border area on the Assam side) 'by demarcating/identifying a particular stretch from the international boundary in the riverine area and provision of identity cards to villagers there'.

The issuing of identity cards was something that I had suggested as far back as 2000 in an earlier book and in many writings.[52] This approach was backed by the prime minister's National Security Advisory Board[53] of 1999–2000 when it discussed the issue of internal security threats and put the suggestion in its official report to the government. In addition, the work permit idea was specifically supported by the highly respected Prakash Singh, a police officer who had earlier been head of the police in Assam and Uttar Pradesh and retired as head of the Border Security Force. But for well over a decade, this suggestion has gathered dust in the files of the Ministry of Home Affairs under both BJP and Congress-led governments. It's too much of a political hot potato for either side to touch, let alone pick up, for fear of being seen as favouring the 'immigrant' or worse, the Bangladeshi.

Upamanyu cited the primary reason for illegal migration as hunger for land—though this is true, it is also facile. While the pressure on land is acute in Bangladesh, and will grow as climate change and rising sea levels send millions of Bangladeshis further inland, we have seen that there are factors why emigration to India is falling. These include better economic and social conditions in Bangladesh which have been remarked upon by the World Bank among others.

Without looking at this issue or considering the larger picture, the commission recommended 'a restriction in the transfer of land—whether by way of sale, purchase, gift or any other such transaction, or by way of allotment from the government or any other agency—only to those who have been citizens of India in the year 1951 and their descendants'.

In that one sentence, the report clarified its intent—it did not want those who came after 1951 to get citizenship. As a result, the issue of illegal or informal migration becomes mixed with illegal settlement of lands—the latter is a problem across the region, not just Assam, and numerous groups are involved, many of them bona fide citizens. The two issues are quite separate yet often are muddled up in public and media perceptions.

The argument about descent from those of 1951 stock runs into trouble: is such a position acceptable when there is a tripartite agreement going back to 1985 between the then agitating student leaders, the Government of Assam and the Government of New Delhi that defined the cut-off year as 1971? Those who came between 1966–1971, mostly Hindu refugees fleeing pogroms, were to be disenfranchised for ten years and their names then restored to voting lists. This has been passed by Parliament and has the sanction and stamp of law-making.

Why repeat a double infliction on a group especially after the BJP said, to much opprobrium in Assam, that it would take 'Hindu' refugees from Bangladesh but not Muslim migrants? Of course, it also tried to widen the net by being a little more equal saying that refugees from neighbouring countries, be they Sikh, Jain, Buddhist, Christian or Zoroastrian, would be welcome as Indian citizens. Muslims were left out of the list.

The report made another critical demand: the implementation of statutory restrictions on transfer of land to non-tribals in existing tribal belts in Assam, which has been made a mockery of by revenue officials and politicians, should be extended to non-tribal areas as well to stave off illegal migrants from acquiring land.

Foreigners acquired land, Upamanyu declared, 'through all means, the favourite mode being to pose as flood and erosion affected persons from other districts with the aid and assistance of a complicit and corrupt administration'.

The report claimed that the influx could reduce the Assamese to a minority by 2047. But it failed to address the contentious issue of who is an Assamese, the very point over which nationalists and sub-nationalists have long battled. For decades after the 1985 agreement, both the Assam government and AASU, which signed the accord, have failed to define the profile of an Assamese as many of the plains tribe groups have rejected the view that they were either 'Assamese' or Axomiya or part of a larger Assamese cultural and social identity. The report forgot that it was the Muslim migrants who accepted Assamese as their mother language in the 1950s, abandoning, officially and politically, their mother tongue, Bangla. This has assured Assamese dominance in the state as it faces competition from the large Bengali population as well as the smaller groups which together make up a majority of the state's population. Today, the number of Assamese speakers has fallen.

According to the 2001 Census of India, there were 13.1 million Assamese speakers in the state in a population of 26.6 million. The number of Bengali speakers, the second largest linguistic entity, was 7.3 million. In other words, the two major language groups comprised about 70 per cent of Assam's population. But Assamese speakers by themselves were in a minority in their own state, 48.8 per cent of the total population. This was a drop from the 57.8 per cent of 1991 while the Bengali population had risen from 21 per cent to over 27 per cent. During the 2001 census, of the total population of 26,655,528, 13,010,478 persons were Assamese speakers and 73,43,338 were Bengali speakers. In the 1991 census the total number of Assamese speakers was 12,958,088 (57.81 per cent) and the Bengali speakers 4,856,532 (21.67 per cent). The number of Bodo speakers in Assam in the

2001 census was 1,296,162.[54]

The growth in Bengali numbers was jarring as was the decline in Assamese speakers, primarily because it was so large.

In 2011, the population had risen to 31.1 million with a decadal growth rate of 16.9 per cent or significantly lower than the national figure of 17.3 per cent. Population density was up from 340 per square kilometre to 397. The Muslim share of the population went to 34.2 per cent, up from 30.9 per cent, a change of 3.3 points as compared to the national average of 0.8. But this cannot be explained away facilely as 'immigration' of illegals. It has everything to do with the high fertility rates among Muslim couples in the areas where the minority group dominates.

Although the Census Commission of India has not released the national 2011 language data for Assam,[55] what was obvious even as far back as 2001 was that there had been a switch. Did a significant number of Assamese speakers of the 1991 era choose to return to Bengali as their mother tongue ten years later? The reasons are yet to emerge clearly. What cannot be ruled out is that many Assamese speakers of Bengali origin, whether out of loyalty to their original tongue or frustration at what was happening in the state, had chosen to go back to Bengali. Others of different ethnic persuasions similarly, it could be surmised, preferred to give their own 'home' languages as their mother tongue.

This is happening not because of the migrants but because those who were for long in the tight grip of the larger Assamese fold want out, and want to be comfortable in their smaller ethnic formations: whether it is the Bodos, Tiwas, Karbis, Cacharis or Rabhas. Each seeks its own space, territorial, linguistic and political. It appears more to have been the failure of the core Assamese middle class and caste Hindus which have failed to have a respectful relationship with the 'others' as well as their hold that these smaller groups resent.

The Upamanyu Hazarika report spoke of a 'big influx' which had 'created a huge immigration population which competes for jobs, in government institutions with Indian citizens, without verification of the antecedents of such non-Indians'.

Upamanyu pushed for eviction of squatters and encroachers especially from the lands of the Vaishnavite satras, the medieval-origin monasteries where celibate monks live, working farms, praying, writing, making masks and other handicrafts, singing devotional music and performing religious plays. Indeed, the election campaign of the Assam legislature elections in 2016 saw demonstrative support to the party from the influential Vaishnavite centres[56] of learning and religious belief. That their lands have been encroached upon is not the question.

The question is who has done so. Is it the ubiquitous 'Bangladeshi' or are these Indian citizens, old Muslim groups of Bengali origin or other tribal and non-tribal factions? What is the evidence behind the sweeping charges, apart from oral accusations, second-hand information and a feeling of angst among the Assamese, of being let down by their leaders? Facts are mixed up in the reports.

Thus while the report recommends legislation for Assam similar to that which has torn Manipur since 2015, saying that this would stop not just encroachment but also settlement by 'illegal aliens', it fails to see that in Manipur the objective of three controversial legislations aimed at stopping settlement and possession of immovable property is targeted at non-Manipuri Indians or 'outsiders' from other parts of the country, such as enterprising, hard-working mercantile communities like the Marwaris, Gurkhas, Biharis and Punjabis.

The three bills, the Protection of Manipur People Bill, 2015; the Manipur Land Revenue and Land Reforms (Seventh Amendment) Bill, 2015 and the Manipur Shops and Establishments (Second Amendment) Bill, 2015, have the cumulative effect of taking away the 'unique' land-holding rights of the hill groups. In addition, the laws would enable people from the Manipur Valley to settle in upland areas, something that had not been possible earlier. This is being furiously opposed by hill tribes. However, hill groups have always been able to settle in the valley, a grouse locally held against them by the Meiteis. The former say the implementation of the laws will destroy their identity, cohesion and traditions, disrupting tribal control over agriculture, territory and tradition. More significantly, this could strike at the heart of core homeland demands which have characterized the politics of the past decades by the Nagas, Kukis and other, even smaller, ethnic groups. Such a defanged political condition would be unacceptable both to the armed factions as well as the mainstream political groups in the hills. It would strike at the very heart of the unique identity that they have long spoken of, emasculating the idea of a special and separate land for their own people.

If such laws were to be drawn up for Assam, it would surely run into stiff and angry resistance from Indian groups who have lived in Assam for over a century. It would also push the focus of the debate away from 'illegal settlers' from a foreign land to settlers from within India who have a constitutional right to migrate and live anywhere they wish in the country. There are exceptions to the rule in specific areas such as Nagaland,

Mizoram and parts of Meghalaya or in Jammu and Kashmir and parts of Uttarkhand and Himachal Pradesh where 'outsiders' are barred by special laws from purchasing land and accumulating immovable property.

There are several issues that Upmanyu's four reports running into over 120 pages raise, including one where they allege that fifty lakh (five million) is the illegal migrant figure as of 2001. This is a staggering number for it is one-sixth of the population of the state alone and just under one-eighth of the entire region. On what basis are such figures trotted out? For that number of people to have come into Assam, they would have had to cross the border every year at not less than 1,00,000 per year for fifty years. Is this humanly possible especially after Assam's borders shrank from over 800 kilometres with Bangladesh to less than 300 kilometres by 1971 with the creation of the new state of Meghalaya? This meant that the 1,00,000 illegal migrants would have to squeeze through over one-fifth of the original length of the border, which includes not less than some 30 to 40 kilometres of riverine areas—rivers, streams, sandbanks and floods during the summer rains. The logical question arises—if these numbers were so large, this means that more than 270 persons would have to cross every twenty-four hours to make that target achievable. Also we need to take into account that until a few years ago, when a non-lethal weapon policy was declared by the Indian government after a series of killings of civilians on the border and a furious outcry in Bangladesh, it was the norm to shoot first and ask questions later. In the space of less than a decade, over 800 persons were killed by the Border Security Force, mostly Bangladeshis, cattle rustlers, petty smugglers and thieves, but migrants and local villagers, including Indians, were also among the dead.

One good suggestion is to tighten security not just by increasing and closing the gaps in the fencing but by installing sensors and providing additional identity cards to local residents so that they are not harassed. Special sensors have been installed in Jammu and Kashmir along the international border to stop infiltration by armed Kashmiri militants sponsored by the Pakistani government. But they still manage to get across, although the numbers have dropped.

However, the Upamanyu Hazarika report gets into quicksand when it asks why lethal action should not be taken along the borders to curb cross-border migration. This is cynically seeking to militarize the border, brush aside the rule of law and international obligations of the Indian state. It would, in addition, empower border guards with powers of life and death. Using phrases like 'continued aggression of illegal migrants', the report says it finds the 'issue of human rights of those who illegally attempt to cross the border...incomprehensible'. This is the essence of the argument—solve an economic problem with brute force and never mind the legal consequences. Or the impact on bilateral relations. It's interesting that the central government has been quiet on a number of the points that the commission raised, obviously aware of the sensitivity of the matter and how it could harm Indo-Bangladesh relations.

The resumption of 'lethal force' would certainly extinguish human lives. Such a policy goes against the basic tenets of fundamental rights to which all humans, not just citizens, are entitled. These have been underlined by ringing verdicts of the Supreme Court itself,[57] in one of which it declared: *'The right to live includes the right to live with human dignity and all that goes along with it.'* Yet it is surprising that the demand for killing people on the border by an officer of the court—for that is the definition of a lawyer—has not been challenged by either the judges or senior lawyers. Activist groups have been silent and the media, of course, appears to have had no time to read over 120 pages of four reports which go into considerable detail on the issues.

It is also clear from all the affidavits and memoranda the one-man commission has submitted to the Supreme Court that there isn't a single contesting claim or counter-memorandum seeking to outline the position of the 'other'. How can a commission tasked to find out the facts on such a sensitive issue do so without talking to all groups across the political and social spectrum including those accused of illegality? A number of them are distinguished professionals and lawyers, scholars, writers and activists in their own right. There are politicians and bureaucrats from the nether regions of the state but they are silenced in the report. Only one view has prevailed and it is important to understand this for it plays into an old recurrent fear in the Assamese psyche, one that has existed for nearly a century—that the local people will be overwhelmed by outsiders.

There are facts which cannot be wished away: there is extensive encroachment on government lands, forests, sanctuaries, 'revenue forests' (the domain of the forest department which permits, for a fee, private contractors to log trees for timber) by a wide range of groups. These are no respecters of the law or of environmental, ethnic or political boundaries. They include heavily armed insurgents, well-organized local business groups with networks reaching across the region and into Myanmar and Bangladesh.[58]

'There is one significant fact which emerges from the fact finding undertaken since May 2015 and resulting in the four reports, including the present one,' Upanmanyu intoned. This was: 'that there is an established institutionalized mechanism which enables a Bangladeshi national to freely come into the country, acquire citizenship rights and more importantly voting rights, which is where their strength lies'.[59]

But despite all the fuss, it has emerged[60] that the Doubtful Voters concept developed by the Election Commission years back has empowered the state government to set up not less than six detention camps in Assam. There are 489 detainees living there, out of which apparently 310 have been identified as belonging to Bangladesh and are ignorant of their place of origin. *The Wire* quoted the *Assam Tribune* as saying that this number included twenty-eight convicted Afghan nationals. So, essentially, it appears to be a fact sheet of all foreign nationals under trial or in detention. The centres created in six district jails with space for D voters, have been in place since 2016 (before the state elections which brought the BJP to power) and land has been allocated in Goalpara district of lower Assam for the first ever detention camp of 'foreigners'.[61]

> Fact that it is a porous border (admitted by both the governments), no verification of any person being enrolled as a voter, no verification of any person getting rights over land, rather settling as an encroacher upon government land, forest land and grazing reserves and subsequently conferred land rights with procurement of fake certification being the norm.

The report referred to a judgment of the Guwahati High Court which noted that a man who had been deported returned to file an affidavit. The state government had been so lackadaisical that it did not even bother to file a response for six years. Upamanyu concluded that 'there is a large scale racket in procurement of fake certificates and which is carried out with the aid and connivance of government personnel'.

However, he made few new recommendations although he did suggest that there should be a major enquiry to study the 'immigration' and connect the dots as it were between 'personnel' involved in the process, those entering and how they had been settling and establishing themselves with official connivance. I doubt whether new investigations will turn up anything that hasn't been reported earlier. The number of Bangladeshis who travel out of that country is far more substantial across the West Bengal border and on the sea routes to Southeast Asia[62].

There are opposing views to those of Upamanyu and others who propagate the fear of large-scale Bangladeshi immigration. Nilim Dutta[63] of

Guwahati argues that there are compelling reasons 'to view with scepticism the claim of illegal immigrants "hiding" among their co-religionists in the Muslim majority districts in Assam as even at the time of independence, population density in these districts were considerably higher making competition for land and the meagre opportunities of livelihood inevitably more intense'. He points out that with competition over land resources, conflict and litigation among immigrants over land is rampant. 'Why would they encourage, let alone facilitate, continuous illegal immigration that would put their own economic survival at peril?' Dutta argues. 'The concentration of Muslims in the areas where the Bengali Muslim immigrants have traditionally settled, underscores the reality that they are mostly likely to be the descendants of those immigrants, and hence legitimate Indian citizens, and not illegal immigrants who have allegedly continued to arrive till now.'

The immigrants then move across India and other parts of the subcontinent, especially to Pakistan, hoping for a conduit to West Asia and the oil-rich kingdoms, sheikhdoms and republics of the Middle East. Detecting them is rough and sending them back even more challenging.

M. S. Prabhakara, the doyen of reporters from the Northeast and long time correspondent of *The Hindu*, who was based in Guwahati for many years, points out that over 300,000 illegal migrants were deported from Assam between 1962 and 1984 under the Foreigners Act, 1946.[64] However, only 1,501 were deported from 1985 to 2003 under the Illegal Migrants (Determination by Tribunals) Act, 1983 (IMDT Act), which was eventually declared to be 'ultra vires the Constitution of India' by the Supreme Court. Interestingly, the Government of West Bengal deported about half a million illegal migrants under the Foreigners Act, 1946, without any agitation and without any IMDT Act.

For the Bangla out-traveller, the effort is either to merge into the Bengali diaspora in India or to get to Pakistan and hopefully to the Middle East, by land, sea or air.

To explain how dangerous a crossing across the India-Bangladesh border can be, let us turn to the example of Felanee. Perhaps that will help courts and lawyers, committees and nationalists understand what has often happened and what is likely to happen if lethal force is placed in the hands of border guards who are then provided legal protection from efforts to bring them to book by the victim's family.

◆

For five hours, the body of the fifteen-year-old girl hung on the barbed wire fence. Blood streaking her clothes in the January chill, her hair falling down in a macabre flow. She was shot while climbing over from the Indian side in West Bengal to Bangladesh and was going for her own wedding. Her father had managed to get over unscathed but the child, whose name was Felanee, did not make it. That was in 2011. That Felanee was Bangladeshi was uncontested but the killing of an unarmed child sparked a furious outcry against shootings of civilians by the BSF on the international boundary.

As a result of this incident, Indian border patrols were instructed not to fire live ammunition on suspected intruders (mind you, the BSF failed to tackle the real infiltrators, those of armed groups who had skipped across for years, creating mayhem, until the Bangladesh government cracked down and handed over ULFA, NDFB and Manipuri insurgent leaders to India). Nearly 1,000 persons had been killed in a ten-year period or one death every four days. An article in *The Guardian*[65] commented sharply on this, pointing out the double standards in violence sanctioned by authority at the border: No one has been prosecuted for any of these killings, in spite of evidence in many cases that makes it clear the killings were in cold blood against unarmed and defenceless local residents.

Shockingly, some Indian officials endorse shooting people who attempt to cross the border illegally, even if they are unarmed. Almost as shocking is the lack of interest in these killings by foreign governments who claim to be concerned with human rights. A single killing by US law enforcement along the Mexican border makes headlines. The killing of large numbers of villagers by Indian forces has been almost entirely ignored.

Those who died included both Bangladeshis and Indians, cattle rustlers, petty criminals as well as children, suspected migrants or people who were shot while going about their daily business.

Cattle smuggling is a major business along the border, as Upamanyu's report points out. Of this, there's no doubt or dispute. It has been studied extensively by Bangladeshi scholars as well as Indian economists. In 2002 the World Bank conducted seven surveys on the issue and came up with the assessment that the smuggling of live animals into the country was valued at not less than $100 million.[66] This was defined as the biggest single item of informal trade at the time into Bangladesh from India. However Indian estimates were over 2.2 times the Bangladeshi one but the bank's study attributed that to a limited survey scope.

Whatever the details, cattle smuggling is doubtless a large income earner for a wide range of people. A well known Indian study by the Indian

Council of Applied Economic Research commented caustically as far back as 1995: 'Once in a while, either due to a breach of the understanding or to demonstrate efficiency or agility of the law enforcing staff (to meet anti-smuggling targets, if any), some seizures are stage managed and the petty operators bear the consequences.'[67]

The criminal gangs which flourish on either side of the border are unlikely to do so without official connivance.

Bangladesh's improved economic performance as well as social indicators may not have ended migration. But they may have just moved it to a different level. While an outflow into India will continue, just because of its size and opportunities and the fact that it happens to be next door, the out-movement is changing, seeking to meet greater aspirations and fresh economic opportunities.

Felanee's short life and fatal last journey showed the danger in these dark and proscribed travels and what pulls people to this implacable destiny. The situation is not limited to India but sweeps across the high seas and continents as people embark on desperate efforts to improve their lives.

From the 1970s to the 1990s especially, Bangladeshis (earlier as East Pakistanis)[68] moved extensively, seamlessly and regularly across porous borders. At the time, there were no fences and although anti-migrant rhetoric was sharp, border patrolling on the Indian side was light. The outposts at fixed points were fortified and exchanged fire from time to time with their counterparts. But, on the whole, guarding was a profitable business.[69]

These days, descriptions of the flight of Bangladeshis across the Bay of Bengal speak of the flourishing people-smuggling trade in their troubled country—and also the pull and responsibilities of destination states to the south, whose economies have boomed in part because of low-wage immigrant labour.[70]

A stressed Bangladeshi woman spoke to a reporter as she waited for word of her brother and his friend who had set out on a boat journey, seeking employment in Malaysia. They ended up in Myanmar instead where Saiful Islam landed in jail, Bangladeshi police informed his sister, Mansura Begum.

The downside for the Bangladeshi migrants was obvious, should they survive the journey. Many of the jobs they end up in are dangerous, poorly paid and may even amount to forced labour or enslavement, as several reports on Thailand's fishing fleet have alleged. In April 2015, the EU issued Bangkok with a 'yellow card' [71] over standards in its fishing industry, carrying the threat of sanctions against hundreds of millions of euros of Thai seafood exports.

'Sailors contact the traffickers and the small boats get 40,000 per person. So that's 40,000 times 700, then the big trafficker gets 180,000 times 700...it's great business, a lot of money,' a trafficker who helped organize the movement told *The Times*.

Bangladeshis who risk all at sea are escaping not just poverty but a demographic bulge that has squeezed job opportunities and made their country one of the world's most densely populated.

While Bangladesh's fertility rate has fallen in recent years to 2.21 children per woman in 2012—compared with India's 2.50 and Pakistan's 3.26—it hosts 1,203 people per square kilometre, fifteen times more than in neighbouring Myanmar. At the same time, political upheaval in Bangladesh over the past few years has stalled previously buoyant foreign investment.

'The ASEAN countries are a tempting destination for Bangladeshis because of the historically high levels of migrant labour that have powered economic growth there—even if several of the states who have benefited have since been turning migrant boats away.'[72]

Thus, the issues are far more complicated than are understood, certainly in India, but also in other parts of Southeast Asia where one would have thought that improved economic performance would have created greater social openness. This does not seem to be the case. Oversimplification and exaggeration have been driven especially by aggressive right-wing political parties in India which have seen opportunities for large, long-term voting gains among Hindus and retention of political power at different levels. This, tied to a noisy visual print media and troll-abundant social media, has made a major difference in the growth of political misunderstanding. The challenges are exacerbated and nuances completely glossed over.

In 2015, when hungry and desperate Bangladeshis and members of the Muslim minority Rohingya group from Myanmar turned up in Thai, Malaysian and Indonesian waters, the response they got was neither tepid nor welcome. It was downright hostile, even inhuman, as officials initially turned the boats away, triggering comparisons with the way refugees from Syria and Iraq were welcomed in Europe as they fled the pogroms of the Islamic State in those countries. Europe, especially Germany with its record in World War II, felt it had a moral and political responsibility to take care of the Syrian refugees.

In Southeast Asia, a photograph captured the image of emaciated men, women and children, looking more like figures from the dust bowl of a tragic African nation, their vessel adrift in Thai waters off the southern island of Koh Lipe. The photograph of Rohingyas, by Christophe Archambault of Agence France-Presse, captures the haunting fear on the faces of scores of people packed into the boat.

The great heave of migration has defined history, ecology, economy and national identity, as well as the sum of its parts. This has been seen time and again, and emphatically this past century, whether it's the partitions of the subcontinent (1947 and again 1971) or political refugees flooding safe havens in Europe as well as Southeast Asia, the tide of movement into the United States from Mexico and the Southern American nations or the flows that have ebbed and raced across Africa, both human-induced or by natural catastrophe such as drought and famine.

◆

But what of the others? What of their voice or voices? Are they more sinned against than sinning? I want to focus on the perception of those who feel they've been treated unfairly in their homeland. This is not a perception we see very often or that we are familiar with. So, in their own words, here are some voices. They reflect the view of many, perhaps not all—and it is important to pay heed to those who speak with moderate words and tones especially in light of the extreme radicalism that has reared its head in Bangladesh.

In 2016, a series of killings by radicalized young Muslims brought the growing threat within Bangladesh to the attention of the world and sent alarm bells ringing through the border states of Assam and West Bengal. In those incidents, the number of diners at a restaurant (a majority of whom were Italians and Japanese, but included one Indian girl and two courageous young Bangladeshis), raised the level of security concerns within that country as well as a heightened sense of alert nearby.

This is a long-burning issue and needs to be considered with logic, sensitivity and understanding especially in places like Assam, other parts of the Northeast as well as West Bengal. A heightened sense of grievance, stoked by anger over discrimination, poverty, lack of opportunities and a feeling of oppression, could also fuel such fires on the Indian side. But more of this later.

Shalim Ahmed, who is doing his PhD at Jamia Millia Islamia, is from a char or small island on the Brahmaputra. His home is in Goalpara district where his family has lived for generations, at least since the turn of the last century when, first, the British encouraged settlement by people from East Bengal to clear the wastelands and develop agriculture. And later the Muslim League under Sir Syed Muhammad Saadulla, premier of Assam, urged more influx in an effort to change the demographic and political composition of the state so that the League could dominate substantial pockets.[73] Subsequently, Gopinath Bordoloi, Saadulla's bête noire and Congress leader, along with stalwarts in the party, thwarted a British plan to pull Assam into a constitutional abyss: the proposal by the Cabinet Mission Plan of Sir Stafford Cripps sought to link Assam to Bengal, create a Muslim majority province which could force Assam into Pakistan. As we have seen, the plan fell through because Bordoloi was supported strongly by Mahatma Gandhi, who helped the rebellious Assam party stand up to Nehru and Patel.[74]

Stout and kind-faced, with a hesitant smile, Shalim helps out with occasional teaching and assignments in the English Department at Jamia. He shared his concerns and perspectives in frank and moving words:

> When our ancestors arrived in Assam in the late nineteenth and early twentieth century, they settled in the char-chaporis (riverine islands and river banks) and were called charuwa (residents of the chars) or pamua (settler). A small (though significant in numbers) portion of these people climbed the social ladder over time and settled permanently in villages away from the chars, thus invalidating the terms 'charuwa' and 'pamua'. Not all of us are from Mymensingh: thus, the now outdated word Mymensinghia doesn't define the entire community. So what do we call ourselves then? If and only if it is impossible for us to be known simply as Indians or Assamese let us be called 'Miya'. The difference between Miya and Bangladeshi must be clearly demarcated.

The word itself comes from the street. In other parts of India, 'Miya' is a polite, respectable form of address but in Assam it is a derogatory term used for a specific community—Assamese Muslims of Bengal origin.

> 'Miya' is a matrix within which fall descendants of people who migrated from Tangail, Pabna, Mymensingh, Dhaka and other districts of present-day Bangladesh. However, there is a class angle to the equation too. An educated Bengal-origin Assamese Muslim who also speaks Assamese might be able to camouflage his 'Miyaness'.
>
> Since I am university educated and speak decent Assamese, I might not be called a Miya, at least until I make it explicit. My cousin, on the other hand, who drives a cycle-rickshaw in Guwahati, will always be one. My class privilege might immunize me from the feelings of disgust reserved for my cousin.

◆

The poet Khabir Ahmed wrote in 1985, two years after Nellie:

> I beg to state that
> I am a settler,
> a detestable *Miya*.
> Whatever be the case,
> my name is Ramzan Ali, or Majid Miya
> Subject: I am an Assamese Asomiya.[75]

But even that narrative is changing. In May 2016, when I visited Nellie, I talked with a young, tired-looking man on the main road to Bhagduba Habi village. Farukh Hussain spoke of moving to Thrissur in Kerala, where he said 'not less than 10,000' from Assam work in factories. Most of them are Muslims. Farukh worked as a machine operator in a factory in Thrissur for ten years. He came back to take charge of the family land as well as to get married. He now has a family and was on his way to the local moneylender to pay back his loans. 'He's a good man, he will get into trouble if we don't pay in time,' he remarked. But he says he is determined to return to Kerala. 'There's nothing here, we grow one crop, there aren't many good schools and we can't even spend a few rupees for them.'

In Kerala, the Assamese merge with a larger influx of other migrants into the coastal state on the edge of the Arabian Sea. There are, according to one estimate,[76] around 2.5 million (25 lakh) migrants in Kerala to deal with its labour gap. They are from all parts of the country, including Uttar Pradesh, West Bengal and Assam. And they're flowing in at the rate of 2.5 lakh every year. They go into all trades from carpentry and farming to plywood factories, hotels and beauty parlours, making up for the large outflow from the state to the Middle East since the 1970s.

Yet, even in Kerala, the nazar (gaze) of the insider towards the outsider is no longer the kindly, tolerant one of an earlier time. A growing crime rate in the country's most educated state has seen accusing fingers pointed at migrant groups instead of people regarding the cases as individual incidents. 'Local' groups are falling into an age-old trap that has impacted communities and individuals across the world, blaming outsiders for crimes and, in some cases, meting out punishment on their own terms.

In one well-known case,[77] a young Muslim of Bangla origin from Assam was accused of the sensational rape and murder of a young woman. In other cases, when Kerala police tracked alleged criminals and went to investigate or arrest them in their villages, over 1,500 kilometres away, they spoke of surprising but positive developments in the midst of grim stories. They also found, apart from their quarry, 'neat, well-tended toilets as in Kerala'.

The movement across India is part of a huge churning of migrants that the World Bank and the UNDP speak of—some 300 million people are on the move in this vast subcontinent of a nation, travelling by bus, train and ferry, on foot and by air, in searing summers, chilly winters and flooded monsoons, seeking new lives.

◆

If Upamanyu Hazarika's efforts marked one aspect of the quest to establish markers and definite spaces for the Assamese, the Government of Assam had opted for a slow yet seemingly more rigorous effort to establish or reject citizenship claims. This was the bid to upgrade and update the hoary National Register of Citizens of 1951, where technically, many of those who were long time residents of Assam could trace their ancestry through a parent or grandparent.

Many in Assam of Bengali descent, including those of antiquity and some more recent, know that their hopes of permanent citizenship and settlement in the state (and by extension India) are riding on the findings of an elaborate exercise run by a quick-talking, efficient official of the Assam government and his huge team of surveyors, data analysts and officials.

Since 2013, Prateek Hajela and his unit have designed, developed and implemented what is called the revision of the National Register of Citizens, which is regarded as the country's most authentic record of citizenship. The NRC, as it is simply known, is to be found in every state and certifies the ancestry of the generations of those born after Independence in the country. It provides the names, ages and origins of those who were residing in India that year in each state. Generations trace their heritage to that document.

Bowing to the orders of the Supreme Court, which ruled on the need to untangle a legal mess and authenticate the ancestry of those living in Assam and hence qualifying their 'Indianness' or citizenship, the Assam government under Tarun Gogoi, then chief minister, began this vast exercise.

Hajela, the man picked for the job, had been a deputy commissioner of Nagaon and mission director of the National Rural Health Mission. From 2014 onwards, he and his team worked on designing a process that would be foolproof and withstand both judicial and political scrutiny as well as allegations of bias. They developed an original idea to define the basis of citizenship or claims to citizenship: each applicant had to provide a family tree.[78] The legacy data depended on people submitting any one of fourteen documents which would then be scrutinized 'where name of self or ancestor appears (to prove residence in Assam up to midnight of 24 March 1971)'[79]. In addition, another document was required should the name on the first list be of a forebear and the applicant. This should, the NRC office said, establish the connection between the purported ancestor and the applicant and worked through software developed specifically for the purpose. The key date was 24 March 1971, which marked the brutal army crackdown in East Pakistan by West Pakistan and its Bangla collaborators that drove an estimated nine million refugees into India. The viciousness of the violence was such that it snuffed out, according to one estimate, at least half a million lives[80] while hundreds and thousands of women were raped.[81]

At one point, in addition to a small core team in Guwahati, Hajela's data enumerators, who were trained by Wipro, the vast software corporation based in Bengaluru which also developed the software, were nothing short of an army. He described them as nearly 10,000 data operators on local contracts provided by Wipro, and a large number of part-time Assam government staff. 'You need an official to do that final check,' he said,[82] it could not be left to enumerators, no matter how capable.

In a separate interview,[83] Hajela, who was officially designated as the state coordinator for the NRC exercise, said:

> Out of 38 lakh people who visited [the NRC Seva Kendras] up to May 21, 34.5 lakh have got their names in lists. The success rate is 91%. 40.19 lakh legacy data codes have been issued online (all voter lists till March 24, 1971 and the 1951 NRC are called legacy data). That is about 75 lakh in all who have already got their records. It's very reasonable [to expect] that the other 9% can get any of the other documents like land records. Even today electoral rolls do not contain the names of everybody.

Hajela also clarified that those who probably did not have full documentation were 'in all likelihood those who have originally been staying here for hundreds of years. They may not have bothered to keep documents' but others who had come since 1971 were cautious and likely to have substantive documentation of their presence. This, of course, was not a closed deal for it does not necessarily work this way. Many who have cultivated the habit of gathering sheaves of documents include those whose relatives were slaughtered at Nellie and they say that a number of them go back to pre-Independence days, some as far back as 1938.

The number crunchers who have sifted through millions of documents relating to residents of Assam 'are being scanned, digitised and the data cleansed. People on those lists and their verified descendants will be recognised as Indian citizens'.

He also said that the entire population of the state has been covered in the exercise, with a total of 68.21 lakh (6.821 million) families applying for inclusion in the updated NRC, involving around 3.27 crore (32.7 million) persons with 6.67 crore (66.7 million) documents submitted. The task of NRC update is 'mammoth' with the verification works involving unprecedented volumes of physical verification, computerization and digitization.

Hajela added that '4.94 crore (49.4 million) documents out of targeted 5.96 crore (59.6 million) documents have already been verified. The documents verification process adopted is the first of its kind wherein all documents are being verified through comparison with the original records/ backend available with the issuing authorities.'

When the draft revised by NRC was published towards the end of 2016, the BJP-led government of Sarbananda Sonowal was expected to brace itself for an outcry and agitation from those left out. The goal was to ensure that the relief and satisfaction felt by a vast majority whose documents were in order would counter the opposition. Hajela was clear that there could not be discrimination on the basis of religion. 'It would support those who were innocent' and work against those who had come since 1971.

Another problem was that not all electoral lists were available because under existing laws, old lists were usually scrapped every six years and replaced by new, revised ones. However, because of the tripartite 1985 Assam Accord between the All Assam Students Union (AASU), the state government and the centre which set the cut-off date for deportations at 1971, many of these documents remained in the possession of the government.

Deportation, Hajela agreed, remained a challenge that had not been sorted out. It was also the call of the central government, not of the state, for it could adversely affect bilateral relations with Dhaka and India is keen to continue its collaboration with that country on security and economic matters as these directly impact the Northeast and the rest of the country, including sensitive states like West Bengal, a recipient of labour outflows from Bangladesh.

But like a good bureaucrat, he fended off the question. After all, it was not the NRC's responsibility. Its goal was singular and simple: to finalize the citizenship of people of Assam. Deletion from electoral lists, detection, displacement and deportation—these would be left to other agencies. He stressed that while the officers and government at every level of the state government were implementers of the project, their role halted at a particular constitutional wall—where the centre took over as a protector of the state and its people, whether it was in terms of citizenship or deportation.

What this has basically meant is that despite the huge exercise, little could really be done to push out 'Bangladeshis', post 1971. No matter how angrily the Supreme Court's justices ruled or how charged up the BJP rhetoric was, a simple fact remained—as it has for nearly fifty years: Bangladesh won't accept anyone who is pushed across the border as an 'infiltrator' or Bangladeshi by the Indians unless there are substantive documents to prove that charge. Until that changes—and it is most unlikely to happen—India and especially Assam will have to live with the troubled legacy of the 1971 war with Pakistan. The most that could happen is the distribution of those identified as post-1971 migrants to other parts of India. But another question then arises: which state would accept them with open arms? The answer probably would be a negative one: none.

The NRC data is to be published, I hear, in December 2017 and may cause a fresh upsurge in Assam. It is not possible to cover this development just as I haven't addressed the Rohingya developments in India because these are taking place as the book is being printed.

Additionally, there's a problem of definition. This was well described by the Japanese scholar Makiko Kimura in her detailed study of the Nellie massacre:

> I noticed that the top student leaders used the word 'foreigner' to denote the target of their political mobilization. However, local student leaders used the terms 'minority' and 'Muslim' while in rural areas such as Nellie, people often used the term Miyas or Mymensinghias. It is important to see the transformation of the terms—how the local leaders—usually located in the smaller towns—as well as the villagers in the rural areas interpreted the movement and the violence.[84]

While the 'Bangladeshi' issue, as much as anything else, has become Assam's defining problem and a larger 'Indian' issue, there is another which pits the state's small nationalisms against its bigger ones. And it leapt out of an agreement that was aimed at ending one set of agitations. This was the Assam Accord of 1985 between the state government, the anti-immigrant agitators and the centre which set down a list of goals that were aimed at bringing growth, stability and peace to the state. One of the clauses was constitutional protection for the 'Assamese' people, to provide them political assurance. For over thirty years, government after government, group after group, one well-meaning negotiator after another has tried to undo the Gordian knot of defining who is Assamese. Each effort has ended in failure. There is much opposition to the concept of a homogenous Assamese identity that would seek to assimilate smaller tribal, linguistic and religious groups into it. Thus, it appears that while the definition of an Indian in Assam may be completed during the NRC update, defining who is an Assamese may take longer as it appears to be far more complex to unravel than the making of a simple Indian citizen.

◆

The warning signals from Bangladesh are clear. Matters are not going to be helped by naïve statements by the government saying that building better fences would keep pro-jihadists out as would tracking such elements from the Bangladesh fringe. What many tend to forget is the challenge within India's borders, within the system, especially in vulnerable areas across Assam and other states. Muslims and other religious groups whose feelings of hurt and frustrations have been exacerbated over the decades, can be tapped by those who believe in a militant brand of justice, justifying extreme acts of violence. Such feelings find fertile soil in vulnerable areas such as middle and lower Assam where populations are large, poverty is high, a sense of grievance and non-realization of dreams is palpable and bitterness at being left out, of being turned upon, of continuous neglect and discrimination, is growing.

The sense of victimhood is writ large on the Muslim groups of Bangla origin. That, in my view, makes for a potentially dangerous especially in an area awash in illegal weapons situation. That it hasn't happened so far is not reason for the state to be complacent. It cannot react with a sense of hysteria—as is evidenced in the responses of West Bengal and Assam which claimed to have 'sealed' their borders after the Dhaka murders in July 2016 by young radicalized Bangladeshis from middle class and wealthy families. Nor should it respond with overkill.

It is unacceptable that some advocate driving migrants out by force. Others have urged for an end to the non-lethal use of force on the India-Bangladesh border. As I have argued earlier, that is advocating a militaristic solution for what is essentially a tragedy of the human condition, a problem caused by a complex mesh of economic, social and political crises. And let's not forget that many of the people living along the border on our side of the boundary are more likely than not to be Indian. They may be Muslims of Bangla origin but they are Indians.

Such campaigns could not only result in confrontation but even to bloodshed in the future. It would go beyond deepening suspicions and hatreds, leading to a sharper radicalization of both younger and older Muslims who feel alienated and outraged by the assaults they face on a regular basis. In a strange way, this sense of alienation and anger is something that those from the Northeast can surely empathize with since many with 'non-Indian' looks and oriental features find themselves the butt of an ugly joke, the object or subject of racist abuse, nasty behaviour and discrimination elsewhere in the country.

To me it is surprising that the obvious danger in the reaction to persistent prejudiced conduct does not seem to be understood by leaders or even the intellectuals and others of Assam. It's staring us in the face and yet we refuse to see it. It reminds me of what we in the region have often complained of—New Delhi's 'ostrich approach' to the issue of migration, of burying its head in the sand when an uncomfortable issue is raised or difficult conditions persist. And here we are doing exactly the same thing!

Although the Rohingya issue is beyond the scope of this book, it is a good example of how pushing a community to the wall sharpens radicalization and push back—in Myanmar there is now an armed insurrection driven by Islamic rebels. It's taken nearly a half century to get there—but it has come.

Greater armed force from the state, more surveillance and sharper policing can be part of an overall approach. However, that larger perspective has to include the following: energized, improved health and education processes and policies (Assam has the worst maternal mortality ratio in India despite many innovative and robust efforts). There would also need to be creation of jobs and up-skilling of livelihoods.

Ideas can't be blocked by walls or fences. Nor can the government's shutting down of social media sites and banning angry voices of preachers and their followers help. If the engagement with such ideas is to happen positively, the following need prioritization: ensuring service delivery, better education, creation of jobs and a clearer understanding of the world around us. In such a situation, improved security measures would be relevant but not as stand-alone measures.

◆

In Bhagduba Habi, many still live with their memories, unwilling to rouse the angers and fears of the past. The past is closed, one wizened man says. Another doesn't agree: he lost his wife, his children and a brother in the killings. 'Of course I remember them every day, who would not, their images haunt me.' And they still haven't received compensation, leave alone justice.[85]

Yet to me it seemed that the survivors and their progeny felt that some things were best left undisturbed. It's part of the knife-edge that communities in Assam and elsewhere in the Northeast often walk every day to avoid conflict and harm.

The graves by the edge of the flooded fields bear testimony to this approach. Nearby, men and women worked furiously to save their rice crops and dry them in a weak sun.

Memories don't die. They fade away as a younger generation, overcoming the fears of the past, seeking to leave behind the sting of mistrust, ventures to the other end of the country, to Thrissur in Kerala, to find work and peace.

It's not easy, reflected Farukh, as he talked on the narrow broken mud road leading to Nellie. 'The railway ticket collectors want to see our documents all the time, they're from north India, they're hefty fellows, not like us, you feel scared of them.' Then there are the police who keep wanting more and more identity cards until the passengers pay them off, he said.

But he wanted to leave, perhaps with his family. He would first go back to Thrissur. He had to repay some debts here. After that, he would migrate: 'There's nothing here for us anymore.'

Chapter 7

A WANDERING HORSE, UPLAND AND BORDER STATES, A PRINCE AND A COMMUNIST

Legend has it that it was the wandering of a horse that led to the foundation of one of the most religiously influential and politically sensitive monasteries to straddle the Himalayan saddle between India and China.

The story goes that in the latter half of the seventeenth century, the fifth Dalai Lama of Tibet dispatched one of his faithful followers, a man called Mera Lama or Lodre Gyatso, to set up a large monastery in the region. To get away from the troubles caused by rival Buddhist factions, the monk entered a time of meditation.

It was during this period of acute reflection that his steed went on a walkabout. When the monk came out of his trance, he went in search of the elusive horse and found it grazing at a particular spot. Taking this as a divine signal, Lodre Gyatso decided to locate his monastery there.

The full name of the monastery is Tawang (Ta means horse and wang is defined as chosen) Galdan Namgye Lhatse or Paradise Celestial Divine. Accounts of the time say that the Dalai Lama gave the monastery a religious painting, the manuals of rules for lamas and deputed a learned monk as the abbot, with two monastic officials as his aides or stewards. The dzongpen or governor of Tsona in Southern Tibet was directed to supply provisions. Tawang was connected to the Drepung monastery and the practice of the Dalai Lama selecting the abbots continued till 1951.

The year is important because that is the time that Tawang officially became a part of India. Therein hangs another tale, involving a young and energetic Naga officer from Manipur and a zealous Assam governor keen to expand the frontiers of a young nation-state.

In *The North-East Frontier of India*,[1] Alexander MacKenzie, administrator and historian, wrote of the influence that Lhasa, capital of Tibet (which he referred to as Thibet and to Lhasa as Lassa), wielded over Tawang. Referring to the Bhutanese (Bhutia) chiefs who controlled trade to Assam, he said:

'they were the subordinates of the Towang Raja, a tributary of Lassa'.[2] The Towang Raja was also known as the Deb Raja or Towang Deo.

The British, with their penchant for lines and boundaries, placed a frontier on the map that defined the territory of the Tawang Raja:

> In 1872–73 the boundary between Assam and the Towang Bhutias was formally laid down from the Deosham river to the west to the Rowta river on the east. The line proposed by the British officers was readily accepted by the Bhutias and by certain Thibetan officials who came down to inspect it.[3]

Thus, if we are to believe Mackenzie, who is regarded as one of the major documenters of Assam and its neighbourhood during the colonial era, a boundary was actually developed and given sanction at the time which placed Tawang outside the official map of India. However, he is quick to elaborate that only 'certain' Tibetan officials accepted the boundary without saying if the higher Tibetan authorities were also in consonance. But those Tibetan officials who helped with defining the border were dressed in monk-like robes and 'appeared' to be men of consequence, according to a British official, Major Graham. It was Graham who proceeded to create the new border along with these four men. However, their significance emerges in another description where they are spoken of as having come from Lhasa on 'a tour of inspection', underlining the Tibetan view of the area as part of its southern periphery. They were able to conduct the boundary delineation because the local population of the Monpa tribe accepted their overlordship.[4]

The area was also defined as follows by F. W. Bailey, who was part of the British armed intervention of 1904 into Tibet: 'Mönyul [sic] is the comparatively low-lying district of Tibet which is governed by the Lamas of Tawang.'[5] Bailey was no ordinary British babu but one of its most widely travelled explorers and administrators who spoke Tibetan fluently and put his name on the history of that area: it was he and another colleague who, through an arduous trek, officially confirmed that the Yarlung Tsangpo and the Brahmaputra were the same river.

In his paper titled *The Centenary of the McMahon Line (1914–2014) and the Status of Monyul until 1951–2*, Lobsang Tenpa writes that the policy veered towards expansionism from the British side, worried as it was about growing Russian influence in Asia, the emerging role of China and the possibility that the latter could not only directly influence Bhutan but also make a thrust into the Bengal plains through the easily accessible trade route between Bhutan and the Tawang area. There are references to Miri, which according to Tenpa, stands for 'the rest of Arunachal Pradesh region, excluding the districts of Tawang and West Kameng'.[6]

Hence, a line was proposed to be drawn that would flow directly east of the northern point of the Bhutan border with Tibet. The main reason for securing the northern border, including the key post of Monyul, was to ensure the strategic protection of British India's commercial interests in Tibet, Bhutan and Assam.

A North East Frontier Tract was established with the Balipara Tract covering Tawang and the Sela sub-agency looking after the affairs of Kameng. A small Assam Rifles post kept an eye on the situation. This tract of land was regarded as strategic for the Indians, the Tibetans and the Chinese.[7]

Despite the reorganization of the Tawang area under the British, at the time of Independence, Monyul was not under the direct control of the Indian government. It remained under the de facto rule of Tibetan ecclesiastics appointed by the Dalai Lama and, in the words of one Indian official about whom we shall hear shortly, for he is responsible for bringing what is now known as Arunachal Pradesh into the Union of India, one very obstinate treasurer. This Tibetan probably controlled the collection of taxes from local subjects and their dispatch to the Tibetan treasury. The officer, Ralenglao Khathing, a Tangkhul Naga of Manipur, was to note that 'the Nyertsang or Accountant of the monastery, who is Deputy from Lhasa may become the only thorn in the administration of the monastery in future [and notes that] he is cunning and well informed'.[8]

The trigger for a proactive Indian approach into the area was the Chinese military takeover or 'liberation' of Tibet in 1950 which prompted the Government of India to advise the Assam government to incorporate the Balipara and Sela region into the Union.

While there are various accounts of who actually authorized the takeover of Tawang, what is clear is that Khathing led the march under instructions of the Assam governor, Jairamdas Daulatram. The latter, in turn, had been so advised by the home ministry in New Delhi. Khathing, who served in the Assam Regiment, was known to the British simply as Bob since they found his first name such a tongue twister. After Independence, he joined the Assam Rifles and served in the Balipara tracts before being appointed assistant political officer based at Sadiya, which had been crushed by the 1950 earthquake.

Khathing was ordered[9] to march to Tawang with 200 troops from the Assam Rifles. They were later joined by a large unit of porters to carry food, supplies, fuel, weapons and ammunition. The march began on 17 January 1951 and after a halt at Dirang Dzong[10] where they were received by a Tibetan officer (who obviously did not oppose their entry), on 26 January, the first anniversary of India adopting a republican constitution, Khathing hoisted the Indian flag. He went on to make brief stops at Chakupru, Sela Pass (one of his daughters is named after the pass) and Jang before reaching Tawang on 7 February.

A show of arms ensured that the reluctant monks and elders agreed to meet with Khathing who told them in no uncertain terms that the days of Tibetan control were over. An order was issued saying that the people of the area were no longer to follow the dictates of Tibetan officials or edicts issued from Lhasa.

A new order had begun but there were still some glitches.

Neeru Nanda, who served extensively in Arunachal Pradesh and has a deep affection for the area and its people, has written fascinatingly about Khathing's role in Tawang's entry into India. One of the stories she told me is one of the most delightful and also perhaps among the least known.

After Khathing's arrival, the elders of Tawang observed the working of the new administration quietly for some time. One day, Khathing found a delegation wanting to see him. 'What is the problem?' the alarmed officer asked. Well, the leader said, while they liked the work of the new government there was something that they couldn't quite understand. Khathing was getting more uneasy. 'What is it?' he demanded.

The response was simple: you don't levy taxes.

Khathing almost burst with relief. He drew himself up to his full height and launched into an oration about India's great democracy and how it didn't exploit others. The delegation listened patiently.

And then they responded, Nanda said, with a riposte that left him speechless:

> After he had delivered his sermon, they folded their hands, again bowed before him and said, 'Well, sahib, all this is very good. But the villager is illiterate, foolish and ignorant. He will not understand a government that abstains from taxation—so even if it is a very petty amount, you must take a tax.'

A system of house-tax was instituted with each household paying ₹5 annually to the government.

That's the other story of how Tawang came to be part of India, part of the legend of Bob Khathing who went on to become chief secretary of Manipur and Indian ambassador to Burma. It's a sore point for China, which is never a good loser on the political, legal or military front.

There's another reason why Tawang is important to the Tibetans: it's the birthplace of the sixth Dalai Lama. Thus, an invisible but unbreakable bond exists despite the Khathing intervention.

◆

Today, Tawang's—and Arunachal Pradesh's—connectedness to India is unchallenged, except by China. In 1987, provoking outrage and tirades from Beijing, Prime Minister Rajiv Gandhi conferred statehood on Arunachal. Refusing to recognize it as part of India, Chinese maps still show the state as Southern Tibet while defining it in international discussions as 'disputed territory'.

The following year, the two countries were in an eyeball to eyeball confrontation with some 400,000 troops mobilized on either side after a Chinese intervention and occupation of a strategic site. Ultimately, the tension abated but it showed how raw the issue was on both sides and how easily a standoff between two nuclear powers could be provoked. The difficulties between the sides surface in different ways.

For example, when Indians from Arunachal Pradesh seek Chinese visas, they're not rebuffed, just treated as non-Indians. The Chinese Embassy in India issues visas not on their passports but on separate sheets of paper, which both the individuals as well as the Indian government refuse to recognize. It's at best an irritant—though it could be worse.

Despite China's refusal to acknowledge the physical existence of Arunachal in India, it's a hefty chunk of territory, difficult to ignore as it sprawls over mountains, valleys and forests sweeping across 83,743 square kilometres, the largest state of the Northeastern region (second is Assam with 78,438 square kilometres) and one-third of the area of the entire Northeast (262,230 square kilometres).

The population is tiny compared to its vastness, a bare 1.38 million, or one-fortieth (2.5 per cent) of the total population of the eight states of the region. To make things more complicated, there are over twenty-six major tribes and numerous smaller ones. Each tribe takes fierce pride in its own culture, dialect, dress, social structure and traditions. There are accounts of polygamy among some tribes, and they follow a range of Hindu, Buddhist and animist beliefs, the latter known as the Donyi-Polo who follow a blend of what appears to be Bible preaching with congregations holding holy books and the Vaishnavism popularized in Assam by Srimanta

Sankaradeva. The main ethnic groups include Monpas, Sherdukpens, Apatani, Wanchos, Noctes, Tangsas, Singphos, Khamptis, Mishmis, Mijis, Galos, Padams, Miwongs, Tagins and Puroiks.[11]

Arunachal still springs surprises: one tribe, the Koro, was discovered recently in the tradition of the good old eighteenth- and nineteenth-century foreign explorer.

A *National Geographic* team of scientists, officials and cameramen with their support staff plunged through deep jungles, forded rough rivers and climbed hills to reach the settlement of the tribe of 1,000 persons, one of the smallest language groups in the world.

Thus, even as changes have begun to visibly alter the urban settings and lifestyles of people, especially of younger Arunachalis, there are still hidden stories to be unearthed and discoveries to be made, a bit in the nature of the fabled Beyul or the hidden paradise of Tibet, somewhere in the caves, forests and mountains of the Tsangpo.

As a burst of modernity hits the towns and rural communities hard, with many younger people from villages moving to the growing urban centres, new issues are confronting the land which Bob Khathing brought into the Indian Union and which the brilliant and sensitive anthropologist Verrier Elwin wrote about perceptively in his policy papers which Nehru accepted and sanctioned as official policy. Elwin and Nehru both saw the need to protect and ensure that the remote hill tribes were able to develop at their own pace without being pressured by more powerful groups or even the government which may seek a different way.

Nehru[12] was to declare unambiguously in his foreword to Elwin's classic *A Philosophy for NEFA* (North East Frontier Agency as Arunachal was known till its formation as a union territory in 1972 with a new name), that he felt:

> ...alarmed when I see—not only in this country but in other great countries too—how anxious people are to shape others according to their own image or likeness, and to impose on them their particular way to living. We are welcome to our way of living, but why impose it on others? This applies equally to national and international fields. In fact, there would be more peace in the world if people were to desist from imposing their way of living on other people and countries.

But then, Nehru being Nehru, there was always a need to introduce a bit of confusion and ambiguity to what he had just said. So he added:

I am not at all sure which is the better way of living, the tribal or our own. In some respects I am quite certain theirs is better. Therefore, it is grossly presumptuous on our part to approach them with an air of superiority, to tell them how to behave or what to do and what not to do. There is no point in trying to make of them a second-rate copy of ourselves.

Elwin,[13] a British-born scholar and social scientist who took Indian citizenship after Independence, was far more prescient. Talking about what he had learnt from Gandhi and his experiments with truth, Elwin spoke of how the father of the Indian Independence movement avoided luxurious and unnecessary innovations, and concentrated everything on a few fundamental and essential needs. Yet another lesson was the importance of the 'individual'.

He added, bluntly:

> The tribal folk are not 'specimens' or 'cases'; they are *people*; they are human beings exactly like ourselves in all fundamental ways. We are part of them and they are part of us; there is no difference. They live under special conditions; they have developed along certain special lines; they have their own outlook and ways of doing things. But the ultimate human needs, aspirations, loves and fears are exactly the same as ours.

To Elwin this was not a classroom subject or a theory to push but a deep and passionately held belief which he followed rigorously in his own life and professional work while he also sought to bring political figures, government babus and others, including his own peers and colleagues in the world of anthropology (although several resisted his ideas fiercely), into his sphere of influence.

Elwin may have been prescient but even he probably did not anticipate how swiftly those changes would come as young and older Arunachalis embraced power and wealth with energy and enthusiasm, especially as New Delhi, in the 1980s and 1990s, leaving behind the Nehruvian legacy, hurled cash, projects and politics, not necessarily in that order, into the state. Part of it stemmed from India's disastrous defeat at the hands of the Chinese in 1962 and the need to strengthen connections to the centre.

The events of 1962 meant many things: apart from destroying Nehru and his visions of a greater Indian role in international affairs, it provoked the government to act on a number of fronts. For one, it triggered the founding of the Indo-Tibetan Border Police Force (ITBP), which included some of the Khampa guerrillas who had fought so bravely against the Chinese in Tibet, increasing the size of the Special Security Bureau (SSB), which the intrepid Bob Khathing had founded to keep an eye on the border but also if necessary to do a hop, step and jump into Tibet to check what the Chinese were up to. The army presence was beefed up and more Assam Rifles posts were set up. Of course, the eye in the sky these days makes physical presence—and risk—less necessary.

A people and a region in hibernation went into fast-forward mode, new townships came up, Hindi became the state language, and the first cabinet under P. K. Thungon as the chief elected member of the union territory took over the administration as the first generation of graduates began exercising political and official muscle in the state.

In the space of a few decades, Arunachal became known as a place of unstable politics with entire governments and their party followers leaping overnight to new parties, just to retain power or capture it. In the process, communities which had not known anything beyond a barter economy became owners of motorcycles, then fancy SUVs, and posh homes with the latest fittings and furniture.

A slow stream of infrastructure projects began to take shape with numerous helicopter landing strips and short landing grounds for aircraft (though, as we have seen, even in the twenty-first century places like Gelling were supplied essential goods by Indian Air Force helicopter sorties), roads linking remote villages to the 'mainland' and to each other, encouraging the Ramakrishna Mission and the Rashtriya Swayamsevak Sangh to work in the area with schools and training centres. Bridges across the Siang (earlier known as the Dibang) were built and then came the game changer, the mother of all moneymaking projects—hydropower dams were conceived and starting coming up.

Vast monies changed hands, impacting not just the fortunes of an elite but the lifestyles of many inside and outside the state. In Dibrugarh, a clutch of private medical centres sprang up paying special and highly profitable attention to patients from neighbouring Arunachal. Communities and individuals who had lived by the sanction of community traditions and laws laid down by village heads became extremely litigious, discovering the joys and horrors of the Indian Code of Criminal Procedure, the Indian Penal Code and other legal facilities. The beneficiaries, an Assamese lawyer once told me in Tinsukia, were lawyers like him and his colleagues in the smaller townships who were able to advise litigants on the intricacies of the law.

Corruption grew rapidly. Gegong Apang, the chief minister, found

himself arrested for organizing a racket of fake receipts for providing supplies
to remote outposts by creating fictitious accounts of porters and suppliers
who did not exist and goods that were never delivered. The investigating
unit described it as a ₹1,000 crore fraud[14] in the state's public distribution
system (PDS). The chief minister was produced initially before a court in
Lakhimpur, Assam, as some of the illegalities had taken place in Assam,
involving business figures in the state. Apang, a friendly and garrulous man,
had been chief minister for twenty-five years.

Arunachal's political instability became legendary after years of one-man,
one-party dominance when three chief ministers were ousted and replaced
in 2016, two in the space of a few days, thanks to the machinations of both
the BJP and the Congress. One of the discards, Kaliko Phul, ended up dead
soon after he was tossed out of office, apparently having committed suicide.

But it was during Gegong Apang's time that the dam gold rush began.

By 2009, Arunachal Pradesh had signed 153 memorandums of
understanding (MoUs) to generate over 43,000 megawatts of electricity,
pushing aside environmental concerns and the risks posed by clustering
dams. Six dams, for instance, were proposed on the Lohit, a tributary of
the Brahmaputra.

The omnipresence of the Chinese remained: when the World Bank in
Washington planned to be involved in the financing of the dam sector, it
was told by the Chinese representative at the institution in no uncertain
terms that Arunachal Pradesh was a disputed area and Beijing was totally
opposed to the bank's role. The organization was told to back off.

Both the Indian and the Chinese approaches to water underscored
the economist Kenneth Boulding's amusing ode to the most vital resource
on earth:

> Water is far from a simple commodity
> Water's a sociological oddity
> Water's a pasture for science to forage in
> Water's a mark of our dubious origin
> Water's a link with a distant futurity
> Water's a symbol of ritual purity
> Water is politics, water's religion
> Water is just about anyone's pigeon
> Water is frightening, water's endearing
> Water's a lot more than mere engineering
> Water is tragical, water is comical
> Water is far from the Pure Economical.[15]

Tragic or comical, economic or political, Boulding, like a traditional economist, left out ecosystems in his effort at poetry, though this is hardly surprising seeing his paper was written over half a century ago when environmental concerns were not a top priority nor were global warming or climate change.

Years after announcements were made on a range of giant, large and intermediate projects, work on many is yet to take off. In 2015, the then chief minister, Nabam Tuki, said that the state had signed pacts with power developers to execute 160 projects with a total capacity of 46,948 megawatts. Tuki said directions had been given to power developers to start work but admitted that several MoUs and memorandums of association had 'been cancelled'.

This was hardly unexpected since many of the MoUs had been rushed through without going through a detailed project report process or a rigorous environmental impact assessment and transparent public hearings; many hearings were arbitrarily adjourned, postponed or cancelled when public resentment began to show and local officials and dam builders were discomfited by questions they faced.

A senior officer from a government power corporation told me in Shillong that the private companies were being asked to pay money up front to politicians in Arunachal Pradesh. Such a state of tension obviously could not last. Ten years after that conversation, many of the major players had withdrawn from their commitments.

The bubble may not have burst but it was leaking badly. 'The frenetic rush, it seems, is over with private companies that had earlier queued up to build dams in the state losing interest and asking the public sector National Hydel Power Corporation (NHPC) to take over their projects', wrote Azera Praveena Rahman in the *Third Pole*[16] (Tibet and the Himalayas are regarded as the greatest reservoirs of fresh water in the world after the two better known poles), an independent web-based environmental news site which looks at developments in the Himalayan region.

A senior official of the NHPC told the reporter: 'Private companies have approached us to take over their projects or work in association (with them) on their hydel power projects. Their main concern is that they now don't see these projects as cost-effective, and therefore want to pull out.'

The official pointed out that the focus was on two projects (out of the scores once tom-tommed), 'a 1,400 megawatt project in Tawang and a 2,000 megawatt project in Subansiri.' The Subansiri project has drawn huge public flak and anger among environmentalists as well as the media and the Assam government, who regard it as an unacceptable intervention that will harm farming, ecosystems and drainage downstream. Groups like the Krishak Mukti Sangram Samiti, which leads a pro-peasant movement, and its allies blocked the transportation of large turbines for the Lower Subansiri project by stalling the movement of ferries carrying the equipment docked at Tezpur port. The fears of catastrophic floods in the event of an earthquake, which could trigger dam collapses, are real.

Thus, according to the *Third Pole*, Jindal Power Limited which had three large projects that were supposed to generate about 5,500 megawatts of power, now says that it is looking at 'prudent avenues of association to unlock shareholder value' or simply, a way to get out of this mess.

Other groups say that lack of roads and power, frequent protests and regulatory hurdles have delayed projects. Constant delays have led to cost overruns, reducing the attractiveness of the dams.

◆

In January 2016, a tipping point came. After years of sullen and angry protests in both Assam and Arunachal, Buddhist monks were mobilized by one of their own and joined by members of the public in a large demonstration of anger against plans to build thirteen large dams in the Tawang area. The incidents shed light both on the arbitrary nature of the Indian state, the local administration and power merchants.

The demonstrators said the proposed dams would irreparably devastate Tawang's unique environmental, cultural and strategic location. There were already twenty-five small and mini hydropower projects in the district; if these were run efficiently, there would be no need for big dams. This is clearly not something to the liking of the power and money lobby. Would they care about the future of the highly endangered snow leopard or clouded leopard, the red panda or the mountain goat? Would they bother about the impact on the Manas National Park, recovering from years of abuse and brutality inflicted by Bodo and other militants?

There were other reasons for public resentment: about one quarter of the entire district is under the control of the army and security forces. Another quarter, according to the journalist Urmi Bhattacharjee,[17] is with the civil administration. The population did not want to lose any more land to major infrastructure projects that were seen to benefit the elite.

On 2 May 2016, the unthinkable happened.

Two men, including a Buddhist monk, were shot dead in police firing on an agitated crowd which had surrounded the local police station, calling for the release of their leader, Lama Lobsang Gyatso. The police apparently panicked and opened fire.

Gyatso is the main force behind the Save Mon Region Federation (SMRF) which is protesting the dam projects. He was earlier arrested on charges that had nothing to do with the anti-dam movement but everything to do with monastery politics: questioning the nationality of the head abbot of Tawang monastery. Gyatso was released after the firing. He later said that he had never insulted the religious elder, only underlined that since the latter was from Bhutan 'he would not understand the sentiments of the local people and hence should stay out of the dam issue'. Guru Tulku Rimpoche, as the revered abbot is addressed, had banned the monks from participating in the agitation, the rebel monk declared.

It was the first time in the half century after the 1962 India–China war that the hills around Tawang had heard the crackle of gunfire. To add insult to injury, the army was called out to 'restore' law and order after the local superintendent of police had been suspended, a move that angered the town's citizens even more. Many harked back to the 1962 war and Bob Khathing's historic march into Tawang.

Jaideep Mazumdar, who writes for *Swarajya*, noted that it was 'incumbent for the Arunachal government to sit with bodies like the SMRF and take their concerns into account'[18] while resolving the issue.

The BJP threw its weight behind the agitation, especially after the firing. The party 'wants to make it tough for Khandu [Dorjee Khandu was chief minister from 2007–2011] in his hometown of Tawang'[19] especially as it was 'still smarting from Khandu's U-turn', when he switched from a BJP-backed government in Arunachal to the Congress.

This brings to light an interesting aspect of what otherwise could have been just a simple environmental issue. A senior Indian government official based in Shillong, who investigates major cases of fraud and illegality, said that the confrontation in Tawang owed much to the late Dorjee Khandu, when he was chief minister.

Khandu, a Monpa tribe legislator who was elected from the area and professed to be a devout Buddhist, died in a helicopter crash while flying from Tawang to the state capital of Itanagar. The officer said that Khandu had pushed hard to garner support for the hydel projects.[20] When he died, his eldest son Pema—who succeeded him as the local MLA and then five years later as chief minister—along with another sibling and cousin controlled the three legislative posts from the district and wielded enormous clout. The anti-dam lobby was running up against them as well and had a formidable task before it, one in which it was unlikely to succeed and certainly was unlikely to get any political support from the government.

The official,[21] who did not want to be identified, said that divisions in the Tawang monk body were a fallout of the tussle between Gyatso and the Rimpoche, a direct appointee of the Dalai Lama. The Rimpoche left his post to take shelter in distant Dharamsala, the headquarters of the Dalai Lama and of the Tibetan government-in-exile.

The protests in Tawang have encouraged activists across not just Arunachal but the entire Northeast to ratchet up their agitations.

Ankush Saikia, the novelist from Shillong, points out in an essay that huge funds pouring in from New Delhi, arrogant developers and ambitious politicians made for a lethal mix. In the process, Saikia stressed repeatedly in his piece, much tension grew unnecessarily since local communities were offended at the outset by being shut out of development plans. He also had heard that NGOs were being paid to disrupt projects: a senior scientist told him that 'some NGOs involved with the anti-dam lobby were taking money from groups that wanted to block hydel projects. He told us about how the hearing for the Lower Siang project around four years ago was disrupted by people from the Upper Siang valley.'[22]

I'm sure that this cuts both ways: the pro-dam groups are paid to strut their stuff; those opposing them, frankly, have little access to the funds of their foes but can smartly court and mobilize media and publicity, if not local public opinion.

Saikia is quick to point out that hopes of a boom in generation and hence improved financial capacity are likely to be belied: only about twenty of the 150-odd projects are likely to see the light of day. Of these, barely five, mostly run by private players, are on track.

New Delhi's planners want to develop Arunachal Pradesh so that it provides the national power grid with an unending flow of energy, feeding the hunger of industry and burgeoning urban demands. The gigawatts of power that the nation state demands from its distant resource pool, which still is known for its greenery and rich ecosystems, can transform Arunachal into the kind of hellish dump that Itanagar has turned into, a wreck of a town that looks as if it has been transported or transplanted from any small size city in the north Indian plains.

◆

The Tawang incident involving the activist monks raises the larger issues of development, energy, public inclusion or exclusion in these processes by state actors and the politics that play out, often harming—as in the case of armed movements and agitations which seek to represent public grievances, real or otherwise—those in whose name they claim to speak. This pattern is repeated ad nauseam across India and South Asia. It raises questions on the rules of engagement and disengagement, of dialogue between the state and other stakeholders and of the role of organized civil society groups as well as the media. For it is the latter, during these days of a swiftly interconnected globe that carries news rapidly—correctly or otherwise—in nanoseconds from laptop to mobile and into millions of hands, homes and minds in a vast array of languages, penetrating divergent cultures and geographies.

What is clear is that in the situation that has existed in Arunachal Pradesh, confrontation and disruption of society and life will grow if formal and informal and transparent dialogue does not. The face-off between those who seek to 'develop' and others who oppose or want a more rational and low-key approach, the two conflicting lobbies, can become far worse and more menacing than the insurgency troubles in the two eastern border districts of Changlang and Lohit where the National Socialist Council of Nagalim's different factions have bases and units, moving between Myanmar and India as well as extorting from officials, professionals and others.

The manufacture of political consent on an issue such as the large dams is not acceptable, especially when it is done by such obviously fraudulent means as public hearings where people are barred from entering or speaking. Such attempts will lead to acute disruptions even by men of the cloth, who are deeply frustrated by the failure of local administrators and the state government to address the core issue of heeding public voices and understanding their angst. It cannot be done by suppression or by undermining popular movements by trying to buy them off or brush them aside. It will be not just divisive but downright dangerous in a highly sensitive border state that is disputed, at least in the eyes of China, and sought after by both Asian giants.

I have focused at length on this issue for to me it is one of the most crucial facing Arunachal Pradesh, on which hinges its future. Although I find myself often in considerable disagreement with some radicals on the issue of dams, I am at one with groups, individuals and demands that seek inclusion of ordinary people, of their voices, communities and representatives in the process of decision-making. Those who have no voice—sentient beings or the creatures of the wild, in the air, of the mountains, forests, waters and below earth—their survival and future must also be taken into account while decisions are made. Our earth is not just for one species,

the human, which has been around for a few million years and has been
the most dominant, dreaded and malignant species to inhabit our globe,
destroying other species at will and often without reason, barring greed
and ego, if these can be called reasons at all.

What is important in places like Arunachal is the need to have a kind
of early warning system in the political sense, as exists in the case of a
hurricane or a tsunami. Each district needs to have a grievance redressal
mechanism which may be headed by the top administrative official such as
the deputy commissioner, with representatives of different political groups
and community organizations.

Such redressal units need to have a list of the main environmental/
political/social issues in the area and an understanding of where different
groups stand on these. Dialogue partners need to be identified along with
common spaces and themes and sub-themes of engagement. These need to
be worked out at the local levels through the existing panchayats but also
using representative, robust, civil movement groups. Once a problem—such
as that in Tawang—is identified as building up, the process of engagement
needs to be activated so that dialogue and peacemakers take the lead, not
troublemakers and confrontation, which benefit none.

An area which I foresee could trigger such tensions is the plan to
build major four-lane highways across the valleys of the state, connecting
one part to the other, a good idea but not only hugely expensive but also
ecologically potentially as disastrous as the interlinking of rivers. Given
the gargantuan size of the project, it also has the potential to generate
vast levels of corruption and malfeasance at every level in a state that is
already known for a welter of corruption scandals. It would be better to
build short landing strips and invest in small flights that can carry people
at low cost to their destinations (this is a project that international or
bilateral funders could consider supporting) while well-maintained (which
the current ones are far from being) two-lane highways could carry large
consignments up the hills.

The need for such a group was driven home when the first train to
Arunachal Pradesh was launched with much fanfare from Dekargaon in
Assam to Naharlagun, a short distance from the capital of Itanagar. Within
a month, the train was cancelled after strident opposition from student and
other groups who said that the service would enable 'outsiders' to flood the
state. The railways later said that only passengers with reservations would be
allowed on the train, an effort to control in-migration and placate local fears
about hundreds of people descending on the place without the mandatory

Inner Line Permits (ILPs), which allow 'outsiders' to live, work and travel in specific areas. Two more lines are proposed, including one to Tawang.

Such confrontations are avoidable for they are also predictable in such situations. The centre could have seen this coming if it had simply studied the situation over a period of time. In many such situations, it's simply a question of better preparedness linked to common sense.

◆

It's better to improve what we have instead of launching ambitious projects that would lead to endless corruption, delays, frustration, growing anger and confrontation and massive destruction of irreplaceable species. We have no right to do that.

The creation of such incubation and dialogue units would also reduce the possibilities of political instability, which only helps those who are inimical to the state's interests. I can think of only one country that is interested in such conditions and it lies on the other side of the Himalayas from our country.

That is why the early warning units or grievance redressal cells or dialogue partner groups—call them what you will—that I have spoken of can become a key to ensuring that the crackling tension is not just reduced but converted to positive gain. Ill will can be banished and goodwill can grow only if we do away with the ham-handed, corrupt and ill-conceived process of manufactured consent. Win-win can then be more than a cliché, it can be the way to conduct sensible politics and good governance, involving communities and giving ordinary people a sense that their voices count, that their opinion matters.

It would be barefoot democracy at work. We can have barefoot doctors, activists and engineers without borders. Why not barefoot democratic engineers, who would also be developing social engineering by bringing organized dialogue and debate to the grassroots? Not the confrontationist brigades but dialogue makers? This is entirely possible given the seriousness with which numerous civil society groups and scholars lead research and conduct fieldwork in the region. That number is growing, although whether it is growing fast enough is a question. There are more institutions on the ground in academia as well as out of it but these need to be more robust as well as reflective, involving local communities. There are opportunities here since growing numbers of younger people from rural areas are moving to urban spaces, enrolling in colleges and universities. In the process, they come under different and at times contradictory pressures which accompany such movements into urban areas in the twenty-first century. Thus, ethnic associations such as tribe-specific student bodies may seek solidarity on issues that impact local culture, politics and livelihoods such as some of those we have outlined as well as individual ones, such as more jobs, hostels and scholarships for specific groups. The state government and politicians may exert pressure on ethnic-based organizations to follow a particular line with the promise of economic opportunities. Then there's the challenge of preparing communities for the future. Part of this lies in what former president A. P. J. Abdul Kalam once described as 'ignited minds'. But those minds would need to be ignited by good preparation and life experiences which will enable them to play a constructive role for the dialogues that can bridge the challenges which have been outlined.

This is where education and especially the out-migration from Arunachal to other states of the country and its metros can have a huge beneficial impact. Much also depends on the experiences they face in the metros and outside the state. The kind of racial discrimination faced by people from the Northeast often triggers the wrong responses, as we have seen. That is why it is so critical for the process of engagement and dialogue to move out of official systems—the government can't handle these non-formal processes, the nature of the state is not designed to cope with it with flexibility or speed. This is again where those who have been trained or studied outside their own areas can have a crucial role in preparing for such a task as well as the social and educational institutions where they have been housed.

Universities may be the playground of ideas but they are also laboratories of experiences that shape lives and careers. New centres for Northeastern studies are coming up in colleges and universities. Instead of just focusing on the region's history, traditions, rights, conflicts and governance, they need to focus also on first building understanding of divisions which fracture the region and designing networks that can bridge those divides. The new cross-cutting papers at the master's level at central universities offered in the social sciences and in history can create space for such multidisciplinary approaches by designing a paper specifically related to these issues of social tension, cohesion and change.

The issues and history of the region must find space in the history, political science, sociology and social work departments of universities so that younger people from other parts of India begin to 'know' the area better as well as vice versa. It's sixty plus years late although brief teaching about the area exists in school curricula at the central level.

The gap is huge at the college and university levels and that is where 'ignited' minds can take off, not in incendiary but constructive ways. It is not that these will be full-time dialogue makers or partners but those who have gone through such nurturing can become resource persons who may be in different professions but can be called upon to play a calming role in difficult conditions. Right now, this is a huge gap with too much dependence placed on governments or a few ethnic associations. The depth and bandwidth of such organizations needs to grow. Such a directory of persons trained in dialogue would be a huge resource base for each state and the region as well as New Delhi.

The state and its networks need to understand that national security can be better assured by enabling such a process, not opposing it directly or through underhand strategies. That's a tougher call, knowing New Delhi's suspicion of activities on the borders and in a border region. It is easier to be suspicious than to be open, especially if the approach is security driven. Arunachal's political and social stability as well as those of 'national interest' mesh and merge at every point in this distant border state.

It may not be the Elwinian dream of helping the tribes to move at their own pace but it would certainly be better than the current aggressive nightmare that is tearing societies apart.

Chapter 8

A LOST KINGDOM, A PLATEAU AND THE PLAINS: WATER, WORDS, WILL

The drive from Bagdogra airport in the steaming plains of north Bengal to Gangtok—a stretch of about 125 kilometres—takes anything between four to six hours. The extra one or two hours depends on how bad the two-lane road is at critical places with popular names like 9th Mile[1] or 29th Mile, which are characterized by sinking land, large landsides and rock avalanches. Things are not made any easier by the occasional earthquakes that jolt the countryside or the vast traffic jams that torment travellers as they inch through the new Jalpaiguri-Siliguri corridor leading to the hills.

The road is bumpy for much of the way and my last visit during the writing of this book was during a very wet July in 2016. In the dry season, dust and vehicle emissions make some stretches extremely trying. During the July trip, when it rained incessantly, friends warned us about being stranded and worse with horrendous tales of travellers being stuck overnight as a result of roads caving in or landslides, cars being crushed by falling debris or hit by a rock and toppling into the Teesta below. Luckily, we came through unscathed, although there were several points on the return journey where vehicles slowed and stopped for long periods.

This is the highway to Sikkim that is supposed to be part of the Look East/Act East Policy that is to take trade in a range of products to Tibet and back. Most of the vehicles appear to be modified SUVs and buses carrying tightly packed passengers who appear, for the most part, to be 'local' travellers. There are goods vehicles but not too many of them.

There's also a helicopter service from Bagdogra, which the Sikkimese novelist Prajwal Prajuly cheerfully recommends. He is probably a far braver person than I am, especially when it comes to trusting rusty flying machines. The government-run helicopters, owned and operated by Pawan Hans, have had a bad safety record and a history of crashes in the region including at least one in Arunachal Pradesh that killed a chief minister, and another in Meghalaya which took the lives of an opposition legislator and others.

It is not just the state of the roads which is troubling but the fate of a great river that runs beside it. With dam after dam, the roar of the mighty Teesta has been subdued to a whisper. Large stretches of the river, as one drives to Gangtok, are still and stagnant. In the dry months, it shrivels to barely a trickle below the dams and can easily be forded by car or on foot except when the engineers release the waters held behind the cement wall. What happens to those dependent on the river in the plains below, in West Bengal and Bangladesh, their livelihoods, what happens to the fish populations and the farms and those who ply their livelihoods by boat? What happens to the beautiful Gangetic dolphins, the xihus or sishus—how will they survive without food?

And all because politicians, engineers and bureaucrats have decided that the Teesta and its sister, the Rangit (which incidentally is sacred to many Sikkimese), must be dammed to produce electricity. No fewer than twenty-six dams have been built or are being constructed or are proposed to be built. They will produce a large amount of electricity for both urban and rural users, largely for industrial use. But few surveys exist of their cumulative impact downstream on crops, farms, lives and livelihoods as the nutrients are cleansed from the river water where tens of millions of people lived. On the one hand, the projects seek to improve living conditions. On the other, they ruin ecosystems of millions of silent creatures while also snatching the livelihoods and incomes of those on farms and river-dependents without giving them an alternative. This is neither equitable nor just nor sustainable. And it's also contradictory because several of the lower dams are in the territory of West Bengal which stands to lose the most in this process.

I wrote about this in anger as a friend and I drove by the Teesta in March 2016:

> The Teesta is dead
> Killed with rocks and dynamite
> Killed by cement and brick
> The winds howl no more
> Thundering down its valley
> Instead a simpering sad whisper
> Touches a leaf or two of the dusty dried up trees
> Lining the hills
> Looking down in tired despair…

Will you take to arms, my friends
Or even raise your arms, and wave the flags
Of protest...?

The Teesta's death won't make it
To the front pages or dear Arnab's news hour
Because it's only a river after all
And a river has no voice...

But do you?

Yet, let's remember Sept 2011
Here, my friends,
The earth shrugged
Hills collapsed, houses fell
Trees crashed, roads broke
The earth split, people died.
So maybe you won't need to take to arms
Or raise them
For all it needs is
For the earth to shrug once more.

It doesn't make economic sense for a government to put all its eggs in the hydro basket. Of course, Sikkim does commendable work on homestays, tourism, including treks and climbing, and has started organic farming to cash in on a niche product and niche markets. The latter have a long way to go although Sikkim tourism has established itself not just on the Indian but also the world market with references in *Condé Nast Traveller* and other major travel and fashion magazines. But for nature to be seen as a source of resources to be extracted and commodified militates against any sense of sustainability and reflects only short-term gain.

The brilliant scientist Jayanta Bandyopadhyay of the Indian Institute of Management at Kharagpur, near Kolkata, has been regularly calling for the need for solutions based on good environmental science to resolve the issue of floods. He correctly brushes aside the 'natural disaster' syndrome that politicians and policymakers as well as many activists jump upon to explain flood disasters every year. Bandyopadhyay is a gruff-spoken man with twinkling eyes and an encyclopedic knowledge about rivers and water resources that is as intimidating as it is vast. As far back as 2008, he noted that while the summer months of the monsoon bring 80 per cent of India's rainfall, rivers carrying huge amounts of water, energy and sediment need space and time to stabilize themselves.[2]

He then proceeds to underscore that our knowledge of science, hydrology and geomorphology is limited. What Bandyopadhyay and other experts like Chandan Mahanta of the Indian Institute of Technology in Guwahati are saying is that we're rushing into physical interventions in sensitive zones like the Himalayas without knowing enough about the terrain in which we are treading.

Bangopadhyaya remarks:

> Owing to unexplained governmental reservations on disclosing detailed data on these rivers, related river research has not been taken up in the public domain. It will not be unfair to say that the management of these rivers is going on without much contact with the advances in interdisciplinary knowledge on river systems made in the recent decades.[3]

In other words, the water data of the rivers flowing down from the Himalayas is a classified secret (for what earthly reason no one has divined nor, of course, have the Government of India and the mandarins of its Ministry of Water Resources bothered to explain). Scholars and professionals don't have access to such data and hence can only extrapolate on the basis of what they know in limited detail. This is not the basis for either good research or teaching and certainly not policymaking. Nor is it a sound foundation for reporting. Bandyopadhyay posits that interventions are taking place without coordinating relevant information that has developed in several fora, spanning borders and valleys. All this is pointing to human-induced catastrophes on a significant scale. But is anyone listening?

The Sikkim government apparently is unlike those in Uttarakhand, Uttar Pradesh and Arunachal Pradesh which have bulldozed expert panels and environmental groups opposing large storage dams. In 2008, Gangtok cancelled four hydropower projects on the Teesta after relentless opposition by Buddhist monks and public bodies led by the Concerned Citizens of Sikkim (CCS), which had resisted the plans since its formation in 1995. The CCS decided to continue its opposition to the remaining dams although it said it 'applauded and welcomed' the government decision on the four dams. A scholar said that the anti-hydel projects in the state underlined 'the reassertion of Lepcha and Bhutia (tribal) identity in Sikkim', an issue that had been buried for nearly forty years after the merger of Sikkim, an independent kingdom ruled by a Bhutia-Lepcha elite, which looked to India for defence and direction in foreign policy.

Till 1975, Sikkim was not part of India but a protectorate, governed by a monarchy which was over 300 years old and whose territory once reached into the Chumbi Valley of Tibet. In the 1960s, it was the stuff of fairy-tale romance when Hope Cooke, a nineteen-year-old New York debutante, met and fell in love with the chogyal (the title of the kingdom's ruler). A couple of decades later, Cooke left Sikkim and her husband, unable to deal with scheming opponents, as her king lost his kingdom to a vicious campaign by politicians determined to grab power and New Delhi's unrelenting drive to control, capture and absorb the kingdom, using every possible subterfuge from crude censorship and simple snooping to intimidation and physical force.

What I have found amazing is the silence on Sikkim. Another aspect that surprises me is the lack of books by Sikkimese authors which have gone into this period in any detail. Yet there is a robust literary tradition in fiction and poetry, which is showcased in the small but enterprising and energetic Converse series of gatherings every year in Gangtok, organized by local poets and writers. And there's the delightful Rachna Book Store, owned by Raman Shrestha, which is at the heart of all such activity, with music, song, readings, interactions and coffee. Later in the evenings of Converse gatherings, whisky, wine and food flow as generous, talkative hosts and guests mingle.

Although the silence on political issues is not new, it is only a matter of time before a Sikkim writer gives us a powerful narrative of his land's story and the year before and after it was embraced by India.

◆

On 15 May 1975, Sikkim became a state of India, shedding (or was it disrobed?) its protectorate status, and its earlier nomenclature of a Himalayan kingdom. Little is known in the public realm about how it happened although there are academic tomes on its society and culture.

The late B. G. Verghese, a great editor and scholar, called the event an 'annexation'—he lost his job at the *Hindustan Times* after writing stinging editorials on the subject, attacking New Delhi for betraying a smaller neighbour.

Perhaps absorption would have been a better word? 'The worst suspicions about the manner in which the protector has reduced its helpless and inoffensive ward, with some genuine and much synthetic drama, will now find confirmation,' the editorial on 30 August 1974, titled 'Kanchenjunga, here we come', blazed. To say that it was not annexation would be 'self-deception and compound dishonesty with folly'.

There are two major books on Sikkim, the first was by the editor and columnist Sunanda K. Datta-Ray, whose *Smash and Grab: Annexation of Sikkim* reads like a thriller. Datta-Ray saw the action from up close and was a correspondent for two influential newspapers, *The Statesman* in India and *The Observer* in London. His views are slanted in favour of the chogyal and *Smash and Grab* came close to being banned. The book disappeared from the market when its author and publisher were slapped with a defamation case. But decades later, Datta-Ray came out with a new edition which should be recommended reading for every student and faculty of history and political science, for every Member of Parliament and the state assembly of Sikkim and the other states of the region.

The other book which places before us a larger canvas and a compelling, encompassing narrative is *Requiem for a Himalayan Kingdom*, by the British journalist Andrew Duff,[4] who tries to balance India's strategic and political concerns with the deep anxieties and compulsions faced by the last royal ruler, Thondup Namgyal, chogyal of Sikkim. Duff traces his interest in Sikkim to a colonial connection—a beloved set of grandparents who travelled there.

By the time Duff got around to publishing his 380-page tome, the Sikkim of the chogyal, Hope Cooke, Datta-Ray, Kazi Lendhup Dorji and his wife, the Kazini, and their assorted relatives, advisers, supporters and opponents, including brusque Indian officials and diplomats, had vanished. In its place is a robust state, under the rule of a farmer's son, Pawan Chamling, whose Sikkim Democratic Front has won five consecutive elections, increased the per capita income of his small population, ensured high qualities of health, connectivity and education with national-level universities like Manipal springing up along with five-star resorts where stars like Richard Gere visit, a network of hotels and restaurants in the overcrowded but spankingly clean capital of Gangtok which are a huge draw for chattering tourists from the plains as well as not so well-heeled international hikers and travellers.

There's a garland of guest houses and spartan but well-designed resorts in distant valleys and hills, adding to the allure of the place. There's a central university and a young population, energetic and bustling along its streets and markets.

How Sikkim's world has changed in the past forty years is seen through the eyes of my friend and veteran journalist Tarun Basu who waxed ecstatically about a visit where he dived deep into Gangtok away from the clamour, filth and rush of daily city life in India.

Gangtok's development is a surprise, especially since one was coming here after some decades. The streets are clean and litter-free (littering invites deterrent fines), traffic is organised and disciplined (overtaking during peak hours on narrow hill roads also invites heavy fines of up to ₹5,000) and the well-planned city centre with its pedestrian walkways, well maintained over bridges and tubular connectors, a nearly kilometre-long tiled pedestrian shopping plaza, bisected by fountains, flowering plants and benches, makes one feel one is in some Southeast Asian city, not India. Gangtok Municipal Corporation is one civic body that seems to be doing its work, quite unlike slothful municipalities in the rest of the country.[5]

Then he strikes a sore point for Sikkim and one which resonates in many other parts of the Northeast—why is a state that appears to run quite efficiently and has a number of distinctions to its credit, including being an organic state and home to the cleanest hill station (Gangtok), 'so little known and talked about?'

In New Delhi, people even ask if Sikkim is part of India and in many parts of the country a Sikkimese is looked upon as a foreigner. A recent article in Sikkim Express, written by a local commentator, Jiwan Rai, summed up the angst of the Sikkimese:

It would be interesting to know how much the rest of India knows about us. How much interest or concern do we generate in the domain of public communication in mainstream India?

Only when an earthquake hits hard enough to crumble a few buildings is a little more visible nationally. That's Sikkim in India.

All those who visit do is chatter and walk about the mall, pack its clean streets and overwhelm its little shops, restaurants, monasteries and other spaces which have become part of the tourist trail. It's a quick getaway for people in the sweltering Bengal plains or the Assam Valley nearby and summertime is full of loud visitors, a phenomenon that the quiet Sikkimese are getting used to but obviously do not enjoy.

Yet basic challenges remain for India's least populous state, with its mountainous, landlocked geography which makes agriculture (only 11 per cent of its 7,000 square kilometres land area is available for cultivation), transportation and communication tough.

Yet devolution of power is significant and visible, including gender equality with women—50 per cent of panchayat seats are reserved for women—taking leadership roles in panchayats which spend 70 per cent of the rural development budget. Survival for Himalayan states like Sikkim and Arunachal revolves around water and the access that people have to it. The management of water and its easy availability—or lack of it—will determine the future of political players, their parties and governments.

Joydeep Gupta, South Asia Director of *The Third Pole*, the environmental magazine, says one specialist points out that while hydropower potential in the countries that shared the Hindu Kush Himalayas and the rivers that flowed down from this range totalled 500 gigawatts, 'the electricity flows from the mountains to plains without providing commensurate benefits to the people who live in the mountains'.[6]

'These benefits have to go beyond compensation (for displacement) and mitigation,' the expert, Aditi Mukherji,[7] says. Mukherji is with the International Centre for Integrated Water Mountain Development (ICIMOD) in Kathmandu which surveys the entire Himalayan range from west and east. All the countries which abut the Himalayas are members of ICIMOD.

Studies in Uttarakhand in India and Nepal showed that though there are laws that compel hydropower developers to pay compensation for any damage, this money usually ends up in the government treasury rather than benefiting the affected population. But conditions were different in Nepal, although it was wracked by seemingly incessant political instability and at least one decade of a brutal civil war.

Mukherji said that the difference was caused by village development committees which negotiated most of the benefits with project developers. Unlike in other countries, the central government did not enter the picture.

'Our experience is that in Nepal communities feel far more empowered; in India communities feel powerless,' Mukherji said. A new Uttarakhand law, which says the compensation paid by hydropower developers should go directly to panchayats, could be the way to go—not through the muscle power and financial clout exercised by private players.

◆

The past always intrudes into the present here and elsewhere in the Northeast.

Some years back, during a wet September, I had gone trekking in Sikkim in the Barsey Rhododendron Sanctuary. From Gangtok, we travelled in a sturdy jeep on a narrow but smooth country road, moving towards hills crowned by forests. Where the road ended, we walked through plantations of giant cardamom (Sikkim's prime commercial crop), shadowed by high trees, to a homestay.

It was spectacularly beautiful. While chatting with a guide, I remarked on four things: one, the country road we had been on was in remarkably good shape even during the monsoons, unlike many hill roads in Assam, Manipur and Nagaland which assume a state of collapse after the first fierce burst of rains. Two, there were cobbled village paths leading to homesteads at 6,000 feet and later, as I discovered, even at 11,000 feet. Three, there was electricity; four, running water.

This was an extraordinary achievement for any state, especially a Himalayan one with the huge challenges of connectivity mentioned earlier. A villager told me: 'The roads were originally built by the chogyal and his administration. By getting villagers and local people involved, people had a stake in these roads, that's one reason they were built well.'

They credited the current government of Chief Minister Pawan Chamling (as mentioned, he is now into his fifth consecutive term as head of government) with other benefits—electricity, drinking water and village paths. There was a basic point here, in the perception of that villager—that the foundations of good governance were laid by former royalty.

The chogyal would have been surprised by the view of his oldest and most relentless foe, Kazi Lendhup Dorji. In 1997, the kazi, who led the movement which overturned the monarchy, made the state a part of India and cost Verghese his job as editor of the *Hindustan Times*, made an astonishing turnaround. Perhaps frustrated and embittered at ninety-one, the old man declared that Sikkim should govern itself outside the framework of the Constitution of India and demanded that New Delhi 'immediately restore to us—the people of Sikkim—the status of "Protectorate State" guaranteed...by the India-Sikkim Treaty of 1950'.

◆

Humans can live for days, even weeks, without food. But few can survive more than five days without water. Less than 1 per cent of the world's fresh water supply is available to seven billion people. Most of the fresh water is locked in glaciers and ice while 97 per cent of the water available on earth is salt water, from the oceans and seas.

Climate change is bringing dramatic changes to life-sustaining resources like water in nation after nation, dismissing national borders with impunity. Private companies are 'privatizing' water by capturing water sources with their funds by creating what they call water banks; others give these groups a sharper and I believe a more accurate description of what they really are—'water mafia'.

The water mafia comes in all shapes and sizes; in places like New

Delhi and Mumbai, Hyderabad and Chennai, they own fleets of large and small water tankers which carry the precious commodity to affluent neighbourhoods and to poor slums. Everyone who wants water pays; some places have a fixed monthly rate for residents to pay for this private water supply because the local corporation or government supply system cannot meet basic needs. Of course, in addition to that, everyone still pays a water cess to the government for a service they don't get.

Before the 2016 monsoons, India's reservoirs—created by dams—had average water levels of 29 per cent while across southern and western India there were extensive reports of wells drying up in rural areas.

In places like Meghalaya and Assam, which receive large amounts of rain every year—this varies because of changing climate conditions but it's still far greater than what the rest of parched mainland India gets—small shiny red tankers holding 1,000-2,000 litres are a common sight in summer as they buzz busily up and down roads and through neighbourhoods. It's clearly a booming business and may be a tribute to private enterprise. But it's also a stinging indictment of the local government whose water supply department is funded both by the centre and local tax collections to deliver that very service.

A closer examination shows that power-broking, moneymaking, environment exploitation and traditional systems and processes are all caught up and bound together in this mesh. Otherwise, how else can one explain the fact that large parts of Shillong, which gets an annual average rainfall of about 2,167 centimetres (or just above 85 inches)[8] spread over the summer depend on frantic calls to water tanker companies?

In the 1980s, despite an intermittent conflict between Indian forces and the Mizo National Front, an intervention by the United Nations Development Programme saw the spread of water harvesting methods which captured rainwater through pipes and drums placed outside homes or in underground storage ponds under houses. A common sight, that of Mizo women and children balancing buckets and jerrycans on their heads or on homemade wooden sleds as they trudged wearily home, became a thing of the past. That image was replaced by large drums of reinforced plastic or PVC or in some cases cement which sprouted on rooftops or by the sides of the houses. Mizoram became one of the first states in India to develop access to drinking water and potable water for cooking, washing and bathing despite the geographical challenges of high hills and low-lying streams. It is not that the supply is adequate or even regular. A recent report that the Centre for North East Studies and Policy Research produced on drinking water and sanitation in Mizoram and Assam, based on pilot studies, indicated, for example that in one village poor electricity supply disrupted the pumping of water from a low-lying stream to large tanks on the hillside above the village. As a result, 'in Sangau village in Mizoram, for example, the villagers got only two hours of water per week, whereas the basic need of an individual is estimated at 40 lpcd [litres per capita per day] of water per day'.

Water harvesting is the natural, cost-effective way to handle water shortages—especially in a water-rich state like Meghalaya instead of investing in dams, which have become a scourge of the hills. A town like the Garo Hills capital of Tura, lush green in parts with cashew and coconut home gardens, need not depend on private water tankers or pump water up from polluted streams to fill empty household tanks. The heavy rains can be captured in large tanks on the hills at low cost. After filtration, it can be released at times of need using simple gravitational pressure to ponds in the town. The state government, district administration and autonomous district council need to develop a policy of encouraging every household to adopt a 'good green policy' of conserving water by storing it, as in Mizoram, by capturing rainwater and placing it in tanks and drums.

It is the basic failure of government to provide simple amenities that also encourages if not provokes public revolts against the state. But in Meghalaya, the seamless way in which power rests with a few among a few, elite within elite, is seen in the control of water sources.

Such sources are regarded as traditional common property of the village where it is located, with the headman—be it the rangbah shnong in the Khasi Hills, the doloi of the Jaintia or the nokma of the Garo—being overall in charge. The headman in turn picks a particular unit from the community which has specific responsibilities for ensuring against the misuse of the water source, either in terms of pollution or access. Today, although water points with pipelines to common bodies have been installed in a large number of villages, a study in the state showed that many of these were dysfunctional because the settlements lacked a maintenance engineer who could be easily trained for the job. Instead, they have to wait for days for a plumber or an engineer to come from the nearby large town or city to fix a problem that could have been resolved locally, quickly and cheaply.

But money power is bringing about sweeping changes in traditional systems and local governments. Thus, in the locality of Laban, in Shillong, where a stream flowed past homes located on hillsides, new houses have come up on the creek itself, killing it. In the event of a flash flood, a sudden storm or an earthquake, there's no prize for guessing what happens to these structures built on the most ecologically sensitive part of the small vales. The contestation is about water and who controls it. Thus, though Meghalaya is the only state to take a strong local initiative that has created a Meghalaya River Basin Authority and involved media, civil society groups as well as politicians, technicians and bureaucrats, money power in places like Shillong is still buying out water sources, often in connivance with local traditional bodies.

Natural resources and exploitation seem to go hand in hand, whether it's water or coal. In the Jaintia and Garo Hills of Meghalaya, coal has been far more in the news than water. Powerful barons like Vincent Pala, owe their provenance to coal. He rose from a petty government officer to coal mine owner and then rose through the local Congress Party to seize its parliamentary seat for Shillong. In the process, he became one of the wealthiest persons in the state, was appointed a minister of state for water resources (rather ironic, considering that the massive exploitation of coal had so polluted water sources and streams in the Jaintia Hills that the water turned lethally blue and undrinkable).

As a Member of Parliament, Pala, an elegant dresser and graceful talker, spoke equally warmly with visitors from New Delhi as with villagers from his constituency. He would send the latter away with some cash, usually a bundle of rupee notes. 'They expect it, they need it,' he said once when I dropped by his new home, which is the old residence of the director general of the Assam Rifles. The paramilitary had rented the mansion from the Ahmed family, one of whose members, Fakhruddin Ali, became president of India in 1974. Pala bought it off the Ahmeds although he has at least two other sprawling homes in Shillong.

In her inimitable, blistering style, the columnist and editor Patricia Mukhim of Shillong spoke of systems and communities that have been corrupted. Noting that land and resources were in the hands of a fraction of the population, Patricia bristled:

> Why is land today owned only by a handful of people? How did the process of land privatisation start?... What happened to the Khasi customary practice of community land ownership? That was how we ensured that every person who was starting a family was allocated a plot for a homestead (this included a home and kitchen garden for subsistence). Families were also allocated jhum plots by the village council.[9]

She approvingly quotes a member of the National Green Tribunal, Ranjan Chatterjee, that the Constitution—and not segments of it like the Sixth Schedule which is supposed to protect tribal rights—will be the deciding factor in issues of environmental management. The Sixth Schedule gives local councils power over local streams, water bodies, forests and roads but Chatterjee said that it cannot be used to conduct 'environmentally hazardous activities such as sand banking or reckless quarrying, mining, leasing out of rivers etc.' The Sixth Schedule, he noted, as well as other similar elements of the Constitution originally sought to protect hill groups from assumed predation of the Indian State and plains. But now, it's the powerful, the elite and 'the landed gentry among tribals that are the real predators conniving with (private) companies in land alienation. The elite tribal are doing harm to their less privileged brethren including poisoning of the Lunar and Lukha rivers in Jaintia Hills, from which they used to get their quota of fish,' said Patricia.

She added:

> The poor as a community are voiceless whether in the Dorbar[10] or with Government. It is the powerful (educated, middle class elite) within the community whose voice is heard. Now, whichever way we look, the poor are losing their resources. They have no land for farming or for a home, their water sources have gone into private hands, the rivers they use for washing, fishing and other human activities have turned toxic. The forests that supplied them with food have diminished. So what do the large majority of the poor in Meghalaya own? They own nothing. Sometime last year I had proposed that Meghalaya pass a legislation on land ceiling so that no one possesses too much land at the cost of others who the system has impoverished economically. An MLA, now in the opposition, said he agreed with me and we should start doing something. It ended with that.

Those in politics and positions of power may not agree with her. But the issue of natural resources and conflicts over their use, abuse and misuse appear to me to be the key drivers and pressure points which will erupt here and elsewhere. That is why I have chosen to focus on these questions, rather than on the usual law and order problems, the so-called 'conflicts', the extortion and brutalization of villagers. Armed groups can be dealt with by the might of the state and its uniformed praetorian guards. Ideas fomenting discontent and uprisings, nourished by ideologies of the left or right, can be handled through constitutional means and dialogue. But the challenges raised by water stress and degradation of environmental systems by poor management and thoughtless government interventions pose a far greater threat to our lives, the communities we love and the lands we treasure, than perhaps any other single reason.

We don't have to search very far to understand that forests and nature resources are centres of acute conflict which will shape political narratives in nations where these confrontations are playing out—places as far removed as the Niyamgiri Hills of Bastar, the Jaintia Hills of Meghalaya in India, the copper belt of Papua New Guinea, the coal mines of South Africa and Kentucky in the US. The Centre for International Forestry Research informs us that conflicts have remained significant in the forests of Colombia, Cote d'Ivoire (Ivory Coast), Democratic Republic of the Congo, Liberia, Mexico, Myanmar, Nepal, the Philippines, Solomon Islands and Uganda.

The Food and Agriculture Organization of the United Nations (FAO) noted in its State of the World's Forests report in 2016 that governments and stakeholders need to move with extreme caution and inclusiveness when changing laws that declassify forest lands to agricultural or industrial use. Citing a parliamentary commission which investigated the sanction of forty-two special purpose agricultural business leases in Papua New Guinea, it said that the lawmakers came to the conclusion that 'only four had proper landowner consent and viable agricultural projects. The remainder, or more than 90 per cent, was obtained through fraudulent or corrupt means.'

It would not be surprising if this was also the case in other parts of the 'underdeveloped' world. Yet governments are also waking up to the catastrophic results of unmitigated deforestation and corrupted forestry programmes. Some countries, the FAO reported, understand that 'innovative investments in forests can help achieve major policy and economic goals, such as mitigating climate change, combating land degradation, promoting landscape-scale restoration, enhancing the resilience of agriculture and providing additional incomes and jobs for local communities'.[11]

Page after page, the message was the same. There were two important caveats: implementation and inclusiveness. Without the former, good laws, resolutions, studies and intentions would remain toothless and on paper. Remote sensing is another effective tool to check assaults on natural resources.

Without an inclusive approach, which includes dialogues with different sides, common approaches to major concerns may not happen, leading to confrontations as in Tawang and elsewhere.

Effective implementation is the key. The FAO defined it in the following terms—adequate capacity for monitoring or mechanisms for reviews; use of 'institutional instruments' which were capable of detection and deterrence and of 'taking effective action against illegal activities'.

Ten years earlier, it had warned that since the government has long seen forests and their dwellers as of little political significance but of extractive value, these regions have been 'poorly integrated into national political processes and receive few public services'. It added that the dominant ethnic groups have marginalized indigenous and tribal units: 'Given the limited employment opportunities in many forested regions, taking up arms may seem like an attractive way to earn a living.'[12]

The institutional framework according to the 2016 statement must include not just the government departments if it was to legitimize national policies but must also work closely with civil society and the private sector. Dismissive of a bureaucratic approach, it laid down clear guidelines saying that officials must work with 'local communities, civil society organizations and responsible private-sector interests'.[13]

One can only remark here that the approaches of both the private sector and the government machinery, specifically in Meghalaya and in other parts of the Northeast, are far from this ideal outlined by the FAO. Indeed, the use of weapons and illegal arms networks and violent cadres from extremist groups has led to a surge in the poaching of the unique and endangered one-horned rhinoceros. The rhino is the state animal of Assam and deeply beloved in the Brahmaputra Valley. It's a large and easy target for smugglers who traffic in its horn (which is supposed to have aphrodisiac properties—scientists dismiss this belief as completely false because the horn is nothing but a mixture of nail and hair). But this falsehood doesn't stop poachers from running a hugely profitable business with connections across South and Southeast Asia.

A senior police officer described the operation. Hunters from Nagaland and Manipur would be taken to secure hideouts before being led into Kaziranga National Park:

> If they succeed in killing a rhino, they take a night bus to Dimapur where the horn is sold at ₹60-80 lakh. Moreh (the Manipuri town on the border with Myanmar) has also emerged as a hub for rhino horns in recent times. The horn reaches Myanmar via Nagaland and Manipur and is ultimately sold for ₹1-2 crore.

The rhino's vulnerability underlines the dangers facing species which are voiceless and depend on humans for their protection and survival. This vulnerability is shown in the vicious nexus between the illicit and the official: in 2016, police arrested a senior official in the Kaziranga National Park for conniving in poaching and revealed his connections to networks of local and larger gangs with international outreach.

Increasingly, poachers are using automatic assault rifles on the rhinos. Bullets are sprayed at them at close range and their horns hacked off while they are still alive—in some cases, they are mothers with calves—and are left to die, bleeding and groaning in pain.

The murder of such creatures and other sentient beings is not just condemnable but requires a fierce counter-assault by well-equipped state forces, backed by good technology—a battery of drones that can detect and help take out such individuals and groups of killers.

The very weapons used to kill the animals are used by non-state armed groups in their campaigns against government forces and both environmentalists and security officials say that cadres of various groups, including from the Karbi Anglong Hills are involved. So while the FAO report quoted by the Swedish scholar Bengt Karlsson is not far off the mark, it is no longer a question of turning to arms to combat an extractive state. As peace processes spread in the Northeast and armed groups which sign ceasefires are restricted to camps, criminal groups closely involved with other illicit networks are thriving

The insights of Karlsson into the situation are worth repeating. He has worked extensively in Meghalaya and who discusses the commodification of complex natural resources. In his seminal work, *Unruly Hills: Nature and Nation in India's Northeast*, Karlsson speaks of how the pressures on the environment can be a trigger of violence, why frontiers are important spaces to an intrusive and aggressive state, which is set on expanding its presence. The state as represented by the centre and various local elites in this case, arm themselves with a colonial exploitative mindset. In such a situation, what is the role of local groups as 'sustainable resource managers'[14], he asks.

This hypothesis is severely tested in another hard-scrabble area where politics, greed, poverty and vulnerability play out in the world of coal extraction in the Jaintia and Garo Hills. Driving to Cherrapunji, the place which has held the record for receiving the world's highest rainfall, or to Jowai and beyond, in the West Garo Hills district, can fill one repeatedly with a sense of acute despair combined with frustrated rage. Hillside after hillside has been carved into skeletal shapes, looming nightmarishly out of the mist or jutting out under a stark sun and blue sky; a tuft of a bush or a surviving tree sits in forlorn solitude on one side or top. Huge jagged gashes have stripped the hills and replaced forests of pine and temperate bushes with bare stone.

At the base of these violated hills rumble stone crushers and mining machinery, crushing millions of years of geography and history into rubble and dumping sand by the ton into waiting trucks, which then dash to Shillong, capital of this empire of greed. They head for the homes of the very elite that has destroyed them.

At the heart of the mining industry is coal—solid, black gold under the soil of the Jaintia and Garo Hills. Its attraction drew former members of ULFA from Assam to Meghalaya in their new role as businessmen, made ministers out of miners, employed tens of thousands, became a force that no political party or government in the state or the centre could ignore and created fortunes overnight for a large number of people. Countless others, including those who mined the coal, continued to live in penury and ill-health. The environment and water sources have been severely polluted. For decades, Meghalaya remained out of the ambit of national laws on safety, employment and health with these laws being flouted with impunity since both tribal systems and the autonomous district councils provide legal exemption to excavators. The Mines Act, 1952, prevents anyone less than eighteen years of age from being employed in these hazardous workplaces. Yet children, who researchers say are far younger, work these mines; they come from places as far away as Nepal and Bangladesh and also from Assam. Few in government care except when the media occasionally shines the light on these unacceptable practices and NGOs ratchet up the ante.

Children and young men squeeze into little openings in the face of the earth or walk up and down flimsy bamboo stairways into the bowels of the earth to dig, shovel and carry coal. During the making of a documentary on the condition of coal miners, filmmaker Chandrashekhar Reddy gained a stark insight into the lives of those who worked the mines: he passed out while filming inside a dark, unventilated 'rat-hole' coal pit.[15] Those he interviewed spoke casually of life and death: 'You need to leave the fear of death when you come to work down here,' one young Nepali migrant said.

The all-male workers, covered in grime, are paid ₹200 per person when they load a nine-ton truck per day (on a good day, a labourer can help load four or five trucks, making about ₹800–1,000 per day or up to three times the official daily wage rate in India, but they tempt death several times in doing so). They have no insurance or health cover or benefits and live in crammed and poorly ventilated dormitories.

The miners crawl through narrow tunnels to hack at seams some 10 to 60 metres below the surface, with minimal lighting and, as the filmmaker discovered, low oxygen levels. It's been this way for over 150 years, say local residents and miners, from the time the industry began, using local coal fuel demand and export to neighbouring Assam. The tipping point came in the 1970s when the coal belt was connected by highways to Assam which had just begun to develop a few industries as well as to other parts of the Northeast. Heavily loaded trucks, whining and groaning under the weight of coal, crawled their way up and down the hills; many frequently toppled because of overloading, bringing the busiest highway in the region to a standstill until cranes were called to lift them out of the way while a swarm of vehicles patiently waited.

Tony Marak was the principal chief conservator of forests for the state, a quiet, unassuming but clear-spoken man. He wrote:

What is happening here is a story that applies to all of India... We have problems with energy. We have problems with the economy. We have problems with coal mining and environment. We have problems with the government. We have been directed by the leaders of this state government not to look at any of this. They see it as a matter of survival. They tell us, 'Don't touch this.'

The trucks created unending traffic snarls, polluted towns like Shillong whose inhabitants once prided themselves on their spanking clean city, spewed venomous smoke, raised dust and made a lot of noise. But they also made some mine owners so rich, said the reporter, Keith Schneider, as to be able to send their children to Ivy League colleges in the US.

'By the 1980s many more large and deep box mines, and innumerable long tunnels, known as rat holes, formed three distinct coal mining districts— the Jaintia Hills east of Shillong, and the Garo and Khasi Hills west and south of Meghalaya's capital,' he wrote.

The method of rat-hole mining involves digging pits ranging from 5 to 100 square metres into the ground to reach the coal seam, noted the environmental magazine *Down to Earth*. Tunnels are then cut into the seam sideways to extract the coal.

Coal seams are reached by excavating the side edge of the hill slopes and then coal is extracted through a horizontal tunnel. The coal from the tunnel or pit is taken out and dumped on nearby un-mined area, from where it is carried to the larger dumping places near highways for its trade and transportation.

By 1980, the first major riots against 'outsiders' in the state had erupted in Shillong, which was under curfew at one point for nearly ninety days in a row. As migrants began to leave, new settlers took their place and also made homes elsewhere. Members of the Jaintia tribe were on their way to becoming famous across the Northeast for acquiring sudden wealth and stories abounded of their ability to buy land, homes and vehicles. A Maruti showroom owner told me in the 1990s about how a group of Jaintia men wearing flip-flops and looking rather the worse for wear had walked into the showroom. They told the owner they wanted a car each. When the man's face showed his disbelief, they opened a small bag they were carrying and showed it to him—bundles of currency notes. He was speechless. Of course, they couldn't walk away with the cars, there was a fair amount of paperwork to be done in those days when forms in triplicate were the norm. But they did take their cars in a day or two. They also took over buildings, stores and land in some of the most expensive parts of town.

It wasn't as if the quality of the coal was good. It wasn't. But it met a basic need and was cheap.

Schneider's account; though brief, paints a grim, stark picture about underground life in what he calls box mines. It is, he says, 'a fearsome sight', lunging '60 to 70 metres (197 to 230 feet) straight down to the coal seams at the black bottom'. It is 'an almost perfect square of dark, empty air measuring 10 by 10 metres (32 feet)'. And labourers just go straight down on rickety stretches of bamboo or wooden steps abutting each other in L-shapes, steps that become slimy and slippery in the long wet season, making walking and working riskier.

It sounds like an account straight out of hell. There have been many deaths in this process and the number of mines is unaccounted for: there hasn't been a complete estimate although there are said to be more than 5,000. What's worse is that since many of the labourers were not 'local' it didn't even become an issue for the state government or for many rights campaigners and others, barring one who made it her mission to publicize, shame and put pressure on the mine lobby.

Hasina Kharbhih, of an organization called Impulse, has worked for years with teams in the rat-holes of the state, drawing fury from the mining lobby for her statements about child labour and a utter silence for years from the state government which was tacitly if not implicitly involved in the racket. She says that children as young as five have worked these mines, that many have died and no one was bothered until Impulse began its campaign. However, her figures of 70,000 child workers in the mines were often dismissed as exaggerated and aimed at generating publicity for the issue as well as for her NGO, a charge she denies.

'Children have been dying in these rat holes and the dead bodies are not actually being taken back because it's not possible. There's no way they can get them out. And they are not being reported because in the context of our state, they're illegal migrants,' says Kharbhih,[16] who is always cheerful despite the struggle she has embarked upon. The reference to illegal migrants is related to alleged Bangladeshi and Nepali men and boys who work here although many are also from neighbouring Assam. Many families, she said, were still looking for their missing children. She and other child rights advocates want modern machinery in these mines so children never run the risk of losing their childhood or lives.

It was a view that met with withering rage from those who spoke for the mining lobby, saying that the appalling conditions painted by activists were false and that the industry was creating jobs and bringing in much needed foreign exchange into the country.

'We have the stock of minerals that is God-gifted in our own private land,' Dolly Khangbah of the International Exporters Chamber of Commerce of Meghalaya told the Al Jazeera reporter who interviewed her while she was surrounded by pro-mining protesters waving placards. 'With this we are exporting to Bangladesh, we are fetching foreign exchange for the Government of India, we are paying royalty. We are fetching revenue for the state government. We are providing employment to all the boys and girls.'

The protesters were pro-mining not anti, speaking for a lobby that is not just immensely wealthy but politically powerful. One of the lobby's chief proponents is Vincent Pala, who, as mentioned earlier, rose to become a central minister for water resources in New Delhi and enjoys enormous clout as a person who influences state politics and politicians as well as street protests and campaigns.

Political power and coal are close companions.

Meghalaya's suave chief minister Mukul Sangma, a hit at dinner parties in New Delhi or Shillong with his ability to sing well (as could Neiphiu Rio, former chief minister of Nagaland) owns large tracts of land in the Garo Hills as do his wife and daughter, according to a statutory filing of assets with the State Election Commission. His wife says she has coal mines and agricultural land while his daughter had a fleet of thirteen vehicles including a Mitsubishi Pajero and an earthmover.[17] Her father's assets grew from ₹3 crore in 2008 to ₹14 crore in 2013, an increase of 323 per cent, according to the Association for Democratic Reform, the independent group which monitors the growth index in the wealth of politicians during and after elections. He's not alone on this affluence curve. In Meghalaya alone: 'All the candidates who contested the 2008 assembly election were "lakhpatis" and in five years most of them became "crorepatis", which means politicians are getting richer while the people in the state are not,' Meghalaya Election Watch said, noting that the 'growth rate' in the wealth accumulation of 111 politicians was 252 per cent. The GDP level for the state, it said, averaged about 15 per cent per year.

◆

As the wall of wealth, power and politicians seemed to grow taller, Hasina got support in her struggle from an unexpected quarter, a caving specialist named Brian Dermot Kharpran Daly, whose interests lay in ending the commercial exploitation of the coal mines but for a different reason. Daly wanted to save the long silent, dark subterranean worlds of limestone under the surface, often very close to the mines and threatened by the other caving, the commercial rat-holes. Pre-history lives here in underground caverns and streams with insects, fish and creatures yet to be discovered with over 1,200 caves of which only two-thirds have been explored. There are Heteropoda spiders and plenty of 'snotgobblers' (web-building fly larvae), a speleologist's delight.

Some 360 kilometres of cave passages have been mapped, including India's longest cave: the Krem Liat Prah-Um Im-Labit System, estimated to be 31 kilometres long. Meghalaya also has the country's deepest cave.[18]

International caving groups and mountaineers, environment organizations and tree huggers grew interested because of the threat to the limestone caves. Limestone is another huge extractive industry in these areas but it doesn't draw the kind of critical response that coal does. Daly had been battling for years, leading a media campaign that focused attention on the cement factories coming up at Cherrapunji. 'Everything will go, the history, the distinctive cave life, the beautiful stalagmites which can tell you the history of the past climate dating back to over 100 years,'[19] he said. The 2015 campaign was against the setting up of a cement plant near the spectacular Siju caves in the Garo Hills.

The environmental push meshed with another battlefront that opened up against the mining lobby. A few years later, the National Commission for Protection of Child Rights (NCPCR), the official body empowered by

Parliament to protect the rights of children, responding to Hasina and others sent an official team to investigate conditions after persistent complaints from Impulse of child abuse and inhuman working conditions. That was in 2009. There was no response from the state government to the commission's report. Two years later, the commission sent a second team which delivered a stinging indictment. The team got the same reaction from the government— no response. In 2012, it sent a third team and found clear evidence of collusion between the government and the mining lobby. Wherever it went, the children vanished. The government was hand in glove with the miners.

> On the way to the coal mines of Rymbai road area, the team could not find any children working on the road side coal depots. When the team approached the depot, the children were reportedly sent away to the jungle area. In one of the coal crushers at Byndihati the manager informed the team that he was being directed by the District administration to send all the children as some inspection team was expected. He stated that all the children engaged in the crusher are sent to the nearby jungle. The NCPCR [National Commission for Protection of Child Rights] team was surprised to know the fact that the District administration is colluding to promote the child labour instead of curbing the same.[20]

A member of the team decided to go down in a makeshift wooden crate which usually carried miners into the depths. It was controlled by a pulley and chain system. He got more than he bargained for of life under the surface.

> There was a makeshift ladder, built by using tree trunks, leading to the pit which looked very risky. One of the members of NCPCR (Dr Yogesh Dube) went inside the pit to have a first hand experience of being in the coal pit. He tried to go inside the well along with a person from Doordarshan on a crane. The well was about 200 feet and after going down halfway, Dr Dube felt suffocated and instructed the person accompanying to climb back. Mr Vinod Kumar Tikoo, Member, NCPCR who entered a rat hole enquired with the Mine Engineer if he has ever entered a rat hole on the side ways of the coal mine wherein gas, fumes were emanating and it was too dark and eerie. The response was in negative. The member even offered incentives to the Mine Engineer but he refused saying that it was too dangerous. Then he was asked how did his department allow the pits to operate without any safety measures risking the lives of children

to extreme risks. The gaseous fumes even affect the respiratory system
of the body and that explained the increased number of medical
emergencies in the area.

The NCPCR had a range of consultations with the state government and
local NGOs and put together a set of recommendations for not less than
five interlinked departments, ranging from labour and health to education
and social welfare.

The state government provided a striking statistic: it had come across
only 222 cases of child labour in the Jaintia Hills where the investigating
unit had visited, and was working on correcting the situation. It took an
easy route out of responsibility, blaming a mess created by private ownership
of land and resources as guaranteed by the Sixth Schedule and customary
processes for the lack of implementation of policy.

On 17 April 2014, all this came to an emphatic head when a new
constitutional body charged with implementing environmental law cracked
the whip. The Special Circuit Bench of the Eastern Zone of the National
Green Tribunal (NGT) banned coal mining in Meghalaya as hazardous
to humans and the ecosystems which sustained human and the natural
systems. Writ large over this sharp denunciation was the state government's
lackadaisical approach as well as the energy of the activists. Sustained media
focus which turned the spotlight on issues and people involved, as well as
the overwhelming evidence gathered by the NCPCR of the Government of
India, were an impetus to the tribunal's own powers and role as mandated.

Within weeks of the 2014 judgment, the mines were abandoned by
labour, young and old, who slipped away to other states to find work.
Small mine owners expressed apprehension about the future. Land prices
in Shillong crashed. The government began seizing trucks and filing cases
against those found transporting coal against the tribunal's orders.

The bench's order was issued by Justice P. Jyothimani and called for
compliance by the state government chief secretary and police chief. The
following month, orders were issued to stop the mining and clear the coal
which had been extracted but not transported from collection sites. When
miners challenged the verdict, the tribunal dismissed their petition saying
they had not provided any compelling reason for the decision to be changed.
The miners said that the tribunal's ban would throw tens of thousands out
of critical jobs, jeopardize the livelihoods of the poor, create economic and
social chaos and throw many into the pit of poverty and despair.

The tribunal's first national chief was Justice Swatantra Kumar, who
had retired from the Supreme Court. The circuit bench for the Eastern

Region responded to concerns and issues of this specific area.

When the miners filed another appeal to the national bench of the tribunal, it called a special session in Shillong presided over by Justice Swatantra Kumar. The bench blasted the state government and showed no leniency to the miners either, citing them for wilful negligence and trying to evade responsibility. Weighbridges would need to be installed, fines paid and deposited in a Meghalaya Environment Protection and Restoration Fund.

In its 25 March 2015 ruling, the NGT slammed the mining system in Meghalaya as 'rampant, illegal, unscientific and life threatening', adding: 'Truly, it was unregulated, uncontrolled and unchecked.'

It faulted the government for its failure, despite several orders and instructions, to develop a policy on mining: 'The formulation of such policy and guidelines for the State has yet to see the light of the day.' It brushed aside a weak defence by the state government citing lack of forces to deal with counter-insurgency measures and also implement the tribunal's earlier orders, citing its 'incapability for compliance'.[21] The NGT said that another request to the centre seeking exemption from central laws which mandated protection and rights for coal workers was not acceptable, saying the state could not take shelter behind the Sixth Schedule. Essentially, it was saying even such systems came under the larger rubric of fundamental rights enshrined in the basic structure of the Constitution. In other words, the pillar of fundamental rights in the Constitution was greater than a specific clause providing special treatment to one group or one geographical area.

The activists were ecstatic, the miners and their patrons in politics and government were shaken.

The NGT decision followed a petition by the All Dimasa Students' Union (ADSU) from the Dima Hasao district in Assam. The ADSU claimed that the mining in the coal belts and coal stockpiles in the Jaintia Hills area were polluting streams and rivers downstream in Dima Hasao district. The students based their charge on a study conducted by Professor Sumarlin Swer and Professor O. P. Singh[22] of North Eastern Hill University (NEHU) in Shillong, which tested the quality of water in the rivers in the Jaintia Hills district and found high sulphur content from coal which makes the water acidic. These rivers merge with the Kopili River which flows from Meghalaya to Dima Hasao district carrying acidic water with it. The paper concluded:

> The rivers and streams of the Jaintia Hills, Meghalaya are the greatest victims of the coal mining. Contamination of acid mine drainage (coloured acidic seepage originating from mines and spoils), leaching

of heavy metals, organic enrichment and silting are some of the major causes of water pollution. Degradation of water quality in the area is evidenced by low pH (in the range of 3-5), high conductivity, high concentration of sulphates, iron and other toxic metals, low DO and high BOD. Mine drainage is affecting aquatic life from elimination of all but the few tolerant species.

As a result, the rivers and streams which had supported extremely rich biodiversity and traditional agriculture, and were sources of potable and irrigation water in the area, now carry polluted water. The level of pollution has reached to the extent that water has become unfit for human consumption and irrigation, and toxic to plants and animals. Consequently, the same rivers and streams that supported human life and activities, and rich biodiversity including many species of fish, amphibians, aquatic insects etc. have now lost their life sustaining role and become nearly devoid of aquatic life.

'The polluted water not only kills aquatic life, but also renders it unfit for drinking or agricultural use,' said a news report.

The river had turned blue with toxicity, the deep blue colour of bruises on a human body; the surrounding land had turned a bright rust red. The impact of another man-made intervention is just being uncovered but not spoken of enough. Thus, the report went on to say that the acidity is damaging equipment in the dam on the Kopili (Bhupen Hazarika, the beloved bard of the Brahmaputra, wrote and sang of the river in: 'Kopili, o Kopili, Ram Dhenur Suwali, alop u morom u nain—Kopili, o Kopili, child of the rainbow, why do you have no love?')

At the 275 megawatt hydro electric project run by the North East Electric Power Corporation Limited (NEEPCO), officials find it tough to counter the acidity in the reservoir. The government of Meghalaya has been informed of the acidic corrosion of metallic parts and the resultant frequent failures of underwater parts—first noticed in 2006—but no action has been taken.

It has also had another impact, which underlies many issues in the region. The growth of coal turned out to be a bonanza for another extractive industry—armed militants. Protection money for every truck of coal that left a mine rose from ₹15,000 to ₹25,000. Mine owners would have to pay ₹50,000 for every mine dug. Some fear that although the prices are negotiable and the demands by armed groups can be beaten down, a ban that came into place in 2014 on coal mining could provoke younger people to 'take up arms or get involved in smuggling coal'. That's another aspect of the FAO report cited earlier—those who feel they are losing the most, and in this case, it is ironically those who have benefited the most from the coal industry, could turn against the very system that sustained and supported it for decades.

Yet illegal coal mining continues despite the legal verdicts and government crackdown. Implementation of good laws continues to be the stumbling block, despite good intentions. An important and encouraging change factor is the growing involvement of ordinary people in tackling environmental collapse as seen in a report, 'JAC formed to rein in illegal coal transporters', in the *Shillong Times* on 27 August 2016:

> ...six villages in Ri-Bhoi have formed a joint action committee (JAC) to rein in illegal coal transporters in the district. The villagers of Mawlyndep, Umbir, Umniuh, Umraleng, Mairung and Umsawlum, along with members of the Lad Umsaw Taxi Drivers' Association, met Umsning MLA Celestine Lyngdoh on Thursday and apprised him about the decrepit Mawmaram-Umsawlum road frequented by heavy vehicles transporting illegal coal and charcoal.

Thus there are grounds for hope just as there is overwhelming evidence for despair. The latter is seen in the stark and continuing demolition of hills and hillsides, deforestation and extraction of another precious product—rock and sandstone. The NGT hasn't cracked its whip yet on this brutal rape of Meghalaya's landscape. But it's time for schoolchildren and college students to get involved, to come out onto the streets and demand environmental justice from their parents and peers—for their future. It is this generation that can retrieve the future by using technological tools—Google Maps, drones and social media skills—as well as emulate restoration practices in other parts of the world which have worked. This could restore, protect and preserve their living traditions.

As I have said, I have chosen to focus on these issues in Arunachal Pradesh, Sikkim and Meghalaya and not the extortions or killings especially in the Garo Hills or even the campaigns against outsiders because these are enmeshed with each other because law and order issues can be dealt with by enforcement agencies. But the greater issues of life and livelihoods, of survival, of water, land and forest management need the greater involvement of people, not just of those in authority.

◆

As far as a people-inclusive approach is concerned, there appears to be only one working idea in action—and even that is limited in its approach and impact. This is a process promoted by the International Fund for Agriculture Development, a branch of FAO, started in a handful of villages where natural resource management authorities were created locally, involving men and women of a village. An elected body was picked by the general body of adult villagers—whether it was a Sixth Schedule area or not—to protect, preserve and ensure democratic use of water bodies and forest spaces.

The key has been involvement of the community, an idea that was well understood by the International Fund for Agricultural Development's first director, Phrang Roy, a Shillong native who had quit the IAS to join the UN. His knowledge of Meghalaya helped set up a network that began small but has now expanded to more than 1,000 villages in five states. Yet even this seemingly democratic process is having problems. Challenges are thrown at it by members of other elected bodies, there are efforts to pressure staff and direct the use of funds. Such limitations show the need to always innovate and bring in practices which could ensure continuity but also the involvement of the principal stakeholders, the people, through a process of continuous dialogue. Without it, rising anger and aspirations, politicians who seek advantage and the subterranean groups which are always waiting to burst into the open seeking more money, publicity and power, are bound to mesh in a self-perpetuating and exploitative cycle. Corruption will grow, governance will fall; fury will rise, delivery will fail. Systems will become as diseased as the deadly blue waters of the Jaintia Hills, leading to frustration and a surge of social explosions against the established order. The old ways of business as usual will not work at all. Only inclusiveness will.

◆

The scarring of the earth is as brutal as the violence inflicted on people in these and the neighbouring hills. This is not just with the child-miners and other youth who came and frittered away their lives in the holes punched into the earth but also with ordinary, working class Indians who have lived in the state or come there in search of livelihoods and incomes.

There has been ongoing political tension between the 'locals' and the dhkars, or outsiders, as those from the plains are often called derisively. Even those from other hills find themselves in tough spots—a well-known poet from Kalimpong in the north Bengal hills spoke recently at a gathering of writers about how he and a colleague were chased one day by a group of young men in a Shillong neighbourhood in the 1980s. There was no explanation and the panicked men did not understand what it was about—but this was at the height of the local-dhkars tensions in the 1990s when attacks and occasional counter-attacks were commonplace. The two Nepalese men managed to find security in a stranger's house.

In the last decades of the twentieth century, riots would erupt sporadically, often without warning. At times, they were extremely brutal. In 2013, a young trader was set ablaze in a crowded market during an agitation against 'outsiders' while another died from 50 per cent burn injuries.

The pugnacious Patricia Mukhim was among the few voices who spoke with fearlessness, calling a spade a spade, noting that some of the non-tribals had been in the area for three generations:

> I would think that mutual respect and a shared objective is likely to achieve more for Meghalaya than the constant bitching about losing out to non-tribals. And like I have said in the past our narratives which are built around fear need to be unbundled. What is it that we fear? Why do we fear? Who do we fear? It's time to analyse this irrational fear on which politicians take a joyride.
>
> Can we claim to be completely self-reliant in our day to day transactions? Don't we need other people to be of service to us? When we need a good doctor do we check his tribe, caste, class or do we repose our faith on his expertise and his credentials? The same is the case with a good teacher or lawyer! So if we are inter-dependent then is it not fair to share a slice of the cake with those who strive to build Meghalaya as much as the tribals do? We also perhaps forget that the Indian Constitution guarantees certain fundamental rights to all citizens irrespective of their caste/creed/tribe. We the tribes already enjoy special protection under the Sixth Schedule of the Constitution.[23]

Devjani Bodepudi, who grew up in Shillong, noted: 'The memories of certain generations of Bengalis release mutterings of riots, curfews, oppression, unfairness and bigotry.'[24]

Subir Bhaumik[25], former BBC correspondent for Eastern India and a no-holds-barred commentator, cites cases of Bengali localities being attacked in the 1980s and notes that riots would often break out during or just before the major Bengali celebrations of Durga Puja. This went on for years until better sense prevailed in the mid-1990s.[26]

There's hardly been a major riot since although reports of intimidation keep trickling in. Discrimination is visible in the treatment to 'others' of the lower middle class while professionals, senior officials and scholars are largely untouched. As an Assamese I haven't experienced a single incident of bias through or since school in Shillong. I could put it down to many factors but essentially to good friends and my mother's love for the city: she couldn't bear the heat, dust and traffic of Guwahati although the smaller towns were okay, up to a point. There are of course other influences: privilege or the lack of it, education and upbringing (the schools you went to and who you went to school with are as critical in smaller towns like Shillong as they are in New Delhi, Kolkata, Mumbai or Chennai).

◆

'There is a dwindling non-tribal population, of late, according to the 2011 Indian Census, from 20% in 1971, to 13%, and the exodus, some people feel, is because of "being denied rights in one's own land" with the Meghalaya Land Transfer Act 1971.'[27]

The Act ensures that local lands can't be alienated by sale to a non-tribal; only a tribal is entitled to buy land here which is completely the opposite of what the Indian Constitution says: that all citizens are free to move, settle and purchase property wherever they wish.

Are the rights endowed by a section of the Constitution—in this case the Sixth Schedule—greater than the rights given on the whole by the initial ringing clauses of freedom, equality and fraternity? I don't think so. I can understand the concerns of the small majority in small states and among small populations—that they could be overwhelmed by influx and the need to curb that. But groups opposing in-migration from other parts of India should not confuse the issue with illegal migration from neighbouring countries like Bangladesh. The former are citizens of the country, with every right to a decent and dignified life. No one has the right to take that away from them, whatever the concern. Can there be a possible via-media? Could these families who have been in Meghalaya and other parts of the Northeast for decades not be allowed to continue to live in perpetuity and sell their property to whomsoever they wish? This would mean making changes to laws but could provide a sense of security, an anchor to those who love Shillong and all of these lands with a fierceness that matches that of any 'local'. It would be rewarding the stakeholder, not the trespasser.

My father, Dr Chaitanya Nath Hazarika, came to Shillong in 1949 and worked and lived there till his death in 1969; my mother came as a young bride and both my brother Suzoy and I were born there. Naturally, we would like our future generations to inherit these lands and settle. This would not harm the indigenous struggle, for all of us are indigenous, in one space or another.

Those of the Northeast demand, and rightfully so, to be treated and recognized as equal Indians, no matter what the colour of the skin, ethnicity, faith, language or the way we look. Similarly, it would be unjustifiable and unacceptable to discriminate against others from different parts of India on these very grounds.

◆

Subir Bhaumik is a large and visible presence, both in girth and volume. He makes his points vigorously and loudly, wagging a finger for emphasis at times, brooking little interference. As a young journalist, he cut his teeth in the backwaters of Tripura, his home state, and then Guwahati and Calcutta, where he worked with *The Telegraph* and later joined the BBC. He returned to Assam for a brief stint with the ill-fated *Seven Sisters Post*, which drowned in the corruption and scams of its owners, but left before the paper's collapse. Now a correspondent with the Bangladeshi channel bdnews.24 and a prolific writer, Subir thunders out his four-point mantra on New Delhi's failure to engage with the states of the region and more important, the people.

'The Indian state has been using Kautilya's four principles of statecraft— sham (reconciliation), dam (monetary inducement), danda (stick) and bhed (split) in varying mix to control and contain the violent movements in the Northeast.' Subir tosses these four words out with relish especially at public events, enlivening discussions and prompting much laughter at the irreverent description.

These views resonate through his writing and experiences, for his home state Tripura has excelled in all four, despite its tiny size. And one of the key players of this approach is the mild-mannered chief minister Manik Sarkar, one of the calmest political leaders that I have seen. Sarkar, who is always seen in public in the Bengali Hindu middle class man's trademark uniform, a white cotton dhoti kurta, has implemented to near perfection these four principles of statecraft that the ancient Indian equivalent of Machiavelli enunciated.

First, with a combination of guile and pressure, he broke the back of the two armed groups that had plagued ordinary life and kept the security forces on their toes for over two decades. These were the All Tripura Tiger Force (ATTF) and the National Liberation Front of Tripura (NLFT), which like other 'insurgent' groups of the region proclaimed their determination for independence from India. They took over a campaign that had been first driven by the Tripura National Volunteer Army (TNVA), led by Bijoy Hrangkhawl. After eight years of life in forests and in exile in Bangladesh, Hrangkhawl decided he had had enough. He signed an agreement with Rajiv Gandhi, among a spate of goodwill accords that came from that young leader's term before his assassination in 1991. Hrangkhawl joined the 'mainstream' and even launched a pro-tribal party that was closely allied with the Congress Party. This was the Indigenous Front of Tripura (IFT), whose fortunes waxed and waned with those of the Congress.

But as Manik Sarkar realized early on in his tenure, a policy of appeasement was certainly not going to deal either with insurgency or bring about confidence among the dominant Bengali Hindu population or the tribal minority. The two groups had bases in the hill areas of the state but also slipped in and out of Bangladesh where they had camps and safe houses. Taking them on was turning out to be a thankless job.

Bhaumik's essay[28] in a book he edited has detail, drama, blood and gore. He tells in detail how Sarkar and his CPI-M predecessor, the veteran Nripen Chakravarty, worked out a strategy with the police, intelligence officials and the army to take out insurgent elements based in Bangladesh. During an earlier time, the Congress leader of the 1960s, Sachindra Lal Singa, who was chief minister, cultivated his contacts with Sheikh Mujibur Rahman, later founder of Bangladesh, to support the Awami League. Sheikh Mujib was charged by Pakistanis in what was known as the Agartala Conspiracy case, where he and others were accused of plotting to overthrow the government in Dhaka. The case was later dropped, but Bhaumik says it had its origins in a secret mission led by Sheikh Mujib to the Tripura capital to ask Singa for armed assistance should they need it.

But in the first decade of the twenty-first century, Manik Sarkar, according to Bhaumik, decided to design his own external security policy, with minimal contact with New Delhi. He supported his head of police, a much reviled officer in Assam called G. M. Srivastava, his chief secretary V. M. Tulidass and an army intelligence officer in creating a strategy that would hit the rebels quickly and hard. The killing of Sarkar's senior ministerial colleague, Health Minister Bimal Sinha, was probably another trigger for the crackdown.

Between 2003–2006, special units launched around twenty attacks on militants based across the border in Bangladesh, using a mix of rebels who wanted to surrender (but were instead asked to attack their former colleagues) and local Bangladeshi gangs and thugs, who were enticed with funds and the promise of more.[29] In 2008, Sheikh Hasina came to power in Dhaka in an overwhelming electoral victory and the rebels in Assam, Manipur and Tripura, who had lived there for years without a worry, found that their days were numbered.

Hasina authorized strong assaults on ATTF and NLFT, which were already under pressure from across the Indian side. Within a matter of time, the rebels, softened up by body blows from both sides, found their local political bases crumbling as CPI-M cadres returned to the hills to assert the party's presence and determination to take the rebels on politically. Election after election saw the growing clout of the leftists and the diminishing hold of the insurgents; each group was said to be aligned to either the Congress or the Marxists.

This triple thrust—military on either side of the border and political pressure—resulted in large-scale surrenders and the dismantling of the terror machinery, which had created a system of abducting businessmen as well as officials for ransom to sustain their operations. The armed movements shut down, trade and businesses in this Left bastion boomed as Bangladesh opened up land routes, allowed shipments of equipment and food grains, improved rail connectivity and opened up an Internet gateway to improve communications in the Northeast.

India's Prime Minister Narendra Modi announced a $2 billion line of credit[30] as Hasina delivered on promises which put Northeastern insurgents in her country on the mat. Modi also promised quick implementation of the earlier line of credit of $800 million and full disbursement of $200 million. The Prime Minister remarked in Dhaka that connectivity between India and Bangladesh by road, rail, rivers, sea, transmission lines, petroleum pipelines and digital links would increase. 'Today, we have unveiled some of the pathways to this future,' he said.

A combination of military pressure and political sagacity had achieved what two decades of standard anti-insurgency, manufactured consent and bursts of rebel surrenders and bouts of conflict had failed to achieve. Manik Sarkar's rethinking of policies where he converted a major local problem into an opportunity with bold initiatives on both the security and political front was the key.

Sarkar 'merely insisted that he was the small leader of a small state facing huge problems from across the border which the centre had failed to tackle'.[31]

But the upturn in Tripura's politics went beyond dealing with insurgency and improved economic conditions. Sarkar felt confident enough to take a dramatic and far-reaching decision on which the Government of India had refused to bend for nearly six decades and which few of his fellow chief ministers were sure of. He recommended to the centre, run by the BJP, a security-conscious and -driven party, the lifting of the Disturbed Areas Act and its companion, the AFSPA.

He faced no opposition as the internal conflict was virtually zero; peace was not a mere slogan but a lived reality, it wasn't at hand but visible in daily conditions.

Ten years after the Justice Jeevan Reddy Committee had submitted its report, at least one state government, smart, small but gutsy and known for competence, had agreed to remove a law which enshrined inequality, injustice, impunity and immunity and send the security forces back to where they belonged—the barracks and the borders. This it has done on the strength of its own record and the vision of its leaders.

Manik Sarkar lifted the application of the laws—he can't repeal them as they are a central legislation and can be repealed only by Parliament—and did so without the social and political pressure of a powerful hunger striker like Irom Sharmila or activist bodies like the Naga Mothers Association or the human rights groups in Manipur or Assam and Nagaland. He did this on his own. That makes it all the more remarkable.

'In view of the significant taming of terrorism in Tripura, the council of ministers today (Wednesday) decided to withdraw the AFSPA from the entire state,' Sarkar told the media, noting that it was no hasty decision but one that had come after much deliberation involving all departments. 'The security forces recently exhaustively reviewed the law and order situation in the state. Considering the reports of the security forces, the council of ministers decided to recommend to the union home ministry to issue a notification to withdraw the AFSPA.'

Insurgency activities in the state 'are now reduced almost at zero', he concluded.

It came a decade after Thangjam Manorama died fleeing from her captors.

◆

As we have seen elsewhere, insurgency related violence in the key states which saw armed rebellion have diminished. More people die in road accidents in the Northeast than in state-rebel conflicts. There are more killings in internecine ethnic clashes than in the latter. Militant groups do play a role in such attacks and counter-attacks but they do so without threatening the structure of the state or harming internal security.

What started as a revolt against the 'idea of India' has become a law and order problem.

Tripura had flagged the opportunities that grow out of good governance and a mix of political and military sensibility. The question that hangs before the centre and the other states and their people is why they cannot follow the Tripura example, not the doctrine advocated as foreign policy but the trinity of internal resilience, strong political interventions and sensible government which enabled Manik Sarkar to do what he did on 27 May 2015. It took place after eighteen years in Tripura—Nagaland and Manipur have waited for nearly sixty. That surely is a long time. Manorama's family and thousands of others will testify to that.

◆

To build an area of peace in the region is especially important at a time when the centre's Act East Policy is taking shape and the government wants a closer relationship with the so-called 'economic tigers of Southeast Asia'. In the long run India wants to emerge out of the confines of the stagnating and divided South Asian Association for Regional Cooperation (SAARC) to tap the economic potential of ASEAN, register itself as a regional power and to try and balance China's growing influence in the region Former prime minister Manmohan Singh stated that it is.

> not merely an external economic policy, it is also a strategic shift in India's vision of the world and India's place in the evolving global economy. Most of all it is about reaching out to our civilisational neighbours in South East Asia and East Asia.[32]

If this is to happen, then the Northeast needs to break the shackles of many controls which hold it back and which divide the region from the rest of India. Repealing AFSPA is central to the plan to open up and reach out. The region needs to be at peace within, with adequate infrastructure and trained and capable human resources, if it is to play the role of a bridgehead to South and Southeast Asia.

STRANGERS NO MORE: THE NEW INDIANS

In February 2013, a young man from Arunachal Pradesh entered a shop in Lajpat Nagar, New Delhi, wanting help in locating a relative's address in the neighbourhood.[1] What happened inside and outside that shop resulted in his death and forced many Indians to look at and rethink ideas and issues of racial discrimination and viciousness towards those from the Northeast and towards people who just happen to 'look different'.

Eighteen-year-old Nido Taniam walked into Rajasthan Paneer Bhandar to ask for directions. The shopkeeper made fun of his hair, which was streaked blonde. Furious at the insult, Taniam smashed a glass counter in the store. Such insults were not new for those from the Northeast who, despite Supreme Court edicts, government diktats and assertions by human rights groups were still often treated as second-class citizens, snubbed as 'Chinkies' because of their facial structure and regarded as promiscuous because they mingled easily with each other. They complained of often being overcharged for apartment rents since there appeared to be a general sense that they came from wealthy families and could afford to pay steep rents.

In Nido's case, angered by the youth's reaction, the shopkeeper, his assistants and others in the store attacked him with their fists; varying accounts say that there were between three to seven men in the group. This did not happen in the darkness of night but in broad daylight.

When the police were summoned, they took both sides to the police station. The battered Nido agreed to pay ₹10,000 for the damage to the shop. According to a friend, the matter did not end there because the police dropped Nido back at the same spot where he had been picked up. Some men again cornered him in the evening and beat him with a stick.

Again the police were summoned, written apologies were extracted from both sides and the matter seemed to be settled. A deeply agitated Nido went to his friend's place where he was living (he was a student at a private university in Jalandhar, Punjab). He was restless and could not sleep. His friends advised hospitalization. He apparently refused. Not going for a medical check-up including a CT scan was a deadly mistake. It could have saved Nido's life.

Nido died of excessive internal bleeding the next day. A relative of the youth said: 'This is surely about racism. Everybody in Delhi discriminates against us based on our looks. We are living in India, but we don't know whether we are actually living in India or not.'[2]

Of all incidents of reported racial discrimination against individuals from the Northeast, this was perhaps the worst. There had been alleged beatings and molestations before, suicides and unsolved deaths in New Delhi, Bengaluru and other towns. But few assaults or cases of discriminatory conduct had resulted in death.

Yet, like other incidents of discrimination this could have perhaps petered out but for two reasons: Nido's father was a member of the state's legislative assembly and also a junior minister in the state government. The shaken family rushed to New Delhi and raised the issue with Prime Minister Manmohan Singh and Congress President Sonia Gandhi. Secondly, the anger back home and across the Northeast as well as in New Delhi over the tragedy, channelled through the visual media and mobilized by local leaders of various Northeast associations, had snowballed into an agitation demanding justice for Nido and action against discriminatory treatment.[3]

By then, three men had been arrested—shop owners Akram and Farhan as well as an assistant, Praveen.

Nido's family demanded a detailed investigation into the tragedy. Political leaders started dropping by the demonstration centre at Jantar Mantar to express support. The politicians included Rahul Gandhi and Arvind Kejriwal, the anti-corruption fighter who later became chief minister of Delhi. Arun Jaitley[4] of the BJP tweeted that 'The death of a northeast student in New Delhi after being beaten up is barbaric and condemnable.'

Kapil Sibal, the then national human resource development minister, called a meeting of various student associations, scholars and professionals to discuss the issue. Top officials were present from his ministry, which handles education. Among the decisions taken at the meeting was the designing and development of programmes to sensitize the Delhi police force to the concerns of young settlers and visitors from the region.[5] Sibal himself was taken aback, as a lawyer, to find that such sensitization had not taken place over the years despite the fact that many incidents of abuse had been reported.

Nido's was not a solitary incident. There was a spate of events before and after his death. The challenges of discrimination do not appear to have been curbed but there appears to be both greater awareness, especially in the media, and a deeper determination among young people from the region who seek to affirm their rights and dignity as Indians.

In addition, a number of academic institutions and research groups have conducted studies on the ugly face of discrimination. What one of them, developed by the C-NES (Centre for North East Studies and Policy Research) at Jamia Millia Islamia, discovered was the determination of younger people to keep coming to the metros in search of better prospects in terms of jobs, opportunities, education and incomes. A new generation of younger people from the Northeast was engaging with India and Indians, not as fighters against Delhi's Raj but as equals seeking acceptance of these rights and entitlements. Perhaps it is here that the core conditions of the region have changed—that a generation of young Indians from this area, exhausted by conflict and bloodshed, by ill will and stress, now seek to carve a new way for themselves based on the laws and systems of 'mainland' India. This is a remarkable change from an earlier time when their forebears, perhaps even their parents, were involved in political and armed fights for independence or autonomy against India.

It is a decision that is not mandated by the power of the gun or by the force of sheer numbers but by a growing realization that the rest of India is moving ahead, even what was once known as BIMARU (Bihar, Madhya Pradesh, Rajasthan and Uttar Pradesh) states such as Bihar, and their lands and communities which had fallen way behind because of conflicts and poor governance, internal feuds, vast corruption and external interventions. Health and education indices have fallen as have incomes. The composite state of Assam was once the fourth from the top in terms of GDP at the time of Independence. Today, it is ranked below the group of BIMARU states while other states such as Tamil Nadu, Rajasthan, Maharashtra and even Orissa (Odisha) have forged far ahead.

The Jamia study stressed this point. One of its key findings was that a striking 80 per cent of the women who were interviewed[6] said that although they had faced verbal and physical discrimination, they would still encourage their relatives and friends to migrate to a metro like New Delhi to scour for opportunities and set new goals. Hope or even the chance to hope is in itself a major driver not just of change but of out-migration.

These concerns about differences, of being different, having different perceptions of 'us' and 'them' and the feeling of separateness are not new. They have existed for hundreds of years and have long driven a wedge between the rulers and people of this region and those of other Indian lands. Nido Taniam was just the latest victim of this clash of identities and ideas.

◆

The sense of discrimination is to be found in many histories by visiting scholars.

In the seventeenth century, the Mughals launched a massive campaign to secure Assam, the country that had so far eluded and even exhausted them. Its rulers were the Tai-Ahoms, who had migrated from the northeastern Burma/China border in the early part of the thirteenth century.

Although Turkish and Persian historians like Minhaj al-Siraj Juzjani, Ziauddin Barani and Abul Fazal wrote extensively of flourishing village life, of various tribes like the Koch and Mech (a sub-tribe of the Bodo), of fortifications, culture, language and religion, all were not that well-disposed. The Persian chronicler Shihabuddin Talish, who accompanied the Mughal general Mir Jumla in his campaign, wrote in elegant prose of the times and the people in his *Fathiya-i-Ibriyya*. While praising the bravery of the Ahoms, the principal opponents of the Mughals, he also lavished warm words on the beauty of the region, the culture and conduct of its people as well as the geography of the area. Clearly, Shihabuddin shared the trials and tribulations of the campaign and so exhausted was he by its stress that he exclaimed in exasperation at one point that Assam[7] was 'a region apart from the land of men'. His descriptions are extensive about the beauty of the kingdom of Koch Behar, the passage to Assam, and he also admonished its king[8] for being so enamoured of wine, women and music that he failed to protect his kingdom.

Strangely, he claimed that the men and women are greenish in colour— this is one of the first assertions of racial difference between the people of the region and the 'outsider' who sees himself as the natural lord of all that he surveys, rather similar to the Government of India of the day. The army's archers, he says, use deadly poison on their arrows. He talks of the prevalence of witchcraft and how there are those who read magic words onto water and give the potion so influenced to the sick, who then miraculously recover. He talks about a fort in Assam which is built of mud bricks and is amazed by its height and the determination of the inhabitants to do battle:

> No one saw its depth but through conscience
> No one could get its height but through imagination.

But as the long campaign took its toll on the general Mir Jumla (who ultimately died of malaria on a boat and is buried in Dhubri), his men and the campaign, the poet and chronicler also became weary of it all and of this land that did not seem to know the word 'surrender'. He wrote:

> In short, every army that entered the limits of this country,
> Made its exit from the realm of Life;
> Every caravan that set foot
> On this land, deposited its baggage of residence in the halting-place of Death...
> And as no one who entered this country,
> Like visitors to the realm of
> Death, ever returned, and the manners of its natives
> were never made known to any [outsider],
> The people of Hindustan used to call the inhabitants of Assam sorcerers and magicians
> And consider them as standing outside the human species,
> And enter the name of this country in [their] spells and counter-spells.
> They say that whosoever visits this country is overcome by charms and never comes out of it.

Even Mir Jumla's death is blamed on Assamese sorcerers: Talish says that the fatal 'sickness was the result of witchcraft practised by the Rajah of Assam'.

The Assamese were 'savages', Talish declared and then burst into poetic song about this wild area:

> Through the force of Fate and the aid of the Divine will,
> Took place [our] journey in Assam, which lies on the border of China and Cathay.
> It is another world, another people and other customs;
> Its land is not like [our] land, its sky is not like [our] sky.
> Its sky sends rain down without the [originating] cause of clouds;
> On its ground the green grass sprouts up without any aid from the soil.
> It stands outside the circle of the Earth and the bowels of the [enveloping] sphere.
> It has been separated from the world, like the letter alipb.
> The seasons all begin [here] at the time of their conclusion [elsewhere];
> Here there is heat in [our] winter and chill in [our] summer.
> The Rajah of Assam brought to the field an army
> Whose large number became a cage on earth;

[They are] tumult-raising and sudden [in attack] like the eyes of the
fair sex,
Hurling arrows and [other] missiles, and making a [firm] stand in the
battlefield
Its rivers are deep
Like the thoughts of a wise man.

It's worth noting that Talish's observations and condemnations include what
Hindus in other parts of the country are supposed to have said about
the Assamese—that they were sorcerers and were considered outside the
pale of human civilization or species. It was not blind abuse of Hindus or
those of other faiths by Muslim rulers: Hindus in other areas of Hindustan
themselves held such blind and discriminatory beliefs. At the time, many
Assamese were outside the Hindu faith and a large number professed
Buddhism. Other accounts speak of the 'poisonous air of Assam', which
surely cannot be blamed on the Ahoms alone. Perhaps it could be described
as one of the first examples of literary prejudice based upon Mughal failure
to bring the people of the Brahmaputra valley to heel.

But it was not always thus. The ancient Indian text, the magnificent
Mahabharata, one of the great epics of good and evil, power and powerlessness,
statecraft, love, deceit and betrayal, speaks of Chitrangada, the beautiful
princess from Manipur, who married the great Pandava warrior, Arjuna,
during his long travels through the Himalayas and the eastern region. Their
son was Bhubhruvahana, of whom not much is heard during the epic. A
blogger[9] describes Manipur as 'mystical and exotic' through Arjuna's eyes.
But Uloopi, Arjuna's second wife, was a Naga princess and a widow who
became infatuated with the soldier-prince, drugged him and had him carried
off 'to her realm in the netherworld'. This is clearly not meant to have any
connection to any Naga ethnic group.

There are places where the epic is not kind to Assam either. The
province was also known as the legendary Pragjyotishpur (compared to
which the present-day Guwahati is a pathetically unpleasant and disorganized
set of neighbourhoods). The Mahabharata speaks of Assam as the realm of
Nakasura, the powerful demon king, who had abducted 16,000 princesses
and threatened to attack Krishna's abode. Of course, Nakasura was vanquished
and Krishna had little choice but to marry the 16,000 women as he couldn't
very well send them away. This too has been absorbed into public memory
especially by Hindus.

Moving from myth to history, the indefatigable Chinese traveller and
documenter of his times, Hiuen Tsang, talked in the seventh century of

the Assam kingdom as 'low and moist' with a good climate and its ruler (Bhaskardeva Varman) being a patron of learning whose subjects were likewise inclined. Learned men, the Chinese scholar intoned, came from many parts of the world to discuss, debate and study in Assam.

But let's leave aside historical treatises, myths and accounts and move to the present. Step by step, brick by brick, walls of difference, discrimination and division were meticulously built. Thus, over the past 150 years, the Northeast has been kept aside not by people from the region but by successive governments in New Delhi, and earlier Calcutta (the former capital), first by the East India Company which was the wealthiest and most powerful corporate house in the world that ran the political system and economic life of a subcontinent. Company Raj was followed by British Raj and then by the government of free India. In his compelling book about the Company, *The Corporation that Changed the World*[10], Nick Robbins dwells on the vast extent of not just its riches but how it intervened to shape political history in India, China and Africa by dealing in cotton, tea and opium apart from spices and other goods. It was a model (albeit ultimately a failed one) for the modern multinational.

Each successive government created more complex networks of legal control over its peripheral areas. In the process, the foundations of acute divergence between the region of Assam and the rest of the country was laid.

As far back as 1874, the British recognized customary laws among different tribes and followed this up with the Assam General Clauses Act which endowed special status on tribal groups, ensuring that the laws of the plains would not apply to the hills. This was the first statement of difference, though it was wrapped in the mask of protection.

The Montagu-Chelmsford Reforms Act, 1919, strengthened the differences. They were cemented by the Simon Commission's[11] recommendations, which were written by members who included Sir Clement Attlee, the future prime minister, agreeing to the protection of tribal rights.

This was followed by the Government of India Act, 1935, which divided the hills into excluded and partially excluded areas and declared that no central or provincial legislation would apply to them unless the governor decided, in pursuance of his discretionary powers, that they were appropriate and would help maintain peaceful conditions. The 1935 Act was the precursor of the Sixth Schedule developed by the Gopinath Bordoloi Sub-Committee[12] during the drawing up of the Indian Constitution.

According to Fernandes, Pereira and Khatso: 'These provisions had originated in the colonial need for peaceful trading relations in the Hill areas that were allowed to govern themselves without a direct daily role for the foreigner. Despite such isolation colonial intervention did destabilise tribal lifestyle, so most tribes resisted it.'[13]

Thus, the major effort of the colonial system was not to protect the tribes or upland people but to protect the extraction and plantation industries upon which the Raj depended. In the process, they kept the hill groups at a great distance from plains communities and the mainland, keeping normal intercourse to the barest minimum, making the hill districts feel they were separate and different, providing them with autonomous political powers and creating a system of administration that was not answerable to the provincial or state government but only to New Delhi through its representative, an all-powerful, all-seeing, supposedly wise but often arbitrary governor.

Thus when the Nagas and then the Mizos launched their respective insurgencies, separated by a full decade (1955–1966), the consequences were disastrous for the hill people who had had hardly any form of detailed contact with the Indians of the plains. The assault by the Indian Army on the rebels took the shape of a massive crackdown against ordinary villagers, their families and homes, their livestock and granaries. For the former and the latter, as noted earlier, it was their first historic encounter as people, face-to-face, and they met as bitter foes—barring the battles of Kohima and Imphal, where the Nagas and a large Indian contingent had fought on the side of the British against the advancing Japanese Army which was supported by elements of the Indian National Army of Netaji Subhas Chandra Bose.

It could not have been a worse meeting. The Indian Army—comprising thousands of soldiers from the north (Sikh, Jat), the west and south (Maratha and Madras Regiment), the Gurkhas, the Assam Regiment and Assam Rifles—swarmed into the jagged hills, narrow valleys, high villages and deep jungles. The bitter lore of those events lives on—of rape and massacres, of torture and extortion, of the burning of entire villages, strafing of towns, displacement of tens of thousands of rural folk. It is a wretched story for which amends have not been made though it is so deeply necessary.

The problems and alienation caused by the non-stop application of AFSPA and the Disturbed Areas Act along with other laws such as the Nagaland Security Regulations Act have created a huge gap of mistrust between individuals and communities in the states caught up in this trouble and the central government and its representatives. Way back in 1996, writing about the deficits faced by the Northeast, the Shukla Commission,[14] which was set up by the then prime minister H. D. Deve Gowda to look at the

challenges before the region, made some trenchant comments. Couched in
the inimitable style of the veteran editor B. G. Verghese,[15] it declared: 'The
Northeast tends to be seen as a distant outpost, some kind of land's end. Yet
it was until recently a crossroads and a bridge to Southeast and East Asia,
with its great rivers ending in ocean terminals at Calcutta and Chittagong.'
The report's introduction defined the core challenges: 'There are four deficits
that confront the Northeast, a basic needs deficit; an infrastructural deficit;
a resource deficit; and, most important, a two-way deficit of understanding
with the rest of the country which compounds the others.' It said that while
the region's exclusive dependency on the centre for development funding
was hurting it, what was needed was 'a more rapid pace of growth (which)
would generate larger internal resources. This could perhaps be enlarged
through the additionality of private investment, Indian and foreign, within
a well-defined framework.'

Noting that the area was a latecomer to development, it underlined
that 'the Northeast must be enabled to grow at its own pace and in
accordance with its own genius. It cannot be treated merely as a resource
region, market dump and transit yard.' It pulled no punches:

> There is strong resentment over what is seen as an earlier phase of
> 'colonial exploitation' in which its wealth was extracted for others'
> enrichment. Such a path of development is not advocated. On the
> contrary, the people of the Northeast must feel that they are equal
> partners in a process of culturally friendly, equitable and sustainable
> development. This must be the thrust. Yet delay would be denial.

The authors of the report were Verghese, the banker and economist
Jayanta Madhab from Assam who had served long years with the Asian
Development Bank, and the Mizo administrator Sainghaka; the chairman
was the respected Indian Administrative Service official, S. P. Shukla, a
member of the Planning Commission and former telecommunications
secretary.

The team presented a vision for the region that resonated with hope
at a time of acute turbulence and violence, when insurgencies were at
their peak, the pressure of the state on ordinary people was enormous, and
helplessness and a sense of despair held the land in their grip. A few months
later, the secret talks leading to a major breakthrough in the Naga conflict
and the ceasefire between Muivah and Swu's organization and New Delhi
was to create a surge of fresh hope. But in March 1997, there was little
that ordinary men and women could aspire for, in terms of a 'normal' life,

peace and stability in at least four of the seven states—Assam, Manipur, Nagaland and Tripura—while Meghalaya was wracked by communal and rebel violence (Sikkim was not yet a member of the North Eastern Council and thus officially was not a part of the region).

However, visionaries are not bound by the present. They look at the future with fresh eyes and the knowledge of experience, rich but challenging. So, the words of the commission ring out from decades back:

> ...with the recent softening of geo-political rigidities following understandings with China, then Myanmar and, most especially, with Bangladesh, the Northeast is no more a burdensome peripheral region somewhere out there, but is poised once again to resume its dynamic role as a bridge to the booming economies of Southeast Asia and Southwest China to mutual benefit. No surprise that proposals to construct a Trans-Asian Highway and Asian Railway have been revived.

These words hold true today for India and its neighbourhood: the abysmal levels of trust and collaboration between these countries have to be dealt with. The effectiveness of the country's foreign policy and the capacity of its Ministry of External Affairs mandarins and the political leadership have to be augmented. It was left to Prime Minister Narendra Modi, twenty-eight years after the Shukla Commission submitted its report, to push through a series of rapid changes and initiatives in policy and approach that could have transformed the region in those three decades. Modi, a man who had made his mark for governance in Gujarat despite bitter controversy that rages about his alleged role or lack of it in the anti-Muslim riots in the state in 2002, became the poster boy of the BJP in the Lok Sabha elections of 2014. As has been noted, he led the party's spectacular capture of office with a majority on its own (something no party had achieved since 1984) and plunged delightedly, like a veteran and not the rookie that he was, to foreign policy, into shaping the country's muscular advocacy of issues in international affairs.

Modi tweaked the Look East Policy, making it, given his predilection for short, effective-sounding phrases, the Act East Policy, promising action, not words.[16] The original policy predated the Shukla Commission by five years but, despite many research tomes, academic articles as well as seminars and workshops, it had, in nearly thirty years, barely even registered on the region. Nor did it make any difference to Myanmar, the large neighbour on the east, or to issues of connectivity to Southeast Asia.[17]

Over the years, the failure to deliver on promises, to structure the

vision set out in black and white,[18] continuing episodic bouts of bitter
violence on both communal and ethnic lines, apart from the struggling
rebellions whose leaders slipped into middle age with the realization that
they were still without a home and far from achieving anything close to
their proclaimed goals of independence, had bred a sense of sullenness
and depression. The faltering economy, destruction of habitat and species,
and extensive deforestation added to agricultural stagnation and propelled
a historic change. A new pattern became visible in the mobility of people
from the region: from being a major migrant-receiving region, the Northeast
became a migrant-producing area for perhaps the first time in centuries. In
other words, people were leaving—they were fed up of the lack of prospects
at home, fearful of local conflicts, tired of extensive corruption and the
rentier economy of freebooters and local elites, dissatisfied with constant
closures and protests, bitter about poor educational facilities with decaying
colleges and fractured school systems. Many did not see a future back home.

So they left. Those who came from wealthy families went to the fancy
public schools and private universities in northern and western India; some
were even sent by their parents, corrupt officials and politicians, to schools
in Australia and the United States. Others began working in sweatshops
in the cities, as store and office assistants, as security guards and in beauty
parlours, restaurants and business process outsourcing jobs. Farmers from
central Assam areas such as Nagaon work as carpenters and labourers in
Kerala and Karnataka, telling those who used to hire them for daily labour
in their home district that they are paid double what they get at home.
'I told them "I can't pay you more",' said my cousin, Romu Baruah of
Nagaon's Amolapatty neighbourhood, when he spoke about trying to hire
labour to maintain their once celebrated garden. Others like Bubu Barooah
of a nearby village talk of how they throw in a lunch but it's not enough
for the Miyas and other daily wage earners who either go to Kerala or
other southern states or to one of the hundreds of brick kilns which now
dot the once prosperous farmlands of Morigaon and Nagaon districts.

The kilns leach their poisonous chemicals into the soil, making
it uncultivable for life, wafting their ash onto the homes and fields of
neighbouring farms, laying an ugly coat of grey over them. The reason
workers go to the kilns is the same as going to Kerala—they earn much
more than as a farmhand. The only difference is that in Kerala they have to
work—at the kilns, they are paid even if there isn't any work. Apparently,
the demand for construction material during the dry season is so huge
that they make enough for the rest of the year.

Those from states and backgrounds with English language skills are luckier and have better chances of survival in the big cities. The migration began in the 1950s with officers from Assam who were working in New Delhi, their children and their friends. The children of politicians, business families and professionals began moving to the capital and other cities. Their friends came too. With the growth of education opportunities, scholarships and jobs, the trickle became a steady flow. Conflicts and violence saw the rise of new privileged elites from the government and pro-government classes as well as those opposed to them. Businessmen, especially Marwaris and 'outsiders' with connections to all these groups and the government, made fortunes overnight. A slow process of shadowy networks, privileges and connections began to take shape, built up with safe conduits for funds and easy money. Funds paid in Shillong would emerge in New Delhi or Kohima or Aizawl or vice versa through these businessmen who became a new class of trustees, providers and power brokers.

The children of Naga underground cadres and leaders lived in Shillong in the 1990s, with the full knowledge of local police, a kind of truce that existed before an official ceasefire came into place in 1997.

But a different group also began to take shape, those from the middle class and affluent backgrounds be they in Nagaland, Manipur, Assam, Mizoram or Meghalaya, who wanted to study, compete and get ahead. It was here that the differences between those who 'looked' Northeastern and others who didn't, developed—at least in the eyes of the beholder.

The term 'Northeastern' came to mean a person of oriental appearance. People come up to Utpal Borpujari, the film critic and filmmaker, as well as to me and others and say: 'You can't be from the Northeast, you don't look like the others.' And we have to explain that indeed a majority of people from the region—in fact nearly 65 to 70 per cent of the entire population—are actually those who don't look 'Northeastern' but as if they are from other parts of India. Yet, such is the visibility of those who look oriental in the public eye that the region is constantly identified with them. This is true because of the sense of conflict and the reality of anti-India violence that has long dominated not just headlines but also a sense of what the area is all about.

The 'Northeastern' look is seen in the appearances and cultural traditions of many small hill communities and a few larger plains communities which are largely tribal or from what are officially designated as Scheduled Tribes by the Indian Constitution. The larger pan-Indian-looking populations dominate the plains of Assam and Tripura, the two largest states of the region.

◆

Information and education would go a long way in dispelling the belief of the Northeast being 'different' from the rest of India, but sadly there is nothing in the Indian education system that actually teaches anything about this vast region in a sustained manner, apart from a few pages in the Central Board of Secondary Education approved curricula that were inserted after 2000.

I remember stopping a few young schoolchildren trotting back from school near the town of Along, above Pasighat in Arunachal Pradesh. They were about to dash across a sprawling suspension bridge, about half a kilometre long, spanning the Siang River. It was about a hundred feet above the level of the fast-flowing waters below and they were about to run across it with their school knapsacks without a thought. I asked a couple of them if I could take a look at their books and flipped through a history lesson—it was all about Akbar and the Mughals. Another was about the East India Company. Of course, these are interesting topics to help students understand India's past. But there was nothing about Arunachal Pradesh or the Northeast nor an explanation of how Assam and Arunachal were connected to each other and the rest of India. It struck me at the time—how on earth could mandarins in the education department in New Delhi expect children near the China border to understand what they were doing in this vast country if school lessons did not even tell them a thing about their own communities, states and neighbouring cultures but tried to 'educate' them about matters which seemed most alien? For much of the hill peripheries of the Northeast, it is not just that in New Delhi's perception, they are far away. To them, New Delhi has always been far.

So for all groups, there comes a tipping point, a threshold beyond which tolerance does not work or even feigned tolerance towards blatant discrimination. For how long do people swallow insult and harm? It's gone beyond a nasty comment, a brutish shove and sexual groping. It has culminated, as under AFSPA and the first face of discrimination, into a disappearance here and a killing there. However, the shelter of impunity no longer exists. Under AFSPA, abusers and killers are not called to account. But here they can be.

◆

In 2012, the central government acted after a burst of derogatory references to people from the region were discriminated via the internet, especially hate mails and bulk SMSes, following anti-Muslim riots in Assam. This had forced an outflow of frightened people from the region who were living in Karnataka and Andhra Pradesh. The Ministry of Home Affairs amended the Scheduled Castes and Scheduled Tribes (Prevention of Atrocities) Act in an effort to curb the use of slurs such as 'Chinki', which were used to describe people of oriental appearance, especially from the Northeast. Little action was taken against those 'breaking' the law although *The Telegraph*[19] was to comment that: 'Activists have long protested the derogatory use of the expression against people with Mongoloid features. People from India's Northeast often encounter such taunts outside the region, especially in Delhi.'

There is of course a problem with the use of words like 'Mongoloid'. Prominent academics such as the Himalayan linguist Georg van Driem of Switzerland contest such terms created by the German scholar Christoph Meiners over 200 years back, saying that the latter was 'imaginatively trying to make sense of human diversity, though he had no expertise or specialist knowledge to do so'.

There is a long and painful history to the 'Chinki' saga: those who came from places like Manipur, Nagaland and Mizoram, apart from Sikkim and Arunachal Pradesh, especially faced its sting. But until the beginning of the twenty-first century, concerned by their own minority status and lack of numbers, few dared to speak out, unsure of whether they would get support even from their peers. A senior academic in Delhi University spoke to me of how as students he and others faced this conduct—'It was seen as normal behaviour, this name-calling. They thought we were from Nepal. We just had to grin and bear it.'

Not any more.

That is why when Nido Taniam reacted in fury to an insult and paid for it with his life, the outrage and mobilization at his death was spectacular. It was also a perception that many other younger Indians, rebelling against conservatism, choosing different, more liberated lifestyles and sexual preferences, could identify with and support. Those who joined the protests were not merely from a group of eastern states but from across the country.

Within a few weeks, the centre had agreed to set up a committee to look at issues of discrimination against people from the region under the respected administrator Madan Prasad Bezbaruah.

It was a good choice: Bezbaruah, the elegant scion of a prominent Assamese family of upper Assam, was well known as a former central tourism secretary in New Delhi and had served as home commissioner in

Assam. He had also served in the Mizo Hills district during the insurgency. Bezbaruah had retired from government service but headed this committee of largely retired government officers, an exception being the senior Delhi police officer Robin Hibu of Arunachal Pradesh.

Under pressure from voluble agitators who were in the media eye as organizers of the protests at Jantar Mantar demanding justice for Taniam, the government expanded the committee to include the victim's mother and a few activists. Some of the latter, with little experience of government functioning or knowledge of the law, with their high-octane conduct, became stress factors for the Bezbaruah team. 'Hulostuliya karbar (a lot of noise)' was how one committee member was to later describe their conduct.

Despite these internal problems and a short pause with the change in government—the Lok Sabha elections of May 2014 saw the rout of the Congress and the United Progressive Alliance and the return of the BJP under Narendra Modi—the Bezbaruah group resumed its work and its chairman submitted his report in January 2015. Within a few weeks, the Modi government announced its acceptance of all major recommendations in an effort to reach out to the region and assert the primacy of law: it also declared at a press conference[20] that constables would be recruited from all eight states (ten men and twenty women from each) to serve in the Delhi police in an effort to help the local police handle the discrimination issue. I had my doubts about this plan.

In fact, I told a senior police official afterwards that it would probably be more effective if 160 to 200 members of the Delhi police from all ranks were sent to the Northeast every year on a regular basis for two to three months to work, observe and learn from local law enforcement units in the different states. They would learn much more about the area, its people, their culture and society, their sensitivities and the challenges faced by ordinary people and the police. It would be an experience that would stay with them for life. Such an approach would achieve much more than having 160 beat constables spread over a vast city of over 15 million where attitudes of discrimination and abuse do not have the word 'Northeast' printed on them but are inflicted on men, women and children of all ages.

Responding to my idea, the official said the suggestion would be conveyed to the police commissioner and other colleagues but nothing came of it. This is hardly surprising: it is a far tougher task to change deeply ingrained attitudes within a force by doing something truly innovative and challenging than by winning some public support and catching media headlines by giving employment to a handful. The latter is a freebie but the media, for the most part, is too shortsighted to see this, so charged are its many channels with the desperation of competition and outshouting the other.

To address the issue of verbal abuse, racial incitement and physical harm or intent to harm based on a person's appearance or way of life (which would include dietary preferences), the Bezbaruah Committee proposed a major amendment to a section of the Indian Penal Code which dealt specifically with discrimination. This was Clause 153, which looked at issues of 'heinous' crimes such as murder and rape—the suggestion from the influential think tank, the Delhi Policy Group, was that when such crimes were inflicted on those from the region, they should be put under the rubric of racial discrimination. The committee also cited the Delhi High Court's ruling on 14 January 2014 which urged the government to bring in legislation that would prevent 'the natives of one state, in any manner, harassing the migrants from any other Indian state or from indulging in hate crimes against them'. This, the court said, could either be in the form of amendments to the Protection of Civil Rights Act, 1955, and the Scheduled Castes and Scheduled Tribes (Prevention of Atrocities Against) Act, 1989.

But there was a problem: epithets such as 'Chinki', 'Momo' and 'Chi Chi Chu Chu', while being offensive were possibly not 'in themselves violative of the law'. This was one of the most common points for anger among those who complained to the committee. How could it make the legal response to such abuse so stinging as to stop people from using those words?

It came out with proposed amendments to the IPC and the CrPC, the other law used in dealing with law enforcement nationwide. For Section 153B of the IPC, it substituted the word 'racial' (which was not defined) with a set of clauses that made both the crime and its punishment precise.

Thus, efforts to abuse and intimidate or physically harm people on the basis of their 'racial origin' could be punished with a prison term of five years. Section 509 of the IPC should be amended so that anyone using a word or phrase that abused a person on the basis of their looks, appearance, customs or place of origin could be fined and face a prison term of three years.

The CrPC also was to be changed, Bezbaruah said, on this basis, using the reference to the IPC. The offences under 153 and thus more 'heinous' were to be non-bailable; the verbal taunts were not.

Years after Nido Taniam's murder, the government has had other 'pressing issues' to handle in Parliament where the Lower and Upper House have been stalled by a boisterous Opposition over issues as critical as the general sales tax and the plans of Modi's right-wing government to acquire vast powers that would enable it to take over farmland on the pretext of the state's requirement for infrastructure such as road building and even commercial use. Apart from the Opposition, there's been a huge outcry and resistance from farmer's groups, trade unions and the media.

This is not yet law; you can snub, molest, abuse and murder anyone from the Northeast and the special treatment either for the victim or the crime perpetrators is nowhere in sight.

That's the level of central commitment to the rule of law and equality of citizens, despite its claims, whether it is a centre ruled by the Congress or the BJP.

All this is happening at a time when many from the Northeast—to quote one Member of Parliament, some 35,000 of them, many of them from Assam but also large numbers from Manipur, Mizoram and Nagaland apart from Arunachal and Sikkim—are migrating to other parts of the country in search of work, education and livelihoods. They are joining a vast stream of internal migration in India, estimated by UNESCO and UNICEF[21] at some 309 million nationwide who are moving for the same purpose—to construction sites and malls, to government and colleges, to schools and profitable farms, to work at semi-skilled and skilled jobs as carpenters, plumbers, hotel receptionists, chefs, flight attendants, beauticians and spa staff as well as owners. The larger figure is a staggering one quarter of India's population—those from the Northeast are a tiny fragment of this hustle seeking better lives. They need to be competitive and on the lookout for themselves and their own. The competition for jobs is another reason why they become targets.

The Internal Migration in India Initiative (IMII) of UNICEF and UNESCO talks of larger issues before migration in the country, issues that were not addressed in any detail by the Bezbaruah Report. Among these concerns, the UN agencies say:

> In India, internal migration accounts for a large population of 309 million as per Census of India 2001, and by more recent estimates, 326 million according to NSSO [National Sample Survey Organisation] 2007–2008, nearly 30 percent of the total population. Internal migrants, of which 70.7 percent are women, are excluded from the economic, cultural, social and political life of society and are often treated as second-class citizens.
>
> The constraints faced by migrants are many—lack of formal residency rights; lack of identity proof; lack of political representation;

inadequate housing; low-paid, insecure or hazardous work; extreme vulnerability of women and children to trafficking and sex exploitation; exclusion from state-provided services such as health and education and discrimination based on ethnicity, religion, class or gender.

The difficulties faced by internal migrants in India are dismissed on the grounds that the Constitution does not restrict free mobility within the country. In the absence of proofs of identity and residence, internal migrants are unable to claim social protection entitlements and remain excluded from government sponsored schemes and programmes. Children face disruption of regular schooling, adversely affecting their human capital formation and contributing to the inter-generational transmission of poverty. Further, migrants are negatively portrayed as a 'burden' to society, discouraged from settling down and excluded from urban planning initiatives.

Most internal migrants are denied basic rights, yet internal migration is given very low priority by the government in policy and practice, partly due to a serious knowledge gap on its extent, nature and magnitude. A growing misunderstanding of the migratory phenomenon is often at the root of misconceived policies or inaction regarding migration.

This is happening at a time when the region is reaching out to the rest of the country, to whatever is understood as the 'idea of India', to the 'mainstream' as it is crudely put—they are working as professors and as security guards, as government officers and waiters, as construction workers and top-end fashion designers and chefs.

So while the Northeast, shedding decades of insularity, anger and total revolt against New Delhi, has begun turning to engagement, its people still feel the sting of being 'the other', of not quite being fully Indian, as the gazes that follow them in malls and roads, markets and offices make them feel. Those with the English language 'convent education' do better.

Lalthanhawla, the veteran Mizoram politician (who's outlasted all his opponents as chief minister, as we have seen), once asked a conference of business leaders: 'What is an Indian supposed to look like? Does he wear a turban, a dhoti, a veshti, a kurta?' Although the gathering broke into good-natured laughter, the pain of being slighted was evident in the remarks of this easy-going leader, who is fondly called Pu Hawla. He once told me of how he had been asked to produce his passport at a five-star hotel in Mumbai and the receptionist would not believe him when he repeated that he was an Indian. There's little likelihood of a repeat of this incident happening in today's India or at least at a top hotel—the chances are that at least one of the receptionists or a supervisor would be from the Northeast.

There is a remarkable passage from a major leader of South Asia which seems to ring true of these conditions.

'We are different beings, there is nothing in life which links us together. Our names, our clothes, our foods—they are all different; our economic life, our educational ideas, our treatment of women, our attitude to animals... We challenge each other at every point of the compass.' Those words were spoken by none other than the founder of Pakistan, Muhammed Ali Jinnah,[22] to a British journalist in January 1944. Nearly fifty years later, a man who rose to become prime minister of India echoed similar sentiments although he was speaking of the similarity of the Northeastern Region to Southeast Asia and, without allusion, its complete difference from the rest of India.

'The food we eat, the languages we speak, the dresses we wear' were indicative of close connections between the people of Southeast Asia and India. But Inder Kumar Gujral, diplomat, veteran Congress Party leader and later Janata Dal (U) leader who became external affairs minister and subsequently prime minister, could not have been speaking of his native Punjab or central or south India. His phrases could only have relevance to the Northeast where scores of communities have these connections spanning hill ranges and international borders.

◆

The differences between those who 'looked' different and the 'mainstream' Indians in the twenty-first century lay at the heart of the Bezbaruah Report. The key lies in the pages which look at the legal aspects in detail. The report stresses how the government has failed to sensitize police forces to the needs and concerns of communities from this region despite repeated home ministry circulars on the subject stressing the need for orientation and training of police forces.

This is where, in almost every sector, India falters and fails—in the question of implementation of good ideas into time-bound programmes with responsibility for shortcomings being fixed on politicians and bureaucrats. The committee spent much detail on the need for developing cultural, information and educational[23] spaces as well as sports connectivity—but these are long-term programmes which need detailed planning and investments.

When I was at Jamia Millia Islamia's Centre for North East Studies and Policy Research, we developed a history paper for undergraduates—we have to start somewhere to correct a teaching system where, as earlier recounted in this chapter, schoolchildren on the edge of the country's border with China are reading about colonial rule and the Partition of Bengal by Lord Curzon but not about their own world. This paper could be used at the senior school and undergraduate levels across the country and then in a master's course at universities. The absence of the region's connections or history has long been a sore point for leaders of all communities as well as media and activist groups. Here is one way in which these gaps in information and knowledge can be bridged. But both the university and other centres have been slow in taking up the paper, which we designed in collaboration with more than twenty historians and social scientists from other fields, over detailed sittings involving scholars of and from the region. This is another example of the slippage of good programmes and ideas; if they are not institutionally sustained, they do not last.

But, above all, what is most required is visible, stinging affirmation of the rule of law and the assertion of the equality of all before and below it, especially those from the Northeast.

We cannot forget that a number of those who have left have fled the instability of the region and not just its inadequate educational, infrastructure and employment facilities. The fear of being targeted either by security forces or by non-state armed groups, of having their studies and work disrupted by unending agitations for various causes, which draw in communities and individuals, especially young people, only to leave them stranded and without hope is common, leading to greater resentments. The extensive use of AFSPA cannot but have had a huge impact on generation after generation and triggered part of the out-migration. The attitudes of fear and resentment, moulded by experiences suffered over decades, has preceded this movement and remains at the heart of the angst of those who have moved and those who continue to stay back. After all, as we have seen in earlier chapters, discrimination is enshrined and legalized through AFSPA.

The children of prominent social, cultural, political and bureaucratic leaders from the states of the region, including human rights activists, editors, those from the police and civil services, live in Mumbai and Bengaluru, Kolkata and Chennai, Bhopal and Delhi. They're also in Australia and the United Kingdom, Europe and the United States. Some have taken the citizenship of the land of their adoption. The list is long. In India, the settlers have purchased houses and apartments in metros. This is ironic: the younger generation clearly feel safer in these 'Indian' cities than in their home towns, despite the energy with which their parents and non-state groups agitate over local issues or assert their rights at the expense of the 'outsider' from other parts of the country, even though these persons may have lived longer in the neighbourhood or town than those proclaiming their 'local-ness'.

◆

Younger people from the region appear determined to do well if not integrate. There's a remarkable example from the village of Song Song on the edge of Mao Gate, the highest point along the Imphal-Kohima route. It's on the Nagaland-Manipur border and in a beautiful setting. Richly glowing golden fields of rice, ready for harvest, a sprawling potato farm, forests, streams and rice terraces cut into a steep valley, as the brooding Naga Hills look down, while trucks painfully groan their way up the high slopes.

Song Song is important historically for a bunch of reasons: it was one of the key points of World War II where the Allied Forces pushed the Japanese back from Kohima. It's also where the first public protests demanding a free Naga land were fired upon in 1948, killing a handful of rallyists. A little hillock with a stone slab in the heart of this town marks that moment and it was near here that Th. Muivah and his Naga supporters faced off with the Manipur police and government in his failed effort to travel to his ancestral village, Somdal, in Ukhrul district. That standoff led to a Naga blockade of food and consumer goods for Manipur, lasting over two months, with the connivance of the state government under Neiphiu Rio. Cooking gas cylinders were priced at ₹2,000 at the height of the blockade while petrol sold at ₹500 per litre. The Meiteis survived, switching to wood fires for cooking, cutting back local transport and working out of their homes, bringing in supplies literally through the back door on their east (Myanmar) and south from Assam. Ultimately, the blockade was lifted but the damage had been done: the bitterness between the Nagas and the Meiteis of the valley had grown as had their suspicions of each other.

Song Song and Mao Gate are also major points for extortion—they're funding or collection centres (from trucks and businesses) for the NSCN (I-M). Automatic weapons and the fancy Glock pistol are easily available for a fee, I am told. The region is awash in the illegal arms trade, a legacy of nearly fifty years of non-stop conflict and uncertain peace as well as the presence of well-armed armies and well-connected arms dealers just across the border in Myanmar. Over fifty years, that country too has fought its large rebel armies to a standstill but now with the advent of democratic icon Aung San Suu Kyi to power, the question of what their role will be in a democratic nation remains an open question. Weapons come from various points on the Myanmar border through Nagaland and Manipur but also through Mizoram, where getting across is easier partly because Indian patrols are fewer.

Yet, from Song Song, the village of a young friend, the tall and cheerful Kaisii Kokho of Jamia's Centre for North East Studies, comes a story of hope, sustainability and investment in India. It is a story that Kokho tells with a smile.

Song Song is prosperous, despite the extortion and its troubled history. People have left the village to work in Nagaland, Manipur, New Delhi and elsewhere. Some have returned to be in a place where the air is fresh, where their families are comfortable, and where, despite the challenges they face every day, life is more relaxed than in New Delhi and Bengaluru. Concerned about reports from New Delhi which spoke of how youth from the village were facing accommodation problems apart from the other issues of harassment and racial targeting, a group of elders met to discuss what could be done. After a series of parleys, a simple decision was taken: the village would buy land in Burari village of North Delhi, where a number of students and professionals from Song Song lived. They would engage a builder, set up a hostel and provide rooms and a full-time cook to cater to the longing for home food, seasoned with local herbs, vegetables and an assortment of meats.

The funds were assigned, the contractor was hired, the land was purchased and today, a single-storey concrete building stands in the by-lanes of crowded Burari, home to twenty-four young men from Song Song. There's also a cook from the Kom tribe of Manipur, the ethnic group to which the Olympic boxing medalist Mary Kom belongs. And, yes, he does prepare Naga food. The house came up in 2009 and is an example of foresight, determination and engagement. It is also an example of how Naga villagers are prepared to invest in a land they once fought and resented (and probably still do) and engage with India. It may not be the embrace that right-wing Indian nationalists want but it is a daily engagement despite the slurs and challenges that the Nagas and others endure almost on a daily basis.

For many years, the stench of intolerance and inequality has overwhelmed individuals and communities from the Northeast. But they are strangers no longer to India. While retaining their traditional food habits, they have also adapted to eating chapattis, the unleavened wheat bread staple of the north, and the insipid lauki, tinda and other summer vegetables of the land. They go to Hindi films, play and sing Hindi songs—public performances of which are banned in Nagaland and Manipur. And they have friends from across the Indian spectrum. They even live in vegetarian homes in towns like Miraj in Maharashtra. The RSS has organized schooling and vocations for Naga youth and Arunachalis in cities such as Mumbai: the governor of Nagaland, P. B. Acharya, a prominent RSS organizer who has known the Northeast well for decades and worked extensively there, has helped develop such networks and connections. It's part of their effort to 'mainstream' the tribes. They seem to have some luck with the Zeliangrongs of Nagaland, but that is partly due to the influence of the late Rani Gaidinliu and the Heraka cult which has been likened to Hinduism.

Sadly, not all migrants to Delhi and other cities have exactly covered themselves with glory. There are many cases of drunken, loutish behaviour as well as street brawls between groups; and there are live-in arrangements which go sour following which one side ends up complaining to the police. Robin Hibu, the energetic, cheerful senior police official from New Delhi who is from Arunachal Pradesh, often raises his hands in despair and frustration at the number of girls who run away from home, people who are found drunk or others who are cheated of their money and assets because they are either too trusting or just stupid. Hibu has almost single-handedly tried to bring the issues of the people from the region to the notice of his bosses and colleagues.

He's had some major successes and some equally resounding disappointments. But he's unfazed and goes on, setting up a WhatsApp group that's like the first port of call for those in distress, needing or wanting advice. Every day, he sends out a series of ideas, instructions, appeals and advice to anyone who will listen—and even to those who won't or don't. It's a thankless job but he's unrelenting. However, frustration with the processes of government, about its lack of understanding at any depth or acceptance of the need for change, and at his own people from the region, including emotional activists, sometimes comes out.

'Dada,' sometimes he bursts out. 'Ki korim? (Elder brother, what can I do?)' And then: 'Lagi thakigo lagibo. (We have to keep at it).'

Yet, the Government of India is unable to reach out and even push a law through that would protect the rights of some of its most vulnerable people in urban spaces. It speaks often—from the prime minister down—about a muscular and robust policy connecting to the neighbours which they call the Act East policy. Words are easy. Action is the challenge.

Forget about amending or repealing AFSPA, as the Reddy Committee suggested in 2005. No government has the political will to do that;[24] it can't even get the amendments to the IPC and the CrPC, on racial abuse and discrimination, which it had publicly accepted in toto, through Parliament. It should have moved forward with public discussions on them so that lawmakers were under pressure to accept these laws. Another opportunity has been missed; another breach of trust is established.

There is, of course, sleight of hand here. Governments would find it easier to deal with a law that tackles racial discrimination than one that is seen as the bulwark of the state against armed rebellion. That's why the Bezbaruah Committee, despite its excellent recommendations and hard work, remains a diversionary tactic for the centre. Unable to tackle AFSPA—either in terms of getting the political support within and without government for that (the political hue of the party in power is immaterial: they're all on the same page on this one) or from the army brass and the defence ministry babus and even the home ministry and all its intelligence agencies, the centre took up another sensitive issue which was potentially easier to handle legally and process through the system. Even here it came a cropper, trying to take the easy way out instead of facing the problem head on and with maturity.

So, ultimately, we'll be left with another bureaucratic answer to a complicated problem: an annual recruitment[25] of nearly 200 police constables[26] from the Northeast to the Delhi police (which has a total strength of nearly 1,00,000) and a hopeful assumption that they will make the difference by being in the right place at the right time to prevent something bad from happening. This is a farcical approach both to policing and the core issue of discrimination. As I'd suggested, it would be a better investment to send constables and junior officers from Delhi and other metros to where there are significant populations of people from the Northeast, to spend time with local police teams, understand their pressures and share concerns while also interacting with local communities, to learn about their cultures and issues. If the recruitment of those from the region to the metro police is seen as necessary, then an exercise in professional and cultural re-training is also critical to behaving with sensitivity, greater competence and understanding differences.

Maybe it would make more sense to those from other parts of India if we compare what Northeasterners face in metros like New Delhi to what has been reported of assaults, abuse and even killings of Indians in Australia as well as in the United States. The Australian and Indian governments have defined this as unacceptable racial profiling. A flurry of media reports, diplomatic efforts and condemnation by both governments followed the incidents which were investigated with vigour by local police. The same urgency and commitment is missing on the issues discussed here perhaps because policymakers think that the region does not make enough of a bloc to make a difference to the politics of the centre. Those who think so are making a fatal mistake: they have forgotten what the last sixty years of conflict has shown—whether it is the Nagas, the Manipuris, the Mizos or the Assamese, you can't take them for granted for, as many soldiers, officials, organizations and political leaders have learnt to their cost, they are fighters, even for lost causes. They are no pushovers.

New Delhi needs to understand a basic point: a patriarchal approach won't work. The people of the Northeast are no longer strangers. They have become part of the system, are familiar with the intricate processes of government, of business and how to move forward and engage with confidence and sophistication in a globalized world. They are no longer outside the room or house, looking in.

They are the new Indians.

Racism is a fact of life especially when it comes to those of darker or fairer skin or who look exotic like those from the Northeast. African students and business people face it whether in New Delhi, Goa or Bengaluru, stigmatized as drug dealers and amoral.

In a bunch of attacks in 2017 in Delhi and its outskirts, African men were targeted and beaten. A number were hospitalized. A few were thrashed in a private mall, the kind of swanky place that is so different to the India outside the mall, where middle-class families, and people like 'us', go with friends and relatives for an evening out in cool surroundings, to eat food and lose ourselves in the delusion that there are little Europes in our midst and India is shining.

Not so—all we need to do is come out of these little comfort zones to confront the real nation, the grime, the incivility, the underlying violence. And the attack on the Africans took place in one of these bastions of comfort. All it drew was a limp response from the central government and the state government of Uttar Pradesh. But it provoked an unprecedented reaction from African diplomats, outraged by the government's low-key position. The diplomats said they were not just unhappy with New Delhi's response and wanted something that had never been heard of—a UN investigation of the attacks, which they branded as racial, or based on skin colour.

Although there was condemnation of the anti-African attacks and various demonstrations, it showed up our discriminatory approaches. Yet, despite the fact that there has been attack after attack on people of a different colour, men and women, we insist that we are not racist in our attitudes. But the media is awash in ads about lotions that promise lighter, fairer skin. It doesn't take a professor of sociology to tell us what this attitude reflects.

And although we may speak of strangers in our neighbourhood or state, we often forget that we too are strangers elsewhere, in other neighbourhoods and bad things happen to us—and we do bad things to others too, from our own national neighbourhoods.

Old attitudes die last, if they die at all. They sink below the surface, beyond the sight of eye, until an event, a word, an act forces a sudden and at times bloody outburst.

◆

That was what Syed Sharifuddin Khan found to his cost, as had Nido Taniam before him. In two different places, geographically almost as far from each other as they could be in India, two different families, but with the same terrible ending.

Khan ran a small business in the dusty town of Dimapur, which abuts the Assam plains. Dimapur is Nagaland's only railhead and its largest city. It's better known for potholed roads, a place where the ubiquitous 'UG' groups extract, often by threat and intimidation, large and small sums of money (taxes, they call it), and where militant leaders, businessmen, government officials and politicians have built lavish mansions of marble and gleaming ornate fittings, their porches and garages home to fleets of flashy cars.

It's a town where over the years, a new community has sprung up—the Sumiyas, a group produced by intermarriage between Muslims from the plains and Naga women, both Sema (Sumi) and other groups. This started as a rural phenomenon, with migrants from Assam, especially the Cachar Valley, moving to the fertile plains around the town, working first as farm labour in Naga homesteads. Later, as Naga landowners saw the virtue of having hardworking men on their farms, intermarriage was encouraged.

It's something that upper middle class Nagas, including a few who are my friends, can't tolerate. The wife of a friend said that women from poor Naga families of one particular tribe were married off to Muslims. 'You won't get anyone from our tribe or of other tribes marrying like that,' she retorted when I asked about Khan's lynching.

The earlier Muslim settlers came to Dimapur, Nagaland's commercial hub, from Pakistan's Peshawar in the 1890s.[27] They gradually came to control poultry, meat, fish and vegetable businesses besides local transportation and construction work.

'Intermarriage was unobtrusive until the 2001 census revealed the Muslim population had increased by 150% to reach 35,005 against Nagaland's population,' the *Hindustan Times* said. A lingering fear, one that existed among many in the region of being outnumbered and swamped by outsiders, especially so-called 'Bangladeshis', rose. This was an emotion fuelled by the anti-immigrant movement, which swept Assam in the 1980s, as we have seen.[28] The results of those dramatic, bloody and fearful days[29] have left a legacy of suspicion and bitterness, memories which still haunt many in the flat farmlands of the Brahmaputra Valley.

The violence against immigrants is even justified by some scholars who assume, without proof, that these people are Bangladeshis. A second view then emerges that many have gathered 'fraudulent documents such as ration and voter identity cards and driving licence(s)' while travelling via Assam to Nagaland. In a report on illegal immigration into Northeast India, Dr Amarjeet Singh writes: 'Since the immigrants possessed these documents, the local police could do nothing despite suspecting their dubious nationality.' The problem here is that the facts are at variance with these assumptions: Nagaland's population was inflated by the state government and local surveyors of the national census by a whopping five lakh[30] or half a million to try and secure additional funds from the centre.

◆

I stumbled onto this during a detailed household survey of village communities for a North East Vision 2020 project sponsored by the North Eastern Council (NEC),[31] based in Shillong. It was an effort to get an understanding of what ordinary people, largely in villages, would like to see in their future and what should be different. Based on an exhaustive 86-set questionnaire that covered household demographics as well as the social and economic structure of families, this unique effort by twenty partner groups with some 120 enumerators covered all eight states. I was privileged to lead it. We completed the work in a record four months during the monsoons, the worst weather of the region; the data filled seven trunk-loads which were deposited in the office of the NEC in Shillong. In all, some 40,000 households were covered in the survey, perhaps the most exhaustive and largest such effort in the region.

The plan was simple: whenever we visited a village, we would, based on the census data, interview 10 per cent of the population. It was working well when one day our team got a call from Nagaland.

My assistant turned to me after the call. There was an issue in Nagaland, he said. I was worried. Was the underground bothering them? There've been too many cases of extortion from non-governmental organizations, genuine and otherwise, government officials, politicians (the last two give quite willingly). Or was it the government, for some unfathomable reason? It was neither.

The Nagaland surveyors were finding, time and again, that the size of the villages was far smaller than the numbers given by the census. Often the figures were off by as much as four-fifths or in one case by nine-tenths. 'Sir,' said one researcher, 'in one village, there were 19 houses. There were supposed to be 193. How do we calculate 10 per cent of 19?'

◆

Some months later, I had a meeting with the state's chief minister Neiphiu Rio at his office in Kohima. I put the problem to him. He paused for a moment and plunged into his answer: 'You are right, we are having many problems now. I doubt if our population is even 14 lakh (1.4 million); it's difficult to justify all this and answer all the questions that the centre puts to us.'

An enterprising young researcher in Bengaluru picked up the thread and did an extensive project on this very issue, interviewing villagers, local leaders, government officials, cabinet ministers, scholars and statisticians. Vikas Kumar, an intense young assistant professor at Azim Premji University, had done his BTech from the Indian Institute of Technology in Kanpur. His detailed work, with a colleague, Ankush Agrawal, turned up many surprising findings.

Giving a talk at his university on 'Winning censuses: the political economy of Nagaland's demographic somersault', Vikas defined data as the most important element in a nation state. India, he said, knew how large the area of Nagaland was. But it was clueless about the population of the state. He pointed out that Nagaland had consistently officially defied economic and social demographics across the world to show a galloping fertility and decadal growth rate despite high education and health barometers from 1971–1991. Women who were better educated and healthier, as in Kerala or Goa, usually had fewer children than poorer, less educated and less healthy mothers. Then, suddenly, without any explanation, the state's population goes into free fall. In absolute numbers, it fell by over four lakhs.

According to Kumar and Agrawal:

The population of Nagaland grew at the decadal rate of 56.08 per cent during 1981–91 and of 64.53 per cent during 1991–2001. These growth rates were the highest in India and among the highest in the world. In the subsequent decade, however the state's population decreased by 0.47 per cent.[32]

The problem was so acute that Rio was pushed to adopt an extraordinary strategy: he summoned a major consultation on 30 September 2009, four years after his government had officially rejected the 2001 census of the registrar general of India as incorrect. At the meeting were church leaders, Opposition figures, government officials, village elders, educators and student leaders to acknowledge the bad data, to explain that poor data would not just mislead but ensure that development goals could not be met. 'Thirty per cent of the population is unaccounted for,' Kumar said. In the joint paper, the authors added: 'This is the first time that a state in independent India has witnessed an absolute decline in population in the absence of war, famine, natural calamities, epidemical diseases, political disturbance, or any significant changes in the socioeconomic correlates of fertility.'

Rio had told me in the 2005 interview that the inflated figures were a result of political concerns: 'All this is because of competition among the tribes, between districts.... The delimitation commission process [of distributing seats in proportion to population] is also creating problems because some districts are losing seats and Dimapur is gaining five seats. Mokokchung seats are dropping by three, Phek will have one less and so on.'

According to Kumar, even Rio was a bit off the mark. The total population in 2001 should have been 1,686,957, to be exact, the scholar says, not 19 lakh. He brings in the much maligned Bangladeshi here again, saying that this group would account for another 50,000–100,000. But certainly not the huge figures that were being bandied about in the state. The earnest Bengaluru-based academic puts the discrepancy in the census at 303,079, not the five lakh that the then chief minister spoke of.

Kumar and Agrawal spoke of two scenarios which could account for this large gap: one was extensive international migration from Bangladesh (which is some 500 kilometres from Nagaland) and Myanmar (with which it shares a border). This they ruled out as quite unlikely. What they seemed to put their money on was the second: '...a substantial portion of the discrepancy in the 2001 Census could possibly be attributed to the deliberate inflation of population figures to avoid potential loss of seats due to the impending delimitation of electoral constituencies'.

Delimitation has been postponed till 2031, so the issue will have to wait for another generation before it comes close to any resolution. That there was to be a resolution is unsure, given the volatility of Naga politics, the ups and downs of the peace talks and conflicts as well as the relationship between the state and the centre.

Kumar added that immigration, undocumented in Nagaland unlike in Assam and Tripura, was being perceived as a potential threat to the tribal identity. While underscoring the Sumiya phenomenon, he also said estimates of the total population of illegal immigrants in Nagaland varied from 1–3 lakh.

The immigrant issue made the influential Naga Students' Federation put non-Nagas into two categories—Illegal Bangladeshi Immigrants (IBIs) and non-Naga Indians allowed entry with Inner Line Permits.

Individuals and organizations in Nagaland blame Assam for all their influx-related ills. But as an editorial in the *Nagaland Post* said: 'The IBI issue in the Northeast cannot be solved overnight. Even in Assam, the Illegal Migrants (Determination by Tribunal) Act hasn't worked...'

◆

It was into this lethal mix of suspicion, concern and lurid portrayals of outsiders as vile aliens out to grab beti and maata that Sharifuddin Khan fell.

While pointing out that immigrants have at times been involved in crimes such as rape, the *Nagaland Post* said of Sharifuddin's lynching:

> There ought to be questions raised on whether the immigrant issue has been raised to the extent that it has unfortunately or unintentionally only led to hatred being fuelled against one community and played into the hands of communal forces? Certainly, two wrongs do not make a right and the incident should be a lesson.

Khan was married to a Naga but was allegedly having an affair with another woman, also a Naga. The woman reportedly demanded money and threatened to blackmail him. When Khan refused to pay up, she accused him of rape and lodged a case against him. He was arrested and put behind bars in the Dimapur Central Jail, technically under the jurisdiction of the central government.

Furious posts, emails and blogs scorched the airwaves when news of the incident spread. Groups of Nagas were urged to assemble first outside the Dimapur deputy commissioner's office. They appeared to disperse after a discussion with the official who assured them that their concerns would be looked into. Suddenly another burst of e-invective pulled schoolchildren out of their classes and brought thousands of youth to the gates of the jail.

By this time, news of trouble had spread through the commercial capital of the state and shops and storeowners had begun downing shutters while people scurried home. No one was sure what the problem was about. Aochuba, a businessman, had gone to a bakery to pick up some bread but drove home when he saw a growing, menacing mob. 'You don't take chances in that kind of a situation,' said Aochuba, who has lived for decades in Dimapur which, like several other Naga urban centres, has a reputation of being a bit of a Wild West town.

After a brief standoff with prison guards and local police, the mob broke the jail gates, went searching for Sharifuddin who had been whisked away to what the jailers thought was a safe location inside the prison. That location was not known to many people except to one person in the mob, who had served time in jail and was a member of a Naga armed group. The frightened Sharifuddin was pulled out as the jail staff watched, beaten and bloodied before being stripped and dragged outside the prison. He was then tied to a motorcycle and dragged through the streets to the town centre. By then, he was dead.

His corpse hung macabrely from a cell phone tower. The searing picture of that event is of hundreds of cell phones raised and pointed at the limp, grisly bloodied corpse as if gloating in triumph over the death of an unarmed man.

You can see only men in that photo.

Sharifuddin's alleged crime remains unproven.

A news report of the time said:

> The Nagaland government has informed the Union Home Ministry that Syed Sarifuddin Khan, accused of rape and lynched by a mob in Dimapur on March 5, had given a statement to the police claiming that he had consensual sex with the woman who later accused him of rape...and had paid her Rs. 5,000, said an official of the Ministry of Home Affairs.[33]

According to the report, Sharifuddin told the police that the woman established a physical relationship with him and then started demanding more money from him. When he refused to pay up, she allegedly lodged a complaint with the police, accusing him of having raped her.

'The State government has informed us that investigations are still under way. Further probe would be conducted on the basis of forensic evidence and medical examination of the complainant,' said the official. The police have also collected CCTV footage from a hotel where Sharifuddin had allegedly taken the woman.

◆

In the 1980s, Shillong went through curfew after curfew after deadly assaults by Khasi groups against Nepali and Bengali settlers. If the 'Bangladeshis' in Assam and Nagaland were Muslim, in Shillong, Hindu Bengalis were targeted. It made no difference that they were refugees from East Pakistan who had left everything there at Partition, fleeing death, rape, destitution and displacement.

I remember the three straight months of curfew in 1980 when non-tribals were fearful of stepping out of their homes and when CRPF troops with automatic weapons marched regularly through the strangely empty streets of what was then a beautiful hill town. That urban space is now corrupted by buildings of brick and cement, tales of vast corruption by politicians, businessmen and officials, drug and alcohol abuse, unending traffic jams and pollution on its main thoroughfares. It's a place where non-tribals, unless they're wealthy and connected, are often treated with disdain and rarely stand a chance of getting jobs in government positions, colleges and entry to schools. Yet, few could gainsay their contribution to the building up of the state even though there was little question that some of them had abused the trust reposed in them.

My mother, Maya Hazarika, made a substantial contribution to the culture and economy of the town. She lived in Shillong for nearly a half century and never wavered in her commitment to the town, to the Mahila Samity which functioned out of a crumbling house near St Peter's School in Stoneyland. That was in the slice of land owned by the Assam Association and Kristi Kendra. Here, year after year, she and her team of middle aged compatriots taught groups of Khasi and other tribal women and a few non-tribals how to embroider, sew and knit, creating not just clothes but also an income generator. Hundreds of young women passed through their hands since the inception of the Mahila Samity, started new lives and livelihoods. It got no funds from government, no big stars came to raise money or raise its profile. My mother passed away in 2006 and every year since then, my brother and I have given modest contributions to the Samity, including an electric sewing machine, to keep her dream alive.

But in 2015, the rickety building housing them collapsed (they were anyway working virtually out of just one room) and the local Assam association refused to give them any alternative space. Opportunities for hundreds of people, including the poorest and most vulnerable, are being denied despite all the tom-tomming that goes on about Make in India and startups. What about restoring an old 'startup' like the Samity which had been sustained all these years by the dedication of a handful of Assamese and other 'non-tribal' women?

I share this from personal experience to show how people like my mother, without gain or thought for themselves, gave willingly of their time, despite failing health, to Shillong. How many know their stories or value their contribution is not the only issue here. What also matters is that they regarded the town as their true home, loved it and built an amazing network across communities, religions and age groups despite times of trouble.

There were many more, doctors and lawyers, editors and writers, businessmen and hoteliers, booksellers and carpenters, plumbers and masons, teachers and students, contractors, officials and politicians who made this place their home and brought their skills, knowledge and abilities to make the place better. But growing tribal aspirations especially among the Khasi, Garo and Jaintia, the hill state movement under the leadership of Captain Williamson Sangma, B. B. Lyngdoh and Stanley D. D. Nichols Roy in the face of Assam's intransigence despite being blessed with a statesman-chief minister in B. P. Chaliha, soured relations. Yet, the commitment of the tribal leadership to a peaceful resolution of issues carried the day and ensured that the movement did not veer to the extremism of the Naga and Mizo experiences.

The new state of Meghalaya was created, with Shillong as its capital, in 1970. In the next years thousands of Assamese and others from the parent state packed their belongings, sold their properties and shifted to the growing metro of Guwahati in the plains and a new settlement of Dispur. Here, the new state secretariat was set up in temporary sheds and warehouses, eventually giving way to a warren of small bungalows for MLAs and ministers, an assembly, an officers' colony and a ramshackle secretariat. The latter was replaced by a spanking new red stone building of brick, cement and gleaming tiles a few years back.[34]

My mother resisted all suggestions that she should leave. This was her marital home, even though my father, much loved as a good human being in the town and a tuberculosis specialist, had passed away in 1969. Shillong was where she had a greater sense of belonging than anywhere else, where the Mahila Samity and her network of friends made life meaningful and enjoyable as did her beloved garden and collection of orchids. She valued her independence and enjoyed our visits, with Minal, my late wife, and our daughter, Meghna, her only grandchild.

◆

The experience of others is sharply different, especially among the Bengalis. A young journalist from Shillong, who lived and worked in New Delhi and Mumbai before returning home, wrote of being beaten by local thugs as a schoolboy. Later, Samrat X, who discarded his Bengali family surname of Chowdhury, preferring the anonymous letter, recounted one of the more brutal episodes from the city of the past thirty years. In the *Asian Age*,[35] seeing the Bengalis as primary targets 'starting with Assam in 1960', he looks at this specific community:

> The violence spread to Meghalaya in 1979 where local organizations, led by the Khasi Students Union, organised violence that targeted anyone who was not a tribal. The principal targets of attacks were the Bengali and Nepali-speaking minorities. All Bengalis, including those born and brought up in Shillong, were targeted as Bangladeshis.
>
> In Shillong, 1987 was a year the curfews lasted longer than usual. Schools and colleges remained shut through the year. I don't remember if it was that year or some other year—because the violence was an annual occurrence—that Gauri Dey, a married woman, was dragged out of her home, raped and killed by having a stick forced into her. There was no 24x7 television in those days, and no Internet. You won't find a documentary calling her *India's Daughter*. You won't even find a story on Google. The story never got out.
>
> The attacks on Bengalis and Nepalis, marked as 'foreigners', was in truth xenophobia driven by racism.

Samrat had another rough experience as a twelve-year-old:

> I was born and grew up in Shillong. One of my childhood memories is of a day when I was walking to the district library to return two books. Two boys, probably a year or two older than me, confronted me on the street. They asked me if I was Bengali. I knew that the right answer was 'no' but the lie took too long to come out of my mouth. By then they had already punched me in the face. I never told anyone about it.[36]

◆

The resentment of the outsider also drives occasional agitations in Meghalaya and Manipur demanding Inner Line Permits (ILP), a form of a domestic visa regime going back over a century to the colonial period.

These permits seek to regulate the movement and settlement of people from outside the region,[37] so that small local ethnic groups are not diminished. Such eruptions of popular anxieties about being reduced to a minority within one's own 'homeland' are fuelled by anger, suspicion and political mobilization. The simmering antagonism to the 'outsider' is reflected in slogans and rallies demanding 'outsiders go home' or 'Khasi by blood, Indians by accident' or calls for maintaining the 'purity' of the race by blocking intermarriage. The Khasi filmmaker Wanphrang Diengdoh interviews youth leaders who talk tough about this issue in his documentary *Where the Clouds End*.

A young academic in Mizoram said that marrying a vai (outsider from the plains) was regarded as one of the worst social offences in her society.[38] Often, the ill will translates into assaults on and abuse of non-tribals particularly Bengalis and Nepalis although the more prosperous Punjabi, Sindhi and Marwari settlers who came at the time of Partition usually are untouched barring more demands for greater cash, partly as protection money.

Patricia Mukhim, a Khasi, is one of the more courageous commentators and social activists of the region. As editor of the *Shillong Times*, now in its seventieth year of publication, she has denounced mob behaviour and written fearlessly about the climate of hate and bitterness that develops sporadically. In 2013, she blasted the campaign against non-tribals:

> The politicization of ethnicity has been a vote-getting strategy for many since 1979. All the bloodshed and violence of that era can be traced to the desire of a few politicians to acquire political power by stressing on differences and by creating a fear psychosis that the non-tribal would walk away with all our land, our jobs and our women. There were periods when women and girls who were seen walking with non-tribals were shamed and the men were punched. This, even before finding out if there was any connection at all or if the girls and boys were class or college mates. It was a reign of terror ... but few dared to speak up.... So we all kept silent and obeyed the diktat of organisations that acted like social policemen.[39]

Patricia also challenged what she described as local narratives built around fear:

> What is it that we fear? Why do we fear? Who do we fear? It's time to analyse this irrational fear on which politicians take a joyride. I am not suggesting that we entertain influx and permit a Lebensraum in Meghalaya. There should be mechanisms in place to check the menace

of influx. But it is wrong to class even those who are born and brought up here and whose antecedents are known to us, as mynder shi sngi (a roving alien). These are despicable terms...

At times, the forces which drive the pro-ILP campaign are fairly well known even if no one writes or comments openly about these. A powerful Congress legislator from Meghalaya spoke to me of how he had funded an agitation in 2013 in an effort to oust the chief minister of the time. However, the party high command in New Delhi was not interested in a change of leadership so he stopped funding the agitation. Within days, the 'movement' had petered out and despite occasional noises has remained silent and inactive. So, I said, it had nothing to do with protecting indigenous rights or blocking outsiders? 'Of course not,' he laughed. 'It was all about trying to topple Mukul [Sangma].'

Much of the campaign over outsiders is ill-founded and poorly researched, although it has a strong appeal and strikes an emotive chord. In reality, the population of non-locals in states such as Nagaland has fallen. The number of people coming into Nagaland has dropped, while the number of those going out has grown. Kumar and Agrawal point out that the number of net in-migrants resident in the state rose by just over 21,000 in thirty years (65,260 to 86,708), from 1971–2001.[40] As a percentage of the state's population, the scholars said, the ratio of in-migrants from outside Nagaland fell from 6.54 per cent in 1971 to a bare 1.78 per cent in 2001. This pattern is visible also in other towns in hill states or districts, especially those where conflicts have been especially sharp.

The case of Nagaland, as earlier noted, is exceptional when it comes to the faking of data which indicated an abnormal increase and abrupt falls, without official explanations. The statistics here just do not add up: thus, one of India's best performing states with regard to Gross School Enrolment (GSE) while compared to population, Nagaland's education facts undergo a dramatic change when we look at the crucial 0–14-year age group (primary and middle school). This is the key barometer in the area of GSE. Nagaland crashed, according to its own statistics, from 58 per cent enrolment to 35 per cent when the national total at this level went up from 32 per cent to 45 per cent in the same time frame.

◆

There are a few things, however, which give grounds for hope, that outside some of these social structures where confrontations have turned traditional interdependence, especially in farming, into mutual suspicion and dislike, if not worse, people can find friendship again and work together.

A couple of years ago, stepping out for a brisk walk in the morning from the International Centre in Goa, in the town of Dona Paula, I was enjoying the silence and the gentle sun when a man and a woman in front of me hailed each other from across the road. Nothing remarkable in that—except, to my surprise, they were speaking in Nepali.

'Kosto cho? Ramro cho?' (How are you? Are you well?) I smiled and spoke to them in my broken Nepali. They were amused and started chattering in Nepali. At which point I raised my hands and said in Hindi that my Nepali was limited. But, I wondered, what were they doing in Goa and were they 'Indian' Nepalis or citizens of the Himalayan land? They were of the second group: 'What to do, sir, there's very little for us back home,' the man said. 'We have to survive, support our families and that's why we have come here.'

A few hundred metres further, I came to a fork in the road for the Cidade de Goa, a busy major resort. There were three young guards checking vehicles. They looked as if they could be from the Northeast. I looked at the name tags on their shirts to make sure. One was a Bodo, another was a Das, the third was a Koch-Rajbongshi.

They were delighted to speak in Assamese. 'Here you are, working together, while at home, all your groups are fighting with each other and killing each other,' I said. 'The mohaal (atmosphere) is very bad at home, no one trusts each other, but here there is no problem,' one of them said. 'We talk to each other and work together.'

Across Goa and southern India, young men and women from the region are making a name for themselves for good conduct, industriousness, honesty and efficiency. A Goan industrialist told me[41] that 'all of my workers are from Assam, they are very hard-working'.

When they travel home, they take with them stories of wealth and opportunity, good infrastructure and tolerance, safety and facilities. To many in Assam's rural landscape, tottering between a fractured economy, fear, violence and poor service delivery, it sounds like a golden land, perhaps just as the Assam of the twelfth century appeared to the Tai-Ahom explorer and conquerer, Sui-ka-Pha.

Remittances from across the country are injecting fresh funds into poor homesteads and more leave to join the opportunities that beckon. But along with those who make it, there are others who don't and fall prey to duplicity.

Stories of women being trafficked from eastern India and Bangladesh are extensive. Falling for the stories spun by touts from home and elsewhere, women and young girls trade family money for a future of horror, where they are battered by rape, prostitution and drugs. Children from poor families who were taken away to be 'educated' have been rescued from hostels in southern India where they lived in dismal conditions with little food, in insanitary conditions and hardly a change of clothes. These too are a grim reality.

Yet, this has not deflected others from seeking a place in other parts of India. The question is whether a Bora, a Das, an Ahmed, a Sarma and a Bodo who can work and live safely together thousands of kilometres away from home can bring some of these elements back to their own lands. Belief in opportunity can spur a better understanding of equality. The rise of aspirations is tempered by the growth of peace, absent at home. Fear need no longer be the key.

Learning to live with these changes and difficulties is in itself learning a new skill. As many from the region have found to their cost, this does not happen easily or kindly—landlords are often boorish, neighbours are raucous and prying, the local youth think the women are fast and harass them. But it's not as if those from the region are exemplars either. There are cases of drunken brawls and substance abuse. But they seem to be more sinned against than sinning.

The presence of so many from the region in cities like New Delhi, enriches the cities, bringing diversity, complexity, talent, skills and many strengths. The swell of migration, propelling people from diverse cultural moorings and interests to new locations where they share space with different cultures, poses a huge challenge about what 'Indians' are supposed to look like and how they conduct themselves. It forces both sides to better understand how to live with each other, how to forge a new citizenship based on mutual respect.

Laws, while necessary for creating a framework to tackle issues, cannot solve problems or change public culture.

Such change will not be easy nor will it happen soon. It has taken three decades and more for youth from the region to assert that they have a right to the larger space across the country. It may not take that long for the new compact to grow but it will take time, through living together, resolving misunderstandings and conflicts, and daily dialogue and engagement.

The response to this challenge, from neighbours and strangers, associates, employers, peers and the less advantaged as well as police and other arms of

government will shape the region's view and of many of its people towards
'India'. It will influence an association, which can be forged, fractured
and tempered in the decades to come. That racial attitudes also shape our
approach to people of a different colour is extremely obvious, especially in
the fairness creams that film stars advertise asking those of a different colour
to lighten their complexion and hence become more socially acceptable.
Then there is also the way Indians conduct themselves with Africans, whether
in Bengaluru or New Delhi, triggering at least two diplomatic incidents
recently with students from Tanzania and Uganda who were roughed up,
molested and abused. In one case a young woman's blouse was ripped off,
not because she had been involved in a criminal offence but just because
she was passing through a particular neighbourhood two days after another
African had accidentally run over a local woman. Our hollowness as a society
on the upward growth path has never been more completely on display.

No matter how much we Make in India or Look West and Act East,
no matter how much leaders dressed in crisp clean clothes come out for
a few minutes armed with brooms to clean streets, we will always be seen
as a nation that will be also known for its lumpen which harasses and
harms without any idea of what it is doing except that it is a mob and a
mob is always fearless in large numbers. Invariably, the victim is a solitary
individual or a handful of people.

◆

But from the Northeastern side, efforts at bridge building continue
seamlessly, with or without government patronage and largesse. Such
changes can be driven by individual and community social enterprise not
by government diktat. This is where the social capital of the people of the
region and their rhythms of life come into play.

By a quirk of DNA, there are some occupations and abilities which
appear to be more natural to Northeasterners. Thus, sports especially football,
boxing, weightlifting and archery is a stronghold of tribal hill groups of
the Northeast. Fashion designers, restaurateurs and the beauty business,
especially small salons in small districts, are the parish of hill groups. A
chain of beauty salons in Bengaluru is owned by a Meitei woman from
Manipur. One of India's most loved and hated media stars, Arnab Goswami,
formerly of Times Now and now managing director of the news channel
Republic TV, is Assamese.

Popular musicians and writers, filmmakers, actors and sports people
from the region span the stages of the country, whether it is a Seema

Biswas and her gripping portrayal of Phoolan Devi in *Bandit Queen*, or Jahnu Barua, the director acclaimed for his humanist approaches related to ordinary people who has won national and international awards, or 'BK' Borkung Hrangkawl, one of the country's top rap singers who bears the initials of his famous father, the pro-independence Bijoy Kumar Hrangkawl who launched the Tripura National Volunteers Force and transformed from a rebel to a local politician in Tripura.

There are the blues singer 'Baba' Rewben Mashangwa; Alobo Naga and the Band; Lou Majaw; and Bollywood successes Zubeen Garg and Papon (the more popular name for Angaraag Mahanta). There is the renowned Shillong Chamber Choir, which has performed for President Barack Obama and the Pope; there are the blues singers, the group Soulmate from Shillong—Rudy Wallang and his partner Tipriti K. Bangar, who's blessed with a voice that can knock the last row off an amphitheatre. There's Adil Hussain, who plays seasoned roles in Bollywood and Assamese cinema—who says he faced discrimination in his home town of Dhubri where his mother was classified as a D voter or person of Doubtful origin (in Assam that usually means the ubiquitous 'Bangladeshi'). It did not matter that his mother was Hindu.

There are the football stars from Mizoram and Shillong, Nagaland and Manipur who are part of the national side and among the top players for the national league, be it in Kolkata or Goa. The football story started with a small club called Lajong in Shillong, put together by hotelier-architect Prabhat Dey. But it was his son Ming who saw the future in the game and pushed it till it rose to the top ten of Indian football and is now even able to trade a player to a Brazil club!

In recent years, football stars from the region have dominated the Indian Premier Football League. In fact, such is the throbbing talent in the region, that in an all-Northeast final in 2017, a team from Mizoram, the Aizawl Football Club, in its first appearance in a national championship, went on to defeat Lajong of Shillong and win the League. But what their fans did after the final also won many hearts and humbled quite a few—without fuss, without orders from anyone, they cleaned out the trash on their side of the stadium as if it was the most normal thing in the world.

Actually, for Mizos in urban settings like Aizawl, it is. Householders regularly sweep the road in front of their homes, there are regular campaigns there and in Shillong by entire communities to clean neighbourhoods. So, it's not just talent that's around, it's also a discipline which should underline to leaders and led who proclaim the need for Swachh Bharat in other parts of the country what they could learn from tiny Mizoram. The margins are better than the 'mainland' in many ways and it really doesn't matter what you eat or wear, which language you speak or what god you worship. What counts is who you are and what you do, not for yourself and a narrow band of brothers but for your neighbours and others.

Doing the region proud is Mary Kom, the boxer who has won Olympic, World, Commonwealth and national championships and still is able to retain a sense of balance, calm and dignity although a hit Bollywood film about her, starring Priyanka Chopra, catapulted her to greater national fame, winning endorsements from cement corporates and putting her face and boxing gloves on billboards across India.

On the other hand, the less said the better about the weightlifters from Manipur and elsewhere who were caught with dope in their systems, disgraced, disbarred and stripped of their medals.

Writers like Mitra Phukan, Dhruva Hazarika, Kaushik Barua, Ankush Saikia, Temsula Ao, Mamang Dai, Aruni Kashyap, Arupa Patangiya Kalita, Margaret Zama, Easterine Kire and many others are popular across India and beyond, and their works have been translated into several languages.

Ideas, music and sports don't have borders. Neither do the cultures and processes of discord. But citizens do. What is unacceptable is that they find themselves bound by laws and rules which date back to a colonial era and which prevent their movement into and away from certain areas.

Artistes, sportsmen and writers have helped the rest of the country to better understand the 'Northeastern' tag. Yet, as the examples of Nido Taniam and others show, it is not enough.

Another group of out-migrants who are doing well and are well-regarded are those who have focused on their studies and completed their PhDs and MPhils, getting absorbed into the 'national' job market in education, law, media, research and teaching.

A fundamental principle of migration is that people usually, when given the choice, move to safer lands than their own where they feel insecure, whether on one side of a border or a different part of the globe. Although they prefer to be closer to home, they are driven by need to lands with greater perceived safety standards and history, where they can find livelihoods and decent incomes but also where they find similarities of culture, social traditions and religion. Of course, as the Middle East experience for those from Kerala, Bihar, Nepal or Bangladesh shows, that hasn't worked out that well.

Maulana Altaf Husain Hali, the poet-philosopher of the nineteenth century, wrote in his 320 canto epic, *Musaddas e Hali*:

> Until when will you persist with your profligate ways
> Until when will you blindly follow the herd
> Forget the old fable, the tale and the story
> Fight the scourge of bigotry, it's evil, it's fury.

That was in 1879. One and a half centuries later, those lines ring robustly and tragically true. Pride, prejudice and hatred are old markers. They will destroy not just their targets but can bring all of us down.

EPILOGUE

In September 2016, a young man collected a sheaf of photocopies of documents from the Parliament Library in New Delhi, paid the fees for the photocopying and left. He sent one of those documents to me by email later, a copy of an impassioned debate—the first in independent India, on the proposed implementation of the Armed Forces (Special Powers) Bill, precursor of the AFSPA. The debate was in December 1947, in the aftermath of the terrible communal riots which killed hundreds of thousands of people, Hindu, Sikh and Muslim, in the time leading up to, during and after Partition. The man was Venkatesh Nayak, a pioneer of Right to Information (RTI) movement in India whose advice and comments are much sought after by RTI activists, media and policymakers in India and abroad.

Reading those speeches by members of the Constituent Assembly opposing and supporting the bill—then sought to be used to put down communal disturbances especially in the Punjab area—sent a chill of dread and recognition down my spine. The arguments for and against the bill's use (and misuse) were the very same as those that rage today, nearly seventy years later. It was a grim reminder that the past is always with us, shaping our present, defining our future, building on our failure to deal with suspicions, old fears and angers and how little has really changed.

The then defence minister, Sardar Baldev Singh, who introduced the Armed Forces (Special Powers) Bill, said the government wanted to expand its use from the four disturbed provinces of Punjab, UP (then United Provinces), Bengal and Assam to the whole country. It had not, he said, inconvenienced anyone so far. And it would not give the armed forces unilateral powers: they would be empowered only if the state government wanted to use them. The minister was specific on another matter while moving the motion to adopt the bill—it was for a year and would be extended only 'if the communal situation' did not improve. But Pandit Thakurdas Bhargava of East Punjab minced no words: the nature of the ordinance and its provisions made it a 'lawless law', words which echoed in the 1958 parliamentary debate and every discussion that has revolved around AFSPA since.

It was unacceptable, Bhargava said, that the army and the air force were being provided such vast sweeping powers: that they could open fire and kill people, using the clause of 'after giving such warning, if any'. The 'carrying of weapons' phrase again was too vague, the pandit said, a 'danda' (stick) could be a weapon so could a penknife or walking stick. To define the occasion so vaguely so as to enable the officer to fire on someone 'on (his) sweet will' was outrageous. Not just that but to arrest a person on mere suspicion that he was 'about to commit an offence' was too 'great and arbitrary a power'.

The founders of the Constitution knew what they were talking about; the same issues are valid in today's world where such laws are concerned. The protection and immunity that officers would enjoy under the Act were unacceptable, Pandit Bhargava said, because such protection did not extend to other officers of the government who could be prosecuted under the CrPC and the IPC. H. V. Kamath, a socialist who was later elected from Hoshangabad in central India several times, noted that the then government, including Deputy Prime Minister and Home Minister Sardar Vallabhbhai Patel, had declared it was strong enough to 'meet any emergency'[1]. If that was the case, Kamath asked, what was the need to provide 'such astounding powers' to troops? Kamath presciently predicted the nature of things to come and what the attitude of the armed forces was likely to be: '…if they are clothed with these powers and if they start exercising these powers for considerably long period, I fear that might become a habit with them and as the saying goes, habit becomes second nature'. What about searches of premises—would persons on those premises also be searched and what about protection for women during these searches, he asked.

Kamath demanded a pledge from the defence minister that the 'draconian' powers would not be abused and that any member of the armed forces who did so would meet 'the severest punishment' even to the point of a death sentence.

Defence Minister Baldev Singh responded by pointing out that the country was under an Indian government, which was committed to the welfare of the people, unlike a colonial administration. He assured members that the powers would not be abused but that 'extraordinary times' called for extraordinary measures. He added that a state government could revoke the Disturbed Areas Act at any time.

Alas, Kamath was right and Baldev Singh was wrong. In 1972, the centre amended AFSPA so that New Delhi could invoke the Disturbed Areas Act without consulting the states or seeking their approval. The centre was effectively not just accumulating power but also bulldozing and silencing the states. The arbitrariness that both Kamath and Pandit Bhargava had feared was now law.

I have recounted these events and reflected on AFSPA and the nightmare it has become—for both users and those who feel the crack of its whip. That is why I find grounds for hope when I talk to people like General V. P. Malik, the soft-spoken former chief of staff of the Indian Army, who now lives in retirement in Chandigarh. General Malik,[2] a man with kind eyes and a frank demeanour, talks of the need to recognize that conditions have changed and the army and political leaders need to adapt themselves to those changes. 'We need to show flexibility, if making a statement helps a situation, there is no harm,' he says, responding to whether the Indian government should apologize to the Mizos for the bombings and the Rambuai years. If the Japanese could apologize to the Koreans and others for the horrors of World War II, 'then this is our own country and countrymen'.

Brigadier B. S. Gill of the 31st Jat Battalion who saw action in Mizoram also speaks frankly of the insurgency there: 'Whenever an ambush took place, the nearest village had to bear the brunt.' He acknowledges freely that 'a lot of atrocities took place, on women, the elderly, menfolk' and that laws like AFSPA seem to have run their course. 'They need to be suitably modified and restricted to specific areas.'

General Bikram Singh, former chief of army staff, said in a television discussion with Karan Thapar[3] that he 'tended to agree' with my view that AFSPA could be lifted from the Northeast since it was no longer a security issue. He added that 'as far as security dynamics are concerned ... you have more of a law and order problem'. He said that the extremists used 'the gun culture for intimidation for extortion, there is gun running, there is gun trafficking, there is smuggling'. Although the general did hedge his bets, Thapar, one of India's most influential and relentless media voices, summed up his views as follows: that the army chief was 'in favour of lifting the AFSPA from specific areas' to start with and then depending on how the situation developed, expand that experiment further. Bikram Singh did not contradict Thapar nor did he demur.

These positives need to be balanced with the strong defence of the need for the act by Attorney General Mukul Rohatgi, who argued along these lines before the ruling against encounters in Manipur.

In that judgment, the Supreme Court declared that 'the public order situation in Manipur is, at best, an internal disturbance and there is no threat to the security of the country or a part thereof either by war or an external aggression or an armed rebellion'.

Commenting on that judgment, the *Hindustan Times* urged the court to 'not stop at this'. It said: 'Along with keeping up pressure on the State to check the misuse of AFSPA, the court must push it also to put in place a robust mechanism, through which people, even anonymously, can voice their grievances when security forces cross the line or report on an alleged false encounter.'[4]

Rohatgi responded in a later hearing: 'Truth of human rights violations if any can be found through criminal trials. It is a serious situation. Security personnel at a Line of Control (LOC) or during an insurgent operation has to act in a particular way. How else [do] we do it?'[5]

The government also has a tough call to make. That is not in dispute. But there are examples before us that have worked. If Tripura can do it, if former army chiefs can see a way forward, then why not move on the issue, one step at a time? If it is so difficult to remove AFSPA, then why not remove the army and the central security forces from their current operational role in the Northeast and put them back in their bases?

If the army, the most visible representative of the act which Justice Reddy said had become an object of 'hatred', mistrust and suspicion, is removed from the scene, will it not reduce the political harm and other insidious pressures of corruption, malfeasance and abuse of power that has hurt its image and that of security forces over the decades? It's simpler said than done, of course. But not to do it would be disastrous. How can India go on tom-tomming its democratic principles and supposed strengths as the world's largest democracy when it has a situation where, in large parts of the country, people can neither hope for justice nor seek a trial for those accused of heinous crimes, crimes which are otherwise prosecutable in a civilian court of law simply because an archaic sixty-year-old act protects the abuser? Surely just on those two grounds and the length of the existence of this act—ten years less than free India—which deny fundamental access to justice, is enough to force the centre's hand? But obviously, it is not. We have to fight tooth and nail to get the right to access justice recognized as such. It is the cry of ordinary people who say:

> By all means, go after the armed groups and those who attack us, molest us, harm us and also target the security forces—but why come after us who are either bystanders in the figurative and literal sense of the word or simply connected to the underground by the fact of

association: we may be related to a cadre or leader or have a friend there.

That is an accident of birth and of friendship. What is the answer to such a simple query? It only underlines that everyone is a suspect unless proven innocent in the eyes of this act. AFSPA turns not just the law but the concept of justice on its head.

For changes to take place, the centre would need to have not just courage but also an exit plan. This is what businesses do as do leaders of organizations who want to hand over charge to younger people, with newly minted ideas and experiences.

◆

One need only look at two issues to review how the stubbornness of the government can harm its international ambitions as well as its proclaimed objective of meeting basic health and development goals. Many would not connect them immediately to AFSPA but they share a deep and abiding link.

The first is India's soaring and unrequited ambition of being a global power and its goal of being a member of the United Nations Security Council, a task to which it has assigned time, funds, diplomatic finesse and government muscle, persuading and cajoling countries great and small to bend them to this goal. All political alliances and coalitions in the country, whether of the centrist Congress Party or the right-wing Bharatiya Janata Party, share this goal and objective. In which case, when uncomfortable questions are asked—and surely they will be—of the country's commitment to the rule of law, to equality before the law, to punishment of the guilty and the existence and use of draconian legislation that is diametrically opposed to the International Covenant on Civil and Political Rights, how will it respond? Will it merely brush these aside as of no consequence or brazen it out as the actions of a nation seeking to defend its territorial integrity against terrorists (although most of the latter are in peace negotiations with it and have signed peace accords despite which the law prevails)?

Another area that requires attention from the government is its commitment to the UN Millennium Development Goals (MDGs)[6] which were set for all nations falling short of the satisfactory delivery of the basic minimum services which meet the most essential of human needs. There were eight goals, desegregated to twelve targets and thirty-five indicators to be met in 2015. These include providing access to safe drinking water, reducing maternal and infant mortality, ensuring better gender equality, achieving universal primary education, reversing—not just reducing—the

incidence of communicable and non-communicable diseases such as HIV/
AIDS, malaria and tuberculosis, and providing a better quality of life for
100 million slum dwellers. The report card is extremely spotty. While the
government's own report says that there has been improvement on all goals,
barring life for the slum dwellers, in several areas it is far short of the targets.

Obviously, one cannot blame the existence of AFSPA for this failure.
But surely, that and the Disturbed Areas Act have a role in the lack of
outreach in areas which are seen as most conflicted or troubled and where
the MDG goals have been way off-target (the MDGs were succeeded by
the Sustainable Development Goals (SDGs) which cover a range of human
security issues including trafficking, child and gender abuse, poverty and
climate change). The states of Nagaland, Manipur and Mizoram are among
the real laggards and it is no surprise that these are all states where AFSPA
and the Disturbed Areas Act have been in operation for the longest period
in the country. The statistics are damning: apart from the laws we have
talked about, obviously other factors are at work. These include lack of
local governance, poor integrity and extensive corruption as well as lack of
governing and technical capacity since two overall non-insurgency affected
states, Arunachal Pradesh and Meghalaya, are on the list. In the words of
Nagaland legislator Al Ngullie:

> Contrary to lofty rhetoric floated by local politicians about
> development and welfare security, the level of poverty in Nagaland has
> increased. Contrary to the all India scenario, which reflects reduction
> in the intensity of poverty in both rural and urban areas, in the case of
> Arunachal Pradesh, Manipur, Meghalaya, Mizoram and Nagaland, the
> intensity of poverty has actually increased in the rural areas, the report
> says. In fact, the report shows, the Northeastern states of Arunachal
> Pradesh, Manipur and Nagaland are the only ones in the country that
> have shown an increase in poverty levels both in their urban and rural
> areas. The welfare performance of Nagaland can be viewed through
> the Poverty Gap Ratio (PGR). The PGR is the gap by which mean
> consumption of the poor below the poverty line falls short of the
> poverty line.

A research question arises: if AFSPA and the Disturbed Areas Act were taken
out of this equation of bad governance, incapable technocrats, thoughtless,
corrupt politicians and extortionist groups, would these states have done
better? Although the number crunching exercise needs to be gone through
and accomplished in the states which have been affected, I think the answer
to that would be a resounding yes. Conflict and its binaries, including

trauma, poor health, incapacity to work, a constant sense of being conflicted or of living in a conflict zone through strikes, protests and counter-protests shut down normal activity, harm ordinary people and ensure that the vulnerable and needy do not have access to their basic needs—food, education and health care. In this, the non-state armed groups and 'civil society groups' are no less to blame. Their unending protests brutally affect ordinary people, snatching their daily earnings and bread from them, blocking access to health-care centres, offices or schools and colleges. There have been innumerable cases of people having appointments with medical specialists in distant hospitals who have had to suffer the consequences of bandhs and protests; they have had to cancel, delay and reschedule these appointments and suffer the consequences of delay. AFSPA hasn't been of much help to them.

This is not limited to the Northeast. Take the official report of the Government of India on this issue: the highest Primary Health Care Reform (PHCR) is for the state of Chattisgarh (39.93 per cent) followed by Jharkhand (36.96 per cent) and Manipur (36.89 per cent). Jharkhand and Chattisgarh are extensively affected by a pro-Maoist armed movement, exacerbated by brutal responses from the state governments and central paramilitary forces though neither of them, unlike Manipur, have AFSPA. Manipur's hill districts have been under the law since 1958.

The MDG report issued by the Government of India's own Ministry of Statistics is scathing:

> All States, except Arunachal Pradesh, Assam, Bihar, Chhattisgarh, Jharkhand, Manipur, Madhya Pradesh, Odisha and Uttar Pradesh are likely to achieve the national level MDG target by 2015. As per the historical trend, 23 States are likely to achieve their respective MDG target by 2015. Among the remaining States, the States of Delhi, Bihar and Orissa are likely to miss their MDG target narrowly, and the States of Madhya Pradesh, Chhattisgarh and Mizoram are likely to miss their MDG targets by huge margins.

These issues are not new. The latest figures show, as we have seen in an earlier chapter, that Assam's maternal mortality ratio (MMR) level has fallen to 300. But it's still the worst in the country.

I reflected on this:

> ...the statistics actually show that it is more disastrous or dangerous to be pregnant or about to give birth in Assam than any other part of the country because the risk of dying from a motherhood-related issue is

highest here. So, Assam, which prides itself on the dignity, honour and place that women have in society actually allows tens of thousands of its women to die in the process of giving life. How is that acceptable?

The state's MMR was 92 points higher than that of the three next worst performing states of Bihar, Uttar Pradesh and Madhya Pradesh, all of which may have law and order problems but do not face either insurgency or the rule of AFSPA. More rigorous and dedicated research is needed in these fields before one connects the dots and comes to a conclusion. But the trends show that any state, however badly governed and with numerous law and order problems including communal and caste riots, is better off than one facing the twin pressures of insurgency and AFSPA. A state like Kerala which does not have either of these challenges, has a history of peace and better rule and excellent human development indices at levels at par with the West: maternal mortality rate at 8, an infant mortality rate of 12 while its total fertility rate actually met the UN's MDG.

A strong argument can therefore be made in favour of a situation which encourages peace and conditions where fear is absent. The latter is a critical element in assessing truly peaceful conditions and the lack of fear may not be reflected in an absence of conflict. Thus, while peaceful conditions may exist under AFSPA, the question to ask is whether the affected population is without fear, be it of the security forces or non-state armed groups. This is the real test of peaceful conditions—where the lack of fear unleashes the full flowering of individual, group and even stakeholder creativity and capacity. Wherever the act and the armed forces are in place, even in places where conflicts have abated, such a burst of creativity is rarely to be seen, shorn of control. It is muted and diminished, not fully articulated. The entire rhythm of life is disrupted when shops, offices, farming, educational institutions and health centres shut. Access to basic services falters and fails; here the fear of conflict, of the security forces and the underground persists. Only when the overall conditions improve, can the delivery of the MDGs and issues such as PHCR also improve.

◆

In 2014, I climbed to a vantage point on a hill overlooking the village of Zubza in Nagaland and walked to a quiet, dark patch of forest and grass not far from the sharp peak reaching for the sky. It's a short distance from the thicket to the edge of the sheer cliff side, from where you can see the Kohima valley spread out below, with escarpments and terraced fields, transmission towers and highways, hamlets and churches and the haze of

Dimapur in the plains further south. In the mornings, one can see the ridge on a flank of Kohima, the capital, that some have named as the profile of the 'Red Indian', a massive rock face shaped like a sharp nose receding from a proud forehead.

In that thicket, amid the calling of birds and the whisper of the wind, I was shown a grave. It's a sad story, but one touched with the grace of the goodness of ordinary people.

At the peak of the inter-factional fighting between the NSCN (I-M) and Khaplang (K) groups among the Nagas, a young fighter from the K was being pursued across this hill. This was at a height of over 5,000 feet where the paths are narrow and uneven, with rock, grass, trees and shrub impeding swift movement. Both the youth and his pursuers were obviously very fit as they rushed, carrying weapons and rations, one in flight, the others in pursuit.

Villagers further down heard the crackle of gunfire that night. The next day when they came to investigate, they found the body of a young Konyak, one of the larger tribes in Nagaland, in his fighting fatigues. A search of his uniform turned up an address in Tamenglong district, about 200 kilometres from where he had fallen, a place that is among the most isolated and backward in Nagaland, with broken roads and small hamlets. The identity card carried a name and a phone number. After the villagers had buried the fighter and placed a cross on the spot to mark the grave, one of them called the number.

An older man answered the phone on the other side. It was the slain fighter's father. A few days later, he reached the place where his son lay and prayed at the graveside. He told the villagers that he did not want to disturb the body and take his son home. The village had given his son dignity in death and he felt deeply honoured. The family wanted this to be his final resting place, the father said, struggling for words between tears.

◆

In another village, some 50 kilometres away, known for its valour against both the British and the Indian armies, a struggle between three khels or clans defined the early part of the Naga struggle. Hanging on the nose of a ridge with terraced fields around and below, Khonoma commands a spectacular view of the valleys that swarm up to it. Apart from its natural beauty, it is also the home of the legendary leader of the Angami tribe, Angami Zapu Phizo, who proclaimed independence from India and set the Nagas on a collision course with New Delhi, a struggle that is recorded in

the early chapters of this book. That trajectory of violence has begun to ease
and change in the past two decades.

But in 1957 and 1958, the village was split between the anti-India
movement led by Phizo and another group led by his one-time lieutenant
T. Sakhrie, who also wanted freedom but felt that it would have to evolve
in stages. The latter felt that it would not be possible to fight the Indian
Army, even at an early stage of India's independence, without extensive
suffering among the Nagas. He was killed by fellow Nagas in an attack
for which no one claimed responsibility but which divided the movement
and split the village of Khonoma down the middle.

As people took sides and laid claim to their village's history, a number
turned to the enemy and became informers for the army and government.
Khel members were attacked in their homes. A total of twenty-one were
killed in those two bitter, eventful years. Many left the village, unwilling to
return. During their absence, rivals made off with the tin roofs of deserted
homes as well as kitchen utensils and other implements.

'Thinking about it makes us feel deep shame,' said Kevisekho Kruse,[7] an
engineer with the state government's Public Health Engineering Department.
The sense of suspicion and unease was palpable despite the passing of years.
Members of the clans did not visit each other, share meals or intermarry.

The situation was such that whatever one side would propose, the
other would oppose. There was no rationale: 'they would oppose for the
sake of opposing', said Kevisekho, an earnest-looking man who was to play
a key role in the future of the village.

All this while, the discussions between the Naga leadership of Muivah
and Swu and the Government of India were ongoing. Yet, the village of
the forebears of the movement against India remained divided and unable
to play any meaningful role. Of course, by then, much blood had also been
shed with Khonoma residents and Phizo's clansmen falling to the bullets of
the NSCN (I-M). The latter saw the Angami leader's Naga National Council
and the Federal Government of Nagaland as its principal ideological rival
as it sought to establish its suzerainty. The controversial Shillong Accord
of 1975[8] was seen as a sellout by many Naga fighters, especially Muivah,
Swu and Khaplang, who formed their own organization, the NSCN. Over
the years, the NSCN emerged as the more powerful of the Naga factions,
heavily armed with weapons picked up from the international arms bazaar.
Its army recruits came from a growing pool of well-trained young men
and women from Muivah's own tribe, the Tangkhul, who live in the hill
districts of Manipur, and the Konyaks under Khaplang. The NNC suffered

blow after blow and reverse after reverse to superior armed forces.

However, the situation changed in 1988. From that year, as in the 1960s, Naga began fighting Naga instead of battling Indian troops. The NSCN split following a ferocious attack in Myanmar by Khaplang's men on Muivah's fighters. The bitter parting of ways continues to haunt the movement, neither leader has forgiven the other, despite efforts by Church leaders and women's organizations to build bridges and heal the wounds of the past. The enmity played out in clashes between the factions in Nagaland and even Manipur.

That's why the Khonoma experiment is significant because it shows how, in a village, old feuds though so intractable can be resolved. The divisions carry with them emotional, political and historical baggage.

How was it to be tackled? One of the factions, Kevisekho's own khel 'hungered' for a settlement. Eventually, members of all three khels met in 2004 and organized a day of prayer and fasting. A Khonoma Public Commission was set up, comprising twenty-one[9] government officials, village elders, youth leaders, writers and peace activists, all from the village.

The commission held over a hundred meetings amid initial anxiety that the effort would open old wounds. 'Why are you digging it all up again when people were forgetting, why are you trying to spoil it?' the peacemakers were asked. But they were clear, just fasting and praying would not do: 'a superficial ointment on a wound' was how one member of the commission described it. It had to be extraordinary.

'At times, the conversation veered off the track—we were disputing who killed the British officer' in 1879 who had tried to capture the Angami bastion, said Kevisekho, as we talked in the large, empty conference room of Nagaland House in New Delhi's Aurangzeb Road.

For over a decade, step by step, home by home, khel by khel, the commission members talked to the families who had been attacked and their attackers. It did not happen at one time but slowly, and not directly, to start with. Going from family to family took not less than three years—a slow and painful process. The conversations took place indirectly, with the commission as mediator. When members of the commission felt the time was right, that both sides were ready, the family of the attacker went to the home of the victim and simply apologized. In most cases, the commission members handling the particular cases were present to help. The opening remarks would go something like this, the engineer recalled, in a style that was peculiarly Angami and Naga: 'It is so painful to us that this has happened to you and your family and that our father has done this,' a representative of the family would say in Angami. The response could be roughly translated as 'we have forgiven you in the name of God and for the sake of the future of our children'.

The last reconciliation was the most difficult, for it was between the groups where the enmity had started: the families of Phizo and Sakhrie. It went back to the differences between the two charismatic men over how to fight against India—through non-violent means, as Sakhrie advocated, or violent ways. At a secret meeting in the heart of the forest above Khonoma, the two men and their supporters confronted each other. I am recounting the way the situation played out in the words of the protagonists and witnesses because it is only in this manner that it can retain its extraordinary flavour and power. It is sparkling in its simplicity and precise in its description.

> Phizo, while stating the reason why the meeting had been called, vehemently denied the charge (that he was a Communist) Sakhrie had made against him. Raising his voice, he said: 'Such misleading accusations made at a time like this when we are fighting to protect our nation cannot be treated lightly.' Shaking with anger, Phizo stamped his foot and said: 'In times of national crisis a mischief of this kind cannot be tolerated,' a reprimand to Sakhrie and a humiliating experience for a man who had played such a prominent part to nurture and propagate the Naga struggle.
>
> His [T. Sakhrie's] clansmen urged him to go away to Shillong to be with his Khasi wife and their small children and wait out the strong opposition that had built up against him. It was his chance to pursue the strategy he had made known would come. He refused. Not long after that Sakhrie was taken away by two young recruits of the emerging Naga Army from a wayside inn where he had come to rest near the Northern Angami village of Chiechama. It was in an area where the Indian Army had started to operate and to search for him as his virtual expulsion from the movement had become known. The two young men could not keep taking him through the forest ahead of the Indian soldiers. Realizing that they were soon going to be captured they shot Sakhrie to death and went to rejoin their comrades. Sakhrie's death immediately split the movement.

When Sakhrie's body was brought to the village to be buried, Sebi Dolie, Phizo's bodyguard, who admired Sakhrie deeply, was one of those who dug the grave. His clansmen stayed away as they knew how deeply the Sakhrie people felt about the killing.

Many years later, Sebi, who was ninety when I last met him, but was like his village, strong and erect, called a meeting in the village church, a large, sturdy stone building that stands proud and high above the little square that welcomes visitors when they arrive in Khonoma. Members from his Dolie clan and from Sakhrie's clan came. He said as the senior-most man of his clan he had decided to fulfil his responsibility by responding to the commission's challenge to heal the wounds and wrongs of the past and give a new future to the coming generations.

(The young people had told the village: 'Give us a new future where the different khels and clans will work together with goodwill for one another.')

In the church, Sebi said he had been at the meeting up in the mountain forest and heard what his uncle Phizo had said. He felt that 'uncle Phizo had gone too far'. He told the gathering:

> I have always known if I were a Sakhrie I would feel exactly as you have felt all these years about the killing of Theyieu (as he was called), your uncle and our leader. On behalf of my uncle Phizo who is no more and my Dolie clan I want to say to you we are deeply sorry for what happened to Theyieu. I ask you to forgive our uncle and our clan, and I ask also that you will ask blessing from God for us so that we prosper again with that blessing through you. I ask also that if there are any other wrongs or hurts done by us that you know and we do not, you tell them to us without hesitation so that there will be nothing to divide us from now on.

Immediately, Tsilie Sakhrie, the senior-most man from the Sakhrie family present, came across to him with his hand outstretched, saying: 'I want to shake your hand right away in response to what you have said. We have stopped expecting to hear anything like that from Dolie men.' Sebi said he was astonished by the response and knew he had done the right thing.

Soon afterwards, the Sakhrie family came out with a cryptic statement which said that the issue 'had been such a cause of pain' but that 'the matter ends here'.

Peace activist Niketu Iralu said that after meeting Sebi, he went to visit Tsilie who had responded with grace to the apology.

> Tsilie listened very carefully. He then said: 'I am very happy with what you are saying to me about your meeting with Sebi this morning. I fully agree with all he has said. I will go to him tonight and I will ring you after that.' The next morning he rang and said, 'I have gone

through everything said at the meeting in the church and we both
fully agree with what you have heard. You can go ahead and tell
Hazarika. We support what he will be saying about this problem which
God has helped us to solve together.'

What does Sebi feel about it all today when he is now nearing ninety, told
Niketu:

That morning when our village declared a day of silence to listen to
God to start the forgiving of one another, I came out to the common
yard in front of my house, I felt something was happening that had
not happened before. Even the pigs and dogs that would normally be
running around and making noise, had disappeared. I knew Khonoma
was doing the right thing and heaven was blessing us. I am ready to
go any day now, at peace in my heart and conscience that I have done
what I should have done to help my village and the Nagas.

◆

Today, if we walk to the alder forest outside of Khonoma, which embraces
us with its coolness, a high rock stands by the side of the road, honouring
Sakhrie and his contribution to the Naga cause. It has been placed there by
the entire village.

Ad shum. It is over, for some.

But for many of Nagaland, perhaps, not yet.

If we can think of the replication of this Khonoma story thousands of
times across Nagaland, Manipur, Assam, Mizoram, Meghalaya and Tripura,
that's how many people without number have suffered, minds have been
battered, bodies tortured, lives lost and youth destroyed.

We can't put a number to it.

To deal with these issues is a task of monumental proportions, tough and
complex, for it deals with raw human emotions, hurtful experiences and a
range of social structures and political processes. That's why Khonoma's story
is akin to the memory stone of remembrance in Kohima, commemorating
World War II:

When you go home
Tell them of us
And say
For your Tomorrow
We gave our Today.

◆

The concept of Nagaland's shared sovereignty, which Muivah claimed had been agreed with the Indian government, has been around for decades. It's seen in the practice of constitutional functioning every day in this country. There is nothing new about that. It's just a new phrase for an old process. Trust the mandarins in Delhi to cook up something as sweet-sounding as this. But the taste can't be terrific and it's taken more than a year to digest.

Is it all about a republic within a republic? Or is there something more? It boils down to a simple question of how we live with others. This is especially challenging in a predominantly rural society where 80–90 per cent of the population lives in villages where groups and individual family units depend on each other for help and interaction, both economic and social. One of the byproducts of urbanization, structured living, with guilds, religious and state origin groups as well as ethnics dominating specific neighbourhoods, is still a slow phenomenon. The issue of living peacefully with one's neighbours, whether close or distant ones, is an issue that engaged the ancient Romans and Greeks, the Indian and Chinese civilizations and people like the Native Americans, Africans and Aborigines.

It is so simple, yet so critical and difficult.

In distant New Delhi, twenty years after the negotiations began, impatience is growing among the followers of Khaplang's rival Muivah. So is hunger for power and the fruits of politics. A younger colleague of the collective leadership,[10] as Muivah and Swu are known, snapped quietly but fiercely: 'Ah, these old people! We have to settle and move ahead.'

This is why Khonoma's experience resonates and sends a powerful message to all sides: that individual and community reconciliation is critical to a long-term political solution. Without it, a settlement is possible but a resolution of the issues won't be sustainable. A decade earlier, Niketu, Charles Chasie and others were involved in a Naga Reconciliation Commission. It fell apart within a few months under huge pressure from the NSCN (I-M); the latter felt that the efforts for reconciliation among the tribes tried to steal their mandate and weaken them politically. After that failed effort, several rounds of frank consultations were held between Muivah and Swu with different Naga civil society groups in Bangkok, New Delhi and Chiang Mai.[11] Muivah and his aides believed the time was not right for such a rapprochement since they were still walking a difficult road with the Indian government. They did not want to be weakened by parallel efforts.

It was the Forum for Naga Reconciliation under a Baptist theologian from the Ao tribe which picked up the threads. Reverend Wati Aier, who was deeply respected by all sides, including the I-M, brought together a team which included a few from the ill-fated Reconciliation Commission but left Niketu and Charles out.

With incredible tact and patience, Aier (pronounced Iyer as the Tamil Brahmin surname) and his team, which included Akum Longchari, the left-leaning editor of the *Morung Express,* and others counselled, chatted, listened to and visited members of the different armed factions to try and bring them closer together. There were times when it seemed as if they were succeeding but at the last minute an ill-placed or untactful word, gesture or act would take the moment away. But after years of trying, they finally managed to get lower rung leaders of the I-M and Khaplang groups to sit together, in the same room, face to face.

One of the best days of the movement was a football match that the Forum for Naga Reconciliation organized between the groups and civil society members. Aier himself, agile and fit and a fine footballer from his younger days, ran circles around his opponents, many of whom were younger but fatter and quickly ran out of steam and breath.

But all these efforts seemed doomed to failure, despite intense prayers, successive dialogues, the breaking of ice between the K and I-M leaders— new players emerged on the block as the K group split with his key aides on the Indian side of the border turning against him, saying he was out of touch with reality. This was the KK or Khole-Kitovi group. Then there was another, the Unification Group, with less than a hundred men under arms.

Phizo's proud and powerful movement, which had fired the first challenge to the Indian government and fought the army at times to a standstill and earned the respect of its foes, was hopelessly splintered in six directions, including the two big groups. The smaller groups are the NSCN (Khole-Kitovi), NSCN Unification, NSCN Reformation, with Phizo's daughter, Adino, still holding on to the rump of her father's nationalist unit, the Naga National Council.

The Forum for Naga Reconciliation warned time and again that without unity, there could be no real future for the Nagas. The divisions appeared at times to escalate and then narrow, like the ebb and flow of the tide, but without the latter's certainty. Each side accused the other of being in the pocket of the government.

During this time of uncertainty, a group of former officials, business figures and others created a sturdy organization with an unwieldy title but which spoke out against corruption and the repressive taxation by the armed groups. This was the Action Committee Against Unabated Taxation

(ACAUT). It infuriated the Naga armed groups especially the I-M, which accused its members of being government stooges and worse. But they did not, as they would have in earlier days, harm the opponents of extortion. Started by a team that included Kekheyi Sema, a former government official and graduate of the elite St Stephens College in Delhi, ACAUT has taken the armed factions head on, accusing them of milking the Nagas dry and enabling New Delhi to exploit differences.

In November 2013, it organized a public meeting of people fed up with the daily extortion—ranging from tea-shop owners and professionals to former government officials and businessmen. The NSCN (I-M) 'banned' the meeting but over 25,000 defied the diktat to hear speakers rail against intimidation. It was a phenomenal turnout for a state where the fear of the gun and the underground had long held sway. The 'underground' groups in Nagaland are a very visible presence, in government-supplied vehicles, media statements and offices. Under its banner of 'One tax,[12] One government', ACAUT wants all the armed and political factions to unite and take the discussions with New Delhi forward.

ACAUT's story, Khonoma's reconciliation and other examples represent the missing factor in talks that have eluded settlement: consulting civil society which has mobilized for a common cause.

◆

This factor is visible in a home off the highway to Kohima, on a rough path that at times can be as bumpy as a continuous stretch of Delhi speed breakers. This was among the places where the Khonoma Public Commission met to deal with stalemates, a home of stone and wood, with gleaming polished floors and wooden pillars, and a sense of abundant calm, not far from Kohima. Designed by one of the state's top architects who gave his services free, and built by contractors who barely charged for their work and materials, this is the home of two of the most remarkable people I know. They may be unsung in the media but are a legend among their colleagues and contemporaries.

Niketu Iralu and his wife Christine have made their abode in Kerünyü Ki Sabang, the house of listening, in the Angami village of Sechü-Zubza, a good kilometre or two off the busy Dimapur-Kohima highway.

I have written elsewhere[13] that they have created a welcoming environment that embraces dialogue between differing groups and Niketu has been steadfastly and selflessly plugging away at mediating, offering advice, pressing for conversations between conflicting groups, often at the risk of becoming an object of the anger of those who are thus challenged to change, both in the armed non-state groups and within the state machinery as well.

These past decades, with the critical and equally courageous support of Christine, who's a wonderful hostess, kind companion and trained professional singer, he's been working with other civil society leaders, men of the cloth and women of the Naga Mothers Association among others, to bring some of the healing that wafts through Kerünyü Ki Sabang to the Naga people and their bloodied, buried but living past.

You can't see the home until you drive off the hill road and get onto an even bumpier dirt path; a final jerk of the vehicle and there it is, carved quietly into the hillside. Kerünyü Ki Sabang is filled with music and laughter. The aromas of cooking of many meals merge with talk as visitors sit, chat or stand around its warm hearth, stone counters, wooden tables and stools. Friends, associates and well-wishers contribute to its upkeep; villagers come with sacks of grain, others bring meat, some send fresh vegetables. Young Nagas come to share problems, political leaders drop in as do powerful bureaucrats, grizzled village elders and church figures. Bodo activists from Assam share their concerns, as do Manipuri editors, human rights workers and Assamese scholars.

For many years, Niketu, from one of Nagaland's illustrious clans, and Christine have worked tirelessly to build a fabric of reconciliation between communities, binding up the wounds of conflict in a place that is breathing peacefully after half a century of bloodshed. Their stories prompted a friend from Delhi to remark in wonder: 'I find it hard to believe that people like you exist in this world.'

◆

This is not an isolated trend: across the Northeast, described only too glibly by media as 'troubled' by fear and hatred; the Iralus and others are part of a growing band of quiet foot soldiers working for peace, discussions and the restoration of rights. A group with which I am closely associated organizes boat clinics for those with no access to healthcare on the islands of the Brahmaputra, partnering with the National Health Mission to provide health care,[14] helping reduce the deadly maternal mortality rate in Assam.

A former army doctor and his wife have set up a network of Bodo women weavers which spreads the message of productive peace; an inventor wins prizes for simple new creations that peel vegetables and fruits; an unlettered villager has single-handedly created a forest.

They are among the many who work for peace and people-oriented growth, demanding inclusion in policies and strategies. There are women activists of the Naga Mothers Association (NMA)[15] who struggle to heal divides between factions, battle human rights violations as well as the new enemies of drugs and alcohol; there's the North East Network which works for 'peace and collaboration'; there's the centrist and pro-peace All Bodo Students Union; and the Young Mizo Association (YMA), which says it's the largest non-government organization in the world with over half a million members (that's half the population of the state of Mizoram) and works for the public good—from rescuing people in disasters to organizing funerals for those who can't afford them. Of course, there are those who are highly critical of the YMA's ideology and tactics, saying it also functions undemocratically and is often high-handed with those who disagree with its views.

Many are not noisy activist groups seeking change through confrontation but instead seeking transformation through dialogue. Of course, there are also outspoken organizations such as the NMA, and Manipur's Mera Paibis, the women activists who are feared by those in and out of uniform. As we have seen in an earlier chapter, there's the resolute Irom Sharmila who closed her seemingly unending hunger strike against AFSPA and impunity in the summer of 2016.

People like Niketu and Irom Sharmila march to the beat of an invisible drummer, seeking justice, dignity, equality and peace. There are others, who seek these very goals but work differently.

I think of G. K. Pillai, the former home secretary, who first read detailed accounts of the army and paramilitary sweep across villages in the Oinam Hill area of Manipur, where villagers were beaten mercilessly, held in custody, houses and property damaged, after an Assam Rifles post was attacked, its occupants slain and the armoury looted by the NSCN (I-M) in one of its most daring attacks. Several villagers were killed in the furious vengeful offensive; the civil administration was prevented from visiting the area until the security forces felt that their job had been done.

In his first avatar and engagement with the Northeast, Pillai, a Kerala cadre Indian Administrative Service officer, was given the unenviable task of joint secretary in the Ministry of Home Affairs with specific responsibility for the region. He did something that most senior officials don't do—he started reading the files on specific issues going back decades, for files, like governments, have a long institutional memory. Much is written and marked on them that can throw light on new and emerging issues and Pillai remarked that a detailed look at some of these documents helped to clarify issues for him. It was to play a part in making him one of the most popular, open and firm home secretaries at the centre, especially when it came to issues of the Northeast.

As a joint secretary, he travelled extensively and even stayed in villages and interacted with ordinary people, not just bureaucrats and politicians. A joint secretary's is a crucial post especially in the Government of India—it's basically the level at which policy decisions are designed. Unlike more senior officials who are transferred frequently, a joint secretary usually has a tenure of three to five years at the centre.

Having read about Oinam, Pillai travelled there. Once in Oinam, he did something truly courageous and extraordinary, something that could have cost him both his job and short-circuited his outstanding career. 'I apologized to them, I said to them, "I come here on my own behalf and on behalf of the Government of India, and I am sorry about what happened so many years ago. We can't change the past but we can make a better future with trust."'

That was a transformative moment for the tall, upright, bespectacled officer with a ready smile, and for the people of Oinam.

Pillai afterwards told me that 'we have to go beyond the ordinary' as far as groups like the Nagas and others are concerned, especially those who had suffered so brutally at the hands of the security forces. It will 'restore their faith' in the system but above all it will appeal to their sense of dignity and justice, that a senior person has recognized that a great wrong was perpetrated on them.

I don't know of any other IAS officer at that level or top politician who has had the courage to apologize for what has happened to many other Oinams in other districts and states. Think of the difference it could make, the uplifting of spirits, the end of depressive and oppressive bitterness and suspicions.

Much good has happened but there has also been much brutality and violence, as we have seen. It would be naïve to paint a rosy picture and gloss over the sharp realities that confront us at every step, every day.

◆

The porous Myanmar border brings in many things, from drugs and a vast range of Chinese-made goods, to clothes, mobile phones and electronic items. It also is a major conduit for illegal weapons which can be picked up easily in Nagaland and Manipur. All one needs is a contact. 'You could pick anything for a price—an AK-56, a revolver or even a Chinese-made grenade which is cheaper than potatoes of equivalent weight,' said a villager from the Nagaland-Manipur border.

Officials in Mizoram say that they can capture only 25 to 30 per cent of the illegal weapons and drugs which are smuggled through the Burmese side. They don't have the manpower to make the interceptions. But at times, they get lucky, with the cooperation of foreign governments.

Thus, Thai arms smuggler Wuthikorn Naruenartwanich alias Willy Na, who was brought to India in December 2015 for running a hugely profitable business of supplying arms to insurgent groups through Myanmar, is said to have developed a network that took across AK-series rifles, machine guns and M20 pistols of Chinese origin. Crucial evidence grew against Na when the NSCN (I-M) army commander Anthony Shimray, who was picked up in Kathmandu, reportedly told captors that he had paid some US $800,000 to supply arms from China. The list of weapons supplied is long and lethal and it includes rocket launchers, grenades, assault rifles and ammunition.

Although the NSCN leadership protested Shimray's arrest and claimed that he was part of the negotiating team (he had been involved in several rounds of talks between the Government of India and the Nagas), it was clear that the NSCN was keeping its powder dry and using funds to organize weapons to fight the very government with which it was negotiating a peace treaty.

◆

The central government also appears to be uncertain on the issue of tackling the Khaplang group of the NSCN. The latter broke its fifteen-year ceasefire with the centre and launched a series of audacious attacks on security personnel in Nagaland and Manipur, the most devastating being an ambush in June 2015 which killed twenty-two army soldiers who were heading home after a stint in Manipur. This was the worst reverse that the army had suffered in civil conflict in India in over forty years.

The central government went into overdrive, asserting that no such attacks from armed groups based in the neighbourhood would be tolerated. Meetings in the defence and home ministries as well as the Prime Minister's Office involving not just top officials but also the leadership of the government discussed and finalized plans. A 'robust' response was called for was the sense, a 'lesson' had to be taught.

Late one night, helicopters dropped commandos of the Special Forces from the elite 21 Para on the Indo-Myanmar border, not far from the suspected camps, opposite Northern Nagaland. They slipped across the border under cover of darkness and attacked. *The Hindu* reported:

> The commandos...equipped with assault rifles, rocket launchers, grenades and night vision goggles, were airdropped at around 3 am on Tuesday from Dhruv helicopters, just inside the Indian territory near the border with Myanmar, security sources said.
>
> Once on the ground, the contingent of the special forces split into two groups and headed for two camps being run by NSCN (K) and KYKL [Kanglei Yawol Kanna Lup], who are believed to be responsible for the deadly ambush on June 4, they said.[16]

The teams trekked through the thick jungles for at least 5 kilometres before they reached the training camps and then attacked, according to the report, with deadly precision.

The operation, cleared by Prime Minister Narendra Modi and supervised by National Security Adviser Ajit Doval, an old Northeast hand, was hailed as a huge success by both the centre and the media.

The Myanmar government, which had deliberately not been informed of the operation, was upset as it was told of it only when offices opened in Naw Pyi Taw, the capital, after the counter-assault was over. Although it was very lightly covered in the official media in Myanmar, the then Indian ambassador Gautam Mukhopadhaya, one of the country's finest diplomats, was told in no uncertain terms that such incidents should not occur and reminded of Myanmar's sovereignty.

The figure of thirty-eight insurgents killed seemed to be rather far-fetched for the camp was already largely deserted by those who had ambushed the army troops. 'They were not going to wait around for a counter-offensive,' said one official. However, the media went ballistic: crowing, with jingoistic broadcasts and reports, without any sense of balance or research, quoting the defence minister, security officials and others. They hailed the event in graphic detail, fed by official sources, of how the commandos went about their business. The death toll inflicted on the guerrillas, according to initial fanciful accounts in the media, soared to nearly a hundred. Papers published a photograph of a group of celebrating soldiers claiming this was the group that had carried out the strike. Later, the army disclaimed responsibility for the photo and it was withdrawn as misleading and unrelated to the event.

The facts are that between five to seven persons were shot in or in the vicinity of the camp in Myanmar. No more. A former insurgent with good connections in the area told me that his friends had called from across the border and said that they had counted seven graves. His information, he said, was that one of those was a cook.

The media scaled down the deaths and the story vanished from the front and even the inside pages. But during the days that the story was hot, Major Rajyavardhan Singh Rathore, the former Olympian ace shooter who contested elections in 2014 and won on a BJP ticket and was made minister of state for information and broadcasting, stirred up a controversy by claiming that the government could consider hot pursuit even on the western border. The remark infuriated the Pakistanis, quick to anger and sensitive to needling. It bears repeating that Pakistan is a nuclear power which will resist any major incursion into its territory (although the attack by Indian Special Forces on terrorist camps on 29 September 2016 across the Line of Control in Jammu and Kashmir appeared to have taken them by surprise).

Khaplang, who died in June 2017, broke off talks with the Indian government in 2015 and abrogated a ceasefire, shuttling between a hospital in Yangon where his care was handled by the military and the government in Myanmar, and his camp in the Naga semi-autonomous area near the India-Myanmar border.

With the Myanmar authorities keeping a close watch, the Khaplang camp also has groups of the renegade ULFA under Paresh Baruah, NDFB's Songjit and clusters of Manipuri rebels with fresh arms. However, Khaplang, the wily old soldier, was ahead of both the game as well as his compatriots turned rivals on the other side of the border. On 9 April 2012, he signed a bilateral ceasefire with the Burmese Army; the districts of Lahe, Leshi and Nanyun were placed in a Naga self-administrative zone under the 2008 Constitution. It was the first time that the Nagas had been officially recognized as a significant ethnic group in Myanmar. He secured five seats in the national Parliament for the Nagas, one of which is in the lower house.

◆

In Myanmar, there are grounds for hope on this front and better economic and political relations with India and its Northeast especially after democratic voices under Aung San Suu Kyi and her National League for Democracy (NLD) stormed to power in the November 2015 general elections that swept the military junta aside. Once the NLD gained power, it used its landslide majority to easily win the president's position. Then it did something that caught the military unawares. Although the military retained its 25 per cent quota in the government under the 2008 Constitution, it was confident that Suu Kyi, given the various clauses that barred Burmese nationals with foreign spouses or with children who had taken the citizenship of other countries from holding the office of president, it was caught napping by the adroit way she and her advisers brilliantly used a constitutional clause that enabled the appointment of a state counsellor by the president. Suu Kyi became state counsellor, foreign minister and party president, all rolled into one, a most formidable combination, keeping control over the government and the party.

But her challenges are not over as she walks a very careful line, ensuring she doesn't alienate the military which has been the only functioning institution that Burma has known for over fifty years. By appointing Kofi Annan, former UN secretary general, as her special envoy, she used his political wisdom to handle one of the most troubled issues facing her nation: resolving the future of the Muslims of the Arakan and trying to resolve an extremely messy imbroglio which has stirred up Buddhist nationalist sentiments. This in turn has led to riots and major assaults against the Muslim minority there, known internationally as Rohingyas, but whom the Burmese government under the military refused to acknowledge as citizens of the state but denounced as foreigners and illegal immigrants from Bangladesh, a sentiment that finds resonance in Assam.

Many Rohingyas live in camps, ineligible to vote or get access to basic services such as education and health. Many are fleeing in despair, by boat and over land to Southeast Asia in search of livelihoods. A handful revolted in the 1990s and took to arms, setting up the Arakan Liberation Army,[17] which had safe houses and transit camps in Mizoram's southern edge.

In the summer of 2017, the situation took a turn for the worse with an estimated 400,000 fleeing an army sweep to seek refuge in Bangladesh, just across the border. They fled in boats, trekked in groups and individually. The exodus was triggered by a well coordinated attack on army and police posts by the Arakan Rohingya Salvation Army (ARSA), which timed its assaults on the day that Kofi Annan released his report, undrlining the need for reconciliation, respect for human rights and good conduct by the armed forces. The ARSA is led by a shadowy group of men who have seen action in the fighting zones of the Middle East and Central Asia, including Rohinguas who have lived in Palistani and Saudi Arabia for long. They have recruited and trained over 500 young men in the use of weapons and tactics in camps and jungles of the Arakan to avenge what they regard as decades of discrimination, abuse and oppression by the Myanmnar state. Differences between the Rohingya Muslims, whose ancestors came to the Arakan in the fifteenth century from what is today the Chittagong area of Bangladesh, and local Buddhists have persisted for as long as the former have been there. Into this mix, throw in pockets of Hindus and resentments.

The ARSA attacked not just the army but also little-known Hindu villagers, targeting the men including neighbours they had known all their lives. Hindus were a target partly perhaps because they were better off than the Rohingya and also appeared to have a comfort level with the government. A Hindu association alleged that women were kidnapped.

Reports of these incidents as much as the security threat to Myanmar had a hand in the Government of India's decision in August 2017 that 50,000 Rohingya—mostly poor and working as daily labourers and in unskilled jobs—who had taken refuge in India over the years would be deported. They were, it said, a 'security threat' and state governments, wherever the immigrants were located, should move to identify and then arrange for their deportation. Easier said than done. This provoked an outcry from civil society groups and earned a rebuke from international leaders and the media. Naturally, the BJP threw its weight behind the government along with friendly media voices, calling for the expulsion of 'terrorists'. An entire community was being branded as 'radical' or 'extremist' without any research or discussion but just because it had been so decided. A legal challenge to the move was placed before the Supreme Court with two of the country's top lawyers, Fali Nariman and Colin Goinsalves, arguing the case.

What was hidden from most writing and talk about the Rohingya was that 14,000 of them had already been classified as refugees by the UNHCR in a quiet, painstaking process lasting years. They were genuine cases fleeing persecution and harmful conditions. The government's position, outlined by Minister of State for Home Affairs, Kiren Rijuju, received flak from the United Nation's top figure for the protection of human rights. Zeid Ra'ad el-Husseini, a member of the Jordanian royal family, denounced New Delhi's view as untenable. The UN High Commissioner for Human Rights cited Rijuju's remarks, without naming the minister, that India was not bound to accept the Rohingyas since it had not signed the Geneva Convention on Refugees as a complete misinterpretation of the country's international obligations under the UN Charter.

> ...by virtue of customary law, its ratification of the International Covenant on Civil and Political Rights, the obligations of due process and the universal principle of non-refoulement, India cannot carry out collective expulsions, or return people to a place where they risk torture or other serious violations.

And anyway, despite the centre's brave utterances, where would the overstretched, understaffed and overworked state home departments and police in different states send the refugees? Not to Myanmar, where they were regarded as non-citizens—until Suu Kyi, in an international broadcast, grudgingly agreed to accept them back after verification. That process was to be defined weeks after her speech. Bangladesh would not accept them; they couldn't be dispatched to Nepal or Bhutan? Nobody wanted them. And at the heart of the matter, that's the unending tragedy of the Rohingya.

Salil Tripathi, author and journalist who has extensively worked on Bangladesh and is familiar with Myanmar's border politics, wrote that after playing to its home constituency, India realized the danger of alienating its staunch ally, Bangladesh. Sheikh Hasina was reportedly extremely cut up with Modi's fulsome praise of Myanmar and its battle against extremism during his official visit there and at meetings with Suu Kyi. However, India could not take a position which was opposed to the Bangladeshis, whose officials and politicians spoke of ethnic cleansing, genocide and army terror on Muslim Rohingya. So when New Delhi decided to send provisions and supplies for the beleaguered refugees and their hosts, it was a visible signal that the Government of India was changing course on the issue. It even agreed to abide by the Supreme Court's decision on whether the Rohingya in India should stay or go.

Tripathi, who is knowledgeable on human rights issues and has worked with Amnesty International, wrote:

> Not only did the view (about the Rohingya being extremists) have few takers in the international community, but also by endorsing it, India risked alienating Bangladesh—a valuable ally in the region... many see the assistance now being provided...as India softening its stand, after having shown little understanding of a complex and sensitive issue.[18]

Tripathi pointed out:

> India has strong economic and defence ties with Bangladesh, and needs the country's support to deal with militancy in the Northeast. Even if India's relations with Bangladesh may get prickly from time to time, Hasina is India's best friend in Dhaka. Bangladesh is set to hold a general election next year, and a new national leader who is hostile to India would only make matters worse.

The scale of stress on Bangladesh and the Rohingya is huge. More than half the entire population of the Rohingya have fled Myanmar; nearly half a million have fled after August 2017 and live in squalid, unhealthy refugee camps on the border with Myanmnar, just across the Naf River. At least another 250,000 had come earlier in successive waves fleeing successive military strikes, starting from 1978; some are in UNHCR camps near Cox's Bazar on the Chittagong coastline.

Suu Kyi accepts that many had fled the country but her position fell far short of the standards that western democrats and several Nobel Peace Prize winners had set for her. She did not condemn the military but only said they had to be told to uphold the law and respect human rights. She used the word Rohingya once, when she referred to the armed group which her government has banned as a terrorist organization.

It would have been difficult for her to live up to the world's expectations. After all, governing a multi-ethnic country of the size of Myanmar, scarred by decades of civil war between warring factions and the Burmese military, running the politics of the country with the military breathing down her neck and also pressing forward with democratic reforms and economic changes is a compelling but daunting task.

The army remains a power unto itself, committed to protecting its interests and what it regards as its divinely appointed role as custodian of Myanmar's integrity under the 2008 Constitution. That document placed the army commander in chief virtually above the president for he reports to no one, except perhaps to General Than Shwe, Burma's long-time shadowy ruler ensconced in his palatial home in Naw Pyi Taw, albeit now in retirement. Than Shwe and the current army commander are in touch with Suu Kyi and they appear to be on the same page, at least for now. Which means that the army too is on her side.

Emerging like a butterfly from nearly a quarter century of detention and harassment by the military, General Aung San's daughter has finally found her place though only the practice of political wisdom and dialogue over the next years will show whether she has found the levers of power and position to bring about the changes that she and her people want. As in the case of Irom Sharmila, depending on one person may not be a good thing: the years of struggle show on Suu Kyi's magnetic face. By the time the next elections come around, in 2020, she will be seventy-five. Much could happen in between.

Myanmar's political future also hinges on the way major and minor ethnic groups, winding down many years of conflict, collaborate with her and the army to develop a new framework of federalism, a process that the military has so far resisted. Yet, without sharing power, a sustained and longer peace is unlikely in a multi-ethnic land as large as Myanmar. Suu Kyi has taken the first steps through the gathering called the 21st Century Panglong, an agreement which she hosted for seventeen of twenty main ethnic armed groups including the United Wa Army, the Shan groups and the Kachins and Karens; the last two have had repeated clashes with the military even in the months leading to the agreement, with thousands of villagers displaced by the bitter fighting.

The first Panglong Agreement was signed in 1947 by Suu Kyi's father, General Aung San, who signed it with ethnic chiefs at the town of Panglong. General Aung San is revered as the father of modern Burma. He fell to a hail of bullets by an assassin who stormed into a cabinet meeting the following year. That earlier agreement fell apart soon after the assassination with ethnic groups accusing successive governments, mostly military, in Yangon of bad faith and disinterest in a federal structure for Burma which would involve sharing power with the ethnic groups.

A top diplomat says that the new agreement underlines Suu Kyi's political lineage and reinforces her clout. What is also significant is that all of the ethnic groups which have battled Yangon to a standstill are no longer speaking of breaking away: they simply want to be autonomous, federal units in a federal set-up, an arrangement that would suit them well since they have extensive control of major mineral and other natural resources including forests and rivers. In turn, this control over resources plays into a fascinating web of power sharing with local Burmese military commanders as well as China, with large payoffs to those facilitating the illegal export of precious stones such as rubies.

The peace has been in place longer in the western sector, where India's clout is greater, barring the NSCN and its satellite wings. The eastern border with China has been 'hot' for decades. This is where the Wa—who are ethnic Chinese—have an army that is nearly 30,000 strong; the Shan and the Kachins have large armies and good relations with the Chinese as well as their security agencies.

The next years will severely test Suu Kyi's capacity as a patient leader of a complex nation rising out of poverty and fifty years of military dictatorship. Myanmar is pushed and pulled in many directions by often contradictory pressures and forces. But one of the key elements of success lies in how she is able to manage relations not just with the ethnics but also with the embittered and lonely Rohingya people, non-citizens in the only home they know.

◆

Fundamental challenges before the Northeast continue to be complicated, hypersensitive and explosive. The vulnerability, rawness and confusion that exist on many issues are exemplified by an incident in August 2016 when twelve persons were killed in a market in Kokrajhar, western Assam. After varying reports that spoke of several armed killers and then finally zeroed in on one, there was still lack of clarity on why a Bodo, the ethnic identity of the alleged shooter, had targeted members of his own community, something that had rarely happened in a cycle of assaults and counter-assaults that has continued over decades.[19]

The killer, who used an AK-47, was apparently shot by a policeman and the stories around the episode show how confusing life and death can be in this part of the world and why nothing is quite what is seems, sounds or looks like, even if it is told or presented as 'truth'. That's how difficult it is to decipher the facts and unpeel the many layers which are so frustratingly embedded in every story.

◆

Another more familiar flashpoint emerged on 19 September 2016, as excavators, forest personnel and police armed with rifles, automatic weapons and tear gas moved to evict hundreds of villagers from Banderdubi village on the edge of Kaziranga National Park. It was part of a drive authorized by the Guwahati High Court to clear the area, which had been occupied for over fifty years by Muslim settlers of Bengali origin. As the forces moved in, villagers and protesters hurled stones triggering use of force with the police firing tear gas, rubber bullets and finally live bullets to disperse the crowd. Two people, a teenage girl and a young man, died in the violence.

In Guwahati, the BJP crowed over the 'success' of evicting illegal settlers; the original stone in this battle had been cast by a party leader from the town of Golaghat (part of the park falls in this district), asking for the dispossession of illegal settlers. One of the concerns expressed was that poachers slipped through inhabited areas on the edge of the park to carry out their task of slaughter of innocent animals and trade in their bodies.

Many of those evicted said they were legal tenants, paying tax to the state government and holding official documents which established their presence before Kaziranga became a national park.

The court order did not recognize this but emphasized the environmental sweep of geography and which areas formed part of the park's natural ecosystems and the need to protect these. The villagers had, through their lawyer, contended in arguments before the Guwahati High Court earlier that 'the petitioners are all residents of the forest area since the 1950s and pattas have been granted in their favour in the year 1962. The summary eviction of the petitioners cannot be done without inquiry and without ascertaining their rights over the land in question.'[20] They prayed for protection under the clauses of the Scheduled Tribes and Other Traditional Forest Dwellers (Recognition of Forest Rights) Act, 2006, including the Sanctuaries and National Parks, which protected the rights of forest dwellers. Lawyers clarified that although social forestry schemes were originally proposed in Banderdubi and a nearby village, the then Congress state government permitted the settlement and the conversion into revenue tax paying villages, thereby legalizing their stay.

The High Court tossed that argument out relying on previous Supreme Court rulings which made it very clear that no state government could arbitrarily change the nature of specified lands in a national park without the centre's consent. This had not happened. In addition 'the petition averments do not anywhere assert or disclose that the petitioners are Scheduled Tribes or other traditional dwellers of the forest'.

Yet, it is worth asking why the Assam government released only 19 per cent of the funds of the annual plan of operations between 2011–2012, why not a single forest guard was sent for training between 2008–2013, and why a measly ₹2.5 lakh (about US $12,500) was the total expenditure between 2010–2013 on intelligence gathering, a key element in anti-poaching efforts, when the volume of illegal trade dwarfed this tiny amount?[21] That's where the question begs itself: was the government or elements in the government or even the park complicit in the trade? This turned out to be the case when a senior park official's home was raided and tiger skins, elephant tusks, rhino horns and cash and jewellery were found. When the protector turns predator, who can save those in need of protection? One group alone cannot be blamed for the challenges faced by the park. The problem of illegal encroachment and the need to evict the settlers figure in the report, years before the Government of Assam finally acted. But the lack of capacity among staff, lack of upgradation of weaponry and poor levels of funding are equally responsible for the mess.

◆

These issues need to be handled with greater tact and assurances of compensation and a sense of justice instead of confrontation, which makes the Muslim community feel targeted and more vulnerable even if this government is heeding a court order. The timing is strikingly unfortunate.

The BJP government in Assam came through this test, though singed by it, partly because it did what no government had been prepared to do till then—implement court orders and audit reports. However, it will need to show its mettle by demonstrating as much alacrity as it did in Kaziranga by tackling urban encroachments which have ruined the green heritage of riverside cities like Guwahati. Urban demolitions and evictions could slash at its own urban middle-class and lower middle-class base.

This will be a real challenge—an even-handed approach to groups which either oppose or support it, despite belonging to different religious groups. This larger concern about justice and how minorities are treated is reflected in a new symbolism that is emerging through poetry, Miya poetry.

One of its proponents is Shalim Hussain. Writing about this phenomenon, the poet and activist Nabina Das says:

> What was once considered hate speech is now a proud badge a literary practitioner can wear. Miya poetry and performance is the new trail being blazed by a group of young scholars, teachers and professionals. The common force between them is that they are poets and writers, and very angry.

She quotes a journalist, M. Reyaz, who says that Muslims in Assam:

> ...have been at the centre of politics for all the wrong reasons. They have grown up being labelled 'foreigner' or Bangladeshi. Past their own struggles and repercussions from hate mongering, the July–August 2015 Bodo-Muslim clashes was the last straw for them. It was the maximum that the new generation of Muslims could take.

The photojournalist Nikhil Roshan who has travelled extensively in Assam writes: 'Several hundred sandy islands, known locally as chars, pepper the surface of the Brahmaputra. This archipelago, inhabited by a largely Bengali-speaking Muslim population—seen by many as illegal immigrants—has become a pivotal element in the politics of Assam.'[22] Noting that identity politics, especially that of the Muslims, will remain at the core of Assam's political dilemma, Roshan underlines one major reason why. 'Every year, the precarious geography of the chars, with periodic changes in the river's levels, pushes the residents to migrate inward into the more stable ground. Access to healthcare and education is limited, as are sources of revenue.'

There is growing concern too about the way anti-Muslim feelings were stoked in Assam before the state elections in 2016, with rhetoric ratcheted up against 'Bangladeshis' by the BJP and its allies. To many in Assam and the neighbouring states, a 'Bangladeshi' is usually taken to mean a Muslim of Bengali origin, such as the ill-fated Sharifuddin Khan of Dimapur, regardless of whether they came pre- or post-Partition or the creation of Bangladesh in 1971.

This is a tinderbox of hate and suspicion that threatens to erupt, not just against the Muslims as against other religious and ethnic groups, which may be in a minority among the followers of Islam. The danger of radicalism is growing with the spurt of the Islamic State in the Middle East, of it springing up in Europe and of the reality that young Indians are being radicalized and being picked up by state agencies. Much of this is happening in India to lower middle-class youth and middle-class Muslims, either tutored or changed by the bitter experience of discrimination and underdevelopment.

The sense of being left out of the growth story—whatever there is of it in a state like Assam—is evident when one visits the chars and saporis, apart from the restless, landless and dispossessed groups of small farmers that peasant mobilizers and agitators like Akhil Gogoi of the Krishak Mukti Sangram Samiti pull onto highways and urban streets to paralyze communications, administrations and economies. The islands of the Brahmaputra are the most exposed and vulnerable to the vagaries of climate change, highly dependent on a once stable but now irregular agricultural cycle.

The loss of economic opportunities and diminishing of livelihoods is driving hardy peasants away to the mainland, from the Assam and Barak[23] valleys to the main towns and to places across the country, within and outside the Northeast.

There are indications that some of this is happening in the soft underbelly of the Northeast, on the border with Bangladesh. As individuals and groups migrate, they come face to face with new realities and negotiate living spaces in those situations.

One of the new realities is a burst of freedom both in the social and economic spheres. Freedom does strange things. There are times when it can make us very unfree. Take the growth of social media. In many languages and with tens of millions of users in this country, social media has a fierce and aggressive way of mobilizing anger and suspicion and taking them to different dimensions, creating fearsome energies. It binds people down to positions, to words they may have spoken in anger or spite and rallies others to gather around symbols of suspicion, brutality and resentment. It makes many users intimidated, even fearful, of speaking their mind for fear of a backlash not just in terms of a tongue lashing from unknown trolls but a sudden attack by unknowns triggered to anger by a post or position.

The nazar of the searching eye, of the Islamic State and the radical Islamic right-wing is always looking for new places to invest in, new battles to fight, new generations to motivate and conquer. It will require great sobriety on the part of the region's leaders, and I am not excluding the media, activists, scholars and writers from this larger list, to calm things down. It is not an issue of handling a mere law and order problem; it could explode like a pressure cooker in a small enclosed space with devastating effects. And it could assume massive proportions, because basic issues of human security and dignity have been ignored or even abused for so long, that it could put the Naga and other insurgencies in the shade.

How long and how far can people be abused, targeted, discriminated against and spat upon? There comes a time when their threshold too is crossed by a word, an act, an event, an incident. They will seek, first, as the poets do, to assert their dignity and rights as citizens and human beings. If that fails, will they too take recourse to the guns of war and the words of hate as have many groups which have felt oppressed in Assam and the other states of the region?

If such a tipping point is reached, there may be no turning back. We have seen how a steadfast refusal to engage with the 'enemy' has harmed the people of Jammu and Kashmir and Indian strategic interests there. The Rohingya situation is the most recent and visible. Look at the Chakmas in Bangladesh. The writing is on the wall and we would be either very stupid or very blind not to recognize and see it.

If it is not tackled through a mix of dialogue, development and security measures, especially on the India-Bangladesh border areas, we could be looking at a disaster in the making which Indian security institutions would be hard put to handle.

What happens now? Or in the next years? Or what could happen? How will the undercurrents of anger and bitterness play out? Much depends on how the local government in Assam handles this angst. Stir it and feed it with more confrontation and violence—the results could be a bloody, uncontrollable mess. Islamic radicalism has soared in Bangladesh, it is reaching many parts of India and other parts of South Asia.

Security measures and eviction efforts won't deal with it. That's the lesson to be drawn from every such conflict in the world. Have we learnt from them? I don't know. The only thing that would work is friendship, dialogue and acceptance of the 'other' as an equal. Perhaps it is not too late.

These are difficult times and we need to tread very carefully—for we could be treading not just on someone's toes but on their graves. Take the example of Churachandpur in Manipur where nine bodies have lain in a morgue since 2015. The bodies are of those who were shot dead by Manipuri police during an agitation against laws passed by the state assembly that empowered the majority Meitei to settle in the hills. Although communities of the hills can settle in the valley, they felt threatened by this approach since they are smaller in number than the majority Meitei and fragmented in terms of tribal affiliations. The Churachandpur campaign is controlled by the Kuki tribe and the confrontation has split Manipur down the middle, between hill and plain. There is a counter-movement in the valley which wants all Meiteis, including many upper caste Hindus, to be declared a Scheduled Tribe. This obviously has both proponents and opponents and has placed Manipur into a quagmire.

As in other places and spaces, the only way forward is through difficult but essential dialogues, finding an answer to that core question: how can people of different ethnicities, religions and world views live together peacefully?

♦

Some afterthoughts to close with...

For a start, where does the 'Northeast' figure in the public imagination? Of course, it is there in PhD theses, lectures, seminars and workshops, in books, essays and formal papers, press statements and articles. But where is it in the public imagination? For in the region we call the Northeast, few people think of it as a whole, as a package. It remains an artificial construct, which is emphasized in official approaches and ideas of the regin and its connect to the neighbourhood. But in the eyes and imagination of ordinary people, say in Assam, there is an Assamese or Bodo or Bangla or Mishing imagination, or a Chakhesang, Ao, Sumi, Angami or Tangkhul imagination among the Nagas, or a Manipuri imagination for the Meiteis. These are just examples of how people think—to think for the region is something left to some politicians, officials, intellectuals and media figures who when they go home return to their original identities.

More than thirty years after the North Eastern Council was founded and a quarter century after the launch of the Look East and Act East Policies, the national government still hasn't understood this basic precept. How people see themselves lies at the heart of their worldview. Statist-driven definitions and dialogue remain impositions.

This region is Asia in miniature, a region where different races mingle and merge, where India ends and Southeast Asia begins—and also the converse, where India begins and Southeast Asia ends. It remains uniquely disadvantaged by Partition and the legacy of colonial rule but with new policies of economic opportunity and regional cooperation opening up, this could change dramatically in the next decades.

◆

The region has been one of the most globalized parts of the subcontinent for well over a century. It was where the prosperous tea gardens and companies in the Assam and Barak valleys were set up, connecting to the international markets especially in London. Steamers and ferries took goods and people from as far as Dhaka and Kolkata to Dibrugarh in upper Assam and back. Large reserves of oil and gas were discovered here in the nineteenth century and still supply a substantial part of India's energy needs. Partition and the India-Pakistan wars shut down the river route and it is only in recent years that Bangladesh and India are negotiating legal instruments of reopening trade, commerce and navigation on what remain the lifelines of both Bangladesh and its neighbour, the Northeast.

A sense of political, economic and historic alienation has added to the fault lines of geography and ethnicity; this in turn has ensured that distances have grown in every sense of the word between the Northeast and the rest of India. In a number of cases, this alienation has taken the shape of violent movements against the state seeking independence or much greater autonomy, although these appear currently to be winding down, as much because of public fatigue and exasperation with frequent shutdowns and economic deceleration as the security heavy-handedness that has come to characterize life in one of Asia's most ecologically diverse and rich areas.

Economic development is failing to keep up with rising expectations. The large majority of the population of the region is rural-based (in Assam, this figure is as high as 90 per cent) although there has been a sharp degree of urbanization in pockets such as Mizoram, on the border with Myanmar, where one-third of the entire state lives in and around the capital of Aizawl.

There has been a growth in the incidence of rural poverty although incomes in urban areas have improved substantially, leading to a sharp and visible spatial inequity. New malls, houses and construction are on an aggressive upward spiral in a handful of cities, indicating the growth of disposable incomes. In addition, local governments have become major sources of employment—such as for teachers and police recruits. The land-person ratio is falling and barring some areas, there has been a drop in farm productivity.

The primary sector has not grown for a number of reasons, not least linked to the lack of governance and the problems of conflict. Nearly seventy years after Independence, infrastructure remains creaky at best although there has been an improvement in railway services and road transport connections. States like Assam suffer as much as 13 per cent or more damage to their net sown area from floods and most states are importers of food. Oil and gas are major economic drivers although the tea economy has suffered setbacks in the past years.

As they look at this region and the challenges for growth here, Indian planners take encouragement from the experience of the Association of Southeast Asian Nations and hope that regional integration and closer cooperation with neighbouring countries can inspire growth and change in its Northeast.[24]

There is much to be done, many challenges and opportunities that beckon. The question is whether we have the time, the energy, the vision and determination to make sure these changes happen on the ground and not in offices and files far from the scene of action.

◆

The changes that have spread out from distant eastern borders are evident even in metros. Naga, Meitei and Mizo restaurants can be found not just in Guwahati but also in New Delhi and they are always full, especially those with top-end clientele like the elegant Karen Yepthomi's Dzukho Tribal Kitchen. Another entrepreneur has opened a chain of Nagaland's Kitchen restaurants. They're always busy, catering to the metropolitan Indian, whose tastes in clothes and food is changing and who is not afraid to experiment.

From the region, students, professionals, academics, activists, cultural performers, sports persons, government officials and businesses continue to flow into the metros, carving out a niche in the system. Delhi may not yet be the ninth state of the Northeast but it is well on its way there.

In Goa, I find Bodos, Assamese, Bengalis and Koch-Rajbongshis working together in hotels and stores. One sees more of this in Hyderabad and Bengaluru and across the country. This reflects both adaptation as well as the levelling of difference through distance and the need for livelihoods. The *Imphal Free Press*[24] talked about this but I think the lived reality is the opposite of what the paper defined as 'ethnic identity ... articulated by an assertion of differences and uniqueness, making the evolution of a common framework for governance next to impossible'.

As we have seen in place after place, example after example, that framework begins to shift with distance, time and the need and recognition of the need for collaboration, mutual respect and coexistence.

That finds resonance in Bhupen Hazarika's rendition of an American civil rights song:

> We're in the same boat, brother,
> We're in the same boat, brother,
> And if you shake one end, you gonna
> Rock the other
> It's the same boat, brother.

As we face the contradictions between traditions and political institutions, between what is promised and what is delivered, the creation of entrenched elites, arms and drug syndicates as well as the larger social upheavals under way—economic change, ingress and the processes of globalization and opening up to Southeast Asia—we find that migratory flows are redefining the political and economic structures of regions as are climate change and the devastating environmental pressures of greed combined with business-politics.

◆

The world of the Northeast has seen some good and much bad. We've looked at some of these factors, which have shaped and reshaped life and society, politics and power, driven by passion and determination, by geography and history, insensitivity and stupidity, by plain common sense, by brutality and by kindness.

In my search for words to close this book, a poem of Easterine Kire's strikes a chord:

> We are using words today
> Not because words are more powerful than guns
> But because we want to rise above guns because all that
> They do is kill
> And we want to rise above killing
> Let us be done with that.
> We will try to understand
> We must for it is the only way
> We can all stop dying...
> Shake off the curse, my brothers
> We will not be damned, we will not be damned.[25]

But there are other words too, words of hope and anger, sadness and conciliation and they flow from the lips of singers and musicians. Music is the channel that embraces change, brings lightness and enjoyment, and creates cultural connectivity and understanding of other cultures more quickly and energetically than any other medium. Especially when it's shared through social media, whether it's Facebook, WhatsApp or any other format.

So, it's apt perhaps to close with one of India's best hip-hop singers, Borkung Hrangkhawl, who speaks of an event that scared and scarred him. It became a life-changing experience:

'I think it was 2006... I was poked in my chest with a small knife. They poked me three to four times, but it didn't go in by God's grace. I asked them why they tried to do it. They said it's their job. I told them there is no use in doing all this. They thought I was from Nepal.' Borkung, better known as BK, recovered from that ugly episode of extreme prejudice but found himself undecided whether to choose to stay or go home. He stayed and wrote the fierce lyrics for what has virtually become his signature anthem, *Never Give Up*, the words of which he hurls at cheering, ecstatic audiences in every part of the country:

> I'm not giving up
> My life, my dreams
> Give up: Never!

Reconciliation and change can happen not because they're the 'right things' to do—but because we want them to happen.

We cannot give up.

ACKNOWLEDGEMENTS

I have gone back time and again to the same sources and persons I relied on for *Strangers of the Mist* and many more: new ones as well as old friends and contacts whom I have approached in the past years.

First, the newer ones: to the Rockefeller Foundation for awarding me the Practitioners Residency in the spring of 2011 at Bellagio, above Lake Como in Italy; to Pilar Palacia, managing director of the Rockefeller Center at Bellagio, and Elena Ongania, for their efficiency, consistent good cheer and willingness to help. The stint at Bellagio, a place of enduring beauty, though short, got me started on this book.

The East West Center in Washington for permitting me to use excerpts from 'The State Strikes Back: India and the Naga Insurgency', a monograph that Charles Chasie and I wrote together.

My membership of the Justice Jeevan Reddy Committee, which reviewed the Armed Forces (Special Powers) Act, opened my eyes to new areas of understanding the nature of the state as well as those who resist and seek to change it. I have deep respect for Justice Reddy's even-handed approach and his vast knowledge. I owe a debt of gratitude to him and the other committee members: Lieutenant General Vasantha Raghavan, a gentleman-soldier; P. P. Shrivastav, former member of the North Eastern Council; and Professor S. B. Nakade, former vice chancellor of Marathwada University. Prime Minister Manmohan Singh picked me for that task although his government failed to seize the opportunity of changing AFSPA, a moment that has come and gone several times since.

Sherman Teichman and Heather Barry, founders of the Institute for Global Leadership team at Tufts University, for being insanely determined to change the world, always brilliant and steadfast. They gave me a fellowship to start working on issues relating to this book in 2006 after my mother's sudden passing, provided a lovely space to work and live and looked after me when I fell ill with a bout of pneumonia in Cambridge.

Many high-ranking army officers, officials in Delhi and the states of the Northeastern Region, spoke to me on the basis of confidentiality;

many are still in service—cabinet ministers and MPs, intelligence officials and diplomats.

The late Prime Minister P. V. Narasimha Rao, who entrusted me to be an initial conversationalist with Thuingaleng Muivah and Isak Chishi Swu (who passed away during the writing of this book).

All those who gave me a chance to write and share my views in *The Statesman*, where I launched the Northeast page as consulting editor; Ravindra Kumar and Ishan Joshi; editors at the *Hindustan Times, Indian Express, Times of India, Assam Tribune, The Tribune, Outlook, Tehelka*; thanks are due to M. J. Akbar, who launched the *Sunday Guardian* (and major papers like *The Telegraph* and *Asian Age*) and carried my columns; to anchors and editors at different channels for letting me spout my views, especially Barkha Dutt, Sonali Singh, Nidhi Razdan, Vikram Chandra, Rajdeep Sardesai.

In the US, Professor Sumit Ganguly of Indiana University, Dr Satu Limaye of the East West Center, Washington DC and Hawaii.

The British Library, London, where I spent many hours.

I wish to acknowledge the following whose work I have used or relied upon for my book:

Mrinal Talukdar, Utpal Borpujari and Kaushik Deka for material used from *Secret Killings of Assam*.

Subir Bhaumik for use of material from his lead essay in 'The Agartala Doctrine'.

Kishalay Bhattacharjee for excerpts from *Blood on My Hands: Confessions of Staged Encounters*.

Anubha Bhonsle for her enchanting description of Irom Sharmila and her friend in a world of their own in *Mother, Where's My Country?*

Rajeev Bhattacharyya's long interview with Paresh Baruah, mystery figure and army chief of ULFA, in *Rendezvous with Rebels*, uncovered many aspects of his interviewee's thinking and experience.

In her book, *The Nellie Massacre of 1983: Agency of Rioters*, Makiko Kimura posited an alternative approach to that tragedy.

Shalim Hussain for his work on island communities and the new genre of Miya poetry.

I have also looked through the lens provided in *Shadow behind the Throne, My Tryst with Assam Administration*, by Jatin Hazarika, veteran administrator.

Fiction that left an impact on this writer of non-fiction: Arupa Patangia Kalita for *The Story of Felanee*; Aruni Kashyap for *The House with a Thousand Stories*; and Janice Pariat for *Boats on Land*, which had a strong narrative on the outsider-insider relationship in Shillong.

Thanks are overdue to:

London: Jaimini and Rita Bhagwati, who hosted me at their home in the UK, the splendid residence of the Indian High Commissioner in London, as I worked in the British Library; Pralab Baruah and Munu in London, Guwahati and Delhi for friendship; Prasun Sonwalkar.

Germany: Malte and Ursula Bremer of Schwenningen; and Dr Nirode K. Barooah of Koln.

Bhutan: HM Jigme Singye Wangchuck, the fourth king of Bhutan who led the Royal Bhutan Army in its fight against armed militants from Assam; his wife, the Queen Mother Ashi Dorji Wangmo; Jigme Yoezer Thinley, the former and first prime minister of the mountain kingdom; Khandu Wangchuk, former foreign minister; Kinley Dorji, founder editor of *Kuensel*, the first newspaper of Bhutan; and the organizing committee of Mountain Echoes, the literary festival in Thimpu.

Nepal: Kanak Mani Dixit, brave editor and battling activist, his family and *The Himal* team; Dhrupad Chowdhury of the International Centre for Integrated Mountain Development.

Bangladesh: Professor Rehman Sobhan, one of the country's founders; Imtiaz Ahmed of Dhaka University and now with the Regional Centre for Strategic Studies in Colombo; Mahfuz Anam, editor and publisher of the *Daily Star*, and his activist wife Shaheen; Latifur Rahman, generous and thoughtful friend, founder of Transcom Industries and owner of the *Daily Star*; Pankaj Saran, former Indian high commissioner to Dhaka; the singer Maqsoodul Haq of Dhaka, his lawyer-wife Lira and little Mihika.

New Delhi: Jamia Millia Islamia and the four vice chancellors—Professor Mushirul Hasan, Najeeb Jung, Professor S. M. Sajid (officiating) and Professor Talat Ahmad—for their support through their tenures during my time there, setting up the Centre for North East Studies and Policy Research (C-NES) in the university from February 2009 to September 2016 when I left to join the Commonwealth Human Rights Initiative as director. My team at C-NES at Jamia: Kaisi Kokho, always willing to listen and speak frankly; Amarjeet Singh; the cheerful Anamika Debroy; Nizamuddin Ansari, who kept our office in order including the accounts; and R. Yusuf, who attended to many issues. Professor Savyasaachi, Professor Asaddudin, Professor Mukul Kesavan, Professor Ajay Behara were supportive friends as were Professor Rizwan Kaiser and Professor Gopinath at the Department of History; Bulbul Dhar from the Department of Political Science and earlier head of the Sarojini Naidu Centre for Women's Studies;

Sultan from the AIS Library. C-NES trustees Gopal K. Pillai, former home secretary; Jayanto Chowdhury, IPS (retired), friend and former DGP of Assam police and the National Security Guard; P. C. Haldar, IPS; the late Lieutenant General V. K. Nayar, who taught me that there is so much more to a soldier than the uniform he dons; and Chaman Lal, IPS, former DGP Nagaland and former trustee, C-NES, for his courage in adversity, battle for human rights and clarity of principles. The UNICEF and UNHCR offices (New Delhi and Guwahati) especially Jeroo Master and Dr Ajit Rane, who ran UNICEF's operations in Assam and were always kind and supportive to me and my team; Onno Ruhl, former head of World Bank operations in India, and Sona Thakur, the bank's communications officer; Axel Harneit-Sievers, Chok Tsering and Sudeepa Aich of the Heinrich Boll Stiftung (HBS); Monica Banerjee of the National Foundation of India; Dr Poonam Muthreja and Alok Bajpayee of the Population Foundation of India (PFI), whose personal and institutional support made many projects, travels and writing as well as two films (*A Measure of Impunity* supported by HBS and *Where There Are No Roads* by PFI possible, giving me a deeper insight into the stories of the region and its people; Gopal and Neiru Tandon, kind neighbours, always game for a chat and chai; Shib Shankar Chatterjee and Priyamrita Chatterjee; Siddarth Vardharajan, formerly of *The Hindu* and now publisher-editor of *The Wire*; Borkung Hrangkhawl, hip-hop singer and son of the former insurgent leader of Tripura, Bijoy Hrangkhaw; Upamanyu Hazarika, Supreme Court lawyer, for providing court documents on the issues of migration and illegal settlement. My colleagues at the Commonwealth Human Rights Initiative (CHRI) for being patient teachers of the law and rights issues; they have asserted upholding the rule of law as well as access to information and justice fearlessly for years, thanks to a leader and mentor in Maja Daruwala, who I succeeded as CHRI director in 2016.

Sikkim: P. D. Rai, MP from Sikkim, and his wife, Jean, for many conversations, meals and years of friendship; Rajendra Gurung, of the Ecological Society of Sikkim; Raman Shrestha of Rachna Books, the amazing book store in Gangtok where everyone has a story, as well as his cabal of friends from that fabulous town, especially Pankaj Thapa and Professor Tanka Subba, vice chancellor of Sikkim University.

Assam: Tarun Gogoi, former chief minister; Himanta Biswa Sarma, Gogoi's former aide turned bête noire and minister for health, education and other portfolios; Dr Milan Baruah; Swaraj and Preeti Das; Babu and Bublu da; Giti and Subrata Barooah; Manju Barua of Wild Grass Resort, Kaziranga;

Moromi and Maan Barua (Oxford); Lonie Chaliha, Rita and Aziz of Chaliha B&B, home to weary travellers, centre of many gatherings, their place was a refuge as I wrote part of this book; Ajant Bhuyan; many friends in the police and civil administration as well as political parties. I think of Himanghsu Shekhar Das and C. K. Das, Naba Das; Dileep Chandan, editor of *Asom Bani*; Manoj and Vineeta Jalan of Jalan Industries, Dibrugarh; Rattan da (Saikia) and his bar in the iconic Mona Lisa Hotel; former members and leaders of the United Liberation Front of Asom (ULFA); Promod Boro, president of the All Bodo Students Union; Dr Ashok Babu, IAS, of the National Health Mission and his team; IAS officers Dr John Ekka, Prateek Hajela, Ashutosh Agnihotri and Sanjay Lohia; Professor A. C. Bhagabati, Professor Monirul Husain, M. S. Prabhakara of *The Hindu* (based in Kolar, Karnataka).

Meghalaya: Dr Sandi Syiem, healer of minds and trusted friend, and his wife, Nola; Patricia Mukhim, editor of the *Shillong Times*; my classmates and friends from St Edmund's, always curious, helpful and warm: Darryl Feegrade, Harish Mardani, Ankush and Farah Saikia and the rumbustious Riu; Professor Pramode Saikia and his wife Moinee, Shillong's best baker; Sanjib Kakoty, patient listener and profound thinker, his wife Achong, his veterinarian doctor brother Tridib, our own James Herriot with a delightful collection of stories about animals and people, his wife Namrata, the energetic Kakoty kids and the matriarch, Chikon Kakoty. Ram Muivah, secretary of the North Eastern Council; Arm Sangma, Bruce Marak and their families; my brother Suzoy and his adopted granddaughter Aneera and the late Monica.

Mizoram: Denghnuna, old friend and former IAS official; the late Brigadier T. Sailo and his wife; the cheerful L. R. Sailo, press adviser to the chief minister, for decades of friendship and conversation; Lalthanhawla, chief minister; Lal Sangliana, MNF leader and aide to Laldenga, for innumerable hours of conversation; Biki Laldenga, wife of the late MNF president, and her family; Lalkhama, former chief secretary; Vanlalngaia, former MNF intelligence chief; Professor J. V. Hluna; Isabella Rothangi; Margaret Zama of the Department of English, Mizoram University; David Zama; Dr Joy Pachhua of Jawaharlal Nehru University; Professor Vanlal Chawna, Department of Economics, Mizoram University; Professor H. K. Laldinpuii Fente, Department of Psychology, Mizoram University; Dr L. Sailo, associate professor, Department of History and Ethnography, Mizoram University; Professor R. Thangvunga of the Department of Mizo, Mizoram University; Dr Lalthantluangi Sailo, Department of English, Pachhunga College; Josephine L. B. Zuali; Colonel John Zama; Dennis

Hralte, owner of Floria Hotel, and his staff; David Thangliana, joint director, Directorate of Information and Public Relations (DIPR); Pratap Chetri, DIPR; Mapuia Chongte, filmmaker from Lunglei; Lalkhawliana, former MNF finance secretary who conducted the famous treasury raid; villagers of Sialsuk especially its women singers; translators Audrey and Opu Dutta Chowdhury; Central Young Mizo Association (YMA); Mizo Zirlai Pawl (Mizo Students' Association); Mizoram Upa Pawl (Mizo Elders Association); ex-MNF and former government staff at Sialsuk; K. Liankimi, former MNF cadre; Lunglei C. Ronghinglova, former Mizo National Army officer; Champhai; Reverend C. L. Hminga; Lathangmawii Chhangte, Lunglei; R. K. Thanga, Aizawl; Vanlalruata, general secretary, Central Young Mizo Association, Aizawl; Remruata Varte, proprietor, *Zolife* magazine; officers of the Assam Rifles, Aizawl; staff at Tourist Lodge, Durtlang, Aizawl, Tourist Lodge, Lunglei, and Tourist Lodge, Champhai; Customs Office, Zowkathar (Indo-Myanmar border); our redoubtable driving team in Mizoram: Pu James and Pu Sanga. Dr Malsawmdawngliana ('Sawmtea') and Mahmingi Rohmingmawii, whose role was critical to research and translation.

Nagaland: Niketu and Christine Iralu, who walk to the beat of an unseen drummer, as do all those who fight injustice and indignity, and are among the most amazing people I know. Neichute Duolo of Entrepreneurs Associates; Charles Chasie; Alobo Naga and the Band; Monalisa Changkija and Ben; Jesmina Zeliang; Rosemary Dzuvichu, teacher and feminist; Temsula Ao, writer and chronicler; Brigadier Marwah, then of the Assam Rifles; Reverend Wati Aier; members of the Naga Hoho and the Naga Mothers Association; Neingulo Krome of the Naga People's Movement for Human Rights.

Tripura: Jayanta Bhattacharyya, indefatigable reporter; Sukendu Dev-Burman, historian; and Bijoy Hrangkhawl.

Manipur: Babloo Loithangbam, human rights activist; Yambem Laba, journalist; Pradip Phanjoubam, founder editor of the *Imphal Free Press*; the family of Kaisi Kokho of Mao Gate and Song Sang; Justice N. Koteswar Singh of the Manipur High Court; Dr Vijayalakshmi Brara of Manipur University; Professor Irene Salam and Rajesh Salam.

Arunachal Pradesh: Mamang Dai, Ozing and Yanne Dai; the late S. K. Singh, former governor; Monii Riba, cultural archiver and activist.

Chandigarh: General (Retd) V. P. Malik, former chief of army staff; Brigadier (Retd) B. S. Gill, Jat Regiment.

Kolkata: Professor Ranabir Samaddar; Dr Paula Banerjee, Professor Samir

Das and the other indefatigable members of Manibaran Calcutta Research Group; Lieutenant General J. N. (Johnny) Mukherjee.

Mumbai: Arundhati Nanavati; Rajendra and Rupal Desai; Ramesh Shah, Suresh and Ranjan Shah, Hemali, Vidhi and Vishal; Kalpana Sharma.

Bhopal: Kirpal Dhillon and his wife Sneh for their hospitality, understanding and wisdom born of rich experience.

My film team of director Maulee Senapati, editor Bikash Dutta, cameraman Hiten Thakuria and camera assistant Raju Baruah for their work in Mizoram, Assam and Nagaland.

Mehfuz I. Borah, ever patient and always willing, who worked with the Centre for North East Studies and Policy Research (C-NES) in New Delhi, dived into information and pulled out documents and discovered the full text of Nehru's 1962 'farewell' speech to Assam which is reproduced in full in the Appendices. My team at C-NES (www.c-nes.org) in Guwahati and Delhi—Ashok Rao, Manik Boruah, Dr C. R. Hira, Bhaswati Goswami, Chandana Bora, Milan Bora, Vicky Das, Pinku, Deepak and Nitya were ever patient, loyal and kind. And the magnificent staff of the boat clinic units across the Brahmaputra Valley, every one of them, the doctors, nurses, lab technicians, pharmacists and the courageous crews, led by the one and only Kapilash. Bhaskar Bhuyan and his dynamic group at the Brahmaputra Community Radio Station, an award-winning group without a background in reporting but with some training emerged as stars: my life has been so enriched by just being with all of you.

Over the years, my chartered accountant, Praveen Jain, partner, Jagdish Chand & Co, New Delhi, has been a valued friend along with his helpful team of Ravi Goel and Manish Kumar.

My conversations with the late Isak Swu and Thuingaleng Muivah of the National Socialist Council of Nagalim (NSCN) in Bangkok, Amsterdam, the Hague and New Delhi helped me understand their passion and commitment while talks with others in Nagaland and Manipur made me appreciate the views of those opposed to them.

The home in Shillong remains a sanctuary and space for reflection and writing, conversation and argument, and the beautiful woods above where I walk and run, alone with my thoughts, soaking in the beauty of the silence around. My brother, Suzoy, has now shifted there with little Aneera and the place has gained energy and a real presence. May it remain unchanged, even as Shillong's skyline and that of every metro across the country changes.

Understanding has grown from extensive travel to every corner of the region, to its neighbouring lands, Bangladesh, Bhutan, Nepal, Myanmar, Tibet and China. Those who have been part of this journey are too many to name, too wonderful to forget, each deserving of a chapter if not a book in themselves.

I remember and feel deeply the absence of those who have left me: Minal, companion of decades; my mother, Maya; and Lea, my beloved Labrador, whose joyous bark welcomed us every day.

I am deeply grateful to my old friend, David Davidar, who published my first book on the Bhopal gas disaster, and *Strangers of the Mist* over twenty years ago, for his infinite patience and belief that the book would eventually be done. Aienla Ozukum at Aleph too has been a long-suffering editor. I am thankful to Delshad Karanjia for her felicitous editing.

Meghna, my daughter, has given me understanding, taught me compassion and courageously challenged my views and conduct; Ralf, my calm and generous son-in-law, has shown great patience and support.

This book would be incomplete without Preeti, who helped me negotiate the difficult paths, overcome stumbles and occasional falls with laughter, affection, firmness, tact and generosity.

EXCERPTS FROM THE REPORT OF THE JUSTICE JEEVAN REDDY COMMITTEE TO REVIEW THE ARMED FORCES SPECIAL POWERS ACT (ASSAM AND MANIPUR), 1958

PART-IV
Recommendations

The Committee has carefully considered the various views, opinions and suggestions put forward by the representatives of organisations and individuals who appeared before it as also the presentations and representations made by the concerned departments of the governments, security agencies and other organisations and individuals.

2. While devising a solution to the problem referred to the Committee, it has to bear in mind the following three basic conditions viz.,

ONE—The security of the nation, which is of paramount importance. Security of the nation involves security of the States as well. The very first entry in the Union List in the Seventh Schedule to the Constitution speaks of defence of India and every part thereof which means and implies that it is the power and obligation of the President, the Parliament and the Union Government to ensure the defence of India and of every part thereof. Though purporting to be a division of legislative powers between the Union and the States, the Seventh Schedule to the Constitution, it is well accepted, does represent the division of powers between the Union and the States. Even if a law is not made under and with reference to a particular entry / legislative head, the executive power would still be available under that entry. Lists-I and II set out the legislative heads / powers of the Union and the States respectively while List-Ill sets out the legislative heads, with reference to which both the Parliament and the State Legislatures can make laws, subject, of course, to the rule of parliamentary predominance recognised by Article 254. For ensuring the defence of India and of its every part, the Parliament can make such law and / or the Union government can take such executive action, as may be found necessary or proper. Some of the ways in which the Union government performs the said obligation are mentioned in Articles 352 to 356, (as pointed out

in Chapter II of Part I I of this Report. Article 355, which places an obligation
upon the Union to protect every State against external aggression and internal
disturbance and also to ensure that the Government of every State is carried on
in accordance with the provisions of this Constitution, has also been referred to
at some length in the said part of this Report). It is necessary to clarify that the
Constitution does not contemplate that the obligation to protect the States in the
Union shall be carried out by the Union Government only by invoking Article
352 (external aggression or internal rebellion) or Article 356 (to ensure that the
government of every State is carried on in accordance with the provisions of the
Constitution); the said obligation can be performed in such manner as may be found
appropriate, without of course violating the spirit and letter of the Constitution.
Now, coming to Article 355, it may be reiterated that the obligation created by
Article 355 includes the duty to protect every State against internal disturbance as
well. "Internal disturbance", as pointed in Part II of this Report, represents a very
serious, large scale and sustained chaotic conditions spread over a large area of the
State. It is no doubt the power and obligation of the State Government to maintain
public order as is evident from Entry 1 of State List in the Seventh Schedule to
the Constitution. However, the said entry read with Entry 2A of the Union List
means that (a) where the State Government finds that it is not able to maintain
public order and it is of the opinion that the aid of the armed forces / forces
under the control of the Union is necessary for maintaining or restoring the public
order, it can request the Union Government to send the armed forces to maintain
and restore the public order; (b) even where the State Government does not so
request but the Union Government is satisfied that for protecting the State from
"internal disturbance" i.e. to save it from domestic chaos or internal commotion,
it is necessary to deploy armed forces of the Union, it can do so under Art.355.

TWO—It is equally the duty of the Union and the States to not only respect
the fundamental rights conferred upon the citizens of India by Part III and other
provisions of the Constitution; they are also under an obligation to ensure the
conditions wherein the citizens can enjoy and avail of the fundamental and other
rights available to the citizens. In particular, Article 21 of the Constitution expressly
declares that no person shall be deprived of his life or personal liberty except in
accordance with the procedure established by law. Article 14 in Part III of the
Constitution ensures to its citizens equality before law and equal protection of laws
within the territory of India which means that no citizen or group of citizens shall
be discriminated vis-à-vis any other citizen or group of citizens. Article 19 confers
upon the citizens six valuable freedoms viz., freedom of speech and expression;
freedom to assemble peacefully and without arms; freedom to form associations
or unions; freedom to move freely throughout the territory of India; freedom to
reside and settle in any part of the territory of India and the freedom to practise
any profession or to carry on any occupation, trade or business - subject of course
to such reasonable restrictions thereon as may be placed by a law made by the

Parliament or State Legislatures under clauses (2) to (6) of the said article. Clauses (1) and (2) of Article 22 confer equally valuable rights upon the citizens of India. Clause (1) declares that no person who is arrested shall be detained in custody without being informed, as soon as may be, of the grounds for such arrest nor shall he be denied the right to consult, and to be defended, by the legal practitioner of his choice. Clause (2) declares that every person who is arrested and detained in custody shall be produced before the nearest Magistrate within a period of 24 hours excluding the time taken for journey from the place of arrest to the nearest court of the Magistrate. Inasmuch as no law has been made by Parliament under Article 33 of the Constitution (as pointed out in Part II of this Report), the above mentioned rights remain sacrosanct and effective even where the armed forces of the Union are deployed to restore public order and/or peace or to protect a State against internal disturbance. Articles 25 to 30 ensure the freedom of religion and ensure to every religious denomination or any section thereof to manage its religious affairs; they ensure freedom of worship, right to conserve one's own culture and also confer a right upon the minorities to establish educational institutions of their choice.

THREE—The armed forces of the Union viz., the army, navy and the air force are meant to ensure the defence of the Union and all its parts. In other words, the armed forces are meant to guard our borders against any aggression by any foreign power or foreign agency, irrespective of the manner in which such aggression is perpetrated. The armed forces are trained and are equipped for this purpose. May be that in an emergency like a flood or other natural calamity, armed forces are also called in to provide relief and help the people but that is only a temporary phenomenon. The Union Government has also been creating and indeed expanding various para military forces under various enactments like the Border Security Force Act, Assam Rifles Act, Indo-Tibetan Border Police Act, CRPF Act, CISF Act and so on. The Union Government has also created what is known as "India Reserve Battalions". Though these para military forces have been created for certain specific purposes, yet, on account of the disturbed situation in certain parts of the country, the Union Government has been obliged to deploy, from time to time, these forces as well as its armed forces to redress these situations. It must be recognised, at the same time, that the deployment of armed forces or para military forces of the Union to restore public order in any part of the territory of India, or to protect a State from internal disturbance is, and ought to be, an exception and not the rule. The deployment of armed forces for the said purposes should be undertaken with great care and circumspection. Unless it is absolutely essential for the aforesaid purposes, the armed forces of the Union should not be so deployed, since too frequent a deployment, and that too for long periods of time, carries with it the danger of such forces losing their moorings and becoming, in effect, another police force, a prey to all the temptations and weaknesses such exposures involve. Such exposure for long periods of time may well lead to the brutalisation of such forces - which is a danger to be particularly guarded against. This concern applies no less in the case of other armed forces of the Union as well. All this means that as soon as the public order is restored or the internal disturbance is quelled, the forces have to be withdrawn to their barracks or to their regular duties, as the case may be. This very concern and consideration underlies Sections 130 and 131 of the Code of Criminal Procedure, which have been referred to and dealt with in Chapter IV of Part II of this Report. These sections of the Code of Criminal Procedure make it repeatedly clear that where it is necessary to call in the army to disperse an unlawful assembly endangering public security, the armed forces so called in shall act according to the directions of the Magistrate though the manner in which the armed forces perform the task entrusted to them lies within their discretion. Even where the armed forces are called in for meeting a more serious threat to public order or public security, or where the deployment of the armed forces is required on a fairly long-term basis, this concern remains equally valid. It has also to be ensured that the legal mechanism under which they function is sufficiently clear and specific and accords with the spirit and provisions of the Constitution as adumbrated herein above. While providing protection against civil or criminal proceedings in respect of the acts and deeds done by such forces while carrying out the duties entrusted to them, it is equally necessary to ensure that where they knowingly abuse or misuse their powers, they must be held accountable therefor and must be dealt with according to law applicable to them. It is not unusual that there will be some indisciplined individuals in these forces as well, but their wrong actions should not be allowed to sully the fair name of the armed forces and the para military forces. While our armed forces are one of the most disciplined in the world, situations may arise when they are deployed outside their regular duties, i.e., when they are deployed for maintaining public order or for quelling internal disturbance in a part of the territory of India, when certain members thereof may seek to take advantage of their power and position to harass or otherwise trample upon the rights of the citizens of this country. The legal mechanism should ensure that such incidents do not take place and should also ensure that adequate remedial measures do exist where such incidents do take place.

3. Bearing the above considerations in mind, we have to proceed ahead. At this juncture it would be appropriate to recall the terms of reference given to this Committee. They read as follows:

"Keeping in view the legitimate concerns of the people of the North Eastern Region, the need to foster Human Rights, keeping in perspective the imperatives of security and maintenance of public order to review the provisions of the Armed Forces (Special Powers) Act, 1958 as amended in 1972 and to advise the Government of India whether:

(a)   To amend the provisions of the Act to bring them in consonance with the obligations of the Govt. towards protection of Human Rights; or

(b)   To replace the Act by a more humane Act.

The Committee may interact with representatives of social groups, State

Governments and concerned agencies of Central Govt./State Govt. legal experts and individuals, as deemed necessary by the Committee in connection with the review of the Armed Forces (Special Powers) Act, 1958 as amended in 1972.

The Committee will meet as often as required and visit the North Eastern Region, if felt necessary."

4. The Committee finds that there are four options available for it to adopt viz.,
   (a) to recommend the repeal of the Armed Forces (Special Powers) Act, 1958;
   (b) to recommend that the present Act should continue as it obtains today or with such amendments as may be found appropriate;
   (c) in case the repeal of the Armed Forces (Special Powers) Act, 1958 is recommended, to recommend that it should be replaced by an appropriate legislation;
   (d) in case of recommendation for repeal of the Act, to recommend insertion of appropriate provisions in an existing /cognate enactment

5. Keeping in view the material placed before us and the impressions gathered by the Committee during the course of its visits and hearings held within and outside the North-Eastern States, the Committee is of the firm view that:
   (a) The Armed Forces (Special Powers) Act, 1958 should be repealed. Therefore, recommending the continuation of the present Act, with or without amendments, does not arise. The Act is too sketchy, too bald and quite inadequate in several particulars. It is true that the Hon'ble Supreme Court has upheld its constitutional validity but that circumstance is not an endorsement of the desirability or advisability of the Act. When the constitutional validity of an enactment is challenged in a Court, the Court examines (i) whether the Act is within the legislative competence of the Legislature which enacted it and (ii) whether the enactment violates any of the provisions of the Constitution. The Court does not - it is not supposed to - pronounce upon the wisdom or the necessity of such an enactment. It must be remembered that even while upholding its constitutional validity, the Hon'ble Court has found it fit and necessary not merely to approve the "Dos and Don'ts" in the instructions issued by the Army Headquarters from time to time but has also added certain riders of its own viz., those contained in clauses 8, 9 and 14 to 21 in para 74 of its judgment (at pages 156 and 157 of the judgment in NAGA PEOPLES' MOVEMENT OF HUMAN RIGHTS v UNION OF INDIA - (1998) 2 SCC 109). The Committee is of the opinion that legislative shape must be given to many of these riders. We must also mention the impression gathered by it during the course of its work viz., the Act, for whatever reason, has become a symbol of oppression, an object of hate and an instrument of discrimination and high-handedness. It is highly desirable and advisable to repeal this Act altogether, without, of course,

losing sight of the overwhelming desire of an overwhelming majority of the region that the Army should remain (though the Act should go). For that purpose, an appropriate legal mechanism has to be devised.

(b)   The Committee is also of the firm view that it would be more appropriate to recommend insertion of appropriate provisions in the Unlawful Activities (Prevention) Act, 1967 (as amended in the year 2004) - which is a cognate enactment as pointed out in Chapter III Part II of this Report instead of suggesting a new piece of legislation.

6. The reasons for adopting the course of introducing requisite and appropriate provisions in the Unlawful Activities (Protection) Act are as follows:

ONE—The ULP Act defines "terrorism" in terms which encompass and cover the activities of the nature carried on by several militant/insurgent organisations in the North-east States. Use of arms and/or explosives so as to cause loss of life or property or to act against a government servant, with intent either to threaten the unity, integrity, security or sovereignty of India or to strike terror in the people or any section of the people in India or in any foreign country (as provided by Section 15), the kind of activity carried on by various militant / insurgent organisations in the North-east, falls within, the four corners of Section 15. It is terrorism within the meaning of the Act.

TWO—The ULP Act not only defines 'terrorism' in expansive terms but also specifically lists some of the organizations engaged in militant/insurgent activity in Manipur, Tripura, Nagaland and Assam as terrorist organizations in the schedule appended to the Act. In other words, the Act recognizes that the activities carried on by the schedule mentioned organizations fall within the definition of 'terrorism' and 'terrorist activity' as defined by the said Act. Furthermore, as pointed out in Chapter III of Part II of this Report, the ULP Act does contemplate, by necessary implication, the use of armed forces of the Union as well as the other para military forces under the control of the Union to fight and curb the terrorist activities in the country. It is for the said reason that it has expressly barred, in Section 49, any suit, prosecution or other legal proceedings against "any serving or retired member of the armed forces or para military forces in respect of any action taken or purported to be taken by him in good faith, in the course of any operation directed towards combating terrorism". In this sense the ULP Act, as it now obtains, does provide for deploying the armed forces or para-military forces for fighting the militant/ insurgent/terrorist activity being carried on in some or all North-eastern States[*]. The Act is designed to curb the terrorist activities of not only the organisations

---

[*]As a matter of fact, it can be said that there are two enactments for fighting militant/insurgent /terrorist organizations, groups and gangs in the North-eastern States viz., the Armed Forces (Special Powers) Act whose application is limited to the North-eastern States alone and the ULP Act which extends to the whole of India including the North-eastern States.

mentioned in the schedule but any and every terrorist activity.

THREE—a major consequence of the proposed course would be to erase the feeling of discrimination and alienation among the people of the North-eastern States that they have been subjected to, what they call, "draconian" enactment made especially for them. The ULP Act applies to entire India including to the North-eastern States. The complaint of discrimination would then no longer be valid.

FOUR—The ULP Act is a comprehensive law designed to (i) ban unlawful organisations; (ii) to curb terrorist activities and the funding of terrorism; and (iii) investigation, trial and punishment of persons indulging in terrorist acts, underline the Armed Forces (Special Powers) Act which deals only with the operations of the armed forces of the Union in a disturbed area. After the proposed amendments, ULP Act would be more comprehensive in the sense that it would expressly permit redeployment of armed forces and para-military forces of the Union to achieve its object viz., curbing terrorism. In other words, operations of the armed forces of the Union would be one of the ways of curbing terrorism. It would also mean that persons apprehended by the armed forces of the Union would be made over immediately to the nearest police station and would be tried in accordance with the procedural laws of the land. The prosecution too would be quicker and more effective because of the special provisions contained in Sections 44 (protection of witnesses) and 46 (admissibility of evidence collected through interception of communications). At the same time, the accused would also get the very important safeguard contained in Section 45 of the Act which provides that no court shall take cognizance of any offence under the Act unless previous sanction therefor is granted by the appropriate government, in case the prosecuting agency proposes to proved against him for any offence in Chapter IV or Chapter VI of this Act. We may clarify that in law it lies within the discretion and judgement of the investing officer to decide, after due investigation, whether to proceed against the accused or to drop the proceedings and in case, he decides to proved against the witness, the determine the offence with which the accused is to be charged. In short, just because, a person is arrested by the armed forces acting under this Act, and is made over to the police, the police is not bound to proceed against him only for offences under this Act, the police is free, depending upon the evidence/material gathered during investigation, to file a charge sheet for offence under this Act or under IPC or such other appropriate enactment, as may be applicable.

7. As stated hereinabove, the ULP Act does contemplate, by necessary implication, use of armed forces or para-military forces to conduct operations and to take steps to fight and curb terrorism. It does not, however, contain any provision specifying their powers, duties and procedures relevant to their deployment. It does not also provide for an internal mechanism ensuring. accountability of such forces with a view to guard against abuses and excesses by delinquent members of such forces. It is this lacuna, which is to be supplied by inserting appropriate provisions in the

ULP Act. The provisions so introduced should be clear, unambiguous and must specify the powers of the armed forces/para military forces while acting to curb terrorist/insurgent activities.

8. We may also refer in this connection to the necessity of creating a mechanism, which we may designate as the "Grievances Ceil" - over the years many people from the region have been complaining that among the most difficult issues is the problem faced by those who seek information about family members and friends who have been picked up and detained by armed forces or security forces. There have been a large number of cases where those taken away without warrants have "disappeared", or ended up dead or badly injured. Suspicion and bitterness have grown as a result. There is need for a mechanism which is transparent, quick and involves authorities from concerned agencies as well as civil society groups to provide information on the whereabouts of missing persons within 24 hours.

9. To ensure public confidence in the process of detention and arrest, grievances cells are proposed to be set up in each district where armed forces are deployed. These cells will receive complaints regarding allegations of missing persons or abuse of law by security/armed forces, make prompt enquiries and furnish information to the complainant. Where, however, the complainant is not satisfied with the information furnished and is prepared to file an affidavit in support of his allegation, it shall be competent for the Cell to call upon the State level head of the concerned force or organization to enquire into the matter and report the same to the cell as early as possible, not exceeding in any event, one week. The State level officers from whom these Grievances Cells seek information shall immediately make necessary enquiries and furnish full and correct information to the Grievances Cell as early as possible, not exceeding in any event one week. The Grievances Cells will be composed of three persons, namely, a senior member of the local administration as its chair, a Captain of the armed forces/security forces and a senior member of the local police. These will have dedicated communications, authority to obtain information from concerned authorities and have facilities for recording and responding to complaints. They shall locate their offices in the premises of the Sub Divisional Magistrate or in the premises of the District Magistrates, as the case may be. Such a mechanism is absolutely essential to achieve the two equally important purposes viz., (a) to infuse and instill confidence among the citizenry that the State, while deploying the armed forces of the Union to fight insurgency/terrorism has also taken care to provide for steps to guard against abuses/excesses with a view to protect the people and to preserve their democratic and civil rights; and (b) to protect the honour and the fair name of the forces.

11. While deploying the forces under sub-section (3) the Central Government shall, by a notification published in the Gazette, specifying the State or the part of the State in which the forces would operate and the period (not exceeding six months) for which the forces shall operate. At the end of the period so specified,

the Central Government shall review the situation in consultation with the State Government and check whether the deployment of forces should continue and if it is to continue for which period. This review shall take place as and when it is found necessary to continue the deployment of the forces at the expiry of the period earlier specified. It shall be permissible for the Central Government to vary the part of the State where the forces are deployed in case the earlier notification is in respect of a part of a State. Every notification extending the period of deployment of forces or varying the area of the State, as the case may be, shall be laid on the table of both the Houses of Parliament within one month of the publication of such notification.

12. A draft of the Bill, which is recommended to be incorporated as Chapter VI A of the Unlawful Activities (Preventive) Act, 1967 is enclosed herewith. The draft bill is meant to serve as a guide in drafting the legislation to be introduced in the Parliament. We may also mention that the Appendix to the draft incorporates the Do's and Don'ts issued by the Army and which have been approved by the Hon'ble Supreme Court of India in its decision report in Naga People's Movement for Human Rights Vs Union of India (A.I.R 1998 Supreme Court 431) as well as the additional directions given by the Hon'ble Supreme Court. However, those directions which have been already incorporated in the Bill are not repeated in the Appendix.

13. A separate note submitted by Sri Sanjoy Hazarika, a Member of the Committee, is also enclosed at Annexure-XIV.

NOTE FROM SHRI SANJOY HAZARIKA ON AFSPA

Note from Shri Sanjoy Hazarika, Member
At the end of a long night, there is a dawn ...

When introducing the Armed Forces Special Powers Bill (1958) in the Lok Sabha, the then Home Minister Shri Govind Ballabh Pant declared that "certain misguided sections" of the Nagas were involved in "arson, murder, loot, dacoity etc." He added, "So it has become necessary to adopt effective measures for the protection of the people in those areas. In order to enable the armed forces to handle the situation effectively whenever such problem arises hereafter, it has been considered necessary to introduce this bill."

Some members of Parliament, especially from Manipur, and elsewhere opposed the Act; one of them, L. Achaw Singh of Manipur, described the proposal as "unnecessary ... an anti-democratic measure ... a lawless law."

AFSPA in the North-East has continued for 47 years. The Committee's essential recommendation, as laid out in both its conclusions and the proposed changes to the Unlawful Activities (Prevention) Act, 1967, (as amended in 2004), is that AFSPA must be repealed forthwith; the gains of the law are extremely moot, its negative impacts have been overwhelming.

Many of the security problems of the region can be tackled by local police and commando forces, with the assistance of the armed forces where essential. But the dependence of the states on the army must be reduced to the minimum and armed forces should be deployed only as a last resort.

Numerous representations from the public as well as from the army, paramilitary and police have informed the Committee that political problems must be addressed politically and not militarily. These must include the processes of development of participative planning, involving local traditional groups in the role of self-governance, instead of sheltering behind the army and other forces. As we have noted earlier, there has been a sustained and systematic failure of governance; without the restoration of governance and the faith of the public in the ability of governments to rule justly and provide security to their citizens, the problems may become more acute.

This is a long and difficult task and the pressures are enormous. The Committee does not underestimate the scale of the challenges. But there is no option for the Indian State or the states of the Union. Faltering and even failing, at times, the states of the Union, and especially the North-east, must strengthen their own systems of governance, restoring the confidence of the people and providing the basics of governance.

What started as a political demand and insurgency in the Naga Hills, now Nagaland, has developed into a number of militant armed uprisings in not less than five other states – Manipur, Tripura, Meghalaya, Assam and Arunachal Pradesh. These have international connections with various armed groups and forces inimical to India and democratic forces. In addition, there are the problems of illegal migration into the region, especially Assam. The intensity of the challenges are immense: these range from ethnic standoffs and struggles for land and space as well as political rights.

In the past half century, another major change has affected the violence: on both sides of the "barrier", the lethality of weapons and their easier availability has transformed the power and quality of the fighting. RDX, AK-56s, machine guns and sniper rifles are used extensively. The immediacy of communications has also effectively changed the profile of these organizations as well of fighting: people can see, hear and even communicate with them by email!

A consequence of such long-drawn out conflicts has been the collapse of governance in a number of the states; the security of the citizens is at extreme risk, from security forces and the militants. During this period, there have been some positive gains – awareness of human rights has increased in India and the world, the media is stronger as are non-government organizations and civil society groups. Violations of human rights by state forces and by non-state armed groups cannot, in these days of instant information, be hidden any longer.

The upsurge in Manipur after the death of Ms. Manorama Devi last June in the custody of the Assam Rifles is a demonstration of this awareness, although there are official views that the agitation was also orchestrated by the underground groups. The latter are not the concern of this Committee, which was appointed last November, as a democratic response by the Central Government to a democratic demand by the people of the state for the repeal of the Act. After a detailed process of hearings in Manipur, Nagaland, Assam, Meghalaya as well as New Delhi and interactions in Arunachal Pradesh and extensive internal deliberations, the Committee has reached a conclusion which is detailed in this report.

It is my view that the army must be deployed in the rarest of rare cases – not as a knee-jerk reaction of governments at the Central and state levels. The army and security forces have, despite obvious shortcomings as are documented and well-known, tried to do their best and upheld their country's honour and integrity.

We have been encouraged by the openness with which people approached the committee and spoke their views without fear or favour, despite many pressures. We also are encouraged by the fact that many of the armed groups in the North-east are in the process of negotiation or seeking conversations which can bring armed confrontations to an end and restore dignity to civil society and the rule of justice and law.

The United Nations Secretary General Kofi Annan said in March 2003 that "respect for human rights, fundamental freedoms and the rule of law are essential tools in the effort to combat terrorism – not privileges to be sacrificed at a time of tension."

We hope that the report of the Committee will help in the process of reconciliation and democratization in the North-east, create a space for dialogue and discussion, reducing conflicts and helping the region write a new chapter of peace, change and happiness in its troubled history. We also hope that it strengthens the county's unity, integrity and security and creates an atmosphere for people to live in dignity, honour and peace.

At the end of every dark night, there is a dawn, however delayed. And for every day, there is a dawn, whether we see it or not.

Sanjoy Hazarika
New Delhi
30 May 2005

Appendix c

SUPREME COURT OF INDIA
on
Armed Forces (Special Powers) Act, 1958

Writ petition (Crl) 550 of 1982 with Writ Petition (C) Nos.
5328/80, 9229-30/82, Civil Appeals Nos. 721 to 724 of 1985,
2173-76/1991,2551/81 and Writ Petition (C) Nos. 13644-45/84

Naga People's Movement of Human Rights, etc. - Petitioner
vs.
Union of India - Respondent

Before J.S. Verma, CJI and other four Judges
27 November, 1997

—

Operative Part of the Judgement (Relevant extracts)

74. In the light of the above discussion we arrive at the
following conclusions:

(1) Parliament was competent to enact the Central Act in exercise of the legislative power
conferred on it under Entry 2 of List I and Article 248 read with Entry 97 of List I. After
the insertion of Entry 2A in List I by the Forty Second Amendment of the Constitution,
the legislative power of Parliament to enact the Central Act flows from Entry 2A of List I.
It is not a law in respect of maintenance of public order falling under Entry I and List II.

(2) The expression 'in aid of the civil power" in Entry 2A of List I and in Entry 1 of List
II implies that deployment of the armed forces of the Union shall be for the purpose of
enabling the civil power in the State to deal with the situation affecting maintenance of
public order which has necessitated the deployment of the armed forces in the State.

(3) The word 'aid" postulates the continued existence of the authority to be aided. This
would mean that even after deployment of the armed forces the civil power will continue
to function.

(4) The power to make a law providing for deployment of the armed forces of the Union
in aid of the civil power of a State does not include within its ambit the power to enact a
law which would enable the armed forces of the Union to supplant or act as a substitute
for the civil power in the State. The armed forces of the Union would operate in the State
concerned in cooperation with the civil administration so that the situation which has
necessitated the deployment of armed forces is effectively dealt with and normalcy is
restored.

(5) The Central Act does not displace the civil power of the State by the armed forces of the Union and it only provides for deployment of armed forces of the Union in aid of the civil power.

(6) The Central Act cannot be regarded as a colourable legislation or a fraud on the Constitution. It is not a measure intended to achieve the same result as contemplated by a Proclamation of Emergency under Article 352 or a proclamation under Article 356 of the Constitution.

(7) Section 3 of the Central act does not confer an arbitrary or unguided power to declare an area as a 'disturbed area". For declaring an area as a 'disturbed area" under Section 3 there must exist a grave situation of law and order on the basis of which the Governor/Administrator of the State/Union territory of the Central Government can from an opinion that the area is in such a disturbed or dangerous condition that the use of the armed forces in aid of civil power is necessary.

(8) A declaration under Section 3 has to be for a limited duration and there should be periodic review of the declaration before the expiry of six months.

(9) Although a declaration under Section 3 can be made by the Central Government *suo motto* without consulting the concerned State Government, but it is desirable that the State Government be consulted while making the declaration.

(10) The conferment of the power to make a declaration under Section 3 of the Central Act on the Governor of the State cannot be regarded as delegation of the power of the Central Government.

(11) The conferment of the power to make a declaration under Section 3 of the Central Act of the Government is not violative of the federal scheme as envisaged by the Constitution.

(12) The provision contained in Sections 130 and 131 Cr.P.C. cannot be treated as comparable and adequate to deal with the situation requiring the use of armed forces in aid of civil power as envisaged by the Central Act.

(13) The powers conferred under clauses (a) to (d) of Section 4 and Section 5 of the Central Act on the officers of the armed forces, including a Non-Commissioned Officer, are not arbitrary and unreasonable and are not violative of the provisions of Articles 14, 19 or 21 of the Constitution.

(14) While exercising the powers conferred under Section 4(a) of the Central Act, the officer in the armed forces shall use minimal force required for effective action against the person/persons acting in contravention of the prohibitory order.

(15) A person arrested and taken into custody in exercise of the powers under Section 4(c) of the Central Act should be handed over to the officer in charge of the nearest

police station with least possible delay so that he can be produced before nearest Magistrate within 24 hours of such arrest excluding the time taken for journey from the place of arrest to the court of magistrate.

(16) The property or the arms, ammunition etc., seized during the course of search conducted under Section 4(d) of the Central Act must be handed over to officer in charge of the nearest police station together with a report of the circumstances occasioning such search and seizure.

(17) The provision of Cr.P.C. governing search and seizure have to be followed during the course of search and seizure conducted in exercise of the power conferred under Section 4(d) of the Central Act.

(18) Section 6 of the Central Act in so far as it confers a discretion on the Central Government to grant or refuse sanction for instituting prosecution or suit or proceeding against any person in respect of anything done or purported to be done in exercise of the powers conferred by the Act does not suffer from the vice of arbitrariness. Since the order of the Central Government refusing or granting the sanction under Section 6 is subject to judicial review, the Central Government shall pass an order giving reasons.

(19) While exercising the power conferred under clauses (a) to (d) of Section 4 the officers of the armed forces shall strictly follow the instructions contained in the list of 'Do's and Don'ts" issued by the army authorities which are binding and any disregard to the said instructions would entail suitable action under the Army Act, 1950.

(20) The instructions contained in the list of 'Do's and Don'ts" shall be suitably amended so as to bring them in conformity with the guidelines contained in the decisions of this Court and to incorporate the safeguards that are contained in clauses (a) to (d) of Section 4 and Section 5 of the Central Act as construed and also the direction contained in the order of this Court dated July 4, 1991 in Civil Appeal No. 2551 of 1991.

(21) A complaint containing an allegation about misuse or abuse of the powers conferred under the Central Act shall be thoroughly inquired into and, if on enquiry it is found that the allegations are correct, the victim should be suitably compensated and the necessary sanction for institution of prosecution and/or suit or other proceeding should be granted under Section 6 of the Central Act.

Source: A.I.R. 1998 SUPREME COURT 463-464

AN EXCERPT FROM THE JUSTICE VERMA COMMITTEE REPORT, 23 JANUARY 2013

Offences against women in border areas/conflict zones

10. We now address a very important, yet often neglected area concerning sexual violence against women—that of legal protections for women in conflict areas. Our views on this subject are informed by the plight of a large number of women from areas in Kashmir, the North-East, Chhattisgarh, Odisha and Andhra Pradesh who were heard at length in the course of preparing our report. We are indeed deeply concerned at the growing distrust of the State and its efforts to designate these regions as 'areas of conflict' even when civil society is available to engage and inform the lot of the poor. We are convinced that such an attitude on the part of the State only encourages the alienation of our fellow citizens.

11. At the outset, we notice that impunity for systematic or isolated sexual violence in the process of Internal Security duties is being legitimized by the Armed Forces Special Powers Act, which is in force in large parts of our country. It must be recognized that women in conflict areas are entitled to all the security and dignity that is afforded to citizens in any other part of our country. India has signed the International Convention for the Protection of All Persons from Enforced Disappearance106, which has to be honoured. We therefore believe that strong measures to ensure such security and dignity will go a long way not only to provide women in conflict areas their rightful entitlements, but also to restore confidence in the administration in such areas leading to mainstreaming.

12. To this end, we make the following recommendations for immediate implementation:

    a) Sexual violence against women by members of the armed forces or uniformed personnel must be brought under the purview of ordinary criminal law;

    b) Special care must also be taken to ensure the safety of women who are complainants and witnesses in cases of sexual assault by armed personnel;

    c) There should be special commissioners—who are either judicially or legislatively appointed—for women's safety and security in all areas of conflict in the country. These commissioners must be chosen from those who have experience with women's issues, preferably in conflict areas. In addition, such commissioners must be vested with adequate powers to monitor and initiate action for redress and criminal prosecution in all cases of sexual violence against women by armed personnel;

d) Care must be taken to ensure the safety and security of women detainees in police stations, and women at army or paramilitary check points, and this should be a subject under the regular monitoring of the special commissioners mentioned earlier;

e) The general law relating to detention of women during specified hours of the day must be strictly followed;

f) Training and monitoring of armed personnel must be reoriented to include and emphasize strict observance by the armed personnel of all orders issued in this behalf;

g) There is an imminent need to review the continuance of AFSPA and AFSPA-like legal protocols in internal conflict areas as soon as possible. This is necessary for determining the propriety of resorting to this legislation in the area(s) concerned; and

h) Jurisdictional issues must be resolved immediately and simple procedural protocols put in place to avoid situations where police refuse or refrain from registering cases against paramilitary personnel.

(pp. 149-151 of the report)

MIZORAM SECRET AGREEMENT

The Government of India under the leadership of the Prime Minister Rajiv Gandhi has brought about a situation where in the long years of disturbed conditions in Mizoram are being brought to an end. The Memorandum of Settlement is being signed between the Government of India and Shri Laldenga, President of the Mizo National Front to give shape to this effort to usher peace and prosperity in Mizoram within the framework of the Indian Constitution. Shri Laldenga has pledged to bring the M.N.F. into the mainstream of the Indian polity and irrevocably committed it to strive for a strong and united India.

In order to further strengthen this resolve and to enable a smooth and orderly transition, the Indian National Congress (I) and the MNF headed by Shri Laldenga agree to form a coalition Government. This decision shall be implemented in the following manner soon after the members of the MNF who are underground lay down their arms and join the national mainstream.

On a date agreed to between Shri Laldenga and the Government of India, Shri Lalthanhawla, the present Congress (I) Chief Minister will submit his resignation and Shri Laldenga will be elected the leader of the Government of Mizoram and be sworn in as the Chief Minister there.

Shri Lalthanhawla, the present Chief Minister, will be sworn as the Dy Chief Minister. In addition to the Dy. Chief Minister, four members of the Congress (I) Party shall be made Ministers of the new Government.

In addition to the Chief Minister, three members from the MNF Party will be made Ministers. The name of the Ministers will be nominated by the respective political parties and the Chief Minister will propose to the Lt. Governor. All issues concerning the formation and induction of this new Govt, will be decided mutually by the Chief Minister and the Dy. Chief Minister.

In order to smoothen the function of the coalition Government, a Coordination Committee will be constituted consisting of the following:

(a) Shri Laldenga — Chaiman
(b) Shri Lalthanhawla— Vice Chairman

Two members of the Congress Party, Two members of the MNF Party.

This committee will take into consideration all matters concerning the party and the Government which either of the political parties may deem necessary to bring for its consideration in order to help smooth functioning of the Government and to bring better coordination between the Congress (I) and the MNF.

This Coalition Government will continue to MP function till such date when the President is satisfied that the normalcy has returned and the holding of elections has become feasible. In the event of any difference arising between the two parties in the functioning of the Government or relationship between the parties they would seek the help of the Hon'ble Prime Minister to resolve the same.

(Signed on 30 June 1986)

NOTES AND REFERENCES

INTRODUCTION

1. Susan Conway, *The Shan Culture: Art and Crafts*, Bangkok: Riverbooks, 2006.
2. Later to lose its independence in 1975 and be incorporated into the Union of India through a swift political and military push. For details, see Sunanda Datta-Ray's *Smash and Grab: Annexation of Sikkim*, New Delhi: HarperCollins, 2012, where he minces no words in criticizing India.
3. 'Slitting Throat' (in) *Strategic Affairs*, which describes itself as India's largest circulated military affairs publication <http://strategic-affairs.com/details. php?task=special&&id=53.
4. British Library, South Asia Section, file no 702 1/ps/7/214> [accessed 27 March 2015] on Chumbi Valley (Arunachal/Sikkim), original file no 704.
5. The Viceregal Lodge is now the prestigious Indian Institute for Advanced Studies (IIAS) where senior scholars work on issues of interest, write books and research papers. The room where the accord was signed is well-preserved—visitors are taken on tours and explained its historic significance.
6. The McMahon Line was agreed to by Britain and Tibet as part of the Simla Accord, a treaty signed in 1914. It is the effective boundary between China and India, although its legal status is disputed by the Chinese government.
7. Sir Olaf Kirkpatrick Caroe was foreign secretary in the external affairs department of the Indian government from 1939 till 1946, bringing an incisive mind and a scholarly, objective, non-discriminatory approach to this sensitive post. He was then briefly governor of the NWFP having served in Balochistan for several years. An obituary in *Asian Affairs*, Volume 13, issue I, 1982, described him as one of the 'few remaining great pro-consuls of the former British Empire'.
8. Letter of 8 February 1943, British Library, London.
9. 29 December 1943.
10. Chan, Chai-fong, 'British Colonial Policy in the Naga Hills: With Special Focus on Control Area Policy', *Komaba Journal of Area Studies*, No. 3, Tokyo: University of Tokyo, 1999, pp.167–187.
11. This is where the North East Frontier Agency originated, as the area came to be known after Independence till the creation of Arunachal Pradesh.
12. The latter's accession has always drawn furious protests in Manipur with the day marked as a Black Day, with black flags, banners and even public protests; many have long said that the then maharaja was put under house arrest in Shillong until he capitulated after several days and signed the Instrument of Accession. But the investigative journalist and indefatigable human rights warrior Yambem Laba says otherwise in the article he published. He says that the maharaja was purchased by the central government. No one from the royal family, the state government of Manipur or the centre has issued a retraction.

13. Later extended to Tripura in the Tripura Tribal Autonomous District Council (TTADC) and the Bodo areas of Western Assam in the Bodoland Territorial Council (BTC); the latter was an exception to the rule of these being located in upland regions. It was legislated as part of an accord to close an armed movement for greater autonomy by the Bodoland Tigers Force and give the Bodos, a minority of about 28 per cent in the demarcated areas, control of political and economic rights in virtual perpetuity.

14. See Pankaj Mishra's interview in the *Hindustan Times*, 25 May 2015.

15. Jawaharlal Nehru, statement to Parliament, 20 November 1950.

16. Sardar Vallabhbhai Patel, letter to Nehru, 7 November 1950.

17. The 17-point agreement was repudiated as 'null and void' by Tibet's temporal and religious head, the Dalai Lama, as soon as he escaped his colonized homeland to freedom in India on 31 March 1959.

18. The Panchsheel Agreement (see Swaran Singh in *Across the Himalayan Gap*, edited by Tan Chun, New Delhi: Indira Gandhi National Centre for the Arts, 1998) signed between India and China in April 1954 at Beijing was essentially 'desirous of promoting trade and cultural intercourse between the Tibet region of China and India and of facilitating pilgrimage and travel by the people of China and India'. The five principles were defined as:
    - Mutual respect for each other's territorial integrity and sovereignty;
    - Mutual non-aggression;
    - Mutual non-interference in each other's internal affairs;
    - Equality and mutual benefit; and
    - Peaceful coexistence.

19. Zhou Enlai's letter of 23 January 1959 to Nehru.

20. That solitary person happened to be me.

21. See Sarvepalli Gopal, *Jawaharlal Nehru: A Biography*, Volume 3, 1956–1964, New Delhi: Oxford University Press, 1984.

22. W. F. Van Eekelen, *Indian Foreign Policy and the Border Dispute with China*, Springer-Science-Business Media, 1964, quoted by A. G. Noorani in *India-China Boundary Problem, 1846-1947*.

23. Document accessed at the British Library, Asia Collection, 13 July 2013.

24. See Claude Arpi, 'The Sumdorong Chu Incident: a strong Indian stand', <http://www.indiandefencereview.com/the-sumdorong-chu-incident-a-strong-indian-stand/>. Some details of the incident are provided below. In its obituary (Bhashyam Kasturi, 'Warrior as Scholar', 22 February 1999) of General K. Sundarji, then army chief, *India Today* wrote: 'Sundarji's place in history will probably rest on the lesser-known Operation Falcon. Spooked by the Chinese occupation of Sumdorong Chu in 1986, Sundarji used the air force's new air-lift capability to land a brigade in Zimithang, north of Tawang. Indian forces took up positions on the Hathung La ridge, across the Namka Chu River, the site of India's humiliating 1962 defeat and manned defences across the McMahon Line. Taken aback, the Chinese responded with a counter-build-up and in early 1987 Beijing's tone became ominously similar to that of 1962. Western diplomats predicted war and Prime Minister Rajiv Gandhi's advisers charged that Sundarji's recklessness was responsible for this. But the general stood firm, at one point telling a senior Rajiv aide, "Please make alternate arrangements if you think you are not getting adequate professional advice." The civilians backed off, so did the Chinese.' In October 1986, Deng Xiaoping warned India that China would have to 'teach India a lesson'. This

was conveyed by the US defense secretary. In the meantime, in December 1986, Arunachal Pradesh became a full-fledged state of the Indian Union. This angered China further. In the spring and summer of 1987 media reported heavy troop movements on both sides of the border. The *Tibetan Review* said: 'All recent visitors from Tibet report fresh and hectic Chinese military activities on the Tibetan frontier adjoining India. A large number of troops are being sent there as what is being termed "troop replacement operation". However, so far no one has witnessed corresponding withdrawal of troops already stationed there. The Chinese military and civil personnel are given a call to proceed with three top-priority preparations: to prepare urgently for a military offensive; to stockpile foodgrains and other necessary materials; and to be ready for construction projects. More and more unemployed but able-bodied young Tibetans are being recruited for heavy manual work. They are paid 300 yuans (about US $60) a month and told their services will be called when the need arises. China is said to have moved in 20,000 troops from the 53rd Army Corps in Chengdu and the 13th Army in Lanzhou in the first months of 1987 along with artillery and helicopters. By early April, it had moved 8 divisions to eastern Tibet.' India continued her build-up during the first months of 1987 with a massive air-land exercise known as Exercise Chequerboard which involved several divisions of the army and several squadrons of the IAF. The Indian external affairs minister's visit to China in May 1987 helped to lower the tensions. Beijing and New Delhi reaffirmed their desire to continue the ongoing talks on the border. A few months later, the Indian and Chinese troops began to slowly withdraw from their positions in the Sumdorong Chu area.

25.   Apart from taking positions along predictable lines of anti-colonialism, anti-Zionism (read anti-Israel) and general support to organizations and movements fighting for subjugated peoples, foreign policy issues in the Congress were largely left to a small group headed by Nehru and Subhas Chandra Bose (till his ouster from the party in 1939) and others with a strong understanding of international affairs.

26.   I use both the official name for the country, Myanmar, as well as the one by which it was and remains better known to its people and to the world.

27.   For a remarkable account of this and other situations that have a bearing on the current conditions in Nagaland and Burma, I recommend Bertil Lintner's path-breaking *Land of Jade* (Bangkok: Orchid Press, 1990), where Lintner undertakes an extraordinary two-year trip from Nagaland to the Thai-Burma border with his wife and daughter. His wife was a former cadre of the Shan National Army and his daughter was born at the start of the journey.

28.   James C. Scott, *The Art of Not Being Governed: An Anarchist History of Upland Southeast Asia*, New Haven: Yale University Press, 2009.

29.   Neichute Duolo, interview with author, Kohima, March 2005.

30.   Bengt G. Karlsson, *Unruly Hills: Nature and Nation in India's Northeast*, New Delhi: Orient Blackswan, 2011.

31.   Review of James C. Scott, *The Art of Not Being Governed: An Anarchist History of Upland Southeast Asia* by Christopher Coyne, F. A. Harper Professor of Economics, Mercatus Center at George Mason University <http://www.ccoyne.com/Review_of_James_Scott.pdf> [last accessed 3 October 2017].

32.   I discuss this in detail in Chapter 1.

33.   George van Driem, 'Paragliding across languages in the Eastern Himalaya', Presentation at international conference on the Eastern Himalaya: Climate Change,

Livelihoods and Poverty, Jamia Millia Islamia, New Delhi, February 2013.

34. My way of describing residents of the non-structured but palpably present Zomia.

35. Panchsheel or the Five Principles of Mutual Coexistence were developed at the Bandung Asian Conference of 1956 and launched by Pandit Nehru, Chinese Premier Zhou Enlai and Indonesian President Sukarno.

36. According to Xi, China and India have been active practitioners of the five principles, based on which the two neighbouring countries have explored a path of harmonious coexistence and common development. Guided by the five principles, China would like to work with India to push their relations of strategic cooperation and partnership oriented toward peace and prosperity to higher levels. 'We are also willing to work with all nations in inheriting and carrying forward the Five Principles of Peaceful Coexistence, adhering to sovereign equality, realizing a win-win outcome in cooperation, seeking common security, safeguarding impartiality and justice, advocating a multi-polar world, jointly sharing development achievements, and jointly ushering in an excellent future,' Xi was quoted as saying by Xinhua. Quoted in Press Trust of India, 'Presidents of India, China and Myanmar greet each other on 60th anniversary of Panchsheel Treaty', *Indian Express,* 28 June 2014 <http://indianexpress.com/article/world/neighbours/presidents-of-india-china-and-myanmar-greet-each-other-on-60th-anniversary-of-panchsheel-treaty/> [accessed 7 October 2015].

37. Stephen E. Flynn, 'The role of border technology in advancing homeland security', written testimony before a joint hearing of the US Senate Judiciary Subcommittee on Technology, Terrorism, and Government Information and the US Senate Judiciary Subcommittee on Border Security, Citizenship, and Immigration, 12 March 2003 <http://www.cfr.org/pub5708/stephen_e_flynn/the_role_of_border_technology_in_advancing_homeland_security.php>.

CHAPTER 1

1. (Other references)

     n pl, -ties

     • exemption or immunity from punishment or recrimination
     • exemption or immunity from unpleasant consequences: a successful career marked by impunity from early mistakes
     • with impunity
       a. with no unpleasant consequences
       b. with no care or heed for such consequences
       c. from Latin *impunitas* freedom from punishment, from *impunis* unpunished, from *im-* (not) + *poena* punishment)

2. *Nandita Haksar and Naga Peoples Movement for Human Rights (NPMHR) vs the State* in which the Supreme Court upheld the constitutional validity of AFSPA but instituted a code of conduct that it urged personnel to follow during operations, including treating women with dignity and sensitivity.

3. When women officers are not part of the team, authorities say that they are difficult to get at night (though these raids are planned well in advance).

4. One of the soldiers wrote to his wife saying that he was 'traumatized' by the event and its aftermath and pleaded with her to believe that he was innocent of the rape accusation (conversation with former Assam Rifles Director General, Lieutenant General Bhopinder Singh, Shillong, November 2004).

5. For details see <htttp://ucdp.uu.se/#country/750,   http://www.pcr.uu.se/

research/ucdo/definitions/>.

6. Preeti Gill, *The Peripheral Centre: Voices from India's Northeast*, New Delhi: Zubaan Books, 2005.

7. Parts of this chapter are excerpted from Chasie and Hazarika's *The State Strikes Back: India and the Naga Insurgency*, Washington DC: East West Center, 2008, with permission of the publishers (Policy Brief 54, pp. 15–25).

8. Until 2006, there was no formal attempt to separate the executive and the judiciary in Nagaland, and district administrators, by virtue of their executive posts, became magistrates.

9. Unlike civil law, the proof of innocence or seeming innocence under AFSPA depends on the gaze of the beholder, not on his or her understanding of the issues of rightness and wrongdoing. Thus, the suspect must prove his innocence beyond *reasonable* doubt, since the authority under which he or she lives and functions has powers not just to search and detain but also to kill. So, just as the rights of the person protected by AFSPA (in this case the security forces) are absolute, the rights of the persons negatively affected by the act are completely vulnerable to the whim and feelings of the officer or authority.

10. See Sanjoy Hazarika, *Strangers of the Mist: Tales of War and Peace from India's Northeast*, New Delhi: Penguin Books India, 2012, p. 99, where I speak of the fate of Sakhrie who tried to make Phizo and his group understand that it would not be possible to fight India and win the war. Sakhrie was killed for his beliefs, the first victim of the internecine conflicts that have plagued the Nagas since the 1950s.

11. Sanjib Baruah, *Durable Disorder: Understanding the Politics of Northeast India*, Chapter 'Governors as Generals', New Delhi: Oxford University Press, 2007.

12. Jamir has survived four assassination attempts by his underground foes, including a road ambush in Nagaland and a 1993 attack at his suite at Nagaland House, the official hostel for government visitors and guests from the state in New Delhi (Chapter 3). North East News Agency wrote in 2007: 'Governor of Goa S. C. Jamir escaped unhurt when his 30-vehicle convoy was ambushed 11 kilometres away from Changki village towards Mariani in Mokokchung district. There were nine Improvised Explosive Devices (IEDs) planted in the ambush area. There were six explosions while three of the IEDs remained unexploded. This is the fourth time that an assassination attempt has been made on the life of Jamir. He was travelling to Dimapur from Mokokchung, and was also accompanied by his wife Alemla Jamir. According to reports, unidentified gunmen fired at the convoy and the personal security escorting Jamir retaliated immediately and in the exchange of fire, a security man was injured. "Mr. Jamir appeared unruffled by the attack and directed his convoy to keep proceeding," DC Mokokchung R. Lotha said. Later Jamir reached Dimapur and took the flight out to Kolkata. This is the fourth time Jamir has had a providential escape since 1993 when he was seriously wounded in an attack at Nagaland House, New Delhi. Another abortive attempt on his life was made in Kohima town in 1995. In 1999, he escaped once again an ambush carried out at a place 30 kilometres from Kohima. Two members of his personal security were killed in the attack. Meanwhile, the shell of an unexploded two-inch mortar was also recovered at the site. Police also recovered a modified .303 rifle with ten live rounds. No casualties were reported except for projectiles let off by the explosion causing a minor injury to an APSI of the 9 IRB in the convoy. The Assam Rifles, who were the first to rush to the scene, detonated the unexploded IEDs... "In spite of the fact that S. C. Jamir has been under threat

because of the ban imposed on him by the NSCN (I-M) to enter Nagaland and in spite of the fact that he is in the Z-Plus Category of the threat perception, the state government has totally failed to protect him," Leader of Opposition and CLP Leader I. Imkong said in a statement.' NENA, *Major Events* Vol 3, Issue no 39, 1–15 December 2007, 'Jamir survives another attempt on his life'.

13. S. C. Jamir interview with Charles Chasie in Kohima, 20 February 2007.

14. The committee's report includes a note by me, saying in essence that the repeal of AFSPA could create political space for negotiations, dialogue and peace in the Northeast. Reddy Committee Report, Annexure VII, p. 120.

15. 'Challenges to Governance', lecture by Chief Minister Lalthanhawla, at the Centre for North East Studies, and Policy Research, Jamia Millia Islamia, New Delhi, 14 September 2010.

16. Hazarika, *Strangers of the Mist*, 'A Stepmother in Delhi', p. 249.

17. For details of the Mizo movement, see Chapter 4, 'A Troubled Peace in Mizoram'.

18. Ten years later, in August 2015, Th. Muivah, fresh from a tête-à-tête with Prime Minister Narendra Modi, took the salute from a contingent of Naga soldiers of the NSCN (I-M) and raised the Naga flag on Naga Independence Day at Camp Hebron, the headquarters of the organization near Dimapur. Little appeared to have changed despite Modi's glowing description of a 'historic accord' with the Nagas though it was barely a few sentences long and contained little beyond a declaration of general principles of future negotiations. For good reason, the government and the NSCN (I-M) kept this document as secret as possible because the shallowness of it all would have caught them wrong-footed. At eighty, Muivah was nobody's fool and no stranger to negotiations with prime ministers; Modi was the sixth he had dealt with in twenty years. At the Hebron rally, he rubbished claims that he had sold out the Nagas and given up on the core claims on sovereignty and territorial integration of Naga-inhabited areas in Manipur, Assam and Arunachal Pradesh with Nagaland, both highly sensitive issues, the first unacceptable to India, the second to the states involved. Little indeed had changed, despite face-saving rhetoric by the government's interlocutor (or was he more of an interloper, to confuse and divide, a well-known Kautilyan ploy of the Centre?) that he could not be held responsible for the statements of others involved in the negotiations.

19. These issues are further discussed in Chapter 9: 'Strangers No More—The New Indians'.

20. Shrivastav was additional home secretary, holding charge of issues relating to the Northeast, in the 1990s.

21. A research visit with Preeti Gill to Kohima in October 2003.

22. A decade later, Dr Sentisungla Longchar, who teaches psychology at Lady Shri Ram College, New Delhi, was to recount a similar story at a discussion on 'Understanding Diversity'. Responding to my remarks on AFSPA, Sentisungla talked about how the sudden entry of an Indian Army patrol into her home, 'the knock on the door', the fear inspired by their presence and manners, still remained an enduring and unhealed memory.

23. General R. K. Sawhney, former director general of military operations, in that same programme acknowledged that the army had made mistakes and targeted civilians in the early years but hastened to add that their villages were no longer being burnt and that human rights violations did not take place any longer. Of course, the army has its own apologists in the media and among so-called 'intellectuals'.

24. Praveen Swami, 'Immunity is not Impunity', *Indian Express*, 18 September 2015.

25. Lieutenant General Umong Sethi, 'Armed Forces Special Powers Act—The Way Ahead' in *Armed Forces Special Powers Act: The Debate*, Vivek Chadha, editor; Institute for Defence Studies & Analysis, Lancer Publishers, New Delhi, 2013, pp. 38–56.

26. Armed Forces Special Powers Act, Jammu and Kashmir, Wajahat Habibullah in *Armed Forces Special Powers Act: The Debate*, Vivek Chadha, editor, Institute for Defence Studies & Analysis, New Delhi: Lancers Publishers 2013, pp. 22–30.

27. The peace was broken by the Khaplang faction of the NSCN in the summer of 2015 with a series of attacks on security personnel, including one in which at least eighteen soldiers were killed in an ambush, the largest number of casualties that the army had suffered in an insurgency in two decades.

28. *NPHMR vs Union of India*, 27 November 1997.

29. Praveen Swami, 'Immunity is not Impunity', *The Hindu*, 18 September 2015.

30. Interview with author, November 2004, Dimapur.

31. Tripathi was speaking in New Delhi at the 4 February 2016 launch of his book *Detours: Songs of the Open Road*, New Delhi: Tranquebar Press, 2016.

32. Soumik Dutta, 'Useful enemies: How politicians in NE India profit from rebel unrest' <https://100r.org/2015/04/useful-enemies/> [accessed 21 April 2015].

33. 'Meghalaya High Court asks centre to consider enforcing AFSPA in Garo Hills', *The Telegraph*, Kolkata, 3 November 2015, <http://www.telegraphindia.com/1151103/jsp/frontpage/story_51203.jsp#.Vj88-EvGDZs> [accessed 3 November 2015].

34. Northern Ireland (Emergency Provisions) Act, 1996.

35. Email from Ambrish Kumar, adviser, Planning Commission, Government of India, to the Health Steering Committee, received by author on 13 May 2011 for a meeting of the National Steering Committee on Health (I was a member of this group) under the aegis of the Planning Commission, Government of India, now known as the Niti Aayog.

36. 'Bearing witness: the impact of conflict on women in Nagaland and Assam', Sanjoy Hazarika and Preeti Gill, eds, New Delhi: Centre for North East Studies and Policy Research, supported by the Heinrich Böll Stiftung, Introduction 2011 (for the full report, access www.c-nes.org).

37. *The Hindu* online is the first website to publish the full report of the AFSPA Review Committee nearly ten years after it was handed over to the government; it remains on its website.

38. The reference here was to Dr Manmohan Singh, who made the pledge in Imphal in 2004.

39. See Chapter 7, 'A Wandering Horse, Upland and Border States, a Prince and a Communist'.

CHAPTER 2

1. Pradip Phanjoubam, Opinion, 'A Defeat Foretold', the *Indian Express*, 20 March 2017 <http://indianexpress.com/article/opinion/columns/irom-sharmila-afspa-manipur-elections-ibobi-singh-4576612/> [accessed 2 April, 2017].

2. Imphal Free Press, 22 August 2015.

3. According to the website E-Pao, the Ministry of Home Affairs on 24 July 2015, issued a rule that 'anyone including members of NGOs, companies, media and academics who intended to visit a prison for the purpose of undertaking research, making a documentary or interviewing the inmates or any other similar research

activity may be required to submit a security deposit of ₹1 lakh by way of a demand draft/local bankers' cheque in the name of Jail Superintendent. However, the State Governments and Union Territory (UT) Administrations may dispense with or modify this requirement in case of research studies undertaken by students. The guidelines were issued under advisory No V-11018/3/2010-PR and says that the visitor(s) may submit an application to the Jail Superintendent of the State/UT Government at least 30 days before the date of visit. Foreigners must submit such application 60 days before. In the case of article by print media, the application may be submitted 7 days before. For foreigners, the State/UT Government is advised to consult the local units of Intelligence Bureau (IB) and/or may also consult Ministry of External Affairs (MEA) or Foreigners Division of MHA.' On receiving the application, the guidelines said the jail superintendent should send the application to the home or prison department of the state along with 'his comments' for seeking permission and the competent authority to grant such permission. However, the guidelines also say 'in case of visitors of Indian nationality, the state/UT government may delegate this function to the head of the prison department that is DG, ADG/IG etc. specifically but not to any other lower level. If the permission is granted in case of newspapers, magazines, web-based articles, the visitor shall follow the journalistic conduct and prescribed norms of Press Council of India before preparing the material for publication. Beside this, for those who wish to make documentaries or conduct interview, they may be allowed to carry Handy Cam/Camera/Tape Recorder or equipment directly connected with the purpose of the visit but tripod, stand mounted cameras or equipment should not be allowed, including mobile phone, papers, book or pen. However, the final version of the documentary, film, research paper, articles or book to be released or published should be submitted to the State Government or head of the prison department for final No Objection Certificate. And in case of violations of guidelines issued by the MHA, the Jail Superintendent shall forfeit the security deposits and initiate suitable legal action. "Visiting Irom Sharmila for interview may require ₹1 lakh security deposit', *Hueiyen News Service*, 7 November 2015, *E-Pao.net*, <http://e-pao.net/GP.asp?src=23..081115.nov15 > [accessed 13 December 2015].

4.   'Shoot and pay: why compensation for encounter killings has begun to feel like hush money', Ipsita Chakravarty, *Scroll.in*, 25 August 2015 < https://scroll.in/article/749256/shoot-and-pay-why-compensation-for-encounter-killings-has-begun-to-feel-like-hush-money> [accessed 9 September 2015].

5.   Kishalay Bhattacharjee, *Blood on My Hands: Confessions of Staged Encounters*, New Delhi: HarperCollins India, 2015.

6.   See 'A Culture of Impunity: Protecting the Killers in Punjab', Human Rights Watch, Washington, 2009, http://www.hrw.org/reports/2007/india1007/3.htm. Also see the work of human rights activist the late Ram Narayan Kumar, who uncovered, along with lawyers in the Punjab, thousands of extrajudicial deaths in the state (this could be as high as 20,000). Kumar wrote a seminal work: Kumar, Amrik Singh, Ashok Agrwaal and Jaskaran Kaur, *Reduced to Ashes: The Insurgency and Human Rights in Punjab* (Kathmandu: South Asia Forum for Human Rights, 2003). 'Many of the bodies had been cremated—6,000 bodies in one district alone. The lawyer who helped Kumar uncover the murders, Jaswant Singh Kalra, was abducted by the police on 6 September 1995, secretly detained, tortured for almost two months and murdered in late October 1995. His body was dumped in a canal.

Six police officers were convicted of charges relating to his murder and abduction in November 2005, although a petition calling for charges against former DGP Gill has lasped with the latter's passing.' Another extract from the report: 'The United States government described the Punjab police practice of faked encounter killings in 1993: In the typical scenario, police take into custody a suspected militant or militant supporter without filing an arrest report. If the detainee dies during interrogation or is executed, officials deny he was ever in custody and claim he died during an armed encounter with police or security forces. Alternatively, police may claim to have been ambushed by militants while escorting a suspect. Although the detainee invariably dies in "crossfire", police casualties in these "incidents" are rare. In the majority of cases, the police abducted the victims of extrajudicial executions or "disappearances" in the presence of witnesses, often family members. Family members of the victims further experienced multiple forms of abuse. A recent study conducted by Physicians for Human Rights (PHR) and the Bellevue/NYU Medical Center Program for Survivors of Torture revealed that family members of the "disappeared" were also tortured in over half of the cases they investigated.'

7.   Bhattacharjee, *Blood on My Hands*, pp. 143–148.

8.   Restricted Area Permits (RAPs), also known as Protected Areas Permits (PAPs), apply to the hill states of Nagaland, Arunachal Pradesh and Mizoram as well as to Manipur. All state governments have long demanded the scrapping of both though they want controls on Indians, enforced through the ILP or Inner Line Permit, to stay.

9.   *The Telegraph*, Kolkata, 16 May 2011 < https://www.telegraphindia.com/1110517/jsp/northeast/story_13990741.jsp>

10. I would regard a central periphery would be that which the central government, publicly or otherwise, regards as a region which may be on a geographical edge of the country, physically distant but, through agitations and public movements and processes, is able to force the centre to take political or security-related action (often reluctantly) which the latter would not otherwise do. The central periphery could be, as in the case of the Northeastern states or Jammu and Kashmir, small in size and population as well as far from the political power and decision-making in New Delhi, but carry influence disproportionate to these because of local abilities to mobilize along lines of ethnicity, religion, language or otherwise, to strike with weapons as through an armed movement or through legal processes, acts of non-violence like hunger strike by the anti-AFSPA protester Irom Sharmila or literary and cultural events that draw public attention and sympathy to an idea or ideas, social conditions, a cause or causes. This is also well defined in *The Peripheral Centre* (ed. Preeti Gill).

11. Bimol Akoijam, professor at Jawaharlal Nehru University, 11 May 2014, on his Facebook wall.

12. Esha Roy, 'Flashback to a killing in Imphal', *Indian Express*, 28 January 2016.

13. Ibid.

14. 'CHRI: Manipur killing is 'obstruction of justice;, calls for investigation of nexus, 30 January 2016 <http://www.humanrightsinitiative.org/press-releases/chri-manipur-killing-is-obstruction-of-justice-calls-for-investigation-of-nexus-press-statement-new-delhi-30-january-2016> [accessed 31 January 2016].

15. Pradip Phanjoubam, 'Under Siege, On Edge', *Indian Express,* Opinion, 22 December 2016

CHAPTER 3

1. One speech was at a public reception at the Indira Gandhi Indoor Stadium and the other was at the first convocation of Nagaland University, both on 28 October 2003.

2. The speech writer had asked to meet with me. What should the prime minister say, he asked, that will help the Nagas respond? 'Speak to them from his heart, speak of honour and dignity, of the innocent lives lost, of a past that shames all of us,' I said. 'Can you write these down and send it to me?' he asked. I did. These lines are from that set of notes. Then he had another question: 'We're told that the weather may not be good when he lands at Dimapur for a helicopter to take him to Kohima. How should he go?' I must have looked a bit blank because, really, didn't the PMO know there was a national highway between Dimapur and Kohima? Of course, we won't speak of its condition much of the time. He must have seen the expression on my face. 'How's the road?' the aide asked warily. 'Well,' I smiled, 'if the prime minister asks please tell him it's the best road in Nagaland.' Sure enough, Vajpayee referred to this in his speech at the public reception: 'Speaking of roads in Nagaland, I have to say that I had a first-hand experience yesterday. Mother Nature wanted me to take the road journey from Dimapur to Kohima. I was told that, of all the roads in the state, this is the best. If this is the best, it is difficult to imagine how bad is the worst.'

3. Interview with a senior Angami tribal leader in Kohima, April 2015.

4. For details of Khonoma and its role in the Naga movement and history, see Hazarika, *Strangers of the Mist*, p.86.

5. Kevichusa was later to become a leader of the Naga Nationalist Council and then the United Democratic Front, which had close relations with the founder of the Naga sovereignty movement, A. Z. Phizo. He is regarded as one of the founders of Nagaland state, and was elected a Member of Parliament in 1971 and two of his sons, Chalie and Tubu, were to fall victim to the bullets of assassins from a rival Naga group.

6. The Maos are one of a number of Naga tribes living on the Nagaland-Manipur border. The other tribes on this chunk of hilly land include the Pumai and Maram. I remember an amusing story about the Maos which also tells of the ignorance of many well-educated Indians. At a meeting of members of the Planning Commission and staff some years back, I remember speaking about the range of ethnic groups in the Northeast and mentioned the Mao. At which point, a member of the commission, a former vice chancellor of a prominent central university, asked how Mao Zedong had gotten to Manipur. I thought he was joking but saw he was extremely serious. That's a tribe in Manipur, I told him.

7. This is substantially drawn from Prof Mao's seminar paper: 'The Naga struggle for sovereignty: Its past and the probable future', Xavier Pfokrehe Mao, at the national seminar on Peace, Non-Violence and National Interest, Shillong, 26–28 July 1999.

8. Then an extra assistant commissioner in Mokokchung and later Member of the Indian Parliament.

9. W. G. Archer, 'Manuscript notes made by W. G. Archer between 1946 & 1948, and miscellaneous papers and letters', *www.digitalhimalaya.com* <http://himalaya.socanth. cam.ac.uk/collections/naga/record/r66668.html> [accessed 8 September 2015].

10. The Battle of Kohima, celebrated as Britain's greatest military victory and a key to the outcome of World War II, was fought on the tennis courts of his official bungalow, a bitter, bruising, bloody struggle with hand-to-hand combat, snipers and trench and foxhole struggles.

11. Lt. Colonel (Retd.) M. Ranjit Singh, 'Reflections on the fourth Naga peace agreement, part 2', *E-Pao.net*, 28 October 2015 <http://e-pao.net/ epSubPageExtractor.asp?src=news_section.Naga_Peace_Process_Indo-Naga_ Talks_2012.Reflections_on_the_fourth_Naga_peace_agreement_Part_2_By_M_ Ranjit> [accessed 11 November 2015].

12. See Epilogue.

13. On 26 May 1953 the Act received the Assam governor's approval and was published in the *Assam Gazette* on 3 June 1953.

14. Over the past decades, the rise of ethnic nationalism has been linked to growing tensions among various communities. This in turn has escalated into gruesome conflicts in different states, particularly in Assam and Manipur, further complicating the security scenario. Indeed, the range of complexities leads planners in New Delhi to view the region as a perpetual national security challenge.

15. In 1972, AFSPA was amended to enlarge the scope of its operation to other states.

16. The Padma Bhushan is one of several national awards given by the Government of India, technically on the recommendation of an awards committee but actually swung by recommendations of political figures with clout in different arenas, including social work, literature, culture and sports.

17. For details see Hazarika, *Strangers of the Mist*; Nirmal Nibedon, *Nagaland: the Night of the Guerrillas*, New Delhi: Lancer Publishers, 1983.

18. At the time there was no television and only one radio service, the official All India Radio, with its scattered stations across the country, including the Northeast. There were a handful of English-language and Assamese papers in Assam, which physically was almost all of the Northeast, while the major Indian dailies from Delhi and Calcutta posted a correspondent at the outpost of Shillong, the regional capital and the heart of its larger politics, in much the same way as administrators were posted at the frontier a century earlier. Being a correspondent for the 'Indian press' was a powerful position; they were supposed to have the ear of governments, both in New Delhi and in Shillong, and men like Hamdi Bey of *The Statesman* of Calcutta were extremely influential and their writing, as those of others, was closely followed. They also reflected the concerns of those in power, with references to 'senior' or 'informed sources' in their work when they reported on government policies and views. All of this as well as the fact of their presence and reporting played into the larger picture of a land apart and a nation separated from its periphery.

19. Mahatma Gandhi to a Naga delegation in New Delhi, 1947, see Hazarika, *Strangers of the Mist*. p.97

20. Udayon Misra, *The Periphery Strikes Back: Challenges to the Nation-state in Assam and Nagaland*. Shimla: Indian Institute of Advanced Study, 2000.

21. Professor H. K. Barpujari, *A Political History of Assam*. Assam: Departmentt. for the Preparation of Political History of Assam, Government of Assam, 1977.

22. Name changed at author's discretion.

23. I was wrong—at least to a degree: some seven years after that conversation with the Naga legend, a small group of young Assamese met at Rang Ghar, the sixteenth-century amphitheatre in Sivasagar, seat of the Tai-Asom kingdom which ruled Assam for 600 years until the British seized control, and decided that they needed to fight the Indian state to carve out an independent nation of Asom. That was the United Liberation Front of Asom (ULFA) and their armed struggle began in the 1980s and continued with surges and failures until the end of 2009, when

virtually the entire leadership of the organization was in Indian captivity, thanks to some sharp work by Bangladesh that year. Earlier, in 2004, a furious assault by the Royal Bhutanese Army on insurgent camps within Bhutan devastated the organization and killed hundreds of cadres (see Chapter 5). The government of King Jigme Singye Wangchuck had been outraged by ULFA's arrogant statement, when requested politely to leave since their presence in Bhutan was causing pressure from and tension with India, that it would stay in the Himalayan kingdom in 'perpetuity' or at least until such time as they carved out an independent nation from India. ULFA's leadership thought, foolishly, that the small nation, wedded to Buddhism and the pursuit of an intriguing notion called Gross National Happiness (GNH), not Gross National Product as the wealth of a nation is normally measured in international financial jargon, would never strike at them. Sovereignty and nationalism or rather nationhood were obviously more important than GNH; or perhaps the latter is, in the eyes of the Bhutanese, connected to the first two.

24. I had been intrigued by Narasimha Rao's interest in the Naga matter. This was whetted by a brief conversation with a senior member of his staff where he mentioned something that was the very stuff of mystery novels. The official was pretty sure that during a visit to Paris in 1995 Swu and Muivah had been slipped in to meet the prime minister. There was no official engagement recorded in the PM's diary but it was during those periods when no programme had been fixed in the afternoon and when Rao was supposed to rest. It was a fifteen-minute meeting and the official had had a glimpse of the men when they went in. I'm pretty sure he knew more than that but was not letting on. So whatever either side may say, both direct and back-door channels were on and functioning in discreet ways.

25. Perhaps that comparison was made without knowing of the disastrous political and economic consequences that overwhelmed China when the Great Helmsman, as Mao was also known, led it through the time of Let a Thousand Flowers Bloom, when other viewpoints as well as cultural freedom was welcomed and then crushed; the Great Leap Forward, when agriculture suffered a disaster that drove China to famine and about three million to starvation deaths; and the Cultural Revolution, when millions of teachers and professionals as well as suspected government officers and party cadres were dispatched to the countryside for 're-education'. Buddhist monks in Tibet were among the worst sufferers, suffering beatings and displacement while their ancient priceless texts, paintings and artefacts, not to speak of the temples themselves, were destroyed.

26. Lintner, *Land of Jade*.

27. The bitterness between the two sides goes back to 1988, when Khaplang, furious at a report that his colleagues were planning a deal with India, a charge they deny just as furiously, authorized a major attack by his commandos on Muivah's camp. Some 200 Tangkhuls were killed, some beheaded, a gruesome experience and memory that has seared Muivah's anger and suspicion. Yet, they had worked together for nearly twenty years, when Khaplang, then heading the Eastern Naga Revolutionary Organization, had facilitated Muivah's trip to China and enabled connections with the Kachin Independence Organization, a relationship that stood them in good stead till the mid-1980s, with the KIO and the KIA offering shelter and training as well as arms, of course, for a price. That was until India's external intelligence arm, the Research and Analysis Wing, established contacts with the Kachins and offered them funds and weapons if they would stop supporting the Indian rebels. By this time, both ULFA and some of the Manipuri underground groups had developed

a comfortable business relationship with the Kachins. The Indian initiative snapped that connection and forced the Northeastern groups to collaborate with each other as well as forge their own independent paths of growth.

28. In an interview at Bhubaneswar, Odisha, Jamir said that fellow Nagas were asking for copies of a document he had published in 2001 called the 'Bedrock of Naga Society', where he had denounced the demand for sovereignty and strongly asserted Nagaland's role within India, saying there was no future for separation. The monograph was sharply attacked; Jamir said his underground detractors got copies burnt. 'But now people want to read it because they think I was correct,' chuckled the political veteran, still dapper at eighty-five, in a conversation on 10 April 2017. He was then governor of Odisha and the interview took place at his office in the stately Raj Bhavan.

29. Indian Army leaders and the Ministry of Defence are strongly opposed to any cohabitation with the Naga fighters in the armed forces but are open to the Nagas either merging with one unit of the central paramilitary forces or New Delhi creating a new unit of just the Nagas.

30. Symbolic though it may be, each state flew its own flag before the merger of the princely states with India. Many of them have their own state anthem and a flag would win emotional and political brownie points, a symbol of independence and distance from Delhi.

31. The Naga writer Easterine Kire one of the finest storytellers of such stories, explains the umbilical connections between tribes like the Nagas and their villages and lands. Her books include *When the River Sleeps* , which won the 2015 Hindu Literary Award, and *Bitter Wormwood*. Another writer of note is Temsula Ao (*These Hills Called Home*).

32. I look at this issue in the Epilogue.

33. Sangeeta Barooah Pisharoty, 'Nagas apprehensive about lasting peace as they bid farewell to a beloved leader', *The Wire*, 30 June 2016.

34. Vijaita Singh, 'NSCN has not given up on sovereignty, says Muivah', *The Hindu*, 8 July 2016 <http://www.thehindu.com/news/national/nscn-has-not-given-up-on-sovereignty-says-muivah/article8820302.ece [accessed 20 September 2016]>.

35. Kharingyo Shimrah, 'Shared sovereignty between India and Nagalim', *The Sangai Express*, 1 March 2016 <http://www.thesangaiexpress.com/shared-sovereignty-between-india-and-nagalim/> [accessed 1 March 2016].

36. 'Part XXI: Temporary, transitional and special provisions, 371A. Special provision with respect to the State of Nagaland', *Constitution Society* <http://www.constitution.org/cons/india/p21371a.html> [accessed 13 November 2016].

CHAPTER 4

1. Brigadier Thenphunga Sailo, AVSM (*Ati Vishisht Seva Medal*), *A Soldier's Story*, self-published, 2001. p. 86.

2. In a strange way, Sangliana was following in his father's footsteps—the latter too had been a guerrilla in 'enemy' territory.

3. Moral Re-Armament, an organization that promoted the idea that societal change could only start from change from within an individual. Led by Rajmohan Gandhi, the grandson of the Mahatma Gandhi, it had a large following in the 1960s and 1970s, and later changed its name to IofC or Initiatives of Change.

4. See Hazarika, *Strangers of the Mist*, p. 97, 346.

5. L.T. Pudaite, *Mizoram and Look East Policy*, New Delhi: Akansha Publishing,

2010, Appendix C 3, Memorandum Submitted to His Majesty's Government, Government of India and its Constituent Assembly through the Advisory Sub-Committee by the Mizo Union, pp. 68–74.

6. The story of Bosnia-Herzegovina, Serbia, Macedonia and the fragmenting Balkans is not one that the United Nations or the Western Alliance can be proud of. Nor is it a story that should be repeated. It is a shameful bloodstained history of massacres and deep-rooted historic and religious prejudice.

7. 'Problem of Peace Making in Mizoram', Lal Hmingthanga, edited by J. V. Hluna, New Delhi: Concept Publishing House, 2013, pp. 129, 132, 133

8. Ibid.

9. Ultimately, the Mizo Army had fallen to about 2,000 at the time of the 1986 peace accord.

10. Nearly fifty years later, the two men sat across a conference table in an Aizawl hotel, both smiling while remembering the moment as Denghnuna, a tall man with a ready grin, said with a characteristic laugh, 'This man, this man, he ordered my arrest!'

11. It can be argued that all of Mizoram and most states on the east of the Northeast border Burma.

12. The Malaysian experience of dealing with insurgency is partly drawn from a detailed article by T. Dugdale-Pointon, *historyofwar.org*, 26 August 2007, *The Malayan Emergency (1947–1960)*, <http://www.historyofwar.org/articles/wars_malaya.html> [accessed 30 July 2015].

13. Ibid.

14. It is widely believed that Chaliha, among the most sagacious of Indian political leaders at the time, had approved the dispersal of funds to Laldenga in an effort to keep the MNF under control. In addition, the Assam government was soft on the MNF leaders when they were captured in December 1963 and then released at the Indo-Pakistan border in Cachar district when returning from a training and preparatory mission in Dhaka.

15. Sajal Nag, *Contesting Marginality: Ethnicity, Insurgency and Subnationalism in North-East India*, New Delhi: Manohar Publishers and Distributors, 2002.

16. Manekshaw was yet to win major glory as the liberator of East Pakistan, in its bloody struggle against West Pakistan, with his blitzkrieg that outflanked enemy generals, crushed the Pakistani Army and forced the surrender of over 90,000 Pakistani soldiers. Before the Indian intervention, which led to the creation of the independent nation of Bangladesh and Pakistan's dismemberment, the place was bathed in blood, ravaged by the rape of women and massacres of university professors, students and ordinary citizens. But before he won laurels in that conflict, Manekshaw was, as the general officer commanding in chief at Fort William, Calcutta, the head of the army's operations and administration in all of Eastern India. He had taken part in action against the Nagas and was a veteran of the 1948 and 1965 wars against Pakistan as well as the 1962 border conflict with China.

17. Dr J. V. Hluna and Rini Tochhawng, *The Mizo Uprising: Assam Assembly Debates on the Mizo Movement, 1966–1971*, London: Cambridge Scholars Publishing, 2012, Introduction, p. xxii.

18. Chief Minister Bimala Prasad Chaliha's statement in the Assam Assembly, 5 April 1966.

19. Stanley D. D. Nichols Roy, Assam Assembly Debates, 5 April 1966.

20. Cherrie Lalnunziri Chhante, in 'The Mizo insurgency movement and terror lore'.

Paper was presented in the at the 29th Indian Folklore Congress and National Seminar on Oral Discourse and Ancient Knowledge Systems of North East India at NEHU, Shillong on September 20-22, 2006.

21. Chief Minister B. P. Chaliha's statement of 1 April 1967, Assam Assembly Debates, March session, 1967, Volume I (pp. 367–373); substantial parts of this section are drawn from this statement.

22. 'Hostiles' was commonly used by the government and the media (including independent media) to refer to anti-government fighters both in Nagaland and the Mizo Hills.

23. Assam Assembly Debates, 7 June 1967, Vol II No. 16.

24. Ibid.

25. The reference is to Gulzarilal Nanda, then home minister of India.

26. The officer is not named and Jafa, a war horse of Assam, Meghalaya and Mizo administration with thirty years of service, credits his wife, Jyoti Jafa, with taking the extensive notes which give us the excruciating first-person account, which is also the story of a penitent destroyer.

27. Lalkhama, *A Mizo Civil Servant's Random Reflections* (self-published), 2006, pp. 177–181. Also see Vijendra Singh Jafa, 'Counterinsurgency warfare: The use & abuse of military force, *South Asia Terrorism Portal* <http://www.satp.org/satporgtp/publication/faultlines/volume3/Fault3-JafaF.htm> [accessed 29 April 2017].

28. These remarks were made during conversations in 2011. We were to meet again in the winter of 2015 to conduct a detailed interview but he passed away on 30 November 2015.

29. The section about R. V. Pillai's kidnapping is drawn from a telephone interview on 2 February 2016 with the former official and a subsequent email note from him on 10 February 2016 responding to a number of questions.

30. 'Brief Review of Mizo Literature' by Margaret Ch. Zama and C. Lalawmpuia, p. 85, unpublished report, Centre for North East Studies and Policy Research, under a grant from the Heinrich Boll Foundation, 2015.

31. The Mizoram Accord was signed by representatives of the Government of India, Home Secretary R. D. Pradhan, the president of the MNF Laldenga, and Lalkhama.

32. Ajit Doval rose to become the director of the Intelligence Bureau and, when Narendra Modi led the BJP to a sweeping victory in the 2014 general elections, was made national security adviser.

33. In all, not fewer than one million people were slaughtered, some 3,00,000 women were raped and nine million East Pakistanis driven into refuge in West Bengal, Assam, Meghalaya and Tripura. (The facts are a bit unclear on the rape figure; it is said that this figure draws upon a slip of the tongue by Sheikh Mujibur Rahman, who wanted to say 30,000 and instead inadvertently came out with the 3,00,000 figure during an interview.)

34. Later, he was to propose Sangliana's execution although no one was prepared to carry out this order, for the young Mizo had won his spurs and was deeply respected and liked.

35. See media reports of 3–15 August 2015 on the peace accord, which did not furnish details, between the Government of India's interlocutor R. N. Ravi and NSCN (I-M) general secretary Th Muivah.

36. Recounted by Sangliana, interview with author, Aizawl, 24 June 2015.

37. Ved Marwah, *Uncivil Wars: Pathology of Terrorism in India*, New Delhi: HarperCollins, 1995, p. 266.

38. Lalkhama, *A Mizo Civil Servant's Random Recollections*, self-published, 2006, p. 170.

39. Sanjay Gandhi was seen as the heir apparent, the crown prince of India's oldest and most influential political dynasty, although he was also regarded in New Delhi's political circles as reckless and ruthless.

40. That assault in the summer of 1984 to flush out Sikh extremists holed up in the Golden Temple outraged the community and was eventually to lead to the assassination of Indira Gandhiby her own Sikh guards and unleash a series of anti-Sikh pogroms in New Delhi and other cities in October–November 1984. Rajiv Gandhi's statement at a large rally at the Boat Club lawns (I was present at the event) that 'the earth shakes when a great tree falls', a reference to the riots, did not go down well with many people.

41. Much of the anti-alien campaign, decades after the Assam Accord, remains couched in similar language and framed in an anti-Muslim mould. The suspicion, hatred and discrimination against this group remains sharply intact as does the latter's resentment and rancour at being shut out of economic and political processes.

42. Interview with the author, Aizawl, 24 August 2015.

43. There is even a Zomi National Army and a Zomi National Force/Front (ZNF), which are led by Burmese nationals although they live on the Indian side. The seamlessness of the politics of the border, not just the people on either side of it or the border itself, was revealed by one story. I was meeting a leader of Burma's National League for Democracy in Aizawl in an exiled Myanmar MP's home when a burly man strolled in. He was the finance secretary of the ZNF and was accompanied by two hefty men, clearly his minders. In the course of a conversation in the home below Burra Bazar, it transpired that he was staying at the State Guest House, which is where, as the name suggests, guests of the state are accommodated. My natural curiosity as a researcher and journalist was piqued. How could a leader of an underground group be a formal guest of the Mizoram government? He came up with the real story: some months earlier, a group of technical officers had been kidnapped from a hydroelectric construction site in Manipur by the People's Liberation Army of that state. These included a couple of Mizos. The Manipur government was worried and desperate. It contacted Zoramthanga, the then Mizo chief minister. Could he do something? Zoramthanga set into motion a series of simple steps: the involvement of the state government was not an option. But he considered his network of contacts in the underground, for these were people his police and the military stayed in close touch with, to get a sense of what was going on in Myanmar. A call went through to the ZRF and its finance secretary. Could they mount an expedition to rescue the officials? They could, but it would cost the Mizoram government a specific fee. The government responded that it was happy to meet their demand. So, late at night soon after, having tracked down the location where the men were being kept hostage, the ZRF stormed the PLA camp, killed at least four Manipuris and freed the hostages. They suffered some wounds and a fatality, if the accounts were to be believed. But the men were freed and handed over to a relieved Manipur government and desperate relatives. The ZRF's fee for the operation: at least ₹2 crore. The PLA was furious with Zoramthanga and the ZRF but could not hit back. Worse, they had lost face at home and outside.

44. Bhupen Hazarika was perhaps the greatest Assamese lyricist and musician of the twentieth and twenty-first centuries. Folklorist and poet, he put the angst and pain of millions of people to paper and transformed them into powerful, anthemic songs. *Manuhe Manuhe Bhaabe* (If humans don't think for each other) was written

at a time of fierce language riots in the state in 1964. Hazarika went from place to place with a small troupe, singing this song in an effort to bring peace and douse the flames of hate.

CHAPTER 5

1. Dzongkha is the Bhutanese name for a district.

2. Population of about 7,40,000, 'The World Bank in Bhutan', *The World Bank*, <http://www.worldbank.org/en/country/bhutan/overview> [accessed 24 July 2016].

3. There are conflicting reports about how many persons were in the camps. Some accounts give a figure of 3,000, others speak of a presence of 2,000.

4. National Socialist Council of Nagalim was headed by S. S. Khaplang until his death in June 2017. This was known as the NSCN (K) to distinguish it from the NSCN (I-M) which was run by Isak Chishi Swu and Th. Muivah. The NSCN (K)'s vice chairman Khango Konyak took over leadership of the group following Khaplang's death.

5. At one time, much of the lower part of the Assam Valley was under the sway of the Koch-Rajbongshis, especially in the fourteenth to sixteenth centuries. The Koch kingdom reached its height at the time of Maharaj Nar Narayana who was assisted by his younger brother, the redoubtable general Bir Chilarai, who defeated the Ahoms. Till such time as the Koch kingdom was strong, the Ahoms, despite their formidable skills and reputation as sailors and soldiers who had crushed the Mughals and local kingdoms, could never go beyond central Assam. As the Koch kingdom waned, the Ahoms grew in strength and their kingdom expanded.

6. The last meeting between the Bhutan government and ULFA took place in October 2003, and with NDFB the following month.

7. Anand Swaroop Verma, 'The military offensive against United Liberation Front of Assam', *revolutionarydemocracy.org* <http://www.revolutionarydemocracy.org/rdv10n1/assam.htm> [accessed 24 July 2016].

8. Literally, hidden beneficiaries or individuals who gained financially from their connections without being formally listed.

9. See Bhimkanta Buragohain's interview with Ripunjoy Das of *The Telegraph*, Kolkata, 'Bhutan attack was betrayal, says Ulfa leader—7 years to the day, mama relives Operation All Clear', 15 December 2010, <http://www.telegraphindia.com/1101215/jsp/frontpage/story_13302722.jsp> [accessed 24 July 2016].

10. Shankhadeep Chowdhury, 'Bhutan king visits Ulfa camp for negotiations', *Times of India*, 27 March 2002.

11. From a conversation with Shimray in Bangkok where I had gone to meet Muivah and Swu in April 1999.

12. Queen Mother Ashi Dorji Wangmo Wangchuck is the third of four sisters and the mother of the current king. The king had married four sisters from a prominent Bhutanese family and has children by all of them. Patrick French etched a detailed portrait in *Vanity Fair* of this much loved monarch who handed over power to his son at the age of fifty-three, 'Enter the dragon king' <http://www.vanityfair.com/culture/2009/05/bhutan-king200905> [accessed 27 July 2016].

13. G. Vinayak, 'Bhutan books 22 abettors of Indian militants', *rediff.com* <http://www.rediff.com/news/report/bhutan/20040722.htm>, [accessed 25 July 2016].

14. 'Bhutan cracks down on anti-India militants', *The Hindu*, 16 December 2003, <http://www.thehindu.com/2003/12/16/stories/2003121606380100.htm>

[accessed 27 July 2016].

15. Basumatary's own film was *Raag* but she also played the role of the mother of Olympian boxer Mary Kom in the film of the same name, which starred Priyanka Chopra in the title role. The Kom is a tiny tribe in Manipur.

16. Anirban Kalita, 'Missing ULFA leaders in secret custody of Bhutan', *Times of Assam*, 13 May 2011 <https://www.timesofassam.com/headlines/missing-ulfa-leaders-in-secret-custody-of-bhutan/> [accessed 13 May 2011].

17. Aruni Kashyap, *The House with a Thousand Stories*, New Delhi: Penguin Books India, 2013.

18. Arupa Patangia Kalita, translated by Deepika Phukan, *The Story of Felanee*, New Delhi: Zubaan, 2011.

19. Interview in *A Measure of Impunity*, a documentary film produced by me and directed by Maulee Senapati (released 2011), on the impact of conflict on women in Nagaland and Assam.

20. Angshuman Choudhury, 'Justice: contours of the Assamese insurgency', *Hard News*, 19 July 2016 <http://www.hardnewsmedia.com/2016/07/justice-contours-assamese-insurgency> [accessed 30 July 2016]. Choudhury's account of the development of SULFA is the base for its description here.

21. Arabinda Rajkhowa's family title was Rajkonwar and his first name was originally Rajib. He changed both names after joining ULFA and becoming its political head.

22. For more details, see Hazarika, 'The Boys in Business', *Strangers of the Mist*.pp.137

23. Mrinal Talukdar, Utpal Borjpujari and Kaushik Deka, *Secret Killings of Assam*, Guwahati: Nanda Talukar Foundation, Human Rights Law Network, 2009, p. 100.

24. Bhaumik worked with the BBC and earlier with *The Telegraph* before editing the *Seven Sisters Post*, a newspaper in Guwahati which collapsed after its owner was arrested for a major scam, and is now an editor at bdnews24.com.

25. In the book, Srivastava is referred to as having been accused of engineering the controversial 'secret killings' and of running an extremely effective Unified Command over which he presided. The police boss also used Tripura, Bhaumik said, as the launching pad for attacks on rebels from the state living as far away as Dhaka or in safe locations elsewhere in Bangladesh 'using a combination of surrendered militants and Bangladeshi mafia'. In this strategy, he had the full support of the central intelligence agencies including the military intelligence as well as paramilitary units. More than twenty attacks on the Tripura rebels followed, forcing them to move from safe houses near the border to further inland, disrupting easy access. It also demoralized the armed groups, leading to a number of surrenders. Tripura's insurgency, characterized by kidnappings for ransom and fierce attacks, waned and collapsed eventually with civilian casualties falling by one-fourth from nearly 400 in 2003 to 94 in 2007. The number of security forces killed in the same period dropped from thirty-nine to six while the number of rebels killed also came down from fifty to eighteen, a reflection of the peace that was slowly being restored to the area.

26. *The Agartala Doctrine: A Proactive Northeast in Indian Foreign Policy*, edited by Subir Bhaumik, New Delhi: Oxford University Press, 2016.

27. Majuli, a sprawling land mass that is being eaten away steadily by the river which engulfs it every year during the monsoon flooding, eroding its sandy banks, is home to a network of influential medieval satras or Hindu Vaishnavite monasteries and a large Mishing tribal population.

28. Alee Command translates in Naga to the foreign legion or essentially the unit that

handled international arms purchases.

29. 'Further probe, IO change ordered', *Daily Star*, <http://www.thedailystar.net/news-detail-71972> [accessed 5 April 2004].

30. Brigadier Gurmeet Kanwal, a respected former director of the Centre for Land Warfare Studies, the Indian army's think tank, and Monika Chansoria wrote: 'Using Bangladesh as an exit point, the ULFA managed to establish contact with arms dealers in Thailand and as far as Romania. This was possibly the beginning of contacts with arms dealers in Cambodia, from whom ULFA started accessing huge numbers of weapons. At Cox's Bazar, ULFA cadres coordinated their arms acquisition and operational strategies with the NSCN and other insurgent groups that were based in the area.' Issue Brief, Centre for Land Warfare Studies (CLAWS), Gurmeet Kanwal and Monika Chansoria, 'Small Arms Proliferation in South Asia: A Challenge for National Security'. In the same article, they said that from 2000 onward, ULFA and the NDFB were closely in touch with Pakistan's ISI and the Afghan Mujahideen.

31. Hiranmay Karlekar, 'The great Chittagong arms haul and India'. *Daily Pioneer* <http://www.dailypioneer.com/columnists/edit/the-great-chittagong-arms-haul-and-india.html> [accessed 8 February 2014].

32. 'Nizami, Babar among 14 to hang', *The Daily* Star, 30 January 2014. <http://www.thedailystar.net/nizami-babar-among-14-to-hang-9132> [accessed 30 January 2014].

33. Muhammad Ali Bukhari interview with Bertil Lintner, 'Bangaldesh is in "Great Game"', *The Daily Star*, 12 February 2014 <http://www.thedailystar.net/bangladesh-is-in-great-game-10905> [accessed 12 February 2014].

34. Press Trust of India, 'NSCN (IM) leader gets bail as NIA says it is in interest of peace talks', *Indian Express*, 4 August 2016 <http://indianexpress.com/article/india/india-news-india/nscn-im-leader-gets-bail-as-nia-says-it-is-in-interest-of-peace-talks-2953887/> [accessed 25 April 2017].

35. Rajeev Bhattacharyya, *Rendezvous with Rebels: Journey to Meet India's Most Wanted Men*, New Delhi: HarperCollins India, 2014.

36. Ashwani Gupta, 'Alliances between insurgent groups in North East: Is it a source of concern', *Claws.in*, 5 January 2014. <http://www.claws.in/1133/alliances-between-insurgent-groups-in-north-east-is-it-a-source-of-concern-ashwani-gupta.html> [accessed 2 January 2014].

CHAPTER 6

1. Akin to Prashant Kishor who masterminded the Bihar victory of Nitish Kumar. Read B. Vijay Murty, 'Prashant Kishor: Man behind Modi LS campaign crafts Nitish win', *Hindustan Times*, 9 November 2015. <http://www.hindustantimes.com/india/prashant-kishor-man-behind-modi-ls-campaign-crafts-nitish-win/storyfgqyNqnz6MSVwerb86OHdJ.html> [accessed 9 November 2015].

2. The alliance and its results gave the AGP, a once powerful force in Assam and the Northeast, a fresh lease of life after being moribund for a decade.

3. Even on a crucial issue like the definition of Assamese, the BJP took a safe position. It simply picked up a crucial clause of the 1985 Accord or Memorandum of Understanding between the Government of India, the Government of Assam and the All Assam Students Union, which had led the agitation of the 1980s. It said that the troublesome Clause 6 sought to bestow 'Constitutional, Legislative and Administrative' safeguards in the social, cultural, linguistic identity and heritage of

Assamese people. This has been unimplemented for over thirty years and is perhaps not implementable because there is robust disagreement among all sections of people about who or what an 'Assamese' is or is not. Thus many plains and hill tribes such as the Bodos, the Karbis and the Mishings oppose the concept of a pan-Assamese or Axomiya identity. Muslims and Hindus of Bangla origin have the same problem and in the Barak Valley, Bangla not Assamese is the language of official communication. It perhaps requires a bit of legislative sleight of hand, a simple amendment to the accord through a parliamentary process that could make the definition broader yet simpler. It could perhaps be along the lines of 'residents of Assam' with a caveat that these would be as identified by the NRC and relevant documents, making it clear that the person was an Indian national.

4.   As many as twenty-two agreements were signed during his July 2015 visit including a $2 billion line of credit and a crucial accord to enable freight and passenger traffic on their shared waterways, which would open up markets and opportunities in Bangladesh to traders and investors in West Bengal and the Assam hinterland and beyond as well as vice versa. According to *The Hindu*: 'Bangladesh and India exchanged 162 adversely-held enclaves on August 1 at the stroke of midnight, ending one of the world's most complex border disputes that had lingered since seven decades. One hundred and eleven Indian enclaves measuring 17,160 acres became Bangladesh territory and similarly, 51 Bangladesh enclaves measuring 7,110 acres became Indian territory. All the Indian enclaves are located in West Bengal's Cooch Behar district. The exchange of enclaves was made possible under the Land Boundary Agreement signed between the two countries recently. Although 14,000 people staying in Bangladeshi enclaves in India have opted to stay in India, only near about 979 have opted to return to India out of the estimated 37,000 people living in Indian enclaves in Bangladesh.' Press Trust of India, 'Security, a prime concern after enclaves exchange', 3 April 2016 <http://www. thehindu.com/news/national/indiabangladesh-land-boundary-agreement-security-a-prime-concern-after-enclaves-exchange/article7491756> [accessed 3 April 2016]. This was the logical settlement of a 2011 border agreement between the two countries signed by Modi's predecessor Manmohan Singh and Sheikh Hasina Wajed of Bangladesh which said that the protocol would result in a 'demarcated boundary in all the un-demarcated segments, exchange of 111 Indian enclaves in Bangladesh with 51 Bangladesh enclaves in India and a resolution of all adversely possessed areas. In the exchange of enclaves, India will transfer 111 enclaves with a total area of 17,160.63 acres to Bangladesh, while Bangladesh would transfer 51 enclaves with an area of 7,110.02 acres to India. While on paper, the exchange of enclaves between India and Bangladesh may seem like a loss of Indian land to Bangladesh, the actual scenario is quite different as the enclaves are located deep inside the territory of both countries and there has been no physical access to them from either country. In reality, the exchange of enclaves denotes only a notional exchange of land as the protocol converts a de facto reality into a de jure situation. The inhabitants in the enclaves could not enjoy full legal rights as citizens of either India or Bangladesh and infrastructure facilities such as electricity, schools and health services were deficient. Further, due to lack of access to these areas by the law and order enforcing agencies and weak property rights, certain enclaves became hot beds of criminal activities.' See *India and Bangladesh: Land Boundary Agreement,* Ministry of External Affairs, Government of India <https://www.mea. gov.in/Uploads/PublicationDocs/24529_LBA_MEA_Booklet_final.pdf> [accessed

22 May 2016], India and Bangladesh Land Boundary Agreement.

5. For ULFA it was the second stunning punch in less than seven years after the 2003 Operation All Clear launched by the Royal Bhutan Army led by the fourth king, Jigme Singye Wangchuck, and his son, the then crown prince and now fifth king.

6. 'Gross enrolment ratio, primary, both sexes (%)', *The World Bank* <http://data.worldbank.org/indicator/SE.PRM.ENRR/countries/BD-8S-XN?display=graph> [accessed 22 May 2016].

7. Secondary Education in India: Development and Performance, P. Geetha Rani, paper at the 43rd Annual Conference of the Indian Econometric Society (TIES), Indian Institute of Technology, Mumbai, 5–7, January 2007.

8. Kounteya Sinha, 'Average Indian's life expectancy up 4.6 years', *Times of India*, 2 October 2012. <http://timesofindia.indiatimes.com/india/Average-Indians-life-expectancy-up-4-6-years/articleshow/16633612.cms> [accessed 2 October 2012].

9. Dr Numol Chandra Borah, chairman of Guwahati Neurological Research Centre Hospitals, <http://gnrchospitals.com/assam-lags-40-years-behind-india-average-in-senior-citizens-state-of-health/> [accessed 25 May 2016].

10. With barbed wire fences which were to be finished by the end of 2016, Home Minister Rajnath Singh was quoted as saying: 'As soon as the border is sealed permanently, the infiltration trend will stop automatically. Plus we will create awareness among the people to prevent infiltration.'

11. 'When the final draft of the updated National Register of Citizens is published it will be clear who are the citizens and infiltrators will get identified.'

12. Sarbananda Sonowal vs Union of India & Anr on 12 July 2005, Supreme Court of India <https://indiankanoon.org/doc/907725/> [accessed 25 May 2016].

13. Ibid.

14. Sonowal had then stepped into the shoes of Mahanta as AASU chief and later became state chief minister in 2016.

15. *Sarbananda Sonowal vs Union of India & Anr* on 12 July 2005, Supreme Court of India <https://indiankanoon.org/doc/907725/> [accessed 25 May 2016].

16. Ibid.

17. 'White paper on foreigners issue', Home and Political Department, Government of Assam, last updated 22 May 2015 <http://assam.gov.in/web/home-and-political-department/white-paper1> [accessed 25 May 2016].

18. Amalendu Guha, *Planter Raj to Swaraj: Freedom Struggle & Electoral Politics in Assam*, New Delhi: Tulika Books, 2014, Chapter 8.

19. For details on this, highly recommended reading is Nirode K. Barooah's *Gopinath Bordoloi: The Assam Problem and Nehru's Centre*, Guwahati: Bhabani Print and Publications, 2010; also Barooah, Gopinath Bordoloi, *Indian Constitution and Centre-Assam Relations, 1940–1950*. Guwahati: Publications Board, 1990.

20. For details of this and the fight to keep Assam in India, as well as the classic tussle between Bordoloi and the central Congress leadership and between him and Sir Mohammed Saadullah of the Muslim League, see Sanjoy Hazarika, *Strangers of the Mist*.

21. Seventy years later, that fear is still so substantial that it enabled the BJP to win a convincing victory in 61 out of 126 seats and propelled its allies to wins in 25 others.

22. Siddhartha Bhattacharyya. His father was the charismatic, courageous but spartan Gauri Shankar Bhattacharyya, a determined socialist who led the attack on Chief Minister B. P. Chaliha's government for its failure to handle the Mizo imbroglio

and the human rights violations of ordinary people.

23. Telephone interview with the author, Guwahati, 20 May 2016.

24. T. S. Eliot, *The Wasteland*, bartleby.com <http://www.bartleby.com/201/1.html> [accessed 11 June 2016].

25. Visit to Nellie with Dileep Chandan, editor of *Asom Bani*, Guwahati, and Parag Tamuly, a local reporter from Jagiroad, the nearest large town, on 27 June 2016.

26. The Kopili dam hydroelectric project was built by NEEPCO, the North Eastern Electric Power Corporation, and has a capacity of generating 275 megawatt of power; it takes its name from the river which flows down the Karbi Hills on Assam's eastern edge, dividing the state from Meghalaya though the hills actually are a continuation of the Khasi and Jaintia Hills.

27. From the former East Bengal district of Mymensingh (now in Bangladesh); settlers were encouraged to come to Assam by the Muslim League government of the 1930s and 1940s to clear and cultivate large expanses of wasteland and forests as well as settle in many areas. The resentment and fears of local communities to this large ingress has remained since that time. The Bangladeshi sentiment has its roots in this bunch of suspicions which spilled over into an irregular campaign against new settlers who have come illegally as well as the older group.

28. In addition to Bhagduba Habi, the villages of Basundhara and Hathigaon.

29. I really don't know why media, especially visual media, makes such a big fuss about anniversaries. For those who have to live with any kind of horror and pain, every day is a remembrance, an anniversary.

30. See Hazarika, *Strangers of the Mist*.

31. 'Lord Wavell, A Viceroy Remembers', see Hazarika, *Strangers of the Mist*.

32. Jatin Hazarika, *Shadow behind the Throne: My Tryst with Assam Administration*, Guwahati: Lawyers Book Stall, 2016, p. 184.

33. Details of the election results in this section are drawn from the official website of the Election Commission of India. 'Statistical report on general election, 1983 to Legislative Assembly of Assam', New Delhi: Election Commission of India <http://eci.nic.in/eci_main/StatisticalReports/SE_1983/StatisticalReportAssam83.pdf> [accessed 17 June 2016].

34. The only time a party came close to the 91 seats pocketed by Saikia in 1983 was when Tarun Gogoi captured 78 seats in 2011. Five years later, when the BJP and its allies swept to power in Dispur, they got a total of 84 seats. The BJP alone won 61, two short of an absolute majority in the 126-member legislature.

35. Hazarika, *Strangers of the Mist*, p. 187.

36. The two words, Miya and Bangladeshi are not interchangeable.

37. Warisha Farasat, 'The State did it', *Indian Express*, 12 November 2014. <http://indianexpress.com/article/opinion/columns/the-state-did-it/> [accessed 12 November 2014].

38. Press statement by civil society groups, 'Civil society condemns the massacre in Assam, demand immediate arrest of Pramila Rani Brahma, safety of Muslims in BTAD', *India Resists*, 5 May 2014 <http://www.indiaresists.com/civil-society-condemns-the-massacre-in-assam-demand-immediate-arrest-of-pramila-rani-brahmasafety-of-muslims-in-btad/> [accessed 25 April 2017].

39. Abhijit Saha, 'Violence in Assam: will we ever learn', *India Resists*, 14 May 2014. <http://www.indiaresists.com/violence-in-assam-will-we-ever-learn/> [accessed 14 May 2014].

40. The BLT's cadres joined the BPF while the NDFB continues to exist.

41. Author's interview with senior Assam police official, Guwahati, December 2012.

42. There were explosions at the parking lots of the senior administrator or deputy commissioner of Kamrup district (in which Guwahati falls) and a judicial official.

43. '61 killed in serial blasts across Assam', *rediff.com*, 31 October 2008. <http://www.rediff.com/news/2008/oct/30blasts.htm> [accessed 31 October 2008].

44. Praveen Swami, 'Assam terror bombing trail leads to NDFB', *The Hindu*, 10 November 2008. <http://www.thehindu.com/todays-paper/assam-terror-bombing-trail-leads-to-ndfb/article1373055.ece> [accessed 10 November 2008]. At the time, he was a correspondent with *The Hindu* newspaper.

45. Krishn Kaushik, 'The Spectre: Politicians play on the fear of immigrants in Assam', *Caravan*, 1 April 2016 <http://www.caravanmagazine.in/reportage/the-spectre-assam-elections-immigrants-fear> [accessed 1 April 2016].

46. Ibid.

47. Tata Tea's top officials were arrested and the company hauled over the coals by the central government for opening negotiations with ULFA in Bangkok and cutting a deal with the rebels to buy peace. Upamanyu wasn't the key lawyer but he assisted the top shots. The Tatas were represented by Fali Nariman, among the most learned and respected lawyers in the country, and Jaitley.

48. Upamanyu's maternal uncle was Ashok or Roon Saikia, the delightful, generous and blunt top aide to Prime Minister Vajpayee who died during a botched heart surgery. Saikia was known to have unique access to Vajpayee whom he had known from his days at Delhi University and to whose house he was a frequent visitor. Upamanyu and his sister, Pahi, a railway services officer, also visited the premier's residence to attend events and family gatherings.

49. Guwahati is now a burgeoning metro with every kind of clothing, gadgetry and food store.

50. Anuraag Baruah, 'No stake in resources for B'deshi illegal migrants: Hazarika Panel', *The Quint*, 22 June 2016. <http://www.thequint.com/opinion/2016/06/22/deprive-bangladeshi-illegal-immigrants-of-land-and-jobs-in-assam-national-register-of-citizens-sarbanand-sonowal>[accessed 22 June 2016].

51. The last report was filed on 4 November 2015 and the four documents included many representations from various groups.

52. See Sanjoy Hazarika, *Rites of Passage: Border Crossings, Imagined Homelands, India's East and Bangladesh*. New Delhi: Penguin India, 2000.

53. I was a member of that initial NSAB and proposed the work permit regime at the time.

54. Sushanta Talukdar, 'Less than 50 percent Assamese speakers in Assam', *The Hindu*, 9 January 2008.

55. Until 26 April 2017, when the Census of India's data relating to this issue (see Linguistic Survey of India) was last accessed.

56. Several satra adhikars or heads of these institutions were given a place of honour at the swearing in of the new BJP-led government in Assam at a public ceremony in May 2016.

57. 'Article 21 of the Constitution of India—Right to Life and Personal Liberty', Riya Jain, UILS Panjab University <https://www.lawctopus.com/academike/article-21-of-the-constitution-of-india-right-to-life-and-personal-liberty/> [accessed 30 April 2017]. In *Sunil Batra v. Delhi Administration*, the Supreme Court held that the 'right to life' included the right to lead a healthy life so as to enjoy all faculties of the human body in their prime conditions. It would even include the right to

protection of a person's tradition, culture, heritage and all that gives meaning to a man's life. It includes the right to live in peace, to sleep in peace and the right to repose and health... In *Maneka Gandhi v. Union of India*, the Supreme Court gave a new dimension to Art. 21 and held that the right to live is not merely a physical right but includes within its ambit the right to live with human dignity. Elaborating the same view, the court in *Francis Coralie v. Union Territory of Delhi*, observed that: '*The right to live includes the right to live with human dignity and all that goes along with it, viz., the bare necessities of life such as adequate nutrition, clothing and shelter over the head and facilities for reading, writing and expressing oneself in diverse forms, freely moving about and mixing and mingling with fellow human beings and must include the right to basic necessities of life and also the right to carry on functions and activities as constitute the bare minimum expression of human self.*'

58. On a trip through Myanmar in 2002, I remember seeing several trucks, thickly covered with tarpaulin, being driven across the broken Burmese roads. At a stop, I asked one of the drivers what they were carrying, 'Ah', he said, 'just forest produce, herbs from Manipur and other places', but he refused to let me have a look. I would not have been surprised if there were large consignments of the flourishing illegal trade in wildlife parts and rare plants as well as insects.

59. PTI Report, 'Hazarika Commission final report on illegal migrants submitted', *NDTV*, 21 November 2015 <http://www.ndtv.com/india-news/hazarika-commission-final-report-on-illegal-migrants-submitted-1245991> [accessed 21 November 2015].

60. Shaheen Ahmed, 'Transitory citizenship and the plight of the 'illegal' immigrant in Assam', *The Wire*, 4 August 2016 <https://thewire.in/56412/assam-national-registry-of-citizens/> [accessed 4 August 2016].

61. Ibid.

62. From Bangladesh, large numbers reportedly have moved to Malaysia and Thailand, and further to Japan and Indonesia. Separately, there is a flow of the Muslim Rohingyas from the Arakan Province of western Myanmar where they face acute discrimination, are denied citizenship and basic rights and are under constant threat of violence and intimidation from right-wing Buddhist groups. The *Financial Times* wrote: 'Their flight highlights the flourishing people-smuggling trade in their troubled country—and also the pull and responsibilities of destination states to the south, whose economies have boomed in part because of low-wage immigrant labour.'

63. Nilim Dutta, 'The myth of the Bangladeshi and violence in Assam', *Kafila*, 16 August 2012.

64. I have stressed this point earlier in this chapter; see the table on Foreigners Tribunal Cases.

65. Brad Adams, 'India's shoot-to-kill policy on the Bangladesh border', *The Guardian*, 23 January 2011. <https://www.theguardian.com/commentisfree/libertycentral/2011/jan/23/india-bangladesh-border-shoot-to-kill-policy> [accessed 23 January 2011].

66. 'Chapter 8: Informal and illegal trade: dimensions, trends, composition, and the role of domestic indirect taxes', *The World Bank* <http://siteresources.worldbank.org/SOUTHASIAEXT/Resources/223546-1168296540386/ch8.pdf> .

67. Sudhakar K. Chaudhari, *Cross Border Trade between India and Bangladesh*, New Delhi: National Council of Applied Economic Research (NCAER), 1995, p.27.

68. Bangladesh became an independent nation after a bloody struggle against a brutal

Pakistani crackdown in 1970 which killed more than a million people and left many more traumatized with physical and mental wounds, with extensive incidents of rape and torture. In a dramatic comeuppance for the Bengali collaborators who were associated with the killings and oppression of religious minorities (read Hindus), intellectuals, pro-Awami League figures (thus pro-independence in the eyes of the Pakistani establishment) and women, were tried and hung for their war crimes. It's the first such trial in a South Asian nation and drew huge support from young and old, the former discovering their bloody roots.

69.   Interviews with various officials, activists and researchers. Professor Imtiaz Ahmed of Dhaka University (who also joined the Regional Centre for Strategic Studies in Colombo as executive director) has often spoken of how border posts used to be 'auctioned' and the number of cattle corridors that are facilitated by security forces and smugglers on either side to support a flourishing smuggling trade in meat and skins.

70.   This part about human trafficking is woven from a number of accounts including the author's own experiences and understanding as well as the following publications: Joseph Allchin and Michael Peel, 'Southeast Asia's economic surge lures Bangladeshis to sea', *Financial Times*, 12 June 2015 <https://www.ft.com/content/23014cb6-0dc1-11e5-aa7b-00144feabdc0?mhq5j=e6> [accessed 12 June 2015]. Michael Peel, 'Malaysia finds 139 graves at migrant camps', *Financial Times*, 25 May 2015 <https://www.ft.com/content/6e09b892-02a4-11e5-b31d-00144feabdc0?mhq5j=e6> [accessed 25 May 2015], Simon Tisdall, 'South-east Asia faces its own migrant crisis as states play "human ping-pong"', *The Guardian*, 14 May 2015. <https://www.theguardian.com/world/2015/may/14/migrant-crisis-south-east-asia-rohingya-malaysia-thailand> [accessed: 14 May 2015].

71.   'Thailand says EU has not taken any decision on fishing ban' *Reuters*, 23 May 2016. <https://www.reuters.com/article/us-thailand-fishing-eu/thailand-says-eu-has-not-taken-any-decision-on-fishing-ban-idUSKCN0YE0TP> [accessed 23 May 2016].

72.   Joseph Allchin and Michael Peel, 'Southeast Asia's economic surge lures Bangladeshis to sea', *Financial Times*, 12 June 2015<https://www.ft.com/content/23014cb6-0dc1-11e5-aa7b-00144feabdc0?mhq5j=e6> [accessed 12 June 2015].

73.   See Hazarika, *Strangers of the Mist*.

74.   For details, see Hazarika, *Strangers of the Mist* and Nirode K. Barooah's *Gopinath Bardoloi: The Assam Problem and Nehru's Centre*, Guwahati: Bhabani Print and Publication, 2010.

75.   Binito Nibedon Ei Je' ('I Beg to State that'); the last two words have a double emphasis on being Assamese: they are a repetition of being Assamese.

76.   Minu Ittyipe, 'Who's that man in the Angadi?' *Outlook*, 27 June 2016. <https://www.outlookindia.com/magazine/story/whos-that-man-in-the-angadi/297328> [accessed 27 June 2016].

77.   Ibid.

78.   Interview with Prateek Hajela, 13 July 2016, see also the website of the National Register of Citizens Assam <http://nrcassam.nic.in/faq06.html>. There are several other links there which help understand the complex NRC revision process.

79.   National Register of Citizens Assam <http://nrcassam.nic.in/admin-documents.html>.

80.   Mark Dummett, 'Bangladesh war: The article that changed history', *BBC*, 16

December 2011 <http://www.bbc.com/news/world-asia-16207201> [accessed 16 December 2011]. News of the initial massacres were broken by a Pakistani journalist of great courage and of Goan descent, Anthony Mascarenas. I remember reading his stories in London as a young journalism student and being shaken and moved by them, watching breathlessly later in the year the strafing runs of the Indian Air Force over Dhaka and the swift lightning strikes of the Indian army against their Pakistani foes. Within a couple of weeks it was all over as Pakistani General 'Tiger' Niazi surrendered his troops and East Pakistan to Lieutenant General J. S Arora. The Bangla leader Sheikh Mujibur Rahman was flown back from detention to a bloodied but jubilant country as Bangladesh became free. Mascarenas's thunderous articles in the *Sunday Times* captured the horror of Pakistani atrocities and is believed to have changed international opinion against Pakistan and in favour of India and the freedom movement in the then East Pakistan. It was headlined simply: GENOCIDE. One of the most compelling pieces that I have ever read and arguably among the most influential in the making of the history of South Asia, it opened thus: 'Abdul Bari had run out of luck. Like thousands of other people in East Bengal, he had made the mistake—the fatal mistake—of running within sight of a Pakistani patrol. He was 24 years old, a slight man surrounded by soldiers. He was trembling because he was about to be shot.' More than forty years later, the BBC, recalling that crackdown, wrote in *Bangladesh war: The article that changed history*, Mark Dummett, BBC News: 'nobody knows exactly how many people were killed, but certainly a huge number of people lost their lives. Independent researchers think that between 300,000 and 500,000 died. The Bangladesh government puts the figure at three million.'

81. Hazarika, *Rites of Passage*; see also 'The demons of 1971' *Rediff.com* <http://www. rediff.com/news/2007/jan/04spec.htm> [accessed 13 March 2014].

82. Interview with author, Guwahati, 13 July 2016.

83. E. Seetharaman, 'NRC in Assam: State coordinator Prateek Hajela on why not all voter lists till 1971 can be made available', *Economic Times*, 14 June 2014, <http://economictimes.indiatimes.com/opinion/interviews/nrc-in-assam-state-coordinator-prateek-hajela-on-why-not-all-voter-lists-till-1971-can-be-made-available/articleshow/47657765.cms> [accessed 14 June 2014].

84. Makiko Kimura, *The Nellie Massacre of 1983: Agency of Rioters*, New Delhi: Sage Publications Pvt Ltd, 2013, p. 109.

85. For a detailed narrative, see the documentary film, *What the Fields Remember*, by Subasri Krishnan. Krishnan describes the events of Nellie and their impact on the survivors and tells the story of Khairuddin, who remembers the events of that day in vivid detail. 'Thirty-two years later, the Nellie massacre remains all but forgotten', *Caravan*, 18 February 2015 <http://www.caravanmagazine.in/vantage/thirty-two-years-later-nellie-massacre-remains-all-forgotten#sthash.xjnZQ6jO.dpuf> [accessed 16 May 2016]: 'The manner in which the mob set fire to his house, while he tried to escape with both his sons on his back; encountering his daughter's lifeless body as he was running, and his inability to spend even a moment to grieve in his haste to get his other children to safety; the injury that he sustained on his head when someone hit him, just before he watched his younger son being hacked to death; and how he lost his older son while trying to swim away from the mob, across the river Kopili. The Central Reserve Police Force (CRPF) eventually rescued him and his wife, but she succumbed to her injuries at the Jagiroad police station—there was a severe paucity of doctors and she did not

receive the medical attention she needed. In one day, Khairuddin had lost two sons, a daughter, his wife, his parents and four of his brothers along with their families.' Krishnan spoke of the views she encountered during a year of interviews. These ranged from 'exhaustion and cynicism from victims who had waited in vain for justice'. In addition, she says that there was a sense of indifference in Assam from those who were convinced that the massacre was a part of their collective past that should not be revisited if their society was to move on. Khairuddin can't move on—'I wake up at 3 am every morning. I cannot sleep at nights. Even today, when I close my eyes to sleep, I see the faces of my dead children.'

CHAPTER 7

1. First published in 1884 as *History of the relations of government with the hill tribes of the north-east frontier of Bengal,* New Delhi: Mittal Publications, 1989.
2. Ibid, p. 16.
3. Ibid, p. 18.
4. See Lobsang Tenpa, 'The Centenary of the McMahon Line (1914–2014) and the Status of Monyul until 1951–2', *Academia.edu* <http://www.academia.edu/6685351/Lobsang_Tenpa_2014_The_Centenary_of_ the_McMahon_Line_1914-2014_and_the_Status_of_Monyul_until_1951-2> [accessed 21 August 2016].
5. Monyul was how the Tibetans referred to the Tawang Tract and Kameng Valley.
6. Tenpa, *Centenary of the McMahon Line*, p. 85.
7. It was no mistake that the Chinese made their devastating lightning thrust in 1962 in this very sector, to emphasize a political point.
8. See Tenpa.
9. This and the following paragraph are drawn on senior journalist Yambem Laba's article, 'Bob Khathing and the taking of Tawang' in *Kangla Online* and reproduced in Nitin Madhavan's blog <http://mnitin73.blogspot.in/2014/05/the-taking-of-tawang-facebook-post.html> [accessed 21 August 2016].
10. Dzong in Tibetan and Dzongkhag in the languages of Tibet and Bhutan means fort, usually a fort that houses both civil authority and a military garrison.
11. See 'Arunachal Pradesh's tribal groups', *Rough Guides* <http://www.roughguides.com/destinations/asia/india/northeast/arunachal-pradesh/arunachal-pradeshs-tribal-groups/> [accessed 25 August 2016].
12. Verrier Elwin, *A Philosophy for NEFA* (Arunachal Pradesh), Shillong: North-East Frontier Agency, 1958.
13. Elwin was a lapsed Christian theologian turned Gandhian, whose pioneering work among the Santhals and tribes of central India informed his work in the Northeast and deepened his empathy for communities who were often treated like dirt by the people of the dusty plains who controlled power, politics and resources in the rest of India.
14. See 'Gegong Apang arrested in Rs. 1,000-crore PDS scam', *The Hindu*, 24 August 2010 <http://www.thehindu.com/news/national/other-states/gegong-apang-arrested-in-rs-1000crore-pds-scam/article591598.ece> [accessed 25 August 2016], and 'Gegong Apang held for ₹1,000 -cr PDS scam', *Business Standard*, 25 August 2010 <http://www.business-standard.com/article/economy-policy/gegong-apang-held-for-rs-1-000-cr-pds-scam-110082500097_1.html> [accessed 25 August 2016].
15. Kenneth Boulding, 'The economist and the engineer', pp. 82–92 in *Economics and*

Public Policy in Water Resources Development, ed S. C. Smith and E. N. Castle, Ames: Iowa State University Press, 1964.

16. 'Private dam builders back out of Brahmaputra dams', *Thethirdpole.net* <https://www.thethirdpole.net/2016/02/25/private-dam-builders-back-out-of-brahmaputra-dams/> [accessed 25 August 2016].

17. 'Seat of ancient Buddhism threatened by fifteen proposed dams', Urmi Bhattacharjee, *International Rivers*, 15 January 2013, < https://www.internationalrivers.org/blogs/259/seat-of-ancient-buddhism-threatened-by-fifteen-proposed-dams> [accessed 26 August 2016].

18. 'Tawang deaths – India loses moral ground', Jaideep Mazumdar, *Swarajya*, 6 May 2016 <https://swarajyamag.com/politics/tawang-deaths-india-loses-moral-ground> [accessed 26 August 2016].

19. Sandeep Phukari, 'Floor Test Cleared, Khandu Government Faces First Political Challenge', *NDTV*, 24 July 2016 <http://www.ndtv.com/india-news/floor-test-cleared-khandu-government-faces-first-political-challenge-1435495> [accessed 28 August 2016].

20. In July 2016, after a series of dramatic moves and counter-moves by the BJP and the Congress after a Supreme Court intervention, Khandu's son Pema Khandu, was picked as chief minister. The following month, he announced his support for continuing the major hydel projects in the state.

21. Author's conversation with the central government official in Shillong, 27 August 2016.

22. 'Arunachal's great hydro games, the damming of a state and its discontents', Ankush Saikia, *Fountain Ink*, February 2016, <http://series.fountainink.in/arunachals-great-hydro-game/> [accessed 28 August 2016].

CHAPTER 8

1. Such name markers appear extensively across the region: thus, Guwahati has its 6th Mile and a 13th mile as does Tuli in Nagaland.

2. 'Everyone loves a good flood', Jayanta Bandyopadhyay, *The Telegraph*, 23 September 2008.

3. Ibid.

4. Andrew Duff, *Sikkim: Requiem for a Himalayan Kingdom*, New Delhi: Vintage Books/Random House India, 2015, p. 380.

5. Tarun Basu, 'Sikkim: A strategic Indian border state sets a development paradigm', *South Asia Monitor*, Society for Policy Studies <http://southasiamonitor.org/detail.php?type=sl&nid=17877> [accessed 1 September 2016].

6. 'Melting glaciers may impact hydropower plans', *Thethirdpole.net*, 2 September 2016 <https://www.thethirdpole.net/2016/09/02/studies-of-melting-glaciers-urgently-needed/> [accessed 2 September 2016].

7. Benefit sharing and sustainable hydropower: Lessons from Nepal, ICIMOD.

8. Sourced from the Indian Meteorological Department's Climate Date for Shillong (1971–2000).

9. Patricia Mukhim, 'Whose land, whose forests, whose rivers, whose water?' The *Shillong Times*, 24 January 2014 <http://www.theshillongtimes.com/2014/01/24/whose-land-whose-forests-whose-rivers-whose-water/#4jYtxjQVie8m15VS.99> [accessed 4 September 2016], republished in *The Citizen* webpaper, 28 March 2014.

10. Traditional council of elders and mantris (ministers) in the court of a Khasi syiem or king. There are local durbars also at the village and neighbourhood levels.

11.   State of the World's Forests 2016, FAO, p. 42.

12.   Bengt G. Karlsson, *Unruly Hills: Nature and Nation in India's Northeast*, New Delhi: Orient Blackswan Pvt Ltd, Social Science Press, 2011, p. 290.

13.   FAO report, 2016, p. 47.

14.   Keith Schneider, 'India's treacherous coal mines in Meghalaya', *Water News*, 15 May 2014   <http://www.circleofblue.org/2014/world/meghalayas-treacherous-coal-mines/> [accessed 6 September 2016].

15.   Srestha Banerjee, 'Meghalaya suspends rat-hole mining', *Down to Earth*, 19 May 2014   <http://www.downtoearth.org.in/news/meghalaya-suspends-rathole-coal-mining-44432> [accessed 6 September 2016].

16.   Karishma Vyas, 'The child miners of Meghalaya', *Al Jazeera*, 7 October 2013 <http://www.aljazeera.com/indepth/features/2013/10/child-miners-meghalaya-2013103132125749825.html> [accessed 6 September 2016].

17.   According to *myneta* website which publishes the assets etc. of all legislators, the chief minister owned a Mitsubishi Pajero, a Maruti Gypsy and a Fiat Palio while his wife listed at least five coal mines in West Khasi Hills district and Garo Hills apart from a bamboo plantation. For further details, see <http://myneta.info/meghalaya2013/candidate.php?candidate_id=277> and the website of the ADR for documents relating to the wealth and assets of political candidates across the country, <http://adrindia.org>.

18.   'A caver's sojourn', *The Hindu*, 18 September 2010 <http://www.thehindu.com/features/magazine/a-cavers-sojourn/article674358.ece> [accessed 7 September 2016].

19.   Bidhayak Das, 'Caving towards disaster', *The Telegraph*, 17 January 2005 <http://www.telegraphindia.com/1050117/asp/northeast/story_4263921.asp> [accessed 7 September 2016].

20.   'Child labour situation in coal mines, pits & rat holes of Jaintia Hills, Meghalaya', Visit Report by: Dr. Yogesh Dube and Sh. Vinod Kumar Tikoo, members, NCPCR, Dr. Ramanath Nayak, senior consultant, NCPCR, *NCPCR* <http://www.ncpcr.gov.in/view_file.php?fid=30> [accessed 6 September 2016].

21.   This segment on the complaint by the ADSU is based on a report in the *Hindustan Times*, Furquan Ameen Siddiqui, 'Curse of the black gold: How Meghalaya depends on coal', 2 March 2015 <http://www.hindustantimes.com/india/curse-of-the-black-gold-how-meghalaya-depends-on-coal/story-EJdAsvmMJhtztTK1BusDYM.html> [accessed 6 September 2016].

22.   Sumarlin Swer and O. P. Singh, 'Status of water quality in coal mining areas of Meghalaya, India' (in) Proceedings of the National Seminar on Environmental Engineering with special emphasis on Mining Environment, Eds. Indra N. Sinha, Mrinal K. Ghose and Gurdeep Singh, NSEEME-2004, 19-20, March 2004. <http://www.indiaenvironmentportal.org.in/files/Status%20of%20water%20quality(meghalaya).pdf> [accessed 6 September 2016].

23.   Patricia Mukhim, 'Non-tribals in Meghalaya, non-citizens or half-citizens', *The Shillong Times*, 22 March 2013 <http://www.theshillongtimes.com/2013/03/22/non-tribals-in-meghalaya-non-citizens-or-half-citizens/> [accessed 22 March 2013].

24.   Devjani Bodepudi, 'Politics & Society', *Kindle Magazine*, 9 October 2014.

25.   Subir Bhaumik, *Troubled Periphery, The Crisis of India's North East*, Sage Studies on India's Northeast, New Delhi: Sage Publications, 2009

26.   By the 1980s, a major out-migration of Nepali speakers had taken place, setting

the stage for the rise of Subash Ghising in the hills of North Bengal and the call for Gorkhaland, seeking a place which the Gorkhas or Nepali speakers, could call their own *bhoomi* in India. Ghising's long bandhs and agitations crippled life in those hills for long years till the West Bengal government ceded his demand for an autonomous territory in the hills without allowing a separation from the state.

27. Devjani Bodepudi, 'Guns and roses', *Kindle magazine*, 9 October 2014.

28. Subir Bhaumik (ed), *The Agartala Doctrine: A proactive Northeast in Indian Foreign Policy*, Introduction, 'Agartala Doctrine: the "Tripura line of Appropriate Response in Foreign Policy"', New Delhi: OUP, 2016.

29. Ibid.

30. Press Trust of India, 'PM Narendra Modi announces fresh line of credit worth $2 billion to Bangladesh', *Economic Times*, 6 June 2015 <http://economictimes. indiatimes.com/articleshow/47567101.cms?utm_source=contentofinterest&utm_ medium=text&utm_campaign=cppst> [accessed 7 September 2016].

31. Bhaumik, *The Agartala Doctrine*.

32. Prime Minister Manmohan Singh's address to Asia Society Corporate Conference, Mumbai, 18 March 2006.

CHAPTER 9

1. The events relating to Nido Taniam (also spelt as Tania) are based on several news reports of the incident including an interview with the Arunachal Pradesh resident commissioner in New Delhi, Avinash Mishra, which appeared in the *Hindustan Times*, http://www.hindustantimes.com/india/delhi-arunachal-mla-s-son-beaten-to-death-autopsy-report-awaited-3-detained/story-qglDekr5heakOlMwk1KvcN. html, accessed 24 December 2015 and in the *Indian Express*, http://indianexpress. com/article/india/india-others/nido-taniam-arunachal-student-northeast-protest-at-lajpat-nagar-market/, accessed 24 December 2015. All states have resident commissioners or the state's principal representative in New Delhi, a coordinator between the centre and states for projects, meetings and the like.

2. Ibid.

3. It is not as if all people from the region face harm and discrimination. It has everything to do with the appearance and occasionally the dress code and what to conservative, middle-class minds caught in a time warp, appear to be unconventional lifestyles. It is what Bimol Akoijam, the perceptive scholar from Jawaharlal Nehru University and Manipur, calls 'the nazar'. I've lived and travelled across India much of my life and I haven't faced any discrimination. Probably, with my beard, I could pass for any 'general' Indian. It is the hill and plains tribal groups from the region (be they Naga, Mizo, Arunachali, Kuki or Bodo), as well as majority groups like the Gurkhas of the Darjeeling belt and Meiteis of Manipur, who face the brunt of abuse. Their ancestry and connectivity to communities across Southeast Asia, Bhutan, Nepal, Tibet and even Southwest China can be traced. Because so many of them have migrated to the metros of India and are extremely visible, be it in the Delhi region or Bengaluru, a perception grows that the tribal groups are a majority in the region. This is far from being the case: the reality is that because of traditions and government regulations, tribals inhabit two-thirds of the region's land mass. However, non-tribals make up nearly 70 per cent of the area's population despite the fact that there are several small states like Nagaland, Mizoram and Meghalaya which are tribal-majority.

4. Later finance minister under Narendra Modi's government.

5.   It was, some of us remarked—as did his officials—the first such meeting between an education minister and a representative group of younger people from the Northeast, showing how wide the information gap was, having widened over the decades.

6.   The survey, conducted in 2013–2014 for the National Commission for Women, focused on the challenges that women from the region faced in four metros of New Delhi, Mumbai, Kolkata and Bengaluru.

7.   Written as Asham in his chronicles.

8.   The Koch raja at the time was Pran Narayan, who fled to Bhutan.

9.   S. A. Krishnan, 'Arjuna and Uloopi', *Stories from Hindu Mythology*, 16 May 2012 <http://hindumythologyforgennext.blogspot.in/2012/05/arjuna-and-uloopi-part-2-of-3.html> [accessed 24 March 2016].

10. Nick Robbins, *The Corporation That Changed the World: How the East India Company Shaped the Modern Multinational*. Hyderabad: Orient Longman, 2006.

11. See Introduction.

12. Ibid.

13. Walter Fernandes, Melville Pereira, Vizalenu Khatso, 'Customary laws in North East India: Impact on women', published by the National Commission for Women: 'Repression was the first official reaction to their efforts to protect their livelihood by resisting the colonial policies. The next step was to isolate them from their neighbours but exploitation continued. Then came compromises, at first in the form of isolating them further with the Inner Line Permit (ILP). Though presented as protection from the plainspeople, its real purpose was to protect the planters from their raids. Besides, the British rulers considered the Northeast a buffer zone against China and Burma (Doley 1998: 15-16). When resistance continued even after these measures, the colonialist introduced more changes some of which continued after independence. For example, in Assam the Sixth Schedule was introduced in Karbi Anglong and NC Hills as a compromise when their tribes demanded a State of their own or showed a desire to join Meghalaya formed in 1970 (Phukan 1990: 8-9). Thus, through their resistance the tribal leaders led the region towards protective measures. After 1947 they were the state's reaction to the nationalist struggles and subsequent negotiations (Fernandes 2005a: 97-98).'

14. 'Transforming the Northeast: Tackling backlogs in basic minimum services and infrastructural needs', High Level Commission Report to the Prime Minister, Planning Commission, Government of India, 7 March 1997 <http://planningcommission.nic.in/reports/genrep/ne_exe.pdf> [accessed 14 May 2016].

15. One of Asia's most distinguished editors (winner of the Magsaysay Award), commentators and writers, the late Boobli George Verghese had a long and abiding affection for the Northeast. Verghese was editor of the *Hindustan Times* and the *Indian Express* and author of numerous books including *India's Northeast Resurgent* and *First Draft*.

16. At a seminar on Look East in Kolkata in February 2015, a former Myanmar diplomat said publicly, to a burst of laughter from the audience at the Oberoi Hotel: 'You have been looking at us for so long, surely you must know what we look like by now. When are you going to go beyond looking?'

17. At a lecture in New Delhi, Surin Pitsuwan, the energetic former secretary general of the Association of South East Asian Nations (ASEAN), asked why India wanted to look east when Southeast Asians want to look west (to India) whose economy was growing rapidly. He was speaking at Jamia Millia Islamia where he

was delivering the Dr Saifuddin Kitchlew Annual Lecture on 7 March 2013 on 'Building a New Asia: India, China and ASEAN'.

18. This includes the North East Vision 2020, released by Prime Minister Manmohan Singh in 2008 and in which academics and policymakers as well as civil society organizations were involved and which advocated a people-centric inclusive approach to development in the region.

19. Nishit Dholabhai, 'Call to ban "chinky" in racism fight', *The Telegraph*, 7 February 2014 <http://www.telegraphindia.com/1140207/jsp/nation/story_17909815. jsp#.Vow7l0vGDZs> [accessed 6 January 2016].

20. Minister of State for Home Affairs Kiren Rijiju at the Delhi Police Headquarters.

21. 'Internal migration in India initiative', UNICEF, UNESCO two-day workshop on Internal Migration and Human Development in India, New Delhi, 6–7 December 2011 <http://unesdoc.unesco.org/images/0022/002214/221486e.pdf> [accessed 10 January 2015].

22. 'Qaid-i-Azam Mohammed Ali Jinnah Papers', Vol. 10, pp. 119–124, cited by Nisid Hajari, *Midnight's Furies, The Deadly Legacy of India's Partition*, New Delhi: Penguin Viking India Ltd, 2015.

23. The Press Trust of India quoted Minister of State for Home Affairs Kiren Rijiju as saying in Guwahati that 'the Delhi University colleges and Jawaharlal Nehru University were further asked to construct hostels reserving 50 per cent of their seats for N-E students with the money for construction provided by the government, he said. Besides, a Northeast Centre in Delhi would be constructed for celebrating occasions with people from other parts of the country to popularise the region, showcase its culture and promote harmony.' 'Special security cell put in place for Northeast people in Delhi: Kiren Rijiju', *Ibnlive.com*, 3 June 2015 <http://www.ibnlive.com/news/india/special-security-cell-put-in-place-for-northeast-people-in-delhi-kiren-rijiju-1001068.html> [accessed 10 January 2016].

24. Interview with General (Retd.) V. P. Malik, former chief of army staff, Chandigarh, 9 January 2016.

25. Police jobs in the region are much in demand and getting one often involves paying large bribes to politicians and officials.

26. Kiren Rijiju, minister of state for home affairs, to PTI, 'Delhi Police to annually induct 160 people from North Eastern states', *The Economic Times*, 30 December 2014 <http://articles.economictimes.indiatimes.com/2014-12-30/ news/57528996_1_delhi-police-hilly-states-chief-ministers> [accessed 11 January 2016].

27. Rahul Karmakar, 'Nagaland case: It's about immigrants, and politics adds fuel to fire', *Hindustan Times*, 8 March 2015 <http://www.hindustantimes.com/india/ nagaland-case-it-s-about-immigrants-and-politics-adds-fuel-to-fire/story-IN0FLkCNSVWVWoyzANfZ1H.html> [accessed 19 January 2016].

28. See Hazarika, *Strangers of the Mist* and *Rites of Passage*.

29. The agitation sparked numerous clashes between different ethnic and religious groups including massacres in roughly hewn patches of land in the state, between Hindu attackers and Muslim victims of Bengali origin at Nellie, between Assamese caste Hindus and Bodo tribes in Gohpur, in a central district not far from Tezpur town, in Goreswar, between plains tribes and Bengali Hindus. The list was endless. To this day, no one knows how many were killed. The toll overall for those brutal days in a valley of luminous beauty is estimated at not less than 3,000. A former senior intelligence official told me that it could not have been less than 10,000.

What is known is that in Nellie, some 1,800 men, women and children were slaughtered on its paddy fields as they fled, all Muslims of Bangladeshi origin. What is also known is that virtually no one was prosecuted for the murders, the investigations by commissions of inquiry were never made public, and many of the files, in official terminology, were 'closed'.

30.   Dr Amarjeet Singh, 'Illegal immigration into North East India: A Case of Nagaland', publication by Institute of Defence and Strategic Analysis (IDSA), New Delhi, 2009.

31.   The NEC is the regional planning body for the eight states of the region, and is a part of the Ministry for the Development of the Northeastern Region (MDoNER). Before this ministry's creation in 2002, the NEC was under the Ministry of Home Affairs. That is a story in itself because it was first meant to coordinate economic growth and security matters for the central government in collaboration with the states. Angry resistance from state leaders to the security aspect of the NEC meant that the post of security adviser was finally done away with, as the states objected to the efforts to control them through Delhi-appointed bureaucrats as well as the ongoing presence of the army, paramilitary forces and the centre's overriding powers with AFSPA.

32.   'Nagaland's Demographic Somersault: An Empirical Investigation', Ankush Agrawal, Vikas   Kumar,   http://www.isid.ac.in/~pu/conference/dec_12_conf/Papers/ VikasKumar.pdf, accessed 24 January 2016.

33.   'Lynched Dimapur man said it was 'consensual sex', The Hindu, 11 March 2015. http://www.thehindu.com/news/national/no-rape-but-consensual-sex-nagaland-govt-tells-mha/article6982750.ece

34.   Interestingly, the old building, which had many significant records, caught fire mysteriously and burnt to the ground even as the switch to the latest abode was going on.

35.   Samrat X, 'Fluid Identities', Asian Age, 11 March 2015,; article provided by author.

36.   Samrat Choudhury, 'After amnesia', RAIOT, 8 December 2015 <http://raiot.in/ after-amnesia/> [accessed 8 December 2015].

37.   See Introduction.

38.   Interview with a student of Pachunga College, Aizawl, August 2015.

39.   Patricia Mukhim, 'Non-tribals in Meghalaya: non-citizens or half-citizens, The Shillong Times, 22 March 2013 <http://www.theshillongtimes.com/2013/03/22/ non-tribals-in-meghalaya-non-citizens-or-half-citizens/> [accessed 2 February 2016].

40.   Agrawal, Kumar, 'Nagaland's Demographic Somersault: An Empirical Investigation' <http://www.isid.ac.in/~pu/conference/dec_12_conf/Papers/VikasKumar.pdf> [accessed 3 February 2016].

41.   Interview at a conference in Dona Paula, Goa, 29 January 2016.

EPILOGUE

1.   From parliamentary records.

2.   Interview with author, Chandigarh, January.

3.   'Is it time to lift AFSPA from parts of Kashmir?' To the Point, India Today news channel, General Bikram Singh, Karan Thapar and me, 27 July 2016 <http:// indiatoday.intoday.in/programme/is-it-time-to-lift-afspa-from-parts-of-kashmir/1/725713.html>.

4.   Editorial, 'The State must follow SC's tough ruling on AFSPA in letter and spirit',

Hindustan Times, 8 July 2016.

5. Press Trust of India, 'Human Rights Violations by Security Forces a Matter of Concern: SC', 7 September 2016, *Indian Express*, 7 September 2016 <http://indianexpress.com/article/india/india-news-india/human-rights-violations-by-security-forces-a-matter-of-concern-sc-3018952/> [accessed 11 September 2016].

6. Millennium Development Goals India Country Report 2015, Chapter 1. <http://mospi.nic.in/Mospi_New/upload/mdg_26feb15.pdf> [accessed 19 September 2015].

7. The story of the Khonoma reconciliation is based on a two-hour discussion with Kevisekho Kruse on 2 February 2016 and on reports from Khonoma by village elders or dispatched to me by email but I have followed it from the beginning with interviews over several years with several others intimately involved in the process.

8. See Hazarika, *Strangers of the Mist*.

9. Exactly the number of those who died in the internecine killings, although Kevisekho said this was not deliberate.

10. This is a hangover from Muivah's leftist track although Swu was a deeply religious Christian who, as we saw in an earlier chapter, was fond of saying grace and was an ordained priest. They're also known as the Mamas (uncles) and a wag talks about the I-M as the Mama party.

11. These were primarily funded by the Indian government especially its security establishment although organizations like the Quakers Association of London also took part, meeting various groups as well as the government in New Delhi and Nagaland.

12. Nagas and most hill tribe groups in the Northeast are not covered by income tax.

13. 'Not confrontation but transformation', Sanjoy Hazarika, the *Hindustan Times*, 1 July 2014.

14. See www.c-nes.org.

15. The Naga Mothers Association ran into a huge confrontation in Nagaland in early 2017 when riots broke out in Dimapur and Kohima after opponents of a state government decision to reserve seats in the urban bodies' elections in a clutch of towns went on a rampage. The trouble died down after the imposition of curfews, violence in which at least two persons were shot and the elections were postponed. Though the latter is seen as a victory for patriarchal forces, many male-dominated groups say it is not that simple. They want the complete protection of Article 371A which gives Nagas control of land and natural resources; it also ensures that no law passed by Parliament would apply to the state unless it was approved by the local assembly. In the case of the women's bill, this had been done. It still takes much persuasion to make groups understand that the proposed reservation for women in a non-traditional body (the municipal councils) would not in any way adversely affect Article 371A. These changes will take years to come for there is clear opposition to ideas that challenge male domination of Naga social structures. I personally find it fascinating that two contesting groups, which had opposed the idea and Constitution of India, are today using that very Constitution to argue against each other. One of them, the NMA, has gone to court to press for reservations although it backed out of the case following the rioting and handed over that responsibility to the Peoples Union of Civil Liberties (PUCL). This has, rather predictably raised another reaction—why should an 'Indian' group meddle in an issue that Nagas felt only they should have the right to decide. There is a strong body of opinion that feels that were the Nagaland Assembly to independently

develop a reservation formula that had no connection to court edicts or earlier parliamentary enactments, that would have a better chance of public acceptance.

16. 'Myanmar operation: 70 commandos finish task in 40 minutes', *The Hindu*, 10 June 2015, <http://www.thehindu.com/news/national/myanmar-operation-70-commandos-finish-task-in-40-minutes/article7302348.ece> [accessed 18 February 2016].

17. I have met and interviewed members of the Arakan Liberation Army and other Burmese ethnic insurgent groups in visits to Mizoram from 1996–2002.

18. Salil Tripathi, 'The case of the reluctant philanthropist, India's untenable position on the Rohingya crisis', New Delhi: *Caravan*, 1 Oct 2017 <http://www.caravanmagazine.in/perspectives/india-untenable-position-rohingya-crisis> [accessed 3 October 2017].

19. For more details, read Ankush Saikia <https://www.facebook.com/notes/ankush-saikia/death-in-the-marketplace-what-really-happened-at-balajan-tiniali-on-august-5th/10155227941929126?pnref=story>.

20. In the Guwahati High Court (the High Court of Assam, Nagaland, Mizoram and Arunachal Pradesh) PIL (suo moto) 66/2012, 67/2012, and WP(C) 648/2013 and 4860/2013; the case was filed by Mrinal Saikia against numerous state and central government departments and officials, details in <http://ghconline.gov.in/Judgment/PIL662012.pdf> [accessed 23 September 2016].

21. 'Performance audit of Kaziranga National Park—issues and challenges', Report of the Comptroller and Auditor General of India, Government of Assam, Report No 2 of 2014, Government of Assam.

22. Nikhil Roshan, 'The River Between: The Bengali Muslim Community of Western Assam', *Caravan*, 10 April 2016 <http://www.caravanmagazine.in/vantage/the-river-between-dhubri-bengali-muslims-assam> [accessed 24 September 2016].

23. Rajah Rasiah, Abul Quesem Al-Amin, 'Integrating Myanmar with its western and northern neighbors: A shared vision through the promotion of sustainable agricultural development', Tin Htoo Naing, Research Paper, 2011.

24. *Imphal Free Press* editorial, 2 February 2016.

25. '*What Happened in the Jungles of Burma, My Brothers?*', Easterine Kire, Biblio, May–June 2008.

BIBLIOGRAPHY

Ao, Temsula, *These Hills Called Home: Stories from a Warzone*, New Delhi: Zubaan Books, 2005.

Barpujari, H. K., *A Political History of Assam*. Assam: Departmentt. for the Preparation of Political History of Assam, Government of Assam, 1977.

Barooah, Nirode K., *Gopinath Bordoloi: The Assam Problem and Nehru's Centre*, Guwahati: Bhabani Print and Publications, 2010.

Baruah, Sanjib, *Durable Disaster: Understanding the Politics of Northeast India*, New Delhi: Oxford University Press, 2007.

Bhattacharjee, Kishalay , *Blood on My Hands: Confessions of Staged Encounters*, New Delhi: HarperCollins India, 2015.

Bhattacharyya, Rajeev, *Rendezvous with Rebels: Journey to Meet India's Most Wanted Men*, New Delhi: HarperCollins India, 2014.

Bhaumik, Subir (ed.), *The Agartala Doctrine: A Proactive Northeast in Indian Foreign Policy*, New Delhi: Oxford University Press, 2016.

————, *Troubled Periphery: The Crisis of India's North East*, New Delhi: Sage Publications, 2009.

Bordoloi, Barooah Gopinath , *Indian Constitution and Centre-Assam Relations, 1940–1950*, Guwahati: Publications Board, 1990.

Chadha, Vivek (ed.), *Armed Forces Special Powers Act: The Debate*, New Delhi: Lancer Publishers in association with Institute for Defence Studies and Analyses, 2013.

Chaudhari, Sudhakar K., *Cross Border Trade between India and Bangladesh*, New Delhi: National Council of Applied Economic Research (NCAER), 1995.

Chun, Tan, *Across the Himalayan Gap: An Indian Quest for Understanding China*, New Delhi: Indira Gandhi National Centre for the Arts, 1998.

Conway, Susan, *The Shan Culture: Art and Crafts*, Bangkok: Riverbooks, 2006.

Datta-Ray, Sunanda, *Smash and Grab: Annexation of Sikkim*, New Delhi: HarperCollins India, 2012 (revised edition).

Duff, Andrew, *Sikkim: Requiem for a Himalayan Kingdom*, New Delhi: Random House India, 2015.

Elwin, Verrier, *A Philosophy for NEFA*, Shillong: North-East Frontier Agency, 1959.

Eekelen , W. F. Van, *Indian Foreign Policy and the Border Dispute with China: A New Look at Asian Relationships*, Leiden: BRILL, 2015.

Gill, Preeti, *The Peripheral Centre: Voices from India's Northeast*, New Delhi: Zubaan Books, 2005.

Gopal, Sarvepalli, *Jawaharlal Nehru, A Biography, Volume 3, 1956–1964*, New Delhi: Oxford University Press, 1984.

Guha, Amalendu, *Planter Raj to Swaraj: Freedom Struggle & Electoral Politics in Assam*, New Delhi: Tulika Books, 2014.

Hajari, Nisid, *Midnight's Furies, The Deadly Legacy of India's Partition*, New Delhi: Penguin Viking India Ltd, 2015.

Hazarika, Jatin, *Shadow behind the Throne: My Tryst with Assam Administration*, Guwahati: Lawyers Book Stall, 2016.

Hazarika, Sanjoy, *Strangers of the Mist: Tales of War and Peace from India's Northeast*, New Delhi: Penguin Books India, 2012 (revised edition).

————, *Rites of Passage: Border Crossings, Imagined Homelands, India's East and Bangladesh*. New Delhi: Penguin Books India, 2000.

————and Chasie, Charles, *The State Strikes Back: India and the Naga Insurgency*, Washington DC: East West Center, 2008.

———— and Gill, Preeti (eds.), *Bearing Witness: The Impact of Conflict on Women in Nagaland and Assam*, New Delhi: Centre for North East Studies and Policy Research with support from the Heinrich Böll Foundation, 2011.

Hluna, J. V. (ed.), *History and Ethnic Identity Formation in North-East India*, New Delhi: Concept Publishing House, 2013.

————and Tochhawng, Rini, *The Mizo Uprising, Assam Assembly Debates on the Mizo Movement, 1966–1971*, London: Cambridge Scholars Publishing, 2012.

Karlsson, Bengt G., *Unruly Hills: Nature and Nation in India's Northeast*, New Delhi: Orient Blackswan, 2011.

Kashyap, Aruni, *The House with a Thousand Stories*, New Delhi: Penguin Books India, 2013.

Kimura, Makiko, *The Nellie Massacre of 1983: Agency of Rioters*, New Delhi: Sage Publications India Pvt Ltd, 2013.

Kire, Easterine, *When the River Sleeps*, New Delhi: Zubaan Books, 2015.

————, *Bitter Wormwood*, New Delhi: Zubaan Books, 2011.

Kumar, Ram Narayan; Singh, Amrik; Agrwaal, Ashok and Kaur, Jaskaran, *Reduced to Ashes: The Insurgency and Human Rights in Punjab*, Kathmandu: South Asia Forum for Human Rights, 2003.

Lalkhama, *A Mizo Civil Servant's Random Reflections* (self-published), 2006.

Lintner, Bertil, *Land of Jade: A Journey from India through Northern Burma to China*, Bangkok: Orchid Press, 1990.

Mackenzie, Alexander. *The North-East Frontier of India*, New Delhi: Mittal Publications, 1989.

Marwah, Ved, *Uncivil Wars: Pathology of Terrorism in India*, New Delhi: HarperCollins, 1995.

Misra, Udayon, *The Periphery Strikes Back: Challenges to the Nation-state in Assam and Nagaland*. Shimla: Indian Institute of Advanced Study, 2000.

Nag, Sajal, *Contesting Marginality: Ethnicity, Insurgence and Subnationalism in North-East India*, New Delhi: Manohar Publishers and Distributors, 2002.

Patangia, Arupa Kalita, *The Story of Felanee*, Phukan, Deepika (trans.), New Delhi: Zubaan Books, 2011.

Pudaite, L. T., *Mizoram and Look East Policy*, New Delhi: Akansha Publishing, 2010.

Robbins, Nick, *The Corporation That Changed the World: How the East India Company Shaped the Modern Multinational*, Hyderabad: Orient Longman, 2006.

Sailo, Brigadier Thenphunga, AVSM , *A Soldier's Story*, self-published, 2001.

Scott, James C., *The Art of Not Being Governed: An Anarchist History of Upland Southeast Asia*, New Haven: Yale University Press, 2009.

Smith, S. C. and Castle, E. N., *Economics and Public Policy in Water Resources Development*, Ames: Iowa State University Press, 1964.

Talukdar, Mrinal; Borpujari, Utpal and Deka, Kaushik, *Secret Killings of Assam*, Guwahati: Nanda Talukar Foundation, and Human Rights Law Network, 2009.

Tripathi, Salil, *Detours: Songs of the Open Road*, New Delhi: Tranquebar Press, 2016.

Verghese, Boobli George, *India's Northeast Resurgent*, New Delhi: Konark Publishers, 2004.

———, *First Draft: Witness to Making of Modern India*, New Delhi: Tranquebar Press, 2010.

INDEX